Comparative Legislative Systems

HERBERT HIRSCH
and **M. DONALD HANCOCK**
EDITORS

Comparative Legislative Systems

A Reader in Theory and Research

THE FREE PRESS, NEW YORK
COLLIER-MACMILLAN LIMITED, LONDON

The Free Press
A Division of The Macmillan Company
866 Third Avenue, New York, New York 10022

Collier-Macmillan Canada Ltd., Toronto, Ontario

Library of Congress Catalog Card Number: 78-136612

printing number
1   2   3   4   5   6   7   8   9   10

Contents

THE INSTITUTIONAL NEXUS

LEGISLATIVE DECISION-MAKING

MAJORITY-MINORITY RELATIONS

EPILOGUE

INDEX

Introduction

LEGISLATIVE SYSTEMS

Legislatures in Systemic Perspective

by HERBERT HIRSCH
and M. DONALD HANCOCK

Legislative research, both cross- and sub-national, has experienced a resurgence. Within the last several years scholars have been increasingly attracted to the legislature both as an important policy-making institution and as a structure within which to test specific theoretical propositions regarding important aspects of political behavior.

Despite this revival of interest, however, little cross-national research exists that is truly comparative and theoretical. Most studies remain descriptive and manifest a rather static conception of legislative processes. Meynaud's lament remains as valid today as it was ten years ago: One sadly notes the lack of theory and the wide "disparities both in lack of data available among systems and approaches to information about legislatures in different political systems."[1]

These difficulties present the student of legislative behavior with grave problems in forming generalizations concerning legislative behavior. In an attempt to facilitate such generalizations we have assembled this selection of published and original material. The volume is both comparative and theoretical, and it is designed to help fill a major gap in existing approaches to the study of legislative behavior. It not only samples some of the best recent work on legislative systems, but it can also serve as a catalyst to stimulate further hypotheses. Our introductory statement, therefore, comprises a critique of the various selections and an attempt to build a framework for analysis that will provide more than simply a heuristic tool that is conceptually useful in structuring our environment.

Yet if this compilation does no more than this it is important, for, as Roderick

---

[1] Quoted in Samuel C. Patterson, "Comparative Legislative Behavior: A Review Essay," *Midwest Journal of Political Science.* For the original study see Jean Meynaud, "Introduction: General Study of Parliamentarians," *International Social Science Journal* 13 (1961): 513. Patterson accurately notes the increase in such comparative endeavors, but the problems remain. These difficulties were neatly illustrated for us when we attempted to fit together the diverse strands of data on recruitment and social background to draw comparisons regarding the process of recruitment in different systems. We were forced to give up in despair owing to the functionally non-equivalent nature of the categories used by different scholars.

Bell observes in the second essay, "theory informs our observations of reality." Bell's paper is an integral adjunct to this introduction. His essay is particularly significant because it provides an example of the process of theory construction, explicates the role of theory in the study of politics, and treats legislative behavior as one more aspect of human behavior rather than as a unique sort of human endeavor.

System Analysis: A Brief Introduction

A considerable number of systemic models have been proposed in contemporary social science literature. Our first step, therefore, is to specify the elements of our systemic conception. We accept Mitchell's definition. According to him, a social system

... consists of *two* or *more* persons who are engaged in a *patterned* or *structured* form of *relationship* or *interaction*, and who are guided by sets of *values* and norms generally called *roles*. It must be noted that the interaction is *relatively persistent*; a chance meeting of strangers on a street cannot be considered as a social system.[2]

Almond and Powell further suggest that a system "implies . . . a boundary of some kind between it and its environment."[3] This boundary enables the observer to determine who is and who is not a member of the system.[4] "The last property of a system . . . is [that] the system tends to establish an equilibrium or balance of the forces that tend both to integrate and disintegrate."[5] Regarding the concept of "equilibrium" or "homeostasis," Loomis notes that it is important not to lose sight of "trends and the dynamic aspects" of the model.[6] According to Ashby

... stability, as defined, in no way implied fixity or rigidity. It is true that the stable system usually has a state of equilibrium at which it shows no change, but the lack of change is deceptive if it suggests rigidity: if displaced from the state of equilibrium it will show active, perhaps extensive and complex, movements. The stable system is restricted only in that it does not show the unrestricted divergencies of instability.[7]

[2] William C. Mitchell, *The American Polity* (New York: The Free Press, 1962), p. 4.

[3] Gabriel A. Almond and G. Bingham Powell, Jr., *Comparative Politics: A Developmental Approach* (Boston: Little, Brown and Company, 1966), p. 19.

[4] Mitchell, *American Polity*, p. 4. It is interesting to observe that Ashby's definition of a system is, in one sense, much less complicated than the elaborate definitions of Parsons and others. Ashby states, "a system is then defined as any *set of variables* that . . . are selected from those available on the real 'machine.' It is thus a list, nominated by the observer, and is quite different from the real 'machine.' " Ashby is evidently making a distinction between the symbolic system and the system operating in the "real" world. The system that we define verbally can be only a symbol of the total system for we are never sure we have isolated all the variables operating in a social system. William Ross Ashby, *Design for a Brain* (New York: John Wiley & Sons, Inc., 1960), p. 16. Easton agrees: "A system was defined as any set of variables regardless of the degree of interrelationships between them." David Easton, *A Systems Analysis of Political Life* (New York: John Wiley & Sons, Inc., 1965), p. 21.

[5] Mitchell, *American Polity*, p. 4.

[6] Charles S. Loomis, *Social Systems: Essays on Their Persistence and Change* (Princeton: D. Van Nostrand Company, Inc., 1960), p. 11. For some early comments on the use of equilibrium models, see David Easton, *The Political System* (New York: Alfred A. Knopf, 1953), pp. 206–366.

[7] Ashby, *Design for a Brain*, p. 55.

When we examine the individual's activity within the system we refer to the concept of role. "The units which make up all social systems, including political systems, are roles."[8] The concept of role can act as a bridge between the individual and the system—between behavior and institution.

Beginning with the concept of role as one of the basic units of a political system, we may speak of a subsystem (for example, a legislative body) as consisting of related and interacting roles; and of the political system as a set of interacting subsystems (for example legislatures, electorates, pressure groups, and courts).[9]

It is a particular group of subsystems—legislatures—that concern us here. For the present purposes the legislature is defined as consisting of those persons directly associated with it in a technical, official and/or administrative capacity.[10]

Inputs into the Legislative System

Systems scholars generally specify two or three general types of inputs: expectations, supports, and demands.[11] According to Mitchell, expectations are

... that rather amorphous group of beliefs that citizens have regarding what the government ought to do and the way its officials and other citizens ought to, or probably will, behave.[12]

Individuals, non-governmental groups, and governmental groups, as well as fellow legislators, have expectations regarding the proper behavior of the individual legislator and the desired output from the system. In fact these expectations are probably important in shaping the legislator's conception of his role.[13]

SUPPORTS

A primary element within the system, supports are similar to expectations and may take various forms.[14] Obviously, without some form of support,

[8] Almond and Powell, *Comparative Politics*, p. 21.

[9] *Ibid.*, p. 22.

[10] Similar definitions have been used in regard to judicial systems: James Herndon, "The Role of the Judiciary in State Political Systems," in Glendon Schubert (ed.), *Judicial Behavior: A Reader in Theory and Research* (Chicago: Rand McNally & Company, 1964), p. 155.

[11] Almond and Powell, *Comparative Politics*, p. 25; Mitchell, *American Polity*, pp. 6–7; David Easton, "An Approach to the Analysis of Political Systems," *World Politics* (April 1957): pp. 383–408; and Easton, *Systems Analysis*, p. 27.

[12] Mitchell, *American Polity*, p. 15.

[13] Owing to a lack of data and the fact that party and constituency influences are often analyzed together, however, we have chosen to place them under the decision-making section. This is not meant to imply that they do not act as input stimuli; they do indeed. It simply refers to the fact that they have been viewed as direct influences on legislative decision making.

[14] Almond and Powell, *Comparative Politics*, p. 26 and Easton, *Systems Analysis*, p. 163 both give numerous examples. For example, Easton says that "as measures of overt support, a variety of activities are typically taken into account: the numbers belonging to organizations; the regularity with which citizens or subjects perform their obligations; manifestations of open hostility such as breaches of the law, riots, or revolutions; and expressions of preferences for other systems through emigration or separatist activities."

institutions could hardly survive. When discussing support for legislative subsystems we are forced to focus our attention on public support. Thus, the Boynton, Patterson, Hedlund article in this volume is primarily concerned with support directed toward a particular institution—the Iowa legislature. Boynton, Patterson, and Hedlund conceptualize support as containing a number of dimensions. "Specific support" is stimulated by certain outputs from the legislature and involves the individuals' perception of how their demands are met. "Diffuse support" is a more general concept referring to

...that reservoir of good will which a system may engender, not dependent upon a particular output, and at the extreme mode typified by unquestioning loyalty or patriotism.

"Overt support involves some kind of action in the form of observable behavior," whereas "covert support" refers to the less behavioristic characteristics such as attitude and sentiment. This seems to us to be a rather weak analytic distinction. If one conceptualizes Boynton, Patterson, and Hedlund's classification of support as a dichotomy, one either acts or one does not act. If their classification is regarded as a continuum, there are numerous shades between overt and covert. Moreover, their discussion seems to confuse lack of action with the absence of an attitude. One can be supportive and yet not take action. The last category of support discussed by the authors of this article suffers from a similar degree of conceptual fuzziness. The distinction between "direct" and "indirect" support does not make clear to the reader whether the authors are referring to a general attitude or to one or a combination of the components thereof.

Support appears to us to refer merely to the individual's attitude toward the legislative institution. If one's attitude is positive it is supportive; if it is negative it may be either non-supportive or some admixture thereof. Given this conceptualization, support could be analyzed in a manner similar to that in which other attitudes are analyzed, *i.e.*, by examining the three basic attitudinal components and the relations between them.[15] We might empirically conceptualize support in the following manner.

SUPPORTIVE ATTITUDES

Feeling		*Behavior*	
		+	−
Positive +		A + +	B + −
Negative −		C − +	D − −

[15] Attitudes are usually conceptualized by social psychologists as being composed of three components: an emotive or feeling component, a behavioral or action component, and a cognitive component. For a simple review of this literature see David Kretch, Richard S. Crutchfield, and Egerton L. Ballachey, *The Individual in Society* (New York: McGraw-Hill, 1962), pp. 137–215. Each of the three components may, in turn, vary in "valence" and in "degree of *multiplexity*." Valence refers to the degree of favorability or unfavorability attached to a particular object. Multiplexity "refers to the number and variety of the elements or parts making up a component." Kretch, Crutchfield, and Ballachey, *Individual in Society*, p. 142. For one application on a particular attitudinal dimension see Morris Rosenberg, *Society and the Adolescent Self-Image* (Princeton, N.J.: Princeton University Press, 1965).

In Cell A the feeling and action components blend together to form an overtly active supportive attitude. In Cell B a positive feeling component does not lead to action and thus we find the covert supporter. In Cell C a negative feeling component is combined with action and we find the non-supportive individual who is probably opposing some specific legislative decision. In Cell D we note the lack of emotional support and the lack of behavior—a category that encompasses the individual to whom legislative politics are not salient. The astute observer will immediately notice that we have omitted the cognitive component from consideration. We do so not because we consider it unimportant, but because we cannot identify its empirical referent.[16]

Despite its minor conceptual problem, the Boynton, Patterson, and Hedlund article does contribute significantly to our understanding of the three areas of support with which it deals, *i.e.*, covert, direct, and diffuse. Using seven attitudinal items to measure support and factor-analyzing their data demonstrate that legislative support in Iowa forms two distinct factors which are labelled "compliance" and "institutional commitment." (These seem to us to be no different from the "specific" and "diffuse" categories put forth earlier. Compliance refers to support for a specific decision, or at least to no resistance to it, whereas institutional commitment refers to the notion that legislatures should continue to exist.) The authors then ask who supports the legislature, and answer by controlling certain basic demographic variables which demonstrate that individuals in the upper socioeconomic brackets are more supportive than those below them in the class structure. Legislative support does not, moreover, differ in rural-urban environments, but is found to be related to knowledge about the legislature (perhaps one portion of the cognitive component of a supportive attitude).

In comparative perspective there is no scholarly work on an equal theoretical plane with that of Boynton, Patterson, and Hedlund. The excerpt from Gerhard Loewenberg's study of the German Bundestag does not attempt to deal explicitly with supportive attitudes. What Loewenberg does demonstrate is that supportive orientations are important, at least as they are perceived by members of the Bundestag. Significantly, German parliamentarians have even instituted a program to improve public knowledge of the legislature. The Bundestag, according to Loewenberg, has been traditionally publicity shy; it began the present program as a means to acquaint citizens with the fact that Germany does indeed have a functioning legislative body. Public response to observing the Bundestag was interesting. As a people not familiar with parliamentary procedures, the Germans were dismayed at the seeming lack of activity within the legislative halls. In response to the public relations program, however, Germans have revealed an increasing awareness of legislative functions and their original cynicism has correspondingly declined.

Loewenberg's findings are most interesting in light of the fact that Boynton, Patterson, and Hedlund found that knowledge about the Iowa legislature was

---

[16] In some cases knowledge has been used as synonymous with cognition. We find this to be somewhat oversimplified and, therefore, because of our inability to cast light on the topic we simply leave it for others to clarify.

related to supportive orientations toward it. Germany seems to have experienced a comparable phenomenon, *i.e.*, the more people know about the Bundestag the more likely they are to manifest supportive orientations toward it. Major differences can be discerned, however, between the two cases. Germans, according to Loewenberg, seem to be oriented more toward local than national governmental units. The Bundestag, therefore, does not provide a connective link between the people and the government—commonly thought to be a primary function of representative institutions. Unlike the United States—where supportive orientations seem to lie with the institution itself—support for the Bundestag is dependent upon its "specific accomplishments." As a result the Bundestag is accorded only "conditional support." Because this dimension was not tapped in the Iowa study, we are unable to make specific comparisons. Suffice it to say that Americans (in at least one state) may be more supportive of their legislative institutions in a diffuse sense, whereas Germans are specifically supportive.

There are a number of possible explanations for this variance. First, it is possible that socialization accounts for the differences. Most obvious, however, is the fact that the German study was conducted with reference to a national legislative body, whereas the Iowa study concentrated on the state level. Since Loewenberg notes that Germans are more likely to look to local governmental units to solve their problems, there might have been greater congruence in supportive orientations had we been able to find a corresponding local or state study of a German legislature to compare with Iowa.[17] Because we know of no such data, further comparative analysis of supportive orientations remains to be done. We hope it is forthcoming.

DEMANDS

Demands comprise the third conceptual classification of inputs. Demands may be an easier category to investigate empirically. According to Mitchell there are several components of demand.[18] First, "What is demanded?" To measure this, one would have to conduct interviews with both lobbyists and legislators in order to get their perception of what is being demanded. Important in this regard is the question of whether legislators perceive demands in light of their content or in terms of the groups who are presenting them.

The second component is, "By whom is the demand being made?" Of particular interest in this context are the number and type of interest groups that operate within the particular legislative context under discussion. For example, Jewell and Patterson provide a gross count demonstrating that Texas far exceeds any other state in the number of lobbyists registered.[19] It is legitimate, however, to ask to what extent this gross type of aggregate counting enables one

---

[17] There is one additional study of support for a legislative institution of which we are aware. It does not, however, deal with the concept in a theoretical manner and is primarily descriptive. See Roger H. Davidson, *et al.*, *Congress in Crisis* (Belmont, California: Wadsworth, 1968), chap. 2, "The Public Looks at Congress," pp. 38–66.

[18] Mitchell, *American Polity*, p. 14.

[19] Malcolm E. Jewell and Samuel C. Patterson, *The Legislative Process in the United States* (New York: Random House, 1966), p. 280.

to separate out the complexities of the demand schedule. Although such a count has some relevance, one needs to delve more deeply into the question of demands. Why, for example, does Texas have so many more lobbyists registered? Is it due to differences in lobbying laws or to differences in the politics and culture of the different states?

The last factor that must be known about the demand schedule is, according to Mitchell, "How are the demands handled?" or "What is the success of the demander?" This appears to be one of the most neglected questions. Are some groups more successful than others either in proposing or blocking legislation? Because it was not possible to find articles dealing with all aspects of the demand schedules, we are forced to concentrate in this volume on the operation and effect of formal associational interest groups. Richard A. Styskal utilizes the concept of demand within the broader context of modernization theory and attempts to assess the relation between demand making and demand development. His study of Philippine legislators demonstrates that citizen demand-making in transitional societies encompasses both traditional and modern behavioral patterns. Traditional demands are "individual oriented, . . . narrow and specific"; they emphasize "personal intimate contacts between citizens and politician" and "lead to highly particularized decision-making." Simultaneously "modern types of demand-making" exist that are "group-oriented." Such "demands tend to be categorical, policy or administrative alternatives."

Styskal's primary emphasis is on the demand system of a transitional society and the mix of traditional and modern structures therein. His findings assume particular significance if one adopts what appears to be a major assumption underlying much of the development and structural-functional literature— namely, that systems in states of transition experience a rapid increase in political demands. If the system is to adapt itself to these new demands, if it is to "absorb them in policy-making and to insure its own continuity in the face of continuous new demands and new forms of political organization," it must devise new methods to cope with the demands. According to Styskal this problem can be resolved only by increasing the development of interest groups and their role in the political process. Attempting to assess the relative influence of organized interest groups as compared with that of "unaffiliated individuals," Styskal hypothesizes that the Philippines, as a system in transition, manifests both forms of demand-making and that the Philippine Congressman can and does distinguish between them. Using interviews with 125 of 128 Philippine congressmen as his data base, Styskal finds that Philippine legislators in general have positive attitudes toward the demand-making roles that interest groups play. Younger representatives viewed this phenomenon more positively than their older colleagues. At the same time, the amount of interaction between congressmen and interest groups and the general congressional ambivalence expressed by politicians regarding the importance of interest groups "warn us against the too-facile conclusion that these groups have reached the importance of similar organizations in the United States." On the contrary, in the Philippines unaffiliated individuals are a "more frequent source of demands" than interest groups and Philippine congressmen view the activity of such individuals favorably. Styskal thus concludes that "the more traditional or informal structure of politics . . . is still predominant in the Philippines." He finds confirmation, therefore, for the "mixed political demand system that exists today in the Philippines."

Harmon Zeigler, on the other hand, does not explicitly address himself to the problem of development. Investigating the effects of lobbying in four states in the United States—Massachusetts, North Carolina, Oregon, and Utah— Zeigler utilizes the concept of interaction as the basic theoretical focus of his study. He asks three fundamental questions: "(1) How much interaction between legislators and lobbyists actually takes place; (2) What is the nature of this interaction; and (3) What is the effect of this interaction?" Incorporating the economic, social, and political characteristics of the four states in his analysis, Zeigler attempts to establish the link between these variables and the strength of interest groups. In so doing he discovers some interesting differences in interaction among the four states. North Carolina is most interesting for comparative purposes.

Characterized as having a "traditionalistic political culture," North Carolina is perhaps the closest approximation to the transitory system found in the Philippines. Zeigler finds that "in North Carolina legislators think little interaction takes place, while lobbyists would 'rank' their state second [in terms of amount of interaction] only to Oregon." Zeigler explains this finding in the following manner: "The essential attributes of such a [traditionalistic] culture . . ." are that "real political power" is confined to a "relatively small and self-perpetuating group drawn from an established elite. . . ." He continues: "If legislators reflect these kinds of attitudes, they would admit very little outside influence. . . ." There are, however, alternative explanations. Elazar lists additional characteristics of what he calls traditionalistic sub-cultures.[20] Among these are an emphasis on personal ties and the consequent eschewal of formal group membership. Thus the fact that legislators perceive interest groups to be less important may be a reflection of a similar cultural situation to that uncovered by Styskal—namely, that the less formal, more personal types of interaction are more salient forms of interaction between the governed and the governors in modernizing or traditionalistic political cultures. Interest groups in North Carolina would, therefore, be of less importance than those in the other three states. This interpretation is suggested as a possible alternative to Zeigler's explanation. Equally likely is that the situation as described by Zeigler would also hold for the Philippines. The interesting point is that the concept of development, if it is to have any relevance, can be applied to certain areas of the United States as well as to other countries.

SOCIALIZATION AND RECRUITMENT

The questions of socialization and recruitment are intimately related. With respect to the legislative sub-system we speak of socialization as it occurs at two stages. The initial period is the one in which the incipient legislator acquires his

---

[20] Daniel Elazar, *American Federalism: A View from the States* (New York: Thomas Y. Crowell Company, 1966), pp. 85–140.

basic world view, *i.e.,* his personality and his attitudes (political attitudes as well as others). In this early period our interest centers on the process of learning in an attempt to explain the life steps that lead the individual to become a political actor. The article by Herbert Hirsch focuses on this period. Possibly the key question, as posed in the Hirsch article, is: "Do individuals marked for an adult political career experience initial political socialization in a manner that increases the probability they will select themselves or be selected for political leadership?" This question is most difficult to answer. Scholars have not been entirely successful in establishing the existence or non-existence of linkages between early socialization and later political behavior. Thus the relation between socialization and recruitment is at best tenuous.

The topic of recruitment has received a great deal of attention from legislative scholars.[21] It is the most thoroughly researched topic on which vast amounts of comparative cross-cultural data are available. Yet when we attempted to combine these data for summary purposes we found the categories to be functionally non-equivalent. Thus we are able only to make general comparative statements, and these are in no sense surprising. Legislators in most of the countries are similar to those in the United States. As members of the dominant ethnic group in each of the countries for which data are available, legislators are, in short, members of the elite.

Recruitment constitutes an important input into the system for the obvious reason that institutions unable to perpetuate themselves by recruiting new members vanish. Recruitment, therefore, is an important step in coöpting individuals into "the system." Following recruitment, the next step in the process involves socializing the freshman legislator. Obviously, when an individual enters a well structured, well institutionalized body with norms and expectations, he learns to adapt to the environment.[22] He is socialized. We hypothesize, therefore, that the process of learning in this case is the same psychological process that the individual goes through as he becomes an adult. The important point to keep in mind is that the psychological processes are probably the same, whereas the agents and content of the stimuli are different.

The essay by Hirsch seeks to posit questions that give a more coherent theoretical foundation to the study of political socialization and also lead one to

[21] The literature on recruitment and background variables is voluminous. For example, see the collection of six articles in the *International Social Science Journal* 13 (1961); Lester G. Seligman, "Political Recruitment and Party Structure: A Case Study," *American Political Science Review* 55 (March 1961): 77–86; Leo M. Snowiss, "Congressional Recruitment and Representation," *American Political Science Review* 60 (September 1966): 627–39; Alan Fiellin, "Recruitment and Legislative Role Conceptions: A Conceptual Scheme and a Case Study," *Western Political Quarterly* 20 (June 1967): 271–87; Donald R. Matthews, *U.S. Senators and Their World* (Chapel Hill: University of North Carolina Press, 1960), pp. 11–46; Jewell and Patterson, *The Legislative Process*, pp. 101–123; Samuel C. Patterson and G. R. Boynton, "Legislative Recruitment in a Civic Culture," *Social Science Quarterly* 50 (September 1969): 243–63; Robert B. Stauffer, "Philippine Legislators and Their Changing Universe," *Journal of Politics* 28 (August 1966): 556–97; Allan Kornberg and Hal H. Winsborough, "The Recruitment of Candidates for the Canadian House of Commons," *American Political Science Review* 62 (December 1968): 1242–57.

[22] Stanton Wheeler, "The Structure of Formally Organized Socialization Settings," in Orville G. Brim, Jr. and Stanton Wheller, *Socialization After Childhood: Two Essays* (New York: John Wiley & Sons, 1967), pp. 51–116.

investigate the important aspect of linkages. Thus, Hirsch asks five questions regarding the socialization process: "What is taught?" "To whom?" "How?" "Under what conditions?" and "With what consequences?"

The answer to the first question involves the content of what is taught and the content of the stimuli involved. Because Hirsch's paper is based on secondary analysis of data, these aspects of socialization could not be investigated. Because the population to be examined was subjectively selected, the answer to the second was built into the analysis. The third question, "By whom?" refers to the agents of socialization and is the primary focus of the study.

Hirsch's analysis suggests that the agents of socialization are intimately related to time. Individuals socialized in childhood were socialized by primary groups, whereas those socialized after childhood were more likely to recall that "other groups" were the primary agents.

Regarding the question of the conditions under which the process occurred, it was discovered that people living in urban areas were socialized earlier than those in small towns and that the status of the family was related to the time of socialization.

In seeking to answer the last question, "With what consequences?" Hirsch found that the source of the legislator's decision to enter politics was related to time. Here we have the first hint that there may in fact be a linkage between early socialization and later behavior. The significance of this study lies not so much in the nature of its findings as in the questions that it opens for future research.

CAMPAIGNS AND ELECTIONS

Before the second aspect of the socialization process can come into play the individual legislator must go through the process of campaigning and getting elected. Campaigns and elections are therefore a central source of input for the legislative sub-system.

One carryover from classic conceptions of democracy, Charles O. Jones observes, is that most people in the United States expect campaigns and elections to be issue-oriented. Jones' major thesis is that in fact they are not. Instead, "the campaign period is a regularly scheduled event in the life of a representative, in which he makes an intensive effort to advertise himself—to project a generalized image of himself as a capable representative—so that he will win. It is not an issue-oriented event, and campaign-electoral conditions are such that the representative need not be bound by the election in his policy-making behavior." He substantiates this hypothesis by examining a number of different types of data. Without reviewing all the incisive statements contained in the Jones article, we will simply mention some that we consider most interesting.

When examining the time that elections occur, Jones finds there is no guarantee that they will fall in a crisis year when great issues are being debated. "In America," he writes, "governments do not fall in time of crisis; they linger on till the first Tuesday after the first Monday of November." This is cited as one example of why one should not expect campaigns and elections to be issue-oriented. Jones further observes that "incumbents win." Most of the time "70–80 per cent of congressional districts will be represented either by the same man or the same party for *five consecutive elections*." During the four years of 1954, 1956, 1958, and 1960, for example, incumbents won an average of 93.9 per cent of the time.

Regarding campaigns, therefore, Jones suggests that "there seems to be no stimulus for a strong, rigorous campaign . . ." because the incumbent usually wins and the voter does not know what is happening. These findings have broad, important implications for our conception of the operation of the legislative sub-system. We have been operating, it seems, on certain unwarranted assumptions regarding the concept, or at least the process, of representation as it works in the United States. An interesting question then asserts itself: Do these findings hold in a country that does not lay claim to a classical type of democracy?

Everything we know about Mexico indicates that it is a much more authoritarian system than the United States. Yet Mexico does have legislatures, and people campaign for election to them. In his study of the 1966 congressional election in Mexico, Karl M. Schmitt suggests that "much of the literature on congressional elections, oriented as it is to the United States, is not readily applicable to the Mexican situation." Because Mexico is an official one-party state and representatives cannot succeed themselves, "the emphasis in the U.S. literature about the campaigns of incumbents and the relationship between policy making and elections are irrelevant." Schmitt finds, however, several interesting parallels between the two countries. Mexican elections are regularly scheduled and provide geographic representation. Moreover, "the purposes of campaigning in both countries are the same: the reinforcement of party supporters, the activation of latent supporters, and the conversion of the opposition. Likewise, the campaigns concentrate more on issues of 'style' than on issues of 'position.'" Schmitt concludes by observing that "the primary function of congressional campaigning in Mexico is nation-building, the creation of a 'civic culture.'" He then introduces the concept of "modernization" as an important aspect to be noted in the comparative analysis of legislative systems. Mexico, interestingly enough, is much more similar to Styskal's assessment of the Philippines than to the United States. Because there is such a striking absence of comparative assessments of campaigns and elections in countries exemplifying different stages of social, economic, and political modernization, we are unable to carry such comparisons too far. We can only urge that such additional analysis be undertaken—perhaps using the concepts of modernization theory as a foundation on which to build.[23]

EXTERNAL INPUTS

The last input that we have identified has been grossly under-represented in the literature. One of the editors of this volume has elsewhere identified external

[23] For an attempt to do so, see Lloyd Musolf and Allan Kornberg, *Legislatures and Developmental Perspectives* (Durham: Duke University Press, forthcoming).

or "international inputs" as an important element in a model of system performance.[24] He defines "international inputs" as referring

to flows of political influence (including consultation with other nations, threats, violence, territorial occupation, or the displacement of domestic actors), the infusion of ideas, and the movement of persons and materials from outside the boundaries of the domestic system.[25]

These seem to us to constitute a potentially important class of input stimuli. Yet we were able to find only one relevant piece of literature. The article by Bruce M. Russett attempts to examine the effect of international communication upon the legislators in Great Britain and the United States. Russett taps the dimension of external inputs by focusing on "various kinds of international transactions . . ." which, he hypothesizes, "contribute to decision-makers' perspectives." Russett's primary emphasis is on "trade in goods and services." Working from a theory of international integration, he mentions the interdependency of today's world. He believes that "trade" or economic exchange between countries could function as a form of international communication— or at least as a mechanism to tie two polities closer together. Moreover, he posits the existence of a linkage between economic interests and political decision:

. . . economic interests may "determine" political decisions or they may merely be used to support those decisions. The question of "priority" is for our purpose irrelevant: interdependence, not determinism, is the concern of the study.

Russett asks three major questions:

(1) whether international contacts make much difference in the way legislators behave, or whether such factors as personality and party loyalty overwhelm international influences, (2) which kinds of contacts are most effective, and (3) whether a legislator with many contacts is likely to behave differently from one who has some personal contacts, but fewer.

Using biographical sources, such as *Who's Who*, for much of his data, Russett discovers that M.P.'s who have ties "of any sort to the United States are more likely to speak up on matters affecting Anglo-American relations than are M.P.'s without ties." Using similar forms of data for United States senators, Russett finds interesting similarities: ". . . a consistent relationship between the possession of personal or economic ties and responsiveness" to Great Britain. For both countries he controls party affiliation which does have quite an effect on the overall relationship. He finds that party affiliation is not, however, so pervasive an influence as to negate the effects of economic and personal ties.

Additional analysis also reveals "some evidence though not enough to be conclusive, that economic ties are more likely to be effective than personal

---

[24] M. Donald Hancock, *The Divergent Evolution of the Two German States.* Paper presented at the Southwestern Political Science Association Meeting, April 3–5, 1969, Rice Hotel, Houston, Texas, p. 4.
[25] *Ibid.*

ones, . . ." and that "the importance of constituency ties in influencing a senator is directly proportional to the weight of the economic interest in the constituency."

We have, therefore, brought into legislative analysis another potentially important source of input stimuli—external inputs. This class of variables has not received much attention from legislative scholars and such oversight needs to be corrected.

In summary, we do not pretend to have identified all classes of input stimuli. We have focused on those that appear most evident to us, and we hasten to add that there are certainly other potential sources of legislative inputs. One could, for example, classify constituency influences as an input. We have done so in the sense that supportive orientations are involved. For the sake of simplicity—and some may have a legitimate quarrel with our conceptualization—we have placed constituency and party influence in the realm of direct stimuli affecting the decision-making process.

The Institutional Nexus

STRUCTURES AND PROCESSES

It is an institutionalized norm that anyone writing on legislatures genuflect in the direction of historical-legal analysis of politics and pay homage to the fact that one is *really* not able to understand the legislative process without rather intimate detailed knowledge of the historical background and structural characteristics of the institution with which he is concerned. Although we do not fully subscribe to this view ourselves, we do believe that the organizational and structural characteristics of legislatures influence the eventual decision-making process. It is for this reason that the article by Lewis A. Froman, Jr. is particularly important. His essay is a partial response to the accusation of some scholars that the field of legislative behavior has produced no body of theory to guide analysis. His aim is to use a specific body of theory as a *post hoc* explanation of "important characteristics of Congress." Obviously, this is a different exercise from using a theory as the basis for research. While such an exercise as this is valuable, it is valuable only if the theory is used to orient future empirical work. We believe that theory should direct research as well as grow out of it.

What is important to note in the Froman article, therefore, is not the thirteen primary characteristics of Congress, but his use of theory to explain them. Froman believes that there are essentially two ways to link empirical findings with "observations" (judgments) about their significance. First, one can talk about consequences of the findings, *i.e.*, what happens because they are true. Second, one may attempt to show *why* the findings are true—what explains them. The first he calls *functional* analysis, the second, *causal* analysis. Froman goes on to state that it is generally accepted that explanation of a given phenomenon must be subsumed under a general law.

Thus, that Congress has a seniority system might be deduced from the following argument: "All organizations with extensive divisions of labor have seniority systems; Congress is an organization with an extensive division of labor; therefore. . . ."

Thus to explain important features of Congress, findings must be subsumed under a set of more general hypotheses. To do this requires that we move away from the view that Congress or other legislatures are totally unique institutions. Our primary need at this time is not for more data but for theory. Froman believes that we have such a theory; for him Congress is an example of a formal organization and can be explained by resorting to organization theory.

In a more descriptive but comparative sense, James L. Payne finds certain structural similarities between the Colombian Congress and the United States Congress. Despite these structural similarities, however, behavioral differences are readily apparent. In Colombia, for example, there is a higher rate of turn-over and little motivation to return; legislators spend less time in committee than do American legislators; rarely do expert witnesses appear; there are no secret (or executive) sessions; the norm of specialization (expertise) is not insti-tutionalized; debates are much more demonstrative than in the United States, and so on. According to Payne, most of these differences are due to the fact that Colombian legislators hold a status incentive whereas American legislators have a program incentive. As a result of their status incentive, Colombian legislators structure their environment to serve their needs. They want

short committee hearings because they are not interested in working out policy; they want floor debates to be interrupted by clamor from the galleries because clamor is what they seek. Congressmen do not have greater technical assistance because they have no use for it. They are not interested in the exhaustive analyses of legislation and its effects.

What emerges, therefore, is a picture of a legislator who is *"indifferent to particular policy outcomes per se."* If program and policy are not important, one's stand on issues can be somewhat flexible. Yet this is not quite true either, for the vote of the Colombian legislator is primarily determined by the faction to which he belongs. Payne thus states that the United States Congress, com-pared to the Colombian Congress, is a model legislature. This is so because in the American Congress certain norms have been institutionalized. The concept of institutionalization, therefore, assumes great importance for comparative analysis.

Nelson W. Polsby notes that the United States House of Representatives is "one of the very few extant examples of a highly specialized political institution which over the long run has succeeded in representing a large number of diverse constituents, and in legitimizing, expressing, and containing political opposition within a complex political system. . . ." Polsby suggests three characteristics of a well institutionalized legislature. First, it is well differentiated from its environ-ment. Second, organization is relatively complex, that is, "there is a division of labor in which roles are specified, and there are widely shared expectations about the performance of roles." Third, there are rules of the game that guide behavior.

After examining operational indicators of each of these characteristics, Polsby concludes that "one of the main long-run changes in the U.S. House of Representatives has been toward greater institutionalization." He then asks three important questions regarding this institutionalization: "What caused it?"

"What follows from it?" and "What can this case tell us about the process in general?" These questions, Polsby emphasizes, are difficult to answer, and any suggested answers are tentative.

What seems important to us is that the United States House of Representatives appears to be more institutionalized, in Polsby's sense of the term, than the Colombian Congress. If the concept is to have any utility, however, additional studies of other countries and of state legislatures are necessary. Polsby suggests that the concept of institutionalization does have utility in that it applies to a "take-off" theory of modernization. Thus, "if one of the stigmata of the take-off to modernity is the rapid development of universalistic, bounded, complex-institutional forms, the data presented here lend this theory some plausibility."

These propositions seem to us to be culture-bound. As utilized in the Polsby article, the concept of modernization takes on a peculiarly Western or American flavor. According to his usage, only those countries whose legislatures approximate the operation of the United States Congress may be classified as wholly modern. Yet there are countries (for example, Iran) where the institutionalization of American legislative norms would not contribute to raising the efficiency of its operation and where in fact these norms would probably not be the result of the cultural patterns of the country. As James A. Bill observes in his essay in this volume, politics in Iran is based on non-associational, personalistic ties. Consequently, to suggest that Iran will reach the apex of modernity when it demonstrates the characteristics of a complex organization is to say no less than that it will probably never be considered modern—at least not politically.[26]

COMMITTEES, NORMS, AND ROLES

From the theoretical viewpoint of this volume, therefore, the seminal article by Richard F. Fenno, Jr. is extremely important. Fenno treats the House Appropriations Committee as a political sub-system. Much of what we have said thus far about legislatures in general applies to these sub-strata. Fenno focuses on the "problem of self-integration," which he suggests is a need of any social system if it is to maintain itself. Integration is important because "differentiation among subgroups and among individual positions . . ." might lead to fissiparous tendencies toward disintegration. "Committee integration is defined as the degree to which there is a working together or a meshing together or mutual support among its roles and sub-groups." Fenno's findings are quite clear; what is most interesting is the hypothesis that the development of consensus and norms on the committee contribute greatly to its integration. Thus Fenno notes a similar finding to Polsby's, only he calls it integration whereas Polsby calls it institutionalization. Or can one say that one indicator of a well institutionalized legislative body is the degree of integration found within its key committees?

Weston H. Agor raises a similar question, although his foci are broader than Fenno's. Agor hypothesizes that standing committees and informal norms "contribute to the integration of the total Chilean political system." Because he

[26] On the informal nature of politics in at least one system see James A. Bill, *The Plasticity of Informal Politics: The Case of Iran.* Paper presented at the Conference on the Structure of Power in Islamid Iran, University of California, Los Angeles, June 26–28, 1969.

adopts Fenno's definition, he and Fenno are theoretically talking about the same phenomena. Agor records a number of interesting findings. In the Chilean Senate interaction within standing committees seems to encourage decreasing partisanship and an increasing tendency toward solutions proceeding toward a common goal. The resemblance between this and Fenno's earlier comments is striking. Agor notes that the norm of expertise is important. Again we have a similarity between the United States and Chile. A number of observers have commented on the role of expertise in the American Senate, but Polsby observes that an increasing division of labor accompanied by norms is an indicator of institutionalization. Is it possible that the Chilean Senate is as well institutionalized a legislative body as the United States Senate and House?

Agor points out additional norms that the Chilean and United States Senates have in common:

1. Senatorial courtesy.
2. Reciprocity.
3. Institutional loyalty.
4. Legislative work.
5. Specialization.
6. Apprenticeship.

The interesting question raised by all the similarities which have been listed is: How do they fit into theories of modernization? Can one maintain, for example, that the United States is the most developed (*i.e.*, the most modern) nation in political terms, when one has just observed the existence of an equally integrated-institutionalized legislative body elsewhere? In other words, what can one use as valid and reliable indicators of political modernity?

Agor concludes by noting the existence of sanctions for violation of norms which may range "from ruling the offending Senator out of order to the extreme of withdrawing his right to speak on the floor for a given period of time." Similar sanctions operate in the United States Senate. Wayne R. Swanson observes that "those liberal Democrats . . . who find it difficult to conform to Senate folkways are frequently passed over when major committee assignments are allocated." Allan Kornberg reports that Canadian legislators perceive the existence of these rules in their Parliament but do not perceive the accompanying sanctions.

The pervasive nature of these phenomena seem to substantiate the discussions of Froman and Polsby. Froman notes the existence of norms as a characteristic of organizations in general, whereas Polsby includes them as an important variable in his conceptualization of institutionalization. This leads us to the not so obvious conclusion that legislatures provide an excellent example of complex organizations. Organization theory should indeed prove a valuable asset in legislative analysis. Certainly Froman's discussion can be extrapolated to other systems—as can Polsby's. The theoretical implications of the above cannot be overlooked in future analyses.

We have just seen that norms probably exist within every legislative body. The same may be said of roles. That legislators associate expectations with their position probably leads to the existence of role perceptions of one type or another in all legislative bodies.[27] If the role concept is to have relevance beyond its descriptive utility, however, it is necessary to demonstrate that the individual's role perception in some way influences his behavior pattern. This has not been done. The two articles on this subject presented in this volume are merely illustrative of the descriptive use of the concept. Further confirmation of its behavioral implications remains a challenge to the legislative scholar.

LEADERSHIP

As is true with roles, we operate under the assumption that all institutional factors we identify contribute in some way to behavioral outcomes. Leadership certainly fits this category. Along with the concept of power, leadership phenomena have a long history in political analyses. Yet numerous questions remain. What are the psychological characteristics of leaders? How do different leadership types emerge? Does leadership affect output? How? The two articles on leadership presented here are introductory statements; neither provides any definitive answers to such questions. Yet each contributes somewhat to a resolution of the riddle.

Heinz Eulau comes closest to examining a psychological theory of leadership. He hypothesizes that the leaders' authority "rests on bases other than their formal position alone." Comparing leaders with rank and file members in four American states, he finds that legislative leaders are perceived in terms of "three criteria—respect, affection, and expertise." Thus the attribution of these three values is central to perception of an individual as a leader.

Because legislative leaders are usually party leaders as well, Ingvar Amilon's presentation provides an interesting comparison. In the case of Sweden, as Amilon points out, collaboration among party leaders has been highly institutionalized in the form of various kinds of leadership conferences. Such conferences serve to engender political cohesion and hence mitigate potentially divisive effects of a multi-party system.

EXECUTIVE-LEGISLATIVE RELATIONS

In most legislative institutions the executive is an important extra-parliamentary source of leadership. The three articles presented here note some relevant comparative aspects of executive-legislative relationships. Focusing on a comparison between Presidents John F. Kennedy and Lyndon B. Johnson, Joseph Cooper and Gary Bombardier point out that Johnson was more successful in pushing his legislative program through Congress than was John Kennedy. They observe, however, that "the critical variable in Johnson's success was the increase in the number of Democrats in general and Northern Democrats in particular." Thus Johnson could maintain the same basic level of support as Kennedy and could win victories that were denied Kennedy. In other words,

---

[27] For two accounts of role perceptions in two additional systems see Arthur B. Gunlicks, "Representative Role Perceptions Among Local Councillors in Western Germany," *Journal of Politics* 31 (May 1969): 443–64; and William H. Hunt, *Legislative Roles and Ideological Orientations of French Deputies.* Paper presented at the Sixty-Fifth Annual Meeting of The American Political Science Association, Commodore Hotel, New York City, September 2–6, 1969.

Johnson owes his success to Barry Goldwater and the ineptitude of the Republican Party at that time. Numerical support is therefore an important condition of executive efficacy in the American system. The executive is consequently tied intimately to the legislature. Karl Dietrich Bracher, on the other hand, finds that the European trend, developing since World War II, is away from legislative influence, whereas James A. Bill describes the general irrelevance and subservience of a legislature to the executive in a non-Western legislative monarchy.

The entire thrust of this section, The Institutional Nexus, has been to examine the organizational and structural features of the legislative institution to determine their relation to the decision-making process. In the final section, Legislative Decision Making, in which we concentrate on the decision-making process, we have chosen to omit a sampling of the rich and sophisticated literature on roll-call behavior. Instead, we have concentrated on party and constituency influences on the decision-making process. For a number of reasons we have also chosen not to examine the societal implications of legislative output. First, the literature exemplified by Dye and the like places undue emphasis, in our opinion, on aggregate data and is riddled with questionable statistical and methodological assumptions.[28] Second, the existing literature concentrates on the American experience; questions regarding the effect of reapportionment and so forth on policy making clearly are not relevant to many other systems. Finally, this omission is consistent with our view of legislatures as sub-systems. We simply stopped with the decisions made within the artificial boundary we have created. Although we view societal implications as important, we leave them to other scholars.

Legislative Decision-Making

The last element of the legislative subsystem that we wish to examine in this reader is the conversion or decision-making process.

PARTY AND CONSTITUENCY INFLUENCES

Hugh L. LeBlanc attempts to extend the discussion initiated by Miller and Stokes which is carried further by Cnudde and McCrone.[29] Examining the effects of party and constituency in twenty-six state senates he finds that party affiliation is clearly related in "varying degrees" to legislative voting behavior in most of the states he examined. He also observes that party is a much more salient predictive variable in the more highly industrialized states of the East and Midwest and was more manifest on issues of "legislative organization and election administration." Constituency influences were likewise most important and were related to party in the most partisan states where "senate-constituency relations . . . reflected the national image of the Democratic party as the party

---

[28] On this matter see Edward R. Tufte, "Improving Data Analysis in Political Science," *World Politics* 21, (July 1969): 641–54.

[29] Warren E. Miller and Donald E. Stokes, "Constituency Influence in Congress," *The American Political Science Review* 57 (1966): 45–56; and Charles F. Cnudde and Donald J. McCrone, "The Linkage Between Constituency Attitudes and Congressional Voting Behavior: A Causal Model," *American Political Science Review* 60 (1966): 66–72.

supported in constituencies of racial and ethnic minorities, the low income, and the poorly educated rather than in constituencies of high income and superior education." In the least partisan states the relation between constituency variables and voting were "more limited and more ambiguous. . . ."

It is important, in our opinion, to keep in mind that LeBlanc's "constituency variables" are aggregate demographic characteristics of the constituency rather than attitudes as measured by exposure to interviews such as used by Miller and Stokes. Consequently, further analysis of the patterns uncovered awaits the large-scale use of interviews on well drawn state samples. State and federal comparisons of party and constituency influences within the geographic boundaries of the United States has not proceeded to a very advanced level. Needless to say, one could draw the same conclusion regarding cross-national analysis of these questions. Thus, George L. Rueckert and Wilder Crane examine only the party dimension. They describe the high degree of cohesion evidenced in the Christian Democratic Union in Germany and find that this cohesion is beginning to break down somewhat. Hence they concentrate on explaining the "deviance." They find that loyalty to the CDU is much greater among upper level party leaders, professional politicians, and businessmen. There is, consequently, little basis upon which to make comparative assessments. Surely this area warrants greater attention from legislative scholars.

MAJORITY-MINORITY RELATIONS

One additional aspect relating to party affiliation, which should be a salient influence upon decision making in legislatures with two or more parties, is the nature of majority versus opposition. David M. Wood, using Guttman scale analysis on the French National Assembly for the years 1956 to 1965, asks "whether or not the apparent trend toward a simplified majority-opposition confrontation in French politics has been evident over the last decade. . . ." Wood finds the beginnings of "real opposition" in 1962 at the conclusion of the Algerian War. Although an effective opposition is a relatively new phenomenon in France, United States legislatures have been confronted with it for some time. As Charles O. Jones observes: "There has usually been an identifiable minority party in Congress. Though it does not always oppose the majority, and cannot be expected to be synonymous with the opposition very often, it does persist." Jones is much more concerned with questions of strategy than is Wood, whose primary task was to substantiate the existence of opposition in France. Jones examines two basic questions: "What are the principal policy making strategies of the minority party? What political conditions determine the range of strategies available to it in any one Congress?" He finds that the minority party's role is not consistent over time but varies according to "external conditions (temper of the times, minority party unity, and presidential power) and internal conditions (procedure, the margin, majority party leadership and organization, and minority party leadership and organization). . . ."

Thus the two articles are not asking comparable questions. Nor do we have much to go on. Legislative systems in different stages of modernization do not have equally well developed or well institutionalized opposition parties. An obvious example is noted by James A. Bill. Besides the fact that there is not an effective opposition party in the Iranian Majlis, political opposition tends to be fundamentally expressed only outside the Majlis. There is also evidence to suggest that in the Iranian legislature the majority-opposition issue is best understood in terms of factions and personal cliques and *not* in terms of parties at all. Thus the discovery of differing patterns of legislative opposition is a significant and fascinating question.

We are, unfortunately, forced to conclude on the same note with which we began. Throughout this essay we have lamented the lack of systematic cross-national legislative research. If it fulfills no other function, this volume will hopefully serve as a catalyst to stimulate the type of inquiry now so sadly lacking.

Notes for a Theory of
Legislative Behavior:
The Conceptual Scheme

by RODERICK BELL

In this essay I shall attempt to lay the groundwork for a theory of legislative behavior—a not inconsiderable chore. To make all of my arguments lucid and persuasive would require a book, not a short essay—hence the title, "Notes." If this essay has any value, therefore, it is probably not so much the substantive theory that is presented as the demonstration of the process of theory construction.[1]

It becomes increasingly clear to me that one of the regrettable costs of the "behavioral revolution" in political science has been the temporary eclipse of a rich tradition in the literature of political theory, namely, a concern with the nature of politics. An immediate consequence of that eclipse is that when we try to explain "legislative" behavior we confront the difficulty of not having adequate ideas about precisely what behavior is to be explained. To put the matter in a trite way: What would a man from Mars see when he looked at the United States Congress? Perhaps the business of pressing buttons to record votes would appear inconsequential, whereas the stately march to the bathroom by some member would seem of paramount importance (indeed, the member in question might agree).

---

[1] I do, however, regard the substantive theory to be finally more important. But it will require more work and research and, no doubt, modification than the present format permits.

At first glance, it may seem that I am inventing an absurd problem: Surely we know what we want to explain, at least roughly, and we know what politics is, more or less. But it is important to remember that in the early history of the natural sciences it was by no means obvious to great minds how to explain the motion of objects (falling bodies and the like), for example, and that was partly because it was unclear as to *what properties of the objects in question were relevant to the explanation.* "Common sense" did not make it immediately obvious that the *size* of the object was theoretically irrelevant, for the contrary appeared to be the case. In modern political science we face analogous difficulties. Indeed, the question whether politics is a special form of behavior which requires its own theory for explanation, or merely an epiphenomenon—a by-product of more basic, universal theories—remains unanswered. My own thinking on the matter convinces me that "politics," properly understood, is a basic phenomenon of human behavior.

Politics is basic, but legislatures are not. That is, we will surely be on the wrong track if we tie our theory to legislatures as such; it is easy to imagine a society without legislatures. On the other hand, I cannot imagine a "non-social system"—I cannot imagine the absence of any social patterns among men, or the absence of any discernible regularities in the relationships between them. Therefore, I intend to treat legislatures as collections of individuals characterized by discernible patterns of relationships—as organizations, if you like. My task will be to suggest systematic connections between some features of these patterns and some forms of individual behavior. Moreover, I shall attempt to indicate what forms of behavior are specifically *political* and how political behavior is a function of the individual/system relationships which I analyze.

Although the bulk of this essay is devoted to the articulation of a conceptual scheme for a theory of legislative behavior, I have digressed occasionally to remark upon methodological issues—issues *about* theory rather than *of* theory—where it seemed to me that one's methodological position would affect the theoretical argument. Unfortunately, at the theory-construction phase one's methodology seems everywhere relevant, even determinate, so I begin with some remarks about theory.

Theory and Legislative Behavior

A theory states what is relevant and the nature of that relevance. That is, theory informs our observations of "reality." There is no need to wonder whether the world is really "out there"—the point is that the special reality that we apprehend affects and is affected by our theory, and we should be self-conscious about this fact. For example, if we persist in thinking of Congress (and the state legislatures as well) as a place where the popular will is somehow transformed into the appropriate laws, we will, I believe, continue to ignore more important factors for the explanation of legislative behavior. As political scientists, we are interested in legislators precisely because they make laws in our political system; as American political scientists, we retain a traditional interest in the question: To what extent is the law-making process in America a democratic one? It appears that such a question misleads us in much the same way that similar questions about the citizen have misled students of voting. Although it becomes increasingly clear that voters do not measure up to an idealized picture of the rational man who votes in his enlightened self-interest, we nevertheless find it difficult to try to explain the voter's behavior in terms *other* than those suggested by democratic theory.[2] Likewise, although it becomes increasingly clear that legislators do not regularly offer themselves up for a thumbs-ups or -down decision by the public, we still find it difficult to avoid asking more questions about "linkages," roles as interpreted in mandate and Burkean theories of representation, and so on. Although I regard such questions as important, in this essay I shall experiment with the tactic of avoiding altogether those "democratic-type" questions, concentrating instead upon the organizational norms of the system with which a legislator may be presumed to identify.

A theory states what is relevant and it affords us some explanation for particular objects or events that we can observe. Powerful theories explain in a particular way: They allow us to *deduce* the thing to be explained or (depending upon our temporal stance *vis-à-vis* the thing to be deduced) predicted. (We should be aware, however, that deduction may not be the goal or useful function of a particular theory. If that is the case, convention would seem to place the burden of proving its usefulness upon the methodologist.) In any event, a theory asserts systematic relations among stated concepts; it does not do more than that.

It is surprising to find the continuing mistaken belief that a really adequate theory would explain and predict everything about the legislative process in which we, as informed observers, might be interested. But we need only remind ourselves that meteorologists have at their disposal very powerful, well tested theories that would, in principle, explain the "weather"; needless to say, meteorologists are not famous for their stunningly accurate predictions. I venture to suppose that confounding factors will wreak no less havoc with any attempts to predict specific behaviors in, say, legislatures, even if we are one day successful in our attempts to develop adequate theories of political behavior.

In my view, then, a theory performs the important cognitive functions of orienting our view of reality (by specifying the nature of reality) and explaining events in the world. It cannot subsume every conceivable observation, however, though any theory of legislative behavior should have non-obvious entailments. Moreover, there should be some theory-specific notion of "political." There is very little reason for us to discuss "legislative behavior theory" if our theories are politically relevant only in the sense that legislatures are "political" mechanisms. We should also be trying to explain the *politics* of the legislative process.

---

[2] Although political scientists and sociologists have struggled to find a way to avoid calling the voters stupid, an economist has shown that models positing rational behavior in the collective interests of large groups of people may be inherently unrealistic. See Mancur Olson, Jr., *The Logic of Collective Action: Public Goods and the Theory of Groups* (New York: Schocken Books, 1968; Harvard University Press, 1965).

Elements of a Theory

Without pretending fully to explicate them here, it may be useful to mention certain strengths and weaknesses of three contemporary approaches to legislative behavior theory. Rational decision-making theories, organization theory, and role theory have been invoked as useful approaches to the study of legislative behavior. Do these theories do what we expect of them?

Bearing in mind that a theory does, among other things, shape our perceptions of the world of experience by specifying relevant observations, we note that theories of rational decision making focus upon choice making as a specific kind of cognitive process. The theoretically relevant thing an individual does is to make decisions, the nature of which can be predicted in a model that operates according to specified rules.

An approach that isolates decision making in a deductive system has the advantage of calling our attention to relevant individual behavior; the disadvantage of such an approach, however, lies in the fact that it often requires assumptions about the cognitive processes of individuals that are probably unrealistic in many situations, as I shall argue later.

Organization theory, although not yet a coherent, confirmed body of systematically related empirical generalizations, is concerned to describe and analyze generic social processes as they are modified by distinctive structural arrangements.[3] Its advantage for the study of legislative behavior inheres in this fact, for it has been argued—convincingly, I find—that congressional behavior has been modified by the increasingly formalized organizational arrangements of that institution.[4] However, even though it is not necessary to do so, investigators are often led by this approach to concentrate upon variables that are not specifically individualistic, thereby losing the advantage of the decision-making approach.

A third approach, role theory, has the advantage of calling our attention to the "relativity problem" implicit in the differences between the first two approaches. That is, recurring problems and bits of evidence suggest that political phenomena of interest take on different aspects depending upon the perspective from which they are viewed. Individual behavior affects and is affected by the social system: Should the phenomenon be regarded as individual behavior (in a relevant environment) or as a feature of the system?[5] Role theory, of course, makes this ambivalence its *raison d'etre*, defining as it does aspects of individual behavior in terms of structurally determined roles. That strong

[3] W. Richard Scott, "Theory of Organizations," in Robert E. L. Farris (ed.), *Handbook of Modern Sociology* (Chicago: Rand McNally and Co., 1964), p. 486.

[4] See, for example, Nelson W. Polsby, "The Institutionalization of the U.S. House of Representatives," *The American Political Science Review*, 62 (March 1968): 144–68; and Lewis A. Froman, Jr., "Organization Theory and the Explanation of Important Characteristics of Congress," *The American Political Science Review* 62 (June 1968): 518–25.

[5] For an interesting discussion and attempted solution to the theoretical problems posed by this perspective problem, see William A. Gamson, *Power and Discontent* (Homewood, Ill.: The *Dorsey Press*, 1968).

advantage seems to be qualified, however, by the non-systematic character of role theory. Typically, role theory describes in a way that seems appropriate, but it is usually not easy to wring deductions of any kind from the descriptive statements. It seems to me that an integration of the advantages of these approaches could be effected by employing a concept of the "self."

A self-concept will be useful in legislative behavior theory for much the same reasons that it is useful to explain motivational behavior as well as many psychological processes. As Shoben points out, "the postulation of self-involvement seems necessary to account for the pursuit of long range goals so typical to human motivation."[6] Self is the product of interaction with the individual's physical and social environment, and is thus developmental and suceptible of change. This process begins in infancy, during which the individual differentiates his body from its surroundings; presently, a complex conceptual system is developed including evaluative categories with associated traits or attributes.[7] The attitudes that compose the self system include, therefore, "the individual's cherished commitments, stands on particular issues, acceptances, rejections, reciprocal expectations (roles) in interpersonal and group relations, identifications with persons or values, and personal goals for the future."[8] These components of the self enter into ongoing psychological processes, resulting in self- or, as it is usually said, ego-involved activity.

The great theoretical advantage of a self concept in the study of legislative behavior becomes clearer when we posit relations between the self and the system. In reply to the question, "Who am I?" individuals ordinarily exhaust social classifications before resorting to idiosyncratic responses. As Sharif points out, "the psychological import of this rather prosaic finding is vast: Each social category . . . [specifies] . . . a self-image whether the individual actually belongs to that category or not."[9] In other words, knowing a good deal about the character of the reference group(s) of an individual tells us much about the self-radius of that individual which, as we shall see, helps to explain his behavior.

Political and social scientists have been talking about "systems" for some time now, and one might suppose that there would be no need to say very much more about the nature of the beast. However, I think that there is a great deal more that needs to be said; here I shall concern myself with the link between the individual and the system. I define a social system as a *set of shared values conducive to action*. Now, political scientists have tended to concentrate their attention upon political systems as concrete entities, hoping thereby to discover the general laws that would explain relations between the parts of the system. I should make it plain that I regard such endeavors as worthwhile; still, we should keep in mind the kinds of concerns that Weber and Parsons have struggled with. When Weber tried to explicate the "bases of legitimacy" which undergird particular types of social organization he was, it would appear, saying

---

[6] Edward J. Shoben, Jr., "Behavioral Aspects of the Self," New York Academy of Sciences, *Annals* 96 (1962): 771.

[7] Muzafer Sherif, "Self Concept," *International Encyclopedia of the Social Sciences* (New York: Macmillan and The Free Press, 1968), vol. 14, p. 153.

[8] *Ibid.*

[9] *Ibid.*, p. 156.

something about the *value system that is conducive to the concrete articulation of a specific type of social organization.* And Mitchell points out that a major task of Parsonian sociology is to discover "how men define their situations, their beliefs, values, norms, motivations, and roles. . . ."[10] The value-component of systems is vital to our understanding of them because it is precisely the internalization of certain shared values by individuals that allows the system to "work." In a sense, every individual has a "system" (or probably several systems) writ small in his consciousness; when aggregates of individuals share a particular set of values of appropriate kinds, one necessary (if not sufficient) condition for the development of a concretized social system is present.[11]

Clearly, as I have admitted above, it is important and worthwhile to study the actual workings of organizations, institutions, and systems. For even as individuals are notoriously capable of attempting to hold contradictory values, so does the institutionalization of norms and goals produce quite unintended or unanticipated results. But surely it is important as well to incorporate an explanation of the mechanisms by which the individual identifies with the system, for it is not at all clear that the "system" has any concrete reality save in terms of the human activity that describes it.

We have seen that individuals' self-attitudes are ordinarily connected to reference groups. An individual appraises himself and others according to norms and standards of the reference group; the reference group itself is subject to appraisal in terms of its relative status in the social organization. It is difficult to overemphasize the importance of such reference sets for the individual, because it is an anchored set of self-attitudes that exerts a stabilizing effect upon performance. It is important to our theoretical argument here to note that the self concept figures as an important determinant of individual behavior, and that self is defined partially in terms of reference groups or sets.[12] Not only does a reference group provide a set of values and norms—a miniature "system"—to which the individual relates, but the reference groups themselves are differentially valued in the larger social system according to the set of values characteristic of that larger system. Thus, as Sherif points out, "the concepts of self as a constellation of attitudes linked with identifiable reference groups and sets provide tools for integrating behavioral (individual) and sociocultural levels of analysis."[13]

To this point in the essay it has not been necessary to speculate beyond the boundaries of already established disciplines (although, obviously, I have taken

---

[10] William C. Mitchell, *Sociological Analysis and Politics: The Theories of Talcott Parsons* (Englewood Cliffs, N.J.: Prentice-Hall, Inc., 1967), p. 9.

[11] Much of the literature on institutions supports this idea; when political scientists talk about the "rules of the game," it seems to me that we are talking about this aspect of social or political systems.

[12] As Rosenberg points out, "our attitudes toward ourselves are very importantly influenced by the responses of others toward us." Morris Rosenberg, *Society and the Adolescent Self-Image* (Princeton: Princeton University Press, 1965). p. 13. But where do those "other" responses come from? "*The process whereby expectations of other individuals are stabilized inevitably involves placement of those individuals in terms of some social scheme or categories.*" Muzafer Sherif and Carolyn W. Sherif, *Reference Groups: Exploration into Conformity and Deviation of Adolescents* (New York: Harper and Row, 1964), p. 73.

[13] Sherif, "Self Concept," p. 156.

the liberty of drawing upon disciplines other than political science). But it is time to argue for systemic connections between specific concepts, and here the evidence is scattered at best. It seems reasonable to hypothesize that the roles that legislators play will be influenced strongly, if not determined, by the extent to which the individual's self-identity is absorbed within the organizational pattern and values of the legislative system. *Ceteris paribus,* extent of identity absorbtion will vary under the influence of two factors: personality characteristics, on the one hand, and system characteristics on the other. An important simplifying assumption, which is in any case a well documented phenomenon, is that self-attitudes are resistant to change in most circumstances. To disturb or change self-attitudes amounts to changing self-identity, "the epicenter of experienced personal stability, even though it may not be an integrated harmonious structure";[14] severe anxiety and pain can accompany such changes.[15]

In order to suggest hypotheses about relations between psychological and systemic variables, and to illustrate the behavioral consequences of those putative relations, we will have to begin with highly simplified conceptual categories. One concept should be systemic—that is, it should name a property of the social or organizational environment, for reasons that I trust are explicit above. Now, as Weber has convincingly argued, different concrete organizational systems will accompany different value systems (bases of legitimacy); here we are concerned to name (refer to) the *degree of institutionalization* of the organizational system. In the United States, we are referring to the degree of institutionalization in a rational-legal system: So long as we limit our analysis to similar legitimacy systems, we can temporarily ignore Weber's other categories.

A second concept should refer to a property of the individual in terms of the systemic concept—*i.e.,* it should be a relational concept. I propose here to refer to the individual's *position in the hierarchy* of the system, recognizing even so that the notion of "position in the hierarchy" drastically oversimplifies the phenomenon I have in mind, and that for two reasons: (1) It is not easy to rank individuals in an organization or social system by intersubjective, operational standards, and (2) in any case, I think that the *organizational specificity* of the individual's function or role is as important for the theoretical argument as his hierarchical rank. For the present, I am in effect making the simplifying assumption that organizational specificity of role increases as hierarchical rank is raised.[16]

Polsby suggests indicators for measuring the degree of institutionalization of

---

[14] *Ibid.,* p. 158.

[15] Perhaps it would lead us too far afield to develop this point in depth; nevertheless, I should like to stress it, for the later arguments about the nature of politicization depend in part upon the acceptance of this premise. Sherif and Cantril point out that "if an individual has identified himself, made part of himself, certain social values which are suddenly and completely upset or destroyed, . . . then that portion of the ego composed of those values may itself be destroyed. . . ." Muzafer Sherif and Hadley Cantril, *The Psychology of Ego-Involvements: Social Attitudes and Identifications* (New York: John Wiley and Sons, 1947), p. 393. The authors go on to analyze the case of one man who "killed himself rather than live on as essentially another person." *Ibid.,* p. 339.

[16] Of course this assumption is not accurate. An individual whose role is that of mechanic probably would be fairly low in an organizational hierarchy; but his function might be to tend a specialized piece of machinery not found in most other organizations, in which case his role would be organization-specific. Nevertheless, considerations of simplicity aside, I suppose that the role of typist transfers from one to another organization more readily than that of, say, sales manager.

the House of Representatives;[17] on that or a similar basis we might classify a given legislative body as "high" or "low" on an institutionalization dimension. If we are willing to accept the simplifying assumption just mentioned, it should be relatively easy to devise some measure of position in organizational hierarchy for any individual so that the individual could be classified "high" or "low" within the organizational structure. Thus a 2 × 2 table of property spaces[18] describing probable role orientations is effected (see Figure 1).

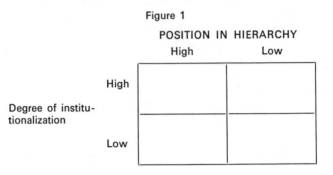

Figure 1

POSITION IN HIERARCHY

Earlier, I indicated that it would be theoretically useful as well as empirically well justified to make the simplifying assumption that self-attitudes are resistant to change in most circumstances. Clearly, then, it will not do to expect the factors specified in Figure 1 wholly to determine role orientations, for individuals' positions in hierarchies and their institutional environment may change rather quickly. Indeed, it seems useful to incorporate into the conceptual scheme some recognition of the fact that different personality types rely in quite different degrees upon reference groups for stable self-anchors. In other words, one sort of individual might well react quite differently from another in the event of a change in his hierarchical position; however, it is precarious to try to generalize about what seems on its face to be idiosyncratic personal characteristics.

In order to proceed with my main arguments, I should like to avoid grappling with all the issues involved here. I propose to adopt a kind of shorthand suggested by David Riesman in his book, *The Lonely Crowd*. For our purposes, his distinction between the inner-directed and other-directed personality seems particularly useful:

What is common to all the other-directed people is that their contemporaries are the source of direction for the individual—either those known to him or those with whom he is indirectly acquainted. . . . This source is . . . "internalized" in the sense that

---

17 Polsby, "Institutionalization of U.S. House of Representatives."

18 The term "property space" only makes explicit what the researcher employing role concepts must assume, namely, that "the property is defined in the conceptual model as complex and multidimensional, and that the measurement scheme for translating such a property into empirical operations must also be multidimensional." Matilda White Riley, *Sociological Research: A Case Approach, I* (New York: Harcourt, Brace and World, 1963), p. 344. (For a general discussion of property spaces, see *ibid.*, pp. 343–48).

dependence on it for guidance in life *is implanted early.* The goals . . . shift with that guidance: it is only the process of striving itself and the process of paying close attention to the signals from others that remain unaltered throughout life.[19]

Without concerning ourselves with Riesman's characterization of modern man in America, we can make use of the categories he develops. In this way we can partially deal with the likely differential among individuals in their propensity to identify with contemporary reference groups. Hence the augmented table of Figure 2.

Figure 2

| Personality Type | | POSITION IN HIERARCHY | |
		High	Low
Inner-Directed	Degree of Institution-alization	High	
		Low	
Other-Directed	Degree of Institution-alization	High	
		Low	

A table of this sort is a simple conceptual scheme. It specifies three concepts whose meanings are to be established (agreed upon) prior to their introduction into a theory. But the choice of variables influences the empirical findings; at the same time, one's pre-theoretical understanding of the phenomena in question influences his selection of variables. The first step toward escaping from this particular squirrel cage is to formulate tentative hypotheses which are susceptible of disconfirmation on the basis of observation.

The Individual in the System

If we begin with the variable, "degree of institutionalization," two problems confront us: First, we will require some operational indicators for the concept; second, we will need to suggest the status of the variable in a putative axiomatic system. (I will not attempt to construct an axiomatic system here; nevertheless, it will be helpful if we can suggest the probable form a full-fledged theory would take. This at least entails an indication as to which variables should be regarded as causally prior.) With regard to the first problem, Nelson Polsby has confronted the "theoretical riches" pertaining to institutionalization. He seems to have survived the ordeal, for he elaborates skillfully three measures of degree of institutionalization: (1) the establishment of boundaries, (2) the growth of

[19] David Riesman, with Nathan Glazer and Reuel Denny, *The Lonely Crowd: A Study of the Changing American Character* (Garden City, N.Y.: Doubleday-Anchor (abridged), 1956), p. 37. (My emphasis.)

internal complexity and (3) the extent of universalistic and automated decision making.[20] Polsby was concerned to demonstrate that the United States House of Representatives has, during its history, moved toward greater institutionalization,[21] but I think one could adapt his measures to a research design for comparing, say, state legislatures in terms of degree of institutionalization.

There exists a fairly sound basis for constructing a research design to measure the degree of institutionalization of legislatures and to test hypotheses which assert determinative relations between the social environment and the degree of institutionalization of those organizations. Both Polsby and Lewis Froman provide arguments and evidence to suggest that relevant organizational characteristics are the product of the social setting—the environment—of the organization.[22] This is important to our argument here, for it allows us to treat as exogenous to the theory those factors affecting one of our three variables, degree of institutionalization. Now the problem becomes that of integrating individual-level of analysis with this system-level analysis.

Richard Scott argues that reference group theory, being relatively undeveloped, encourages *post hoc* interpretations of individual behavior in organizations: "Since there are virtually no constraints on the use of the concept, the investigator can freely select from among the many membership groups the ones that seem most plausible in accounting for the behavior."[23] Scott goes on to say that reference group concepts seem more defensible when a limited number of salient reference groups are specified in advance.[24] I think Scott may misconceive the nature of scientific theory, but in any case it is possible to meet his objection here. It is an easy matter to limit the salient reference groups; in a differentiated organization, we shall consider hierarchical levels of personnel to comprise salient reference groups. In less differentiated organizations, informal factions are likely surrogates. However, in my opinion, it is not the problem of unlimited reference groups that hampers the explanatory power of reference group theory in organizations studies, but the fact that *the mechanisms of attachment to reference sets* are not made explicit. Cognitive dissonance theory is an obvious solution to this problem.

Elliot Aronson describes the core notion of dissonance theory as follows: "Dissonance is a negative drive state which occurs whenever an individual simultaneously holds two cognitions (ideas, beliefs, opinions) which are psychologically inconsistent."[25] Thus, since dissonance is an unpleasant state, the individual attempts to reduce it by adding consonant cognitions or by changing one or both cognitions so that they are consonant with one another. Now, one advantage to dissonance theory is that it has generated a great amount of experimental research, enabling us therefore to speculate with somewhat more

---

[20] Polsby, "Institutionalization of U.S. House of Representatives." The three measures are discussed in order: (1), p. 145ff., (2), p. 152ff., and (3), p. 160ff.

[21] *Ibid.*, p. 164.

[22] Polsby in *ibid.*, and Froman, "Organization Theory."

[23] Scott, "Theory of Organizations," p. 517.

[24] *Ibid.*

[25] Elliot Aronson, "Dissonance Theory: Progress and Problems," multilith manuscript (Austin: The University of Texas, 1966), p. 2.

confidence about its applicability within our conceptual scheme. The results of many of these experiments suggest that it may be more realistic to view man not as a *rational* animal, but as a rational*izing* animal—that is, "he attempts to appear rational, both to others and to himself."[26] However, much controversy about the utility of dissonance theory has been generated, owing largely to a major disadvantage in its use. Festinger said that two cognitions are dissonant if, considering these two cognitions alone, the obverse of one follows from the other.[27] But what does "follows from" mean? As Aronson shows, it is by no means clear in some circumstances whether dissonance *will* occur for an individual, since dissonance apparently results not only from logical inconsistencies based in cultural mores, hierarchies of values, and empirical or experiential beliefs.[28] Aronson's solution of the conceptual difficulties thus posed dovetails with the integrating concept in this essay: "If dissonance exists, it is because the individual's behavior is inconsistent with his self-concept."[29]

If we begin with the assumption (as most experiments on dissonance theory implicitly have done) that individuals generally will have a positive self-conception,[30] then experimental findings suggest a line of reasoning about self-attitudes and hierarchical position. On the reasoning that if people undergo a great deal of trouble to gain admission to a group, they will experience dissonance if the group turns out to be disappointing, experiments have been conducted which confirm the hypothesis that the greater the effort expended to gain admission to a group, the more likely the individual will hold positive attitudes about the group.[31] That is because one way of reducing the dissonance which occurs when an individual feels he has expended great effort toward a worthless goal is to decide that the goal is, in fact, worthwhile; then there is no inconsistency in cognitions. In the case of legislators, we can hypothesize that greater institutionalization results in greater restrictions on hierarchical mobility; greater restrictions on mobility entail greater effort by individuals to ascend the hierarchy. The higher one's position, the greater he values the institution, its norms and its goals.[32] In other words, over time, the individual increasingly defines "himself" in terms of the organization; his identity is given in terms of his

---

[26] *Ibid.*, p. 3.

[27] Leon Festinger, *A Theory of Cognitive Dissonance* (Evanston, Ill.: Row, Peterson), 1957.

[28] Aronson, "Dissonance Theory," pp. 7, 8.

[29] *Ibid.*, p. 34.

[30] More precisely, we assume that individuals *prefer* positive self-attitudes to negative ones, in which case dissonance theory yields satisfactory conclusions. That seems to be a safe assumption: "It can hardly be disputed that, as a rule, people would prefer to have a favorable opinion of themselves rather than an unfavorable opinion." Rosenberg, *Society and the Adolescent Self-Image*, p. 9.

[31] See, *e.g.*, the following experiments that support the hypothesis: Aronson, E., "The effect of effort on the attractiveness of rewarded and unrewarded stimuli," *Journal of Abnormal ana Social Psychology* 63 (1961): 375–80; Aronson, E. and Mills, J., "The effect of severity of initiation on liking for a group," *Journal of Abnormal and Social Psychology* 59 (1959): 177–81; Lewis, M., "Some nondecremental effects of effort," *Journal of Comparative and Physiological Psychology* 57 (1964): 367–72; Zimbardo, P. G., "The effect of effort and improvisation on self-persuasion produced by role-playing," *Journal of Experimental Social Psychology* 1 (1965): 103–20.

[32] Cf. Richard Fenno's observation that the stern apprenticeship undergone by junior members of the House Appropriations Committee seems to produce greater loyalty and positive perceptions of the group on the part of successful "initiates"; Richard F. Fenno, Jr., "The House Appropriations Committee as a Political System: The Problem of Integration," *American Political Science Review* 56 (June 1962): 310–24.

organizational position. As will be seen, this hypothesis provides a basis for predicting the politicization of individual legislators.

There is one sense in which we have been discussing the socialization of individuals to membership in an organization, specifically into a legislature. But I feel that it is important to stress not "socialization" (a term which, in any case, seems to be used interchangeably with "learning" and is, therefore, a theoretical concept too broad in this context) but the mechanisms hypothesized to account for individual identification with systemic roles. If we (not very realistically) confine our attention to "within-system" socialization, cognitive dissonance theory explains the fact that more senior members of Congress, for example, value the norms of Congress especially as they relate to the hierarchical structure. It is suggestive as well of roles that should be compatible with different hierarchical levels:

Figure 3

			POSITION IN HIERARCHY	
Personality Type			High	Low
Inner-directed	Institution-alization	High	Politico	Maverick
		Low	Goal orientation	
Other-directed	Institution-alization	High	Conservative	Conformist
		Low	Faction orientation	

Most attempts to describe role orientations of legislators have suffered from a lack of theoretical guidance, or from being guided by an inappropriate theory. For example, Eulau *et al.* define legislative roles in terms of normative democratic theory; it is therefore unclear what such roles might mean in terms of a theory of human behavior.[33] Figure 3 suggests role orientations for legislators that are defined in terms of our conceptual scheme. Thus Eulau *et al.'s* "politico" can be understood in rather different terms: An inner-directed personality who has attained a position of relatively high rank in an organization characterized by unequally distributed power capabilities (*i.e.*, hierarchical) should be "more sensitive to conflicting alternatives in role assumption, more flexible in the way he resolves the conflict of alternatives, and less dogmatic in his representational style. . . .[34] In the same organizational position, we expect to find the other-directed personality adopting a conservative, conformist style—to challenge the

---

[33] Heinz Eulau, John Wahlke, William Buchanan, and LeRoy Ferguson, "The Role of the Representative: Some Empirical Observations on the Theory of Edmund Burke," reprinted in Heinz Eulau, *Political Behavior in America: New Directions* (New York: Random House, 1966).
[34] *Ibid.*, p. 35.

norms or expectations of the system with which he has identified would entail cognitive dissonance. Individuals in the lower hierarchical levels of an institutionalized organization will be either "mavericks" (characterized by the constant challenging of the norms and rules, and so on) or strong conformists to the norms, depending upon personality type. The reader is invited to satisfy himself that dissonance theory accounts for the change in roles over time and over hierarchical levels.

The situation is problematic for the cells in the "low" institutionalization categories. It is not clear how an individual could be in a relatively high position in the organizational hierarchy when low institutionalization implies little or no formal hierarchy within the organization. In other words, the property spaces do not have empirical counterparts. However, we may speculate that under conditions of low institutionalization the inner-directed personality tends to goal-oriented behavior, whereas the other-directed personality would tend to factionalism. (Factionalism, indeed, is probably characteristic of less institutionalized legislatures.[35] In part, it is a function of the requirement for reference-group identifications on the part of other-directed individuals.)

Politicization

It is remarkable that in all of the behavioral political science literature there are exceedingly few attempts to specify the *nature* of a political act, or of "politicization." (This is owing, one supposes, to a suspicion that such an endeavor characterizes political philosophy—traditional stuff—and that it is unscientific to undertake it.) Schattschneider perhaps comes the closest, arguing that politics is conflict and that conflict is itself contagious. "Therefore the contagiousness of conflict, the elasticity of its scope and the fluidity of the involvement of people are the *X* factors in politics."[36] Schattschneider's well known argument proceeds to examine the questions: Under what conditions are private disputes made public ones? Who controls the process? But I am interested in asking how we can account for conflict at all. We can observe that it is contagious; *why* is it? What happens, "psychologically"? In the language afforded us by this essay's conceptual scheme, we would say that *politicization occurs when the individual's identity is threatened by systemic changes affecting his reference sets.* Thus a change in the rules of advancement in a hierarchy will constitute a threat to the status (and self-esteem) of the individual who has achieved high position by the old set of rules, especially if he is other-directed and has acquired self-attitudes that are anchored in his hierarchical status. Notice that we are not positing a crude "self-interest" hypothesis; there is no question that the individual will lose his job, or take a pay cut, or even lose his rank. What is at stake is the individual's identity; if the social arrangements

---

[35] Cf. Polsby's account of the growth of internal complexity in the U.S. House of Representatives, "Institutionalization of the U.S. House of Representatives."

[36] E. E. Schattschneider, *The Semi-Sovereign People: A Realist's View of Democracy in America* (New York: Holt, Rinehart and Winston, 1960), p. 3.

which have defined the individual's self are altered, then his identity is altered. As we noted earlier, such a change is resisted as it entails severe psychological pain. In general, the other-directed personality is more prone to politicization than the inner-directed type; on the other hand, inner-directed personalities are more likely to *initiate* the kinds of activities that politicize the other-directed type. In a highly institutionalized organization, the inner-directed personality finds his identity threatened in the *absence* of systemic change, which inclines him to politicized activities that in turn politicize the other-directed type.

By the foregoing reasoning, it would appear that the potential for politicization of individuals increases as institutionalization increases, for both personality types will increasingly feel threats to their identity as a function of systemic disturbances. At a societal level there would appear to be some impressionistic evidence to support such a hypothesis;[37] indeed, Weber's contention that highly bureaucratized organizations create instability-producing strains could be interpreted in this light as well. It is interesting to note that in Weber's analysis of the bases of legitimacy, it is the charismatic leader who emerges as the "change factor," so to speak. I think that notoriously difficult concept, "charisma," can be interpreted as the capacity to elicit identity-projection in circumstances that are threatening to individuals' identities. In other words, the charismatic figure is the hero with whom people identify under certain stress circumstances; identity-threatening circumstances are most prevalent in social systems that are very highly institutionalized or that are in transition.

Conclusion

I am well aware that this essay does not contain a theory, properly speaking. I am also aware that, to many, it will not appear that this conceptual scheme could *become* a theory—at least not a theory about legislative behavior. For example, it does not appear to possess the capacity to generate predictive statements about voting (roll-call decisions) in legislatures. Surely we would expect a theory of legislative behavior to do that?

My answer is: No, we should not expect a theory to do that. Of course, it would be of great practical utility for some people to be able to predict legislative outcomes, but notice the theoretical unlikelihood of such an eventuality. The entire behavioral revolution in political science assumes, among other things, that an explanatory theory of politics must treat with the behavior of persons, not the formal structures (institutions, rules, and the like) that may or may not

---

[37] It is nearly commonplace today to note that systemic disturbances are "easier" to effect in a complex, highly interdependent social system such as our own. But I find it crudely mechanistic to explain that fact by reference to "technology," etc., alone, as though we were hooked together by many wires. It seems to me that the proliferation and increasing elaboration or organization makes it more and more likely that any given individual will find his identity threatened by some systemic disturbance; e.g., with the fantastic growth of higher education in America, we have succeeded in capturing quite a lot of people in a rather elaborate hierarchical structure. Neither student nor parent nor professional academic finds it easy to avoid anchoring his identity in this enormous set of hierarchies.

reflect the realities of the situation. In other words, behavioralists presume the necessity for developing theories of human behavior, not descriptions of institutions. Why, then, do we so often select our dependent variables in institutional terms? What theoretical reason is there to suppose that the "end" of human behavior in legislatures is voting? I submit that our interest in practical information has misled us in theory construction.

By analogy, think of the weather. Like the meteorologists, we shall always be faced with the reality of what are for all *practical* purposes random inputs. There is no Theory of Rain in My Backyard, I am sorry to say; neither, I suspect, is there any Theory of Voting for the 1964 Civil Rights Act, no matter how much we would have liked to predict the outcome.

Accordingly, the theorist must attempt to systematize in an economical way what is "going on" in legislatures. I began by attempting to relate individual behavior to changes in the system, or organization, which is the legislature. As I attempted to show, a wide variety of phenomena (best described as role playing and politicized behavior) may be accounted for in terms of just three variables: (1) degree of institutionalization of the legislative system, (2) position of the individual in the hierarchy of the system, and (3) personality of the individual (inner- or other-directed). Although the details of it might vary from researcher to researcher, variables (1) and (2) should present no great measurement (operationalization) difficulties. Variable (3) is more problematic; it may be that I am sweeping rather too much under the rug here, for it might prove fairly difficult to falsify the theory on account of this variable. (*E.g.*, anyone who does not behave as predicted could be called "inner-directed" in a sort of *post hoc* interpretation of the findings.) But difficulties such as these are precisely the reason why theory construction must proceed hand-in-hand with empirical research. It is, after all, an empirical question whether most people are consistently inner- or other-directed.

The most promising research tactics would appear to lie in comparative legislative research, on the one hand, and small group experimentation on the other. Comparative research could begin with the fifty state legislatures in the United States: The independent variable, degree of institutionalization, should be somewhat distributed even in a relatively homogeneous country such as ours. If it is, then the implications of this theory could be tested. Small group experimentation would allow the manipulation of the independent variable and the systematic control of the other variables, thus providing a powerful test of the logic of the theory. Pursuing both lines of research should greatly strengthen the theory's deductive power—or should result in its falsification.

Inputs into
the Legislative System

SUPPORTS

The Structure of Public Support
for Legislative Institutions

by G. R. BOYNTON, SAMUEL C. PATTERSON, *and* RONALD D. HEDLUND

Legislative sub-systems make important functional contributions to political systems. They are involved in the management of tensions in the polity through the mechanisms of deliberation, decision-making, adjudication, and catharsis. They also contribute to the integration of the political system through the supportive processes of authorization, legitimation, and representation.[1] The capacity of the legislative system to make its functional contributions effectively, to cope adequately with demands made upon the political system through legislative structures, theoretically is influenced by the level of public support for the legislative institution.

Easton treats *support* as a major input to the political system. He argues that, in addition to demands, support provides a "summary variable" with which to examine linkages between the political system and its environment. The concept of support has been useful to political scientists, in one way or another, in analyses of processes of public policy formulation. Political parties, interest groups, and leaders, among others, seek to build support for certain political alternatives in order to influence the decision-making processes of the legislature. However, support directed toward the legislature as an institution is not limited to a focus upon specific policy alternatives. Easton points out that

. . .if demands are to be processed into binding decisions, regardless of whose demands they are, it is not enough that support be collected behind them so as to impress the

---

[1] For an elaboration of these notions, see Malcolm E. Jewell and Samuel C. Patterson, *The Legislative Process in the United States* (New York, 1966), pp. 8–15.

Reprinted from "The Structure of Public Support for the Legislative Institution," *Midwest Journal of Political Science* 12, no. 2 (May 1968): 163–80, by G. R. Boynton, Samuel Patterson and Ronald D. Hedlund, by permission of the Wayne State University Press and the authors. Copyright © 1968 by Wayne State University Press.

authorities with the need to adopt them as a basis for decisions. Basically, a large proportion of political research has been devoted to just this matter. Studies of voting behavior, interest groups, parties, and legislative analysis have all sought to reveal the way in which support is distributed, shifted, and mobilized behind varying demands (issues) or behind personalities and leadership groups seeking positions of authority. But if the authorities are to be able to make decisions, to get them accepted as binding, and to put them into effect without the extensive use of coercion, solidarity must be developed not only around some set of authorities themselves, but around the major aspects of the system within which the authorities operate.[2]

The legislative system constitutes one discrete sub-system of the polity around which support may become focused. It may become a focus of support such that legislative decisions can be implemented without resort to extensive coercion. It is this type of support, support directed toward the institution as such, that is the concern of the research here.

Support for political institutions may take a number of different forms. It may be *specific* or *diffuse*. Specific support "flows from the favorable attitudes and predispositions stimulated by outputs that are perceived by members to meet their demands as they arise or in anticipation."[3] Diffuse support is that reservoir of good will which a system may engender, not dependent upon any particular output, and at the extreme mode typified by unquestioning loyalty or patriotism. Easton also suggests that support for political structures may be *overt* or *covert*. The first involves some kind of action in the form of observable behavior; the latter involves attitudes, sentiments, predispositions, or frames of mind. Finally, support may be *direct*, linking the public with the political elite in some immediate way; or it may be *indirect*, mediated by some communication links between public and elite.

Political scientists have relatively little information on levels of support for legislative institutions. In this research we have sought to measure the degree to which a sample of adults in Iowa were committed to the legislative institution in their state political system. Our operationalization of support led us to focus upon those types of support which Easton classifies as covert, direct, and diffuse.

Measurement of Legislative Support

Easton discusses some of the problems associated with the measurement of support.[4] One difficulty he recognizes is that general indices of support may not differentiate political objects toward which attitudes may be targeted. A citizen

---

[2] See David Easton, *A Systems Analysis of Political Life* (New York, 1965), pp. 153–340; the quotation is at pp. 157–158.

[3] *Ibid.*, p. 273.

[4] *Ibid.*, pp. 161–64. Our conceptualization of support also relies on Gabriel A. Almond, "A Developmental Approach to Political Systems," *World Politics*, Vol. 17 (January 1965), 183–214. Both Easton and Dennis have dealt with support in some empirical sense. See David Easton and Jack Dennis, "The Child's Acquisition of Regime Norms: Political Efficacy," *American Political Science Review*, Vol. 61 (March 1967), 25–38; and, Jack Dennis, "Support for the Party System by the Mass Public," *American Political Science Review*, Vol. 60 (September 1966), 600–615. Though they are not really comparable, diffuse legislative support in Iowa appears impressionistically to be less ambivalent than diffuse support for the party system in Wisconsin, the site of Dennis' research.

may be supportive of the political community and the regime, but hostile to the authorities. Our investigation reduces this problem some by focusing on one political sub-system, the legislative, and by examining only its central institutional manifestation, the legislature.

To measure support for the legislature, we constructed seven Likert-type attitudinal statements (shown in full in Table 1). These support items, along with a substantial number of additional questions, provided the survey schedule which was administered to a household probability sample of the adult population of Iowa in November, 1966. We interviewed 1,001 respondents, although complete data for legislative support were available only for 950 of them, and these constitute our working number of respondents.

Although the data arrayed in Table 1 make it clear that large proportions of the Iowa sample expressed attitudes of compliance with the laws passed by the legislature, preference for legislative law-making, and commitment to the existence of the legislature as an institution, some notable variations are evident. The least legislative support was evinced by the question of the governor taking the law into his own hands rather than waiting for the legislature to act; more than a fourth of the sample agreed that there were times when the governor should do this, and only 12 percent strongly disagreed. Nearly one-sixth agreed that sometimes citizens should take the law into their own hands without waiting for the legislature to take action, although more than half disagreed and more than a fourth disagreed strongly.

In contrast, very marked legislative support was indicated by the high proportions in the sample who responded in such a way as to show that they felt citizens ought to comply with laws passed by the legislature whether they agreed with them or not. Less than 3 percent were willing to agree that it was all right to disobey the law. These data suggest that, for some, extraordinary action by the governor or by citizens can sometimes be acceptable substitutes for the legislative process, but outright failure to comply when legislative authority has been exercised rarely is acceptable.

The items involving retention of the legislature and reduction of its powers produced greater difficulty in responding, but the pattern for the three items is quite similar for those who did respond. Across these items, about 12 percent were willing to consider abolishing the legislature or reducing its constitutional powers. More than two-thirds did not wish to reduce legislative power, 72 percent agreed that proposals to abolish the legislature should be defeated, and more than 78 percent disagreed that the legislature should be abolished if it persistently passed disagreeable laws.

These seven attitudinal items provided a workable basis for indices of legislative support. Our hypotheses about the interrelationships of these seven items were two-fold. We first hypothesized that support for the legislature would form a general dimension. In statistical terms, we expected that the individual items would all have high factor loadings on the first factor when subjected to a principal component analysis, and that this factor would account for most of the explained variance. This expectation was adequately borne out in the analysis (see Table 2), which shows that the first factor accounts for more than

Table 1—Attitudes of Support Toward the Iowa Legislature (in percentages)

	Items	DIRECTION OF SUPPORT	LOW 1	Legislative Support 2	3	HIGH 4	DON'T KNOW	TOTAL
1	There are times when it almost seems better for the citizens of the state to take the law into their own hands rather than wait for the state legislature to act.	Disagree	1.2	13.2	51.7	28.0	5.9	100.0
2	If you don't particularly agree with a state law, it is all right to break it if you are careful not to get caught.	Disagree	.8	1.3	52.6	42.1	3.2	100.0
3	There are times when it would almost seem better for the Governor to take the law into his own hands rather than wait for the state legislature to act.	Disagree	.8	25.0	54.0	11.8	8.4	100.0
4	Even though one might strongly disagree with a state law, after it has been passed by the state legislature one ought to obey it.	Agree	.7	2.2	71.7	21.6	3.8	100.0
5	One should be willing to do everything that he could to make sure that any proposal to abolish the state legislature was defeated.	Agree	1.2	12.7	62.6	9.8	13.7	100.0
6	If the Iowa legislature continually passed laws that the people disagreed with, it might be better to do away with the legislature altogether.	Disagree	.4	12.0	62.1	16.4	9.1	100.0
7	It would not make much difference if the constitution of Iowa was rewritten to reduce the powers of the state legislature.	Disagree	.2	11.9	59.2	6.9	21.8	100.0

(N = 1,001)

Table 2—Dimensions of Legislative Support

Items	Principal Component SOLUTION		Rotated Solution COMPLIANCE	INSTITUTIONAL COMMITMENT
	Factor I	Factor II	Factor I	Factor II
1 Times when citizens take law into own hands	.591	− .454	.745	.003
2 All right to break law if you disagree with it	.594	− .349	.679	.116
3 Times when the Governor should take law into his own hands	.575	− .174	.552	.237
4 Ought to obey laws even if one disagrees	− .502	.188	− .505	− .180
5 Ought to do everything to prevent abolishing the legislature	− .482	− .575	.015	− .766
6 If laws people disagreed with passed, do away with legislature	.645	.291	.305	.638
7 Wouldn't make much difference if legislative powers were reduced	.580	.338	.226	.632
Percent of total variance (cumulative)	32.4	45.9		
Percent of explained variance (cumulative)	70.5	100.0		

70 percent of the explained variance, and that six of the seven items have higher factor loadings on the first factor than on the second.

We also hypothesized that this general dimension of support could be divided into two more specific dimensions.[5] The bi-dimensional character of our support items is confirmed when the two factors are rotated using a Kaiser Varimax rotation. The first factor is related to the willingness to comply with decisions reached in the legislative system. Four items have high loadings on this factor. Briefly, they are: (1) There are times when citizens should take the law into their own hands; (2) It is all right to break the law if you disagree with it; (3) There are times when the governor should take the law into his own hands; and, (4) One ought to obey laws even if one disagrees. These four items are directly reflective of compliance with legislative decisions, and we call them together the "compliance factor."

The second factor is related to institutional maintenance. Three items have high loadings on this factor. They are: (1) One ought to do everything to prevent abolition of the legislature; (2) If it passed laws people disagreed with, better do away with the legislature; and, (3) It would not make much difference if legislative powers were reduced. Supportive responses to these items indicate a willingness to maintain the legislative system in the face of a generally unsatisfactory performance, and so we have called this the "institutional commitment factor." As Table 2 indicates, the compliance and institutional commitment factors are

[5] See A. G. Neal and Salomon Rettig, "On the Multi-dimensionality of Alienation," *American Sociological Review*, Vol. 32 (February 1967), 54–64, for a precedent for the use of the principal component solution to establish a general dimension and the rotated solution to specify distinguishable sub-scales within the basic dimension.

very clearly distinguishable. Only one item has a secondary loading as high as .305, while all of the primary loadings are substantially higher.

Using the generalized factor and its two sub-dimensions, we factor scored the respondents in the sample. In order to establish the salient locations of legislative support in different social and political strata, we used indices both from the principal component and from the compliance and institutional commitment factors separately. We will consider first the dimension of general legislative support, and then examine variations brought about by its bi-section into sub-dimensions.

The Location of Support in Different Social Strata

Since we know that legislative support varies in our sample as a whole, we would expect it to have a distribution in social and political strata consistent with the findings of research on the effects of stratification on other political phenomena. Such things as political opinions, voting behavior, political activity, and political influence are likely to differ in different social strata. The implementation of supportive attitudes in the political system will tend to come through linkages between the public at large and the political elite drawn very largely from upper socio-economic levels. It is, therefore, vital to the maturing of a theory of political support to know where most supportive attitudes are to be found in the stratification hierarchy. If our knowledge about other political effects of socio-economic status differences is stable, we ought to find that legislative support is strongest among those high in levels of education, occupation, and income. We have used these as indicators of social stratification, adding size of place to assess the ecological distribution of support. For purposes of presentation we have trichotomized the sample by factor scores for legislative support, but the analysis of variance is based upon the entire range of support scores.

Tables 3, 4, and 5 show our analysis of legislative support in terms of education, occupation, and income. These data indicate the pronounced tendency for support to be located in the higher social strata. Persons with some college education are significantly more supportive of the legislature than are those who have only grade school educational experience. Forty-three percent of those with a high educational level were high in legislative support, while nearly half of those with only a grade school education were low in support. The greatest difference in terms of significant t's occurs between these two groups.[6]

Occupational groups differ significantly in their diffuse support of the legislative institution. The sharpest occupational difference occurs between those in professional and managerial occupations, foremen, operatives, craftsmen and laborers, on the one side, and those who are housewives or retired, on the other.

---

[6] t = − 7.46, p < .001. The t values between all three educational groups are significant. Between college and high school t = − 4.78; between high school and grade school, t = − 4.02.

Table 3—Education and Legislative Support
(*in percentages*)

	Educational Level[b]			
	HIGH	MEDIUM	LOW	TOTAL[c]
Legislative Support[a]	(N = 203)	(N = 499)	(N = 248)	(N = 950)
High	43.4	34.4	23.0	33.4
Medium	35.9	34.7	28.6	33.4
Low	20.7	30.9	48.3	33.2
Total	100.0	100.0	99.9	100.0

F = 28.18   df = 2, 947   p < .001

[a] Trichotomized by dividing the range of factor scores from the principal component solution into terciles, in this and following tables.
[b] High = 13 or more years of school completed; Medium = 9–12 years of school; Low = 8 years or less of schooling.
[c] Responses were available for sufficient items in Table 1 to make it possible to score only 950 respondents on legislative support for this and following tables.

Table 4—Occupation and Legislative Support
(*in percentages*)

	Occupational Groups					
Legislative Support	PROFESSIONAL & MANAGERIAL (N = 215)	FARMERS (N = 176)	SALES & SERVICE WORKERS (N = 88)	FOREMEN, OPERATIVES, & LABORERS (N = 214)	HOUSEWIVES, RETIRED, & OTHER (N = 257)	TOTAL (N = 950)
High	42.3	33.5	35.2	32.7	25.7	33.4
Medium	35.3	33.0	34.1	25.7	38.1	33.4
Low	22.3	33.5	30.7	41.6	36.2	33.2
Total	99.9	100.0	100.0	100.0	100.0	100.0

F = 6.01   df = 4, 945   p < .01

Table 5—Income and Legislative Support
(*in percentages*)

	Income Level[a]			
	HIGH	MEDIUM	LOW	TOTAL[b]
Legislative Support	(N = 254)	(N = 316)	(N = 174)	(N = 744)
High	40.9	38.0	25.9	36.2
Medium	33.5	31.0	30.5	31.7
Low	25.6	31.0	43.7	32.1
Total	100.0	100.00	100.1	100.0

F = 10.75   df = 2, 742   p < .001

[a] High = $8,000 or more; Medium = $4,000–$7,999; Low = $3,999 or less.
[b] Of the 950 respondents who could be scored on legislative support, 206 did not report income levels.

Professionals and managers also are significantly different from farmers in their degree of legislative support. Farmers and sales and service workers differ least, nor are farmers significantly different from craftsmen and laborers or house-wives.[7] Thus, farmers and sales and service workers fall between professionals-managers and foremen-laborers in their relative support for the legislative institution.

Differences in income levels bear a significant relationship to legislative support. Relatively more affluent citizens are much more likely to express supportive attitudes than are those whose incomes are low. As Table 5 shows, more than 40 percent of those who make more than $8,000 a year could be found in the highest third of the scores on legislative support, while only about a fourth of those who make less than $4,000 were in that category.[8]

Table 6—Size of Place and Legislative Support
(in percentages)

	Size of Place					
Legislative Support	50,000 OR MORE (N = 237)	5,000– 49,000 (N = 226)	2,500– 4,999 (N = 61)	UNDER 2,500 (N = 214)	FARM (N = 207)	TOTAL[a] (N = 945)
High	36.3	31.4	23.0	33.6	35.3	33.4
Medium	32.1	34.5	45.9	33.2	29.5	33.2
Low	31.6	34.1	31.1	33.2	35.3	33.3
Total	100.0	100.0	100.0	100.0	100.1	99.9

$F = .60$ $df = 4, 940$ $p > .05$

[a] Five respondents could not be classified as to size of place.

We have established that education, occupation, and income are, taken separately, significantly related to legislative support. In this paper, we consider one additional bivariate relationship, that of size of place and legislative support. Socio-economic differences in support for the legislature could easily have been anticipated, and they occurred. Size of place differences might also have been expected. A rationale might easily be developed to argue the hypothesis of decreasing support with increasing size of place, based upon conventional wisdom about the greater potential alienation of constituents in large communi-ties compared to those in small ones. In representational terms, it might be argued that people in smaller communities or rural areas have greater proximity to their representatives, and thus perhaps might be more likely to support the representatives' institution. Or, it could be contended that, in general, compliance with law and commitment to the established institutional order are better main-tained in smaller, rather than larger, ecological areas. But, as Table 6 plainly

---

[7] The significant t's are: professional and managers/farmers = 2.19, p < .05; professionals and managers/foremen, operatives and laborers = 4.01, p < .001; professionals and managers/house-wives and retired = 4.35, p < .001.

[8] t = − 4.64, p < .001.

shows, size of place and legislative support are not directly associated in Iowa. A similar analysis in a political system with a larger metropolitan center might produce different results. Iowa's largest city, Des Moines, has fewer than 300,000 inhabitants. In any case, support for the legislature is, in Iowa, spread relatively evenly across the state, from city to small town to farm.

Legislative Support and Political Stratification

V. O. Key argued that "the political system is constructed of strata definable in terms of political activity and influence and independent of occupational strata, income levels, and other such readily perceptible indicators beloved of the sociologist and the daily commentator."[9] As indicators of differentiations among political strata, Key used levels of political involvement, political participation, and sense of political efficacy. Political stratification is important for the functioning of political systems because people in different strata have differential influence on the operation of the system, political stratifications are relatively stable over time, and members of different political strata respond to the same situation in quite different ways. Key and others have argued that it is the activity, beliefs, and support provided by the politically active stratum in the United States that makes for a relatively stable and viable political system.[10] In contrast, data analyzed by Converse and Dupeux lead one to suspect that the instability of the party system in France is, at least in important respects, the result of the attitudes of the most politically active stratum of French society.[11] In both systems, the analysts either argue or assume that the politically active stratum has more influence than less active ones, but that the effect of their influence on the systems is quite different.

We used levels of political knowledge and activity as differentia for political stratification. We expected persons who had some modicum of knowledge about the legislative institution, its members, and how it works to exhibit great support for it. We did not ask respondents to be sophisticated in their knowledge about the legislature in order to qualify for categorization as "high" in cognitive level. Our criteria were minimal; we asked them how often the legislature meets and what the term of the representative is. Using this rather low threshold, only 22 percent of the sample could answer both questions correctly, and 27 percent could correctly answer neither question. We used these rudimentary questions and answers to partition our sample in terms of three different cognitive levels (see Table 7).

In fact, knowledge about the legislature, however minimal, is highly associated with legislative support. Nearly half of the respondents in the "high" level of knowledge were high in legislative support, while only a third of those with

[9] V. O. Key, Jr., *Public Opinion and American Democracy* (New York, 1961), pp. 197–198.

[10] For instance, see *Ibid.*, pp. 536–58; and, Robert A. Dahl, *Who Governs?* (New York, 1961), pp. 311–25. Key labeled the highest level of political stratification the "activist sub-culture"; Dahl uses the term "political stratum."

[11] Philip E. Converse and Georges Dupeux, "Politicization of the Electorate in France and the United States," *Public Opinion Quarterly*, Vol. 26 (Spring, 1962), 1–23.

Table 7—Political Knowledge and Legislative Support (in percentages)

| | Cognitive Level[a] | | | |
Legislative Support	HIGH (N = 212)	MEDIUM (N = 478)	LOW (N = 260)	TOTAL (N = 950)
High	48.1	32.0	23.8	33.4
Medium	31.6	36.2	29.6	33.4
Low	20.3	31.8	46.6	33.2
Total	100.0	100.0	100.0	100.0

F = 38.94   df = 2, 947   p < .001

[a] Respondents were asked "Do you happen to know how often the state legislature meets in regular session?" and "Do you happen to know for how long a term are Representatives to the state legislature elected?" High = two correct responses; Medium = one correct response; Low = no correct responses.

"medium" knowledge and less than a quarter of those "low" in cognitive level could be found in the upper, or positive, third of the support scores. Not only are cognition and legislative support significantly related in general (as indicated by the analysis of variance), but also each cognitive level significantly differs from the others.[12]

In a similar vein, we could easily expect citizens who participate in politics to exhibit more positive support for the legislature than those who are not much involved in political activity. As with levels of political knowledge, we chose modest thresholds by way of classifying respondents' political activity levels. Our nominal categories of political participation were based upon whether respondents voted in the 1966 election, and whether they talked to others about candidates or parties. By these criteria, 30 percent of the sample could be grouped as "high" in political participation (they both voted and talked to others about parties and candidates), 41 percent were "medium" (they voted but did not talk politics), and 29 percent were "low" (they reported neither kind of participation).

Table 8 presents the proportions of high, medium, and low legislative support by participation levels. It is clear that participants in the political process, even

Table 8—Political Participation and Legislative Support

| | Participation Level[a] | | | |
Legislative Support	HIGH (N = 282)	MEDIUM (N = 392)	LOW (N = 276)	TOTAL (N = 950)
High	41.8	32.4	26.1	33.4
Medium	36.9	34.7	27.9	33.4
Low	21.3	32.9	46.0	33.3
Total	100.0	100.0	100.0	100.0

F = 19.18   df = 2, 947   p < .001

[a] Respondents were asked "Did you vote this November 8th or did something keep you from voting?" and "Did you talk to any people and try to show them why they should or should not vote for one of the parties or candidates?" High = voted and talked to people; Medium = voted only; Low = neither voted nor talked to people.

[12] High/Medium t = 5.32; High/Low t = 8.82; Medium/Low t = 4.90; all p < .001.

on a modest scale, are considerably more likely to express supportive sentiments than are those who do not vote. Comparing participation levels by degrees of legislative support produces a very significant F-ratio, and the differences between pairs of participation groups also are significant ones.[13]

Our purpose has been to map support for the legislature in social and political strata of the population, and we have handled our data accordingly, using bivariate analysis. However, questions immediately arise about the inter-penetration of the variables considered. We would expect education, occupation, and income to be highly inter-correlated, and would not expect an analysis of occupation or income with legislative support to withstand controls for educa-tion. This turns out to be the case. Further, we have shown that size of place is not significantly related to legislative support in Iowa, and this is the case for each level of education. We have argued that social strata and political strata in the Iowa population are distinct, and have mapped legislative support in each. It might be suspected that the relation between political knowledge and legis-lative support is dependent upon education levels, but this is not the case. When controlled for variations in education, political knowledge and support still are significantly related at the .001 level. Similarly, when the relation between political participation and legislative support is controlled for education, the two are significantly associated at each education level (High, $p < .05$; Medium, $p < .001$; Low, $p < .05$).

Compliance and Commitment

It will be recalled that we defined legislative support in general in terms of principal component loadings for seven attitudinal items. We then showed the bi-dimensional character of our measure of legislative support, presenting the rotated factor solution calling for two factors. We have labeled the factors *compliance* and *institutional commitment*. The foregoing data were presented on the basis of the principal component factor scores because it displayed our findings in the simplest and most direct way. But it is clear that our general measure of legislative support contains two distinguishable sub-dimensions. We noted earlier that the bivariate comparisons made here are not altered funda-mentally when legislative support is partitioned into its two factors. Without recapitulating each comparison in detail, it can be shown that the general pattern of relationships developed with the principal component factor scores for legislative support is not seriously disturbed when scores from the two-factor solution are substituted. Table 9 is a presentation of the F-ratios for each factor with the six descriptive variables considered in earlier tables. We have reiterated the principal component-based F's for purposes of easy comparison. With compliance and commitment separated, all of the variables considered, except for size of place, show a significant relation to support.

[13] High participation/Medium participation $t = -4.08$; High/Low $t = -6.13$; Medium/Low $t = -2.54$. For the first two, $p < .001$; for the latter, $p < .02$. See William N. McPhee and Jack Ferguson, "Political Immunization," in William N. McPhee and William A. Glaser (eds.), *Public Opinion and Congressional Elections* (New York, 1962), pp. 155–179.

Table 9—F-Ratios for Factors of Legislative Support and Other Variables

Variables	Compliance		Institutional Commitment		General Factor	
	F	P	F	P	F	P
Education	26.80	.001	18.95	.001	28.18	.001
Occupation	6.92	.001	2.75	.05	6.01	.01
Income	12.14	.001	5.13	.01	10.75	.001
Size of Place	.79	*	.66	*	.60	*
Cognitive Level	29.42	.001	33.85	.001	38.94	.001
Participation Level	17.22	.001	12.95	.001	19.18	.001

* Not significant.

Although the evidence is great that compliance and commitment are measurably different factors of the legislative support scale, the significant overall relationships (in terms of F-ratios), and the inter-group differences (indicated by t-values), present very much the same picture for income, size of place, political knowledge, and participation when they are related to the factors separately. When variations in compliance and commitment are mapped at different levels of income, political knowledge, and participation, the analysis produces results much like those stemming from comparisons using only the general factor scores (principal component). The F-ratios are high, and the patterns of t-values between groups are very similar. In the case of size and place, as with the principal component analysis, the two-factor analysis confirms the null hypothesis.

Interesting differences between groups appear in the cases of education and occupation. The compliance scores for respondents with college and high school educational experience differed strongly from those with only grade school experience, while college and high school groups were less different. In contrast, commitment proved to be much stronger in the college group, with a lesser difference appearing between the high school and grade school groups. To put it more succinctly, the break for compliance seems to come between high school and grade school groups, while the break for commitment appears to occur between college and high school groups.

We noted earlier that, using principal component scores, differences occurred at the .001 level between professionals and managers on the one hand, and workers and housewives on the other. Also, professionals and managers differed from farmers at the .05 level, applying the principal component scores. Compliance and commitment work somewhat differently between occupational groups. When compliance is taken alone, professionals and managers still differ significantly from workers and housewives, but no longer from farmers. Now, farmers also differ from workers and housewives. When institutional commitment is taken alone, the professional-manager group is significantly different from farmers. And, the differences between the professional-manager group, and workers and housewives, while significant, is not nearly so strong as was the case with compliance.

Conclusion

We measured legislative support using seven attitudinal items administered to a sample of the Iowa population. We indexed the respondents on legislative support in general by the use of principal component factor scores. We also showed that legislative support as measured could be partitioned into two distinct factors, which we called compliance and institutional commitment.

Having measured support for legislative institutions, we asked who supports the legislature most, and who least? Using the general support index from the principal component scores, we showed that persons occupying high socio-economic status are significantly more inclined to express attitudes supportive of the legislative institution than are those occupying low socio-economic status. Educational, occupational, and income groups differ significantly in the support they give to the legislature, the greatest support tending to come from the college-educated, professional and managerial, and high income groups. Grade school educated workers with relatively low incomes have a much lower level of support for the legislature. When compliance and institutional commitment are considered separately, the difference between professional-managerial types and workers is stronger for compliance and farmers make an interesting shift. Farmers in Iowa are more like professionals and managers when it comes to compliance, but more like workers when it comes to commitment. In the case of educational levels, we could show that high school and college educated people differed more strongly from the grade school educated on compliance, whereas commitment distinguished the college educated from the high school and grade school levels. In regard to educational differences, we probably can conclude that the high school educated population is more inclined to be compliant than it is to be committed. The college educated are highly compliant and committed, while the grade school educated are both less compliant and less committed.

How is legislative support distributed ecologically? Is it greater in small towns, on the farm, or in the cities? Our analysis makes it possible to assert that people who live on farms, in small towns, and in cities exhibit positive legislative support in about the same measure. Any speculations which might be entertained about rural-urban differences in legislative support should be tempered by these findings.

Levels of political knowledge and participation are strongly associated with legislative support. Support is strongest among those who have some glimmer of knowledge of the legislature, and who are at least minimally participating in the political process. These findings simply reinforce the growing body of research results which suggest the very great importance of the political stratum in the maintenance and performance of political systems. To the degree that the persistence of the legislative sub-system and its conversion capabilities are dependent upon support, that support tends to come most strongly from the politically knowledgeable and participant segments of the population.

We have reported only simple, bivariate relations in this paper, and have dealt only with a limited array of variables. We believe that these bivariate comparisons are intrinsically interesting from the point of view both of description and theory. Furthermore, we can build our subsequent analyses on these foundations. Although we have shown that people who have relatively high social status and who are more politically involved are more supportive of the legislative system in Iowa, there is no necessary connection between these two variables and positive support. Revolutions are led by those who are highly involved politically, and in the 1930's support for local governmental institutions in the United States may have been lowest among those in the higher strata of the status hierarchy. In our study we have hypothesized that support is related to the extent to which there is congruence between people's expectations about how the political system ought to perform and their perceptions of how it is performing. We will report in later papers on whether this congruence of expectations and perceptions is higher in some strata than it is in others.

The Bundestag and the Public

by GERHARD LOEWENBERG

Public Relations

AMBIVALENCE TOWARD THE PUBLIC

The role which the public deliberations of the Bundestag may play in the political system depends, of course, on the extent to which they receive public attention. But the attitude toward the general public on the part of most Members is ambivalent. In much of their work, Members seek to escape public scrutiny. They lack talent in reaching the public and confidence in public judgment. In the pursuit of specialization and party cohesion, they sacrifice open communication with each other. Their desire to reach the public is, by comparison, occasional, and does not grow out of the requirements of their day-to-day work. It is the desire of party leaders to appeal to the electorate, or of the officers of the House to improve its image, or of the average Member to make a contribution to civic education. But these are weak motives compared to those which constantly impel Members to take refuge from the public in closed committee chambers. And the general public, for its part, hardly clamors for access to those deliberations which take place privately, as long as interest groups within it have adequate information on decisions concerning them. Public interest in the work of the Bundestag suffers from the anti-parliamentary attitudes of past generations, from the unfamiliarity of present institutions of government, and from a general affluence which, ironically, has made the political system uninteresting just because its results have been so satisfactory.

EDUCATION

Aware of its dependence on public interest, yet anxious to preserve ample privacy, the Bundestag has sought to escape its dilemma by a program of public relations designed to improve its rapport with the public without requiring it to

Reprinted from Gerhard Loewenberg: *Parliament in the German Political System.* Copyright © 1967 by Cornell University. Used by permission of Cornell University Press and the author.

change its habits of work. A steady stream of visitors, a large proportion of them students on class excursions, passes through the public galleries of the House in organized shifts. The total during the first four parliamentary terms was five million persons, but nine-tenths of the visitors saw the House empty, because of the infrequency of public sessions. Individual Members, when they are present, meet with groups of visitors to answer questions, and the staff of the Bundestag conducts guided tours or question-and-answer sessions after the visit. An annual budget of DM 250,000 ($62,500) for "the introduction of educational and youth groups into the work of Parliament" helps to defray travel costs of student groups.[1] In many cases, hospitality extends to an invitation to lunch or refreshments in the parliamentary restaurant.

For teachers, a program of week-long seminars is offered in the Bundeshaus in Bonn, under the sponsorship of the Federal Office for Political Education, a government organization supported by the Ministry of the Interior which conducts a great variety of citizenship training programs.[2] Its weekly documentary newspaper, *Das Parlament*, contains extensive excerpts of the parliamentary debates, and is by far the most important medium of their dissemination. With a weekly circulation of nearly 100,000 copies, most of them sent without charge to schools, church and youth organizations, and military units, it largely displaces the official stenographic transcript as a documentary source of the debates for the general public.[3] Less than 1,000 copies of the official debates are purchased by private subscribers, the press run of 4,000 being reserved largely for Members of the Bundestag, each of whom receives one copy, and for Government offices and university libraries.

RADIO AND TELEVISION

The difficulty of a public relations program for a publicity-shy subject is demonstrated by the vacillation of the Bundestag regarding live radio and television transmission of its sittings. Marking the initial decision to broadcast or telecast major debates, Bundestag President Ehlers explained in 1952 that "we must bring the people directly into contact with the work of its Parliament, into contact with its debates, its differences of opinion, and the motives of the various decisions."[4] But the result, especially in some of the heated foreign policy and defense debates of the following years, was not entirely what had been sought. In a public unfamiliar with parliamentary procedure and behavior, observing for the first time a Parliament whose public sessions constituted only a small part of its work, there were some extremely critical responses. The special objects of dismay were the sparse attendance and conspicuous inattention of Members of the House, and the sharp partisanship of the speeches. The

---

[1] *Bundeshaushaltsplan für das Rechnungsjahr 1965*, Einzelplan 02, Tit. 308. Quadrennially, the House appropriates funds—the sum was DM 335,000 ($83,750) in 1965—to distribute the Official Handbook of Parliament (*Amtliches Handbuch des Deutschen Bundestages*) to public libraries, schools, and youth organizations (see *ibid.*, Tit. 874).

[2] *Das Parlament*, Oct. 14, 1964, p. 4.

[3] *Ibid.*, Oct. 25, 1961, pp. 8–9.

[4] Hermann Ehlers, "Die Demokratie im neuen Deutschland," in Friedrich Schramm ed., *Um dem Vaterland zu Dienen* (Cologne: O. Schmidt, 1955), pp. 39–40.

institution of Parliament did not clearly and unquestionably benefit, as had been expected. Furthermore, each party became anxious to gain the best television audience for its speaker, introducing an extraneous factor into the organization of the debate. Finally, and most effectively, the governing party found that the televising of debates subjected it to a new, and unwelcome, source of criticism. The Council of Elders therefore determined, at the beginning of the third parliamentary term in 1958, that live radio and television broadcasts of debates would be abandoned except on those ceremonial occasions "which do not serve parliamentary discussion, but which document the unity of the House."

But growing concern about public disinterest in Parliament led to a new decision five years later: with Presidential approval, now always given, radio and television may record the sessions of the House for later broadcasts, in excerpts, in news and feature programs. In addition, on subjects of major public importance, such as the extension of the statute of limitations on war-crimes trials, and on major occasions, such as debates on declarations of Government policy, live transmission is permitted. During 1965, debates were telecast live on six days, four of them in succession devoted to the discussion of Government policy after the opening of the fifth term of the Bundestag. The SPD, having decided to conduct a more vigorous opposition in debate, favored a general rule allowing live transmission of Bundestag proceedings at the discretion of the broadcast networks. Simultaneously, new efforts were made to explain to visitors, and to the public, the role which public debate has in the total work of the House.

THE PUBLIC IMAGE OF THE BUNDESTAG

These massive efforts to reach the public, and the passage of time, may have contributed to the measurable growth in public awareness of the identity of Parliament, and a decline in the original cynicism toward its work. More than half the population can today distinguish the Bundestag from the other major institutions of government, and nearly half can correctly identify the Member from their constituency.[5] In the decade after 1951, the proportion of the population believing that a Member of the Bundestag needs great competence rose from 39 to 61 percent, and those believing that the public interest was the primary concern of Members rose from 25 to 41 percent of the population.[6] Finally, those who held a fair or better opinion of the Bundestag rose, between

---

[5] In answer to the question, "Does the Bundestag in Bonn represent the *Länder*, the people, or is it the Government?," the responses in 1951 and 1965 were as follows:

	1951	1965
representation of the people	48%	54%
representation of the *Länder*	8	4
the Government	24	28
no answer	20	14

The ambiguity of the concept of "the Government" (*die Regierung*) in a parliamentary system may be a source of some of the confusion (*EMNID Informationen* [Bielefeld: EMNID Institut, 1965], no. 9, pp. 2–3). A satisfactory identification of the Bundestag Member representing the respondent's constituency was given by 43 per cent of respondents in October, 1961. That proportion has risen steadily since 1951, when it was 22 per cent (see E. N. and E. P. Neumann, eds., *Jahrbuch der öffentlichen Meinung* [Allensbach: Institut für Demoskopie], I [1947–55], 161; II [1957], 174; III [1958–64], 262).

[6] *Ibid.*, I, 162–3; II, 176–7; III, 262–3.

1951 and 1965, from 66 to 86 percent of the population, and within this group, those who found it good or better increased from 35 to 52 percent of the total.[7]

Formal knowledge about the institution correlates closely with the educational level of the respondents,[8] suggesting that it will continue to rise with rising educational levels and with special efforts in the field of civic education. But the growing ability to give correct answers to textbook questions about the Bundestag is not matched by a measurably growing interest in or understanding of the work of Parliament. Over 85 percent of the population has not heard anything about the work of its Member in the Bundestag, a figure which has hardly changed from the beginning.[9] In a study comparing the political cultures of the United States, Great Britain, Italy, Mexico, and Germany, Germans alone displayed a greater sense of being able to affect administrative than legislative decisions.[10] Only 12 percent of German respondents indicated that they would try to contact elected leaders (or the press) in an attempt to influence a national political decision, while 44 percent of British and 57 percent of American citizens said they would do so.[11]

Correspondingly, the mail which Members of the Bundestag receive from their constituents is small in quantity and consists mainly of special requests for intervention with ministries, or other kinds of assistance with personal problems. Members from rural areas, particularly those who hold or have held local office, may receive ten to twenty letters daily, and may, in addition, hold weekly or fortnightly office hours in their constituency, where they receive additional requests.[12] Many of them spend a large proportion of their energies on such constituency errands, which can contribute more than anything else to their renomination. On the other hand, Members elected in urban areas receive very little direct mail. In either case, mail expressing the correspondent's views on current issues is rare, and Members, poorly equipped to deal with correspondence, do nothing to encourage it. A steady flow of letters urging particular political decisions comes to the President of the Bundestag, who, in the eyes of the correspondents, is apparently the appropriate authority. The average German is inclined to look to local government officials rather than to his Member of Parliament for a redress of grievances. He is content to allow interest groups to act in his name in expressing demands on national issues.[13] The direct contact between the individual Member and his constituents is weak.[14]

[7] *EMNID Informationen*, 1965, no. 9, p. 4.

[8] While, on the average, 54 percent of respondents could identify the Bundestag correctly (see n. 5, *supra*), 84 percent of those who had completed a college preparatory curriculum (*Abitur*) could do so (*EMNID Informationen*, p. 3). A similar correlation exists with respect to other measures of formal knowledge of the Bundestag (see *Jahrbuch der öffentlichen Meinung*, III, 261–2).

[9] *Jahrbuch der öffentlichen Meinung*, I, 161; II, 174; III, 262.

[10] Gabriel A. Almond and Sidney Verba, *The Civic Culture, Political Attitudes and Democracy in Five Nations* (Princeton: Princeton University Press, 1963), pp. 218, 225–7.

[11] *Ibid.*, p. 203.

[12] For the experiences of two Members, see Heinrich Ritzel, *Einer von Vierhundertzwei* (Offenbach/Main: Bollwerk Verlag, 1953), pp. 55–60, 74; *Die Welt*, Jan. 12, 1963.

[13] Almond and Verba, *op. cit.*, pp. 314, 431–2, 435, 439.

[14] By contrast, a large number of citizens make use of the traditional right to address petitions to the Bundestag, which is guaranteed by article 17 of the Basic Law. Coming in at the rate of 7–10,000 annually, these petitions present a great variety of requests, mostly pertaining to personal affairs. A standing committee of the Bundestag deals with them or forwards them to the appropriate authority,

Table 1—Public Attitudes toward the Bundestag[a]

	Response			
Year	EXCELLENT OR BASICALLY GOOD	FAIR	POOR	NO OPINION
1951	35	31	9	25
1952	30	35	13	22
1953 (May)	46	31	10	13
1953 (November)	59	25	4	12
1954	49	37	10	4
1955	57	33	6	4
1956	46	37	12	5
1957 (September)	55	30	7	8
1958	37	41	16	6
1959	56	30	5	9
1960	52	35	6	7
1961 (December)	55	25	6	14
1963 (May)	46	36	7	11
1965 (January)	52	34	4	10

[a] In per cent of respondents to the question: "What do you think of the Bundestag in Bonn as our representative assembly?" From *EMNID Informationen* (Bielefeld: EMNID Institut, 1965), no. 9, p. 4.

The inadequacy of the Bundestag as an avenue of access to government for the citizen limits its capacity to serve as an instrument for legitimating the actions of government. The comparative study of political cultures reveals a general correlation between a citizen's sense of participation in affecting political decisions and his attachment to the political system. In Germany, not only is the sense of participation relatively low, but so is pride in the political system.[15]

The results of a survey of attitudes toward the Bundestag which has been conducted regularly since 1951 bear this out in several respects. They indicate substantial fluctuations in popular judgments of the institution, in spite of a long-term tendency toward a more positive attitude toward it. (See Table 1.) Furthermore, there is a strong correlation between the fluctuations in attitude toward the Bundestag, and changing attitudes toward the policy of the Chancellor and his Government.[16] Among respondents at any given point in time, attitudes toward the Bundestag vary with party identification. While 75 percent of CDU/CSU adherents thought well of Parliament in the 1961 survey, this was true of only 64 percent of FDP and 45 percent of SPD supporters. Only 1 percent of CDU/CSU respondents thought the Bundestag "poor," but 5 percent of FDP and 11 percent of SPD supporters did.[17] In the 1965 survey, in which, on

reporting regularly to the House on its work and requesting its approval (see, for example, *Dt. Btag.*, 4. W.P., Drs. 459). But in this relationship, the Bundestag serves as one of many agencies providing remedies for personal problems, not as an avenue by which the citizen participates in political decisions.

[15] Almond and Verba, *op. cit.*, p. 103.

[16] Compare the responses between 1951 and 1963 to the question, "Are you by and large in agreement or in disagreement with the policy of Adenauer?" (*Jahrbuch der öffentlichen Meinung*, I, 172–3; II, 182–3; III, 298–305).

[17] *EMNID Informationen*, 1962, no. 8, pp. 3–5.

the average, 38 percent of respondents found the Bundestag "fair" or "poor," this was true of 52 percent of SPD supporters.[18]

The attitude toward the institution of Parliament therefore appears to correlate with attitudes toward the party which has dominated that institution throughout its existence, and with satisfaction with Government policy. The "ins," who have a sense of better access to government and are more satisfied with its decisions, find the institution of Parliament more acceptable than the "outs." Furthermore, the complete party control of the Bundestag's public performance makes it difficult for it to attract support independent of party. For the compromises among parties which are negotiated in the Bundestag, and the procedures by which they are reached, are largely hidden from public view. But the failure of the Bundestag to gain general acceptance as a political institution impairs its capacity to legitimate the decisions of government. In this respect the attitude toward the Bundestag is part—perhaps a decisive part—of the general attitude toward the political system. The available evidence indicates that the support which the system enjoys depends on the specific accomplishments it has so far produced, and that it has failed to gain legitimacy independent of its concrete achievements.[19] Insofar as the Bundestag has been unable to supply substitutes for the symbols of legitimacy which the authoritarian political system possessed, its limits as an agency of legitimation may explain the conditional support given the present system generally.

ALTERNATIVES TO PARLIAMENTARY COMMUNICATION

As an avenue of communication between the Government and the public, Parliament has severe competition. The Government employs press conferences, interviews and planted articles. Interest groups address themselves to ministries and parliamentary committees directly and privately. But the channels of communication which thus compete with Parliament, whatever their advantages to those who employ them, cannot provide a forum in which conflicting opinions confront each other in the open. At best, they permit a flow of diverse demands and responses among specialized publics. They do not exhibit these conflicting opinions to the general public, do not permit an organized debate between opposing sides, and they leave the unorganized interests in society unheard. In short, to the extent that the chief actors in the political system bypass Parliament as a medium of communication, parliamentary debate cannot contribute to the reconciliation of conflicting demands and to public acceptance of the policy result. To that extent Parliament does not perform a representative function in the political system.

[18] *Ibid.*, 1965, no. 9, p. 4.
[19] Almond and Verba, *op. cit.*, pp. 103–5, 247–51; Lucian Pye and Sidney Verba, eds., *Political Culture and Political Development* (Princeton: Princeton University Press, 1965), pp. 141–5.

DEMANDS

Philippine Legislators' Reception
of Individuals and Interest Groups
in the Legislative Process

by RICHARD A. STYSKAL

Demand-making in Transitional Societies

Much has been written about the "mixed," "blended," or "prismatic" character of political systems found in Asia, the Middle East, and Latin America.[1] Through contact in one form or another with Western nations, many of these political systems have been introduced to modernizing processes which have yielded an "admixture," a "fusion," a "mutual penetration" of traditional and modern political structures and values.[2]

Types of citizen demand-making in these "transitional" societies also warrant a mixed designation. Both traditional and modern means exist for making demands of public officials.[3] Traditional types are individual-oriented, emphasizing personal, intimate contacts between citizen and politician. The relation-

---

[1] Gabriel A. Almond and James S. Coleman, *The Politics of the Developing Areas* (Princeton, 1960); Gabriel A. Almond and Sidney Verba, *The Civic Culture* (Princeton, 1963); Fred W. Riggs, *Administration in Developing Countries* (Boston, 1964); Lucian W. Pye, *Politics, Personality and Nation-Building* (New Haven, 1962), pp. 33–38. Of course, as Almond and Verba have observed, all political systems are a mixture of traditional and modern patterns. Nevertheless the distinctiveness of the two polar types appears more clear-cut and prominent in transitional societies.

[2] Joseph R. Gusfield, "Tradition and Modernity: Misplaced Polarities in the Study of Social Change," *American Journal of Sociology*, LXXII (January 1967), 354.

[3] Gabriel A. Almond, "A Comparative Study of Interest Groups and the Political Process," in Harry Eckstein and David E. Apter, eds. *Comparative Politics* (Glencoe, 1963), pp. 397–408; Lucian W. Pye, "The Nonwestern Political Process," *Journal of Politics*, XX (August 1958), 468–486; Riggs, *Administration*.

Reprinted from "Philippine Legislators' Reception of Individuals and Interest Groups in the Legislative Process," *Comparative Politics* 1, no. 3 (April 1969): 405–422, by Richard A. Styskal by permission of *Comparative Politics* and the author.

ship is often one of mutual aid and dependence. The influence of kinship, which centers on primary groups such as the family, is far-reaching. Demands tend to be narrow and specific and lead to highly particularized decision-making. By contrast, modern types of demand-making are group-oriented, stressing the utilization of functionally specific secondary groups. Demands tend to be general, categorical, policy or administrative alternatives.[4]

When speaking of mixed demand-making in transitional societies, at least two structural distinctions are apparent. First, the *demand-system* may be a mixture of more or less traditional and modern demand-structures used for influencing public officials.[5] A well entrenched compadre system, for example, may exist side by side with a well differentiated and functionally specific set of interest groups.[6] The empirical problem in describing such a system is to determine the relative weight of the traditional and modern demand-structures within it and their influence on the political system.

Second, the *demand-structures* themselves may be more or less mixed. Here we find the "fusion" of traditional and modern forms of political action with various demand-making structures such as the extended family, interest groups, political parties, the church, the military, and the like. Riggs, for example, speaks of "clects," where membership requirements are based on achievement and ascription and where demands are both particular and universalistic.[7] Again, the problem of describing such structures involves determining the influence of traditional and modern forces.

In this article we are concerned with the first problem—that of describing the demand-system of a transitional society and the mix of traditional and modern structures therein. Although the empirical evidence is slim, students of transitional societies appear to agree that the mix of demand-structures favors traditional or individual-oriented means for influencing public officials. Pye has noted that "in the non-Western political process there are relatively few explicitly organized interest groups with functionally specific roles."[8] Almond and Verba found that membership in voluntary associations was lowest in the two countries out of five that they classified as transitional (Italy and Mexico).[9]

Beyond this evidence, we find numerous statements to the effect that the imbalance which favors traditional means for demand-making in transitional

[4] See Carl H. Landé, *Leaders, Factions, and Parties: The Structure of Philippine Politics* (New Haven, 1964).

[5] "Tradition" and "modernity" are "pure" or analytic types which occupy end points on a continuum along which political systems may be compared. They are widely used in linear theories of social, political, and economic change.

[6] Gusfield, p. 355.

[7] Riggs, pp. 167–69. See also Agpalo, who classifies interest groups in the Philippines according to personalist-impersonalistic and unitarian-pluralian criteria. Remigio E. Agpalo, "Interest Groups and their Role in the Philippine Political System," *Philippine Journal of Public Administration*, IX (April 1965), 87–106.

[8] Pye, "The Nonwestern Political Process," 480. Also see Almond, "A Comparative Study," p. 408.

[9] Almond and Verba, p. 302. In a study of participation in voluntary associations in a Mexican city, Dotson found less participation at all levels of socioeconomic status (with the possible exception of the highest) than would be expected for similar strata in the United States. Floyd Dotson, "A Note on Participation in Voluntary Associations in a Mexican City," *American Sociological Review*, XVIII (August 1953), 380–386.

societies must be corrected. Many argue that with increasing specialization of the economy and differentiation of the society, political demands increase at a rapid rate. This increase in new demands poses a central problem for the continued "political modernization" of a society. As Eisenstadt states, this problem centers on the ability of the political system to adapt itself to changing political demands, to absorb them in policy-making, and to insure its own continuity in the face of continuous new demands and new forms of political organizations.[10] The problem can be resolved only by increasing the development of interest groups and their role in the political process.[11]

However, before these arguments can be fully considered, it is essential that several prior questions concerning the *relative weight* of traditional and modern patterns of demand-making in transitional societies be answered. This study, by examining the role of interest groups and unaffiliated individuals in the Philippine legislative process, attempts to shed light on one of these questions.

In more specific terms our problem is (1) to describe the attitudes of Philippine congressmen toward the role of interest groups and unattached individuals in the legislative process, and (2) to compare the amount of contact that congressmen have with interest groups and with unattached or unaffiliated individuals.

A major assumption is that direct contacts with elected officials by individuals who are unattached to or who do not represent interest groups *approximate* traditional means for making demands. It is also assumed that contacts with elected officials by interest groups or their representatives approximate more modern methods for making demands. In making these assumptions, we are not denying the validity of the distinction made above that interest groups themselves are a mixture of traditional and modern characteristics. Rather, we are positing that two types of demand-structures exist in the Philippines regardless of the traditional-modern mixture of their internal organization; that one type is individual-oriented and the other is group-oriented; and that Philippine congressmen can and do readily distinguish between them.[12]

---

[10] S. N. Eisenstadt, "Political Modernization: Some Comparative Notes," *International Journal of Comparative Sociology*, V (March 1963), 3–24.

[11] These arguments usually involve assumptions about the mediating effects of interest groups in the political process. For example, interest groups facilitate the interjection of new claims and new ideas into the political system making for development or "modernization" rather than stagnation. Eisenstadt, 3–24. Interest groups act as politicizing agents through the mobilization of broad and diverse strata of the population into the political sector of the society. The result is a broadening of the representational capability of the government and an increase in the political integration of a society. Almond and Verba, pp. 310, 318; Fred W. Riggs, "Bureaucrats and Political Development: A Paradoxical View," in Joseph LaPalombara, ed. *Bureaucracy and Political Development* (Princeton, 1963), pp. 120–67; Clifford Geertz, "Primordial Sentiments and Civil Politics in the New States," in Clifford Geertz, ed. *Old Societies and New States* (London, 1963), pp. 105–57. Interest groups act as countervailing forces in the policy-making process, offering competing goals and thereby reducing the threat of dictatorial regimes. Remigio Agpalo, pp. 87–106. Interest groups reduce the flow of diverse, direct, and highly personal demands by incorporating them into a lesser number of group demands, thus reducing the threat of demand overload and eventual breakdown of the government. David Easton. *A Systems Analysis of Political Life* (New York, 1965). For a general discussion of the mediating effects of interest groups, see Richard A. Styskal, "Strategies of Influence Among Members of Three Voluntary Associations in the Philippines" (unpub. Ph.D. diss., University of Oregon, 1967).

[12] We recognize, of course, the argument that Philippine congressmen may identify individual interest groups by their particular leaders or officials. This is commonly the case not only in the

Congressmen—rather than administrators or other public functionaries—were chosen for study for two reasons: first, their attitudes and behavior, perhaps more than those of any other group in the Philippines, reflect and in turn influence the degree of legitimacy which is accorded interest groups; second, they offer the most parsimonious and direct means for measuring both interest group and unattached citizen activity in the authoritative decision-making process.

Before turning to the findings, it would be helpful to note some of the characteristics of the Philippine political system that influence demand-making.

The Philippines: A Bifurcated Political System

The Philippines has, in effect, two operative political structures—one formal, the other informal.[13] The formal structure closely approximates the group-based model of modern Western democracies. Values and norms associated with this model of government support and encourage interest group demand-making. The formal structure consists of the Philippine constitution and other written and unwritten rules and regulations which have been borrowed largely from the United States. To a great extent this system of government has been super-imposed over traditional means for settling disputes and distributing resources, first in the form of laws applied by the United States to its then colonial territory and later as incorporated into the 1946 constitution.[14] It is based on the general assumption that there will be a degree of personal and social distance between the elect and the electors. Under this structure, a central function of the legis-lature is the "accommodation" of interest group demands in the legislative process.[15]

The formal structure has provided the Philippines with some of the political refinements of the more developed and industrialized societies of the West: a highly formalized political role structure; an emphasis on the desirability of public deliberation over and production of formal rules and regulations; a degree of elite accountability through regular elections; and the orderly succes-sion of elected officials from independence to the present which, comparatively speaking, is somewhat of a rarity among the less-developed countries.

The informal political structure is heavily influenced by traditional Filipino norms and values which emphasize strong familistic loyalties, reciprocal rela-tions between the landed aristocracy and the peasants, and village and regional parochialism in governmental affairs. The basic unit of the informal structure is

---

Philippines but in the more developed Western democracies. See, for example, Dayton D. McKean, *Pressures on the Legislature of New Jersey* (New York, 1938), Ch. 3. However, it seems difficult to conceive that a politician will not distinguish an approach by an unattached individual from an approach by an official of an organized group with the full weight of the membership behind him.

[13] Much of this discussion is indebted to Carl H. Landé's analysis of Philippine politics. See Landé, pp. 2–3, 141–48.

[14] Georges Fischer, "The Political Evolution of the Philippines," in Saul Rose, ed. *Politics in Southern Asia* (New York, 1963), pp. 254–55.

[15] John C. Wahlke, Heinz Eulau, William Buchanan, and LeRoy C. Ferguson, *The Legislative System* (New York, 1962), p. 342.

the dyad, essentially a relationship of mutual aid and dependence between two individuals. It usually evolves from primary group influence sources.[16] The "framework of action" is individualistic rather than group-oriented and, as one student of Philippine politics describes it, is generally alien to the concept of voluntary associations where numbers of people are organized for specific purposes.[17]

Most students of Philippine politics agree that the informal or traditional structure currently predominates in Philippine politics. Landé notes that Filipinos lack loyalty both to associations or interest groups and to political parties.[18] The great majority of Filipino people emphasize primary group values and interests, they have difficulty seeing individual interests in policy terms. Relationships based on highly personal ties between individuals exist at all levels of political organization from the national to the village.[19] The strength of a typical Filipino politician is based on a network of these personal ties and loyalties[20] which, as a rule, are recruited on other than a categorical basis.[21]

Parties and pressure groups, on the other hand, are "very weak organizations," according to Agpalo.[22] He and others argue that the Philippines, like many other transitional societies, has yet to develop the distinctive social classes and modern economy to support the type of collectivist representation found in the United States and Great Britain. Still, interest group activity is not negligible. Wurfel comments that while Philippine interest groups are less important than similar organizations in the United States, they are more important than interest groups in the other Southeast Asian countries.[23] And, in a recent study, Grossholtz notes that associational interest groups have developed at a rapid rate and are playing an increasingly important role in Philippine politics, particularly in the urban areas.[24]

Finally, recent work on politicians and interest groups in the Philippines suggests that, at best, politicians hold an equivocal view toward such organizations; at worst, they believe them to be dangerous and not in the national interest. Grossholtz states that Filipino politicians are ambivalent about pressure groups: "Most Congressmen deny that pressure groups exist."[25] She adds that "in the Philippine politician's view, pressure groups are evil and illegitimate, for

[16] Landé, pp. 143–44.

[17] Jean Grossholtz, *Politics in the Philippines* (Boston, 1964), p. 243.

[18] Landé, p. 2.

[19] *Ibid.*, p. 7.

[20] David Wurfel, "Individuals and Groups in the Policy Process," *Philippine Journal of Public Administration*, IX (January 1965), 32.

[21] Landé, p. 7.

[22] Remigio E. Agpalo, *The Political Process and the Nationalization of the Retail Trade in the Philippines* (Quezon City, 1962), p. 274.

[23] Wurfel, 34.

[24] Grossholtz, pp. 244–47. See also Robert B. Stauffer, "Philippine Legislators and their Changing Universe," *Journal of Politics*, XXVIII (August 1966), 556–97. But compare Kraus, who found a decline in the ratio of voluntary associations to population at the local and national levels in Manila during the years 1929–1964. However, Kraus did point out that there was an increase in "specific" associations during that period (Kraus defined specific associations as ones which are "distinguishable by the narrowness of membership eligibility." They include such groups as medical associations, associations of wine manufacturers, etc.). Wilma R. Kraus, "Differentiations of Associations in Manila, 1929–1964," *Philippine Journal of Public Administration*, X (October 1966), 343–58.

[25] Grossholtz, p. 240.

they represent demands that he use his public authority for private gain."[26] Landé, by contrast, says that Filipino politicians are highly sensitive to the appearance of any new group with the means and the willingness to press claims for governmental action.[27]

Given these observations about the role of individuals and groups in the Philippine political system—the prevalence of individual-oriented relationships between citizen and politician, the incipient and still relatively weak position of interest groups in the political process, and the ambivalence of politicians toward such organizations—we would expect a relatively low level of congressional receptiveness to interest group demand-making. We would expect just the opposite to be true for attempts at individual-oriented influence. To these questions we now turn our attention.

Legislators' Reception of Individuals and Groups

In attempting to measure the receptivity of interest groups and individuals by Philippine congressmen, we have followed, in a limited way, the approach used by Wahlke, Eulau, *et al.*, in their study of American state legislators' attitudes toward interest groups. Briefly, they maintain that legislators' role conceptions are a crucial factor in governing their behavior and that they affect thereby the access and influence of all groups: ". . . Legislators' role conceptions constitute a determining factor in pressure politics at least as important as the number, size, strategy, skill, or other characteristics of pressure groups themselves, the individual group affiliations and identifications of legislators, or the peculiarities of personality and personal whim of those legislators."[28] More specifically, they suggest that legislators' perceptions and evaluations of pressure groups will determine, in part, the success of such organizations in the legislative process. They conclude, among other things, that ". . . probably the effective performance of the legislative system itself depends to some extent upon legislators' acquiring [group-conciliating] orientations."[29] In other words, legislators must first have favorable attitudes toward interest groups before they can be expected to include such organizations in the legislative process.

In the present study, Philippine congressmen were asked about both their attitudes and their behavior with respect to interest groups and individual demand-makers. Attitudes are interpreted as representing the orientation of congressmen (pro or con) toward the present and future role of individuals and groups in the legislative process. Interaction of legislators with groups and individuals is considered a test of these attitudes as well as a measure of the relative activity of groups and individuals in the legislature. Together they measure Philippine legislators' reception of traditional and modern demand-making structures.

26 *Ibid.*, p. 242.
27 Landé, p. 116.
28 John C. Wahlke, Heinz Eulau, William Buchanan, LeRoy C. Ferguson, "American State Legislators' Role Orientations Toward Pressure Groups," *Journal of Politics*, XXII (May 1960), 206.
29 *Ibid.*, 227.

We should make it clear that we are concerned with legislators' attitudes and behavior toward groups and individuals as *generic* classes of "significant others" rather than with particular group affiliations and identifications or with particular friendships and long-standing contacts with certain individuals.

In the interview procedure, attempts were made to reach all members of both houses of the Philippine Congress that met during the spring of 1966. One hundred and twenty-five out of a total of 128 congressmen were finally interviewed. Interviews lasting approximately one-half hour were taken using a written questionnaire consisting almost entirely of forced-choice questions.

CONGRESSIONAL ATTITUDES TOWARD THE ROLE OF INDIVIDUALS AND GROUPS IN THE LEGISLATIVE PROCESS

Every individual forms meaningful *generalized* attitudes about any object, however complex, just as he develops more *specific* attitudes about the component parts of an object.[30] It seems reasonable then to expect that Philippine congressmen will have both general and specific attitudes about the role of individuals and interest groups in the political system. In this section, we begin by examining the more general and inclusive attitudes.

Two general and opposing statements reflecting normative attitudes toward the role of individuals and interest groups were presented to the legislators. They were asked to indicate their amount of agreement or disagreement on a six point scale.[31] To the statement, "Under our form of government every individual should take an interest in government directly and not through interest group organizations," 95 percent of the congressmen agreed, with 48 percent "strongly" agreeing. The amount of consensus on this statement cannot be overstated. Philippine legislators are much more favorable to individual activity in government than are the American state legislators interviewed in the study by Wahlke, Eulau, *et al.* In response to this same question, 43 percent of the California, New Jersey, Ohio, and Tennessee state legislators "agreed" or "tended to agree," with 3 percent "undecided" and 54 percent "tending to disagree" or "disagreeing."[32]

Yet, 76 percent of the Philippine congressmen "agreed" (while 29 percent "strongly agreed" and 22 percent "disagreed") with the opposing statement that "working through interest group organizations is the best way an individual can participate in his government." The agreement here, although less than found in the previous statement, is nevertheless impressive. Discounting the possibility that congressmen interpreted "should take an interest" in the first statement to mean preferred strategy and "best way" in the second statement to mean effective strategy,[33] the two responses at first glance seem contradictory. But are they? A possible clue to the answer may lie in the bifurcated nature of the

[30] Theodore M. Newcomb, Ralph H. Turner, and Philip E. Converse, *Social Psychology* (New York, 1965), pp. 53–54.

[31] Response categories to these questions were "agree strongly," "agree somewhat," "agree slightly," "disagree slightly," "disagree somewhat," and "disagree strongly."

[32] Wahlke, Eulau, *et al.* "American State Legislators' Role Orientations," 208.

[33] Interviewers were instructed that these statements, and others like them, were normative "ought to" or "should be" statements and that they should so inform the respondent during the interview.

Philippine political system. As noted above, implicit in the formal structure of Philippine government are democratic ideals or "constitutional myths" which put a premium on *common* political identity and the response of public officials to group- rather than individual-supported policies and goals. Public officials in fact take pride in Philippine democracy which they regard as more successful than in most other developing countries. As Wurfel notes, the consensus over these ideals is widespread. "The politician in the Philippines must continually cultivate a democratic image."[34]

However, most citizens with whom Philippine politicians must deal are an undifferentiated, unorganized mass largely devoid of common interests and unable to perceive their individual interests in policy terms. In dealing with politicians, family, personal skill, and social status are more important than are concepts of organized groups, community, and nation.[35]

Table 1—Working Through Group Organizations Is the Best Way an Individual Can Participate in His Government

	Representatives				Senators			
	NEW		OLD		NEW		OLD	
	%	N	%	N	%	N	%	N
Agree strongly	45	20	24	14	15	2	0	0
Agree	16	7	58	34	69	9	90	9
Disagree	25	11	12	7	8	1	10	1
Disagree strongly	11	5	5	3	0	0	0	0
No answer	2	1	0	0	8	1	0	0
Total	99	44	99	58	100	13	100	10

The politician, then, is faced with the existence of two sets of political values in the Philippine society. He is obliged to recognize, if not to act upon, the values of both individual and group political action. Below, we may be able to tell more clearly the extent to which congressional behavior reflects these attitudes.

What about differences *between* congressmen with regard to the desirability of working through group organizations (statement two, above)? According to Wahlke, Eulau, *et al.*, since commitment to legislative purpose increases with increasing service in the legislature and since, further, the legislature is the primary agency responsible for the adjustment of group conflicts, then "legislators with most tenure would tend more than those with little tenure to be facilitators" (approving) of interest groups.[36]

In Table 1, we have divided congressmen by office and tenure.[37] Response

---

[34] Wurfel, "Individuals and Groups," 42.

[35] Grossholtz, p. 9. For a general discussion on politicians and undifferentiated publics, see Pye, "The Nonwestern," 477–82.

[36] In the Wahlke, Eulau, *et al.* study, this hypothesis was upheld in all but one case. *The Legislative System*, p. 341. Also see Oliver Garceau and Corinne Silverman, "A Pressure Group and the Pressured: A Case Report." *American Political Science Review*, XLVIII (September 1954), 672–91.

[37] Forty-four members of the House of Representatives at the time of their interview had been in office slightly more than three months, while thirteen members of the Senate had been in office four years or less.

categories have been collapsed to four alternatives. The data clearly reveal that, regardless of tenure, representatives are more "strongly" favorable toward interest groups than are senators. More striking is the fact that, contrary to the predictions of Wahlke, Eulau, *et al.*, concerning American state legislators, the younger Philippine legislators within both houses of congress are more "strongly" favorable toward interest groups than are the more seasoned members, with the notable exception of 36 percent of the "new representatives" who "disagree" with the statement.

This finding suggests a competing hypothesis, at least within the framework of the statement given to Philippine legislators. That is, seasoned politicians may tend to be more cautious or suspicious of new changes in demand-making than are newcomers who, because they are younger and more inexperienced, may be more open and receptive to groups. This may be especially true during recent

Table 2—As a Legislator, Do You Attach More Importance Groups or Individuals in the Legislative Process?

	Representatives		Senators	
	%	N	%	N
Individual	24	24	30	7
Group	26	26	9	2
Both are important	24	24	26	6
Depends on issue	28	28	35	8
Total	102	102	100	23

years. Younger Filipinos are entering congress during a period of growth in the Filipino middle class and during increasing entrepreneurship which in turn is strengthening both labor and business.[38] On the other hand, inexperience that takes the form of parochial attitudes may also account for the 35 percent of the "new representatives" who are unfavorable to group action.

We next turn to the more specific question of the attitudes of congressmen toward the importance of the role of groups and individuals in the legislature. Congressmen were asked, "As a legislator, do you attach (more, less, the same) importance to the individual who represents himself before you as a *member of a group such as the Chamber of Commerce* than you do to the *individual who is not a member* of any specific interest group?"

In Table 2, congressmen are divided by office.[39] We find that roughly equal proportions of representatives favor individuals, favor groups, feel that both groups and individuals are important, or feel that their answer to the question would depend on the issue at hand. By contrast, only two out of twenty-three senators feel that groups are more important than individuals, while seven (of whom five are "old" senators) feel that individuals are more important. These responses appear to compliment the more cautious senatorial responses shown

[38] On the question of labor groups in the Philippines, see Grossholtz, pp. 256–61.
[39] There was little difference between old and new members within the two houses of congress.

in Table 1, thus lending support to the thesis that congressional veterans and senators are more conservatively oriented toward interest groups.

Why do Philippine legislators attach more importance to individuals than to groups or vice versa? And why do some congressmen attach equal weight to both? Comments by individual congressmen are revealing. For those who favor individuals at least three major reasons stand out. The first of these might be called *paternalism*. The comment of a senator with nineteen years' congressional experience illustrates this attitude: "In the Philippines, the individual who is not a member of an organized group is often left out, and it is up to the high-ranking government members to pull this individual up." Secondly, a number of legislators feel that *individual demand-makers are more representative* of the public's interests than are interest groups or their representatives.[40] For example, a member of the lower house for twelve years responded that "the individual who represents no group has more things to request for the country's interest. The individual who represents a group is asking for the group's interests." Finally, some congressmen do not favor individuals so much as they *disfavor groups*. A member of the House of Representatives explained that "individuals purposely attached to a group merely represent their own interests when they come to me." In a later question he defined a "non-legitimate" request of a legislator as one "that is limited to a group."

By way of contrast, a member of the House for fifteen years who favors interest groups stressed the importance of *community* in his statement: "They [groups] are grouped together for a certain purpose; they have a certain purpose for their group. They are responsible to the community; their interests are in consonance with the interests of the community in which they live." And, finally, a freshman representative who favored neither individuals nor groups pointed out that "if I think the individual is representing more the public interest than any group, I give more weight to him; however, if I think the group is more representative than the individual, then the former has my support. My only basis is, are they representing the interest of the public or not?"

It should be noted that for these and numerous other statements offered by Philippine legislators both for and against interest groups, there is a great deal of emphasis on the "public welfare," the "general interest," the "will of the people," and the "good of the country."[41] It is possible that such modern-sounding values can be realized in the Philippine polity through individual as well as group demand-making; in other words, particularized demands of individuals may be converted into policy objectives that benefit the "public welfare." On the other hand, such comments may merely represent the "public voice" of politicians. Interesting as these speculations are, it is impossible in the present study to calculate their probability. We can, however, be more specific

---

[40] Cf. Wurfel, who states that " ... particularistic demands have little impact on the policy process." 32.

[41] Cf. Grossholtz, who states that the Filipino politician does not " ... perceive an objective 'public interest' as meaningful; rather he seeks a synthesis of the subjective demands of the people important to his status. It is these more direct considerations that condition his behavior." Grossholtz, p. 9.

about legislators' attitudes toward the role of relatively broad "publics" as represented by interest groups in the legislative process. Let us next consider these attitudes.

Congressmen were asked for an evaluative judgment of the role of interest groups regarding two particular activities: gaining support for bills and drafting bills and amendments.[42] Both statements were drawn with little change from the study by Wahlke, Eulau, *et al.*[43]

Congressmen agreed by a ratio of more than eight to one with the first statement that "interest groups give politicians valuable help in lining up support for their bills." Little difference was found between congressmen divided according to tenure or office held. Nearly four out of five congressmen agreed with the statement that "legislators get valuable help in drafting bills or amendments from interest groups or their agents." Division according to tenure and office held reveals much the same difference found in Table 1. Greater proportions of "new" representatives both "agreed strongly" and "disagreed" with the statement. That is, there was a more distinct polarization among "new" representatives with regard to the role of interest groups than was the case among the other three legislative groups. And this polarization "favored" the increased role of interest groups in the legislative process. It is significant that attitudes remained constant toward both general and specific aspects of the role of interest groups. It provides added support to the thesis that *newer* congressmen are more open and receptive to change among types of demand-making structures.

The close similarity between the language of the last two measures and the Wahlke, Eulau, *et al.*, items provides an opportunity for comparing the *degree* of Philippine and American support of interest groups.[44] These figures are compared in Tables 3 and 4, where for both studies the response categories have been collapsed.

The data indicate that Filipinos are more accommodating to interest group activity than are Americans. Differences of twenty percentage points for each statement appear fairly substantial even when granting dissimilarities in wording and the comparison of state and national legislators at two different time periods. In addition, for *both* congressional groups, agreement seems high, suggesting that the differences obtained between them are more real than apparent. More specifically, Philippine legislators' support of interest group activity is higher than we would expect, given available information on the Philippine political system. Similarly, American agreement is high, particularly when weighed against the statement by Garceau and Silverman in their study of the Vermont legislature that "the most striking fact that emerged from the interviews as a whole was the extremely low level of recognition of interest group activity."[45]

[42] Respondents could agree or disagree strongly, somewhat or slightly.

[43] In the Wahlke, Eulau, *et al.* study, these statements were used as behavioral rather than attitudinal indicators. See "American State Legislators' Role Orientation," 215.

[44] The Wahlke, Eulau, *et al.* statements read: "I get valuable help in drafting bills from interest groups or their agents" and "interest groups or their agents give me valuable help in lining up support for my bills." *Ibid.*, 214 footnote.

[45] Garceau and Silverman, p. 260.

Table 3—Interest Groups Give Politicians Valuable Help in Lining Up Support for their Bills

	Wahlke, Eulau, et al.	Philippines
	%	%
Agree	69	89
Disagree	31	11
Total	100	100

Table 4—Legislators Get Valuable Help from Interest Groups in Drafting Bills and Amendments

	Wahlke, Eulau, et al.	Philippines
	%	%
Agree	55	78
Disagree	45	22
Total	100	100

These conclusions must, of course, remain tentative until rigorous comparisons can be made between more evenly matched congressional groups.

In summary, our investigation of congressional attitudes toward interest groups, although far from complete, reveals that such organizations are accorded a comparatively favorable role in the political process. We found that substantial majorities of Philippine legislators hold favorable attitudes toward both *general* and *specific* roles of interest groups in the political system.[46] It seems reasonable to assume that such positive norms will encourage the development of interest group functions in the exercise of authority. And, providing they stay in office, the attitudes of the newer congressmen, particularly the representatives, should aid this development.

We also found that congressmen looked favorably upon individual demand-making strategies, particularly upon the *general* role of individuals. Together with the findings on interest groups, this receptiveness to individuals indicates that, in general, congressmen tend to favor *both* traditional and modern demand-structures in Philippine politics.

The consensus disappears, however, when the *importance* of individuals and groups in the legislative process is considered. Nearly 50 percent of the congressmen felt that only one type of demand-making structure was important. Thus, congressmen may agree on the types of demand-making action that are important for the citizen, but they disagree on their significance in the legislative process. The extent to which this particular "mixed" set of attitudes is reflected in congressional behavior will be examined in the next section.

CONTACTS OF CONGRESSMEN WITH INTEREST GROUPS AND UNATTACHED INDIVIDUALS

In order to compare the frequency of individual and group contact with legislators, congressmen were asked how often *individuals* not representing a

[46] See Tables 1, 3, and 4.

group came to them with demands—that is, personally sought them out for help in solving personal problems. Next, they were asked how often groups or their representatives came to them for help with group problems.

These questions do not measure the type of congressional contact (for example, direct or indirect), nor do they distinguish the type of individual or group problem involved in the interaction. Rather we aimed for a *general estimate* of congressional contact with the structural vehicles for demands—individual and group—located "outside" the government.

In Table 5, the forty-four members of the House of Representatives who had been in office slightly more than three months at the time they were interviewed are tabulated separately because of their relative inexperience in congress.

Table 5—How Often Do Individuals, Groups, Come to You for Help ?

| | Individuals | | | | Groups | | | |
| | NEW REPRE- SENTATIVES | | SENATORS AND REPRESENTATIVES: TWO OR MORE YEARS IN CONGRESS | | NEW REPRE- SENTATIVES | | SENATORS AND REPRESENTATIVES: TWO OR MORE YEARS IN CONGRESS | |
	%	N	%	N	%	N	%	N
Very often	89	39	95	77	7	3	36	29
Somewhat often	7	3	1	1	25	11	30	24
Not too often	2	1	3	2	27	12	23	19
Very seldom	0	0	1	1	23	10	7	6
Never	2	1	0	0	18	8	3	2
Depends	0	0	0	0	0	0	1	1
Total	100	44	100	81	100	44	100	81

Table 5 shows the greater frequency of individual over interest group contact reported by the legislators, regardless of their tenure. Dividing by tenure, we find that nearly three times as many seasoned congressmen were approached "very often" by individuals rather than groups. Yet the overall extent of interaction with groups, although less frequent than with individuals, is widespread. Only 3 percent of the veterans said that they had "never" been approached by interest groups, while 66 percent said they were contacted "very often" or "somewhat often." This last is a sizeable proportion, individual contacts notwithstanding.

On the other hand, only half as many "first termers" as seasoned congressmen were contacted "very" or "somewhat often" by interest groups. This difference is not unexpected. Undoubtedly one of the major reasons for the newer legislators' lack of contact with groups is their short time in office. What is somewhat unexpected is that after only three months in office nearly 90 percent of the new representatives said they had been approached "very often" by individuals seeking help with personal problems. Large numbers of constituents, it seems, take quick advantage of their newly elected representatives.

As a further measure of contact with unaffiliated individuals, congressmen were asked: "How often do your constituents ask you for personal favors?" Table 6 shows ample evidence of the traditional relationship between politician

Table 6—How Often Do Your Constituents Ask for Personal Favors ?

	%	N
Very often	90	113
Often	5	6
Sometimes	4	5
Not very often	1	1
Not at all	0	0
Total	100	125

and citizen that is often called "personalism."[47] None of the congressmen is immune to favor-seekers, with 90 percent of them saying they were "very often" approached. Congressmen replied characteristically to this question that they were continually swamped ("every day," "very, very often," "my constituents come here every minute") by constituents both in and out of congress who sought financial assistance, jobs, legal aid, and advice and help with other personal problems.

Although these questions reveal that the frequency of individual contacts with congressmen is much greater than the frequency of contacts by organized groups or their representatives, what happens with more specific requests of legislators, particularly those dealing with policy issues rather than personal or group problems? Asking a congressman to vote pro or con on a pending bill is a type of demand that might be considered issue-oriented.

Legislators were asked both whether and how often individuals and members of groups "such as the Chamber of Commerce, the PTA, the Market Vendors

Table 7—How Often Do Individuals, Groups, Ask You to Vote a Certain Way on a Political Issue ?

	Individuals				Groups			
	NEW REPRE-SENTATIVES		SENATORS AND REPRESENTATIVES: TWO OR MORE YEARS IN CONGRESS		NEW REPRE-SENTATIVES		SENATORS AND REPRESENTATIVES: TWO OR MORE YEARS IN CONGRESS	
	%	N	%	N	%	N	%	N
Very often	20	9	47	38	7	3	34	28
Somewhat often	18	8	17	14	9	4	16	13
Not too often	23	10	16	13	11	5	5	4
Very seldom	9	4	4	3	5	2	5	4
Never	25	11	15	12	55	24	27	7
Depends	2	1	1	1	2	1	9	22
No answer	2	1	0	0	11	5	4	3
Total	99	44	100	81	100	44	100	81

[47] On "personalism-paternalism" as a "mode" of politicization see Daniel Goldrich, "On the Concept of Politicization," in Robert S. Cahill and Stephen P. Hencley, *The Politics of Education* (Danville, 1964), pp. 189–202.

Association and other groups" ask them to vote a certain way on an issue. Their answers are shown in Table 7.[48]

Again, contacts with individuals outnumber contacts with interest groups. Yet, when compared to Table 5 above, we find that the ratio of individuals to groups, who both new and veteran legislators say approach them "often," has narrowed considerably: from 10:1 to 3:1 for new representatives, and from 3:1 to 1.5:1 for veteran legislators. These changes result almost totally from the drop-off in the number of congressmen who reported contacts with individuals. If we add to this the evidence of Table 7 that the number of legislators who have "never" been contacted by individuals has increased considerably, it then seems reasonable to conclude that *individual* demand-making is substantially more "personal-problem" (and thus particularistic more than categorical) than it is "issue"-oriented.

Table 8—Have Interest Groups Supported You in Your Campaign for Office?

	Representatives				Senators			
	NEW		OLD		NEW		OLD	
	%	N	%	N	%	N	%	N
No	32	14	24	14	8	1	10	1
Yes, recently	59	26	66	38	77	10	70	7
Yes, in the past	7	3	5	3	8	1	20	2
Don't know/ no answer	2	1	5	3	8	1	0	0
Total	100	44	100	58	101	13	100	10

In a more limited sense, much the same conclusion may be drawn with regard to *interest groups* when the data in Tables 5 and 7 are compared. On the basis of the reports of legislators, Philippine interest groups appear to be more "group-problem-oriented" than "issue-oriented." Beyond this, further conclusions would be speculative. We have no way, for example, of telling definitely whether "group-problem-type" contacts with legislators largely involve categorical or particularized demands.[49] However, it is enough for our purposes to reveal the difference between individual and group contacts with congressmen.

In a final measure of the relations of legislators with groups, congressmen were asked whether interest groups (other than political parties) had encouraged and supported them to run for political office. The results appear in Table 8.

---

[48] It should be noted that these figures represent the frequency with which individuals and groups approach legislators about voting on issues in general. It seems clear that the demand-making activity of organized groups and unattached individuals may vary with the particular issue under consideration. Unfortunately, because of considerations of time and the overall requirements of the research project, legislators were only asked about the activities of interest groups on a few selected issues. These issues, because of their very great importance for certain groups but not others, would have presented a biased picture of interest group activity in general.

[49] See Grossholtz, who mentions the tendency of group members to utilize their own personal relations to advance their interests (with, in this case, administrative bureaus) to the detriment of the group. Grossholtz, p. 245.

In Table 8 senators are tabulated separately from representatives because of the different electoral procedures which, we suggest, may affect their associations with groups. Unlike representatives, who are chosen by districts, Philippine senators are elected at large. Their constituency is, in effect, nation-wide, covering eleven large islands and numerous smaller ones. This fact prevents a candidate for the senate from concentrating exclusively on any one area for raising electoral support and, moreover, demands a great deal more campaign organization and expense than is necessary for representatives.[50] If this interpretation is correct, then, on the basis of campaign financing alone, it seems probable that senatorial candidates would find it more advantageous than would candidates for the House to rely on interest group support. The data in Table 8 suggest that this is indeed the case. Only 8 percent and 10 percent of new and old senators, respectively, have never been supported by interest groups, while 24 percent of the old and 32 percent of the new representatives report no such support.

More important, though, is the ample evidence that a substantial majority of the members of congress, regardless of tenure and office, have utilized interest groups in their campaign for office. Because political campaigns in the Philippines are expensive, it is highly likely that the congressmen themselves requested aid from interest groups. If this is the case, we find the dependency relationship just the reverse of that found in the traditional patron-client dyad: here, the politician is the client and the interest group the financial benefactor. As campaign costs in the Philippines increase, the politician may very well become even more beholden to interest groups.

To summarize this section, contact with individual "personal-problem" demand-makers is widespread and frequent among legislators, whereas contact is less frequent with individuals making voting demands. The picture that unfolds shows Philippine congressmen being besieged by their constituents with personal requests. Eighty-nine percent of those congressmen in office for only three months said they were approached "very often" by individuals who wanted help with personal problems. At first glance, these findings seem to reinforce the commonplace notion that public officials in transitional countries are often harassed and annoyed by individual demands. If, however, our evidence of the favorable attitudes of legislators toward the general role of individuals is correct, this interpretation is questionable—at least in the case of Philippine legislators. Such favorable attitudes suggest accommodation rather than inhibition of traditional means for making demands.

Legislator contact with interest groups was significantly lower than contact with individuals. This difference is obviously accounted for by both the comparative weakness in number and organization of Philippine interest groups and the great intensity of individual demand-making. But it seems likely that the latter factor is the more important reason for such a difference. Interest-group activity, measured by the number of influence attempts, would appear to be always less than individual action, even in more developed countries such as the

---

[50] *Ibid.*, 119–120; Wurfel, 32.

United States. In the United States, where "the informal role of private organizations . . . has been so intensive that observers constantly . . . refer to government by pressure groups,"[51] V. O. Key notes that "even in legislation, government continues to deal, more often than is commonly recognized, with the individual case rather than with the rights and duties of categories of persons."[52]

Legislator contact with interest groups was also lower than expected, given the extent of favorable attitudes toward the general and specific roles of these organizations. This difference between attitudes and behavior suggests there may be a reservoir of good faith toward interest groups. Unquestionably, the attitudes may be partly explained by lip-service to the strong constitutional myth in the Philippines. But we should be aware also of the possibility that many of these attitudes toward groups are sincere, particularly in view of the extent to which interest groups are involved with congressmen in their campaign for office.

Conclusion

We have attempted to describe and compare the attitudes and behavior of Philippine legislators with respect to the role of interest groups and unattached individuals in the legislative process. We have assumed that in a transitional society such as the Philippines, interest groups approximate modern, while unaffiliated individuals approximate traditional, demand-making structures. We have paid special attention to groups and individuals as generic classes of "significant others" rather than singling out particular groups and specific individuals. Although our data are incomplete, several important, if tentative, conclusions are suggested.

Perhaps the most important conclusion is that Philippine legislators have positive attitudes toward the general *and* specific roles of interest groups in the legislative process. This approval is heightened by the comparatively enthusiastic reception of interest groups by the newer representatives. When we view the variously tenured congressmen in quasi-longitudinal fashion, it appears that their favorable feeling toward the role of interest groups in Philippine politics is increasing. Supporting this conclusion is the relatively widespread use of interest groups by congressmen in their political campaigns. Such a change of attitudes is evidence of an openness and receptivity to change in demand-making structures that may lead toward a greater share in decision-making for groups outside formal government and, ultimately, to the increasing dispersion of power in the Philippines. At the same time, the ambivalence of politicians over the *importance* of interest groups in general (see Table 2) and the evidence of their rate of interaction with such organizations (see Tables 5 and 7) warn us against the too-facile conclusion that these groups have reached the importance of similar organizations in the United States. There, as Wahlke, Eulau, *et al.* note,

[51] Bertram M. Gross, *The Legislative Struggle* (New York, 1953), p. 23.
[52] V. O. Key, Jr., *Politics, Parties and Pressure Groups* (New York, 1952), pp. 171–172 footnote.

if interest groups were "removed or prevented from influencing legislative action, the authority of the legislature would be found unacceptable."[53] In the Philippines, this central importance may be true of the "sugar bloc" of the landed elite,[54] but it does not yet hold for Philippine interest groups as a whole.

A more frequent source of demands on legislators are constituents—individuals unaffiliated with groups—who come in large numbers to press their representatives for help with personal needs and wants. Moreover, our findings suggest that congressmen view such activity with favor, at least generally speaking. The data appear to support previous findings to the effect that the more traditional or informal structure of politics, as we have called it, is still predominant in the Philippines. Further, the evidence we and others have amassed suggests that the intensity of individual demand-making will not subside and that Philippine politicians will continue to accommodate and favor this activity. There is no lack of support for this conclusion in studies of other countries. Goldrich, for example, states that "although many social scientists have expected personalism and paternalism in Latin America to diminish with economic development and urbanization, these orientations continue to be widely manifested in the cities, even in those most industrially advanced."[55] Yet we cannot go so far as to say that individual demand-making is more *important* than interest group demand-making in the Philippines. The ambivalent attitude of congressmen toward the importance of both individual and group demands (see Table 2) cautions us to be wary of such a conclusion. It also invites further study of what is and is not important (and influential) in legislative demand-making and, indeed, how one defines such a quality.

More generally, the findings describe the kind of mixed political demand system that exists today in the Philippines. *Attitudinally*, Philippine legislators are generally receptive to *both* traditional and modern forms of demand-making. These values are not necessarily contradictory, nor are they necessarily in conflict; on the contrary, traditional values can supply sources of legitimation that can be used to pursue new structures and new processes.[56] On the other hand, more modern-sounding values may be used to lend a measure of legitimacy to traditional practices. Neither are these values mutually exclusive. Certain traditional values—such as the ceremony resulting from the meeting of politician and citizen in the Philippines—no doubt always will remain, no matter how modernized the political process becomes. Such an agglomeration of values may provide a clue to the orderly adaptation of the Philippine political system (and other transitional political systems as well) to new and changing political demands.

The picture that emerges with respect to the *interactions* of congressmen with demand-makers shows clearly that the traditional-modern "mix" is weighted heavily in favor of tradition. That this rate of interaction may, in fact, never favor interest groups we have discussed above. Yet at least three factors suggest

[53] Wahlke, Eulau, *et al.*, "American State Legislators' Role Orientation," 203.
[54] Wurfel, 35.
[55] Goldrich, p. 198.
[56] Gusfield, p. 355.

that there will be a change to a more balanced picture, a picture that includes increased demand-activity from interest groups. First are the increasingly favorable attitudes of legislators toward groups. Second is the fact that interest groups, in their involvement in the electoral process, have begun to establish stronger bargaining positions *vis-à-vis* elected officials. Third is the increasing differentiation and specialization of the Philippine economy, particularly in the industrial and commercial sectors. This growth of interest group activity, if it develops as hypothesized, does not necessarily mean a corresponding decline in individual demand-making activity—in so-called personalistic politics.[57] On the contrary, as the society develops, and with a commensurate increase in politicization, such influence attempts are likely to increase also. If these speculations are sound, political scientists may need to take a new look at the "blends" and "mixtures" of traditional and modern forces in transitional societies and their contribution to political development.

[57] See Pye, *Politics, Personality and Nation Building,* who argues against the idea that there should be a quantitative decline in traditional forms of behavior and a corresponding increase in behavior consistent with the modern pattern. P. 37.

The Effects of Lobbying:
A Comparative Assessment

by HARMON ZEIGLER

Adherents of the group theory of politics would consider it heretical to wonder what would happen to the legislative process if there were no interest groups and lobbyists. Yet, such a question is not unreasonable, especially when one considers the fact that most case studies of "interest groups in action" *begin* with the assumption that the group model is correct. However, recent studies of the lobbying process in Washington, notably those of Milbrath and Bauer, Pool, and Dexter, suggest that the policy outcomes of Congress would not have been very different if lobbyists were eliminated from the decision-making process.[1]

The serious questions raised by these studies need further exploration on a comparative basis. If it is true that lobbyists are not very influential in Washington, why is this so? One would suspect that there are certain structural conditions in Washington, not the least of which is that the legislator has other sources of information, that reduce the influence of lobbyists. The purpose of the research reported here is to offer an assessment of the strength of interest groups in four states: Massachusetts, North Carolina, Oregon, and Utah.[2]

---

[1] Raymond A. Bauer *et al.*, *American Business and Public Policy* (New York: Atherton Press 1963), p. 398. Lester Milbrath, *The Washington Lobbyists* (Chicago: Rand McNally, 1963).

[2] Interviews were conducted during February and March, 1966. Efforts were made to interview each legislator and lobbyist. For the legislators, the percentage of completed interviews is: Massachusetts, 87%, North Carolina, 97%, Oregon, 94%, and Utah, 94%. For lobbyists, the percentage interviewed is more difficult to assess. In Utah, there is no list of registered lobbyists and in the other states it was found that some lobbyists do not register. In Massachusetts and North Carolina, the number of completed interviews exceeds the number of registered lobbyists. In Oregon, 94% of the registered lobbyists were interviewed. In Utah, since we first had to construct a list based upon preliminary interviews with experienced legislators, newspaper reporters, and more visible lobbyists, no percentage calculation can be given.

Reprinted from "The Effects of Lobbying: A Comparative Assessment," *The Western Political Quarterly* 22, no. 1 (March 1969): 122–40, by Harmon Zeigler. Reprinted by permission of the University of Utah, copyright owners, and the author.

The theoretical focus of the study centers around the concept of interaction. We need to know: (1) how much interaction between legislators and lobbyists actually takes place; (2) what is the nature of this interaction; and (3) what is the effect of this interaction. Finally, having offered an assessment of the effects of interaction, it is necessary to speculate as to possible explanations for variations in effect. This is a difficult task, and any number of explanations might be as valid as the one suggested in the conclusion to this article. Nevertheless, a beginning of a revised theory of the role of groups in the political process should offer some speculation as to why groups are powerful in some systems and not in others. Of course, one can argue that the political systems themselves, rather than the interaction of participants *within* these systems, are the crucial explanatory factor. Taking this approach, one might link the strength of interest groups to the economic, social, and political characteristics of a state. It will be necessary to consider this argument after first presenting an alternative explanation.

Frequency of Interaction

To be effective, lobbyists have to interact with legislators on a regularized and frequent basis. State legislators are busy, and the sources competing for their time are many. Therefore, the beginning of an assessment of interest group strength must be frequency of interaction. Legislators and lobbyists were asked how many contacts (of any kind) occurred per week during the legislative session.[3] Table 1 indicates, first, that there are substantial interstate differences

Table 1—Mean Interactions Per Week as Reported by Legislators and Lobbyists

	Mean	N
Massachusetts		
Legislators	7.8	244
Lobbyists	10.7	185
North Carolina		
Legislators	8.5	164
Lobbyists	25.9	132
Oregon		
Legislators	34.0	84
Lobbyists	31.0	193
Utah		
Legislators	16.0	90
Lobbyists	18.5	134

and, second, with regard to interstate differences, that the perceptions of legislators and lobbyists differ. It seems quite clear that both legislators and lobbyists report more contact in Oregon. More interaction takes place in Oregon than in

[3] It is obviously better to *observe* the number of interactions than to ask the participants to recall them, but to do so would have been impossible both in terms of comparative research and in terms of time involved. The table should be interpreted as an estimate.

any other state, regardless of who is making the judgment. It also is clear that legislators and lobbyists have the fewest number of interactions in Massachusetts. Utah falls between the two extremes, and again there is substantial consensus. The real problem is North Carolina. In each of the other states legislators and lobbyists are relatively close in their assessment of the extent of interactions, but in North Carolina legislators think little interaction takes place, while lobbyists would "rank" their state second only to Oregon. Here we encounter a basic problem in Eulau's suggestion that both actors in the interaction should be examined. Who is right? One possibility is, of course, that lobbyists are exaggerating their importance, as McAdams has suggested in another context, while legislators, conforming to their perception of the good legislator, believe they are acting "independently."[4] This explanation has the obvious flaw of failing to account for the tendency of legislators in other states to approximate the estimates of lobbyists. In Oregon, legislators see *more* interaction than do lobbyists.

Still, there might be some truth in the explanation. North Carolina is less urban, less industrialized, and less wealthy than the other states. It also has the lowest rate of political participation. These conditions generally contribute to the strength of the interest group system, but at the same time might contribute to the reluctance of legislators to discuss interest groups, or to the failure of legislators to be able to offer accurate assessments. North Carolina has, according to Elazar, a *traditionalistic political culture*. The essential attributes of such a culture are "a paternalistic and elitist concept of the commonwealth." Consequently, such a culture confines "real political power to a relatively small and self-perpetuating group drawn from an established elite" who have a "right" to govern.[5] If legislators reflect these kinds of attitudes, they would admit very little "outside" influence, whether from party, interest group, or constituents. Eulau's evaluation of Tennessee—a state with essentially the same political culture as North Carolina—is suggestive of this conclusion. There are more 'trustees" in Tennessee than in any of the other states examined.[6] Trustees define their legislative role as that of free agent, relying on their own conscience and principles rather than the advice of any external forces. Therefore, they would be reluctant either to place much reliance on lobbyists or, perhaps, to *admit* that they do so.

The fact that interest groups seem to be such a minor part of the Massachusetts legislative system might be a function of the strong party cohesion in that legislature. Further, Massachusetts is a populous, ethnically diverse state which might, on the one hand, produce more demands for legislative action, but at the same time increase the number of competitors for rewards (still, there are fewer registered lobbyists in Massachusetts than in Oregon).

In addition to the strength of party, Massachusetts has nearly three times as many legislators as does either Oregon or Utah, making the task of interaction

---

[4] Alan K. McAdams, *Power and Politics in Labor Legislation* (New York: Columbia U. Press, 1964), p. 193.

[5] Daniel Elazar, *American Federalism: A View From the States* (New York: Crowell, 1966), p. 93.

[6] Wahlke, *et al.*, *op. cit.*, p. 281.

difficult purely on the basis of the ratio of legislators to lobbyists.[7] Boston is a large city in which one can easily submerge oneself in anonymity; Salem, Oregon, is a small town with the legislature as the main focal point of activity. Salt Lake City, between Boston and Salem in population, yields an interaction rate also between these two extremes. Of course, one can hardly maintain that the size of the capital city, *per se*, is a basic contributor to the rate of interaction, but, coupled with the limited visibility of interest groups in comparison to the strong political parties of Massachusetts, it might be a reinforcement. The weakness of groups in North Carolina and Massachusetts appears easier to explain than the strength of groups in Oregon and Utah. As the explanation develops, attempts will be made to correct this deficiency.

The fact that legislators and lobbyists have different perceptions of the extent of communication might be indicative of actual *patterns* of interaction. Both sets of judges might be correct. Assuming this is true, we might conclude that in the states in which legislators perceive more communication than do lobbyists, the bulk of the contact comes from a *few* lobbyists trying to communicate with a large body of legislators. The target of communications might be large. The best examples of this possibility are Oregon and Utah. The larger targets of lobbyists might reflect the relatively open decision-making structure of these legislatures. Neither strong parties nor traditionalistic cultures would restrict the number of legislators who might be viewed as useful targets for communication. The strategy would thus be to contact as many legislators as possible, whether or not they hold important party or legislative positions. Yet, since a relatively small proportion of lobbyists are full time "professionals" who make lobbying a business, this relatively large body of legislators would interact with a smaller proportion of lobbyists. In Oregon, in contrast to Utah, more lobbyists are "professionals" and put in longer hours on the job. In this state, therefore, there is both the necessity of contacting a larger body of legislators and a larger number of lobbyists trying to interact.

Two contrasting patterns are presented by North Carolina and Massachusetts, neither of which has broad target areas. In Massachusetts, few legislators interact with few lobbyists. In North Carolina, many lobbyists interact with few legislators. Thus, the rigidity of party control in Massachusetts might eliminate the rank-and-file from the communication process, while the traditionalism and value placed upon experience might do so in North Carolina. In North Carolina, however, the case for a restricted target zone appears strengthened because of the greater activity of lobbyists. North Carolina brings to mind the research of Garceau and Silverman, which suggested that many Vermont legislators are unaware of intense lobbying activity, and of Wahlke, Eulau, Buchanan, and Ferguson, who find Tennessee legislators uninformed, but draw a different sort of conclusion: that there not much lobbying takes place. It is clear, in North

---

[7] The idea of the difficulty of the lobbyists' job being related to the size of the audience can be explored by examining the interaction rates of the state senates, which have fewer members. In Massachusetts and Utah there is substantially more interaction in the Senate than in the House. However, in North Carolina, there is substantially less contact in the Senate, while in Oregon the interaction rates are virtually the same.

Carolina, that most legislators are not involved in the lobbying process, but this does not necessarily mean that little lobbying takes place.

The problem would not have existed had only legislators been interviewed, but the description emerging from a single set of interviews would have been less valid. One approach to the problem is to find out what *kinds* of lobbyists and legislators are most likely to interact. For instance, it may be that interaction increases with the experience of both or either of the sides. In the case of lobbyists, it may take time to locate key decision-makers, become familiar with the rules of the game, learn the technicalities of legislation, establish a reputation, and get on friendly terms with legislators. Legislators might have increased contact with lobbyists if they have had considerable legislative experience and if their position in the legislature is sufficiently important to attract the attention of lobbyists. Since turnover in the ranks of both groups is fairly high, perhaps a minority really get involved. To some extent these speculations are supported by the data, but not in a clear fashion. In all states except Utah, the experienced lobbyists do interact more with legislators than do the novices. However, the Oregon novice lobbyists interact with legislators as much as do the experienced lobbyists in North Carolina. Thus, intense interaction is limited in North Carolina but is more "open" in Oregon. In Utah, the novice lobbyists actually have more contacts with legislators than do the experienced ones. Assuming that the experienced lobbyists know more about their jobs, this suggests that a better strategy is to limit contact. Both North Carolina (52 percent) and Utah (44 percent) have a higher proportion of experienced lobbyists than Oregon (30 percent) and Massachusetts (29 percent).[8] However, in spite of the relative experience of their lobbyists, the two states differ markedly with respect to intensity of interaction.

A similar pattern emerges for legislators; those with the most experience have the greatest contact with lobbyists, except for North Carolina, which is a puzzling development. We have described North Carolina as a relatively "closed" state in which only the more experienced lobbyists actually get into the act of contacting a few legislators. But the experienced legislators do not absorb the bulk of the efforts of lobbyists, as they do in other states. Nor do committee chairmen or party leaders receive more communications from lobbyists than non-leaders, as is generally true.[9] The structure of power in North Carolina's legislature—insofar as it can be ascertained from the efforts of lobbyists—is totally unrelated to the formal structure of the institution.

On the basis of interaction—without concern for the *effects* of interaction, Oregon and Massachusetts stand at opposite ends of a continuum with North Carolina (depending upon the judges) and Utah falling in between. Of course, interaction need not be an indicator of effect. Perhaps one contact by a good lobbyist is worth 100 contacts by an amateur. Also, perhaps the greater the contact—indicating a more intense set of demands—the less effective any one contact is likely to be. Further, intensity of interaction might simply be a function of how busy legislators are. The more bills there are to consider, the more

[8] The cut-point for experience is eleven years (the mean).
[9] From data to be reported in the future.

frequent will be the interaction (assuming that interest groups are the basic communicators of demands). Such an assumption clearly does not work because Massachusetts, with its low rate of interaction, considers almost twice as many bills per day (19) as does Oregon (10).

Although the explanation of the reasons for varied rates of interaction is divided at this point, let us proceed to the next step in the argument. The question is: to what extent does frequency of interaction provide clues both about the nature and effects of the interaction?

What is the Nature of the Interaction?

Although a communications model may be too weak, communicating with legislators is what lobbyists are supposed to do. It is certainly true that the purpose of *any* communication is to change behavior, yet the communications

Table 2—Percentage of Legislators and Lobbyists Classifying Their Roles As:

	Persuader	Informant	Both	N
Massachusetts				
Legislators	30%	42	28	244
Lobbyists	54%	18	28	185
North Carolina				
Legislators	20%	53	27	164
Lobbyists	45%	29	27	132
Oregon				
Legislators	26%	55	19	84
Lobbyists	48%	34	19	193
Utah				
Legislators	29%	57	14	90
Lobbyists	38%	36	25	134

and mechanistic models offer markedly different interpretations of the nature of communications. The supporters of the communications model believe that lobbyists transmit *information* to legislators. The consequences of this assumption are: (1) most interaction occurs between two partisans: "Its [the interest group] role became that of an auxiliary service bureau for a senator with whom it was in complete agreement";[10] and (2) successful lobbyists are those upon whom legislators know they can rely for accurate information, preferably information which is available most conveniently (or exclusively) from lobbyists. One lobbyist phrased the job of the informant in these words: "I try to establish a reputation for having certain . . . technical information which is otherwise unavailable to them [legislators]."

The assumptions of the mechanistic model are fundamentally different. Lobbyists have as their fundamental goal the *persuasion* of legislators. Subscri-

[10] Bauer, *et al., op. cit.,* p. 357.

bers to the mechanistic theory believe: (1) lobbyists communicate with opponents or undecided legislators, and (2) successful lobbyists are those able to convert opponents into supporters and firm up waverers. According to one such lobbyist: "Well, I may as well be honest about it. We are trying to influence votes on certain measures. We spend most of our time trying to influence votes on legislative measures."

Just as Eulau argues that neither the mechanistic nor the communications models are entirely correct, it is reasonable to assume that there is a bit of truth in the behavioral consequences which flow from either model. Certainly the data suggest that this is the case (Table 2).

Legislators and lobbyists are categorized according to whether they spend more of their time sending or receiving messages with a content either primarily informational or persuasive.[11] Obviously, such a categorization of the nature of communication is ideal. Information is certainly an instrument of persuasion, and most messages are probably a "mix." Nevertheless, respondents were able to decide what the perceived essential purpose of a message was. Table 2 is illus-

Table 3—Interaction Rates of Legislators and Lobbyists Devoted to Persuasion or Information

	Persuasion	Information
Massachusetts		
Legislators	.25	.33
Lobbyists	.46	.22
North Carolina		
Legislators	.09	.17
Lobbyists	.33	.22
Oregon		
Legislators	.21	.30
Lobbyists	.37	.25
Utah		
Legislators	.23	.38
Lobbyists	.33	.32

trative of some fundamental concepts in the examination of the interaction process. The evaluation of an encounter will be based upon self-perceptions and perceptions of the other person. The nature of the interaction is seen quite differently by the two participants. The pattern is quite consistent from state to state. In every case, a higher proportion of lobbyists are classified as persuaders and a higher proportion of legislators define their role as receivers of information. These contrasting perceptions of the encounter can be expected to have an impact upon the behavior of the actors. As we have argued, the nature of the encounter is defined by the perceptions of the participants. It stands to reason that the more congruent the perceptions of the participants, the less ambiguous

---

[11] The categorization is derived from the "purposive" and "nonpurposive" distinction found in the literature of communications. See Bruce H. Westley and Malcolm S. Maclean, Jr., "A Conceptual Model for Communications Research," in James H. Campbell and Hal W. Helper (eds.), *Dimensions in Communication* (Belmont, California: Wadsworth Publishing Co., 1965), pp. 61–62.

will be the encounter. In this case, the effectiveness of the lobbyist should be related to the extent of harmony between his perceptions and that of the legislator. In other words, the clearer the mutual expectations, the more effective will be the lobbyist.

Table 2 provides categories based solely upon whether or not one type of communication outweighs another. To get an idea of the extent of congruence, let us examine the rate of interaction spent in either informational or persuasive communication (Table 3). We can now see that the greatest congruence concerning perception of persuasion occurs in Oregon, followed by Utah, North Carolina, and Massachusetts. Thus, the two states with the highest interaction have the greatest congruence. It will be argued shortly that Oregon and Utah are the states with the strongest groups, thus supporting the ideas of the relationship between congruence and effectiveness. Further, the fact that there is greater congruence in states with high interaction indicates that stereotypic perceptions probably dictate the terms of an *initial* encounter, but that more accurate images develop as the interactions become more frequent. Hence, Massachusetts and North Carolina, with the lowest rates of interaction, also have the least congruence and the least effective lobbyists. Notice also that there is uniformly greater congruence concerning informational communication. This may indicate a greater acceptance of the legitimacy of this type of communication and, incidentally, suggest an introductory chapter to a textbook for beginning lobbyists.

The Effects of Lobbying

Measuring the effects of lobbying is especially difficult in view of contrasting perceptions, and because of the existence of at least two functions of lobbying. If lobbying is persuasion, we need to know how often this goal is achieved. If lobbying is information, we need to know how much confidence is placed in this information. The point to be made is that a single measure of influence is not able to account for the *ends* attached to various lobbying *means*. Mention was made earlier of the report by Zeller.[12] Political scientists were asked to describe the influence of interest groups in their states as "strong," "moderate," or "weak." The defects of this method are apparent. The panel of judges is, at best, questionable. Asking people to evaluate the effects of interest groups in terms of such an ambiguous concept as "power" compounds the felony. A better method was devised by Wahlke, Eulau, Buchanan, and Ferguson. Their measure was based on questions dealing with both the legislators' awareness of interest groups and their acceptance of the legitimacy of lobbying. By combining legislators' attitudes (as measured by a series of scales) and awareness (as measured by ability to identify certain organizations), legislators were classified into three role-orientations: facilitators, neutrals, and resistors. Thus, in no case is anybody simply asked about the power of interest groups. However, as we noted earlier, there are some problems with this scheme. The classifications are only minimally

---

[12] Belle Zeller (ed.), *American State Legislatures* (New York: Crowell, 1954), pp. 190–91.

behavioral. They do not deal with the effects of actual interaction but only with attitudes. Wahlke reasons that legislators can be expected to behave according to their role definitions and that the behavioral consequences follow naturally from role definitions.

Whereas this assumption may be correct, no actual behavior is described.[13] Our data do indicate, in support of Wahlke, that the extent of contact, effect of contact, and attitudes toward lobbyists are clearly interrelated. However, one of the conclusions of *The Legislative System,* that percentage of resistors declines as legislative experience increases, is challenged. It was found that, whereas the *attitudes* of legislators toward lobbyists become more favorable as experience increases, legislators *do not* become more persuadable. The lack of connection between behavior and attitude is illustrated by Wahlke's discussion of the potential for interest-group politics in the various states, avoiding a discussion of what happens in favor of an estimate of what might happen. Finally, the potential and the actuality are gradually merged until the distinction is lost.

There is no clear way out of these dilemmas. The approach offered here is to consider lobbying as both a persuasive and informational process and to assess the effects of both attempts, relying upon reports of behavior more than upon assessment of attitudes.

Initially, we might observe some apparent differences between lobbying in the states and lobbying in Washington, D.C. In Washington, where informational lobbying seems typical, lobbyists talk to sympathetic legislators. In the states, where there is more persuasion, opponents seem to have considerable contact with each other. It is true that more contact takes place among like-minded lobbyists and legislators than among those who do not see things in the same way, but in all states at least a third of the legislators and lobbyists indicate substantial contact with opponents. In Oregon, to use a slightly atypical case, about the same number of contacts take place among those with conflicting points of view as between those in agreement. In fact, lobbyists tend to lean toward contacts with legislators whose position is unclear. In short, lobbyists appear to "lobby" in the traditional stereotype more in the states than in Washington. Concerning stereotypes, the younger lobbyists are more likely to talk to opponents and to define their role as persuader than are the older lobbyists; hence, they fit the stereotype more easily. There is a sort of professionalization process which reduces the stereotypic behavior of lobbyists as they begin to learn the rules of the game. Such a process of professionalization is certainly related to the number of interactions. The greater the number of interactions, the more realistic become the actors' images of each other. Hence younger lobbyists who do not get "into the game" very much have not had the opportunity to correct their stereotypes.

Another aspect of stereotypic behavior which is probably related to extent of interaction concerns the notion of "pressure." According to popular and some scholarly characterizations, pressure groups do just what the name implies. No

---

[13] Since this analysis is based upon reports of behavior rather than independent observations of behavior, the point of the objection is questionable. Nevertheless, in using reports as a surrogate for behavior, the effort to describe behavior is made clear.

one is really sure what pressure tactics are available to lobbyists, and the research in the Washington setting of Milbrath and Bauer, Pool, and Dexter suggests that "information groups" is a more appropriate appellation. Nevertheless, the image persists. To legislators and lobbyists, pressure is an undesirable connotation. When a legislator says that he is being pressured, he means that he perceives the lobbyist to be trying vigorously to overcome his resistance by any available means.

The perceived incidence of pressure varies from state to state and between legislators and lobbyists. Massachusetts lobbyists, who report very little contact with legislators, believe that they engage in pressure tactics far more than do the lobbyists of the other states. In Massachusetts, as is true for the other states, legislators tend to see less pressure than lobbyists, but the discrepancy between the perceptions of the two judges is substantially greater.[14]

Table 4—Percentage[a] of Legislators and Lobbyists Believing That They Have (Have Been) Influenced to the Extent of:

	Questioning a previously held opinion	Leaning more toward the views of the lobbyist	Changing from one position to another	N
Massachusetts				
Legislators	34	31	20	244
Lobbyists	51	39	26	185
North Carolina				
Legislators	22	20	18	164
Lobbyists	76	70	39	132
Oregon				
Legislators	45	42	51	84
Lobbyists	79	52	41	193
Utah				
Legislators	32	38	42	90
Lobbyists	77	66	48	134

[a] Percentages are of those who indicate that a particular event has occurred "frequently" or "occasionally."

By contrast, Oregon, which appears to have the greatest interaction, also appears to have the lowest perception of pressure tactics on the part of both legislators and lobbyists. The general rule seems to be that interaction and perceptions of pressure exist in a functional relationship. The greater the interaction between legislators and lobbyists, the more favorable become the evaluations of the encounter. The exception is Utah, which is a high interaction state with high perceptions of pressure. Indeed, Utah legislators believe themselves to be more pressured than the legislators of any other state. As will become evident shortly, although Utah and Oregon seem to be the two states in which interest groups are most active, the attitudes of legislative participants in these states is quite different. There is a general reluctance on the part of legislators in Utah to accept

14 See p. 83.

interest groups as legitimate, even though they come into frequent contact with them. It can be demonstrated that, whereas the interaction frequency in Utah is slightly less than that in Oregon, the effects of interaction are somewhat less in Utah.

Effectiveness of lobbying is measured by three questions based upon the assumptions of Guttman scaling. Legislators were asked, first, whether they could recall being influenced by a lobbyist to the point of questioning their position about any given issue. Next, they were asked if they could recall being influenced by a lobbyist to the extent of changing their opinion on an issue so that the positions of legislator and lobbyist were not as far apart as they were initially. Finally, legislators were asked if they could recall being influenced to the extent of reaching total agreement with the position of the lobbyist. The first question represents minimum effect and the last question represents maximum effect. Lobbyists were also asked these questions with appropriate modification in wording so that the legislators became the object rather than the subject of persuasion. The assumptions require that the frequency of success would

Table 5—Differences in the Effects of Communication As Reported by Legislators and Lobbyists

	Questioning a previously held position	Leaning more toward the views of the lobbyist	Changing from one position to another	Average
Massachusetts	− 17 [a]	− 8	− 6	− 10
North Carolina	− 54	− 50	− 21	− 42
Oregon	− 34	− 10	+ 10	− 15
Utah	− 44	− 28	− 6	− 26

[a] Entries are differences between the percentages reported in Table 4. Negative signs indicate a higher percentage of lobbyists reporting on effects; positive signs indicate the reverse.

decrease with the difficulty of the task. The assumptions held true for lobbyists. In terms of what they think they are doing, the more difficult the task, the fewer the favorable responses. According to lobbyists, they are able to produce "questioning" and "leaning" responses more often than they are able to produce a "conversion" (Table 4).

With legislators, the assumptions are not so neatly fulfilled. In both Oregon and Utah, more legislators indicate that they have changed positions more often than they have undergone more moderate forms of persuasion. The table confirms pretty well what we have learned so far about the four states under examination. Massachusetts lobbyists are far more skeptical about their ability to achieve successful results than are the lobbyists in any other states. This pessimism is shared to some extent by legislators, although the gap between perceptions is far less severe than it is in North Carolina. North Carolina lobbyists see their influence as far greater than do legislators. Indeed, the difference between the North Carolina lobbyists (whose legislators consider them impotent) and the Oregon lobbyists (whose legislators consider them powerful), is minimal and in one case the North Carolina lobbyists appear to be more optimistic. The table also firms up the argument that Oregon and Utah appear to be strong lobbying states, whereas Massachusetts and North Carolina appear to be weak lobbying states, especially if we consider the attitudes of legislators.

Naturally, lobbyists exaggerate the impact of their efforts. However, there is one exception to the rule of lobbyists' overestimation which deserves mention. In Oregon, more legislators than lobbyists believe that conversion has occurred. The difference in Oregon is especially striking. In this particular case, lobbyists are underestimating substantially the impact of their communications. The difference in the perceptions between legislators and lobbyists is least in Oregon and in Massachusetts, with both judges in Oregon agreeing that lobbyists are

Table 6—Percentage[a] of Legislators Reporting Influence Related to the Extent of Interaction Initiated by the Legislator

	Questioning a previously held position	Leaning more toward the views of the lobbyist	Changing from one position to another	N[e]
Massachusetts				
Low [b]	28	26	24	156
Medium [c]	51	42	44	41
High [d]	47	53	60	15
North Carolina				
Low	19	18	15	130
Medium	32	32	23	22
High	38	13	38	8
Oregon				
Low	29	33	42	24
Medium	63	53	57	30
High	46	50	63	24
Utah				
Low	24	32	44	50
Medium	39	46	39	26
High	60	50	50	10

[a] Percentage indicating that an event had occurred "frequently" or "occasionally."
[b] Less than five contacts per week.
[c] Six to twenty-five contacts per week.
[d] Twenty-six or more contacts per week.
[e] "Don't know's" are excluded.

powerful and both in Massachusetts agreeing that lobbyists are ineffective (Table 5). These sorts of realistic appraisals are, of course, not found in North Carolina or in Utah. The optimism of the Oregon lobbyist is earned, as is the pessimism of the Massachusetts lobbyists. To a lesser extent, the optimism of the Utah lobbyists is realistic, but the optimism of the North Carolina lobbyists is apparently without foundation.

Finally, conversion does occur more frequently than the research on national legislation has suggested. We would expect legislators to underestimate the extent of conversion; but even taking this into account, a slight majority of

Oregon lawmakers and a large minority of Utah legislators indicated that they have been switched from one position to another by lobbyists. Even in Massachusetts, 34 percent of the legislators have been influenced by lobbyists, albeit to the limited extent of questioning a previously held opinion. These data assume, of course, that the job of the lobbyists is that of changing minds. In fact, we have seen that there are two role definitions of the job of the lobbyist: that of persuader and that of informant. Needless to say, these role definitions are not mutually exclusive, making it possible for lobbyists to perform different roles at separate points in time or even simultaneously. Further, the data should not be interpreted to mean that more subtle, less explicit modes of communication cannot have a quite persuasive consequence.

This chapter is not concerned with lobbying strategies, but rather with an assessment of lobbying strengths. Nevertheless, one source of strength, and indeed perhaps a crucial source, is the extent to which legislators accept the lobbyist as a legitimate source of information. Our data indicate that, whereas there is no relationship between the extent of communication *initiated* by legislators and this degree of persuasability (Table 6), legislators who seek out lobbyists are more likely to be persuaded by them in comparison to legislators who do not initiate as much interaction. Consequently, one source of the

Table 7—Attitudes of Legislators Toward Information Received from Lobbyists: Percent Indicating They:

	Depend upon[a] information from lobbyists	Have confidence[b] in information from lobbyists	Find information[c] from lobbyists helpful	N
Massachusetts	50	55	41	244
North Carolina	41	56	28	164
Oregon	83	88	61	84
Utah	80	70	43	90

[a] Percentage reporting they depend upon information from lobbyists "a good deal" or "some" of the time.
[b] Percentage indicating they have "a lot" or "quite a bit" of confidence in information.
[c] Percentage indicating "all" and "most" of the information is helpful.

strength of interest groups in Oregon and Utah might be found in the fact that two-thirds of the legislators in these states indicate that they solicit the opinions of lobbyists when an issue arises about which they have legitimate concern. In contrast, only slightly more than one-third of the legislators in Massachusetts and North Carolina do so.

We would assume that the seeking out of lobbyists indicates an acceptance on the part of the legislators of the legitimacy of interest groups in the legislative process. However, by a variety of measures it appears that the attitude of Utah legislators toward lobbyists is far more hostile than their behavior would indicate. Consider, for example, a question approaching legitimacy from a slightly different angle. Legislators were asked if they believed it was proper to be seen socially with a lobbyist. Whereas 83 percent of the Oregon legislators indicated that it was proper to be seen with a lobbyist, 68 percent of those in Utah indicated that it was proper. Fewer Utah legislators are comfortable in the presence of lobbyists than Massachusetts legislators (75 percent) and are exceeded only by North Carolina legislators (58 percent). Thus, legislators in one of the "strong lobby states" are more circumspect in the presence of lobbyists than legislators in a "weak lobby state."

This pattern can be amplified further by the return to the problem of the relationship between attitudes and behavior. We noted that there was a relationship between the two, but the caveat should be added that this relationship does not emerge very clearly in Utah. For instance, there is no relationship in Utah between the attitudes of legislators toward interest groups and the extent of interaction. Those who have an unfavorable attitude are just about as likely to interact as those who do not. Also, more legislators in Massachusetts than in Utah believe that lobbyists are "absolutely necessary" in the legislative process. A good illustration of the suspicion of the lobbying process in Utah can be seen in Table 7, which presents the attitudes which legislators have toward the information they receive from lobbyists.

It can be seen that legislators in Utah depend upon lobbyists for information almost as much as their counterparts do in Oregon, but that the confidence that they have in this information is substantially less. Also, only a minority of Utah legislators in contrast to Oregon ones find this information especially helpful. Indeed, they appear almost as unimpressed with such information as the Massachusetts legislators. It is clear that the dependence of Utah legislators upon the services of lobbyists is not based solely upon a facilitating attitude. It appears that the interaction of Utah lobbyists and legislators is not entered into in a purely voluntary way. The interaction seemed forced upon each actor, somewhat in the nature of the exception Homans cites to his principle that interaction and attraction are related.[15]

In political systems there are compelling reasons for the continual functioning of a system in spite of private attitude systems; the interaction system is more compelling than the attitude system. Certain things have to be done; laws have to be passed, information must be gathered. There are very few staff services in Utah, and the legislators are very inexperienced in comparison to those in the other states. Thus, attitudes alone do not explain the nature of the Utah legislative system. The Utah legislators' attitudes are perhaps traceable to the fact that two-thirds of them are Mormons (in contrast to less than half the population of the state). Utah is the only state in which a religio-economic group controls a majority of the seats. Since the Mormon church has such total access it is naturally not seen as an interest group. The dominance of the Mormon church probably diminishes the favorable attitude of legislators toward other "outside" groups. In addition, there is a stern moralism associated with the Utah legislature. Perhaps one source of these hostile attitudes is an orientation booklet which tells the beginning legislator:

[15] See George C. Homans, *The Human Group* (New York: Harcourt, Brace and World, 1950), pp. 116–17.

Perhaps the most overwhelming experience for any new legislator is his first contact with the lobbyist—the person representing a special interest. Since each lobbyist is committed to advancing the cause of his own group, the legislator can expect to encounter considerable pressure to vote a narrowly seen "right way." There is nothing wrong with listening to the case presented by a lobbyist. He may provide valuable information. But the legislator should always remember that the lobbyist will volunteer only information which is helpful to his cause; that which is contrary must be learned elsewhere.[16]

In spite of these pressures against lobbyists, Utah still has a strong interest-group system.

Services Provided by Lobbyists

Since we know that a favorable persuasive situation is created when the legislator asks the lobbyist to perform a service for him, we now need to know the nature of the services performed by lobbyists. We have previously discussed the

Table 8—Percentage[a] of Legislators and Lobbyists Interacting for "Influence" Services

	Influencing other Legislators	Mobilizing public support	Participating in planning strategy	N
Massachusetts				
Legislators	11	17	17	244
Lobbyists	22	38	36	185
North Carolina				
Legislators	25	27	39	164
Lobbyists	51	65	73	132
Oregon				
Legislators	53	32	65	84
Lobbyists	55	46	64	193
Utah				
Legislators	46	45	42	70
Lobbyists	68	65	73	134

[a] Percentages indicate those who "frequently" and "occasionally" request (or are requested to) perform a service.

nature of the interaction between lobbyists and legislators in terms of either persuasion or information. A slight modification needs to be made with respect to the kinds of services performed. Here we are dichotomizing services into those involving a display of power or influence and those involving the provision of information. Three kinds of services are selected as being typical of the use of lobbyists as sources of influence by legislators. They are, first, calling upon lobbyists to have them influence other legislators; second, calling upon lobbyists to have them help amass public opinion in favor of a legislator's position; and

[16] *The Utah Legislator's Orientation Manual* (1966), p. 6.

third, including lobbyists in planning strategy in an effort to negotiate a bill through the legislature. The extent to which lobbyists are called upon perform these services are given in Table 8.

Considering only the relative importance of lobbying in the various states, nothing new is learned from this table. Oregon still appears as the most lobbying-oriented state; Utah runs a close second, with North Carolina and Massachusetts bringing up the rear. However, there are some variations both in the kinds of services likely to be performed within a given state and in the extent to which the perceptions of legislators and lobbyists differ. For instance, participation in the planning strategy preceding the introduction of a bill seems relatively more important in Oregon and North Carolina than it does in Utah and Massachu-

Table 9—Percentage[a] of Legislators and Lobbyists Interacting for "Informational" Services

	Communicating with other lobbyists	Researching a bill	N
Massachusetts			
Legislators	25	46	244
Lobbyists	22	43	185
North Carolina			
Legislators	19	47	164
Lobbyists	51	71	132
Oregon			
Legislators	40	89	84
Lobbyists	53	73	193
Utah			
Legislators	49	78	90
Lobbyists	63	63	134

[a] Percentages indicate those who "frequently" or "occasionally" request (or are requested to) perform a service.

setts. At the same time, helping to amass public opinion does not seem as prominent in Oregon as it should be in comparison to the relative utilization of other services. It appears that a greater amount of the services performed by Oregon lobbyists are kept within the internal politics of the legislature. This type of service is not found to the same extent in any other state. Indeed, the amassing of public opinion is the single item on which both sets of judges in Utah "rank" their state higher than Oregon.

The other type of service which lobbyists can perform consists of the provision of information. We consider here two types of such services: the communication to the legislator of the opinions of other legislators or lobbyists, and the actual conducting of research for the legislators for use in the presentation of arguments for or against legislation. The first kind of service is, essentially, the utilization of lobbyists for the "nose-counting" which usually precedes any decision by the legislator concerning strategy. The second kind of service, the actual production of information based upon technical research, is usually performed in Washington by staffs. Since state legislators typically do not have staff assistants, legislators come to rely upon lobbyists more than any other service, as Table 9 indicates.

The tables, considered together, suggest that even though informational services are more frequently provided than are influence-type services, lobbyists apparently do not consider them as glamorous. With the exception of those in North Carolina, the general tendency is for legislators to agree with lobbyists that informational services are typical of the legislator-lobbyist relationship. An examination of the differences between the percentages indicates that there is a mean difference of about 21 percent between the perceptions of legislators and lobbyists with regard to influence services as compared to a difference of 7 percent with respect to informational services (Table 10).

Table 10—Differences in Legislators' and Lobbyists' Perception of the Services Performed by Lobbyists[a]

	Influence	Information
Massachusetts	− 17%	+ 3%
North Carolina	− 37%	− 28%
Oregon	− 5%	+ 2%
Utah	− 25%	+ 1%

[a] Entries are the average differences in the answer of legislators and lobbyists reported in Tables 9 and 10. Negative signs indicate that more lobbyists than legislators believe the service is performed.

Indeed, only in North Carolina do the differences between the perceptions of legislators and lobbyists with respect to informational services approach the magnitude of the difference on influence services. When evaluating influence services, lobbyists exaggerate (or legislators minimize). When evaluating informational services, both legislators and lobbyists see lobbyists' performance in a similar manner. In Oregon and Utah, for example, legislators indicate they call upon lobbyists for research quite a bit more than the lobbyists so indicate. It should also be noted, however, that the differences in perception in Oregon are relatively small no matter whether influence or informational services are being evaluated, indicating a high congruence in perception in comparison to the other states. Nevertheless, it does appear that these answers are somewhat indicative of idealized roles. It appears that legislators look upon lobbyists as providers of information, but lobbyists like to think of themselves as agents of influence.

These findings support the earlier conclusions with respect to how lobbyists spend their time. At any rate, pedestrian though it may be, it is clear that even in weak lobbying states, such as Massachusetts, lobbyists are frequently called upon to provide legislators with facts. In strong lobbying states there is a considerable amount of influence-trading, but even here research is the basic task.

To lobbyists, the prominence of research means that persuasion has to be accomplished by indirect means. We noted earlier that experienced lobbyists are inclined to define their role as that of informant. Concurrently, legislators indicate a substantial preference for the services of experienced lobbyists, especially if they have had previous governmental experience. In all states, these kinds of lobbyists are sought out for services far more than are the inexperienced lobbyists. The experienced lobbyists frequently engage in an explicit attempt to define their role to the legislators. Consider, for example, the following statement:

Last session there were eleven people on the House Financial Affairs Committee. Five of them were freshmen. My first job was to introduce myself to them and let them know that I would be around, be at the Committee meetings, and that I am the fount of all information with respect to the insurance industry and if they have questions they should call on me. Certainly I try to persuade them, but I try to persuade them with information.

In this case the lobbyist is seeking to establish a relationship based solely upon his role as informant. The purpose is to produce perceptions on the part of legislators congruent with the lobbyist's self-perceptions. If successful, this lobbyist would have built a substantial influence base, resting upon the willingness of legislators to seek him out.

Summary and Conclusions

This comparative analysis has probably raised more questions than it has provided answers to existing questions. In the first place, it is obvious that neither the mechanistic nor the communications model are universally applicable, suggesting that less inclusive theories are more useful. There seems to be little question that interest groups are very powerful in Oregon and very weak in Massachusetts. To phrase the conclusions in terms of Eulau's rhetorical question, very little would happen in Massachusetts if there were no lobbies, but the legislature would function in an entirely different fashion in Oregon were this situation to come to pass. On the other hand, in the case of North Carolina and Utah it would be very difficult to say what the consequences would be because the perceptions, especially in North Carolina, are so incongruent. Also, in Utah the high activity and moderate impact of lobbyists is not matched by a favorable set of attitudes on the part of Utah legislators. Attitudinally, Utah is as similar to Massachusetts, as it is to Oregon.

To return to the question about the effect of environmental variables, it appears that they are randomly distributed. The "weak lobby states"—Massachusetts and North Carolina—have little in common. Massachusetts is urban, heterogeneous, industrialized, with a relatively wealthy, well-educated population. North Carolina is the reverse. Massachusetts is competitive, North Carolina is not. Indeed, Massachusetts is more similar to the "strong lobby states"— Utah and Oregon—in its degree of party competition, than it is to North Carolina.

On the other hand, Utah and Oregon seem somewhat more similar. Yet, on a variety of measures they are approximations of Massachusetts. The population of Utah and Oregon is quite a bit more mobile than that of the weak lobby states. Indeed, this is the only characteristic which is consistent.

The socio-economic environment does not appear to affect interaction of legislators or lobbyists and consequences of the lobbying effect, with the exception of mobility. Mobility, however, is in reality an artifact of a more fundamental distinction between weak and strong lobby states which is more *developmental* than environmental. To illustrate this point, let us add to our sample of four states two states examined by Wahlke, Eulau, Ferguson, and Buchanan: California, which is clearly a strong lobby state, and Tennessee, which is clearly a weak lobby state.[17] We can now see that a basic distinction is between the newer, late developing states, and the older, now established political systems.

Table 11—Expenditure and Revenue of Strong and Weak Lobby States

		Strong			Weak	
	OREGON	CALIFORNIA	UTAH	MASSA-CHUSETTS	TENNESSEE	NORTH CAROLINA
Revenue per capita	$257	$251	$251	$185	$171	$183
Expenditure per capita	$260	$254	$255	$190	$164	$171

California, Oregon, and Utah did not develop viable *stakes* for the political game until the twentieth century. By the time that Massachusetts, Tennessee, and North Carolina had developed enough complexity to support an interest group system, the rules of the game of politics had been established and, in a sense, closed to interest groups. In the South, legislators are likely to view *all* "outsiders" (interest groups, parties, constituents) as having doubtful legitimacy. In Massachusetts, interest groups have a difficult time competing with established parties. In both areas, therefore, there is an oligarchical type of politics which does not include interest groups.

In contrast to the old New England or southern states stands the new West. Political systems and interest groups developed simultaneously in a much more open fashion. Interest groups did not have to fight existing political institutions; they shared in the developing of the political system; also, political development coincided with economic development. Lobbyists and politicians "grew up" together. Finally, the western political tradition—non-partisanship, open primaries, a high rate of participation—invites interest groups, along with everybody else, to compete for the stakes of politics.

A further possibility is raised by this notion of the stakes of politics. We have explained high interaction and the effects so far without reference to the obvious possibility that interest groups will be attracted to the arenas where important decisions are being made—where the stakes are the biggest. Do the stakes vary from state to state? Do some states do a "bigger business" than others? If so,

---

[17] Ohio and New Jersey are excluded because their classification is less certain.

how does this relate to patterns of group politics? To anwser this question, consider Table 11, which compares the per capita revenues and expenditures of the strong and weak lobby states. Clearly the strong lobby states have a greater output than the weak lobby states. In the research of Dye, Hofferbert, and others mentioned earlier, the environment influences the output. In this case, a sort of reverse of this suggestion is developed. The magnitude of the outputs influences the pattern of activity accompanying the output.

SOCIALIZATION
AND
SOCIAL BACKGROUND

The Political Socialization of State Legislators: A Re-examination

by HERBERT HIRSCH

One of the most neglected areas of political socialization research involves "learning connected with recruitment to performance of specialized roles, such as bureaucrat, party functionary, and legislator."[1] A possible source of data that could help to remedy this delinquency and provide insights into the problem of linking earlier socialization experiences to later behavior is that collected by the authors of *The Legislative System.*[2]

Chapter 4 of *The Legislative System* constitutes an examination of the political socialization of state legislators from four states. The author of that chapter describes six dimensions: (1) the major sources of political interest (p. 79), (2) the time of earliest political interest recalled by the legislators (p. 81), (3) relatives of state legislators in politics (p. 82), (4) primary groups that influenced the legislator's socialization (p. 83), (5) political interest as a result of external events (pp. 85–89), and (6) personal predispositions and political socialization (p. 91). All these variables are presented in tabular form showing the percentages in each state. Although the description is interesting, it adds little to our quest for theory. If we are going to develop a theory of political

---

[1] Fred I. Greenstein, "Political Socialization," Article written for the *International Encyclopedia of the Social Sciences*, mimeo, p. 4.

[2] John C. Wahlke, *et al.*, *The Legislative System* (New York: John Wiley & Sons, Inc., 1962).

Copyright © 1971 by The Free Press and Herbert Hirsch. The author wishes to thank Professors Malcolm Jewell and Dean Jaros for their comments on an earlier draft of this paper. This study reports data collected by the State Legislative Research Project. For a complete report of the research design and the findings of this study, see John C. Wahlke, Heinz Eulau, William Buchanan, and LeRoy C. Ferguson, *The Legislative System: Explorations in Legislative Behavior* (New York: Wiley, 1962). The data were supplied to the Department of Political Science, The University of Kentucky, through the Inter-University Consortium for Political Research.

socialization, we must know more than state-by-state differences. It is more important, theoretically, to ascertain how variables are interrelated.[3]

Methodology

This paper attempts to suggest answers to a series of questions posed by William Mitchell.[4] He states that

one way of getting at the socialization of citizens is to ask a series of logically related questions which might read as follows: "What is taught?" "To whom?" "How?" "Under what conditions?" "With what consequences?"[5]

The data from *The Legislative System* do not enable us to answer the first question. The second question, "To whom?", is answered by the population that was interviewed—in this case, state legislators. The third question, "By whom?", refers to the agents of socialization. This is the primary focus of the present study. We want to know what agents are salient at what time periods of the legislator's life. Although it is true that socialization does not emerge full blown at a single juncture in an individual's life, for the purposes of this paper we conceptualize socialization as referring to the time of his life in which the respondent first remembers becoming interested in politics. The fourth question, "How?", cannot be answered from the present data, but we shall attempt to suggest answers to the questions of "Under what conditions?", and "With what consequences?" The consequences are, of course, partially known since all of the respondents became state legislators. Additional consequences in which we are interested involve aspirations for further office.

Before proceeding further, it is imperative to establish that we are not pretending to offer final answers to these questions. This study must be viewed as suggestive only.[6]

Political Socialization: Time and Agent

The authors of *The Legislative System* state that the socialization of state legislators seems to take place at an earlier period than it does for the average

---

[3] For a study based on the same data which does examine variable inter-relationships, see Kenneth Prewitt, Heinz Eulau, and Betty H. Zisk, "Political Socialization and Political Roles," *Public Opinion Quarterly*, 30 (1966–67): 569–82.

[4] William C. Mitchell, *The American Polity* (New York: The Free Press, 1962), p. 146; and Greenstein, "Political Socialization," p. 3.

[5] Mitchell, *American Polity*, p. 146.

[6] Several additional caveats must be entered. First, as Eulau emphasizes, the data "... cannot be interpreted in a motivational sense ...," (p. 93). Second, the data are based on the legislators' recollections of when they remember becoming interested in politics. Recall data are, of course, notable for the problems they give rise to, but the only alternative to recall data, for a study of this type, is longitudinal research, which is notable for the time and expense involved. In this case, insights to be gained from the use of recall data outweigh the problems. Third, because the data are not drawn from a random sample, we use gamma only as a measure of the reduction in the proportion of error in predicting the dependent variable from the independent.

citizen.[7] Although there are no data comparing the time of socialization of legislators with that of non-legislators, the earliest political interest for both seems to occur about the time of childhood or grammar school.[8] Using a sample of Canadian and United States' legislators, Kornberg and Thomas, found, moreover, that the time of socialization is strongly related to the agent (G = .98).[9] They further demonstrated that those who were socialized in childhood tend to cite the family as the main socializing agent; those who recall being socialized in adolescence cite themselves as the agent; and those who recall being socialized in adulthood give as the agent "external events and conditions."[10]

In testing a similar proposition this analysis is handicapped by the form in which the data are coded. Each respondent could give five answers regarding the time and agent of socialization. Rather than treat them separately, all five responses are combined and percentages are calculated using the total number of responses as a base. Doing this, and putting the data into a form similar to that of Kornberg and Thomas, demonstrate a finding similar to theirs—although the present gamma is much smaller.

Table 1—Relation between Time and Agent of Socialization

	Time				
Agent	CHILDHOOD	ADOLESCENCE	COLLEGE	AFTER COLLEGE	ZERO HOUR
Primary Groups	38%	11	19	17	8
Other Groups	21	45	42	35	38
Particular Events	15	18	10	19	19
Personal Predispositions	23	22	25	22	29
Socioeconomic Factors	4	4	5	7	5
	101[a]	100	101[a]	100	99[a]
	(N = 310)	(N = 108)	(N = 81)	(N = 121)	(N = 99)

Gamma = .18

[a] Percentage does not equal 100 because of rounding.

Table 1 demonstrates that more of those who were socialized in childhood were socialized by "primary groups," whereas those who were socialized after childhood were socialized mainly by "other groups." Under the broad stipulation, "other," the authors of *The Legislative System* include such widely divergent groups as education groups, political groups, civic or community groups, and occupational groups. These largely correspond to what Mitchell refers to as

[7] Wahlke, *et al.*, *Legislative System*, pp. 80–81.

[8] For studies on the time of socialization of a group of young children, see David Easton and Robert D. Hess, "The Child's Political World," *Midwest Journal of Political Science* 3 (August, 1962): 229–46; David Easton and Jack Dennis. "The Child's Image of Government," *Annals of the American Academy of Political and Social Science* 361 (1965): 40–57; and by the same authors, "The Child's Acquisition of Regime Norms: Political Efficacy," *American Political Science Review* 61, 1 (March, 1967): 25–38.

[9] Allan Kornberg and Norman Thomas, "The Political Socialization of National Legislative Elites in the United States and Canada," *Journal of Politics* 27 (November, 1965): 761–75.

[10] *Ibid.*, p. 766.

formal and organizational agents of socialization as opposed to informal and non-organizational agents.[11] We might suggest, therefore, as a tentative answer to the question of "By whom?" that those who remember first becoming interested in politics during childhood are more likely to be socialized by primary or family groups, whereas those who are socialized in adolescence or afterwards are more likely to be socialized by formal and organizational groups. The question of "By whom?" cannot, therefore, be answered apart from the question of time, for different agents seem to be more important in different periods of the individual's life cycle. This suggests that future studies of political socialization examine agents other than the family, and time periods other than childhood.

"Under What Conditions?"

Because the agents of socialization are related to the time period in which the individual remembers being socialized, it follows that the conditions under which the agents are acting should likewise be related to the time of socialization.

Table 2—Relation between Where Respondent Grew Up and Time of Socialization

	Area Where Grew Up		
Time	CITY	SMALL TOWN	FARM OR RANCH
Childhood	41%	37	30
Adolescence	18	11	14
College	7	12	16
After College	13	19	15
Zero Hour	20	20	26
	—	—	—
	99 [a]	99 [a]	101 [a]
	(N = 179)	(N = 123)	(N = 98)
		Gamma = .12	

[a] Percentage does not equal 100 because of rounding.

Bronfenbrenner suggests that ". . . rural families appear to 'lag behind the times' somewhat in their practices of infant care."[12] If this dynamic extends to political socialization, then we could expect legislators from rural backgrounds to be socialized at a later stage in life than those from urban environments.

The expected relation shows up to a slight degree. There is indeed a relation between the time of socialization and the geographic area where it occurred. Urban dwellers were socialized earlier than farm or small town residents, and Bronfenbrenner suggests a possible explanation. He states that rural families

[11] Mitchell, *American Polity*, p. 159.

[12] Urie Bronfenbrenner, "Socialization and Social Class Through Time and Space," in Harold Proshansky and Bernard Seidenberg (eds.), *Basic Studies in Social Psychology* (New York: Holt, Rinehart and Winston, 1965), p. 358.

"lag behind" because they are isolated from the ". . . agents of change (e.g., public media, clinics, physicians, and councilors)."[13] Also, it is possible that the farmer and small town resident are isolated from political stimuli and from the great issues of the day and that this isolation manifests itself in a lower degree of political interest which is, in turn, transmitted to the rural child and is reflected in his being socialized later in life.[14]

Additional factors may be involved and may prove to be more reliable indicators of the time in which socialization occurred. One possibility is the status of the parent's primary occupation. Kornberg and Thomas found that the higher the occupation status of the father, the more likely the legislator was to be socialized early in life.[15] They trichotomized their variables, and in order to compare findings, we shall use their classifications.[16]

Table 3—Relation between Status of Parent's Primary Occupation and Time of Socialization

| Time | Occupation | | |
	BUSINESS-PROFESSIONAL	FARMER	LOW-STATUS
Childhood	43%	33	32
Adolescence	14	12	20
College	10	14	11
After College	13	23	17
Zero Hour	21	19	21
	101[a]	101[a]	100
	(N = 198)	(N = 110)	(N = 114)
		Gamma = .09	

[a] Percentage does not equal 100 because of rounding.

The relation is not nearly so strong as that found by Kornberg and Thomas whose data showed that 91 percent of those whose fathers had a low-status occupation were socialized late in life.[17] Our data show that those whose fathers were in low-status occupations were socialized later than those whose fathers were business-professional in occupation. The magnitude of our differences are not so great as Kornberg and Thomas found. They observe that the strong relation they found is probably due to the presence of the Canadian legislators whose "fathers' occupations were particularly salient for the manner in which the Canadians were socialized, the magnitude of the correlation for them being approximately three times as great as for the Americans."[18]

[13] *Ibid.*, p. 356.
[14] On the isolation of the small town see Arthur J. Vidich and Joseph Bensman, *Small Town in Mass Society* (Garden City, New York: Doubleday 1960).
[15] Kornberg and Thomas, "Political Socialization of National Legislative Elites," p. 771.
[16] "Low-status occupations include blue collar and low level white collar jobs such as clerks, salesmen, etc. Business-professional include those who were proprietors of their own business, executives of large businesses and professionals such as doctors and lawyers." From Kornberg and Thomas, "Political Socialization of National Legislative Elites," fn. 21, p. 771.
[17] *Ibid.*, p. 771.
[18] *Ibid.*, p. 772.

Using only the American portion of their sample, Kornberg and Thomas found that 41 percent of those American legislators whose fathers were business or professional men were socialized early in life. Our data show that 43 percent were socialized in childhood. Both sets of data indicate that 33 percent of those whose fathers were farmers were socialized early in life. The remarkably similar findings suggest that the occupational status of the father is indeed related to the time of socialization.

In regard to the relation between the conditions under which socialization takes place and the time it occurs, we may say that as a rule most of the legislators were socialized in childhood. Two conditions had a slight effect upon this basic relation. Those legislators who were brought up in urban environments were socialized earlier than those who were raised on farms or in small towns. Legislators whose fathers were business-professional men were, likewise,

Table 4—Relation between Source of Decision to Enter Politics and Time of Socialization

	Source				
					ECONOMIC AND
Time	*FAMILY*	*SELF*	*FRIENDS*	*PARTY*	*OCCUPATION GROUPS*
Childhood	70%	36	30	33	21
Adolescence	4	18	17	7	0
College	13	13	9	13	0
After College	9	15	15	20	36
Zero Hour	4	17	29	26	43
	100	99	100	99 [a]	100
	(N = 23)	(N = 158)	(N = 89)	(N = 54)	(N = 14)

Gamma = .24

[a] Percentage does not equal 100 because of rounding.

socialized earlier than those whose fathers were farmers or had low-status occupations. These findings indicate that future inquiry into childhood socialization should examine the interaction between the time of socialization and the conditions under which it takes place.

The Consequences of Socialization

Given the nature of our data, we are able to give only a rough approximation of an answer to the question of the consequences of early socialization. However, if the study of political socialization is to have any meaning in terms of macro-theory, it must in some way be demonstrated that early socialization experiences do indeed affect later political behavior.

Prewitt asks the key question: "Do individuals marked for an adult political career experience initial political socialization in a manner which increases the probability that they will select themselves or be selected for political leadership?"[19] He then hypothesizes that "What the politician shares with his colleagues is a familiarity with politics that reaches back into his early adulthood, adolescence, or, in many cases, his childhood."[20]

The present data do not enable us to compare the socialization experiences of a group of political actors with a group of non-actors, nor does it enable us to longitudinally follow a selected sample of respondents from childhood to adulthood. We are able, however, to examine the relation between the legislator's source of his decision to enter politics and the time and agents of socialization.

Table 4 demonstrates that the time of socialization is related to the legislator's source of decision to enter politics. Seventy percent of those legislators

Table 5—Relation between Source of Decision to Enter Politics and the Agents of Socialization

			Source		
Agents	FAMILY	SELF	FRIENDS	PARTY	ECONOMIC AND OCCUPATION GROUPS
Primary Groups	59%	23	33	24	11
Other Groups	20	36	41	37	42
Particular Events	2	15	12	11	21
Personal Predispositions	18	25	14	28	26
	99[a]	99[a]	100	100	100
	(N = 44)	(N = 265)	(N = 138)	(N = 90)	(N = 19)

Gamma = .06

[a] Percentage does not equal 100 because of rounding.

who said that the family was the source of their decision to enter politics were socialized in childhood. Although the total number who gave the family as the main source of the decision to enter politics is small, the relatively high gamma indicates that there is, in fact, a relation between the time of socialization and the source of the decision to enter politics, and that this relation accounts for 24 percent of the variance in the data. We suggest, therefore, that individuals socialized early in life are more likely to be steered into political careers by their family than by other sources. This finding is entirely congruent with those of other socialization scholars and provides additional evidence of the family's great influence upon the socialization process in general, and upon the adoption of adult political roles and career patterns in particular.

When we examine the relation between the source of the decision to enter politics and the agents of socialization we find a similar pattern.

Table 5 demonstrates that there seems to be a relation between the source of the legislator's decision to enter politics and the agents of socialization. More of those who stated that the source of their decision was the family were socialized

[19] Kenneth Prewitt, "Political Socialization and Leadership Selection," *Annals of the American Academy of Political and Social Science* 361 (1965): 97.
[20] *Ibid.*, p. 105.

by primary groups, whereas those who said the source of their decision was personal, their friends, a political party, or economic and occupation groups were socialized by other groups. Although we cannot say that the agents or time of socialization enable us to predict who will or will not become a political actor, we can, at least, say that one of the consequences of the time and agents of socialization is that they are influential in stimulating the receiver of their cues to enter politics.

With this in mind, we can now attempt to ascertain whether or not the time and agents of socialization have any relation to the legislator's expectations to run again or to his aspirations for higher office. Intuitively, we suspect that the

Table 6—Relation between Expectation to Continue to Run for the Legislature and Time of Socialization

Time	"Do you expect to continue to run for the legislature?"		
	YES	PERHAPS	NO
Childhood	38%	44	32
Adolescence	17	7	16
College	11	12	9
After College	15	16	19
Zero Hour	19	21	25
	100	100	101[a]
	(N = 240)	(N = 93)	(N = 57)
		Gamma = .06	

[a] Percentage does not equal 100 because of rounding.

earlier socialization takes place, the more likely the legislator is to want to run again or to aspire for further office.

Table 6 demonstrates that there is only a small relation between the time of socialization and the legislator's expectation to continue to run for office. When we examine the relation between time of socialization and a desire to run for other governmental positions, we see the existence of a fairly strong relation.

Legislators who aspire to further office were socialized earlier in life than those who do not so aspire. We suggest, therefore, that a consequence of early socialization is greater motivation for political office.

Although the present analysis does not enable us to answer the key theoretical question of whether or not we can predict, on the basis of socialization experiences, who will become a political actor, we can say with some confidence that the time of socialization does indeed have consequences for later political behavior.

Conclusion

In this paper we have suggested answers to a series of three questions posed by William Mitchell and Fred Greenstein. Regarding the question, "By whom?"

this study suggests that the agents of socialization, the "whom," cannot be separated from the time of socialization, the "when." Those socialized in childhood were socialized by primary groups, those socialized in adolescence, in college, after college, and at zero hour were all more likely to be socialized by "other groups."

In regard to the question of "Under what conditions?" we can suggest that: (1) Those who live in urban areas are socialized earlier than those who live in small towns or on farms, and (2) that the status of the father's occupation is related to the time of socialization. The legislator whose father is a business or professional person is socialized earlier than the legislator whose father is a farmer or in a low-status occupation.

Table 7—Relation between Aspiration for Other Governmental Positions and Time of Socialization

Time	"Are there any other governmental positions you would like to seek?"		
	YES	PERHAPS	NO
Childhood	42%	47	29
Adolescence	17	18	10
College	16	7	8
After College	11	17	21
Zero Hour	14	11	32
	100	100	100
	(N = 149)	(N = 83)	(N = 169)
		Gamma = .26	

On the last question, "With what consequences?" we discovered that the source of the legislator's decision to enter politics is related to the time in which his socialization occurred. This suggests that the time of political socialization could possibly be influential in the selection of a career or in the direction that a political career might eventually take. Further evidence for this possibility is found in the fact that we discovered that the time of socialization is related to aspiration for additional governmental office. Those who are socialized early in life are more likely to seek higher office.

In conclusion, it is hoped that this study will act to stimulate future scholars of political socialization to examine more than the content of what is socialized. Future studies must consider: (1) the agents of socialization, (2) the time period of the individual's life in which socialization takes place, (3) the structural conditions under which the process occurs, and (4) theoretically the most important, the consequences of early political socialization for later political behavior.

CAMPAIGNS
AND ELECTIONS

The Role of the Campaign in
Congressional Politics

by CHARLES O. JONES

A basic assumption of any theory of representative democracy is that there is a link between elections and policy-making. Not all citizens can participate directly in public decisions, so they elect representatives. The representatives act in the interests of those who elect them, when participating in the policy-making process. It is at election time that citizens and representatives come together. In theory, this is the period of accounting: either the representative is instructed further, or he is defeated for malrepresentation, or he is warned, or he is encouraged. The candidate himself reviews his record, if he has one, discusses and clarifies issues, makes promises. If the representative process is designed to accomplish for a modern state what pure democracy cannot, then a key event is the election.

Because the above description is a fair summary of a popular theory of representative government, it is not surprising that many people expect elections to be "issue-oriented" events. Candidates should discuss public problems, possible future solutions, and solutions which have succeeded or failed in the past. Debate should characterize the effort to win elections. If the campaign behavior of candidates and the voting behavior of citizens does not meet these expectations, there are criticisms of both the citizen and the representative-candidate and reforms are discussed and sometimes implemented.[1]

This study focuses on campaigns and elections for the United States House of Representatives in order to cast light on the nature of the relationship between elections and policy-making. What is the role of the campaign in the political

[1] For an extensive statement on what should characterize the good campaign, see Stanley Kelley, *Political Campaigning* (Washington, D.C.: The Brookings Institution, 1960).

Reprinted from "The Role of the Campaign in Congressional Politics" by Charles O. Jones in M. Kent Jennings and L. Harmon Zeigler (eds.), *The Electoral Process*, Englewood Cliffs, N.J.: Prentice-Hall, Inc., 1966, pp. 21–41. Copyright © 1966 by Prentice-Hall, Inc. Reprinted by permission.

life of a representative? Are the campaign and election, in fact, issue-oriented events? Is the Congressman bound by the campaign and election in his policy-making behavior? The major thesis in response to these questions is that the campaign period is a regularly scheduled event in the life of a representative, in which he makes an intensive effort to advertise himself—to project a generalized image of himself as a capable representative—so that he will win. It is not an issue-oriented event, and campaign-electoral conditions are such that the representative need not be bound by the election in his policy-making behavior (though he may, of course, choose to bind himself). Furthermore campaign-electoral conditions are such that one should not expect the representative to bind himself to electoral returns.

There are several sets of data which will be relied on here to describe campaign and electoral conditions. First, it is necessary to have data about elections themselves. Why and when are they scheduled? Is there anything about congressional elections, as events, which should lead one to expect that they will be issue-oriented events that bind the winner? Second, data about interparty competition and turnover are necessary to establish the extent to which constituents actually dismiss incumbents—*i.e.*, vote them out of office. This study will concentrate on incumbents, because they are returned to office in such high percentages. Furthermore, in assessing the impact of the campaign and election on policy-making, it is easier if one is able to study the candidate who already has a record as a representative at the time of the campaign.[2] Third, data are needed concerning voters' awareness of issues. Do the voters demand discussion of issues? Are they aware of issues? Do they view the campaign as a time of accounting? Fourth, it is necessary to examine what the incumbent does in a campaign. How does he organize it? What is his strategy? What does he talk about? What is his over-all purpose? Finally, data are needed about whether a Congressman changes his policy-making behavior because of changes in his margin of victory.

Congressional Elections

Members of the United States House of Representatives must seek re-election every two years. The Constitution states:

[2] There are several situations which may upset a prediction of victory for the incumbent. These are: redistricting, population shifts, or registration of voters previously not registered (e.g., Negroes in the South). It is difficult to measure the effect of the campaign on the nonincumbent winner—it may well be that a representative's first campaign is very influential and he tries to implement promises made in the campaign. Regardless of the influence of the campaign, however, the new member in the United States House of Representatives will be severely limited in carrying out campaign promises. The freshmen Congressman is very busy defining his constituency and his relationship with colleagues, and establishing lines of communication to party leaders, the executive, and interest groups. He cannot expect, nor is he expected, to participate in policy-making to any great extent. There is a published study of a nonincumbent victor wherein it is concluded that the candidate, Frank Coffin of Maine, "projected an image of himself as an able, aggressive young man who 'gets things done.' " See John Donovan, *Congressional Campaign: Maine Elects a Democrat* (New York: Holt, Rinehart & Winston, Inc., 1958), p. 13. It should also be noted that Robert Huckshorn and Robert Spencer are studying defeated candidates for the United States House of Representatives and will have material on the role of the campaign for these candidates.

The House of Representatives shall be composed of members chosen every second Year by the People of the several States. . . . The Times, Places and Manner of holding Elections for Senators and Representatives, shall be prescribed in each State by the Legislature thereof: but Congress may at any time by Law make or alter such Regulations. . . .[3]

In 1845, Congress did pass legislation fixing the first Tuesday after the first Monday in November as the day for choosing Presidential electors and congressional representatives.[4]

There is nothing in the Constitution or the federal statutes which states that congressional elections will occur when there are pressing issues. Elections are by the calendar. Thus, 1929 was a year of great economic crisis—but there were no congressional elections until the following year and no Presidential election until 1932. If major issues do exist at the time of election, it is pure coincidence. In America, governments do not fall in time of crisis; they linger on till the first Tuesday after the first Monday of November.

It is said, and Congressmen have been heard to argue, that though election dates are set, the United States House of Representatives best reflects the American mood on issues because elections to that body are so frequent. This argument is a partial rejoinder to the assertion that American elections are not issue-oriented. If any issues develop, the argument runs, the congressional representative will be aware of them and must attend to them in campaigns, because he returns so often to the constituency for re-election. On the other hand, however, it can be argued that frequent elections de-emphasize the importance of that event in the minds of voters and therefore they often do not vote or, if they do vote, do not view the election as an opportunity for protest or expression.

Finally, there is the problem with the ballot itself. In most states the ballot is long and complicated. The voter may have as many as twenty choices to make. Even if there is a central issue in an election, it is difficult for the voter to determine which choice, at which level, will best express his view on that issue.

In short, there are any number of characteristics of elections which suggest that one should not expect campaigns and elections to be issue-oriented or to bind the victor on policy matters.

Incumbents Win

A "new" Congress is not new at all. It is likely that the membership of one Congress will be made up of 80–90 percent of the membership of the old Congress and that an additional 5–10 percent will be members who belong to the

---

[3] Article I, Sections 2, 4.

[4] There was a provision in the 1845 law that states whose constitutions specified a different day for Congressional elections could continue to hold elections on that day. Arkansas and Maine had such constitutional provisions as did Oregon when it entered the Union in 1859. Maine was the last state to amend its constitution to conform with the rest of the states. Until 1960, Maine held its congressional elections in September.

same party as the previous incumbent from a given district.[5] One can be even bolder and note that 70–80 percent of congressional districts will be represented either by the same man or the same party for *five consecutive elections.*[6]

Of course, in each congressional election there are several incumbents who do not seek re-election (owing to retirement, death, defeat in the primary, decision to run for another office). If one calculates the percentage of incumbents who win among those who actually seek re-election, the advantage of incumbency is seen to be even greater. Table 1 presents the data for the four elections, 1954–60.

Table 1—Percentage of Incumbents Who Win Re-election

Year	Total Incumbents Seeking Re-Election	Won	Lost
1954	401	94.5%	5.5%
		($N = 379$)	($N = 22$)
1956	403	96.5	3.5
		($N = 389$)	($N = 14$)
1958	390	91.0	9.0
		($N = 355$)	($N = 35$)
1960	400	93.8	6.2
		($N = 375$)	($N = 25$)

The percentage of incumbents winning varied little during the four elections —from 91 percent in 1958 to 96.5 percent in 1956 ($\bar{x} = 93.9$ percent). These figures should not be publicized to those candidates challenging incumbents. Good candidates for Congress are difficult to find and recruitment will not be aided if the challenger knows that only six or seven challengers out of every hundred will defeat the incumbent.

---

[5] Lewis Froman, Jr., provides interesting evidence on the extent to which there are differences in roll-call behavior between particular incumbents who represent the same district (i.e., districts which have had more than one incumbent from the same party in a certain period of time). See *Congressman and Their Constituencies* (Chicago: Rand McNally & Co., 1963), Chap. 8; and "The Importance of Individuality in Voting in Congress," *Journal of Politics,* XXV (May 1963), 324–32.

[6] My study of interparty competition shows that there is a trend toward a higher percentage of districts represented by the same party for five consecutive elections. During the three periods, 1932–40, 1942–50, and 1952–60, the percentage of districts represented by the same party increased from 69.9 to 74. to 78.2 per cent. Of course, the percentage varies from region to region. There are a few studies of congressional elections: Donald Ackerman, "Significance of Congressional Races with Identical Candidates in Successive District Elections," *Midwest Journal of Political Science,* I (August 1957), 173–80; Edward Cox, "Congressional District Party Strengths and the 1960 Election," *Journal of Politics,* XXIV (May 1962), 277–302; Edward Cox, "The Measurement of Strength, *Western Political Quarterly,* XIII (December 1960), 1022–42; Cortez A. M. Ewing, *Congressional Elections* (Norman, Okla.: University of Oklahoma Press, 1947); Paul Hasbrouck, *Party Government in the House of Representatives* (New York: The Macmillan Company, 1927), Chap. IX; Malcolm Moos, *Politics, Presidents and Coattails* (Baltimore: Johns Hopkins Press, 1952); Louis Bean, *The Midterm Battle* (Washington, D.C.: Cantillon Book Co., 1950); John Harding, "The 1942 Congressional Elections," *American Political Science Review,* XXXVIII (February 1944), 41–58; W. G. Carleton, "Our Congressional Elections: In Defense of the Traditional System," *Political Science Quarterly,* LXX (September 1955), 341–57; various issues of the *Western Political Quarterly* in which elections in the West are described.

There are regional differences in the percentage of incumbents who win. As might be expected, incumbents are most likely to win in the South—indeed they often do not have challengers at all in the general election. There were challengers in only 35 percent of the congressional elections in the 106 Southern districts during the period 1954–60.[7] Table 2 shows that of the 397 Southern incumbents who ran for re-election during the period measured, only *two* were defeated—in 1954 a Republican defeated a Democrat in Florida's First District and a Democrat recaptured Virginia's Ninth District, which the Republicans had won in the Eisenhower sweep in 1952.

For the other regions, Table 2 shows a rather uniform pattern. The range for individual elections is from 70.8 percent of incumbents winning (New England in 1958—where the low percentage resulted from the fact that all six Connecticut incumbent Congressmen were defeated) to 100 percent (New England, 1956; the South, 1956, 1958, 1960; and the Mountain States, 1954). The range of average percentages for the entire period (see last column, Table 2) is from 86.4 percent in the West Central States to 99.5 percent in the South. Only New England and the West Central States fall below the 90 percent mark. The loss of six Republican incumbents in Connecticut accounts for more than half the New England losses. The West Central region appears to have the greatest flux, much of it resulting from an exchange of seats between Republicans and Democrats in 1958 and 1960 (the case in the following districts—Iowa Second; Kansas Second, Third; and Nebraska Third, Fourth).

The Central States had the largest number of incumbents defeated—though not the highest percentage. Many of these occurred in 1958 as well, but the Republicans were not as successful in regaining them in 1960 in this area as they were in the West Central States. These two regions (Central and West Central) accounted for nineteen of the thirty-five incumbents defeated in 1958.

Discussion of percentages for specific regions should not obscure the central feature of these data—i.e., the incumbent is likely to be re-elected. There are years in which incumbents in certain areas have difficulty, but even during those years it is probable that more than 75 percent of them will be returned to office.

What are the chances of victory for a challenger of the opposite party if the incumbent does not seek re-election? Table 3 shows that, over-all, the incumbent party candidate holds the edge. The percentage of incumbent party candidates winning varies from 67.4 percent in 1958 to 85.3 percent in 1954 ($\bar{x} = 76.6$ percent).

What is the significance of these data for present purposes? The overwhelming majority of winners in congressional elections are incumbents. The campaign and election are events—rather frequent events—in their over-all political life. These incumbents have policy records; they have experience in policy-making; they have continuous political life. And, apparently, they will be re-elected.

---

[7] During this period there were 148 challengers in the 424 elections in Southern districts (106 × 4). Most of these—105 of 148—were in Texas, Virginia, North Carolina, and Florida.

Table 2—Percentage of Incumbents Who Win Re-election, by Region

Region[a]	1954 WON	1954 LOST	1956 WON	1956 LOST	1958 WON	1958 LOST	1960 WON	1960 LOST	Totals WON	Totals LOST
New England (28 seats)	96.3% (N = 26)	3.7% (N = 1)	100.0% (N = 26)	0.0% (N = 0)	70.8% (N = 17)	29.2% (N = 7)	87.5% (N = 21)	12.5% (N = 3)	89.1% (N = 90)	10.9% (N = 11)
Middle Atlantic (87 seats)	96.3 (N = 79)	3.7 (N = 3)	96.3 (N = 78)	3.7 (N = 3)	97.3 (N = 71)	2.7 (N = 2)	95.1 (N = 77)	4.9 (N = 4)	96.2 (N = 305)	3.8 (N = 12)
Central (77 seats)	90.1 (N = 64)	9.9 (N = 7)	97.1 (N = 67)	2.9 (N = 2)	84.1 (N = 58)	15.9 (N = 11)	92.8 (N = 64)	7.2 (N = 5)	91.0 (N = 253)	9.0 (N = 25)
West Central (41 seats)	92.1 (N = 35)	7.9 (N = 3)	94.2 (N = 36)	5.8 (N = 2)	77.1 (N = 27)	22.9 (N = 8)	80.6 (N = 29)	19.4 (N = 7)	86.4 (N = 127)	13.6 (N = 20)
Border (39 seats)	89.2 (N = 33)	10.8 (N = 4)	91.9 (N = 34)	8.1 (N = 3)	86.1 (N = 31)	13.9 (N = 5)	94.6 (N = 35)	5.4 (N = 2)	90.5 (N = 133)	9.5 (N = 14)
South (106 seats)	97.9 (N = 94)	2.1 (N = 2)	100.0 (N = 98)	0.0 (N = 0)	100.0 (N = 102)	0.0 (N = 0)	100.0 (N = 101)	0.0 (N = 0)	99.5 (N = 395)	.5 (N = 2)
Mountain (16 seats)	100.0 (N = 12)	0.0 (N = 0)	93.3 (N = 14)	6.7 (N = 1)	92.9 (N = 13)	7.1 (N = 1)	83.3 (N = 10)	16.7 (N = 2)	92.5 (N = 49)	7.5 (N = 4)
Pacific (41 seats)[b]	94.7 (N = 36)	5.3 (N = 2)	92.3 (N = 36)	7.7 (N = 3)	97.3 (N = 36)	2.7 (N = 1)	95.0 (N = 38)	5.0 (N = 2)	94.8 (N = 146)	5.2 (N = 8)

[a] States included in each region are:
New England: Connecticut, Maine, Massachusetts, New Hampshire, Rhode Island, Vermont
Middle Atlantic: New York, New Jersey, Pennsylvania
Central: Illinois, Indiana, Ohio, Michigan
West Central: Iowa, Kansas, Minnesota, Nebraska, North Dakota, South Dakota, Wisconsin
Border: Delaware, Kentucky, Maryland, Missouri, Oklahoma, West Virginia
South: Alabama, Arkansas, Florida, Georgia, Louisiana, Mississippi, North Carolina, South Carolina, Tennessee, Texas, Virginia
Mountain: Arizona, Colorado, Idaho, Montana, Nevada, New Mexico, Utah, Wyoming
Pacific: California, Oregon, Washington (Alaska, Hawaii)
[b] The Pacific region had a total of forty-three seats when Alaska and Hawaii were admitted to the Union.

Table 3—Percentage of Districts Won by Incumbent Party Candidates (Incumbent not seeking re-election)

Year	Total Districts	Won by Incumbent Party Candidate	Won by Challenger
1954	34	85.3% (*N* = 29)	14.7% (*N* = 5)
1956	32	81.3 (*N* = 26)	18.7 (*N* = 6)
1958	46	67.4 (*N* = 31)	32.6 (*N* = 15)
1960	37	70.3 (*N* = 26)	29.7 (*N* = 11)

The Voter and Congressional Elections

The discussion has thus far established the extent to which incumbents will be the victors in congressional elections. What about their audience? Do the voters attend carefully to the campaigns for congressional seats? Do they know the issues? Indeed, do they know the candidates? The data suggest that congressional candidates need to spend a sizable portion of their campaign time identifying themselves to the voters.

Most studies of voting behavior have concentrated on Presidential elections. Their findings picture the voter as having little demonstrated interest in politics. He does not participate much in politics. He usually is aware of the Presidential candidates, and often has some opinion of both, but he knows little—and apparently cares less—about the issues in the campaign. His principal basis for voting is his traditional party identification (though only about one third of the voters willingly declare themselves to be "strong" party members). He may vote for the other party occasionally, but he maintains a partisan preference.[8]

The point of interest here is the congressional election rather than the Presidential election. Less is known about congressional elections and we are indebted to the Survey Research Center at the University of Michigan for those data which are available.[9]

[8] The principal studies are those by the Columbia group: Paul Lazarsfeld, *et al.*, *The People's Choice* (New York: Duell, Sloan & Pearce, Inc., 1944); and Bernard Berelson, Paul Lazarsfeld, and William McPhee, *Voting* (Chicago: The University of Chicago Press, 1954); and by the Survey Research Center: Angus Campbell and R. L. Kahn, *The People Elect a President* (Ann Arbor, Mich.: Institute for Social Research, 1952); Angus Campbell, *et al.*, *The Voter Decides* (Evanston, Ill.: Row, Peterson & Company, 1954); and Angus Campbell, *et al.*, *The American Voter* (New York: John Wiley & Sons, Inc., 1960).

[9] In 1954, the Survey Research Center conducted a study of voting behavior in congressional elections—Angus Campbell and Homer Cooper, *Group Differences in Attitudes and Votes* (Ann Arbor, Mich.: Survey Research Center, 1956). Further work was done in 1958 and, after a series of interesting papers presented at various conventions of the American Political Science Association, articles are now beginning to appear in the journals. Two in particular will be relied on here: Warren Miller and Donald Stokes, "Constituency Influence in Congress," *American Political Science Review*, LVII (March 1963) 45–56; Donald Stokes and Warren Miller, "Party Government and the Saliency of Congress," *Public Opinion Quarterly*, XXVI (Winter 1962), 531–46. Other works include: William McPhee and William Glaser, *Public Opinion and Congressional Elections* (New York: The Free Press of Glencoe, Inc., 1962); Joan Moore, "Social Deprivation and Advantage as Sources of Political Values," *Western Political Quarterly*, XV (June 1962), 217–26; and those works cited in n. 6.

If the voter has a low degree of interest and involvement in much of what happens in a Presidential campaign, then he is very nearly apolitical when it comes to congressional contests. According to a 1958 study by Warren Miller and Donald Stokes, well over half the constituents interviewed in congressional districts where there was a contest between the two parties had not read or heard anything about either candidate. Less than one in five had read or heard anything about both. Of those who voted in 1958, 46 percent had not read or heard anything about either candidate and only 24 percent knew something about both.[10]

Miller and Stokes have data which complement data presented in the discussion of incumbency. The number of voters who knew something about incumbent candidates was considerably higher than the number of those who knew something about the challenger. As noted above, 24 percent knew something of both. An additional 25 percent knew something about the incumbent but not about the challenger—a total of 49 percent knowing something about the incumbent. Five percent knew something about the challenger but not about the incumbent—a total of 29 percent who knew something about the challenger.[11]

Thus, it appears that even the incumbent has a problem in identifying himself to the voter. The challenger, however, has a monumental task. And the voters' awareness of the candidate makes a difference in voting. Miller and Stokes found that, where voters were aware only of their own party's candidate, 98 percent of them voted for him; where they were aware only of the other party's candidate, 60 percent voted for their own party's candidate; where they knew both candidates, 83 percent voted for their party's man; and where they knew neither candidate, 92 percent voted for their party's man. Any knowledge of the opponent seems to mean increased deviation from party voting.[12]

The results of these data again substantiate the advantage of the incumbent. He is more likely to be known and thus benefits from the higher percentage of votes for the man who is known. On the other hand, he probably benefits also from a straight party vote by those who know neither candidate because it is likely that his party has a majority of the registered voters in the district.

What about the voters' awareness of issues in congressional elections? Miller and Stokes note that "of detailed information about policy stands, not more than a chemical trace was found."[13] In fact, the electorate's knowledge about Congress as a whole is severely limited. When asked which party controlled Congress, 1957–58, only 47 percent of those interviewed knew that it was the Democrats.[14]

---

[10] Miller and Stokes, "Constituency Influence in Congress," *American Political Science Review*, 53–54.

[11] *Ibid.*

[12] Stokes and Miller, "Party Government and the Saliency of Congress," *Public Opinion Quarterly*, 541.

[13] Miller and Stokes, "Constituency Influence in Congress," *American Political Science Review*, 54. See also V. O. Key, Jr., *Public Opinion and American Democracy* (New York: Alfred A. Knopf, Inc., 1961), pp. 482–83, and Norman Thomas and Karl Lamb, *Congress: Politics and Practice* (New York: Random House, 1964), pp. 33–38.

[14] Stokes and Miller, "Party Government and the Saliency of Congress," *Public Opinion Quarterly*, 536.

The conclusion from these first sets of data is that a Congressman is relatively free from his constituency. As Miller and Stokes put it: "He knows the constituency isn't looking." His chances of re-election are excellent. The chances of his suffering at the polls as a result of his stands in Congress or his party's overall posture are so slight as to be inconsequential.

The Campaign

Based on the discussion so far, what type of campaign might be expected from the incumbent? The data suggest that no real campaign is necessary. There seems to be no stimulus for a strong, rigorous campaign. The incumbent will probably win, and most of the constituency will be unaware of what is going on if he does campaign. It cannot be assumed, however, that the incumbent candidate knows he will win just because most incumbents do. No good politician is overconfident. Nor can it be assumed that he wins because he has already won before, although that does seem to be a factor in and of itself. He wins because more voters are familiar with his name than are familiar with his opponent's name. And more voters are familiar with his name, in part, because his party is probably predominant in the district,[15] he campaigns vigorously, and is the incumbent (which of these many factors is most important is difficult to measure).

To demonstrate what incumbents do in campaigns, let us examine, in some depth, two congressional campaigns for re-election.[16] The two are quite different —one occurs in an almost totally rural constituency; the other, in a totally urban constituency. One constituency is composed of over half of a state's geographical area; the other is measured in city blocks. The campaign techniques of the two incumbents are almost as different as night and day. Both of the incumbents are of the same party, but the rural candidate has a sizable edge in party registration while the urban candidate has a minority of party registrants. Withal, however, the campaign itself plays a similar role for each Congressman. The specific differences between the two campaigns are numerous, but the significant point is the similarity in the role of the campaign in the political lives of these two men. After these two campaigns are examined, the findings of other campaign studies will be summarized. (Several of these studies were presented as papers at a seminar on congressional campaigning sponsored by the National Center for Education in Politics.[17])

[15] Frederick Wirt, in "The 1962 Ohio Fifteenth Congressional District Campaign: A Study in Casual Politics," an unpublished paper presented at the National Center for Education in Politics Seminar for Teachers of Politics, Washington, D.C., September 1–4, 1962, observes that party preference is a basic determinant in explaining outcome in the Ohio Fifteenth District.

[16] I observed much of Mr. Rural's campaign first hand in 1960. I was not able to spend as much time with Mr. Urban in 1962 but I did interview him, his campaign manager, and other assistants; accompanied him on the campaign trail on two different occasions; and followed the campaign in the press.

[17] The seminar was held September 1–4, 1962, in the Sheraton-Park Hotel, Washington, D.C.

Mr. Rural and Mr. Urban Seek Re-election

No candidate who has opposition can ever be certain which is the best campaign technique. The winners are the experts, but even they cannot afford to be confident about why they won. Analysis of almost any campaign effort will show that the candidate relies on the shotgun rather than the rifle. He wants votes on Election Day. Because there is no guaranteed appeal, the candidate relies on as many appeals as he can think of and afford.[18] The slogan for all candidates might well be: "Keep moving, keep firing, and don't look back."

Both Mr. Rural and Mr. Urban followed this advice. They sensed, if they did not know for certain, that victory would come if they worked hard until Election Day. Their efforts were tireless. Despite the differences in techniques, organization, and financial resources, both candidates were trying to establish (or, rather, to re-establish) themselves in the minds of party workers and voters as energetic, knowledgeable, educated, capable, aware representatives of the people. They stressed their expertise. They talked about their record. They enjoyed being asked to unravel complicated issues. If anything, they—not the constituents—were the instructors. Little or nothing occurred in either campaign to convince the candidates to alter their policy-making behavior in Congress.

There were several similarities in the two campaigns. Both candidates conducted a perpetual campaign in the district—making a speaking tour when in the district between elections and maintaining contact with constituents while in Washington. Both candidates had campaign organizations apart from the regular state and local party organizations. And both conducted whirling-dervish campaigns designed to impress voters that they were represented by hardworking, dedicated public servants.

The differences in the two campaigns can be explained by differences in the political, social, and economic characteristics of the two districts. The districts differ in type of economy, geography, size, population density, occupational characteristics of constituents, transportation and communication, racial and ethnic characteristics, and almost every other characteristic one could mention. Thus, the two candidates conducted campaigns which differed according to the differences in their constituencies.

Mr. Urban had an elaborate and well-financed organization. He had a campaign manager, a campaign chairman, a chairman of finance, a treasurer, and an executive committee of ninety-one prominent citizens. He had fifty different groups organized to support him—e.g., Doctors for Urban, Lawyers for Urban, Labor for Urban. He could rely on a large volunteer staff.

Mr. Rural traditionally had carried his organization around "in his hat." In 1960, he finally organized a Rural for Congress Committee, but continued to manage his own campaign. Because, in the candidate's words, "I was never quite

---

[18] William Gore and Robert Peabody offer the perfect phrase *spray of stimuli* to describe this shotgun approach in campaigning. See "The Functions of a Political Campaign: A Case Study," *Western Political Quarterly*, XI (March 1958), 65.

sure how to use it," the Committee was principally used for fund-raising. Rural relied on regular party county chairmen to some extent, but only as advisors and friends.

The costs of the two campaigns differed enormously. Mr. Urban spent more on postage than Mr. Rural did on his whole campaign! Whereas the Congressional Campaign Committee's contribution to Mr. Rural comprised nearly half of his contributions, Mr. Urban (according to his campaign manager) didn't really need the contribution from the Campaign Committee—it was too small. A conservative estimate would be that Mr. Urban's campaign cost between ten and twenty times that of Mr. Rural.

As might be expected, on the basis of differences noted so far, the campaign plans of the two candidates differed markedly. Mr. Rural had no well-conceived plan; he operated mostly on intuition and personal relations. A rough pattern evolved as the campaign progressed, but comparatively little time was spent in precampaign strategy meetings.

Mr. Urban's campaign was planned in detail. Almost nothing was overlooked. An extensive campaign manual was prepared for all volunteers, outlining four phases of the campaign. In the first phase an attempt was made to get 5000 signatures on the candidate's petition (750 were needed).[19] During the second phase, the preprimary phase, the organization made an effort to speak to all the voters of the candidate's party and urge them to vote in the primary. The third phase emphasized the registration of voters. The fourth and final phase was devoted almost entirely to visiting every member of the other party and independents to urge them to vote for the candidate.[20] The over-all plan proceeded as outlined.

The media of communication used by Mr. Rural were those designed to cover a large geographical area with low population density. Billboards, television, radio, newspaper advertisements, and direct mailing were all employed. Mr. Urban did not rely on television, radio, or metropolitan newspapers[21] because these are not efficient campaign media for urban congressional candidates. These media give the urban candidate a much larger audience than he needs to have, which means that he has to pay for this large audience but has no guarantee that *his* audience—*i.e.*, his constituents—will identify him as their Congressman. It is much more efficient to rely on personal contact media. Thus, Mr. Urban conducted a program of extensive telephoning, canvassing, and direct mailing. In addition, from three to five social gatherings every night were sponsored by constituents in the final phase of the campaign. The candidate would make a brief appearance at each of the gatherings.

19 Mr. Rural also used this technique. He collected 10,234 names and sent each a letter and campaign literature.

20 The campaign manual also provided information on primary petitions and the primary, interviewing techniques, tips on canvassing for both the primary and general election, details of registration and methods for getting people registered, and general information about the candidate and government at all levels.

21 Mr. Urban did appear on both television and radio, however. He debated his opponent on television on a program sponsored by a local station. He appeared on other such public-service programs as well.

Of course, both candidates relied to a considerable extent on personal hand-shaking and speaking tours of the constituency. Mr. Urban traveled by taxi, however, while Mr. Rural often spent as much time enroute—seeking out constituents—as he did in shaking hands. For example, on one typical day, Mr. Rural traveled 215 miles, spent seventeen hours, and met or talked to approximately 300 people. In the same time, Mr. Urban met or talked to from three to five times that many people and his travel distance was measured in city blocks.

The specific content of speeches and conversations for each candidate differed considerably. Both, however, spoke about local problems—what they had done for the constituency and what might be done. Mr. Urban spoke more about international and national issues; Mr. Rural concentrated on agriculture. Both railed the opposition.

What were they doing in all this activity? Each tried to create an image of himself as a capable representative. The two candidates relied on different techniques because of differences in their constituencies, but both saw the campaign as a period in which they would meet as many people as possible in order to impress voters that they were well represented in Washington. This effort did not require extensive promises, or discussion of a great many specific issues (though issues were discussed).[22] It did require that they appear knowledgeable, able, and trustworthy. Mr. Rural explained it this way:

In rural areas, you don't get large groups involved in a position or discussion of a position. In rural areas, they kind of want to see the man around once in a while. It is not as important how the man votes in Congress. It is all right if they feel he is a steady sort of guy—then the votes are all right. They don't get so excited one way or the other.

His analysis suggests a conclusion about the relationship of the campaign to policy-making. A victorious candidate who views the campaign and election period as a time of judgment, in which voters judge his ability as a representative, is then relatively free to represent his constituency as he thinks best. He is not bound by instructions during the campaign. To him the central question of the election is: "How do you judge me? Should I continue to represent you ably, as I have in the past?" If the answer is affirmative, even by a reduced margin, the Congressman has considerable latitude in policy-making as far as his constituency is concerned. This is not to say that he has complete freedom to act: he will bind himself; he is bound by his associations, however developed; and he is bound by his party. But, it is herein contended, he need not be bound by the campaign and the election.

One might well argue at this point that the campaign-election period is indeed issue-oriented in that the incumbent does discuss his record; he does project an image of an able and knowledgeable representative which has

---

[22] Mr. Rural did note that he enjoyed being asked questions about complex issues so that he could display his expertise. As he put it: "I like to be asked such questions [i.e., about agricultural policy] because I soon lose them all [i.e., the audience] in details." It was evident that Mr. Urban also enjoyed discussing details of issues.

significance for predicting his behavior on issue resolution; he does learn something from another campaign in his constituency (e.g., reaffirmation of his "sense" of the constituency or perhaps awareness of a new problem). This, however, is not what is generally meant by an issue-oriented campaign and it is certainly not what is implied by American representative-democratic theory. For these reasons, it is useful to distinguish between an "issue-oriented" campaign and an "image-oriented" campaign which is "issue-involved." Campaigns for the United States House of Representatives are of the latter type. The candidate who has opposition attempts to project an image from which a perceptive voter can discern an approach to the solution of future legislative issues. There is little exchange between the constituency as a whole and the incumbent on specific issues in the campaign, but there is developed an image which indicates what one may expect from the candidate when he returns to Washington. The fact is that many voters do not care to discover this image—or even the name of the incumbent.

Other Congressional Campaigns

There is evidence, in the few congressional campaign studies which are available, to support the principal thesis of this study. Students of congressional campaigns are impressed with the extent to which incumbents attempt to cast an image of themselves as capable, experienced representatives. The campaign is not seen to be issue-oriented or a time of commitment of the candidate to the constituency.

In her study of the old Massachusetts Tenth District (now abolished by redistricting), Professor Josephine Milburn observes that incumbent Lawrence Curtis "emphasized his experience as 'a proven public official' and his interest in the Tenth District. . . ."[23] He only discussed issues which were of "immediate interest" to his constituency and "he did not attempt to educate the voters, but rather he presented the appearance of reflecting their views and ideas."

Congressman Curtis was apparently successful in his effort, because polls of voters conducted by Professor Milburn's students showed that "Curtis was viewed as an experienced man in Congress, and as a Congressman who kept in touch with his constituency."

Professor Frederick Wirt's conclusions about the incumbent's campaign in Ohio's Fifteenth District are very much the same—though details of this campaign differ from others discussed.[24] Incumbent Moorehead "has absolutely no concept of what issues concern his constituents." In fact, he asked Professor Wirt in an interview "if he [Wirt] could tell *him* what the issues were over which his people were aroused." Wirt describes Moorehead's style of campaign as "casual" and attributes this to constituency characteristics—*i.e.,* "very little is

[23] Josephine Milburn, "The Perennial Congressional Campaigner and His Opposition in the 'Late' Massachusetts Tenth District," an unpublished paper presented at the National Center for Education in Politics Seminar for Teachers of Politics, Washington, D.C., September 1–4, 1962.
[24] Wirt, "The 1962 Ohio Fifteenth Congressional District Campaign. . . ."

moving in the hills of the Fifteenth." Wirt's response to the question: "What is the role of the campaign in the over-all political life of the Congressman?" was:

The campaign seemed to Moorehead to be an almost incidental affair. . . . Moorehead finds little relationship between his role as campaigner and those of representative and legislator. By and large, . . . the campaign is mainly a device whereby he impresses his name and party on the district, with very little place for issues.

In a district which is identified only as "The Mid-Heartland Third Congressional District," Professor David Kovenock provides interesting interview data which distinguishes the campaign role from the legislator role:

Some of my legislative interests and activities are tied to the campaign, but not many. A couple of these are good for something, but it's the *image* that counts. What *you do* up here is important; in politics what *they think* is important.

I campaign all the time. It's just that as the election approaches, decisions have got to be made—like brochures and schedules. . . .

No, in legislation as far as the campaign is concerned, it's the image. I'm trying not to be typecast. I want to be seen as involved, but not with much that's too specific.[25]

Professor Lewis Froman approaches the campaign differently and provides additional evidence for the position taken here. In his book *Congressmen and Their Constituencies*, he emphasizes the setting in congressional campaigns.[26] His argument is that the candidates and the campaign have very little to do with the outcome. He centers his study on Wisconsin's Second District and is persuasive in his analysis. Froman provides further substantiation for the conclusion that the incumbent will win and there is very little that the challenger can do about that. And issues are of very little impact or importance.

Finally, there is a published study of the 1954 congressional campaign in Washington's First District. Professors William Gore and Robert Peabody observe that probably the most effective stimuli to voters were the challenger's "thoughtful, reflective demeanor" and the incumbent's "quiet candor and sincerity." Working with a highly efficient organization, incumbent Thomas Pelly's strategy "was to develop a stereotype of a fair-minded, capable man willing and able to protect and further the interests of all of the people of his district. This theme was directed toward activating motivations based upon the personality and character of the candidate."[27]

[25] David Kovenock, "The Congressman and the Campaign: Excursions Along a Decision-Making Approach to the Study of Congressional Behavior," an unpublished paper presented at the National Center for Education in Politics Seminar for Teachers of Politics, Washington, D.C., September 1–4, 1962.

[26] Froman, *Congressmen and Their Constituencies*, Chap. 4.

[27] Gore and Peabody, "The Functions of a Political Campaign: A Case Study," *Western Political Quarterly*, 66. See also Donald B. Johnson, "The Congressional Campaign and the Off-Year Elections of 1962," *American Government Annual* (New York: Holt, Rinehart & Winston, Inc., 1963).

Elections and Policy-Making

After the election results are tabulated and the incumbent returns to office with either an increased or decreased margin, does he change his policy-making behavior? Because there are no studies which deal directly with this question, some data have been collected here which apply.

Before these data are examined, it should be said that one need only study electoral and policy-making conditions in this country to conclude that it is risky to change policy-making behavior because of variations in election results. Election results are ambiguous. Though thorough analysis of voting in the constituency may reveal which groups of voters have reduced or increased their support for the incumbent, the cause-effect relationship between voter opinion and the incumbent's policy record is more difficult to determine. Yet a representative should know something of this cause-effect relationship if he is to base a change in behavior on election results. If there is an obvious shift of opinion in the district, the representative may try to accommodate it. But the shift is seldom obvious and the representative seldom so flexible. Furthermore, most representatives will probably attribute loss of strength to nonpolicy causes —e.g., overconfidence of his own forces, long and vigorous campaigning by his opponent ("He started in January"), a long session of Congress ("The President kept us in Washington until October"), lack of finances, labor/business support for his opponent. Only a few incumbent representatives can be expected to say, "I lost ground because of my policy record."

In order to provide some measure of the effect of election results, let us examine roll-call behavior on certain issues selected by the *Congressional Quarterly*. In 1959, the *Congressional Quarterly* calculated "Economy Support Scores" (ESS) for all members of the House and contrasted these scores with scores received in the Eighty-fifth Congress. In 1961, they presented "Federal Role Support Scores" (FSS) and contrasted these with scores received in the Eighty-sixth Congress. Thus, it was possible to study changes in scores following the 1958 and 1960 elections.[28]

It so happens that the winning Republican incumbents tended to experience percentage losses in the 1958 elections (only a handful of Democrats had a percentage decrease), and the winning Democratic incumbents suffered percentage losses in 1960 (only seven Republicans had their margins decreased by more than 5 percent). Thus, data will be presented on Republican incumbents for 1958 and Democratic incumbents for 1960.

The representatives studied have been divided into three groups: Group A includes those who lost 5 percent or more in their margins; Group B includes

---

[28] The ESS were developed on the basis of voting for measures which would reduce government spending. The ESS are based on fifty-nine economy issues in the Eighty-fifth Congress and twenty-nine economy issues in 1959. The ESS were developed on the basis of voting for measures which would increase the role of the federal government. The FSS are based on twelve roll-calls in the Eighty-sixth Congress and ten roll calls in 1961. See *Congressional Quarterly Almanac*, XV, 147–54; XVII, 631–37.

those who lost less than 5 percent in their margins; Group C includes those who increased their margins. Those incumbents who did not have opponents in one of the elections have been excluded because a decrease or increase in such cases would not be meaningful. In 1958, there were forty-eight Republicans in Group A, sixty in Group B, and twenty-one in Group C, for a total of 129. In 1960, there were fifty-one Democrats in Group A, forty-eight in Group B, and forty-six in Group C, for a total of 145.

Any conclusions based on these data must be cautiously developed. Only roll-call behavior on certain issues is examined. An incumbent might change his policy-making behavior in any number of ways which would not show up on roll-call analysis. Furthermore, even if change does occur, it is possible only to note the correlation between loss or gain at the polls and change in roll-call behavior. Any conclusions about cause and effect would have to be based on further study.

The procedure used here is simple and was the same for both elections, 1958 and 1960. First, the incumbents were grouped (see the three groups above) according to election results in 1958—contrasting their margin with that in 1956. Then their ESS before the 1958 election in the Eighty-fifth Congress was compared to their ESS after the 1958 election in 1959, and the difference between them determined. A mean difference was calculated for all 129 Republican incumbents, and then for each of the three groups (A, B, C). The process was repeated for the FSS in 1960.

If the campaign and election are not primarily issue-oriented events, then one would expect no significant differences between any one of the groups and the group as a whole. An alternative hypothesis would be that there would be significant differences—*i.e.*, Group A would change significantly as a result of their greater loss at the polls, that Group B would change less significantly, and that Group C would not change because voters have approved their previous behavior and rewarded them with an increased margin.

Table 4—Analysis of Change in ESS for House Republicans, Eighty-fifth Congress and 1959

Republicans	N	Mean ESS [a] 85TH CONG.	Mean ESS 1959	Mean Difference 85TH CONG. → 1959	z [b]
All Republicans	129	50.5	59.7	+ 9.2	
Group A [c]	48	52.6	63.1	+10.5	+ .8
Group B [d]	60	51.6	58.3	+ 6.7	−1.6
Group C [e]	21	43.0	56.2	+13.2	$t = +1.37$

[a] Economy Support Score as developed by the *Congressional Quarterly*. See *Almanac* XV (1959), 147–54.

[b] This test for z is based on the formula: $z = \frac{\bar{x} - \mu}{s/\sqrt{n}}$. See John Freund and Frank Williams, *Modern Business Statistics* (Englewood Cliffs, N.J.: Prentice-Hall, Inc., 1958), pp. 233–37.

[c] Includes members who lost 5 percent or more in the 1958 election.

[d] Includes members who lost less than 5 percent in the 1958 election.

[e] Includes members who increased their margin in the 1958 election.

[f] Since the number in Group C is less than 30, a different formula is used: $t = \frac{\bar{x} - \mu}{s}\sqrt{n}$. See Freund and Williams, *Modern Business Statistics*, p. 236.

The results of this analysis for 1958 are shown in Table 4. As noted in Table 4, none of the means for the three groups is significantly different from the mean of the population at the 0.05 level (*i.e.*, $z > 1.96$). Thus, at least until further proof is available, it is possible to accept the hypothesis that there are not significant differences between the groups and the group as a whole. Indeed, the findings are almost the reverse of what would be expected if the alternative hypothesis is to be accepted: Group A has the least, rather than the most, variance; Group C has the second greatest variance (and the greatest absolute variance from the population mean) rather than the least; and Group B has the greatest variance.

Other, less statistical observations can be made about Table 4. Each of the three groups remained at the same relative level after the election as before. Group A was the most economy-minded, by the *Congressional Quarterly* measure, during the Eighty-fifth Congress and remained so in 1959; Group C was the least economy-minded and remained so; Group B remained in the middle.

The results of the analysis for 1960 are shown in Table 5.

Table 5—Analysis of Change in FSS for House Democrats, Eighty-sixth Congress and 1961

Democrats	N	Mean FSS[a] 86TH CONG.	Mean FSS 1961	Mean Difference 86TH CONG. → 1961	z
All Democrats	145	85.2	89.8	+4.6	
Group A	51	80.2	85.3	+5.1	+ .35
Group B	48	90.1	92.1	+2.0	−1.37
Group C	46	85.5	92.4	+6.9	+1.44

[a] Federal Role Support Score as developed by the *Congressional Quarterly*. See *Almanac*, XVII (1961), 631–37.

Once again, none of the differences between the groups and the group as a whole is significant at the 0.05 level (*i.e.*, $z > 1.96$). And, as with 1958, there is further basis for rejecting the alternative hypothesis, inasmuch as Group A has the least variance, Group C the most, and Group B slightly less than Group C. Finally, Group A remained in the same relative position in 1961 as in the Eighty-sixth Congress (the lowest FSS in both). Groups B and C however, traded places by a narrow margin—Group C becoming the group with the highest FSS in 1961.

On the basis of the caveats noted earlier, there is support in these data for the notion that a representative will not change his policy-making behavior because of the results in his own election.

One final note on these data. In both cases there were changes in over-all scores between the periods of measurement. It may be that an election has an effect on the party as a whole, and that that effect is uniform among individual representatives as pressure is applied by party leaders. Such a proposition should be examined.

Conclusion

This study has presented data on several propositions and contingencies which are of interest to students of the electoral process. The major proposition is that the campaign and election are regularly scheduled events in the political life of a representative in which he makes an intensive effort to project an image of himself as a capable representative—which image is "issue-involved" in that it provides clues as to what to expect by way of policy-making behavior from the Congressman. Elections are not primarily policy or issue events where issues are discussed and resolved or where there is exchange between constituency and candidate. When the representative is returned to office, he is relatively unbound by the campaign and election in his policy-making behavior (though he is bound by other factors not measured here). Basically, and this may be too simple to be accepted, the campaign-election period is a time when the incumbent is re-elected—returned to office to represent as he has in the past.

Supporting propositions and contingencies to the above are as follows:

1. Elections are scheduled by the calendar—not by issue emergence.
2. An overwhelming majority of incumbents are returned to office.
3. Voters are almost totally unaware of issues in congressional elections and a majority are unaware of the candidates.
4. The incumbent's campaign will be designed to identify him to as many voters as possible. His specific campaign activity and techniques will vary depending on the characteristics of his constituency. He will not be committed to specific issue stands during the campaign except by choice.
5. The victorious incumbent will not alter his policy-making behavior as a result of percentage changes at elections.

Most of these statements depend on other propositions about what does influence the policy-making behavior of a representative. Though no extensive treatment of this subject is possible here, it should be said in conclusion that the Congressman is committed to and bounded by his own perception of his constituency, by those groups which have access to him (and to which he allows access), by his legislative party, and by his colleagues (especially those in standing committees of which he is a member). These boundaries to his action become well established for the incumbent and, in a sense, provide further evidence for the contention here. Even if he wanted to change his behavior because of election returns, the incumbent would have difficulty in doing so. One does not easily switch perceptions, group affiliations, and contacts.

Congressional Campaigning
in Mexico:
A View From the Provinces

by KARL M. SCHMITT

On July 2, 1967, Mexican voters elected representatives to the Chamber of Deputies, the lower house of the national legislature. By law the Chamber is completely renewed every three years, and members cannot succeed themselves. Throughout the country, the elections took place smoothly and without serious disturbances. The State of Yucatán, remote and isolated from the major political and economic centers of the country, quietly participated following an election campaign that was reserved and orderly.[1]

Although scholars have made some few analyses of presidential elections in Mexico, they have paid scant attention to congressional campaigns. Given the virtually one-party system of Mexican politics and the predominance of the executive branch, it is not surprising that national congressional campaigns have aroused little interest. Scott notes that the normal characteristics of campaigns in competitive political systems—"the interplay of interests, the balancing of demands and adjustment of differences"—are to be found within the official party, and before the nomination of candidates rather than after.[2] Scott also

---

[1] The only reported trouble was in the town of Seye in the Second Congressional District, where the candidate and his party were greeted with hostility by the local people when he came to hold a rally. This opposition stemmed from a dispute of the previous year over agrarian credits extended to the campesinos by the national government. The candidate of the second district, a high-ranking state official at the time of the dispute, ordered the dispersal of the campesinos when they marched into Mérida.

[2] Robert E. Scott, *Mexican Government in Transition* (Urbana: University of Illinois Press, 1959), pp. 197–98.

Reprinted from "Congressional Campaigning in Mexico: A View from the Provinces," *Journal of Inter-American Studies*, 11 (January 1969): 93–110, by Karl M. Schmitt. Reprinted by permission of the *Journal of Inter-American Studies* and the author.

points out that, because of executive dominance, congressional aspirants are motivated more by a desire for the perquisites of office than by "a hope of influencing policy." Beyond this Scott has little to say about congressional campaigns. He has a few paragraphs on the forces that in the broad national context determine the overall allotment of seats to the official party's three "sectors,"[3] but he has nothing to say about requisite qualifications and recruitment of candidates, the operations of candidate selection and campaigning in the opposition parties, or, more importantly, the function of congressional campaigning for the political system.

Padgett, on the other hand, pays somewhat more attention to the electoral laws, particularly the recent proportional representation enactment. More significantly, he attempts to deal with the functions of elections. In addition to providing for a change in personnel in office, Padgett points out, elections "symbolize at least the goal value of democracy." He also insists that they are useful "in mustering large audiences, propagating the 'gospel' of the regime and stirring a sense of participation in the masses,"[4] but like Scott he has little to say about recruitment of congressional candidates, and nothing on the role of opposition parties in congressional campaigns. It is hard to quarrel with the generalizations of Scott and Padgett. They are moderate and reasoned statements. On the other hand, neither authority cites much empirical data to support his views. It is the purpose of this paper to take a close look at the congressional campaign in a state—Yucatán—uncluttered with accompanying presidential, gubernatorial, or municipal elections.

With a population of about 775,000, Yucatán holds only three of the 178 district seats in the Chamber of Deputies. For the 1964–1967 term, however, the state had four representatives because the candidate of the National Action Party (PAN) in the first district (although he failed to win a popular majority) gained sufficient votes to obtain a seat under the terms of the proportional representation law of 1962. The PAN lost corn for internal consumption. The henequen industry has declined that seat in the 1967 elections.

Small in population and poor in resources, the state has been spared serious economic sufferings only by massive infusions of federal funds for education and welfare as well as for capital investments. The economy rests on an agricultural base consisting largely of henequen for export and has suffered severely in recent decades with competition from foreign natural and artificial fibers. Some Yucatecans have also blamed poor administration, careless planting techniques, and improper care and cutting of the plants following the Agrarian Reform of the 1930's as important contributing factors to the reversals of Yucatecan henequen. Whatever the causes, the Yucatecan economy is stagnant, and continued federal investments and grants seem necessary to keep it afloat. The capital city of Mérida, with well over one-fourth the total population of the state, appears to be relatively well off and thriving, and some of the larger towns such as Progreso and Motul seem to share some of this prosperity. The small towns and villages,

[3] *Ibid.*, pp. 227–28.
[4] L. Vincent Padgett, *The Mexican Political System* (Boston: Houghton Mifflin Company, 1966), pp. 85–6.

however, and the rural areas, where over half of the inhabitants live, suffer from depressing poverty.

Basically, state politics reflects the national scene. The official Institutional Revolutionary Party (PRI), with token opposition at best, completely dominates the state outside the city of Mérida. It has strong organizational control over the labor unions, farm groups, and public employee organizations. Within the capital, however, the National Action Party, somewhat oriented toward Christian Democracy, enjoys a considerable but not well integrated following among those elements dissatisfied for one reason or another with the government and the official party. The Marxist-type Socialist People's Party (PPS) has a skeletal organization and seems to pick up support largely among students and intellectuals and from the personal friends and acquaintances of the candidates.

Given the nature of the Mexican political system—one-party domination, highly centralized authority structure, high degree of party loyalty and discipline —much of the literature on congressional elections, oriented as it is to the United States, is not readily applicable to the Mexican situation. For example, since the official party in Mexico has almost monopolized elective offices for about forty years, and since representatives (or deputies as they are called in Mexico) cannot succeed themselves, the stress in the U.S. literature about the campaigns of incumbents is irrelevant. So is the question as to whether or not the representative is bound by the election in his policy-making behavior—he does not make policy in Mexico. It does not help much either to learn from American studies that incumbents gain re-election about 80 percent–90 percent of the time, or that when incumbents choose not to run, their party is highly likely to win.[5] Mexico can offer no comparisons with this kind of data.

On the other hand there are some striking contrasts and some interesting parallels. Legally and constitutionally Mexican congressional elections are similar to those of the United States except for the limited proportional representation amendment and law of 1962. These elections, regularly scheduled as in the United States, are designed to provide geographic representation by states and equal representation for those entitled to vote, and they are not to provide for representation of collectives or organized groups. It has been demonstrated that in the United States the political campaign provides the latter,[6] but in Mexico the parties, especially the official party with its sociological "sectors," sees to the representation of organized interests.[7] However, some of the purposes of campaigning in both countries are the same: the reinforcement of party supporters, the activation of latent supporters, and the conversion of the opposition. Likewise, the campaigns concentrate more on issues of "style" rather than on issues of "position."[8] That is to say that broad general themes

[5] Charles O. Jones, "The Role of the Campaign in Congressional Politics," in M. Kent Jennings and L. Harmon Zeigler (eds.), *The Electoral Process* (Englewood Cliffs: Prentice-Hall, Inc., 1966), pp. 23 and 26.

[6] William J. Gore and Robert L. Peabody, "The Functions of the Political Campaign: A Case Study," *The Western Political Quarterly*, Vol. XI, No. 1, (March, 1958), p. 55.

[7] Scott, *Mexican Government in Transition*, p. 173.

[8] For the use of the terms "style" issues and "position" issues, see Lewis A. Froman, Jr., "A Realistic Approach to Campaign Strategies and Tactics," in M. Kent Jennings and L. Harmon Zeigler, *op. cit.*, p. 8.

rather than concrete, specific problems constitute the primary discussion materials for candidates. If the explanation for this in the United States is that a candidate's basic support comes from his own party supporters who need reassurances as to the party's general ideological stance, and that it is most difficult to convert the opposition, to whom a strong stand on specific issues might appeal, then the explanation has even greater applicability to Mexico. It is also probable that opinion leaders in Mexican parties are generally more successful in holding the rank-and-file loyal at election time than in the United States. On the other hand, it would appear that the opposition parties in Mexico, with their need to cut into the massive majorities of the official party, would stress specific problems seemingly neglected by the government. In Yucatán in 1967 they did not, possibly for lack of sophistication in the ability to present the case, possibly for a lack of real alternatives, but most likely because the present psychology of Mexican political leaders is to stress party ideological differences and moral superiority whether real or imagined.

The major differences between U.S. and Mexican campaigns lie in the basic function of the campaign and the manner of recruiting candidates. In the United States candidates are recruited by a wide variety of means, whether by themselves, their friends, business associates, interest groups, political parties, or political factions.[9] In Mexico there is only one road, and that is through the party. As to the second point, the differences are even more striking. U.S. campaigns are designed to elect candidates to congressional seats where they will broadly represent the leading interests of their local constituency. In Mexico, on the other hand, with a virtual one-party system, most elections are foregone conclusions, deputies have no independent position *vis-à-vis* the executive, and represent, if only theoretically, national interest groups first and local power centers only secondarily. The campaign in Yucatán bears this thesis out. One may well ask, then, what are the functions of congressional campaigns in Mexico?

The primary function of congressional campaigning in Mexico is nation-building, the creation of a "civic culture." All elections, of course, contribute to the process, and it is significant to note that the staggered nature of elections in the country gives a regular and continuing sense of participation in the political process to the masses who only marginally are aware of the larger developments of Mexican national life. Elections are a part of the educational process in the long and arduous task of nation-building, of turning illiterate campesinos, Indians, and an uneducated and culturally backward people into Mexican citizens. Election campaigns constitute one method of communication, instruction, and indoctrination.

Recruiting Candidates in Yucatán, 1967

Mexican electoral procedures do not provide for primary elections, and Mexican electoral practices do not provide the basis for self-recruitment or for recruitment by friends, associates, or interest groups outside party structures.

---

[9] Gore and Peabody, *op. cit.*, pp. 56–58.

All of the candidates, therefore, of all the parties were recruited within the party organizations, and (within the official party at least) legislative candidates had to be approved by national party headquarters if the initial selection was not actually made there. Furthermore, the campaign teams and financial support were also raised within the parties.

Candidates are nominally chosen by party conventions on the appropriate level (local, state, or national), but candidates are usually selected by an inner group of party leaders prior to the convention, and decisions by lower groups are usually reviewed by higher party authorities. Conventions, supposedly representing the rank-and-file, then simply ratify the selections of the leaders. Internal party discussions (and possibly disputes) over the selection of candidates are rarely open to public view, but within the PAN and the PPS in Yucatán it is not difficult to surmise the procedure. Both parties appear to have only small groups of activists, and within these only a very few would seem to be appropriate as candidates, not only in terms of those who would be willing to stand, but of those who would have at least moderate facility in public speaking, time available, and a modicum of popular appeal. Although the PRI has a much larger base to draw upon than its rivals, in 1967 it imported one of its candidates from Mexico City. There were some indications of rivalry over candidacies in the state, but nothing definite came to light and no evidence was uncovered as to how disputes of this nature were resolved. Again, it may be surmised that, given the degree of *personalismo* that prevails in society at large, decisions were reached to some degree in terms of personal relationships not only in the PRI but in the PAN and the PPS as well.[10]

PAN recruited all three of its candidates in Yucatán for the 1967 elections from the lower middle and middle classes, although it had considerable electoral support from the comfortable middle and upper classes in Mérida. All of its candidates came from humble origins, demonstrated considerable upward striving ambitions, and showed modest success in their endeavors at self improvement. None could be called an intellectual, although one was a medical practitioner; of the other two, one was a retail salesman and the other a semi-skilled day laborer. None was widely known in his congressional district. Only one candidate was a recent recruit to the party, the other two having over ten years of service.

All three PPS candidates, in contrast with those of PAN, were intellectuals (school teachers or university students), of solid middle-class origin. The two younger candidates were recent recruits to the party from Mérida, and only the third, a retired professor, was a founding member who had spent most of his adult life in Mexico City. Like the PAN candidates they demonstrated the middle-class characteristic of upward striving but, unlike PAN members, were motivated far more strongly by ideology. None of the PPS candidates was well known in his district, although the retired professor (who ran in the third district) had some notoriety in and around Mérida for his "radicalism."

[10] The alternate for the first district (Mérida) was a nephew of the current PAN deputy from Mérida.

The PRI candidates had two common features: a rather high degree of achieved status and years of service to the party. Only one had held a prior elective position, although the other two had worked for government at national, state, and local levels either as consultants or in appointive posts. Two PRI candidates with their residence in the state were well known personally in their districts, and the third, although living in Mexico City, was known through the prominence of his family, which was of Yucatecan origin. The extent of popular support for the candidate personally loomed as an important factor in his selection only in Mérida. The other two candidates, with no expected opposition in their districts, were obviously selected to reward able men for years of party service. Although they were fairly close in age (in their forties), in social origin the PRI candidates demonstrated no uniformity; one was of humble background, another of an upper middle-class business and professional family, and the third of a military family that rose to prominence in the bloody phase of the Revolution.

Most striking, however, in a consideration of PRI candidates was the diversity of the career patterns of the three candidates in Yucatán. The candidate of the first district was a technical expert, an engineer, who had worked for most of his career in government service in his chosen profession. The candidate of the second district was a political and party activist without a university education who had seldom if ever held a non-political job—the professional politician. The third district candidate, by contrast, was almost the stereotype of the intellectual—a law professor and author of learned volumes. Perhaps in this eclecticism in the choice of candidates we have an additional explanation for the continued success of the PRI, *i.e.*, its openness to persons from many walks of life to achieve high position in the government and party. Its demands are talent and service, first to the party and through the party to the government and to the nation.

All three parties apparently distributed their candidates according to definite plans. Both the official party and the PAN ran their best candidate in the first district, comprising primarily the city of Mérida. The PPS, for reasons to be explained later, ran its most able man in the relatively remote third district, the eastern two-thirds of the state. All three parties ran their least appealing candidates in the second district, the western third of the state including the port city of Progreso. Obviously PRI and PAN put their best men in the first district since it is the only district in which the opposition gives serious competition to the official party; it is also the only district in which the vote is registered and tabulated with near complete accuracy. For the others, the PPS candidate in Mérida was a bright young university student leader, the PAN candidate of the third district was a doctor in the important town of Motul, the PRI candidate in the second district was a professional physician born in Progreso, and the PRI candidate in the third district was the Mexico City import whose family originated in that area. The PAN and the PPS candidates for the second district were both natives of Mérida and appeared to be simply fill-ins for those slots.

Campaigning—A Nation-Building Process

To some extent all the parties contribute to the nation-building process, but the PRI contributes more than its opponents because of greater resources and the consequent extent of its campaign activities. In this election, as in others, PRI leaders rallied their supporters and obtained the votes of the majority by insistence that the PRI is the only "true" party of the Revolution, by reminders of past accomplishments, and by promises of future rewards. In addition the official party again forced the political opposition to temper its criticism, not only by holding out the possibility of elective offices for opposition parties, but by undercutting opposition attacks on Mexican political practices as undemocratic, simply by holding a fairly honest election. The government and official party have long been sensitive to such attacks on the system since democracy has been a stated goal of the Revolution since 1910. The 1962 proportional representation law was designed to provide additional seats to the larger opposition parties, thus demonstrating the benefits to be gained by continued loyalty to the present political system.

The election campaign also provided important services for opposition parties and their members. It offered opportunities for those parties to propagandize at a time when public interest is most receptive to political argument. However, in 1967 the opposition parties in Yucatán, at least, did not take full advantage of their opportunities to bring their message to the public partly because of their conception of a political campaign and partly because of limited resources. Secondly, the election campaign served as an outlet for political expression by political activists who opposed the official party and government. The election permitted such persons to "let off steam" harmlessly. For the PPS, specifically, the election permitted the party, which in fact for years operated more as a narrow intellectualized interest group, to retain one of the distinguishing characteristics of a political party, *i.e.*, the holding of public offices. For PAN, the election presented some real opportunities to contest PRI hegemony at least in a few areas of the country. It again gave PAN some sense of accomplishment, if not of victory, not only through the winning of one majority seat but also through the winning of party seats. For PAN the slow but steady increase in its total popular vote (12.5 percent for 1967) has meant not only material but moral victories for its members.

Mexican political parties ordinarily make no information available concerning party finances, but all three parties complained about restrictions imposed on campaigning by lack of money. Although the official party was better equipped by far than its opponents, its funds were limited even in Mérida far below what would ordinarily be available to a congressional candidate of the United States in a city of comparable size. It was next to impossible to make estimates of political spending in absolute terms. Some relative assessments, however, were possible from various kinds of evidence.

The official party occupied a spacious, if somewhat poorly maintained, party headquarters in an old rambling building not far from the center of Mérida. Auditorium, meeting rooms, and offices seemed ample to meet the needs of the party. The headquarters, furthermore, gave an appearance of vitality with people and delegations coming and going, the offices bustling with secretaries clattering away at typewriters, telephones ringing, and party officials conferring over the campaign and attending to callers. By contrast the other two parties occupied modest quarters of two or three rooms (also not far from the center of Mérida); until recently they maintained no permanent offices and set up a party headquarters only at election time. Neither opposition party had a professional political staff nor paid secretarial help. During the daytime PAN and PPS headquarters were kept open by a few party members, but practically all business was conducted after 8:00 P.M., when members came off their regular jobs. Furniture was sparse and a single telephone and typewriter were available for party needs. About twenty to thirty people was the maximum number observed at any one time at either PPS or PAN offices.

Party use of paid media also gave some indication of relative expenditures. In the matter of handbills, bulletins, and posters, all the parties distributed thousands, so that comparison was difficult. The PPS, for example, reported that it had 65,000 handbills printed, and the number of these stacked in the office and plastered all over Mérida seemed to bear out this claim. The PRI also distributed posters and handbills in abundance. The PAN apparently used fewer, but anything approaching an exact count was difficult. With respect to newspaper advertisements and the use of radio and television the story was quite different. The advantage of the PRI in this area was remarkable. Whereas the PPS never used paid media at all, and PAN used only the newspapers (and those only three or four times), the PRI used all three, particularly newspapers in which the party publicized its campaigns two or three times a week for at least two months. This advantage was all the more impressive when it is remembered that radio, television, and newspapers reported virtually nothing of candidates or of their political campaigns as straight news items.

TECHNIQUES

Radio and television were used sparingly in the campaign. In fact T.V. was used only once and then by the official party early in April to introduce its recently nominated candidates to the public. Radio was used a few times, again only by the PRI, to make brief announcements of party meetings and functions; radio was never used for speech-making, but one or two public rallies were broadcast statewide. Both PAN and PPS reported that the use of these means were beyond their financial abilities.

Newspapers were far more widely used, but as noted above, primarily by the PRI. Furthermore, the official party devoted far more of its newspaper ads to the candidate of the first district than to those of the second and third districts, where the opposition could be discounted.[11] These items consisted primarily of

[11] There are only two newspapers of any substantial circulation in the whole peninsula, including the state of Campeche and the territory of Quintana Roo. Both of these (*Novedades de Yucatán* and *Diario de Yucatán*) are published in Mérida. A third newspaper of some importance, the *Diario del*

reports with pictures of recent meetings of the candidates with local interest groups or local PRI officials. By contrast the few PAN announcements that appeared in *Novedades* consisted primarily of political editorials by the party's leading theorist in Yucatán. Two others concerned the selection of the PAN candidates, and only one reported political rallies. As stated above the PPS made no newspaper announcements.

All parties used handbills and posters in profusion. These consisted largely of pictures of the candidate and his alternate, with a few party slogans or principles. Seldom did they deal with specific, concrete issues. The PAN and the PPS, particularly the latter, posted these pieces on utility poles, walls, and buildings. PRI with its control of political and economic life placed most of its announcements in store fronts. The official party also passed out in the first district some hundreds of fans with the candidate's picture. In lesser quantity, the PPS and the PAN distributed booklets and manifestos of party doctrines and broad programs.

Mass speeches and rallies were rarely used by any of the parties in Mérida, although the PRI candidates in the other two districts attempted to hold at least one rally in each of the 50-some municipios in their districts. In Mérida the PRI candidate spoke extensively, but his remarks were normally addressed to particular interests such as labor organizations, public employee associations, or business groups. The candidates of the two opposition parties held a few public meetings in their districts, but those for Mérida held no public rallies at all. The PAN candidate in Mérida stated that he expected most of his support to come from voters interested in PAN doctrine and that his primary efforts to increase his strength consisted of personal contacts rather than mass rallies. The PPS candidate also used person-to-person talks to build his strength, concentrating most of his attention on university students, among whom he had his best contacts. In his campaign he also used a loud-speaker attached to an auto to promote his cause.

Personal observation and newspaper reports demonstrated that campaign meetings, whether addressed to a general audience or to a specialized group, had an identifiable format and style. Besides the expected master-of-ceremonies and the candidate himself, most of the rallies had a rather formidable list of speakers. These were usually local political leaders of some importance or officers of the particular group addressed; mercifully, their talks were short. The main speaker himself normally held the platform for not more than thirty minutes (often for less time) and the whole affair lasted approximately an hour. A few rallies of the PRI were interspersed with music and singing, but food and drink were seldom distributed. As might be expected, the crowds were normally supporters of the candidate and the several that I attended had a social, festive air about them. These programs were designed to reinforce the beliefs and loyalty of the

---

Sureste, with a circulation of about one-sixth of the other two, is the official organ of the state government. *Novedades* reported a little pre-election campaign news and had a substantial amount of party advertising; *Diario de Yucatán* carried a few pre-election editorials, but virtually no advertising; and the *Diario del Sureste* concentrated on PRI announcements. As a result this survey of the use of newspapers is confined almost exclusively to *Novedades.*

faithful and to persuade them of the duty and necessity to vote. There was little activity in the campaigning in Yucatán to attract new support by means of public exposure either of the candidates or of the issues.

CONTENT

Legislative campaigning in Yucatán in 1967 was designed more to assert the relevance of the doctrines and principles of one or another of the parties to modern Mexico, than it was to raise and debate concrete issues and problems of the state of Yucatán. Some attention was paid to the latter in all the thousands of words that were printed or spoken, but *in toto* it constituted a relatively small part of campaign propaganda. Seldom if ever did the parties discuss the need for improved port facilities at Progreso, the present high cost of those facilities, the specific methods to achieve agricultural diversification, the soaring birth rate, the need for new markets and uses for henequen, the dispute with the national government over utility rates, and the labor-management dispute that grounded and eventually bankrupted the locally owned airline, Aeromaya. All of these issues were discussed and debated at length in the local newspapers and widely among the informed populace, but were not considered matters of great interest by the candidates and the parties, at least in their public statements. On the other hand, some of the important national issues were given attention, particularly by the PPS.

The PPS—The campaign literature of the PPS consisted of two basic types: (1) handbills carrying the names and (at times) the pictures of the candidates; and (2) manifestos of party principles and programs. The former carried brief general statements of party positions, stressing labor rights and benefits, the extension of social services to campesinos and students, or better working conditions and higher income. The other types of printed material were longer and more detailed statements of PPS views. By their very nature (discursive, highly intellectualized, closely printed) these manifestos apparently had a very limited audience, *i.e.*, among the well-educated already inclined toward the party's positions. It is difficult to understand what function these publications served except to instruct and inform party leaders on local levels as to the decisions of national headquarters on points to be stressed. For mass appeal they obviously needed to be popularized. The contents of these subtypes, however, varied but little. They dealt primarily with party doctrine and national issues (some of them quite specific and concrete) but with little relevance to local needs and problems. The best PPS treatment of local issues concretely appeared in the party booklet *Manifesto to the People of Yucatán*, and here the discussion, lengthy though it was, involved largely the need to make henequen competitive in world markets and to diversify the state's economy.

Although several issues were seriously treated by the PPS, the party did not succeed in getting its message across to any considerable body of potential voters in the campaign. Its lack of newspaper and other media coverage, its failure to discuss the issues in public forums and debates, and the lack of contacts with organized groups and interests meant that the party leaders were largely talking to each other and a handful of the party faithful.

The PAN—The literature of the National Action Party fell into the same two categories as that of the PPS: handbills and manifestos. However, the variety of PAN materials was substantially inferior to that of the socialists. Similar in most respects to PPS handbills, those of PAN, however, carried virtually no statement of party principles or doctrine except to state that PAN representatives would be "free" agents in the legislature. The manifestos originating in national party headquarters in Mexico City concerned themselves with broad statements on large national issues that have been stock-in-trade with the PAN for years. They demanded, among other things, educational reforms that implied assistance to private schools, the freeing of trade unions from political controls, agrarian reform that would give title of the land to the present communal farmer, and the placing of limits on public investments. Most of the positions taken were vague and broad; a few were specific. Rather striking was the absence of any literature dealing directly with the enormous social and economic problems facing the state. Victor M. Correa Rachó, the leading PAN theorist in Yucatán, concerned himself primarily with the larger national interests such as freedom and honesty of elections, the relation of candidates to the electorate, PAN's role in the political system, and the necessity of voting for a party and its ideology rather than for particular candidates. In public rallies, these same general themes were advanced. Many local party leaders were introduced and each spoke for a few minutes, pledging support of his followers and extolling the merits of the candidate and the party. Little time was available to develop any argument in depth, and, as with the published literature, the party depended on its general principles and ideology rather than on its concern for concrete local issues to win it support. As with the PPS, the PAN has difficulty getting its message across, but in Mérida at least it was well known as the major opposition party.

The PRI—The official party, undoubtedly because of its command of far greater resources, distributed a wider variety of campaign literature than either of its opponents, although it used basically the same two types: handbills and manifestos. None of the handbills made any reference whatever to party principles, doctrines, or programs except in the use of the most general terms such as "progress" and "loyalty" to revolutionary principles." The manifestos, however, stressed past accomplishments of the party in the state in terms of recreational, educational, and social welfare projects. The local candidates at times were associated with these achievements, and clear implications were made that more of the same could be expected. A manifesto in the rural third district played on the old theme of participation of the area in the Revolution, and the implementation of the Agrarian Reform. None of these manifestos made reference to current problems, but some conceded that many things remained yet to be done.

Although campaign literature made no reference to specific problems, PRI candidates brought up such subjects occasionally in their speeches. Julio Bobadilla, in one of his last rallies held in Progreso, promised to work toward the renewal of the operations to construct the much needed sheltered port for that city. Victor Manzanilla in the third district admitted to disorganization, dishonesty, and lack of responsibility in the administration of the communal farms (the ejidos) and the agrarian bank, while Rubén Encalada, the first district candidate, on various occasions noted the need for economic diversification and the difficulties of henequen. For the most part, however, campaign speeches and rallies of official party candidates consisted largely of pleasantries, references to past party achievements, and general promises of a better future.

The Election

On Sunday, July 2, election day, good weather prevailed as is normal in midsummer in Yucatán; the turnout was relatively good, but below the national level. By law the polls opened at eight o'clock in the morning, and closed at five in the afternoon. A number of election officials arrived late, a few not at all. Some election officials arrived on time but failed to set election procedures in motion because they did not understand their duties. There were also reports of illegal assistance to voters by official party officers.[12] Overall, however, the infractions seemed to be minor and had no substantial effect on the outcome of the elections. At a polling booth in central Mérida that I observed for several hours, a steady stream of voters filed through in an orderly manner presenting their voter registration cards and casting their ballots with a minimum of difficulty.[13]

The final returns indicated that approximately 194,000 people voted. Out of a voting age population of 349,000 in Yucatán, the turnout represented about 55 percent. This compares with the national vote of 12,340,000, representing over 70 percent of the voting age population nationwide. While the Mexican turnout nationally far surpassed average mid-term U.S. congressional election participation, the discrepancy between Yucatecan and national figures is frequently duplicated in the United States.

The official party won handily in Mérida, and overwhelmingly in the other two districts. Hadad of the PAN received 12,258 votes or about 22.12 percent of the first district ballots.[14] The PPS ran weakly throughout the state, receiving its greatest support in the third district but still placing third. Both opposition parties made their poorest showings in the second district, where they ran their weakest campaigns.

Two questions of importance always raised with respect to election statistics in Mexico should be explored: (1) How accurate were the total figures for election turnout; and (2) how fair and honest was the count? With respect to the first question, we can assume that the statistics indicate only a rough approximation of the level of voter participation; there is undoubtedly some padding of the count in the more rural and remote districts. The official party organization is

[12] I personally heard reports of these problems at PAN headquarters Sunday afternoon when party poll watchers came to report their difficulties.

[13] There were 152 polling booths in the first district, of which 129 were in the city of Mérida proper; 271 in the second district, and 270 in the third district, according to *Novedades de Yucatán*, July 2, 1967, p. 1.

[14] On the first returns from 144 boxes Hadad was credited with 12,674 votes, See *Novedades de Yucatán*, July 3, 1967, p.1. No explanations were made about the downward revisions, and as far as is known the party did not seriously question the count.

well geared to persuade, cajole, pressure, or assist the members of large organizations such as labor unions, campesino groups, and government employee organizations to turn out *en masse*. The vast majority of these cast their ballots for the official party; seemingly they follow the counsels of their leaders who are tied in with the official party hierarchy. Many, without doubt, clearly believe it is to their interest to vote for PRI, and a few perhaps support the party out of fear. Opposition party voters are on the whole rather highly motivated and politically aware individuals who oppose the government and the PRI for a variety of reasons. All in all the total statistics reported represent voter turnout fairly well, but tell us little of motivation, commitment to the system, or the accuracy of the distribution of the vote.

Table 1

Political Party	First District	Second District	Third District	All Districts
PRI				
Candidate	41,274	65,248	60,756	167,278
Alternate	40,162	65,248	60,756	166,166
PAN				
Candidate	12,258	3,708	4,694	20,660
Alternate	12,002	3,708	4,694	20,404
PPS				
Candidate	1,591	203	4,134	5,928
Alternate	1,410	203	4,134	5,747
Other				
Candidate	0	72	351	423
Alternate	0	72	351	423
Totals				
Candidates	55,123	69,231	69,935	194,289
Alternates	53,574	69,231	69,935	192,740

With respect to the question of the honesty of the count, there is undoubtedly a degree of error and distortion, if not outright fraud, as there is in most elections everywhere. Opposition party leaders made some mild remonstrances on these grounds following the election, but no one insisted that the inaccuracies substantially changed the outcome. Qualified informants believed that the "purity of the suffrage" in Mérida was basically unsullied. Less faith could be put in the accuracy of the count in rural and outlying areas. A close examination of the returns in the second and third districts suggested not grand fraud but simply careless counting in a massive victory, and a political deal in the third district. An examination of the returns in the table reveals that the votes for candidates and alternates were dissimilar in the first district, but exactly the same in each party in both the second and third districts. The results of the first district were what might normally be expected, and an informant who served as a polling official related some of the difficulties involved in counting the vote: some voters failed to vote for the alternate; a few split their tickets; one or two voted for Cantinflas, and so forth. Given the lower degree of sophistication in the rural second and third districts it appeared highly suspicious that the returns for candidates and alternates were exactly the same. It also appeared that the returns might well have been padded for these two districts, where the record turnout was substantially higher than in Mérida, where the level of interest and the degree of political socialization is much higher than in the rest of the state. (The population of the state is fairly equally divided among the three districts.) This "stuffing" of the ballot boxes is frowned upon by national party leaders but zealous local PRI officials apparently desire to make a good impression on their superiors. It had no effect on the outcome of the election.

The existence of a "deal" between the PRI and the PPS is largely surmise, but known facts tend to support the contention. First, "deals" between these parties have been reported nationally for years.[15] More to the point, however, were certain events surrounding the campaign and election returns in the third district. Fernando Peraza, the PPS candidate, was an old friend of Lombardo Toledano, the national leader of the party, and one of the co-founders with Lombardo of the PPS in the late 1940's. Peraza had run for deputy before from the Federal District but had never obtained a seat. Now retired from his teaching position from the National Polytechnic Institute in Mexico City, he returned after an absence of more than 20 years to his native state to run for deputy. Why should he have done that simply to lose a race that would engender no interest? The PPS has a number of other local members, such as the two young men it ran from the first and second districts, if it simply wanted to put up a candidate. The first important clue to this mystery appeared on July 10 when the newspapers printed the final returns and Peraza was credited with 4,134 votes. What was surprising was, first of all, that the party should make its best showing in the most rural part of the state when normally it should do best in Mérida with its high concentration of intellectuals. More striking was the fact that the final returns were greatly out of line with preliminary and partial returns that came in during the first few days after the election. No other party in any of the districts showed such spectacular increases. For example, on July 3 from 181 boxes Peraza polled 362 votes; by July 5 from 211 boxes he received 395 votes; but when the final count was announced on July 10 from all 270 boxes, his vote had increased more than ten times.[16] I presumed at the time that a few thousand votes had been credited to Peraza as a local figure who had earned some prominence in the capital, as a friend of Lombardo Toledano, and as an intellectual whom the government might wish to honor in this manner. The impact of the "deal" did not become apparent until the end of August when the Electoral College announced the winners of the seats allotted through proportional representation. Peraza was among the PPS "party deputies."[17] Obviously, his 4,134 votes were insufficient to win him a seat under the terms of the law, but the government several years ago had announced that it was more interested in the spirit than in the letter of the law. That one of the PPS seats was allotted to Yucatán depended not at all on the relative strength of the party in Yucatán,

15 See Padgett, *The Mexican Political System*, p. 78.
16 See *Novedades de Yucatán*, July 3, 1967, p. 1; July 5, 1967, p. 2; and July 10, 1967, p. 2.
17 *Diario de Yucatán*, August 31, p. 1.

but on the fact that the PPS had a Yucatecan it wished to reward with a legislative seat.

A close examination of congressional campaigning in Mexico reinforces some widely held generalizations about elections and candidates and reveals some useful data. It is obvious that congressional elections, despite the impotence of the national legislature *vis-à-vis* the executive, are taken seriously by both the official party and the opposition even in a small and remote state such as Yucatán. Elections, therefore, must perform some functions that are vital to the political system and profitable to the persons and groups that participate. Beyond sending a few people to Mexico City and advancing some individual political careers, elections provide opportunities for conflicting interests to proclaim their views, criticize the opposition, and offer at least in general terms their solutions to problems. Elections, therefore, provide an outlet for opposition short of violence by respecting the expressions of contrary views and by holding out the possibility of political office. Most importantly, perhaps, elections serve to create and fortify a sense of nationality among Mexico's urban and rural masses. To be sure, this process has long been underway and methods other than elections perform this same function. But congressional elections are times when the nation-building instructions are carried out nation-wide. Millions of people are bombarded with the idea that they belong to a community that extends beyond their neighborhood or village, that they are participants in the grand drama called the Revolution that is still being played out, that they must help protect the social and economic gains that the Revolution has accomplished, and that they can contribute to its ultimate fulfillment. Almond and Verba have demonstrated that while most Mexicans by their behavior do not take seriously the last appeal, they do take pride in their political system and have high expectations for future betterment.[18] Elections are devices used to reinforce these attitudes.

Congressmen and congressional candidates have never been scrutinized in Mexico, and this paper offers only a small sample. The PPS has been known for its intellectual leadership, PAN for its upper middle class, Catholic, and business orientation, and PRI for its broad-base support. The PPS candidates in Yucatán fit the basic stereotypes, but the PAN candidates did not, except that all identified personally with the Catholic church. But none of the candidates were upper middle class or businessmen. PAN in Yucatán presented middle to lower middle class candidates and directed much of its appeal to the rural lower classes. On the other hand, it did have strong but not unanimous support among the old upper classes. The PRI candidates were most diverse in terms of social origin, education, and career. All were talented in their chosen endeavors and all had served the party and government in a variety of positions. The career patterns of these candidates offer excellent illustrations of the road of political advancement in modern Mexico, an area of investigation still neglected. Elections and candidates offer a fruitful field of research in political and sociological terms. In Mexico, the field is wide open.

[18] Gabriel A. Almond and Sidney Verba, *The Civic Culture: Political Attitudes and Democracy in Five Nations* (Boston Little: Brown and Company, 1965), pp. 310–12.

EXTERNAL INPUTS

International Communication and Legislative Behavior: the Senate and the House of Commons[1]

by BRUCE M. RUSSETT

The Alleged Effect of Communications

According to the view well stated by David Truman, "The politician-legislator is not equivalent to the steel ball in a pinball game, bumping passively from post to post down an inclined plane" (Truman, 1951, p. 332). Political figures bring to their jobs a set of attitudes, predispositions, ways of looking at the world which, along with such traditionally recognized influences as party, executive leadership, and lobby pressures, affect the way they speak and act. Any explanation of legislative behavior which hopes to be complete must account for variables of personality and personal background.

Various kinds of international transactions contribute to decision-makers' perspectives. One of these, long recognized but seldom analyzed with care, is trade in goods and services. Few writers hold that trade necessarily improves relations between two countries, but some have come perilously close. Richard Cobden told his followers, "I believed Free Trade would have the tendency to unite mankind in the bonds of peace, and it was that, more than any pecuniary consideration, which sustained and actuated me" (Cobden, 1870, p. 421). One finds this sentiment in the most unlikely places. William McKinley, author of the McKinley Tariff, declared, "Good trade insures good will. It should be our

---

[1] This article stems from a forthcoming larger study of Anglo-American relations and the theory of international integration (Russett, 1963).

Reprinted from "International Communication and Legislative Behavior: The Senate and the House of Commons," *Journal of Conflict Resolution* 6 (1962): 291–307, by Bruce M. Russett, by permission of the *Journal of Conflict Resolution* and the author.

settled purpose to open trade wherever we can, making our ships and our commerce messengers of peace and amity" (Leech, 1959, p. 142). Even Nikita Khrushchev, inverting the economic determinist position, stated, "Trade is like a barometer; it shows the direction of policy" (*The New York Times*, September 17, 1959, p. 18).

Most authors, of course, are more moderate, though very rarely do they state their qualifications in detail. To be specific, financial crises and debt defaults can seriously embitter international relations. If two countries are highly interdependent and one suffers from severe economic instability, the other will share the instability. Depression spreads from its origin by cutting other countries' exports. Irritation may also arise when one nation is the world's major exporter of a commodity, for the importing state may feel exploited if the supply is controlled by a monopoly or oligopoly. Even government price supports or production controls, though adopted merely to sustain the income of domestic producers rather than deliberately to exploit the buyers, may nevertheless cause hard feelings.

But if these difficulties are absent, trade becomes an important bond of mutual interest between two nations. Karl Deutsch *et al.* insist that a wide range of mutual transactions is necessary to the growth of a security community. These need not be commercial transactions, for strong economic ties are a helpful but not an essential condition for integration. But they are important, and if not present must be replaced by other transactions. The statement, "The helpfulness of economic ties may lie largely in the extent to which they function as a form of communication and as visible sources of reward," hits the crux of the problem (Deutsch *et al.*, 1957, pp. 157, 169).

Economic interests may be important on matters which do not affect them in any immediate sense. An exporter is likely to have a general interest in the well-being of his market, an interest that transcends the marketing conditions, narrowly defined, for his product. He may become attuned to the needs of the importing country over a great range of noneconomic matters. Daniel Lerner found that, in a sample of French business leaders, support for EDC as opposed to the maintenance of a French national army varied directly with the importance of export trade to the businessman's firm (Lerner, 1956, p. 220). Only in a few cases could any of these businessmen be said to have a direct "economic interest" in the decision.

Commerce thus becomes important as a means of communication, exposing the trader to a wide variety of messages that would not otherwise reach him; he must listen to viewpoints he otherwise would never hear. Trade is a capability by which the needs of one country can be made known to another. It may serve as a direct or an indirect means of communication for a lawmaker. Though he may not be associated with the interest, the constituents, editors, fellow-legislators, lobbyists, and others from whom he gets most of his ideas and information may be. In addition, economic interests tend to bias decisions, and persons who are predisposed to particular decisions will try to mobilize available economic interest groups for the support of that decision. That is, economic interests may "determine" political decisions, or they may merely be used to support those decisions. The question of "priority" is for our purpose irrelevant: interdependence, not determinism, is the concern of the study.

Trade is not the only channel for mutual attention and communication. Contacts between two cultures are likely to be varied and continuing, and include, among many others, migration, tourism, student exchange, telegraph and telephone, newspaper attention, and the exchange of cultural products like books, magazines, and motion pictures. Four of Deutsch's helpful conditions for a pluralistic security-community were related to this matter: unbroken links of social communication, mobility of persons, a multiplicity of ranges of communications, and a compensation of flows of communications and transactions (Deutsch *et al.*, 1957, p. 58). There are of course exceptions, especially when the cultures in question—as of Indian students in the United States—are particularly alien to each other. Communication by itself does not produce understanding or responsiveness; it may merely communicate grievances or differences of outlook. Yet communication is a *necessary* if not a *sufficient* condition for amicable relations between two nations who are affected by the consequences of each other's actions.[2]

The precise effect of international communication has seldom been studied systematically, and never on formal political decision-makers. This paper will examine some of its effects on legislators in Great Britain and the United States. We shall want to know: (1) whether international contacts make much difference in the way legislators behave, or whether such factors as personality and party loyalty overwhelm international influences; (2) which kinds of contacts are most effective, and (3) whether a legislator with many contacts is likely to behave differently from one who has some personal contacts, but fewer.

Analytical Method

The effect of many means of communication, especially the mass media, is difficult to evaluate with respect to individual decision-makers, but quite a number of others can be examined. In analyzing the attitudes of Members of Parliament, I investigated the business and personal connections of a sample of Members in each of three years.[3] Standard biographical sources such as *Who's Who* provided the basic material. Members with economic bonds included those who were officers or directors of firms engaged in exporting to the United States, firms with American subsidiaries, or businesses which were themselves subsidiaries of American companies. Others were M.P.s who owned businesses in the United States, whose firms imported American goods, who were engaged

---

[2] Homans reports that in small-group experiments there is a strong positive relationship between the frequency of interaction and favorable attitudes towards members of the group (Homans, 1950, ch. 5; Homans and Riecken, 1954).

[3] In each case the sample was composed of about 130 M.P.s (over 20 percent of the total membership of the House of Commons) selected at random. Of the years selected, 1890 and 1954 were chosen because they were near the extremes of the timespan covered by the larger study. Since there were so few expressions of opinion on matters of Anglo-American relations in 1890 (see below), a third year, 1938, was added with reference to the needs of the complete study.

in foreign banking, merchant bankers, and owners of shipping lines with vessels that sailed to American ports.[4]

In addition to economic bonds, it seemed essential to identify as many men with personal ties as possible. Into this category fell M.P.s who were born or educated in the United States, who worked there for a while, or who married Americans. Men with this kind of link were said to have "strong" personal ties. There was also a group with bonds that seemed intrinsically weaker; ties which should not be included with the others yet ought not to be ignored. They included people who had received honorary degrees from American universities or American medals for war service in joint causes, who had worked on joint Anglo-American agencies during the World Wars, or who had traveled in the United States. While the influence of their experiences was unlikely to have been as great as that of marriage or education, the fact that they often took the form of rewards might well predispose the men in question to be responsive. In addition, I had data on membership in the Pilgrims of Great Britain in 1938 and 1954 and in the English-Speaking Union in 1954.[5] These associations have the specific aim of promoting closer Anglo-American relations. Unavoidably there must also have been a number of men with ties which could not be identified. The reader will be aware that the class of M.P.s without ties means, in the following tables, merely those with no known links. But even so, we shall see that there is a significant difference between the attitudes of M.P.s whom we know had ties and of those for whom there is no evidence of bonds to America.

I followed a similar procedure with members of the Senate in 1890 and 1954, though in this case it was possible to include the entire membership rather than just a sample. Thanks to the United States Census, which gives figures on agricultural, mining, and manufacturing production by state, I was able to add a dimension not possible for the House of Commons—legislators with "constituency ties." This term was applied to Senators whose home states gained at least 5 percent of their gross income from any commodity of which at least 5 percent of total production was exported to Britain. It seemed likely that producers of this commodity might have a substantial source of influence over their Senators. The cut-off points chosen are unavoidably arbitrary, but I believe the procedure to be justified by the results presented below. I tried various higher cut-off points without significantly changing the findings.[6]

Except for the constituency data, membership in Anglo-American organizations, and travel information (where some supplementary sources were used), all information on legislators' backgrounds was derived from the biographical sketches. Some additional intelligence which might have been interesting was not to be found. Parents' birth, ancestry, and business connections were largely

---

[4] The sources and procedures of identification are described in detail in the longer study (Russett, 1963, ch. 9).

[5] From correspondence with the secretary of the Pilgrims and conversation with the secretary of the English-Speaking Union. In the latter case the records of membership in 1954 had been destroyed, and the secretary gave me the names only of those he was certain were members then. That list is therefore accurate as far as it goes, but is not all-inclusive.

[6] It would have been useful also to have identified M.P.s from constituencies where goods for export to America were manufactured, but there is no information on production by constituency in the United Kingdom.

ignored—not universally, but generally enough that any attempt to draw conclusions from the isolated references found would require subjecting the analysis
to too many unknown biases. Touring was also often unreported.

The task then was to test the role of these influences in affecting legislators'
attitudes. For the House of Commons I chose to analyze public statements on
policy rather than voting patterns. A Member of Parliament virtually *never*
votes against his party, and almost all votes, certainly all on issues even remotely
associated with foreign affairs, are those on which the party takes a partisan
stand. If he does defy the whips, he risks expulsion from the parliamentary party,
abandonment by his constituency organization, and defeat in the next election.
A single lapse may be overlooked, but repeated violations of discipline will
almost certainly end his political career. Even "crossing the floor" to the other
party offers little hope—no member has done so, and been returned at the next
election, since 1945. This is not to imply that British parties are dictatorial and
can march M.P.'s into their lobbies at will. There may be much pushing and
hauling before a policy is settled, and the leadership must always beware of
antagonizing the rank-and-file too seriously. But once policy is set and made a
matter of public record, the Member who attacked it would do so at his great
peril. Thus, an examination of voting records would provide little information
about an M.P.'s true feelings or about the pressures he put on his party chiefs
before the votes.

If an M.P. seldom votes against his leaders, he may abstain from voting
somewhat more freely. Abstention is a recognized way of showing disagreement,
and is unlikely to be punished by the leadership unless done repeatedly. Unfortunately the recording of abstentions (or better, absences) at divisions shows no
significant pattern. Abstention can show those who are really interested how one
feels on a matter—constituents, interest groups, or fellow Members can note
one's abstention, and the leaders against whom one wants to protest will surely
notice it. But even on an important measure there usually are many involuntary
absences due to illness and business or personal demands for M.P.s' presence
elsewhere. One who merely reads the report of a division years after the event,
without knowing the reasons for a particular M.P.'s failure to be recorded, can
rarely discern a significant pattern.

But it is not unusual for a Member, even though he may vote as directed in
the end, to criticize a policy during debate, to ask a hostile question during
question time, or to oppose the policy in a speech to his constituents or another
group. He feels particularly free to do so during the period before an official
party position is adopted. For example, the Labour Party directed its members
to abstain on ratification of the 1954 London and Paris Agreements to rearm a
sovereign West Germany. Yet by the time the vote was taken almost half the
Labour M.P.s had expressed opinions in Parliament, in letters to newspapers, or
in outside speeches reported by a London or major provincial paper. In addition
to providing information on Members' real feelings about matters which come
up for division in the House, this kind of analysis also gives their views on a
great number of issues that are never made a matter of record vote.

Much of this material, and practically all of it for the earlier years analyzed, came from the parliamentary debates themselves. For 1938 and 1954 this could be supplemented by reports of debates at the annual party conferences, and by party publications which cull newspapers and private speeches for statements— particularly those which might embarrass the opposition. These include the Tory *Hints for Speakers* and the *Liberal Magazine.* For 1954 there was also a superb collection of clippings at the Conservative and Unionist Central Office in London, containing a complete file of all reports of M.P.s' statements in the London daily and Sunday press, the most important country papers, and periodicals like the *New Statesman.* Though the files for a few deceased M.P.s had been disposed of, there were still, in 1960, clippings on over 90 percent of the 1954 members of the Commons. Because these supplementary sources were not available for 1890, and only in part for 1938, the following tables record far more expressions of opinion in 1954 than in the two earlier years combined.

A major flaw in this kind of analysis is its implicit assumption that all topics on which an opinion might be expressed are of equal importance, both to the speaker and to the other government in question. Thus an M.P. might criticize the United States for its shipping subsidies, aid to Franco Spain, and lack of civil liberties, but support the American-backed program of German re-armament. Quite possibly the United States government would value the support on German rearmament highly enough to offset the other criticisms, and in an important sense the M.P. would be more "pro-American" than another Member whose attitudes on all four issues were reversed. There might be a serious fallacy in simply counting the number of issues on which the Member supported or criticized American policy. Yet in practice there is no thoroughly satisfactory way to weight the issues. No two observers could agree whether a statement on German rearmament was worth two statements on other policies, or worth four pronouncements, and so on down a list of 20 additional issues.

In the particular case this was not too serious a handicap. For the three years under study, nearly three quarters of the M.P.s expressing opinions did so uniformly—they were either always responsive to the United States or always unresponsive—thus substantially eliminating the weighting difficulty.[7] Still, a more systematic method of solving this problem would be desirable, and it is offered by Guttman scale analysis. The essential principle of scale analysis is that,

The items can be arranged in an order so that an individual who agrees with, or responds to, any particular item also responds positively to all items of lower rank order. The rank order of items is the scale of items; the scale of persons is very similar, people being arranged in order according to the highest rank order of items checked, which is equivalent to the number of positive responses in a perfect scale [Green, 1954, p. 353].

The classic illustration is a group of questions regarding height. If you ask a man if he is over 6′ tall, and he responds affirmatively, you know that he would also answer yes to questions asking if he were over 5′ 10″ in height, and over 5′ 8″.

---

[7] In the interests of economy and of providing a large enough sample to test for statistical significance I have not here discussed attitude patterns on individual issues. Nevertheless the relationships identified do hold for most of the particular issues as well as for the group.

By finding that the issues in Anglo-American relations could be scaled we would side-step the "weight problem." That is, we might find that with regard to responsiveness to the United States, the four issues—Spain, civil liberties, subsidies, and German rearmament—ranked in that order. A man who opposed American aid to Spain would be unresponsive on all other issues. Similarly, if he defended the state of American civil liberties but criticized American shipping subsidies, he would also support assistance to Spain but oppose arming the Germans. We have not solved the weight problem in the sense of saying which issue is more "important," but we have avoided the necessity of worrying about it. We will not have to decide whether support on German rearmament is "worth" opposition on the other three matters, for such a situation will never occur. The procedure gives us a method of ordering legislators from most responsive to least responsive in a meaningful and consistent way.

The result is that we can describe the pattern of responses as "unidimensional" in scale-analysis terms, for the items in the scale measure related attitudes on a particular topic. We cannot be sure what basic feelings are responsible for the statements by the various M.P.s making those pronouncements, but we can be reasonably sure that all the particular measures were regarded as aspects of one general policy by the Members. A man normally highly responsive will not have been unresponsive on one issue because of extraneous factors.

The discussion in the last two paragraphs is, of course, an oversimplification. Hardly ever is unidimensionality so perfect that there are no variations within the scale, no "errors" where a man is responsive when we would expect him to be unresponsive. Other factors do operate to some extent, but the amount of variation must be very limited if we still are to treat the list of issues as forming a scale. By convention, the response of no more than one man in ten may be in "error" on any item, and the total number of "errors" for all items may not exceed ten percent of the number of items times the number of men. Since in fact no one item may have more than ten percent error, and many items show less, this "coefficient of reproducibility" (total nonerrors divided by number of men times number of items) is almost always about .95 or higher. Thus the effect of extraneous variables is kept to a minimum.

The creation of a scale does not eliminate the need for sound judgment on the part of the researcher. One might indeed be measuring a single dimension, but it need not be the dimension which one is really trying to measure. In deciding what issues to try to put into the scale, and in interpreting the meaning of that scale when completed, one must know what the issues signified and have a set of independent criteria for picking them out. In this case I used the following criteria for issues involved in Anglo-American relations. No issues which did not meet these criteria were proposed, and it was essential that at least most of those items which did meet the criteria be capable of incorporation into the scale. (For further information and a list of votes see the Appendix pp. 156-8.)

1. Explicit criticism or approval of the other government or nation. (Criticism of individuals was not included unless it appeared that the speaker meant it to apply to the government itself or to all or most members of the other nationality.

Criticism of President Eisenhower would probably be recorded as an attack on the United States, but remarks about Senator McCarthy might not be.)
2. A call for weaker or stronger ties with the other country.
3. Policies intended to increase mutual capabilities for responsiveness (whether by the creation of common institutions or by such means as eliminating restrictions on travel).
4. Ratification of a treaty signed by both governments.
5. A direct economic interest of the other country (tariffs or foreign aid).
6. Restrictions on the freedom of the government to conclude international agreements (the Bricker Amendment).
7. An expressed desire by the other government.

Much of the evidence needed to apply these criteria was contained in the debates. Outside checks nevertheless seemed necessary, particularly in the last class, to be sure that nothing was missed or inappropriately included. To fill this need I used diplomatic histories and memoirs, editorials in *The Times* of London and *The New York Times*, and, for the two later years, the annual volumes by the Council of Foreign Relations (*The United States in World Affairs*) and the Royal Institute of International Affairs (*Survey of International Affairs*).

These criteria do not produce a list merely of matters of direct economic interest—issues on which one would not be surprised that legislators linked with firms exporting to the other country would be responsive. The concerns are far wider and more indirect. Nor does the list include only major matters where the prestige of a government or a significant element of the other nation's welfare was at stake, but a great number of minor matters as well. Responsiveness is necessary not only at great crises, but in smaller everyday affairs. Many crises or dramatic displays of responsiveness can be avoided by quiet everyday awareness of and, where appropriate, acquiescence to another nation's needs or demands. Thus, I made no effort to choose years in which the most obvious, crucial, and immediate demands were made. Cooperative international relations are dependent on more common stuff.

This procedure made it possible to rank legislators from most responsive to least responsive, and I have applied it to the United States Senate.[8] In most of the following analysis it will be necessary to simplify the results, merely classifying lawmakers into three groups—responsive, moderate, and unresponsive—of as nearly equal size as possible. But the reader should remember that the information was made available through a complete ordering.

Like any other quantitative tool which imposes a certain amount of simplification on a complex reality, this procedure has its faults. It cannot tell us whether a particular legislator holds an opinion firmly or with little intensity. His action may result from deep conviction or strong interest-group pressure, or he may simply be "log-rolling" for support on issues of more importance to him. Perhaps an influential legislator determines the votes of a number of "satellites" on an issue.

---

[8] Guttman scaling requires nearly complete information on attitudes. It therefore could not be applied to the data on Commons, which include expressions of opinion by only a minority of M.P.s on any given issue.

These refinements can be made only with such other approaches as interviewing and examination of legislative debates and other public statements. But
if these two methods (analysis of votes and analysis of statements) are used in
tandem, one can get the benefits of both while avoiding most of the pitfalls
which either alone sets. The analysis of public statements is peculiarly suited to
the House of Commons, where roll call votes are relatively rare and a Member
seldom votes against his party, and the examination of voting patterns is
peculiarly suited to the Senate, where the opposite conditions prevail. If, using
the two techniques, one in each body, we find that similar variables have similar
effects on lawmakers' attitudes, we will have very strong evidence of the validity
of the relationships so identified.

Ties and Responsiveness

The information on Commons is analyzed in two ways. First, every M.P. is
classified either as responsive, unresponsive, or "neutral"; *i.e.*, no policy statement on any of these issues was recorded. Second, it was useful to record the
number of statements on separate issues made by each M.P. Thus, if a member is
recorded as responsive on one issue and unresponsive on two others, he is
treated as, on balance, unresponsive, and a one is entered in the appropriate cell
on the *left*-hand side of the following table. But on the *right*-hand side of the

Table 1—Percentage of M.P.s With and Without U.S. Ties Who Were Responsive, Unresponsive, and Neutral, and of Responsive and Unresponsive Statements

1890

M.P.s With	Res.	Neut.	Un-Res.	Statements by M.P.s With	Res.	Un-Res.
U.S. Ties (N = 24)	8	88	4	U.S. Ties (N = 4)	50	50
No U.S. Ties (N = 118)	0	96	4	No U.S. Ties (N = 5)	0	100

1938

M.P.s With	Res.	Neut.	Un-Res.	Statements by M.P.s With	Res.	Un-Res.
U.S. Ties (N = 31)	16	81	3	U.S. Ties (N = 8)	88	12
No U.S. Ties (N = 101)	8	88	4	No U.S. Ties (N = 19)	79	21

1954

M.P.s With	Res.	Neut.	Un-Res.	Statements by M.P.s With	Res.	Un-Res
U.S. Ties (N = 40)	20	60	20	U.S. Ties (N = 56)	48	52
No U.S. Ties (N = 89)	16	52	33	No U.S. Ties (N = 125)	26	74

All Years Combined

M.P s With	Res.	Neut.	Un-Res.	Statements by M.P.s With	Res.	Un-Res.
U.S. Ties (N = 95)	16	74	10	U.S. Ties (N = 68)	53	47
No U.S. Ties (N = 308)	7	81	12	No U.S. Ties (N = 149)	32	68

table we list individual statements on issues, so a one is recorded under "responsive" and a two under "unresponsive." Tables do not always add to 100 percent because of rounding.

In every subsection of Table 1 the same pattern holds. M.P.s with ties of any sort to the United States are more likely to speak up on matters affecting Anglo-American relations than are M.P.s without ties. And when they speak, they are more likely to be responsive. This is true whether each particular M.P. is characterized as responsive or unresponsive, or whether the statements are examined individually. In many of the above subtables there are not enough cases for the results to be statistically significant even at the .10 level, but they are so in the three with the greatest number of cases. For M.P.s the relationship between ties and responsiveness is significant at the .02 level in the table for all years combined. And for statements, the relationship is significant at well above the .01 level both for 1954 and for all years combined.

Table 2—Percentage of M.P.s With and Without U.S. Ties Who Were Responsive, Unresponsive, and Neutral, and Percentage of Responsive and Unresponsive Statements, With Party Affiliation Controlled, 1954[a]

M.P.s With	Res.	Neut.	Un-Res.	Statements by M.P.s With	Res.	Un-Res.
Conservative (N = 64)	(16)	(67)	(17)	Conservative (N = 44)	(50)	(50)
U.S. Ties (N = 26)	19	65	16	U.S. Ties (N = 20)	70	30
No U.S. Ties (N = 38)	13	68	19	No U.S. Ties (N = 24)	33	67
Labour (N = 62)	(18)	(40)	(42)	Labour (N = 132)	(26)	(74)
U.S. Ties (N = 14)	21	50	29	U.S. Ties (N = 36)	36	64
No U.S. Ties (N = 48)	17	37	46	No U.S. Ties (N = 96)	22	78

[a] Three M.P.s—two Liberals and one Irish Nationalist—are not included.

For 1954 there are enough cases to control for party affiliation and the results are the same. For individual M.P.s the association of ties and responsiveness is as hypothesized, but not to a statistically significant degree. For the analysis by statements, however, the association is significant at the .01 level. The uniformity of direction identified in these two tables, and the high significance often found, form as persuasive a proof as could be expected with these data.

Note that the association between party and responsiveness is also quite strong, as Conservatives are much more likely to be responsive than are Labourites. In the "M.P.s" half of the table, the relationship is significant at the .02 level; in the "Statements" half it is significant at .001, an extremely high level. The relationship between party and responsiveness, in fact, is stronger on both sides of the table than is that between ties to the United States and responsiveness.[9] A Labour M.P. *with* a tie to America is less likely to indicate respon-

[9] For "M.P.s" the contingency coefficient for party and responsiveness is .29 and that for ties and responsiveness just .04. For "Statements" the comparable figures are .25 and .18. Certainly there is no attempt to claim that international contacts are the only variables affecting attitudes on foreign policy, but merely that such contacts are sufficiently important that no adequate explanation can ignore them.

siveness than is a Conservative M.P. *without* an identifiable tie. We can only speculate on the reasons. Much of the difference is surely traceable to differences in ideology and interest-group support. But part of the explanation undoubtedly is that Conservatives tend to get most of their ideas from other Conservatives, and the same with Labourites. Since almost twice as many Conservatives as Labourites have known ties with America, their views probably carry a heavier "weight" in the informal opinion-forming processes of their party. Similarly, the greater "weight" of men with ties in the Conservative Party must give them a better chance of invoking party discipline in their favor. Although discipline is not enforced nearly as stringently in speeches as in voting, it is nevertheless a factor. Possibly a major element lies in ties to America of which we have no knowledge. It seems very probable that Conservatives, having on the whole

Table 3—Percentage of Senators With and Without U.K. Ties Who Were Responsive, Moderate, and Unresponsive

SENATORS WITH	RESPONSIVE	MODERATE	UNRESPONSIVE
1890			
U.K. Ties (N = 49)	37	33	31
No U.K. Ties (N = 35)	9	46	46
1954			
U.K. Ties (N = 23)	48	22	30
No U.K. Ties (N = 73)	27	33	40
Both Years Combined			
U.K. Ties (N = 72)	40	29	31
No U.K. Ties (N = 108)	21	37	42

Table 4—Percentage of Senators With and Without U.K. Ties Who Were Responsive, Moderate, and Unresponsive, With Party Affiliation Controlled

Senators	Responsive	Moderate	Unresponsive
1890			
Democratic (N = 37)	(57)	(43)	(0)
U.K. Ties (N = 27)	67	33	0
No U.K. Ties (N = 10)	30	70	0
Republican (N = 47)	(0)	(34)	(66)
U.K. Ties (N = 22)	0	32	68
No U.K. Ties (N = 25)	0	36	64
*1954**			
Democratic (N = 48)	(40)	(25)	(35)
U.K. Ties (N = 15)	40	20	40
No U.K. Ties (N = 33)	39	27	33
Republican (N = 47)	(23)	(36)	(40)
U.K. Ties (N = 8)	63	25	13
No U.K. Ties (N = 39)	15	38	46

* Excludes one Independent.

more money, are more likely to have traveled to the United States than Labourites, and having more business connections, are more likely to have an economic link with the United States that was not caught in the rather wide-meshed net used to find M.P.s with commercial ties.

We can analyze the same influences on Senators' attitudes. In Tables 3–5 each Senator is classified as responsive, moderate, or unresponsive according to his position on the Responsiveness to Britain scale.

Just as with M.P.s, we find a consistent relationship between the possession of personal or economic ties and responsiveness. For 1890 the relationship is significant at the .01 level; for 1954 and for the two years combined it is significant at the .10 level. A similar pattern emerges when we control for party affiliation.

In two of the cases above the control for party affiliation emphasizes the importance of personal and economic bonds. For Democrats in 1890 and Republicans in 1954 the relationship is marked and highly significant (.01 level). For Republicans in 1890 and Democrats in 1954, however, there is no such relationship. But as we shall show below, the latter finding is due to the fact that in 1954, constituency ties were entirely without effect in promoting responsiveness. If only direct ties, economic and personal, are considered, those 1954 Democrats with them prove highly responsive.

As can be seen from the most cursory examination of these tables, party affiliation was an important variable. Particularly in 1890 party discipline (or perhaps likemindedness, we cannot tell which), was extremely powerful in matters of foreign affairs. We cannot be sure why, but an explanation would undoubtedly include much the same factors as were offered regarding the difference in responsiveness between the Conservative and Labour Parties in Britain. This sheds light on the political situation of the late nineteenth century when the Democratic Party was often accused of being pro-British, despite its dependence on the votes of Irish-Americans. Here is evidence that the Democrats were, in an important sense, much more "pro-British" than their partisan opponents. On every issue affecting Anglo-American relations a majority of Democrats was ranged on the responsive side against a majority of Republicans. Exactly 62 percent of the Senators never voted against their party on these issues—21 Democrats and 31 Republicans. The "moderate" section includes *all* who ever voted against their party.

We can use this information to illustrate the influence of ties in another way. In 24 instances a Democrat voted against his party in an unresponsive manner; in 31 cases a Republican went against his party in order to be responsive. If we distinguish between those Senators with and without ties, and make a ratio of

Table 5—Votes Cast Against Party Per Senator, Senators With and Without Ties to U.K., 1890

Senators With	Responsive Votes	Unresponsive Votes
Ties to U.K.	.73	.33
No Ties to U.K.	.60	1.50

the number of votes against party over the number of Senators in each class, we have the figures of Table 5.

Note that the existence of a tie with Britain has a greater effect in moderating opposition to British wishes (column 2) than as a positive force in promoting responsiveness (column 1).

Kinds of Ties

We also wish to know whether two or more links per lawmaker would be more effective than a single tie. The following table gives data for the House of Commons, with M.P.s possessing two or more links analyzed separately from those with only one.

In the left-hand side of the table we see that Members with two ties were actually *less* likely to be responsive than M.P.s with only a single tie. On the other hand, Members with two or more links tended to speak out somewhat more often, whatever the content of their remarks. In the right-hand half of the table there is a slight tendency, significant at the .10 level, for responsiveness to be more frequent where there is more than one tie.

Examination of the Senate was also inconclusive on this point. In 1954 only two Senators had more than one discernible bond with the British, and both of them were highly responsive, but the cases were obviously too few to give any satisfactory indication. For 1890, however, the results were just the opposite of what one would expect. Though not to a statistically significant degree, Senators with two or more ties tended to be *less* responsive than those with only one. On this evidence, then, we must conclude that the fact of any link at all is far more effective than the reinforcement of that link by one or two additional ones.

Table 6—Percentage of M.P.s With and Without U.S. Ties Who Were Responsive, Unresponsive, and Neutral; and Percentage of Responsive and Unresponsive Statements, With Number of Ties Controlled, All Years Combined

M. P. s With	Res.	Neut.	Un-Res.	Statements by M.P.s With	Res.	Un-Res.
Two or More (N = 28)	21	61	18	Two or More (N = 28)	64	36
One U.S. Tie (N = 67)	13	79	7	One U.S. Tie (N = 40)	45	55
No U.S. Ties (N = 308)	7	81	12	No U.S. Ties (N = 149)	32	68

In addition it seemed necessary to see whether the kind of tie made any difference; whether either economic or personal ties were more efficacious than the other. The following table lists separately all M.P.s with economic ties, all with no economic but "strong" personal ties, those with only "weak" personal ties, those whose only connection with the United States was through the English-Speaking Union or the Pilgrims, and finally those with no known link at all.

The association of responsiveness with economic ties is evident on both sides of the table, and is significant at the .01 level in each case. Among those with various kinds of personal ties to the United States, it makes little difference whether the bonds are weak, strong, or merely of membership in an organization like the Pilgrims. Possibly some differences would show up in a larger sample, but they are not evident here. But there is a *slight* difference, significant (at the ·10 level) only in the right-hand half of the table, between all those with just personal ties and those with commercial bonds. Possibly economic self-interest plays a part. More likely, however, the difference is due to the fact that the ties of commerce are current ones: the legislator has a continuing channel of information and opinion from the United States. Most personal ties, on the other hand, were formed in the past, and it may have been many years since the individual talked to many Americans. As most of the American policies in question, such as German rearmament and China policy, were of relatively recent vintage, it is not surprising that men with past but not current contacts with the United States should fail to perceive American wishes or their justification. Of all the personal ties the only current one applicable to many M.P.s was membership in the Pilgrims or the English-Speaking Union, and one would not expect that to be a particularly high-capacity communications channel.

Notice that men with personal ties to America of any kind are more likely to speak up on matters affecting Anglo-American relations. Only 62 percent of those with personal ties said nothing, whereas 81 percent of those with no ties are unrecorded. They are even somewhat more likely to record unresponsiveness than are those without ties (17 percent to 12 percent). Perhaps this is because men who have been abroad or who have personal contacts with foreigners naturally have more interest in foreign affairs (whether contacts cause interest, vice versa, or it is a mutually reinforcing process is not relevant here). But it may also be that the experiences of these men have in some instances made them "anti-American." Clearly it is a danger to be considered. If a wider experience of foreign contact in a population is likely, in general, to increase responsiveness, it may also result in a certain concomitant increase in the level of hostility as well.

We cannot reproduce the analysis of Table 7 for the Senate, as in the two years under study a total of only five Senators had personal ties of any nature without also having economic ties to the United Kingdom, and this is too few to produce interesting results. But it is possible to compare the effects of all kinds of direct ties, personal or economic, with that of constituency ties. Table 8 lists all Senators with constituency economic ties, those with only direct bonds, and those with none at all.

The number of Senators who have only direct ties to Britain is too small for us to talk of statistical significance, but the figures are interesting nevertheless. They suggest that whereas constituency ties were once very powerful forces in producing responsiveness, they are no longer very important. In fact, in 1954 Senators with no links at all were more likely to be responsive than were those whose links passed through their constituencies. This apparent shift is not surprising when one examines the changes in America's economic structure since the turn of the century. In 1954 no state derived more than 12 percent of its income from a commodity important in Anglo-American trade. But in 1890, no

Table 7—Percentage of M.P.s With and Without U.S. Ties Who Were Responsive, Unresponsive, and Neutral, and Percentage of Responsive and Unresponsive Statements, With Type of Tie Controlled; All Years Combined

M.P.s With	Res.	Neut.	Un-Res.	Statements by M.P.s With	Res.	Un-Res.
Econ. Ties (N = 53)	11	83	6	Econ. Ties (N = 22)	73	27
Strong Ties (N = 15)	20	60	20	Strong Ties (N = 27)	48	52
Weak Ties (N = 19)	21	63	16	Weak Ties (N = 19)	63	37
ESU-Pilgrim (N = 8)	25	63	13	ESU-Pilgrim (N = 10)	50	50
No U.S. Ties (N = 308)	7	81	12	No U.S. Ties (N = 149)	32	68

Table 8—Percentage of Senators With Constituency Economic Ties, Direct Ties Only, and No U.K. Ties, Who Were Responsive, Moderate, and Unresponsive

1890

SENATORS WITH	RESPONSIVE	MODERATE	UNRESPONSIVE
Constituency Ties (N = 46)	39	30	30
Direct Ties Only (N = 3)	0	67	33
No U.K. Ties (N = 35)	9	46	46

1954

SENATORS WITH	RESPONSIVE	MODERATE	UNRESPONSIVE
Constituency Ties (N = 12)	25	25	50
Direct Ties Only (N = 11)	73	18	9
No U.K. Ties (N = 73)	27	33	40

less than seven states—Texas (55 percent), Mississippi (46 percent), South Carolina (41 percent), Arkansas (33 percent), Alabama (32 percent), Georgia (31 percent), and Louisiana (19 percent)—gained more than 12 percent of their income from cotton, and wheat contributed at least that much to three other states—North Dakota (55 percent), South Dakota (29 percent), and Minnesota (17 percent). No wonder, then, that the economic nature of his constituency made so much less difference in the way a Senator voted in 1954 than it did in 1890. Anglo-American commerce has diminished greatly both as a power base and as a means of communication to legislators who are not themselves directly tied in with it. In 1954 the British government deliberately discriminated, for balance of payments reasons, against imports from the dollar area. Possibly its action alienated some Senators from states which produced goods whose export to Britain continued, but in limited quantities. In any case, the above figures provide dramatic evidence of the South's diminished "internationalism," which many writers have noted.

This conclusion, that the effectiveness of constituency ties in promoting responsiveness is directly proportional to the weight of the economic interest in the constituency, rests on scanty evidence, but it can be buttressed with another set of data. For both years I ranked the states involved in Anglo-American trade according to the amount of income derived from goods important in that trade, and then ranked their Senators by degree of responsiveness. For 1954 (when no state derived more than 12 percent of its income from such products), the correlation between the two rank orders[10] was only .14, and not statistically significant. But for 1890 the same procedure produced a correlation of .34 (significant at the .05 level), for Democratic Senators and the astonishingly high correlation of .86 (significant at the .001 level) for Republican Senators. With this evidence it is hard to imagine how the precipitous decline in Anglo-American commerce over the past 70 years could fail to work to the detriment of continued responsiveness from American policy-makers.

To summarize, we have found that: (1) Legislators with economic or personal ties to the other country are more likely to be responsive to the needs of the other country than are legislators lacking those ties. (2) This holds true when party affiliation is controlled, though party is itself an extremely important variable. (3) It makes little difference whether an individual legislator has a number of ties to the other country, or only one. (4) There is some evidence, though not enough to be conclusive, that economic ties are more likely to be effective than personal ones. (5) The importance of a constituency tie in influencing a Senator is directly proportional to the weight of the economic interest in the constituency.

At this point we may consider two possible criticisms of the above findings. One is that we have reversed the chain of causality—people who already look favorably on another country are then willing to develop ties with it, not the reverse, though the association shows up equally in the analysis. With regard to bonds of education, travel, business, and particularly membership in Anglo-American organizations, this objection obviously carries some weight, but with many other ties self-selection is not a factor. A man has no influence over where he is born, and is unlikely to have much more over where or with whom he does military service in wartime. Many of the business firms in question—Lloyds, Macmillan's, Simmons—have international ties that long ante-dated the M.P.s' or Senators' association with them. Nor are they companies whose tie with the other country would be a major factor in attracting the legislator.

Another potential objection concerns the degree to which these findings can be generalized. Although these influences may be important for ordinary legislators, they may not be effective on such others as members of the executive, who must take a wider view and who are subject to immensely more varied pressures. Especially in Britain fifty or more years ago, cabinet members were likely to be rather wealthy landowners, and perhaps were less affected by narrow economic concerns. Joseph Chamberlain in the 1890's, for example, heartily championed an Anglo-American rapprochement, but he may well have had no strong economic interest in the United States. He wanted friendship with America to counterbalance the new threat of German power. The point, however, is that other men also feared Germany's might, but were not necessarily led to embrace the republic across the seas. But Chamberlain did, and it is perhaps no coincidence that he had an American-born wife. There is no attempt to argue cause in this particular case—he may have married an American because he

---

[10] Using the Kendall Rank Correlation Coefficient.

already liked Americans generically; his marriage may have only reinforced an initial liking for Americans; or it may in fact have been no more than a coincidence. Yet since the association of links with responsiveness is so notable for M.P.s and Senators, it may affect cabinet members similarly. This seems particularly plausible because we are *not* arguing that one becomes responsive in any simple, direct way to one's economic stake in another country's welfare, but rather that the existence of an economic or personal link opens a man to messages he would otherwise never hear.

Appendix

I. List of issues in Anglo-American relations on which sampled members of the House of Commons made public statements, with the number of members speaking on each.

1890:
1. The American tariff (3)
2. British restrictions on import of American cattle (3)
3. American adherence to International Sugar Convention (1)
4. The American copyright law (1)
5. American import restrictions other than the tariff (1)

1938:
1. The Anglo-American Trade Agreement (9)
2. Calls for cooperation with America in specific areas (5)
3. General calls for cooperation with America (3)
4. Settlement of British debt to U.S. (2)
5. Imperial Preference (2)
6. U.S. gold policy (1)
7. Restrictions on the import of U.S. films (1)
8. Dismissals of British nationals by American firms (1)
9. U.S. disarmament proposals (1)
10. Visa requirements for travel between Britain and U.S. (1)
11. Exchange of aircraft landing rights in the Pacific (1)

1954:
1. German rearmament (30)
2. Withdrawal from British military base at Suez Canal (20)
3. Trade with Communist countries (19)
4. Alleged U.S. intervention in Guatemala (14)
5. SEATO (12)
6. Policy toward Communist China (10)
7. Actions of U.S. servicemen in Britain (9)
8. Commonwealth Preference and trade with America (8)
9. British defense spending and length of national service (8)
10. Possible intervention in Indo-Chinese war (7)
11. Friendship and cooperation with U.S., general (6)
12. Civil liberties in the U.S. (6)
13. Adoption of standard NATO Belgian-designed rifle (5)
14. U.S. military bases in Britain (5)
15. Anglo-Iranian oil agreement (5)

16. Amount of consultation and information from U.S. (5)
17. NATO (4)
18. American foreign policy, general (3)
19. U.S. activities in British Honduras and British Guiana (2)
20. Call for Summit meeting without U.S. (1)
21. American aid to Spain (1)
22. American shipping subsidies (1)

II A. List of roll-call votes used to form Responsiveness to Britain scale in 1890, in the order in which they appear in the scale (high responsiveness votes first). Numbers are page references to *Congressional Record* Vol. 29, Washington, p. 890. When a vote for the measure is considered responsive, a (+) follows, where responsiveness is indicated by a vote against, a (−) follows.

1. Naval Appropriation Bill. Amendment to strike out appropriation for three long-range battleships. During the debate fears of antagonizing Britain were expressed. (p. 5297) (+)
2. Revenue Bill (Tariff). Conference Report. (p. 10740) (−)
3. Bill to classify worsted cloths as woolens, pay higher duty. (p. 4300) (−)
4. Customs Administration Bill. Evarts amendment regarding importers' rights of appeal on decisions of Customs. (p. 4128) (+)
5. Revenue Bill. Amendment to reduce duty on tinplate. (p. 4128) (+)
6. Revenue Bill. Amendment to reduce duty on band and hoop iron. (p. 8393) (+)
7. Revenue Bill. Plumb amendment to allow free import where domestic supply is controlled by a monopoly. (p. 9911) (+)
8. Customs Administration Bill. Vest amendment regarding importers' rights of appeal. (p. 4121) (+)
9. Customs Administration Bill. Evarts amendment regarding importers' rights of appeal. (p. 4121) (+)
10. Revenue Bill. Amendment to reduce duty on band and hoop iron. (p. 8370) (+)
11. Revenue Bill. Final vote. (p. 9943) (−)
12. Merchant Marine Subsidy Bill. (p. 7188) (−)
13. Customs Administration Bill. Final vote. (p. 4132) (−)

Coefficient of Reproducibility of scale = .962. Where a Senator was absent but either was paired or put his opinion on record, that expression of opinion was counted as a vote. Complete absences were counted neither as errors nor as item responses in calculating the Coefficient of Reproducibility.

At least a score of other roll-call votes, mostly on the Revenue Bill, scaled with these items and could have been included, but as they added no information (the voting pattern, except for absences, was just the same as on one of the votes that was included) there was no point in adding them.

Note that although most of these votes were on tariff questions, a wider range is covered, including the Maritime Subsidy Bill (an Ocean Mail Bill showed exactly the same pattern and so was not included) and the Naval Appropriation Bill. There were a number of other tariff votes that might possibly have been included, but in the interest of keeping to votes which would most seriously affect British manufacturers I decided to include votes only on measures which *The Times* of London listed as likely to injure British producers. These goods were linen, hoops and hoop iron, cutlery, tinplate, and woolens. (See *The Times,* June 2, 1890; p. 11; June 23, 1890; p. 11; and September 29, 1890; p. 9.)

IIB. List of roll-call votes used to form Responsiveness to Britain scale in 1954, in the order in which they appear in the scale. Numbers are page references to *Congressional Record*, Vol. 100, Washington, 1954.

1. International Sugar Agreement. Ratification. (p. 5662) Final vote. (+)
2. Mutual Security Authorization. (p. 13052) (+)
3. Mutual Security Authorization. Long amendment to reduce authorization by $1 billion. (p. 13038) (−)
4. Mutual Security Authorization. Long amendment to reduce authorization by $500 million. (p. 13039) (−)
5. Bricker Amendment. George amendment providing that nontreaty agreements may not take effect as internal law unless implemented by Congressional action. (p. 2358) (−)
6. Bricker Amendment. Final vote. (p. 2374) (−)
7. Bricker Amendment. Ferguson amendment that any provision of an international agreement which conflicts with the Constitution shall not take effect. (p. 1740) (−)
8. Bricker Amendment. Morse motion to recommit. (p. 2267) (+)
9. Atomic Energy Act. Lehman amendment to delete provision that the AEC should give maximum effect to policies contained in international agreements made after enactment of the bill. Lehman said the provision implied that the U.S. would treat "less seriously" agreements (*i.e.*, with Britain) previously entered into. (p. 11954) (+)
10. Bricker Amendment. Knowland amendment to require that the Senate consent to ratification of treaties by roll-call vote. (p. 1782) (−)
Coefficient of Reproducibility = .952.

Although many of these votes were on the Bricker Amendment, a wide range of other matters is also covered. The vote on the Lehman amendment is very particularly related to policy toward Britain. There were no other foreign affairs votes that would have scaled with these items, but there were five other votes that met the criteria set up in the main body of the article. One of these, however, was on reconsideration of the Universal Copyright Convention (p. 9133) which was of little interest to the British Government but of great importance to American printers. A number of liberal and otherwise responsive Senators voted to reconsider this measure because of its effect on labor. The other four votes—one on Mutual Security Appropriations (p. 14507), two on the Bricker amendment (pp. 1916, 2262), and one on extension of the Reciprocal Trade Act (p. 8886)—showed just too many errors (slightly over 10 per cent) to allow their inclusion in the scale, indicating that some other variable or variables affected voting behavior. One of the major values of scale analysis is just this, that it enables us to identify and concentrate on those votes where the variable of interest (responsiveness) is of overwhelming importance.

The Senators located at the two extremes of responsiveness are largely those whom the "common sense" observer would put near the same extremes from an independent knowledge of their opinions. The four highest-scoring Senators were "internationalist-liberals": Hayden, Hennings, Lehman, and Morse; at the bottom of the range were "isolationist-conservatives": Bricker, Butler (Nebraska), Frear, Malone, McCarthy, and Russell.

References

COBDEN, RICHARD. *Speeches on Questions of Public Policy.* JOHN BRIGHT and JAMES E. T. ROGERS (eds.). London: Macmillan, 1870, II.

DEUTSCH, KARL W. *et al. Political Community and the North Atlantic Area.* Princeton, N.J.: Princeton University Press, 1957.

GREEN, BERT F. "Attitude Measurement." In GARDNER LINDZEY (ed.). *Handbook of Social Psychology.* Cambridge, Mass.: Addison-Wesley, 1954, I, 335–66.

HOMANS, GEORGE. *The Human Group.* New York: Harcourt, Brace, 1950.

HOMANS, GEORGE and RIECKEN, H. W. "Psychological Aspects of Social Structure." In GARDNER LINDZEY (ed.). *Handbook of Social Psychology.* Cambridge, Mass.: Addison-Wesley, 1954, II, 786–832.

LEECH, MARGARET. *In the Days of McKinley.* New York: Harper & Bros., 1959.

LERNER, DANIEL. "French Business Leaders Look at EDC," *Public Opinion Quarterly,* 20 (1956), 212–21.

RUSSETT, BRUCE M. *Community and Contention: Britain and America in the Twentieth Century.* Cambridge, Mass.: Massachusetts Institute of Technology Press, 1963.

TRUMAN, DAVID B. *The Governmental Process.* New York: Knopf, 1951.

The Institutional Nexus

STRUCTURES AND PROCESSES

Organization Theory and the Explanation
of Important Characteristics
# of Congress

by LEWIS A. FROMAN, JR.

By and large the Congress of the United States has been studied on its own terms, as a somewhat unique political institution. Studies of Congress are usually considered to be important simply because they shed light on an important institution in the American political system. It is true, of course, that Congress *is* an important policy-making body and does deserve study for that reason. But there is no reason why substantive importance cannot be combined with "importance" in another sense. It is also important, for example, to develop theory within any discipline which will help explain the phenomena under study. Trivial substantive problems can be made interesting because of the theory which they suggest. And because a problem may already be substantively important does not mean that it cannot be made even more significant by theoretical development.

As a result of this substantive focus, research on Congress has produced a very rich body of descriptive data on various components of the institution, including its members and leadership, group structure, committees, party systems, organization, and rules and procedures. Studies have also provided generalizations concerning such things as the decentralized decision-making of Congress and the effects of the seniority rule on the distribution of power within the House and Senate. These descriptive data and generalizations may serve as the content to be explained within the context of a theory. As yet there has been very little effort at theory construction concerning Congress. The data are there —their organization and explication remain.

Reprinted from "Organization Theory and the Explanation of Important Characteristics of Congress," *The American Political Science Review* 62 (June 1968): 518–26, by Lewis A. Froman, Jr. Reprinted by permission of the American Political Science Association and the author.

Characteristics of Congress

Although it is difficult to abstract *the* most important characteristics of Congress which have emerged from these studies, most close observers would agree that the following thirteen accurately reflect some of the more interesting and useful things which may be said about Congress.[1]

I. Impact on Public Policy
  1. Congress is an important political decision-making body which, unlike legislatures in many other countries, makes a significant, independent contribution to public policy.
II. Organization
  2. Decision-making in Congress is highly decentralized, with power widely dispersed among committees, subcommittees, and the formal and party leadership.
  3. Each body has a well-developed system of formal and impersonal rules and procedures, with the rules of the House of Representatives more formal and impersonal than those of the Senate.
III. Members
  4. Members in each body may make large individual contributions to public policy, although some members are more salient than others.
  5. Members of each house have a high commitment and loyalty to the Congress.
IV. Group Structure
  6. There are many subgroups within each body, with the House having a larger number than the Senate.
  7. There is a highly developed specialization of labor and specificity of roles, and more so in the House than the Senate.
  8. Group cohesion in each body is relatively low.
  9. The existence of an active group structure has important consequences for decision-making and public policy.
V. Leadership
  10. Each house has a relatively elaborate and complex leadership structure.
  11. Authority of leadership is relatively low.
VI. Processes
  12. Internal communication within each body is relatively elaborate and complex.
  13. A prevalent form of decision-making within each body is bargaining.

These thirteen generalizations about Congress are obviously not meant to be exhaustive of those which could be made in each category (as well as in additional categories). They are, however, among the more important propositions which aid in the understanding of the congressional process. As far as I

---

[1] Since the literature is so voluminous, and since most of the findings have been replicated and are not controversial, I will not attempt to cite specific references in each instance. For a general bibliography see the latest texts on Congress, William J. Keefe and Morris S. Ogul, *The American Legislative Process: Congress and the States* (Englewood Cliffs: Prentice-Hall, 1964), and Malcolm E. Jewell and Samuel C. Patterson, *The Legislative Process in the United States* (New York: Random House, 1966).

know none are contradicted by any study, and most are supported extensively in the literature. These thirteen propositions, then, will be taken as "given," as true of Congress, and as important enough to be "explained."

Possible Explanatory Theories

There are, essentially, two ways in which one may attempt to link up empirical findings with observations about their significance. One may discuss the *consequences* of the findings, what happens *because* the findings are true; or one may attempt to show *why* the findings are true, what *explains* the findings. The first is called functional analysis, the latter causal analysis.

Occasionally, but unfortunately only occasionally, the rich descriptive data on specific aspects of Congress and the generalizations relating one aspect to another are related further to possible consequences which the data being explored may have on public policy, careers of members, relations with the executive branch, or the American political system in general. Although most researchers on Congress are aware of the importance of demonstrating the effects which the institutional characteristics or processes which they describe have on important outcomes, the difficulty in collecting reliable data on such consequences often prohibits more than speculation.

More rare still are studies which explain *why* the descriptions or patterns which are observed are what they are. With relative infrequency historical references are made as to the genesis of certain features of Congress, but little or no *causal* analysis is attempted. At best one finds ad hoc explanations of special features of Congress, but such explanations are normally intrinsic to the organization itself and therefore difficult to validate in terms of general laws. Comparative data are necessary for this purpose. For example, to explain why power in Congress is decentralized it is not sufficient to point to the existence of the committee system. Multiple units are undoubtedly necessary to a dispersal of power, but not a sufficient condition for it. Are, for example, all organizations with committees decentralized? Undoubtedly not. But raising the general question forces one to think in a context larger than Congress itself, that is, on a comparative basis.

It is commonly accepted in philosophy of science that one achieves explanation of a phenomenon when that phenomenon can be subsumed under a general law. Thus, that Congress has a seniority system might be deduced from the following argument: All organizations with extensive divisions of labor have seniority systems; Congress is an organization with an extensive division of labor; therefore . . . (The soundness of this particular argument is not at issue here, it is the *form* of explanatory propositions with which this paragraph is concerned.)

What is necessary, then, in order to "explain" certain salient features of Congress is to subsume the specific findings under a set of more general hypotheses or laws (whether the former or the latter will affect the *credibility* of the explanation). But to do so requires moving away from the view that Congress is a unique institution and treating it, instead, as an instance of a more general category. What the more general category is will affect the terms of the theory as well as other matters. For example, Congress may be considered as an example of a legislature. If we had a theory of legislatures, then many of the propositions about Congress could be tested within that theory and many of the characteristics of Congress could be explained by the laws or hypotheses of that theory. We do not, however, have such a theory, although the development of one would certainly be useful. We do have the beginnings of general theory in the literature on organizations and it is not unrealistic, in order to use that theory, to label Congress an instance or an example of a formal organization.

If we view Congress as a formal organization, and use the general propositions which have been stated, with more or less validity, about formal organizations, we will be able to avoid strictly ad hoc interpretations of Congressional phenomena and, in their place, substitute a somewhat organized and consistent set of empirical generalizations which have been found to be true of other formal organizations. Such propositions, used in explanation, may be quite powerful and parsimonious and aid immeasurably in our understanding of why Congress is as it is. Dealing with Congress at this theoretical level may also have a number of other payoffs. If we are able to subsume important findings about a political institution under some general laws such an effort would provide significant clues as to what might be involved in attempts to change or reform various features of that organization. When one attempts to make changes in the absence of knowledge about causes, he is often "whistling in the wind," a constant source of irritation by the way to those who, at an intuitive level, are knowledgeable about Congress and who must deal with reform proposals by those who are not.

What follows, then, is an effort to explain the thirteen general characteristics of Congress concerning public policy, organization, members, group structure, leadership and processes, by subsuming these characteristics under general statements which have been drawn from organizations other than Congress. It is in this sense that Congress will be treated as a formal organization, subject to the same "laws" as other organizations, and unique only in the sense that there is only one Congress of the United States although there are many formal organizations.

The major source of these propositions is an article by Stanley Udy, Jr., which is an effort to subsume the extant literature on comparative organizations by the formulation of somewhat abstract generalizations.[2] Udy's definitions will be found in his article, along with the bibliographic references supporting the propositions. In several cases the propositions have been rephrased for clarity, consistency, and relevance. It is to be emphasized, however, that these propositions are designed to encompass organizations in general and that data from legislative bodies had no part in their formulation. The process in which we are engaged in this paper, then, may be described in two ways: (1) an exploration of

---

[2] Stanley H. Udy, Jr., "The Comparative Analysis of Organizations," in James G. March (ed.), *Handbook of Organizations* (Chicago: Rand McNally, 1965), pp. 678–709. Proposition seven comes from James G. March and Herbert A. Simon, *Organizations* (New York: Wiley, 1958), p. 130.

"goodness of fit" of propositions in one literature to the findings in another literature, and (2) an attempt to organize a number of descriptive statements about Congress around a set of explanatory propositions.

Explanation of Major Findings on Congress

The propositions about organizations from Udy and March and Simon may be placed in one of two categories, depending upon the reference of the independent variable: (a) propositions in which the environment of the organization is the independent variable, and (b) propositions in which either the organization itself or its membership is the independent variable. We will first consider three propositions which specify the environment or social setting as the independent variable. These three propositions help to explain seven of the descriptive statements about Congress enumerated at the beginning of this paper. The numbers in parentheses following each proposition refer to the descriptive statements (see above) being subsumed. We will then proceed to discuss four propositions in which organizational factors are the independent variables.

ENVIRONMENTAL DETERMINANTS

1a. *The more highly differentiated the social setting, the more salient the organization itself.*[3] (1)—Since outcomes of legislatures are public policies, this proposition asserts that although any setting undoubtedly affects an organization's output, the more differentiated and less unitary the setting the greater will be the effects of the organization itself in determining the organization's outcomes.

Applying this general proposition to Congress, it has often been suggested that Congress does not simply ratify the requests from its environment (including requests from the executive, interest groups, public opinion, political parties, etc.), but that the organization itself has a major impact on matters of public policy. It is even suggested that the American Congress is probably more powerful *vis-à-vis* the executive than are most other national legislatures. One explanation of this independence, as this first proposition suggests, is that the United States Congress may be classed with those formal organizations which face a relatively more differentiated environment. The social setting of the British Parliament, for example, is a good deal less highly differentiated given the fact that the diversity of interests which exist are already aggregated in a strong, cohesive, majority party which presents the bulk of requests. In Britain, of course, Parliament is not a highly salient political institution in terms of its independent impact on public policy. This observation may lead to a general hypothesis about legislatures: the independent influence which a legislature

[3] This part of proposition one is actually a deduction from two others: The more highly differentiated ... the social setting, the less salient it will be; The less salient the social setting ..., the more salient the organization itself; therefore. ... By "differentiated" is meant dispersed, heterogeneous, plural, non-unitary. By "salient" is meant important as an influence on the output of the organization.

exerts will vary inversely with the centralization of other pressures. The French Assembly under the Fourth Republic could have a greater impact on public policy than the French Assembly in the Fifth Republic. In the former centralization of pressure was rather weak; in the latter it is relatively strong.

1b. *The more highly differentiated the social setting, the more decentralized the decisional apparatus, the greater the amount of internal communication and group interaction, and the greater the expectation of high commitment of members.*[4] (2, 12, and 5)—Part b of this proposition asserts that not only will a diffuse and non-unitary environment make the organization more important as a determiner of its own decisions, but such an environment will also affect how the body is organized and how its members behave. An organization which faces a more unitary environment will be less likely to have an elaborate decentralized decision-making structure. It will also have less internal communication and less commitment of its members to the organization (which may, incidentally, also help to explain why a more centralized decision-structure is necessary).

The fact that Congress is subjected to a wide breadth and diffuseness of external pressures is documented without contradiction in the literature on Congress as well as in the relevant literatures on interest groups, political parties, public opinion, and public administration. The literature, of course, also supports the findings that Congress is highly decentralized, has a large amount of internal communication and interaction, and a high commitment of members to the organization.[5]

It is also interesting to observe that propositions 1a and 1b are probably mutually reinforcing. That is, an organization which has an important independent influence on its own decisions is also an organization where one would expect the commitment of members to be high. Similarly, an organization where commitment of its members is low is much more likely to be hierarchically organized (in order to force compliance) than an organization where commitment is high.

The amount of differentiation in the social setting, then, affects four important variables, some of which also influence (or at least are consistent with) the others.

2. *The . . . greater the amount of pressure exerted on the organization from the social setting, the greater the emphasis on administration.* (10)—In this proposition "administration" may mean at least three things: (1) routine tasks, (2) elaborate rules and procedures, and (3) complexity of leadership structure. Although we are primarily interested in the latter, all three meanings of the term are consistent with congressional findings. Proposition 2, then, asserts that organizations will vary in amount of routine tasks, the elaboration of rules and procedures, and leadership complexity and that one of the factors affecting the extent of "administration" is the amount of pressure exerted on the organization from the environment.

---

[4] These three dependent variables are positively associated with what Udy calls "breadth and diffuseness of external pressure." I take "differentiated social setting" and "breadth and diffuseness of external pressure" to be synonymous.

[5] For discussions and bibliography see Keefe and Ogul, *op. cit.;* and Jewell and Patterson, *op. cit.*

Studies of Congress attest to the large amount of outside pressure which is exerted on its members (from interest groups, constituents, executive agencies, party leaders, etc.) and also to the large amount of time which is spent by Congressmen and Senators on routine tasks (answering the mail, going to meetings, "making a record," etc.), the rather elaborate rules and procedures in both bodies, and the relatively complicated leadership structure.[6] As is suggested by the general proposition, the two sets of factors, amount of pressure and amount of administration, are related in organizations other than Congress as well.

Another way to state this proposition is in terms of work overload. Congressmen and Senators are literally deluged with requests, information, and "pressure." The three administrative responses of routine, rules, and role structure are efforts to cope with this overload.

3. *The greater the degree of conflict with the social setting, the greater the amount of authority exercised at all levels, and the more cohesive the group structure.* (11, 8)—Authority exercised by leaders in Congress is relatively small. Committee chairmen, the Speaker, the Majority and Minority Leaders, etc., are not able to command support although they do bargain for it. The literature suggests that leaders do have rewards and punishments to dispense, but all agree that the size of these resources is relatively small. Similarly, although the group structure in Congress is important and extensive it is not cohesive.[7]

These features follow from the independent variable in the above proposition, that is, Congress as an organization is not in conflict with the social setting. Rather, one would more accurately describe the relationship as being *in league* with the social setting. This comes about in two ways. First, Congressmen and Senators have constituents to court and care for, and they in fact spend an enormous amount of time doing just that. Estimates of time spent on constituency affairs range as high as ninety percent. Congressmen and Senators may, in fact, be in conflict with certain segments of the population, but not a majority of their own constituents (at least not publicly).

Second, it has been pointed out numerous times that although in some senses the executive branch and Congress are in conflict, in most matters legislators work hand in glove with the administrative departments which they oversee. Of course, the amount of cooperation undoubtedly varies in the House and Senate from committee to committee, but by and large relations with executive agencies are cordial and friendly, not hostile.

Another aspect of these same phenomena of lack of strong authority and low

[6] For example, see Robert L. Peabody, "Party Leadership Change in the United States House of Representatives," this REVIEW, 61 (September, 1967); Randall B. Ripley, "The Party Whip Organizations in the United States House of Representatives," this REVIEW, 58 (September, 1964), 561–576; Lewis A. Froman, Jr. and Randall B. Ripley, "Conditions for Party Leadership: The Case of the House Democrats," this REVIEW, 59 (March, 1965), 52–63, and Lewis A. Froman, Jr., *The Congressional Process: Strategies, Rules, and Procedures* (Boston: Little, Brown, 1967).

[7] Lewis A. Froman, Jr., *Congressmen and Their Constituencies* (Chicago: Rand McNally, 1963); David B. Truman, *The Congressional Party* (New York: Wiley, 1959); Alan Fiellin, "The Functions of Informal Groups: A State Delegation," in Robert L. Peabody and Nelson W. Polsby (eds.), *New Perspectives on the House of Representatives* (Chicago: Rand McNally, 1963), pp. 59–78; and John H. Kessel, "The Washington Congressional Delegation," *Midwest Journal of Political Science*, 8 (Feb., 1964), 1–21.

cohesion is the fact that Congress exhibits a good deal of intra-organizational conflict, not only between the parties but within parties as well. It would also be expected that this would be true of other organizations which have non-conflictual environmental relations, a fact which might suggest that relationships between organizational variables in Congress might also be generalizable to other organizations.[8]

These three environmental factors, extent of differentiation, amount of pressure, and degree of conflict help to explain a wide range of congressional phenomena in particular (statements 1, 2, 5, 8, 10, 11, and 12 in the list at the beginning of this paper), and organizational phenomena in general.

ORGANIZATIONAL DETERMINANTS

In the previous three propositions the environment or social setting has been the major independent variable. In this section we will consider propositions in which the independent variable is intra-organizational.

4. *The more permanent the organization, the lower its turnover rate, and the less mechanized the technology, the higher the salience of its group structure.* (9)— One of the features of Congress which has intrigued several recent writers on Congress is the important role which informal groups and group norms have in affecting the way in which Congressmen do their work.[9] It has long been known, since Woodrow Wilson's *Congressional Government*,[10] that committees and subcommittees play an all but overwhelming role in Congressional deliberations. But not only are these more formal groups now recognized as important cogs in the decision-making apparatus, but informal groups such as state delegations, voluntary clubs such as the Democratic Study Group in the House, informal groups of individuals within committees and subcommittees, and even larger groups such as the "conservative coalition," are being given increasingly more attention. Both the House and the Senate have a large number of informal groups as well as formal ones.

Causal proposition 4 asserts that the permanence of an organization, its relatively low turnover, and an unmechanized technology help to produce in organizations generally a highly salient group structure. Congress is certainly a permanent organization. Less well known, however, is the fact that turnover from Congress to Congress is relatively low, averaging about fifteen percent in the House of Representatives every two years.[11] That is, approximately eighty-

[8] See, for example, Samuel P. Huntington, *The Common Defense* (New York: Columbia University Press, 1961), which draws explicit parallels between Congressional processes and decision-making in the Pentagon.

[9] See Richard F. Fenno, Jr., "The House Appropriations Committee as a Political System: The Problem of Integration," this REVIEW, 56 (June, 1962), 310–324; Donald R. Matthews, *U.S. Senators and Their World* (Chapel Hill: University of North Carolina Press, 1960), especially Chapters 1 through 5; Alan Fiellin, "The Functions of Informal Groups: A State Delegation," in Peabody and Polsby (eds.), *op. cit.*, pp. 59–78, and John F. Manley, "The House Committee on Ways and Means: Conflict Management in a Congressional Committee," this REVIEW, 59 (December, 1965), 927–39.

[10] (New York, Meridian Books, 1956.) This book was first published in 1885.

[11] See Samuel P. Huntington, "Congressional Responses to the Twentieth Century," in David B. Truman (ed.), *The Congress and America's Future* (Englewood Cliffs: Prentice-Hall, 1965); Nelson W. Polsby, "The Institutionalization of the House of Representatives," paper delivered at the 1966 Annual Meeting of the American Political Science Association, and Lewis A. Froman, Jr., *The Congressional Process, op. cit.*, Chapter 1.

five percent of all Congressmen remain in Congress from one election to the next. The turnover in leadership positions, of course, is even smaller. In addition Congress is noted for its resistance to mechanization. Even such simple things as the installation of electric voting devices have failed to attract much enthusiasm among Congressmen and Senators. Most members of Congress pick up their information about what is going on as a result of talking with others. Televising the proceedings in each chamber, with closed-circuit outlets in each office would certainly be an aid to the members in determining when their presence on the floor might be desired. Rather than this, however, reliance is placed on word of mouth, and such low mechanization items as the telephone.

In addition to the high salience of the group structure, or more likely as a consequence of it, a number of informal norms have developed which help to protect the members and preserve stability. In a body in which members will be in contact with one another over long periods of time, and in which the technology of the organization is almost entirely social, it is not surprising to find that informal ways of doing things grow up which help to avoid serious threats to the stability and functioning of the organization. The seniority rule, senatorial courtesy, restrained debate, and even the so-called "Senate type," are undoubtedly a product of this. No issue is worth the destruction of the institution— members will have to deal with other members over a wide range of issues and over long periods of time. Legislators are, in effect, socialized into rules which specify that one must not jeopardize his ability to play future games by seriously discombobulating other members.

5. *The greater the need for technical expertise, the more salient the membership.* (4)—Not only is Congress as an organization highly salient (essentially because of its highly differentiated environment), and groups within Congress important (causal proposition 4), but its members may also become significant figures in the development of public policy. Undoubtedly, as this proposition suggests, part of the reason why this is true is the importance attached to technical knowledge about very complicated matters of public policy. Such expertise may lie in a substantive field like housing or tax matters, or in parliamentary skills. In any event members may become influential by the amount of information about a topic which they have at their command.[12]

This factor of technical expertise also helps to explain why some Congressmen are more important than others and why periods of apprenticeship are developed within the institution. A number of norms of behavior, in fact, revolve around the learning of technical expertise. Freshman members are expected not to participate extensively in debate, to speak only about what they know, and generally to watch and listen rather than participate.[13] One source of power in the House and Senate is information and, like other technical skills, it must be learned. Additional support is given to this hypothesis by the deference which is paid to those who have information and skills. Wilbur Mills, Chairman of the House Ways and Means Committee, for example, is an enormously

---

[12] See, for example, Richard F. Fenno, Jr., *The Power of the Purse* (Boston: Little, Brown, 1966).
[13] See Matthews, *op. cit.*, Chapter 5.

respected member of the House, not only because of his formal position but for his technical competence and parliamentary skill as well.

6. *The larger the size of the organization, the greater the number of subgroups in it; hence the greater the overall emphasis on formal and impersonal rules and specificity of roles.* (3, 6, 7)—This proposition helps us in two ways. First, both the House and Senate are relatively large organizations. For example, in 1960 more than ninety-five percent of the 4.7 million business organizations in the United States had less than one hundred employees.[14] Even without counting the large supporting staffs in the House and Senate, each is larger than this figure. We would expect, then, that both houses of Congress would have a relatively large number of subgroups, formal and impersonal rules, and high specificity of roles.

But the fact that membership in the House is over four times that of the Senate would also suggest that the House, as compared with the Senate, would have a larger number of subgroups, a more complex and impersonal set of rules, and greater role specificity. The data indicate that each of these is true. Although the data on social groups is incomplete, in formal group structures the House in the Eighty-ninth Congress (1965–66) had 20 committees and 125 subcommittees, whereas the comparable figures for the Senate were 16 and 99. On the question of role specificity, Representatives are usually members of only one committee whereas Senators normally have three or more committee assignments. In addition fifty-one percent of Senate Democrats have two or more committee or subcommittee chairmanships whereas only twelve percent of House Democrats play such multiple roles.[15] The data on rules and procedures is somewhat more difficult to summarize, but existing evidence supports the contention that House rules are more elaborate, formal, and impersonal than are Senate rules.[16]

7. *The extent of use of analytic processes to resolve conflict is a function of the type of organizational conflict involved. The more organizational conflict represents individual rather than intergroup conflict, the greater the use of analytic procedures. The more organizational conflict represents intergroup differences, the greater the use of bargaining.*[17] (13)—This proposition simply asserts that bargaining as a method of reaching agreement will be prevalent in organizations which have group conflict as opposed to analytic problem-solving devices in individual conflict.[18] The processes of log-rolling, compromise, and side-payments are widely used to reach majority agreement in committees, subcommittees, and on the floor of both the House and Senate.[19] The reasons for intergroup conflict in Congress are, of course, obvious. Disagreements in Congress reflect, generally, the cleavages within society. Such cleavages include

[14] William R. Dill, "Business Organizations," in James G. March, *op. cit.*, p. 1072.

[15] Lewis A. Froman, Jr., *The Congressional Process, op. cit.*

[16] *Ibid., passim.*

[17] This proposition is taken from James G. March and Herbert A. Simon, *Organizations* (New York: Wiley, 1958), p. 130.

[18] A similar proposition is found in Udy, *op. cit.*: "The greater the difficulty of group as opposed to individual problems, the greater the pressures toward social interaction" (p. 701).

[19] See Froman, *The Congressional Process, op. cit.*, Chapter 2.

ideological differences (*e.g.*, over the role of the federal government), religion, race, region, social class, and many others. Small groups of Congressmen and Senators may think somewhat alike on such matters, but putting together a majority coalition with respect to any single policy which touches on one or more cleavages usually results in extensive bargaining.

These last four intraorganizational propositions, then, account for the remaining six descriptive statements about Congress (3, 4, 6, 7, 9, and 13).

Summary and Implications

We began this paper with thirteen major propositions about Congress. Each was subsumed under a more general empirical proposition about formal organizations derived independently of any data on Congress but which fit other formal organizations. We can now briefly summarize, diagrammatically, the major relationships.

In each of the thirteen explanations there is no recourse to factors peculiar to Congress (and hence no problem in proving the validity of unique explanations). In addition several additional findings about Congress were cast in a more general language to suggest that they too may not be peculiar to only one formal organization.

A number of implications for further research are suggested by this tentative beginning in wedding organization theory to the study of Congress.

1. Propositions in organization theory may be very helpful in causal analysis of political institutions other than those usually included in public administration. The executive branch is by no means the only location of formal organizations which may have common features. In addition, the general propositions used here by no means exhaust the list of possible factors which may be included in the study of comparative organizations.[20]

2. There is, of course, no reason why such comparative study should be restricted to the search for causes only. It may also be true that certain organizational characteristics may produce similar consequences in terms of the organization's output. None of the possibilities which readily suggest themselves concerning *functional* analysis have been included here.

3. As suggested at the beginning of this paper, proposals for change in such highly visible organizations as the United States Congress must take into account the "realities" of the organization. Included in a list of such realities would have to be some notion of *why* the organization operates the way it does now in order to make realistic estimates of the likely acceptance and feasibility of changes. To propose changes without taking into account the causal roots of what is being proposed to be changed is to run the risk of being labeled naive, being ignored, or botching the job. Among other things which the 1946 Legislative Reorganization Act purported to do, for example, was to reduce the number of committees in Congress. In fact, counting subcommittees which have

---

[20] Udy's article, *op. cit.*, lists many more general propositions, most of which have to do with technological and psychological relationships.

Summary Relationships

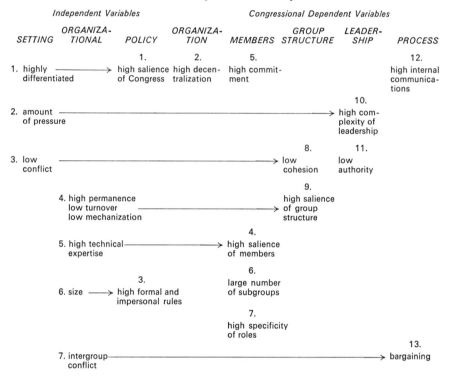

Independent Variables   Congressional Dependent Variables

SETTING	ORGANIZA-TIONAL	POLICY	ORGANIZA-TION	MEMBERS	GROUP STRUCTURE	LEADER-SHIP	PROCESS
		1.	2.	5.			12.
1. highly differentiated	──────→	high salience of Congress	high decentralization	high commitment			high internal communications
						10.	
2. amount of pressure	──→					high complexity of leadership	
					8.	11.	
3. low conflict	──────────────────────────────────→				low cohesion	low authority	
					9.		
4. high permanence low turnover low mechanization	──────────────────────→				high salience of group structure		
			4.				
5. high technical expertise	──────────→		high salience of members				
	3.		6.				
6. size ──→	high formal and impersonal rules		large number of subgroups				
			7.				
			high specificity of roles				13.
7. intergroup conflict	──→						bargaining

vastly increased in number, the number of subgroups in the organization has increased. The analysis in this paper perhaps sheds some light on why this has been the case.

4. The interplay between organization theory and the study of specific formal organizations like Congress need not be all in the direction of organization theory suggesting the more general propositions which will then be applied to a specific governmental institution. In several places in this paper propositions which developed from the study of Congress were thought to have more general application. For example, a greater degree of technical expertise in any organization might produce a more highly extended apprenticeship system, similar to the one developed in Congress. Or organizations which have low conflict relations with the environment might be hypothesized to have a higher degree of intra-organizational conflict. Both of these general propositions were suggested as a result of the study of Congress, and the question being asked is whether these propositions might not be true of other organizations.

5. One of the advantages of relying on comparative data as a source of general propositions is that factors which may be peculiar to only a small subset of institutions may turn out, on reflection, to be special cases of more general rules. For example, although a large number of important propositions about

Congress were discussed, in no case was it even necessary to refer to the fact that Congressmen are elected rather than recruited in some other way. Certainly the fact that they are elected has something to do with the low degree of conflict with the social setting which, it is suggested, is characteristic of Congress. But organizations may, for many different and specific reasons arrive at the same or similar degree of low conflict. Election is one way, recruitment through professional schools may be another. Regardless of the specific nature of recruitment, however, the result may be the same, that is, low conflict with the social setting.

Given these advantages of comparative organizational study, it is hoped that this paper will encourage further efforts in the same direction.

The Colombian Congress

by JAMES L. PAYNE

Q. *Why is attendance in Congress for votes, even apparently important votes, low?*
A. *Well our congressmen just haven't gotten the idea that a vote is important. If I am writing a letter or reading an interesting magazine and they say, "there's a vote; come and vote," I prefer to finish the letter or the magazine. I just can't be bothered. We think Congress is for speeches, not votes.*

> Interview with a member of the Co-
> lombian House of Representatives
> (Bogota, September 2, 1965).

An American observer is easily deceived by the Colombian legislature. At first glance it seems to resemble the American Congress. There are two chambers: a Senate (96 members) and a House of Representatives (184 members). The concurrence of both houses is required for the passage of legislation. Senators are elected every four years and must be over 30 years old; Representatives are elected every two years and must be over 25. Each house elects its own officers and has standing committees to which its members are assigned and to which legislation passes before final disposition is made on the floor.[1]

Aside from these superficial similarities, however, the Colombian Congress stands a world apart from the American body. In virtually all its processes, practices, and underlying characteristics, the Colombian legislature is what the American Congress is not. As it turns out, the many contrasts are consistent with the incentive analysis followed in this study.

One of the many contrasts with the American Congress is the astonishingly

---

[1] There are a few contrasts in formal arrangement with the American body. Colombian Senate seats are apportioned to the departments on the basis of population, instead of a fixed number to each state (two) as in the United States. Also, Colombian representatives are elected from department-wide circumscriptions under a system of proportional representation. In the United States representatives come from single-member districts within each state.

Reprinted from "The Colombian Congress," in *Patterns of Conflict in Colombia* (New Haven: Yale University Press, 1968), pp. 238–67, by James L. Payne. Copyright © 1968 by Yale University. Chapter abridged by the editors.

Table 1—Continuity in the Membership of the Colombian Congress

Base year	Total members	Number returning for second consecutive term	Number returning for three consecutive terms
House of Representatives			
1925	112 (100%)	14 (12.5%)	6 (5.4%)
1935	119 (100%)	24 (20.2%)	7 (5.9%)
1960	152 (100%)	34 (22.4%)	12 (7.9%)
Senate			
1923	48 (100%)	8 (16.7%)	3 (6.3%)
1935	56 (100%)	10 (17.9%)	
1958	82 (100%)	24 (29.3%)	

Source: *Anales del Congreso; Anales del Senado; Anales de la Cámera* (beginning in 1923 these documents contained lists of congressmen elected for each session from which continuity could be calculated).

high rate of turnover. In Table 1 the continuity rates for the Senate and the House have been calculated for three different periods: Conservative rule (1920s); Liberal rule (1930s); and the Frente Nacional (since 1958). In all three cases, turnover is remarkably high, with only about one-fifth of the representatives or senators returning for a consecutive term. Only a very small number of legislators, less than 10 percent, will experience three successive terms. In Table 2, continuity for the United States House of Representatives is calculated for the period 1959–63. Of the representatives elected in 1959, 85 percent returned for a second term; 67 percent returned for three successive terms.

In Colombia between 5 and 10 percent of the representatives in a given year will miss one term and return two years later (Table 3). Returnees from further back in the past will, in quite small numbers, augment the number of experienced representatives present in any given year. But even including all these sources of continuity it seems safe to say that over half of the representatives at any moment have never been in the House before.

Initially we might seek an explanation for high turnover in the intensity of electoral competition. This explanation, however, is at variance with some important facts. First, if it were electoral competition that caused turnover, more legislators would reenter Congress after one term of absence. Being relieved of the supposed distractions of officeholding, the ex-congressman would be free to reactivate his old contacts and devote his full time to getting reelected. There is little evidence, however, that this in-out-in pattern obtains (see Table 3).

Secondly, if a congressman really wants to stay in office, he has many resources which his aspiring opponents lack. He has considerable prestige,

Table 2—Continuity in the U.S. House of Representatives

Base year	Total members	Number returning for second consecutive term	Number returning for three consecutive term
1959	437 (100%)	373 (85.4%)	294 (67.3%)

Source: Compiled from the *Congressional Record.*

Table 3—Alternate Membership in the Colombian House of Representatives (in-out-in)

Base year	Total members	Number of representatives skipping one term and then returning
1925	112 (100%)	9 (8%)
1960	152 (100%)	12 (8%)

Source: Compiled from *Anales del Congreso; Anales de la Cámera.*

governmental connections, a position of greater prominence and publicity. The resources open to other candidates, such as street campaigns and face-to-face politicking are also available to the incumbent *if he is willing to expend the necessary effort*. If it is true that the legislator's desire to stay in is as strong as his desire to get in, then he has a clear advantage over his opponents.

By examining the attitudes of the legislators themselves we discern that electoral competition does not account for turnover, for these men lack the will to return before elections even arrive. Many will frankly voice a desire not to return. Others I interviewed were noncommittal or indifferent: "perhaps," "I haven't thought about it," "if they want me," "we'll see what happens." Being so weakly motivated to return, these men are likely to lose out in the struggle to regain their seats. Getting reelected is generally an exhausting task and demands considerable motivation.[2]

Studies of American state legislatures support the view that motivation and not electoral competition mainly account for turnover. Hyneman observed that turnover was highest in the least party-competitive states (Indiana, Iowa, and Maine) and lowest in the more competitive areas (New Jersey, New York, and California). Simply by noting that less than one third of the legislators not returning ran in primary or general elections he could conclude that electoral competition was not the primary cause of turnover.[3]

Turnover in the Colombian Congress is not the result of electoral competition but, instead, of the status incentive of leaders. Colombian leaders are seeking the prestige inherent in the position of representative or senator. And that prestige adheres to an ex-representative as well as an incumbent. In this sense the office is like a medal or award which, once achieved, is always possessed and requires only proper display and occasional polishing to serve as a status indicator. If it is only prestige one seeks from Congress, then a career in the legislature becomes an unnecessary cross to bear.

The Colombian congressman will, with few exceptions, follow one of two

[2] See, for example, California Representative Clem Miller's efforts to stay in touch with his constituency, which involved a grueling 18-hour day: Clem Miller, *Member of the House* (New York, Charles Scribner's Sons, 1962), especially pp. 74–79.

[3] Charles S. Hyneman, "Tenure and Turnover of Legislative Personnel," *The Annals of the American Academy of Political and Social Science, 195* (January 1938), 21–31. His computations for turnover in ten states combined showed that only 35.4% of his sample of 10,152 legislators were first-termers. This figure is not strictly comparable with ours, but would not be far from showing a 65% continuity rate, compared to the 20% rate for Colombia. Eulau *et al.* discovered greater electoral competition is associated with a greater willingness to return: "Career Perspectives of American State Legislators," in Marvick, ed., *Political Decision-makers*, pp. 218–63.

Table 4—Movement of Representatives to the Senate in Colombia

Base year	Total representatives	Number of representatives who became senators at the next elections
1925	112 (100%)	9 (8%)
1960	152 (100%)	31 (20%)

Source: Compiled fom *Anales del Congreso, Anales de la Cámera, Anales del Senado.*

paths after his first term. Either he will retire, having gained the title he sought, or, depending upon his ambitions and expectations, he will seek to win a higher title and move into the pre-presidential ring of senators, ministers, and governors. A relatively high proportion of representatives move up to the Senate in the next election (between 10 and 20 percent, see Table 4). In Colombia there are basically two patterns of political motion: in and out, or in and up. The career-type pattern of staying in at the same level for long periods of time is extremely rare.

In the United States, by and large, a congressional position is taken seriously as a career. An American congressman gets a continuing satisfaction from defending constituencies and working out policies, and hence wishes to retain his seat. Getting reelected and doing the business of a legislator is indeed taxing, but most American congressmen consider the satisfactions worth the costs. They are just as anxious (if not more so) to be reelected as they were to gain the seat for the first time. . . .

A second remarkable contrast between the Colombian legislature and the American Congress is the presence of a system of alternates and a generally high rate of absenteeism. In Colombia both senators and representatives are elected along with alternates who may be appointed to fill the seat if the incumbent does not wish to serve. As indicated in Table 5, about 20 percent of the representatives elected to hold office give their seats to alternates. Furthermore, about five or ten representatives will simply disappear from the scene, their names (or names of possible alternates) not appearing in any roll call listing. In the votes themselves, even apparently important and close votes, one usually finds only about three-quarters of the representatives or senators voting.

The phenomenon of alternates and absenteeism is a direct consequence of the status incentive of legislators. The position of alternate is, of course, a convenient

Table 5—Use of Alternates in the House of Representatives

Election date	Total members	Number of representatives who were replaced by alternates
March 1937	119 (100%)	20 (17%) July 1937
March 1939	119 (100%)	22 (18%) July 1940
March 1960	152 (100%)	31 (20%) July 1961

Source Compiled from *Anales del Congreso; Anales de la Cámera.*

way to share the prestige of office. But the practice has grown up because congressmen do not mind sharing their seats or simply forgetting about them. Once having obtained the title of representative or senator, Colombian leaders rapidly lose interest in Congress. They are not interested in actually doing the work of a legislator. When asked about their job, they classify being a congressman as *"aburrido"* (boring) or *"pesado"* (dull). It is a job from which they seem to get little, if any, satisfaction. In this way we can explain the curious paradox that Colombian leaders struggle fiercely at election time to become senators or representatives, but once elected they are casual or even reluctant about serving.

In the United States it is doubtful that legislators would ever establish a system of alternates, let alone use it to any great extent. A congressman is elected to *be* the representative; he wants to do the job. The idea of turning his back on Congress after being elected would be distasteful or even incomprehensible to a man with a program incentive. It would be like going to a bridge tournament, registering, and then going home without playing. American congressmen, like bridge players, get their satisfactions from playing the game.

Briefly we may inspect some other areas of legislative life which are affected by the status incentive of congressmen.

COMMITTEES

Prior to 1945 there were no permanent committees in the Colombian Congress. At that time it was perhaps felt that committees were the answer to the age-old cry in Colombia of "congressional decadence." The reformers meant well but nothing substantial was achieved. Each house now has seven formal standing committees. The membership of these committees is large, ranging from about 14 to 38. Subcommittees are apparently never used. Some committees never meet; others meet a few times a session. After making daily inspections of congressional committees I concluded that the typical day (Tuesday, Wednesday, or Thursday; Monday and Friday are congressional holidays) would see the following committee activity:

> 3 committees—met for one or two hours
> 2 committees—met for less than 30 minutes
> 2 committees—had called meetings but no quorum was
>   achieved and hence they did not meet
> 7 committees—did not meet

I estimate that the average congressman in Colombia spends about one hour a week in committee meetings. In the United States, congressmen appear to spend between 10 and 20 hours weekly in committee. On midweek days there will be from 30 to 50 committees and subcommittees meeting in the U.S. Congress. On Mondays or Fridays there will be between 10 and 20 committee meetings.

But even when they do meet, Colombian congressional committees do not resemble their American counterparts. Expert witnesses, with the infrequent exception of top administration officials, are not called. To my knowledge, no committee has ever had an executive (secret) session. The practice of exhaustive committee investigations into particular subjects is virtually unknown. Committee activity generally takes the form of (1) acrimonious debates scarcely connected with policy matters, as twenty or thirty congressmen make political attacks, or (2) boring rubber-stamp sessions in which a few stout-hearted congressmen sit through a reading of some document and drearily vote unanimous approval. In short, Colombian committees are not policy-making bodies. And how could they be policy-making bodies when their members do not wish to make policy?

EXPERTISE AND SPECIALIZATION

When congressmen are not interested in making policy they do not equip themselves to know about the problems of government. Colombian legislators are virtually without research or technical assistance. The Senate Library and congressional archives, with their tiny collections of lawbooks and scattered documents, employ about ten clerks. But even so they are grossly overstaffed, for congressmen seldom use these facilities. Congressmen have no offices and no secretaries. The committees have tiny staffs (usually one secretary and two typists) to handle paperwork, but nothing approaching a research staff.

Finally, few Colombian congressmen have acquired special knowledge on any area of legislation. American legislators have specialized in response to the complexity of governmental problems and the impossibility of knowing about all of them. If one wishes to have a decisive influence on policy, he must know about the policy area. But the acquisition of specialized knowledge requires effort. If legislators have no interest in policy, then they will not inconvenience themselves to become expert on specific policy areas.

FLOOR DEBATES

The House and Senate usually meet from about 6 to 8 or 9 P.M. on Tuesday, Wednesday, and Thursday. At least once a week the chambers will fail to meet, lacking a quorum, so each chamber has approximately five hours floor time a week. Floor time is largely spent either in dreary reading of documents and pro forma voting or in acrimonious debate, the purpose of which is to attract attention. By creating a scene the speaker gains publicity which enhances his status and advances his political career. As a consequence debates are characterized by personal charges, irresponsible attacks and condemnations and, frequently, *zambra* (physical violence). The observers in the galleries are free to cheer and shout down speakers.

Debates are customarily political and strategic, rather than upon substantive policy matters. Political scandals, accusations of corruption, favoritism, and administrative incompetence are favorite themes. Congressmen are as ready to accuse each other and Congress itself as they are likely to attack the administration.[4] Verbatim records of floor debates are not kept (nor of committee hearings); minutes give only a brief summary of what transpired.

These practices are again a product of the status incentive of legislators. Because American legislators have a program incentive, in the U.S. Congress many formal and informal norms are designed to prevent disruptive activity. Fist fights, cheers from the gallery, personal attacks, degradation of the institution, all get in the way of serious policy-making, and the rules of the legislature are intended to prevent such activity. Norms such as courtesy, deference, seniority, apprenticeship, and specialization (speak only on the subject on which you are expert) have developed because they facilitate policy-making.[5] Verbatim transcripts of floor debates and committee hearings are kept because what is said is intimately related to policy-making. Every day congressmen and administrators inspect the wording of testimony and debates to determine precise meanings, to get the facts absolutely correct.

Colombian legislators hold a status incentive and therefore they structure and employ their Congress accordingly. It is easy to imagine what some foreign mission would suggest if given $100,000 to propose reforms for the Colombian Congress: more staff, subcommittees, etc. But such reforms would treat only symptoms. If proposed they either would not be adopted, or if adopted, abused. Congressmen want short committee hearings because they are not interested in working out policy; they want floor debates to be interrupted by clamor from the galleries because clamor is what they seek. Congressmen do not have greater technical assistance because they have no use for it. They are not interested in the exhaustive analysis of legislation and its effects. An illustration of the futility of rules which are in conflict with the incentives of congressmen is the law which states that no congressman should receive his daily salary if he is absent from Congress without an excuse on that day. This rule has been on the books since 1931, but apparently has never been applied.[6]

The Congress and Policy-making

The most important fact about the Colombian Congress is, then, that in general *congressmen are indifferent to particular policy outcomes per se.* All of our inquiries about program differences between the parties (Chapter 4), factional-

---

[4] A sensational attack on Congress from within was made by Representative María Elena de Crovo of the MRL in the session of September 1, 1965. She captivated the House with scathing allegations of congressional corruption using, as props, a whip ("to punish the dishonesty of some parliamentarians") and a pistol ("to shoot the heels of those people who fail to respect me"). *El Tiempo*, September 2, 1965, p. 6, and September 17, 1965, p. 31; *El Espectador*, September 18, 1965, p. 13A; *Contrapunto*, August 26, 1965, p. 3. It was rumored that these colorful attacks were related to her interest in a Senate seat in 1966.

[5] See Matthews, *U.S. Senators and their World*, pp. 92–117; Richard F. Fenno, Jr., "The House Appropriations Committee as a Political System," *American Political Science Review, 56* (June 1962), 310–24; Nicholas A. Masters, "Committee Assignments in the House of Representatives," *American Political Science Review, 55* (June 1961), 345–57; John F. Manley, "The House Committee on Ways and Means: Conflict Management in a Congressional Committee," *American Political Science Review, 59* (1965), 927–39.

[6] In 1946 *Semana* (December 16, 1946, p. 8) noted that this pay deduction "has never been applied."

ism (Chapter 9), party structure (Chapter 10), as well as the above examination of the nature of Congress lead to this conclusion. Because Colombian leaders have a strong status incentive, they have little interest in public policy for its own sake. I think this orientation is accurately reflected in an interview with an ex-representative from Cundinamarca:

Q. But aren't there people in Congress who are defenders of particular programs, who take a continuous interest in a policy . . . or defend. . . . Like agrarian reform, for example?
A. No, actually there are not. No one really has a particular interest. Take agrarian reform [1961]. The gringos [Americans] wanted an agrarian reform, so we did it—to please the gringos. We didn't care one way or the other. These issues come and go; it's all a matter of circumstances.[7]

The observer who seeks to find a Left and a Right in the Colombian Congress is doomed to error if he makes a superficial study and is likely to go insane if he makes a careful examination. The search for a progressive or reactionary segment in the Colombian Congress is about as pointless as attempting to divide birds along the same lines.[8]

What, then, determines the behavior of legislators with a status incentive? How do Colombian congressmen, who have little interest in policy itself, respond to the issues that come before them? Votes are taken and frequently they affect policy. What makes congressmen vote as they do?

The answer is complicated and involves three elements which typically bear concomitantly upon the voting decision:

1. The strategic implications of the issue for the national factions.
2. The popular-demagogic inclination to favor lower strata groups.
3. The ignorance of and lack of interest in specific policies and details of policies.

An important and frequently overriding determinant of a congressman's vote is the strategic implication of the issue for the faction to which he belongs. If it is clear that his faction stands to gain by voting "no," then the congressman will vote "no." In asking members of national directorates and congressmen about faction "discipline" it clearly emerged that they see two types of issues: "political" and "nonpolitical," or in our terms, strategic and program. Leaders defined a political issue as a matter which directly and obviously affected the political welfare of the faction. Illustrations include the election of a presidential designate, electoral laws, approval of high administrative appointments, and withdrawing support from an executive.

---

[7] The reader should not conclude from this comment that Colombian congressmen are "reactionary" or conservative. That considerable attention to "agrarian reform" came from foreigners and not locally probably reveals more about the ignorance of these foreigners in perceiving real political priorities than any conservative tendency of Colombian leaders.

[8] When I argue that Colombian congressmen are basically uninterested in policy, I strongly disagree with Albert Hirschman. Hirschman constructed an interesting model to deal with "reform" in the Colombian Congress based on the proposition that congressmen had strong policy preferences, that indeed they had strong preferences on all policy issues. On this point I believe Hirschman is mistaken and consequently much of his analysis is irrelevant for Colombia. Albert O. Hirschman, *Journeys Toward Progress* (New York, The Twentieth Century Fund, 1963), p. 292 and passim.

Nonpolitical or program issues were, in the view of the leaders, such matters as fiscal and monetary policy or social and economic measures. On strategic issues the leaders stated that faction discipline was expected; on program matters it was not. Leaders repeatedly pointed out that *on program matters directorates did not take positions and were not expected to take positions*. This is significant because it clearly reveals the lack of concern leaders exhibit toward program matters, compared with their concern over private, strategic matters.

In practice a division does exist between strategic and program matters, but Colombian leaders oversimplify the distinction. First, even on purely strategic issues it appears that "discipline" does not account for the cohesion which obtains in the voting patterns. When asked about the punishment of faction members who go against the faction on strategic matters, leaders were surprised and confused as if such a case were incomprehensible. When pressed to give illustrations of how discipline would be applied or to cite cases of punishment, leaders were curiously evasive.

In one interview with a member of a national directorate I finally got to the heart of matter of cohesion:

Q. What happens to the congressman who votes against his faction on a clear, what you call "political" issue?
A. Well . . . Well, it means that he is no longer in the faction; that he doesn't want to belong to the faction.

That is, the failure of a congressman to go along with a faction already indicates that he has shifted loyalties to another faction. He does not see the same risks and opportunities as other faction members and is, de facto, a member of a competing faction. Cohesion obtains within the faction on strategic issues because members share the same strategic perspective.

This cohesion does not represent the "discipline" of some other party systems. Threats and punishments are necessary where participants have prominent policy attitudes and have to be coerced into going along with the leadership on program matters. The carrot-stick technique employed in Great Britain and to a lesser extent in the United States to encourage party unity is necessary because legislators may have program preferences of their own which conflict with those of party leaders. Weapons of discipline are not necessary in Colombia because congressmen and leadership rarely care about program. On strategic matters all faction members have the same attitude; if they did not, they would not be in the same faction.

One matter, for example, which is always strategic is the election of presiding officers for each house of Congress. These three officers, a president and two vice-presidents, enjoy terms of only 60 days and customarily are not reelected. This practice is, of course, a response to pressure for the prestige of these positions; the rapid rotation insures that many legislators will attain the status of these posts. On May 4, 1965, the election for presiding officers of the House produced an interesting but clearly strategic division. The supporters of Carlos Lleras for president in 1966, the Officialist Liberals and Ospinista Conservatives, backed one slate. The opponents of this candidacy, the Lauro-alzatista Conservatives, the Movimiento Revolucionario Liberal, and the Alianza Nacional Popular of Rojas Pinilla, united behind another slate.[9]

Many observers were astounded by this alliance. How could Laureanistas unite with Rojistas when Rojas had deposed Laureano Gómez in 1953 and after Gómez had been bitterly attacking Rojas for years? How could the MRL, which got votes by arousing anti-Conservative feelings of the Liberals, unite with the Lauro-alzatista Conservatives? How could allegedly "Rightist" ANAPO unite with the supposedly "revolutionary Leftist" MRL? Obviously neither historical, nor personal, nor ideological considerations were important. The three groups had a common strategic goal: opposition to the candidacy of Carlos Lleras. Under the circumstances they could advance their common strategic goal by opposing the Llerista slate for House officers.

Strategic issues, however, are not clearly defined but shade into program matters so that virtually every item that comes before Congress has some strategic implications and therefore a tendency toward faction cohesion remains. That is, program issues such as taxes, budgets, labor reform, and public works often have—or are thought to have—strategic overtones. On these issues the directorates almost never take a position, either formally announcing that congressmen are free to vote as they like or simply ignoring the matter altogether. Nevertheless, faction members tend to vote together on such issues.

Typically, the most important strategic implication of program policies will be their impact upon the executive. Each faction adopts an orientation toward the president ranging from almost complete support to belligerent opposition. These strategies are determined primarily by the relative share of participation in the government (ministries, governorships) allotted to the faction, and the calculations made by faction leaders concerning the relative electoral benefits of support or opposition. In general those factions accepting posts in the government are government supporters, those without posts are opposition. However intermediate positions exist: quasi-support (accept ministries but reap electoral benefits from harassing the executive); or quasi-opposition (refuse ministries but tone down opposition to facilitate an alliance with a government-supporting faction or a larger offer from the president at some future date).

Consequently if a measure is supported by the executive and/or it appears that the executive will benefit from a measure, the tendency will be for opposition groups to oppose it and collaborators to support it. Opposition forces seek to disgrace and undermine the regime for electoral purposes. Their cry is that a drastic change, namely themselves, is necessary to rescue the country from chaos. Furthermore, groups outside the government oppose the executive because they must indicate that their support can be bought only at a price—a satisfactory number of government positions to their faction members. There will be an underlying tendency, then, for opposition factions to oppose anything the executive might want or need: monetary or fiscal measures, reforms of one

---

[9] *La República,* April 29, 1965, p. 7, and April 30, 1965, p. 8; *El País* (Cali), May 5, 1965, p. 21; *Semana al Día,* May 7, 1965, p. 9. Since neither side could obtain the necessary two-thirds majority, the House remained with the existing officers.

kind or another. Conversely, those factions participating in the government have been "paid" and consequently will generally support what the government seeks. . . .

Conclusion

This examination of the Colombian Congress supports some findings of Barber's study of freshmen Connecticut State Assemblymen, . . .[10] The group he identified as Lawmakers were individuals whose satisfactions came from working on policy, from translating their preferences into law. In our terms they had a program incentive. As we would expect, these participants exhibited a high willingness to return to the legislature and were active in legislative work.

Another group, the smallest in Barber's sample, were termed Advertisers. They entered the legislature for prestige and contacts. They had, it seems, a status incentive. The Advertisers had much in common with Colombian legislators. They were unwilling to return for a second term. Although they were active in a formal sense, their activity was attention-getting (speeches, for example) rather than on substantive matters. They found the legislature a dull place and regarded legislation as if it were not their job to make it. What would a legislature populated largely by Advertisers look like? I think it might be described by the following hypothesis, drawn from an examination of the Colombian Congress:

H34. A legislature whose members have a status incentive will be characterized by:
1. chronic absenteeism in committees and votes
2. low committee workloads
3. few technical or research facilities for legislators
4. disruptive, conflict-provoking patterns of behavior
5. a popular-demagogic orientation toward program policies

These findings about the Colombian legislature suggest that Americans may be misguided in their criticisms of the U.S. Congress. We are often impatient with such norms as seniority or apprenticeship. At least since Woodrow Wilson wrote *Congressional Government* in 1884 we have been mistrustful of the committees which guard their subject matter so jealously. We are annoyed when congressmen are reluctant to force a bill from committee. We find the club-like atmosphere of restraint stifling if not downright suspicious. We are unhappy to discover that congressmen frown upon colleagues who speak on subjects they have not studied. We are suspicious of the way congressmen use devices to hide their lawmaking activities from the public eye: closed committee hearings, secret markup and conference committee sessions, the teller vote. We vaguely suspect that in these private nooks and crannies corruption is flourishing.

An examination of the Colombian legislature suggests that these criticisms are somewhat misplaced. The above practices have evolved naturally and necessarily from the American legislators' desire to form policy and enact laws.

[10] Barber, *The Lawmakers.*

Working on a program is the reason why most of these men are in Congress and they have seen to it that nothing, perhaps even the electorate, greatly interferes with their goal. As a policy-making institution, as a body of men who examine exhaustively, deliberate calmly, and weigh thoughtfully, the United States Congress would seem a model legislature.

As a legislature sensitive to immediate popular demands, the United States Congress does not rate highly at all. Such sensitivity is inconsistent with the same incentive that makes congressmen such dogged policy-makers. They want to study matters in detail, examine consequences, allow things to "settle down." They want their policies to *work*, and workable policies require much study. American congressmen therefore tend to be cautious, and Congress takes on a conservative cast. And, I need hardly note, the program attitudes of many congressmen are expressed in opposing measures which happen to be popular in an immediate sense.

The Colombian Congress presents the opposite picture. As a policy-making body it is equivocal, clumsy, and superficial in the usual meanings of those terms. But it is extremely sensitive to immediate popular demands. There is little resistance to doing the popular thing immediately, no desire to study, investigate, or hesitate. Colombian congressmen get little satisfaction from devising policies. And they certainly are not inclined to advance policies that are unpopular. Their satisfaction comes from the prestige of office, and the conquest of higher office requires popularity. The Colombian Congress, therefore, becomes a popular-demagogic institution.

The Institutionalization of the

U.S. House of Representatives

by NELSON W. POLSBY

Most people who study politics are in general agreement, it seems to me, on at least two propositions. First, we agree that for a political system to be viable, for it to succeed in performing tasks of authoritative resource allocation, problem solving, conflict settlement, and so on, in behalf of a population of any substantial size, it must be institutionalized. That is to say, organizations must be created and sustained that are specialized to political activity.[1] Otherwise, the political system is likely to be unstable, weak, and incapable of servicing the demands or protecting the interests of its constituent groups. Secondly, it is generally agreed that for a political system to be in some sense free and democratic, means must be found for institutionalizing representativeness with all the diversity that this implies, and for legitimizing yet at the same time containing political opposition within the system.[2]

Our growing interest in both of these propositions, and in the problems to which they point, can begin to suggest the importance of studying one of the very few extant examples of a highly specialized political institution which over the

---

[1] A good recent summary of literature bearing on this point as it applies to the study of political development may be found in Samuel P. Huntington, "Political Development and Political Decay," *World Politics*, 17 (April, 1965), 386–430.

[2] Robert A. Dahl speaks of "the three great milestones in the development of democratic institutions—the right to participate in governmental decisions by casting a vote, the right to be represented, and the right of an organized opposition to appeal for votes against the government in elections and in parliament." In enumerating these three great achievements of democratic government, Dahl also implies that they are embodied principally in three main institutions: parties, elections, and legislatures: Robert A. Dahl (ed.), *Political Oppositions in Western Democracies* (New Haven and London: Yale University Press, 1966), p. xi. See also William Nisbet Chambers "Party Development and the American Mainstream," especially pp. 18–19, in Chambers and Walter Dean Burnham (eds.), *The American Party Systems: Stages of Political Development* (New York: Oxford, 1967).

Reprinted from "The Institutionalization of the U.S. House of Representatives," *The American Political Science Review* 62 (March 1968): 144–68, by Nelson W. Polsby. Reprinted by permission of the American Political Science Association and the author.

long run has succeeded in representing a large number of diverse constituents, and in legitimizing, expressing, and containing political opposition within a complex political system—namely, the U.S. House of Representatives.

The focus of my attention here will be first of all descriptive, drawing together disparate strands—some of which already exist in the literature[3]—in an attempt to show in what sense we may regard the House as an institutionalized organ of government. Not all the necessary work has been done on this rather difficult descriptive problem, as I shall indicate. Secondly, I shall offer a number of speculative observations about causes, consequences, and possible lessons to be drawn from the institutionalization of the House.

The process of institutionalization is one of the grand themes in all of modern social science. It turns up in many guises and varieties: as Sir Henry Maine's discussion of the change from status to contract in the history of legal obligations,[4] as Ferdinand Tönnies' treatment of the shift from *Gemeinschaft* to *Gesellschaft*,[5] as Max Weber's discussion of the development of "rational-legal" modes of legitimization as an alternative to "traditional" and "charismatic" modes,[6] as Durkheim's distinction between "mechanical" and "organic" solidarity in his treatment of the consequences of the division of labor[7] and finally—dare we say finally?—as the central process at work in the unfolding of organizations that are held to obey Parkinson's Law.[8]

Such theoretical riches are bound to prove an embarrassment to the empirical researcher, since, unavoidably, in order to do his work, he must pick and choose among a host of possibilities—not those that initially may be the most stimulating, but those that seem most likely to be reflected in his data, which, perforce, are limited.[9] Thus the operational indices I am about to suggest which purport to measure empirically the extent to which the U.S. House of Representatives has become institutionalized may strike the knowledgeable reader as exceedingly crude; I invite the ingenuity of my colleagues to the task of suggesting improvements.

[3] See for example, Nelson W. Polsby, "Congressional Research and Congressional Data: A Preliminary Statement" (mimeo) delivered at the Conference on Congressional Research, sponsored by the Inter-university Consortium for Political Research and the Social Science Research Council at the Brookings Institution, Washington, D.C., April 3–4, 1964; H. Douglas Price, "The Congressman and the Electoral Arena" (mimeo, 1964); and T. Richard Witmer, "The Aging of the House," *Political Science Quarterly*, 79 (December, 1964), 526–41.

[4] Sir Henry Sumner Maine, *Ancient Law* (London: John Murray, 1908), pp. 220–325.

[5] Ferdinand Tönnies, *Community and Society (Gemeinschaft und Gesellschaft)* (East Lansing: Michigan State University Press, 1957). See, in particular, the introductory commentary by Charles P. Loomis and John C. McKinney, "The Application of Gemeinschaft and Gesellschaft as Related to Other Typologies," *ibid.*, pp. 12–29.

[6] Max Weber, *The Theory of Social and Economic Organization* (Glencoe: The Free Press, 1947), pp. 328ff.

[7] Emile Durkheim, *The Division of Labor in Society* (Glencoe: The Free Press, 1947).

[8] C. Northcote Parkinson, *Parkinson's Law* (Boston: Houghton Mifflin, 1957).

[9] The only successful modern attempt I am aware of that employs a classical theory of institutionalization in an empirical study of something other than a bureaucracy is Harold W. Pfautz's "Christian Science: The Sociology of a Social Movement and Religious Group" (unpublished Ph.D. dissertation, Department of Sociology, University of Chicago, 1954). See also Harold W. Pfautz, "The Sociology of Secularization: Religious Groups," *The American Journal of Sociology*, 41 (September, 1955), 121–28, and Pfautz, "A Case Study of an Urban Religious Movement: Christian Science" in E. W. Burgess and D. J. Bogue (eds.), *Contributions to Urban Sociology* (Chicago and London: University of Chicago Press, 1963), pp. 284–303.

For the purposes of this study, let us say that an institutionalized organization has three major characteristics: (1) it is relatively well-bounded, that is to say, differentiated from its environment. Its members are easily identifiable, it is relatively difficult to become a member, and its leaders are recruited principally from within the organization. (2) The organization is relatively complex, that is, its functions are internally separated on some regular and explicit basis, its parts are not wholly interchangeable, and for at least some important purposes, its parts are interdependent. There is a division of labor in which roles are specified, and there are widely shared expectations about the performance of roles. There are regularized patterns of recruitment to roles, and of movement from role to role. (3) Finally, the organization tends to use universalistic rather than particularistic criteria, and automatic rather than discretionary methods for conducting its internal business. Precedents and rules are followed; merit systems replace favoritism and nepotism; and impersonal codes supplant personal preferences as prescriptions for behavior.

Since we are studying a single institution, the repeated use of words like "relatively" and "tends" in the sentences above refers to a comparison of the House of Representatives with itself at different points in time. The descriptive statement: "The House of Representatives has become institutionalized over time" means then, that over the life span of this institution, it has become perceptibly more bounded, more complex, and more universalistic and automatic in its internal decision making. But can we find measures which will capture enough of the meaning of the term "institutionalization" to warrant their use in an investigation of the process at work in the U.S. House of Representatives?

The Establishment of Boundaries

One aspect of institutionalization is the differentiation of an organization from its environment. The establishment of boundaries in a political organization refers mostly to a channeling of career opportunities. In an undifferentiated organization, entry to and exit from membership is easy and frequent. Leaders emerge rapidly, lateral entry from outside to positions of leadership is quite common, and persistence of leadership over time is rare. As an organization institutionalizes, it stabilizes its membership, entry is more difficult, and turnover is less frequent. Its leadership professionalizes and persists. Recruitment to leadership is more likely to occur from within, and the apprenticeship period lengthens. Thus the organization establishes and "hardens" its outer boundaries.

Such measures as are available for the House of Representatives unmistakably show this process at work. In the 18th and 19th centuries, the turnover of Representatives at each election was enormous. Excluding the Congress of 1789, when of course everyone started new, turnover of House members exceeded fifty percent in fifteen elections—the last of which was held in 1882. In the 20th century, the highest incidence of turnover (37.2 percent—almost double the twentieth century median) occurred in the Roosevelt landslide of 1932—a figure exceeded forty-seven times—in other words almost all the time—in the 18th and 19th centuries. As Table 1 and Figure 1 make clear, there has been a distinct decline in the rate at which new members are introduced into the House. Table 2 and Figure 2 make a similar point with data that are partially independent; they show that the overall stability of membership, as measured by the mean terms of members (total number of terms served divided by total number of Representatives) has been on the rise.

These two tables provide a fairly good indication of what has happened over the years to rank-and-file members of the House. Another method of investigating the extent to which an institution has established boundaries is to consider its leaders, how they are recruited, what happens to them, and most particularly the extent to which the institution permits lateral entry to and exit from positions of leadership.

The classic example of lateral movement—possibly the most impressive such record in American history—is of course contained in the kaleidoscopic career of Henry Clay, seventh Speaker of the House. Before his first election to the House, Clay had already served two terms in the Kentucky House of Representatives, and had been sent by the legislature to the U.S. Senate for two non-consecutive short terms. Instead of returning to the Senate in 1811, he ran for the Lexington seat in the U.S. House and was elected. He took his seat on March 4, 1811, and eight months later was elected Speaker at the age of 34. Three years later, he resigned and was appointed a commissioner to negotiate the Treaty of Ghent with Great Britain. The next year, he returned to Congress, where he was again promptly elected Speaker. In 1820 he resigned once again and left public office for two years. But in 1823 he returned to the House, served as Speaker two more terms, and then resigned again, to become Secretary of State in John Quincy Adams' cabinet. In 1831, Clay became a freshman Senator. He remained in the Senate until 1844, when he resigned his seat. Five years later he re-entered the Senate, this time remaining until his death in 1852. Three times (in 1824, 1832, 1844) he was a candidate for president.[10]

Clay's career was remarkable, no doubt, even in a day and age when the boundaries of the House of Representatives were only lightly guarded and leadership in the House was relatively open to lateral entry. But the point to be emphasized here is that Clay's swift rise to the Speakership is only slightly atypical for the period before the turn of the 20th century.

Table 3 demonstrates that there has been a change over time in the seniority of men selected for the Speakership. Before 1899, the mean years of service of members selected for the Speakership was six; after 1899, the mean rises steeply to twenty-six. Figure 3 and Table 4 summarize the gist of the finding in compact form.

---

[10] On Clay, see Bernard Mayo, *Henry Clay: Spokesman of the New West* (Boston: Houghton Mifflin, 1937); Glyndon G. Van Deusen, *The Life of Henry Clay* (Boston: Little, Brown, 1937); Mary Parker Follett, *The Speaker of the House of Representatives* (New York: Longman's, Green, 1896), pp. 69–82; and Booth Mooney, *Mr. Speaker* (Chicago: Follett, 1964), pp. 21–48.

Table 1—The Establishment of Boundaries: Decline in Percentage of First Term Members, U.S. House of Representatives, 1789–1965

Congress	Year of 1st Term	% 1st Term Members	Congress	Year of 1st Term	% 1st Term Members
1	1789	100.0	45	1877	46.6
2	1791	46.5	46	1879	42.3
3	1793	56.5	47	1881	31.8
4	1795	38.9	48	1883	51.5
5	1797	43.1	49	1885	38.0
6	1799	36.0	50	1887	35.6
7	1801	42.5	51	1889	38.1
8	1803	46.9	52	1891	43.8
9	1805	39.9	53	1893	38.1
10	1807	36.2	54	1895	48.6
11	1809	35.9	55	1897	37.9
12	1811	38.5	56	1899	30.1
13	1813	52.6	57	1901	24.4
14	1815	42.9	58	1903	31.3
15	1817	59.2	59	1905	21.0
16	1819	40.8	60	1907	22.5
17	1821	45.2	61	1909	19.9
18	1823	43.2	62	1911	30.5
19	1825	39.4	63	1913	34.4
20	1827	33.2	64	1915	27.2
21	1829	41.0	65	1917	16.0
22	1831	38.0	66	1919	22.7
23	1833	53.7	67	1921	23.6
24	1835	40.0	68	1923	27.1
25	1837	48.6	69	1925	16.3
26	1839	46.3	70	1927	13.3
27	1841	37.7	71	1929	17.7
28	1843	66.7	72	1931	19.0
29	1845	49.0	73	1933	37.2
30	1847	50.4	74	1935	23.4
31	1849	53.1	75	1937	22.7
32	1851	53.3	76	1939	25.5
33	1853	60.5	77	1941	17.0
34	1855	57.5	78	1943	22.9
35	1857	40.2	79	1945	15.8
36	1859	45.1	80	1947	24.1
37	1861	53.9	81	1949	22.3
38	1863	58.1	82	1951	14.9
39	1865	44.3	83	1953	19.5
40	1867	46.0	84	1955	11.7
41	1869	49.2	85	1957	9.9
42	1871	46.5	86	1959	18.2
43	1873	52.0	87	1961	12.6
44	1875	58.0	88	1963	15.2
			89	1965	20.9

Data for 1st through 68th Congresses are from Stuart A. Rice, *Quantitative Methods in Politics* (New York: Knopf, 1928), pp. 296–297. Data for 69th through 89th Congresses are calculated from *Congressional Directories.*

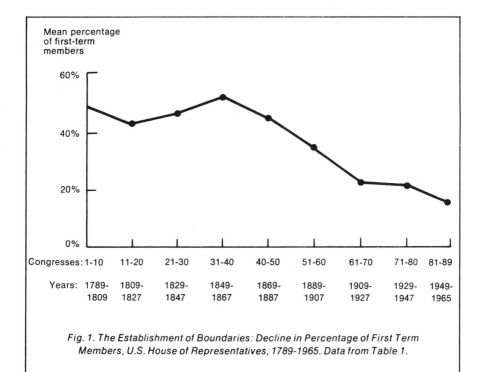

Fig. 1. *The Establishment of Boundaries: Decline in Percentage of First Term Members, U.S. House of Representatives, 1789-1965. Data from Table 1.*

Just as 19th-century Speakers arrived early at the pinnacle of House leadership, many left early as well and went on to other things: freshman Senators, state legislators, Cabinet members, and judges in the state courts. One became President of the U.S., one a Justice of the Supreme Court, one a Minister to Russia, one the Mayor of Auburn, New York, and one the Receiver-General of the Pennsylvania land office. Indeed, of the first twenty-seven men to be Speaker, during the first eighty-six years of the Republic, *none* died while serving in the House of Representatives. In contrast, of the last ten Speakers, six died while serving, and of course one other sits in the House today. Table 5 and Figure 4 give the relevant information for all Speakers.

The importance of this information about Speakers' careers is that it gives a strong indication of the development of the Speakership as a singular occupational specialty. In earlier times, the Speakership seems to have been regarded as a position of political leadership capable of being interchanged with other, comparable positions of public responsibility—and indeed a high incidence of this sort of interchange is recorded in the careers of 19th century Speakers. That this sort of interchange is most unusual today suggests—as do the other data presented in this section—that one important feature in the development of the

Table 2—The Establishment of Boundaries: Increase in Terms Served by Incumbent Members of the U.S. House of Representatives, 1789–1963

Congress	Beginning Term	Mean Terms of Service[a]	Congress	Beginning Term	Mean Terms of Service[a]
1	1789	1.00	45	1877	2.11
2	1791	1.54	46	1879	2.21
3	1793	1.64	47	1881	2.56
4	1795	2.00	48	1883	2.22
5	1797	2.03	49	1885	2.41
6	1799	2.23	50	1887	2.54
7	1801	2.25	51	1889	2.61
8	1803	2.14	52	1891	2.44
9	1805	2.36	53	1893	2.65
10	1807	2.54	54	1895	2.25
11	1809	2.71	55	1897	2.59
12	1811	2.83	56	1899	2.79
13	1813	2.31	57	1901	3.11
14	1815	2.48	58	1903	3.10
15	1817	1.93	59	1905	3.48
16	1819	2.15	60	1907	3.61
17	1821	2.23	61	1909	3.84
18	1823	2.29	62	1911	3.62
19	1825	2.42	63	1913	3.14
20	1827	2.68	64	1915	3.44
21	1829	2.55	65	1917	3.83
22	1831	2.59	66	1919	3.74
23	1833	2.15	67	1921	3.69
24	1835	2.23	68	1923	3.57
25	1837	2.13	69	1925	3.93
26	1839	2.17	70	1927	4.26
27	1841	2.30	71	1929	4.49
28	1843	1.76	72	1931	4.48
29	1845	1.90	73	1933	3.67
30	1847	2.00	74	1935	3.71
31	1849	1.92	75	1937	3.84
32	1851	1.84	76	1939	3.91
33	1853	1.69	77	1941	4.24
34	1855	1.81	78	1943	4.22
35	1857	2.04	79	1945	4.50
36	1859	2.02	80	1947	4.34
37	1861	1.83	81	1949	4.42
38	1863	1.75	82	1951	4.73
39	1865	2.00	83	1953	4.69
40	1867	2.12	84	1955	5.19
41	1869	2.04	85	1957	5.58
42	1871	2.11	86	1959	5.37
43	1873	2.07	87	1961	5.65
44	1875	1.92	88	1963	5.65

[a] Total number of terms served divided by total number of Representatives.

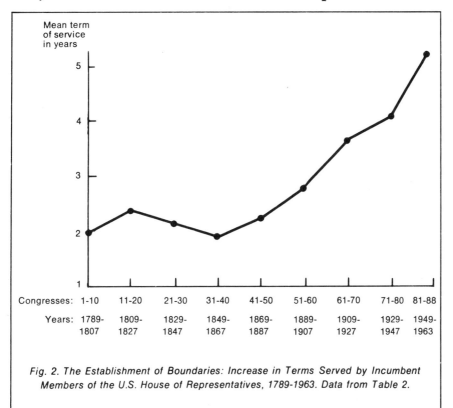

Fig. 2. The Establishment of Boundaries: Increase in Terms Served by Incumbent
Members of the U.S. House of Representatives, 1789-1963. Data from Table 2.

U.S. House of Representatives has been its differentiation from other organizations in the political system, a stabilization of its membership, and a growing specialization of its leaders to leadership of the House as a separate career.[11]

[11] This pattern has been suggested before, by Douglas Price and myself, in unpublished papers (see Footnote 3). It is apparently not unique to the House. David Rothman, on what seem to me to be tenuous grounds, suggests something similar for the U.S. Senate in *Politics and Power: The U.S. Senate 1869–1901* (Cambridge: Harvard University Press, 1966). Consider, for a better example, where the United States gets its military leaders today and compare with this observation on the Mexican war period:

The President [Polk] now undertook to offset this Whig advantage by making a number of Democratic generals. . . . He thereupon proceeded to name numerous Democrats to command the new divisions and brigades. . . . Even this flock of Democratic generals did not erase Polk's fears. After he had committed the command to Scott he considered giving the top authority to a civilian. He wanted to commission Senator Thomas Hart Benton a lieutenant general, and give him overall command. . . .

(Roy F. Nichols, *The Stakes of Power:* 1845–1877, New York: Hill and Wang, 1961, pp. 16, 17.) One would expect civilians to serve high in the officer corps in wars of total mobilization, such as the Civil War and World War II, but not in a conflict involving only a partial mobilization, such as the Mexican War, Korea or Viet Nam. Nevertheless, the full professionalization of our army took place only in this century. During the Spanish-American War, another war of partial mobilization, the business of fighting was still carried on partially by militia and by federal volunteer regiments—irregulars—who fought side by side with, but independently of, regular troops. See Walter Millis,

Table 3—The Establishment of Boundaries: Years Served in Congress Before First Selection as Speaker

Date of Selection	Speaker	Years	Date of Selection	Speaker	Years
1789	Muhlenberg	1 or less	1861	Grow	10
1791	Trumbull	3	1863	Colfax	8
1795	Dayton	4	1869	Pomeroy	8
1799	Sedgwick	11	1869	Blaine	6
1801	Macon	10	1875	Kerr	8
1807	Varnum	12	1876	Randall	13
1811	Clay	1 or less	1881	Keifer	4
1814	Cheves	5	1883	Carlisle	6
1820	Taylor	7	1889	Reed	12
1821	Barbour	6	1891	Crisp	8
1827	Stevenson	6	1899	Henderson	16
1834	Bell	7	1903	Cannon	28
1835	Polk	10	1911	Clark	26
1839	Hunter	2	1919	Gillett	26
1841	White	6	1925	Longworth	22
1843	Jones	8	1931	Garner	26
1845	Davis	6	1933	Rainey	28
1847	Winthrop	8	1935	Byrns	25
1849	Cobb	6	1936	Bankhead	15
1851	Boyd	14	1940	Rayburn	27
1855	Banks	2	1946	Martin	22
1857	Orr	7	1962	McCormack	34
1859	Pennington	1 or less			

Table 4—The Establishment of Boundaries: Summary of Years Served in Congress Before First Selection as Speaker

Term	Before 1899	1899 and after
8 years or less	25	0
9–14 years	8	0
15–20 years	0	2
21–28 years	0	10
	33 Speakers	12 Speakers

Arms and Men (New York: G. P. Putman's Sons, 1956), pp. 167–210. See also a contemporary Washington newsman's report: Arthur Wallace Dunn, *From Harrison to Harding* (New York: G. P. Putnam's Sons, 1922), Vol. I, pp. 240ff, 272–274. Dunn says (Vol. I, pp. 240–41): "From the very beginning politics cut a leading part in the war. The appointments of generals and many other officers were due to influence rather than to merit or fitness. . . . One of these [appointments] was General Joe Wheeler, a member of Congress from Alabama. When he appeared with the twin stars of a major general on his shoulders, he joyously exclaimed: 'It is worth fifteen years of life to die on a battlefield'. . . . 'He will have twenty thousand men under him [remarked a critic] who do not share his opinion, and they will not care to lose fifteen years of their lives to give Joe Wheeler a glorious death.' " See also Samuel P. Huntington, *The Soldier and the State* (Cambridge: Harvard U. Press, 1957), esp. pp. 222–69. Huntington dates the rise of the American military as a profession from after the Civil War.

Consider also the following observation about the U.S. Supreme Court: "In the early years, resignations tended to occur for all sorts of reasons; Chief Justice Jay resigned to assume the governorship of New York, for example. But as the Court's prestige increased, justices found fewer reasons to step down from the bench": Samuel Krislov, *The Supreme Court in the Political Process* (New York: Macmillan, 1965), p. 9. David Danelski has suggested in a personal com-

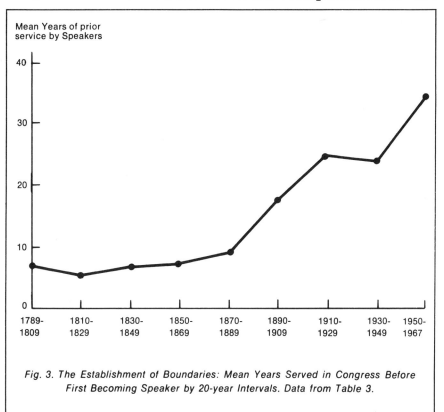

Fig. 3. *The Establishment of Boundaries: Mean Years Served in Congress Before First Becoming Speaker by 20-year Intervals. Data from Table 3.*

munication that while in its earliest years the U.S. Supreme Court was neither a prestigious nor well-bounded institution, it became so more rapidly than the House, as the following table indicates:

Decade Appointed	Number of Justices Appointed	Average Tenure
1789–99	12 justices	10.3 years
1800–09	4	25.0
1810–19	2	29.0
1820–29	3	18.0
1830–39	6	20.3
1840–49	4	18.7
1850–59	3	12.3
1860–69	5	21.0
1870–79	5	18.0
1880–89	7	13.6
1890–99	6	16.1
1900–09	4	14.2
1910–19	7	15.0
1920–29	5	14.0
1930–39	6	20.0 +
		(Black and Douglas still on)
1940–49	8	9.4

It is, of course, not uncommon for students of the Court to view the leadership of Chief Justice Marshall as highly significant in stabilizing the role of the Court in the political system and in

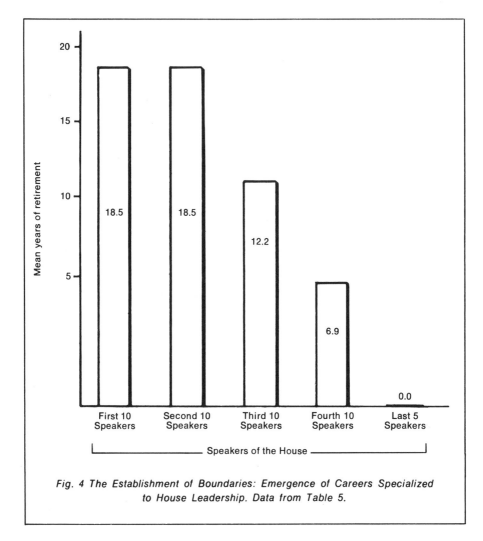

Fig. 4 The Establishment of Boundaries: Emergence of Careers Specialized to House Leadership. Data from Table 5.

enlarging its influence. Other indicators useful in tracing the institutionalization of the federal judiciary might be to study changes in the professional training of persons who have become federal judges, the increase in the number of judges on inferior federal courts, the codification of procedures for dealing with constitutional questions, the routinization of procedures for the granting of certiorari, and the growth of a bureaucracy to administer the federal court system. See, *inter alia*, Mr. Justice Brandeis' dissent in *Ashwander vs. T.V.A.* 297 U.S. 346–48; Edwin McElwain, "The Business of The Supreme Court as Conducted by Chief Justice Hughes," *Harvard Law Review*, 63 (November, 1949), 5–26; Merlo J. Pusey, *Charles Evans Hughes* (New York: Macmillan, 1951), Vol. II, pp. 603–90; Frederick Bernays Wiener, "The Supreme Court's New Rules," *Harvard Law Review*, 68 (November, 1954), 20–94; and Chief Justice Vinson's address before the American Bar Association, "The Work of the Federal Courts," September 7, 1949, reprinted in part in Walter F. Murphy and C. Herman Pritchett (eds.), *Courts, Judges and Politics* (N.Y.: Random House, 1961), pp. 54–58.

Table 5—The Establishment of Boundaries: Emergence of Careers Specialized to House Leadership

Speaker (term)	Elapsed years between last day of service as Representative and death	How Speakers finished their careers
1. Muhlenberg (1789–90, 1793–94)	6	Receiver-general of Pennsylvania Land Office
2. Trumbull (1791–92)	14	Governor of Connecticut
3. Dayton (1795–98)	25	Senator 1805; private life
4. Sedgwick (1799–1800)	12	Judge of Supreme Court of Massachusetts
5. Macon (1801–06)	17	Senate
6. Varnum (1807–10)	10	U.S. Senate and State Senate, Massachusetts
7. Clay (1811–13, 1815–19, 1823–24)	27	Senate
8. Cheves (1814)	42	President, Bank of U.S.; Chief Commissioner of Claims under Treaty of Ghent; private life
9. Taylor (1820, 1825–26)	21	State Senate, New York; private life
10. Barbour (1821–22)	11	Associate Justice, U.S. Supreme Court
11. Stevenson (1827–33)	23	Minister to Great Britain; Rector, University of Virginia
12. Bell (1834)	28	Senate; private life
13. Polk (1835–38)	10	President of U.S.
14. Hunter (1839–40)	40	State Treasurer, Virginia; Collector, Tappahannock, Virginia
15. White (1841–42)	1	Judge, 19th Judicial District, Virginia
16. Jones (1843–44)	3	Representative to Virginia State House of Delegates and Speaker
17. Davis (1845–46)	12	U.S. Commissioner to China, Governor of the Oregon Territory
18. Winthrop (1847–48)	44	Senator by appointment; unsuccessful candidate for Senate, Governor; private life
19. Cobb (1849–50)	11	Secretary of Treasury, Buchanan cabinet; Confederate major general; private life
20. Boyd (1851–54)	4	Lt. Governor of Kentucky
21. Banks (1855–56)	3	Served many nonconsecutive terms *after* Speakership; unsuccessful candidate; private life
22. Orr (1857–58)	14	Minister to Russia
23. Pennington (1859–60)	1	Failed of reelection; died soon after
24. Grow (1861–62)	4	Speaker in 37th; later private life; later still reelected to Congress; declined renomination; private life
25. Colfax (1863–68)	16	Private Life; Vice-President
26. Pomeroy (1869)	36	Speaker 1 day; Mayor of Auburn, New York; private life
27. Blaine (1869–74)	17	Secretary of State; President, Pan-American Congress
28. Kerr (1875)	0	Speaker at his death, 1876
29. Randall (1876–80)	0	House of Representatives
30. Keifer (1881–82)	22	Not renominated to House after served as Speaker; Major General in Spanish American War; Returned later to House; private life
31. Carlisle (1883–88)	20	Senate, Secretary of Treasury; private life
32. Reed (1889–90, 1895–98)	3	Private life; law practice

Table 5 (continued)

Speaker (term)	Elapsed years between last day of service as Representative and death	How Speakers finished their careers
33. Crisp (1891–94)	0	U.S. House of Representatives (nominated for Senate at time of death)
34. Henderson (1899–1902)	3	Private life; retired, House of Representatives
35. Cannon (1903–10)	3	Retired, House of Representatives
36. Clark (1911–18)	0	House of Representatives
37. Gillett (1919–24)	10	Senate; private life
38. Longworth (1925–30)	0	House of Representatives
39. Garner (1931–32)	32+	Vice-President; private life
40. Rainey (1933–34)	0	House of Representatives, Speaker
41. Byrns (1935–36)	0	House of Representatives, Speaker
42. Bankhead (1936–39)	0	House of Representatives, Speaker
43. Rayburn 1940–45, 1947–52, 1955–61)	0	House of Representatives, Speaker
44. Martin (1946–47, 1953–54)	1+	Defeated for renomination, 1966, in his 82nd year and his 44th consecutive year of House service
45. McCormack (1962–67)	0+	House of Representatives, presently Speaker (1967)

The development of a specifically House leadership, the increase in the overall seniority of members, and the decrease in the influx of newcomers at any point in time have the effect not only of separating the House from other organizations in the political system, but also of facilitating the growth of stable ways of doing business within the institution, as we shall see shortly.

The Growth of Internal Complexity

Simple operational indices of institutional complexity and universalistic-automated decision making are less easy to produce in neat and comparable time series. As for the growth of internal complexity, this is easy enough to establish impressionistically, but the most obvious quantitative measure presents a drastic problem of interpretation. The temptation is great to measure internal differentiation by simply counting the number of standing committees in each Congress. This would produce a curiously curvilinear result, because in 1946 the number of standing committees was reduced from 48 to 19, and the number has since crept up only as far as 20.[12]

But the "streamlining," as it was called,[13] of 1946 can hardly be said to have reduced the internal differentiation of the House. On the contrary, by explicitly

[12] The combined totals of standing committees and subcommittees might be a better guide; but reliable information about subcommittees only exists for the most recent two decades.

[13] I believe the word is George Galloway's. See *Congress at the Crossroads* (New York: Crowell, 1946), p. 340.

delineating the legislative jurisdictions of the committees, by consolidating committees with parallel and overlapping functions, by assigning committees exclusive oversight responsibilities over agencies of the executive branch, and by providing committees with expanded staff aid, the 1946 reorganization contributed to, rather than detracted from, the reliance of the House upon committees in the conduct of its business. Thus the mute testimony of the sheer numbers of committees cannot be accepted as an appropriate index of internal complexity. I shall therefore attempt a more anecdotal accounting procedure.

Briefly, the growth of internal complexity can be shown in three ways: in the growth in the autonomy and importance of committees, in the growth of specialized agencies of party leadership, and in the general increase in the provision of various emoluments and auxiliary aids to members in the form of office space, salaries, allowances, staff aid, and committee staffs.

A wholly satisfactory account of the historical development of the House committee system does not exist. But perhaps I can swiftly sketch in a number of plausible conclusions from the literature.

From the perspective of the present-day United States, the use of standing committees by Congress is scarcely a controversial issue.[14] Yet, in the beginning the House relied only very slightly upon standing committees. Instead of the present-day system, where bills are introduced in great profusion and automatically shunted to one or another of the committees whose jurisdictions are set forth in the rules, the practice in the first, and early Congresses was for subjects to be debated initially in the whole House and general principles settled upon, before they were parceled out for further action—fact-finding, detailed consideration or the proposal of a bill—to any one of four possible locations: an officer in the Executive Branch, a Committee of the Whole, a Select Committee formed *ad hoc* for the reception of a particular subject, or a standing committee. Generally, one of the alternatives to standing committees was used.

Of the First Congress, Harlow writes:

The outstanding feature of procedure in the House was the important part played by the Committee of the Whole. Much of the business in the House of Delegates of Virginia was transacted in that way, and the Virginians were influential enough to impose their methods upon the federal House. . . . It was in Committee of the Whole that Congress worked out the first tarriff bill, and also the main outlines of such important measures as the laws organizing the executive departments. After the general principles were once determined, select committees would be appointed to work out

---

14 It certainly is, on the other hand, in the present-day United Kingdom, where purely legislative committees are regarded as a threat to the cohesion of the national political parties because they would give the parliamentary parties special instruments with which they could develop independent policy judgments and expertise and excercise oversight over an executive which is, after all, not formally constituted as an entity separate from Parliament. Thus committees can be construed as fundamentally inimical to unified Cabinet government. For an overview see Bernard Crick, *The Reform of Parliament* (Garden City: Doubleday Anchor, 1965); *The Political Quarterly*, 36 (July-September, 1965); and Andrew Hill and Anthony Whichelow, *What's Wrong with Parliament?* (Harmondsworth: Penguin, 1964), esp. pp. 64–82. See also a most illuminating essay by Robert C. Fried on the general conditions under which various political institutions (including legislatures) are strong or weak within their political systems: *Comparative Political Institutions* (New York: Macmillan, 1966), esp. p. 31.

the details, and to frame bills in accordance with the decision already agreed upon in Committee of the Whole. Considerable work was done by these select committees, especially after the first session.[15]

And Alexander says:

In the early history of the House the select committee . . . was used exclusively for the consideration of bills, resolutions, and other legislative matters.[16] As business increased and kindred subjects became scattered, however, a tendency to concentrate inaugurated a system of standing committees. It rooted itself slowly. There was an evident distrust of the centralizing influence of permanent bodies. Besides, it took important business from the many and gave it to a few, one standing committee of three or five members often taking the place of half a dozen select committees.[17]

It is difficult to disentangle the early growth of the standing committee system from concurrent developments in the party system. For as Alexander Hamilton took control of the administration of George Washington, and extended his influence toward men of like mind in Congress, the third alternative to standing committees—reference to a member of the Executive Branch—became an important device of the Federalist majority in the House.

By the winter of 1790 [Harlow writes] Hamilton was attracting attention because of his influence over Congress. . . . His ready intelligence grasped the truth at once that Jefferson spent more than ten years learning: that not even the Constitution of the United States could keep apart two such inseparable factors in government as executive and legislature.[18]

In the first two Congresses Hamilton is said to have used the Federalist caucus to guide debate in the Committee of the Whole, and also to have arranged for key financial measures to be referred directly to himself for detailed drafting.[19] This practice led, in the Second Congress, to sharp clashes with followers of Jefferson, who

made it perfectly clear that if they should ever get the upper hand in Congress, they would make short work of Hamilton, and restore to the House what they considered to be its constitutional authority over finance.[20]

[15] Ralph V. Harlow, *The History of Legislative Methods in the Period Before 1825* (New Haven: Yale, 1917), pp. 127–28. See also Joseph Cooper, "Jeffersonian Attitudes Toward Executive Leadership and Committee Development in the House of Representatives 1789–1829," *Western Political Quarterly*, 18 (March, 1965), 45–63; and Cooper, "Congress and Its Committees in the Legislative Process" (unpublished Ph.D. dissertation, Department of Government, Harvard University, 1960), pp. 1–65.

[16] On changes in the use of select committees, Lauros G. McConachie says: "Business of the earlier Houses went to hosts of select committees. At least three hundred and fifty were raised in the Third Congress. A special committee had to be formed for every petty claim. A bill founded on the report of one small committee had to be recommended to, or carefully drafted by, yet another committee. But the decline in the number of these select committees was strikingly rapid. In twenty years, at the Congress of 1813–1815 with its three war sessions, it had fallen to about seventy": *Congressional Committees* (New York: Crowell, 1898), p. 124. See also Galloway, *op. cit.*, p. 88.

[17] DeAlva Stanwood Alexander, *History and Procedure of the House of Representatives* (Boston: Houghton-Mifflin, 1916), p. 228.

[18] Harlow, *op. cit.*, p. 141.

[19] *Ibid.*, p. 120–150.

[20] *Ibid.*, p. 151.

The Republicans did in fact gain the upper hand in the Third Congress (elected in 1792) and they restored detailed power over finances to the Committee of the Whole. This did not work satisfactorily, however, and in the Fourth Congress a Committee on Ways and Means was formed. Harlow says:

The appointment of . . . standing committees, particularly . . . Ways and Means, was in a way a manifestation of the Republican theory of government. From their point of view, the members of the House, as the direct representatives of the voters, ought to be the mainspring of the whole system. Hitherto, the Federalists had sold their birthright by permitting the executive to take a more active part in the government than was warranted by the Constitution. The Republicans now planned to bring about the proper balance between the different branches, by broadening at once the scope of the operations of the House, and restricting the executive. It was the better to enable the House to take its assigned part that the new type of organization was worked out. Just as the heads of departments were looked upon as agents of the executive, so the committees would be considered as the agents of the House.[21]

During the presidency of Thomas Jefferson, committees were constituted and employed as agents of the President's faction in Congress which was in most matters actively led by the President himself. Binkley says:

. . . When the House of Representatives had elected its Speaker and the committee chairmen had been appointed it was apparent to the discerning that lieutenants of the President had not appointed them, but his wishes, confidentially expressed, had determined them just as surely as if he had formally and publicly nominated them. Here was the fulfillment of Marshall's prediction that Jefferson would "embody himself in the House of Representatives."[22]

There is, however, some doubt as to Jefferson's absolute mastery over committee appointments, since it is also reported that Speaker Macon was extremely important in constituting the committees, and, in particular, in keeping John Randolph on as chairman of the Ways and Means Committee for some time after Randolph had repeatedly and violently broken with the Jefferson administration.[23]

Recently the suggestion has been made that the direct evidence is slight and contradictory that political parties in Congress went through rapid organization and differentiation in the earliest years of the Republic. This revisionist interpretation lays greater stress upon boarding house cliques, more or less sectional and more or less ideologically factional in their composition, as the heretofore neglected building blocks out of which the more conventionally partisan Congressional politics of the Jacksonian era eventually grew.[24]

[21] *Ibid.*, pp. 157–58.

[22] Wilfred E. Binkley, *President and Congress* (New York: Vintage, 1962), p. 64.

[23] Of Randolph's initial appointment as chairman of the Ways and Means Committee, in the Seventh Congress, Noble Cunningham writes: "in view of the close friendship of [Speaker] Macon and Randolph, it is unlikely that Jefferson had any influence in the choice of Randolph as Chairman of the Ways and Means Committee": *Jeffersonian Republicans in Power* (Chapel Hill: University of North Carolina Press, 1963), p. 73. See also Henry Adams, *John Randolph* (Boston: Houghton-Mifflin, 1886), pp. 54–55, 123–165ff; and Adams, *History of the United States of America During the Administrations of Thomas Jefferson and James Madison* (New York: Boni, 1930), Vol. III, p. 128.

[24] This interpretation is the brilliant achievement of James S. Young in *The Washington Community: 1800–1828* (New York: Columbia University Press, 1966). It harmonizes with Richard P. McCormick's notion of a series of historically discrete American party systems. See McCormick, *The Second American Party System* (Chapel Hill: University of North Carolina Press, 1966).

But even revisionists concede to Jefferson a large influence over Congressional politics; the conventional accounts of the growth of the committee system are pretty much undisturbed by their critique. In essence, by the early years of the 19th century, the House committee system had passed through two distinct phases: the no-committee, Hamiltonian era, in which little or no internal differentiation within the institution was visible; and a Jeffersonian phase, in which factional alignments had begun to develop—these were exploited by the brilliant and incessant maneuverings of the President himself, who selected his lieutenants and confidants from the ranks of Congress *ad hoc*, as political requirements and opportunities dictated. During this period a small number of standing committees existed, but were not heavily relied upon. Their jurisdictions were not so securely fixed that the Speaker could not instead appoint select committees to deal with business that ought to have been sent to them.[25]

The advent of Henry Clay and the victory of the War Hawk faction in the elections of 1810 brought the committee system to its third phase. Clay for the first time used the Speaker's prerogative of appointment of members to committees independently of Presidential designs. There is some question whether Clay's appointment policies were calculated to further his policy preferences or merely his popularity (and hence his Presidential ambitions) within the factionally divided house,[26] but there seems no reason to doubt that Clay won for the Speakership a new measure of independence as a power base in the American political system. Under Clay five House committees were constituted to oversee expenditures in executive departments, the first major institutionalization of the Congressional function of oversight. William N. Chambers writes:

[By] 1814 the committee system had become the dominant force in the chamber. Thus effective power was exercised not by the President, as had been the case with Jefferson, but by factional Congressional leaders working through the speakership, the caucus, and the committees.[27]

For the next 100 years the committee system waxed and waned more or less according to the ways in which committees were employed by the party or faction that dominated the House and elected the Speaker. Figures from the latter decades of the 19th century testify amply to the leeway afforded Speakers— especially new ones—in constituting committees regardless of their prior composition.[28] In part, it was Speaker Cannon's increasing use of this prerogative in an attempt to keep control of his fragmenting party that triggered the revolt against his Speakership in 1910–1911, and that led to the establishment of the committee system as we know it today.[29]

[25] See Wilfred Binkley, "The President and Congress," *Journal of Politics*, 11 (February, 1949), 65–79.

[26] See Young, *op. cit.*, pp. 131–135.

[27] William Nisbet Chambers, *Political Parties in a New Nation* (New York: Oxford, 1963), p. 194.

[28] See Nelson W. Polsby, Miriam Gallaher and Barry Spencer Rundquist, "The Growth of the Seniority System in the Selection of Committee Chairman in the U.S. House of Representatives" (mimeo., October, 1967).

[29] *Ibid.* Chang-wei Chiu says, "The power of appointing committees by the Speaker was a real issue in the attempts to reform the House. In the eyes of the insurgents no change would be of any real and permanent value to the country if that change did not take away from the Speaker the power of appointing standing committees": *The Speaker of The House of Representatives Since 1896* (New York: Columbia University Press, 1928), pp. 71–72.

Under the fourth, decentralized, phase of the committee system, committees have won solid institutionalized independence from party leaders both inside and outside Congress. Their jurisdictions are fixed in the rules; their composition is largely determined and their leadership entirely determined by the automatic operation of seniority. Their work is increasingly technical and specialized, and the way in which they organize internally to do their work is entirely at their own discretion. Committees nowadays have developed an independent sovereignty of their own, subject only to very infrequent reversals and modifications of their powers by House party leaders backed by large and insistent majorities.

To a degree, the development over the last sixty years of an increasingly complex machinery of party leadership within the House cross-cuts and attenuates the independent power of committees. Earlier, the leading faction in the House elected the Speaker and the Speaker in turn distributed the chairmanships of key committees to his principal allies and opponents. Thus the work of the House was centralized to the extent that the leading faction in the House was centralized. But differences of opinion are not uncommon among qualified observers. The Jeffersonian era, for example, is widely regarded as a high point of centralization during the 19th century. Harlow reports:

From 1801 to 1808 the floor leader was distinctly the lieutenant of the executive. William B. Giles, who was actually referred to as "the premier, or prime minister," Caesar A. Rodney, John Randolph of Roanoke, and Wilson Cary Nicholas all held that honorable position at one time or another. It was their duty to look after party interests in the House, and in particular to carry out the commands of the President. The status of these men was different from that of the floor leader of today. . . . They were presidential agents, appointed by the executive, and dismissed at his pleasure.[30]

But another observer, a Federalist congressman quoted by Noble Cunningham, suggests that the Jeffersonian group was not at all times well organized:

The ruling faction in the legislature have not yet been able to understand each other. . . . There evidently appears much rivalry and jealousy among the leaders. S[amuel] Smith measures, experience and great address ought to give him a preponderance in all their thinks his whilst Nicholson evidently looks upon these pretensions of his colleague with contempt, and Giles thinks the first representative of the Ancient Dominion ought certainly on all important occasions to take the lead, and Johnny Randolph is perfectly astonished that his great abilities should be overlooked. There is likewise a great number of other persons who are impatient of control and disposed to revolt at any attempts at discipline.[31]

This certainly squares with the reports of Jefferson's own continued attempts, also revealed in his letters, to recruit men to the House with whom he could work.[32]

Despite Jefferson's difficulties, he was the most consistently successful of all

---

[30] Harlow, *op. cit.*, p. 176.

[31] Cunningham, *op. cit.*, p. 74. The quotation is from a letter from Roger Griswold to John Rutledge, December 14, 1801.

[32] See Jefferson's letters to Barnabas Bidwell and Wilson Cary Nicholas cited in *ibid.*, pp. 89–92. Also Henry Adams, *History, op. cit.*, Vol. III, pp. 166–71.

the 19th century Presidents in "embodying himself in the House of Representatives." After Jefferson, the Speaker became a power in his own right; not infrequently he was a candidate for the Presidency himself, and the House was more or less organized around his, rather than the President's, political interests. There was no formal position of majority leader; the leading spokesman for the majority party on the floor was identified by personal qualities of leadership and by the favor of the Speaker (or in the Jeffersonian era, of the President) rather than by his institutional position.[33]

Later, however, the chairman of the Ways and Means Committee—a key post reserved for the chief lieutenant of the Speaker—became *de facto* floor leader, a natural consequence of his responsibilities in managing the tariff bills that were so important in 19th century congressional politics. Occasionally the chairman of the Committee on Appropriations was the *de facto* leader, especially during periods of war mobilization, when the power of the House in the political system was coextensive with the power of the purse.[34] In the last part of the 19th century, however, the Committee on Appropriations was temporarily dismantled, and the chairman of the Ways and Means Committee began to receive formal designation as party leader.

The high point of the Ways and Means chairman's power came in the aftermath of the 1910 revolt against the Speaker. The power of committee appointments was for Democrats lodged in the Ways and Means Committee. Chairman Oscar Underwood, in cooperation with President Wilson, for a time (1911–1915) eclipsed the Speaker and the committee chairmen by operating the majority party by caucus.[35]

But Underwood's successor as chairman of Ways and Means, Claude Kitchin (majority leader 1915–1919), disapproved of Wilson's war policies; this made it

[33] Randall Ripley, in his forthcoming Brookings study, *Party Leadership in the House of Representatives* (mimeo, 1966) says: "The Majority leader did not become a separate and consistently identifiable party figure until some time around the turn of the century." Ripley also discusses the indeterminacy of the minority leadership in the mid-19th century. Of an earlier period (1800–1828) Young (*op. cit.*, pp. 126–27) writes: "Party members elected no leaders, designated no functionaries to speak in their behalf or to carry out any legislative task assignments. The party had no whips, no seniority leaders. There were no committees on committees, no steering committees, no policy committees: none of the organizational apparatus that marks the twentieth-century congressional parties...." On pp. 127–30 Young argues that although there were a number of party leaders in the House, there was no fixed majority leader. "[W]hile the names of Randolph, Giles, Nicholas and Rodney appear more frequently, at least twenty Republican legislators in the eight years of Jefferson's administration are either explicitly identified as leaders in the documentary record or are associated with activities strongly suggesting a role of presidential spokesmanship" (p. 130).

[34] From 1865–1869, for example, Thaddeus Stevens left the chairmanship of Ways and Means (a post he had held from 1861–1865) to become chairman of the new Committee on Appropriations. See Samuel W. McCall, *Thaddeus Stevens* (Boston: Houghton-Mifflin, 1899), pp. 259–60. McCall says, oddly, that at the time the Appropriations Committee was not very important, but this is hard to credit. From 1895–1899, Joseph G. Cannon was floor leader and chairman of Appropriations. See Edward T. Taylor, *A History of the Committee on Appropriations* (House Document 299, 77th Congress, 1st Session) (Washington, Government Printing Office, 1941).

[35] See George Rothwell Brown, *The Leadership of Congress* (Indianapolis: Bobbs Merrill, 1922), pp. 175–77, 183–84; Oscar King Davis, "Where Underwood Stands," *The Outlook* (December 23, 1911), 197–201. At p. 199: "Every move Mr. Underwood has made, every bill he has brought forward, he first submitted to a caucus.... Not until the last man had had his say was the vote taken that was to bind them all to united action in the House. Every time that vote has been either unanimous or nearly so, and invariably it has approved Mr. Underwood." See also Binkley, "The President and Congress," *op. cit.*, p. 72.

cumbersome and impractical for the leader of the majority on the floor and in caucus to hold this job by virtue of what was becoming an automatic succession through seniority to the chairmanship of Ways and Means. A separation of the two roles was effected after the Democrats became the minority in 1919.[36] Ever since then, the majority leader's job has existed as a fulltime position; the incumbent now holds a nominal, junior committee post but he rarely attends committee meetings. At the same time, the majority leader has become less of a President's man, and the caucus is now dormant as an instrument of party leadership—although it now sometimes becomes a vehicle, especially at the opening of Congress, for the expression of widespread dissatisfaction by rank-and-file House members. Thus, while binding votes on policy matters have not been put through the caucus by party leaders, the Republican caucus has three times in recent years deposed party leaders and the Democratic caucus has deprived three of its members of their committee seniority.

Formally designated party whips are, like the differentiated post of majority leaders, an innovation principally of the twentieth century. The first whips date back to just before the turn of the century. In the early years, the designation seems to have been quite informal, and it is only recently that an elaborate whip system, with numerous deputies, a small staff, and formal procedures for canvassing members, has been established by both parties in the House.[37]

Thus, we can draw a contrast between the practices of recent and earlier years with respect to formal party leaders other than the Speaker:

(1) Floor leaders in the 20th century are officially designated; in the 19th, they were often informally designated, indefinite, shifting or even competitive, and based on such factors as personal prestige, speaking ability, or Presidential favor.[38]

(2) Floor leaders in recent years are separated from the committee system and elected by party members; earlier they were prominent committee chairmen who were given their posts by the Speaker, sometimes as a side-payment in the formation of a coalition to elect the Speaker.[39]

(3) Floor leaders today rely upon whip systems; before 1897 there were no formally designated whips.

A third indicator of the growth of internal organization is the growth of resources assigned to internal House management, measured in terms of personnel, facilities, and money. Visitors to Washington are not likely to forget the sight of the five large office buildings, three of them belonging to the House, that flank the Capitol. The oldest of these on the House side was built just after the turn of the century, in 1909, when a great many other of our indices show significant changes.

Reliable figures, past or present, on personnel assigned to the House are

---

[36] See Ripley, *op. cit.*; Hasbrouck, *op. cit.*, p. 94; and Alex M. Arnett, *Claude Kitchin and the Wilson War Policies* (Boston: Little, Brown, 1937), pp. 42, 71–72, 75–76, 88–89 and passim.

[37] See Randall B. Ripley, "The Party Whip Organization in the United States House of Representatives" this REVIEW, 58 (September, 1964), 561–76.

[38] See, e.g., Alexander, *op. cit.*, pp. 111–114. "[W]ith very few exceptions, the really eminent debaters . . . were in the Senate; otherwise, MacDuffie [who served 1821–1834], Chief of the Hotspurs, could scarcely have justified his title to floor leader," p. 114.

[39] *Ibid.*, p. 110: "In selecting a floor leader the Speaker often names his party opponent."

Table 6—The Growth of Internal Complexity: Expenditures Made by the House of Representatives[a]

Fiscal Year	Expenditures (1000s dollars)	Fiscal Year	Expenditures (1000s dollars)	Fiscal Year	Expenditures (1000s dollars)
1872	1,952	1915	5,081	1961	47,324
1873	3,340	1916	4,917	1962	50,295
1874	2,687	1917	5,400	1963	52,983
		1918	5,331	1964	55,654
1875	2,030	1919	5,304	1965	58,212
1876	2,201				
1877	2,232	1920	7,059	1966 (est.)	65,905
1878	2,183	1921	6,510	1967 (est.)	70,883
1879	2,230	1922	6,001		
		1923	6,588		
1880	2,137	1924	6,154		
1881	2,191				
1882	2,188	1925	7,761		
1883	2,339	1926	7,493		
1884	2,405	1927	7,526		
		1928	7,623		
1885	2,466	1929	7,813		
1886	2,379				
1887	2,232	1930	8,260		
1888	2,354	1931	8,269		
1889	2,416	1932	8,310		
		1933	7,598		
1890	2,567	1934	7,154		
1891	2,520				
1892	2,323	1935	8,007		
1893	2,478	1936	8,377		
1894	2,844	1937	8,451		
		1938	8,139		
1895	2,945	1939	8,615		
1896	2,843				
1897	3,108	1940	9,375		
1898	2,948	1941	9,511		
1899	3,063	1942	9,678		
		1943	9,361		
1900	2,981	1944	10,944		
1901	3,066	1945	11,660		
1902	3,088				
1903	3,223	1946	14,243		
1904	3,247	1947	16,012		
		1948	18,096		
1905	3,367	1949	18,110		
1906	3,517	1950	20,330		
1907	3,907				
1908	4,725	1951	21,053		
1909	5,005	1952	23,474		
		1953	23,622		
1910	4,897	1954	23,660		
1911	5,066	1955	26,610		
1912	4,741				
1913	5,148	1956	34,587		
1914	5,012	1957	36,738		
		1958	39,524		
		1959	43,882		
		1960	44,207		

[a] *Sources:* U.S. Executive Office of President. Bureau of the Budget. *The Budget of United States Government.* Annual Volumes for 1921–1967. Washington, U.S. Government Printing Office.
U.S. Treasury Department. *Combined Statement of Receipts, Expenditures and Balances of the United States Government.* Annual volumes for 1872–1920. Washington, U.S. Government Printing Office.

impossible to come by; but it is unlikely that a commentator today would agree with the observer early in this century who said:

It is somewhat singular that Congress is one of the few legislative bodies that attempts to do its work almost entirely without expert assistance—without the aid of parliamentary counsel, without bill drafting and revising machinery and without legislative and reference agencies, and until now it has shown little inclination to regard with favor proposals looking toward the introduction of such agencies.[40]

Indeed, the only major contemporary study we have of congressional staff speaks of present "tendencies toward overexpansion of the congressional staff," and says that "Three-fourths of the committee aides interviewed" thought that professional staffs of committees were sufficiently large to handle their present work load.[41]

Needless to say, that work load has grown, and, though it is impossible to say precisely by how much, congressional staffs have grown as well. This is roughly reflected in figures that are more or less comparable over time on that portion of the legislative budget assigned to the House. These figures show the expected increases. However, except for the jump between 1945 and 1946, reflecting the new provisions for staff aid of the Legislative Reorganization Act, the changes in these figures over time are not as abrupt as is the case with other of our time series. Nor would changes over time be even as steep as they are in Table 6 if these figures were corrected for changes in the purchasing power of the dollar. So we must regard this indicator as weak, but nevertheless pointing in the expected direction.

From Particularistic and Discretionary to Universalistic and Automated Decision Making

The best evidence we have of a shift away from discretionary and toward automatic decision making is the growth of seniority as a criterion determining committee rank and the growth of the practice of deciding contested elections to the House strictly on the merits.

The literature on seniority presents a welter of conflicting testimony. Some commentators date the seniority system from 1910;[42] others say that seniority as a criterion for determining the committee rank of members was in use well

---

[40] James W. Garner, "Executive Participation in Legislation as a Means of Increasing Legislative Efficiency," *Proceedings of the American Political Science Association at its Tenth Annual Meeting* (Baltimore: Waverly Press, 1914), p. 187.

[41] Kenneth Kofmehl, *Professional Staffs of Congress* (Lafayette, Indiana: Purdue University Press, 1962), pp. 97–99. The quotation is at p. 99. Kofmehl presents a short, nonquantitative historical sketch of the growth of committee staffs on pp. 3–5. See also Samuel C. Patterson "Congressional Committee Professional Staffing: Capabilities and Constraints," a paper presented at the Planning Conference of the Comparative Administration Group, Legislative Services Project, Planting Fields, New York, December 8–10, 1967; and Lindsay Rogers "The Staffing of Congress," *Political Science Quarterly,* 56 (March, 1941), 1–22.

[42] George B. Galloway, *op. cit.,* p. 187; George Goodwin, Jr., "The Seniority System in Congress" this Review, 53 (June, 1959), p. 417.

Table 7—The Growth of Universalism: Violations of Seniority in the Appointment of Committee Chairmen, U.S. House of Representatives, 1881–1963

Percentage of Committees on which the chairman was not selected by seniority, averaged by decades

Congress:	47–51	52–56	57–61	62–66
Years:	1881–89	1891–99	1901–09	1911–19
Average:	60.4%	49.4%	19%	30.8%
Violations of Seniority				

Congress:	67–71	72–76	77–81	82–88
Years:	1921–29	1931–39	1941–49	1951–63
Average:	26%	23%	14%	.7%
Violations				

before.[43] Woodrow Wilson's classic account of *Congressional Government* in 1884 pays tribute both to the independence of the committees and their chairmen and to the absolute discretion of the Speaker in the committee appointment process.[44] It is clear that the Speaker has no such power today. In another paper my colleagues and I present a detailed preliminary tabulation and discussion on the extent to which seniority in its contemporary meaning was followed in the selection of committee chairmen in the most recent 40 Congresses.[45] The central finding for our present purposes (summarized in Table 7 and Figure 5) is that the seniority system—an automatic, universally applied, nondiscretionary method of selection—is now always used, but that formerly the process by which chairmen were selected was highly and later partially discretionary.

The figures for before 1911 can be interpreted as indicating the use of the Speaker's discretion in the appointment of committee chairmen. After 1911, when committee appointment powers are vested in committees on committees, the figures principally reflect the growth of the norm that no one man should serve as chairman of more than one committee. Congressmen often sat on a large number of committees, and senior men rose to the top of more than one committee, but allowed less senior men to take the chair, much as the custom presently is in the U.S. Senate. After 1946, when the number of committees was drastically reduced, this practice died out, and a strictly automated system of seniority has asserted itself.

[43] Chiu, *op. cit.*, pp. 68–72; James K. Pollock, Jr., "The Seniority Rule in Congress," *The North American Review*, 222 (1925), 235, 236; Asher Hinds, "The Speaker of the House of Representatives," this REVIEW, 3 (May, 1909), 160–61.

[44] Woodrow Wilson, *Congressional Government* (New York: Meridian Books, 1956) (First edition, 1884). See, for example, on pp. 85–86: "The Speaker is expected to constitute the Committees in accordance with his own political views . . . [and he] generally uses his powers as freely and imperatively as he is expected to use them. He unhesitatingly acts as the legislative chief of his party, organizing the Committees in the interest of this or that policy, not covertly or on the sly, as one who does something of which he is ashamed, but openly and confidently, as one who does his duty. . . ." Compare this with p. 82: "I know not how better to describe our form of government in a single phrase than by calling it a government by the chairmen of the Standing Committees of Congress. This disintegrate ministry, as it figures on the floor of the House of Representatives, has many peculiarities. In the first place, it is made up of the elders of the assembly; for, by custom, seniority in congressional service determines the bestowal of the principal chairmanships. . . ."

[45] Polsby, Gallaher, and Rundquist, *op. cit.*

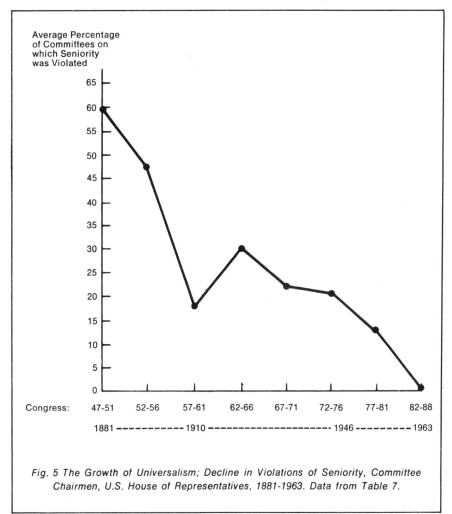

Average Percentage
of Committees on
which Seniority
was Violated

Fig. 5 The Growth of Universalism; Decline in Violations of Seniority, Committee Chairmen, U.S. House of Representatives, 1881-1963. Data from Table 7.

The settlement of contested elections on some basis other than the merits seems in earlier years to have been a common phenomenon. To this point, we can bring the testimony of a number of quotes and anecdotes, widely separated in time. Here are a few examples:

1795: A foreshadowing of future developments arose in the contested election of Joseph B. Varnum, of Massachusetts, in the Fourth Congress. This case became the focus of a struggle for power between the Federalists and the Anti-Federalists. It is an early instance of the triumph of the rule that all too often might makes right, at least in the settlement of election contests in the House of Representatives. Varnum's election was contested on the principal ground that the Board of Selectmen of his home town (of which Board he was a member) had returned sixty votes more than there were qualified voters in the town. Since he had been elected with a certified overall plurality of eleven votes, investigation was warranted. Theodore Sedgwick, leader of the Federalists in the House, suggested that testimony be taken . . . inasmuch as the House alone had the power to compel the town clerk to produce the records containing the names of the illegal voters, if indeed any existed. Varnum, an Anti-Federalist, strongly protested against such a procedure. . . . He proposed . . . that petitioners . . . should present the names of the illegal voters, if they could do so. . . . This was impossible, since only the town clerk had access to the voting records of the town. The Anti-Federalists, who controlled the House at the time, on a party-line vote sustained Varnum's objections . . . in fact, the controlling faction even went so far as to adopt a resolution, again by a partisan vote, declaring that "the charges against [Varnum] are wholly unfounded. . . ." "Thus, amidst an outburst of derisive laughter, the incident closed like a harliquinade."[46]

1860's: I served in my second term on the Committee on Elections. . . . Election cases in the House up to that time were . . . determined entirely by party feeling. Whenever there was a plausible reason for making a contest the dominant party in the House almost always awarded the seat to the man of its own side. There is a well-authenticated story of Thaddeus Stevens, that going into the room of the Committee on Elections, of which he was a member, he found a hearing going on. He asked one of his Republican colleagues what was the point in the case. "There is not much point to it," was the answer. "They are both damned scoundrels." "Well," said Stevens, "which is the Republican damned scoundrel? I want to go for the Republican damned scoundrel."[47]

1869: All traces of a judicial character in these proceedings are fast fading away. . . . Each case is coming to be a mere partisan struggle. At the dictate of party majorities, the Committee [on Elections] must fight, not follow, the law and the evidence. . . . This tendency is so manifest . . . that it has ceased to be questioned, and is now but little resisted . . . [E]fforts . . . to hold the judgments of the Committee on Elections up above the dirty pool of party politics have encountered such bitter and unsparing denunciation, and such rebuke for treason to party fealty, that they are not likely often to be repeated.[48]

1890: The [elections] committee usually divides on the line of party . . . and the House usually follows in the same way. . . . The decision of election cases invariably increases the party which organized the House and . . . appoints the majority of the Committee on Elections. Probably there is not an instance on record where the minority was increased by the decision of contested cases. . . . It may be said that our present method of determining election cases is . . . unjust to members and contestants and fails to secure the representation which the people have chosen.[49]

1895: A most casual inspection of the workings of the present system of deciding election contests will show that it barely maintains the form of a judicial inquiry and that it is thoroughly tainted with the grossest partisanship. . . . When it is alleged that

[46] John Thomas Dempsey, "Control by Congress over the Seating and Disciplining of Members" (unpublished Ph.D. dissertation, The University of Michigan, 1956), pp. 50–51. The final quotation is from Alexander, *op. cit.,* p. 315.

[47] George F. Hoar, *Autobiography of Seventy Years* (New York: Scribner, 1903), Vol. I, p. 268. Hoar claims that during the time he served on the Elections Committee in the Forty-second Congress (1871–73), contested elections were settled on the merits.

[48] Henry L. Dawes, "The Mode of Procedure in Cases of Contested Elections," *Journal of Social Science* (No. 2, 1870), 56–68. Quoted passages are at p. 64. Dempsey, *op. cit.,* pp. 83–84, identifies Dawes as a one-time chairman of the House Committee on Elections. See also C. H. Rammelkamp, "Contested Congressional Elections," *Political Science Quarterly,* 20 (Sept., 1905), 434–35.

[49] Thomas B. Reed, "Contested Elections," *North American Review,* 151 (July, 1890), 112–20. Quoted passages are at pp. 114 and 117. See also Alexander, *op. cit.,* p. 323.

members of a minority do not generally contest seats, a striking tribute is paid to the partisanship of the present system.[50]

1899: The Republican majority in this House [56th Congress] was reduced about fifty from the previous Congress, but before the [first] session closed, a dozen or more Democrats lost their seats in election contests, which gave the Republicans a comfortable majority with which to do business.[51]

1905: Today it is simply a contest between two parties for political influence and the rewards of office, or sometimes a contest between the majority in the House and a constituency of the minority party.... In the period [1865–1905, 39th through 58th Congresses]... the majority deprived itself of seats only nine times, while it deprived the minority of seats eighty-two times.[52]

A journalist writing at the beginning of the twentieth century summarizes the situation as he had encountered it over a twenty-year period:

It may be said ... that there is no fairness whatever exercised in ... contests for seats, especially where the majority needs the vote for party purposes. Hundreds of men have lost their seats in Congress, to which they were justly entitled upon all fair, reasonable, and legal grounds, and others put in their places for purely partisan reasons. This has always been so and doubtless will continue so....[53]

In fact, it has not continued so; nowadays, contested elections are settled with much more regard to due process and the merits of the case than was true throughout the nineteenth century. By 1926, a minority member of the Committee on Elections No. 1 could say:

In the eight years I have served on Elections Committees and six years upon this Committee, I have never seen partisanship creep into that Committee but one time. There has not been any partisanship in the Committee since the distinguished gentleman from Utah became Chairman of that Committee. A Democrat was seated the last time over a Republican by this Committee, and every member of the Committee voted to seat that Democrat.[54]

This quotation suggests a method by which the development of universalistic criteria for settling contested House elections can be monitored, namely, measuring the extent to which party lines are breached in committee reports and in voting on the floor in contest cases. I have made no such study, but on the basis of the accumulated weight of contemporary reports such as I have been quoting, I predict that a time series would show strict party voting in the 19th century, switching to unanimity or near-unanimity, in most cases, from the early years of the 20th century onward.

Attempts to establish legal precedents for the settlement of contested elections date from the recommendations of the Ames Committee in 1791. In 1798 a

---

[50] Report from Elections Committee No. 3, Mr. McCall, chairman, quoted in Rammelkamp, *op. cit.,* p. 435.

[51] O. O. Stealey, *Twenty Years in the Press Gallery* (New York: published by the author, 1906), p. 147.

[52] Rammelkamp, *op. cit.,* pp. 421–42. Quoted passages are from pp. 423 and 434.

[53] Stealey, *op. cit.,* p. 147.

[54] Quoted in Paul De Witt Hasbrouck, *Party Government in the House of Representatives* (New York: Macmillan, 1927), p. 40.

Table 8—The Growth of Universalism: Contested Elections in the House by Decades, 1789–1964

Congress	Number of Contested Seats	Mean Seats in House for Decade	% Seats Contested Per Congress [a]
1– 5 (1789–1798)	16	89.8	3.56
6–10 (1799–1808)	12	126.6	1.90
11–15 (1809–1818)	16	166.4	1.92
16–20 (1819–1828)	12	202.6	1.18
21–25 (1829–1838)	11	230.0	.96
26–30 (1839–1848)	17	231.8	1.46
31–35 (1849–1858)	23	233.0	1.98
36–40 (1859–1868)	73	196.4	7.44
41–45 (1869–1878)	72	273.0	5.28
46–50 (1879–1888)	58	312.2	3.72
51–55 (1889–1898)	87	346.8	5.02
56–60 (1899–1908)	41	374.4	2.20
61–65 (1909–1918)	36	417.4	1.72
66–70 (1919–1928)	23	435.0	1.06
71–75 (1929–1938)	25	435.0	1.14
76–80 (1939–1948)	15	435.0	.68
81–85 (1949–1958)	12	435.0	.56
86–88 (1959–1964)	8	437.0	.90

[a] Column 2 divided by column 3, over the number of Congresses (5 except in last instance).

Sources: Dempsey *op. cit.*, Appendix I, and George B. Galloway, *History of the U.S. House of Representatives* (House Document 246, 87th Congress, 1st Session) (Washington: U.S. Government Printing Office, 1962), pp. 215–216.

law was enacted prescribing a uniform mode of taking testimony and for compelling the attendance of witnesses. This law was required to be renewed in each Congress and was allowed to lapse in 1804. Bills embodying similar laws were proposed in 1805, 1806, 1810, 1813, and 1830. Not until 1851 was such a law passed, which provided for the gathering of testimony forming the bases of the proofs of each contestant's claim, but not for rules concerning other aspects of contested elections. More significant, however, was a clause permitting the House to set the law aside in whole or in part in specific cases, which apparently the House availed itself of with some regularity in the 19th century. With a few modifications this law is still in effect.[55]

The absolute number of contests shows a decrease in recent decades, as does the number of contests in relation to the number of seats. This suggests that the practice of instigating contests for frivolous reasons has passed into history; contemporary House procedures no longer hold out the hope of success for such contests.[56] Table 8 and Figure 6 give the figures, by decades.

[55] See U.S., *Revised Statutes of the United States*, Title II, Ch. 8, Sections 105–30, and Dempsey, *op. cit.*, pp. 55–60. For indications of attempts to routinize the process of adjudication by setting up general criteria to govern House disposition of contested elections, see two 1933 cases: Gormley vs. Goss (House Report 893, 73rd Congress; see also 78 *Congressional Record*, pp. 4305, 7087, April 20, 1934) and Chandler vs. Burnham (House Report 1278, 73rd Congress; see also 78 *Congressional Record*, pp. 6971, 8921, May 15, 1934).

[56] On the relatively scrupulous handling of a recent contest see Richard H. Rovere, "Letter from Washington," *The New Yorker* (October 16, 1965), 233–44. Rovere (at p. 243) identifies criteria governing the report on the 1965 challenge by the Mississippi Freedom Democratic Party to the entire Mississippi House delegation in the following passage: "... the majority could find no way to report favorably [on the challenge] without, as it seemed to them, abandoning due process and their constitutional responsibilities. Neither, for that matter, could the minority report, which went no further than to urge continued study."

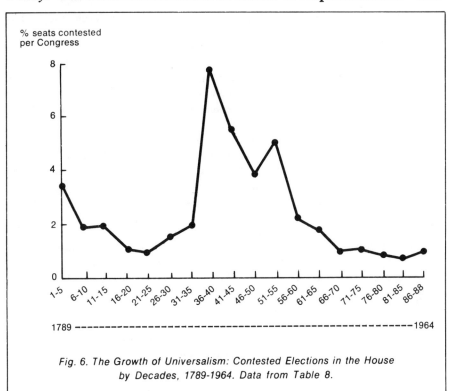

Fig. 6. The Growth of Universalism: Contested Elections in the House
by Decades, 1789-1964. Data from Table 8.

There is today, certainly, no wholesale stealing of seats. If any bias exists in the system, it probably favors the protection of incumbents irrespective of party,[57] and hence (we may surmise not incidentally) the protection of the boundaries of the organization.

Causes, Consequences, Conclusions

It seems reasonable to conclude that one of the main long-run changes in the U.S. House of Representatives has been toward greater institutionalization. Knowing this, we may wish to ask, at a minimum, three questions: What caused it? What follows from it? What can this case tell us about the process in general? It is not from lack of space alone that our answers to each of these questions will be brief and highly speculative.

Not much, for example, is known about the causes of institutionalization. The best theoretical guess in the literature is probably Durkheim's: "The division of labor varies in direct ratio with the volume and density of societies, and, if it

[57] See, e.g., the assignment of burden of proof in Gormley vs. Goss and Chandler vs. Burnham, *loc. cit.*

progresses in a continuous manner in the course of social development, it is because societies become regularly denser and generally more voluminous."[58] "Density" in at least some sense is capable of being operationalized and measured separately from its institutional consequences. For present purposes, the proposition can probably be rendered as follows: As the responsibilities of the national government grew, as a larger proportion of the national economy was affected by decisions taken at the center, the agencies of the national government institutionalized.[59] Another, complementary, translation of the density theorem would be that as organizations grow in size, they tend to develop internally in ways predicted by the theory of institutionalization. Size and increasing work-load seem to me in principle measurable phenomena.[60] Size alone, in fact, seems almost too easy. Until a deliberative body has some minimum amount of work to do, the necessity for interaction among its members remains slight, and, having no purpose, coordination by means of a division of labor, rules and regulations, precedents and so on, seem unlikely to develop. So a somewhat more complicated formula has to be worked out, perhaps relating the size of an organization to the amount of work it performs (e.g., number of work-days per year, number of full-time as opposed to nominal members, number of items considered, number of reports rendered) before the strength of "density" and "volume" can be tested as causes of the process of institutionalization.

A discussion of the consequences of the House's institutionalization must be equally tentative. It is hard—indeed for the contemporary observer, impossible —to shake the conviction that the House's institutional structure does matter greatly in the production of political outcomes. A recent popular account begins:

A United States Congressman has two principal functions: to make laws and to keep laws from being made. The first of these he and his colleagues perform only with sweat, patience and a remarkable skill in the handling of creaking machinery; but the second they perform daily, with ease and infinite variety.[61]

No observer who focuses upon policy results, or who cares about the outputs of the American legislative process, fails to note the "complicated forms and diversified structure" which "confuse the vision, and conceal the system which

[58] Durkheim, *op. cit.*, p. 262. Durkheim in turn cites Comte as describing this mechanism. Weber's notion, that the central precondition for the development of bureaucratic institutions is the money economy, strikes me as less interesting and less plausible. See H. H. Gerth and C. Wright Mills (eds.), *From Max Weber: Essays in Sociology* (N.Y.: Oxford University Press, 1946), pp. 204–09. See, however, Weber's comment (p. 211): "It is obvious that technically the great modern state is absolutely dependent upon a bureaucratic basis. The larger the state, and the more it is or the more it becomes a great power state, the more unconditionally is this the case."

[59] Cf. Young, *op. cit.*, pp. 252–53, who seems to put great stress on public attitudes and local political organization as causes of the growth in the influence of the central government.

[60] George Galloway's *History of the U.S. House of Representatives*, 87th Congress, 1st Session, House Document No. 246 (Washington: U.S. Government Printing Office, 1962), pp. 215–16, has a convenient scorecard on the size and party composition of the House for the first 87 Congresses. Mere size has been found to be an indifferent predictor of the internal complexity of bureaucratic organizations. See Richard H. Hall, J. Eugene Haas and Norman J. Johnson, "Organizational Size, Complexity, and Formalization," *American Sociological Review*, 32 (December, 1967), 903–12.

[61] Robert Bendiner, *Obstacle Course on Capitol Hill* (N.Y.: McGraw-Hill, 1964), p. 15.

underlies its composition."[62] All this is such settled knowledge that it seems unnecessary to mention it here. Still, it is important to stress that the very features of the House which casual observers and freshman legislators find most obtrusive are principal consequences of (among other things) the process we have been describing.[63]

It is, however, not merely the complexity or the venerability of the machinery that they notice. These, in our discussion so far, have been treated as defining characteristics rather than consequences of institutionalization. What puzzles and irks the outside observer is a partial displacement of goals, and a focus of resources upon internal processes at the expense of external demands, that come as a consequence of institutionalization. This process of displacement is, of course, well known to social theory in other settings.[64] A closer look at the general character of this displacement is bound to suggest a number of additional consequences.

For example, representatives may find that the process of institutionalization has increased their incentives to stay within the system. For them, the displacement of resources transforms the organization from a convenient instrument for the pursuit of social policies into an end value itself, a prime source of gratification, of status and power.[65]

The increasing complexity of the division of labor present an opportunity for individual Representatives to specialize and thereby enormously increase their influence upon a narrow range of policy outcomes in the political system at large. Considered separately, the phenomenon of specialization may strike the superficial observer as productive of narrow-minded drones. But the total impact of a cadre of specialists operating over the entire spectrum of public policies is a formidable asset for a political institution; and it has undoubtedly enabled the House to retain a measure of autonomy and influence that is quite exceptional for a 20th century legislature.[66]

Institutionalization has, in the House, on the whole meant the decentralization of power. This has created a great many important and interesting jobs

---

[62] Woodrow Wilson, *op. cit.,* p. 57.

[63] This is not to say, however, that the policy output of the House is exclusively determined by its level of institutionalization. The 88th, 89th and 90th Congresses all represent more or less equivalent levels of institutionalization, yet their policy outputs varied greatly. Nevertheless if the casual observer asked why it took thirty years, more or less, to get the New Deal enacted in the House, and what sorts of strategies and circumstances made the legislative output of the 89th Congress possible, answers would have to refer quite extensively to structural properties of the institution.

[64] See, e.g. Peter M. Blau, *The Dynamics of Bureaucracy* (Chicago: University of Chicago Press, 1955), *passim;* Philip Selznick, *TVA and the Grass Roots* (Berkeley: University of California Press, 1953), esp. pp. 250ff.

[65] See Philip Selznick, *Leadership in Administration* (Evanston: Row, Peterson, 1957).

[66] This position disagrees with Sidney Hyman, "Inquiry into the Decline of Congress," *New York Times Magazine,* January 31, 1960. For the argument that 20th century legislatures are on the whole weak see David B. Truman, "The Representative Function in Western Systems," in Edward H. Buehrig (ed.), *Essays in Political Science* (Bloomington: Indiana University Press, 1966), pp. 84–96; Truman, *The Congressional Party* (New York: Wiley, 1954), pp. 1–10; Truman, "Introduction: The Problem and Its Setting," in Truman (ed.), *The Congress and America's Future* (Englewood Cliffs: Prentice-Hall, 1965), pp. 1–4. For the beginning of an argument that the U.S. Congress may be an exception, see Nelson W. Polsby, *Congress and the Presidency* (New York: Prentice-Hall, 1964), pp. 2, 31–32, 47–115.

within the House, and thus increased the attractiveness of service therein as a career. Proposed reforms of Congress which seek to move toward a recentralization of Congressional power rarely consider this fact. But it is at least possible that some moves to restore discretion to the Speaker, or to centralized party agencies outside Congress, would reduce the effectiveness of Congress far below the level anticipated, because the House would come to be less valued in and of itself, its division of labor would provide less of a power base for subject matter specialists, and the incentives to stay within the organization would sharply decline.

Thus we can argue that, along with the more obvious effects of institutionalization, the process has also served to increase the power of the House within the political system and to spread somewhat more widely incentives for legislators to participate actively in policy making.

A final possible consequence of institutionalization can be suggested: that the process tends to promote professional norms of conduct among participants. Indeed, something like these norms are built into the definition of institutionalization by some commentators.[67] But the built-in norms typically mentioned in discussions of "organization men" have to do with the segmental, ritualized interaction that characterizes organizations coordinated by hierarchical means; slightly different predictions about norms would have to be made for more decentralized, more egalitarian institutionalized legislative bodies.

In fact, there is coming to be a sizeable body of literature about the norms of professional legislative conduct. Time and again, the norms of predictability, courtesy, and reciprocity are offered by professional legislators as central to the rules of the legislative game.[68] Thus, we can suggest a hypothesis that the extent to which these norms are widely applied in a legislative body is a direct function of that body's structural institutionalization. Appropriate tests can be made cross-sectionally, by comparing contemporary legislatures that vary with respect to boundary-maintenance, internal complexity, and universalistic-automated internal decision making. Historically, less satisfactory tests are possible, since a number of vagaries enter into the determination of what is recorded and what is not, and since antecedent factors may account for both structural and normative institutionalization. This makes it hard to estimate the dispersion and importance of norms of conduct.

Nevertheless, the history of the House does suggest that there has been a growth in the rather tame virtues of reciprocity, courtesy, and predictability in legislative life since the turn of the century. Clem Miller describes human relations in the House of today:

---

[67] See Weber, *op. cit.*, p. 69, pp. 330–34; and Gerth and Mills, *op. cit.*, pp. 198–204.

[68] See, for example, Donald Matthews, "The Folkways of the U.S. Senate," this REVIEW, 53 (December, 1959), 1064–1089; John C. Wahlke, Heinz Eulau, William Buchanan, and LeRoy C. Ferguson, *The Legislative System* (New York: Wiley, 1962), pp. 141–69; Alan Kornberg, "The Rules of the Game in the Canadian House of Commons," *The Journal of Politics*, 26 (May, 1964), 358–380; Ralph K. Huitt, "The Outsider in The Senate," this REVIEW, 55 (September, 1961), 566–75; Nicholas A. Masters, "Committee Assignments in The House of Representatives," this REVIEW, 55 (June, 1961), 345–57; Richard F. Fenno, Jr., "The House Appropriations Committee as a Political System: The Problem of Integration," this REVIEW, 56 (June, 1962), 310–24.

One's overwhelming first impression as a member of Congress is the aura of friendliness that surrounds the life of a congressman. No wonder that "few die and none resign." Almost everyone is unfailingly polite and courteous. Window washers, clerks, senators —it cuts all ways. We live in a cocoon of good feeling. . . .[69]

No doubt there are breaches in the fabric of good fellowship, mostly unpublicized, but the student of Congress cannot refrain even so from comparing this testimony with the following sampling of 19th century congressional conduct:

Upon resuming his seat, after having replied to a severe personal arraignment of Henry Clay, former Speaker White, without the slightest warning, received a blow in the face. In the fight that followed a pistol was discharged wounding an officer of the police. John Bell, the distinguished Speaker and statesman, had a similar experience in Committee of the Whole (1838). The fisticuffs became so violent that even the Chair would not quell it. Later in the day both parties apologized and "made their submissions." On February 6, 1845, Edward J. Black, of Georgia, "crossed over from his seat, and, coming within the bar behind Joshua R. Giddings as he was speaking, made a pass at the back of his head with a cane. William H. Hammett, of Mississippi, threw his arms round Black and bore him off as he would a woman from a fire. . . ."

When Reuben M. Whitney was before a committee of investigation in 1837, Bailie Peyton, of Tennessee, taking offense at one of his answers, threatened him fiercely, and when he rose to claim the committee's protection, Mr. Peyton, with due and appropriate profanity, shouted: "You shan't say one word while you are in this room; if you do I will put you to death." The chairman, Henry A. Wise, added: "Yes; this insolence is insufferable." As both these gentlemen were armed with deadly weapons, the witness could hardly be blamed for not wanting to testify before the committee again.

"These were not pleasant days," writes Thomas B. Reed. "Men were not nice in their treatment of each other."[70]

Indeed they were not: Nineteenth century accounts of Congressional behavior abound in passages like these. There is the consternation of members who put up with the presence on the floor of John Randolph's hunting dogs.[71] There is the famous scene on May 22, 1851, when Representative Preston Brooks of South Carolina entered the U.S. Senate and beat Senator Charles Sumner senseless with a cane,[72] and the record contains accounts of more than one such occasion:

When Matthew Lyon, of Kentucky, spat in his face, [Roger] Griswold [of Connecticut, a member 1795–1805] stiffened his arm to strike, but remembering where he was, he

[69] Clem Miller, *Member of the House* (John W. Baker, ed.) (New York: Scribner, 1962), p. 93. See also pp. 80–81 and 119–22.

[70] Alexander, *op. cit.*, pp. 115–16. The internal quotations are from John Quincy Adams' *Diary* and from an article by Reed in the *Saturday Evening Post*, December 9, 1899.

[71] Mayo, *op. cit.*, p. 424; William Parkes Cutler and Julia Perkins Cutler (eds.), *Life, Journals and Correspondence of Reverend Manasseh Cutler* (Cincinnati: Robert Clark and Co., 1888), Vol. II, pp. 186–89.

[72] A motion to expel Brooks from the House for this act was defeated; but soon thereafter Brooks resigned anyway. He was subsequently reelected to fill the vacancy caused by his resignation. See *Biographical Directory of The American Congress, 1774–1961* (Washington: Government Printing Office, 1961), p. 604.

coolly wiped his cheek. But after the House by its vote failed to expel Lyon, he "beat him with great violence," says a contemporary chronicle, "using a strong walking-stick."[73]

With all the ill will that the heat of battle sometimes generates currently, the House has long since left behind the era of guns and dogs, canings and fisticuffs, that occupied so much of the 19th century scene. No doubt this reflects general changes in manners and morals, but it also reflects a growth in the value of the House as an institution capable of claiming the loyalty and good behavior of its members.[74] The best test of the hypothesis, to be sure, remains the cross-sectional one. If American state legislatures, for example, can be found to differ significantly with respect to structural institutionalization, they may also be found to vary concomitantly with respect to the application of the norms of professional legislative life.[75]

Finally, the study of the institutionalization of the House affords us a perspective from which to comment upon the process in general. First, as to its reversibility. Many of our indicators show a substantial decay in the institutional structure of the House in the period surrounding the Civil War. In sheer numbers, the House declined from 237 members in the Congress of 1859 to 178 in the Congress of 1861; not until a decade later did the House regain its former strength. Frivolous contests for seats reached a height in this period, and our rank-and-file boundary measures reflect decay as well. It may be true, and it is certainly amusing, that the strength of the British Admiralty grows as the number of ships declines;[76] but that this illustrates an inflexibly narcissistic law of institutional growth may be doubted. As institutions grow, our expectations about the displacement of resources inward do give us warrant to predict that they will resist decay, but the indications of curve-linearity in our present findings give us ample warning that institutions are also continuously subject to environmental influence and their power to modify and channel that influence is bound to be less than all-encompassing.

Some of our indicators give conditional support for a "take-off" theory of modernization. If one of the stigmata of the take-off to modernity is the rapid development of universalistic, bounded, complex institutional forms, the data

[73] Alexander, op. cit., pp. 111–112. Other instances of flagrant misbehavior are chronicled in Ben Perley Poore, Perley's Reminiscences of Sixty Years in the National Metropolis (Philadelphia: Hubbard, 1886), Vol. I, pp. 394–95; and William Plumer, Memorandum of Proceedings in the United States Senate (Everett Somerville Brown, ed.) (New York: Macmillan, 1923), pp. 269–76.

[74] A report on decorum in the 19th Century House of Commons suggests that a corresponding toning down has taken place, although Commons was palpably a good bit less unruly to start with. Says an ecstatic commentator, "Like so much else that is good in the institutions of Parliament, the behaviour of the House has grown straight, or, like a river, purified itself as it flowed": Eric Taylor, The House of Commons At Work (Baltimore: Penguin, 1961), pp. 85–87. Anthony Barker says: "The close of the 19th Century has been described by Lord Campion as the ending of informality and the beginning of rigid government responsibility for policy in the procedures of the House of Commons": " 'The Most Important And Venerable Function': A Study of Commons Supply Procedure," Political Studies, 13 (February, 1965), p. 45.

[75] Perhaps secondary analysis comparing the four states (California, New Jersey, Tennessee, Ohio) in the Wahlke, Eulau, Buchanan, and Ferguson study (op. cit.) will yield an acceptable test of the hypothesis. This study has good information on the diffusion of legislative norms; it is less strong on structural data, but these might be relatively easy to gather.

[76] Parkinson, op. cit., p. 39.

presented here lend this theory some plausibility.[77] The "big bang" seems to come in the 1890–1910 period, on at least some of the measures.

In conclusion, these findings suggest that increasing hierarchical structure is not a necessary feature of the institutionalization process. Organizations other than bureaucracies, it seems clear, also are capable of having natural histories which increase their viability in the modern world without forcing them into uniformly centralized patterns of authority.

[77] The growth of political institutions does not play a particularly important part in the interpretation offered by W. W. Rostow in *The Stages of Economic Growth* (Cambridge: Cambridge University Press, 1960), see, e.g., pp. 18–19, but these may afford at least as good support for his theory as some of the economic indicators he proposes.

COMMITTEES, NORMS, AND ROLES

The House Appropriations Committee
As a Political System:
The Problem of Integration

by RICHARD F. FENNO, JR.

Studies of Congress by political scientists have produced a time-tested consensus on the very considerable power and autonomy of Congressional committees. Because of these two related characteristics, it makes empirical and analytical sense to treat the Congressional committee as a discrete unit for analysis. This paper conceives of the committee as a political system (or, more accurately as a political subsystem) faced with a number of basic problems which it must solve in order to achieve its goals and maintain itself. Generally speaking these functional problems pertain to the environmental and the internal relations of the committee. This study is concerned almost exclusively with the internal problems of the committee and particularly with the problem of self-integration.[1] It describes how one congressional committee—The Committee on Appropriations of the House of Representatives—has dealt with this problem in the period 1947–1961. Its purpose is to add to our understanding of appropriations politics in Congress and to suggest the usefulness of this type of analysis for studying the activities of any congressional committee.

The necessity for integration in any social system arises from the differentiation among its various elements. Most importantly there is a differentiation

[1] On social systems, see: George Homans, *The Human Group* (New York, 1950); Robert K Merton, *Social Theory and Social Structure* (Glencoe, 1957); Talcott Parsons and Edward Shils, *Toward A General Theory of Action* (Cambridge, 1951), pp. 190–234. Most helpful with reference to the political system has been David Easton, "An Approach to the Analysis of Political Systems," *World Politics* (April, 1957), pp. 383–400.

Reprinted from "The House Appropriations Committee as a Political System: The Problem of Integration," *The American Political Science Review* 56 (June 1962): 310-24, by Richard F. Fenno, Jr. Reprinted by permission of the American Political Science Association and the author.

among subgroups and among individual positions, together with the roles that flow therefrom.[2] A committee faces the problem, how shall these diverse elements be made to mesh together or function in support of one another? No political system (or subsystem) is perfectly integrated; yet no political system can survive without some minimum degree of integration among its differentiated parts. Committee integration is defined as the degree to which there is a working together or a meshing together or mutual support among its roles and subgroups. Conversely, it is also defined as the degree to which a committee is able to minimize conflict among its roles and its subgroups, by heading off or resolving the conflicts that arise.[3] A concomitant of integration is the existence of a fairly consistent set of norms, widely agreed upon and widely followed by the members. Another concomitant of integration is the existence of control mechanisms (*i.e.*, socialization and sanctioning mechanisms) capable of maintaining reasonable conformity to norms. In other words, the more highly integrated a committee, the smaller will be the gap between expected and actual behavior.

This study is concerned with integration both as a structural characteristic of, and as a functional problem for, the Appropriations Committee. First, certain basic characteristics of the Committee need description, to help explain the integration of its parts. Second comes a partial description of the degree to which and the ways in which the Committee achieves integration. No attempt is made to state this in quantitative terms, but the object is to examine the meshing together or the minimization of conflict among certain subgroups and among certain key roles. Also, important control mechanisms are described. The study concludes with some comments on the consequences of Committee integration for appropriations politics and on the usefulness of further Congressional committee analysis in terms of functional problems such as this one.

I

Five important characteristics of the Appropriations Committee which help explain Committee integration are (1) the existence of a well-articulated and deeply rooted consensus on Committee goals or tasks; (2) the nature of the Committee's subject matter; (3) the legislative orientation of its members; (4) the attractiveness of the Committee for its members; and (5) the stability of Committee membership.

CONSENSUS

The Appropriations Committee sees its tasks as taking form within the broad guidelines set by its parent body, the House of Representatives. For it is

[2] On the idea of subgroups as used here, see Harry M. Johnson, *Sociology* (New York, 1960), ch. 3. On role, see specifically Theodore M. Newcomb, *Social Psychology* (New York, 1951), p. 280; see generally N. Gross, W. Mason and A. McEachern, *Explorations in Role Analysis: Studies of the School Superintendency Role* (New York, 1958). On differentiation and its relation to integration, see Scott Greer, *Social Organization* (New York, 1955).

[3] The usage here follows most closely that of Robert Merton, *op. cit.*, pp. 26–29.

the primary condition of the Committee's existence that it was created by the
House for the purpose of assisting the House in the performance of House
legislative tasks dealing with appropriations. Committee members agree that
their fundamental duty is to serve the House in the manner and with the substantive results that the House prescribes. Given, however, the imprecision of
House expectations and the permissiveness of House surveillance, the Committee must elaborate for itself a definition of tasks plus a supporting set of
perceptions (of itself and of others) explicit enough to furnish day-to-day
guidance.

The Committee's view begins with the pre-eminence of the House—often
mistakenly attributed to the Constitution ("all bills for raising revenue," Art. I,
sec. 7) but nevertheless firmly sanctioned by custom—in appropriations affairs.

It moves easily to the conviction that, as the efficient part of the House in
this matter, the Constitution has endowed it with special obligations and
special prerogatives. It ends in the view that the Committee on Appropriations,
far from being merely one among many units in a complicated legislative-
executive system, is *the* most important, most responsible unit in the whole
appropriations process.[4] Hand in hand with the consensus on their primacy
goes a consensus that all of their House-prescribed tasks can be fulfilled by
superimposing upon them one, single, paramount task—*to guard the Federal
Treasury.* Committee members state their goals in the essentially negative terms
of guardianship—screening requests for money, checking against ill-advised
expenditures, and protecting the taxpayer's dollar. In the language of the
Committee's official history, the job of each member is, "constantly and
courageously to protect the Federal Treasury against thousands of appeals and
imperative demands for unnecessary, unwise, and excessive expenditures."[5]

To buttress its self-image as guardian of public funds the Committee
elaborates a set of perceptions about other participants in the appropriations
process to which most members hold most of the time. Each executive official,
for example, is seen to be interested in the expansion of his own particular
program. Each one asks, therefore, for more money than he really needs, in
view of the total picture, to run an adequate program. This and other Committee
perceptions—of the Budget Bureau, of the Senate, and of their fellow Representatives—help to shape and support the Committee members in their
belief that most budget estimates can, should and must be reduced and that,
since no one else can be relied upon, the House Committee must do the job.
To the consensus on the main task of protecting the Treasury is added, therefore,

---

[4] This and all other generalizations about member attitudes and perceptions depend heavily on
extensive interviews with Committee members. Semi-structured interviews, averaging 45 minutes
in length were held with 45 of the 50 Committee members during the 86th Congress. Certain key
questions, all open-ended, were asked of all respondents. The schedule was kept very flexible,
however, in order to permit particular topics to be explored with those individuals best equipped
to discuss them. In a few cases, where respondents encouraged it, notes were taken during the interviews. In most cases notes were not taken, but were transcribed immediately after the interview.
Where unattributed quotations occur in the text, therefore, they are as nearly verbatim as the author's
power of immediate recall could make them. These techniques were all used so as to improve *rapport*
between interviewer and respondent.

[5] "History of the Committee on Appropriations," House Doc. 299, 77th Cong., 1st sess., 1941–
1942, p. 11.

a consensus on the instrumental task of *cutting whatever budget estimates are submitted.*

As an immediate goal, Committee members agree that they must strike a highly critical, aggressive posture toward budget requests, and that they should, on principle, reduce them. In the words of the Committee's veterans: "There has never been a budget submitted to the Congress that couldn't be cut." "There isn't a budget that can't be cut 10 per cent immediately." "I've been on the Committee for 17 years. No subcommittee of which I have been a member has ever reported out a bill without a cut in the budget. I'm proud of that record." The aim of budget-cutting is strongly internalized for the Committee member. "It's a tradition in the Appropriations Committee to cut." "You're grounded in it. . . . It's ingrained in you from the time you get on the Committee." For the purposes of a larger study, the appropriations case histories of 37 executive bureaus have been examined for a 12-year period, 1947–1959.[6] Of 443 separate bureau estimates, the Committee reduced 77.2 per cent (342) of them.

It is a mark of the intensity and self-consciousness of the Committee consensus on budget-cutting that it is couched in a distinctive vocabulary. The workaday lingo of the Committee member is replete with negative verbs, undesirable objects of attention, and effective instruments of action. Agency budgets are said to be filled with "fat," "padding," "grease," "pork," "oleaginous substance," "water," "oil," "cushions," "avoirdupois," "waste tissue," and "soft spots." The action verbs most commonly used are "cut," "carve," "slice," "prune," "whittle," "squeeze," "wring," "trim," "lop off," "chop," "slash," "pare," "shave," "fry," and "whack." The tools of the trade are appropriately referred to as "knife," "blade," "meat axe," "scalpel," "meat cleaver," "hatchet," "shears," "wringer," and "fine-tooth comb." Members are hailed by their fellows as being "pretty sharp with the knife." Agencies may "have the meat axe thrown at them." Executives are urged to put their agencies "on a fat boy's diet." Budgets are praised when they are "cut to the bone." And members agree that "You can always get a little more fat out of a piece of pork if you fry it a little longer and a little harder."

To the major task of protecting the Treasury and the instrumental task of cutting budget estimates, each Committee member adds, usually by way of exception, a third task—*serving the constituency to which he owes his election.* This creates no problem for him when, as is sometimes the case, he can serve his district best by cutting the budget requests of a federal agency whose program is in conflict with the demands of his constituency.[6a] Normally, however, members find that their most common role-conflict is between a Committee-oriented budget-reducing role and a constituency-oriented budget-increasing role. Committee ideology resolves the conflict by assigning top, long-run priority to the budget-cutting task and making of the constituency service a

[6] The bureaus being studied are all concerned with domestic policy and are situated in the Agriculture, Interior, Labor, Commerce, Treasury, Justice and Health, Education and Welfare Departments. For a similar pattern of Committee decisions in foreign affairs, see Holbert Carroll, *The House of Representatives and Foreign Affairs* (Pittsburgh, 1958), ch. 9.

[6a] See, for example, Philip A. Foss, "The Grazing Fee Dilemma," Inter-University Case Program, No. 57 (University, Alabama, 1960).

permissible, short-run exception. No member is expected to commit electoral suicide; but no member is expected to allow his district's desire for federal funds to dominate his Committee behavior.

SUBJECT MATTER

Appropriations Committee integration is facilitated by the subject matter with which the group deals. The Committee makes decisions on the same controversial issues as do the committees handling substantive legislation. But a money decision—however vitally it affects national policy—is, or at least seems to be, less directly a policy decision. Since they deal immediately with dollars and cents, it is easy for the members to hold to the idea that they are not dealing with programmatic questions, that theirs is a "business" rather than a "policy" committee. The subject matter, furthermore, keeps Committee members relatively free agents, which promotes intra-Committee maneuvering and, hence, conflict avoidance. Members do not commit themselves to their constituents in terms of precise money amounts, and no dollar sum is sacred—it can always be adjusted without conceding that a principle has been breached. By contrast, members of committees dealing directly with controversial issues are often pressured into taking concrete stands on these issues; consequently, they may come to their committee work with fixed and hardened attitudes. This leads to unavoidable, head-on intra-committee conflict and renders integrative mechanisms relatively ineffective.

The fact of an annual appropriations process means the Committee members repeat the same operations with respect to the same subject matters year after year—and frequently more than once in a given year. Substantive and procedural repetition promotes familiarity with key problems and provides ample opportunity to test and confirm the most satisfactory methods of dealing with them. And the absolute necessity that appropriations bills do ultimately pass gives urgency to the search for such methods. Furthermore, the House rule that no member of the Committee can serve on another standing committee is a deterrent against a fragmentation of Committee member activity which could be a source of difficulty in holding the group together. If a committee has developed (as this one has) a number of norms designed to foster integration, repeated and concentrated exposure to them increases the likelihood that they will be understood, accepted and followed.

LEGISLATIVE ORIENTATION

The recruitment of members for the Appropriations Committee produces a group of individuals with an orientation especially conducive to Committee integration. Those who make the selection pay special attention to the characteristics which Masters has described as those of the "responsible legislator"—approval of and conformity to the norms of the legislative process and of the House of Representatives.[7]

Key selectors speak of wanting, for the Appropriations Committee, "the

---

[7] Nicholas A. Masters, "House Committee Assignments," this REVIEW, Vol. 55 (June, 1961), pp. 345–57.

kind of man you can deal with" or "a fellow who is well-balanced and won't go off half-cocked on things." A Northern liberal Democrat felt that he had been chosen over eight competitors because, "I had made a lot of friends and was known as a nice guy"—especially, he noted, among Southern Congressmen. Another Democrat explained, "I got the blessing of the Speaker and the leadership. It's personal friendships. I had done a lot of things for them in the past, and when I went to them and asked them, they gave it to me." A Republican chosen for the Committee in his first term recalled,

The Chairman [Rep. Taber] I guess did some checking around in my area. After all, I was new and he didn't know me. People told me that they were called to see if I was— well, unstable or apt to go off on tangents . . . to see whether or not I had any pre-conceived notions about things and would not be flexible—whether I would oppose things even though it was obvious.

A key criterion in each of the cases mentioned was a demonstrable record of, or an assumed predisposition toward, legislative give-and-take.

The 106 Appropriations Committee members serving between 1947 and 1961 spent an average of 3.6 years on other House committees before coming to the Committee. Only 17 of the 106 were selected as first term Congressmen. A House apprenticeship (which Appropriations maintains more successfully than all committees save Ways and Means and Rules[8]) provides the time in which legislative reputations can be established by the member and an assessment of that reputation in terms of Appropriations Committee requirements can be made. Moreover, the mere fact that a member survives for a couple of terms is some indication of an electoral situation conducive to his "responsible" legislative behavior. The optimum bet for the Committee is a member from a sufficient safe district to permit him freedom of maneuver inside the House without fear of reprisal at the polls.[9] The degree of responsiveness to House norms which the Committee selectors value may be the product of a safe district as well as an individual temperament.

ATTRACTIVENESS

A fourth factor is the extraordinarily high degree of attractiveness which the Committee holds for its members—as measured by the low rate of departure from it. Committee members do not leave it for service on other committees. To the contrary, they are attracted to it from nearly every other committee.[10] Of the 106 members in the 1947–1961 period, only two men left the Committee

---

[8] In the period from 1947 through 1959 (80th to 86th Congress), 79 separate appointments were made to the Appropriations Committee, with 14 going to freshmen. The Committee filled, in other words, 17.7 per cent of its vacancies with freshmen. The Rules Committee had 26 vacancies and selected no freshmen at all. The Ways and Means Committee had 36 vacancies and selected 2 freshmen (5.6 per cent). All other Committees had a higher percentage of freshmen appointments. Armed Services ranked fourth, with 45 vacancies and 12 freshmen appointed, for a percentage of 26.7. Foreign Affairs figures were 46 and 14, or 30.4 per cent; UnAmerican Activities figures were 22 and 7, or 31.8 per cent. Cf. Masters, *op. cit.*

[9] In the 1960 elections, 41 out of the current 50 members received more than 55.1 per cent of the vote in their districts. By a common definition, that is, only 9 of the 50 came from marginal districts.

[10] The 106 members came to Appropriations from every committee except Ways and Means.

voluntarily; and neither of them initiated the move.[11] Committee attractiveness is a measure of its capacity to satisfy individual member needs—for power, prestige, recognition, respect, self-esteem, friendship, etc. Such satisfaction in turn increases the likelihood that members will behave in such a way as to hold the group together.

The most frequently mentioned source of Committee attractiveness is its power—based on its control of financial resources. "Where the money is, that's where the power is," sums up the feeling of the members. They prize their ability to reward or punish so many other participants in the political process—executive officials, fellow Congressmen, constituents and other clientele groups. In the eyes of its own members, the Committee is either the most powerful in the House or it is on a par with Ways and Means or, less frequently, on a par with Ways and Means and Rules. The second important ingredient in member satisfaction is the government-wide scope of Committee activity. The ordinary Congressman may feel that he has too little knowledge of and too little control over his environment. Membership on this Committee compensates for this feeling of helplessness by the wider contacts, the greater amount of information, and the sense of being "in the middle of things" which are consequent, if not to subcommittee activity, at least to the full Committee's overview of the federal government.

Thirdly, Committee attractiveness is heightened by the group's recognizable and distinctive political style—one that is, moreover, highly valued in American political culture. The style is that of *hard work*; and the Committee's self-image is that of "the hardest working Committee in Congress." His willingness to work is the Committee member's badge of identification, and it is proudly worn. It colors his perceptions of others and their perceptions of him.[11a] It is a cherished axiom of all members that, "This Committee is no place for a man who doesn't work. They have to be hard working. It's a way of life. It isn't just a job; it's a way of life."

The mere existence of some identifiable and valued style or "way of life" is a cohesive force for a group. But the particular style of hard work is one which increases group morale and group identification twice over. Hard work means a long, dull, and tedious application to detail, via the technique of "dig, dig, dig, day after day behind closed doors"—in an estimated 460 subcommittee and full committee meetings a year. And virtually all of these meetings are in executive

---

[11] One was personally requested by the Speaker to move to Ways and Means. The other was chosen by a caucus of regional Congressmen to be his party's representative on the Rules Committee. Of the 21 members who were forced off the Committee for lack of seniority during a change in party control, or who were defeated for reelection and later returned, 20 sought to regain Committee membership at the earliest opportunity.

[11a] A sidelight on this attitude is displayed in a current feud between the House and Senate Appropriations Committees over the meeting place for their conference committees. The House Committee is trying to break the century-old custom that conferences to resolve differences on money bills are always held on the Senate side of the Capitol. House Committee members "complain that they often have to trudge back to the House two or three times to answer roll calls during a conference. They say they go over in a body to work, while Senators flit in and out. . . . The House Appropriations Committee feels that it does all the hard work listening to witnesses for months on each bill, only to have the Senate Committee sit as a court of appeals and, with little more than a cursory glance, restore most of the funds cut." *Washington Post*, April 24, 1962, p. 1.

session. By adopting the style of hard work, the Committee discourages highly individualized forms of legislative behavior, which could be disruptive within the Committee. It rewards its members with power, but it is power based rather on work inside the Committee than on the political glamour of activities carried on in the limelight of the mass media. Prolonged daily work together encourages sentiments of mutual regard, sympathy and solidarity. This *esprit* is, in turn, functional for integration on the Committee. A Republican leader summed up,

I think it's more closely knit than any other committee. Yet it's the biggest committee, and you'd think it would be the reverse. I know on my subcommittee, you sit together day after day. You get better acquainted. You have sympathy when other fellows go off to play golf. There's a lot of *esprit de corps* in the Committee.

The strong attraction which members have for the Committee increases the influence which the Committee and its norms exercise on all of them. It increases the susceptibility of the newcomer to Committee socialization and of the veteran to Committee sanctions applicable against deviant behavior.[12]

MEMBERSHIP STABILITY

Members of the Appropriations Committee are strongly attracted to it; they also have, which bears out their selection as "responsible legislators," a strong attraction for a career in the House of Representatives. The 50 members on the Committee in 1961 had served an average of 13.1 years in the House. These twin attractions produce a noteworthy stability of Committee membership. In the period from the 80th to the 87th Congress, 35.7 per cent of the Committee's membership remained constant. That is to say, 15 of the 42 members on the Committee in March, 1947, were still on the Committee in March, 1961.[13] The 50 members of the Committee in 1961 averaged 9.3 years of prior service on that Committee. In no single year during the last fourteen has the Committee had to absorb an influx of new members totalling more than one-quarter of its membership. At all times, in other words, at least three-fourths of the members have had previous Committee experience. This extraordinary stability of personnel extends into the staff as well. As of June 1961, its 15 professionals had served an average of 10.7 years with the Committee.[14]

The opportunity exists, therefore, for the development of a stable leadership group, a set of traditional norms for the regulation of internal Committee behavior, and informal techniques of personal accommodation. Time is provided in which new members can learn and internalize Committee norms before they attain high seniority rankings. The Committee does not suffer from the

[12] This proposition is spelled out at some length in J. Thibaut and H. Kelley, *The Social Psychology of Groups* (New York, 1959), p. 247, and in D. Cartwright and A. Zander, *Group Dynamics: Research and Theory* (Evanston, 1953), p. 420.

[13] This figure is 9 per cent greater than the next most stable House Committee during this particular period. The top four, in order, were Appropriations (35.7%), Agriculture (26.7%), Armed Services (25%), Foreign Affairs (20.8%).

[14] The Committee's permanent and well integrated professional staff (as distinguished from its temporary investigating staff) might be considered as part of the subsystem though it will not be treated in this paper.

potentially disruptive consequences of rapid changeovers in its leadership group, nor of sudden impositions of new sets of norms governing internal Committee behavior.

II

If one considers the main activity of a political system to be decision-making, the acid test of its internal integration is its capacity to make collective decisions without flying apart in the process. Analysis of Committee integration should focus directly, therefore, upon its subgroups and the roles of its members. Two kinds of subgroups are of central importance—subcommittees and majority or minority party groups. The roles which are most relevant derive from: (1) positions which each member holds by virtue of his subgroup attachments, *e.g.*, as subcommittee member, majority (or minority) party member; (2) positions which relate to full Committee membership, *e.g.*, Committee member, and the seniority rankings of veteran, man of moderate experience, and newcomer;[15] (3) positions which relate to both subgroup and full Committee membership, *e.g.*, Chairman of the Committee, ranking minority member of the Committee, subcommittee chairman, ranking subcommittee member. Clusters of norms state the expectations about subgroup and role behavior. The description which follows treats the ways in which these norms and their associated behaviors mesh and clash. It treats, also, the internal control mechanisms by which behavior is brought into reasonable conformity with expectations.

SUBGROUP INTEGRATION

The day-to-day work of the Committee is carried on in its subcommittees each of which is given jurisdiction over a number of related governmental units. The number of subcommittees is determined by the Committee Chairman, and has varied recently from a low of 9 in 1949 to a high of 15 in 1959. The present total of 14 reflects, as always, a set of strategic and personal judgments by the Chairman balanced against the limitations placed on him by Committee tradition and member wishes. The Chairman also determines subcommittee jurisdiction, appoints subcommittee chairmen and selects the majority party members of each group. The ranking minority member of the Committee exercises similar control over subcommittee assignments on his side of the aisle.

Each subcommittee holds hearings on the budget estimates of the agencies assigned to it, meets in executive session to decide what figures and what language to recommend to the full Committee (to "mark up" the bill), defends its recommendations before the full Committee, writes the Committee's report to the House, dominates the debate on the floor, and bargains for the House in conference committee. Within its jurisdiction, each subcommittee functions independently of the others and guards its autonomy jealously. The Chairman

---

[15] "Newcomers" are defined as men who have served no more than two terms on the Committee. "Men of moderate experience" are those with 3–5 terms of service. "Veterans" are those who have 6 or more terms of Committee service.

and ranking minority member of the full Committee have, as we shall see, certain opportunities to oversee and dip into the operations of all subcommittees. But their intervention is expected to be minimal. Moreover, they themselves operate importantly within the subcommittee framework by sitting as chairman or ranking minority member of the subcommittee in which they are most interested. Each subcommittee, under the guidance of its chairman, transacts its business in considerable isolation from every other one. One subcommittee chairman exclaimed,

Why, you'd be branded an imposter if you went into one of those other subcommittee meetings. The only time I go is by appointment, by arrangement with the chairman at a special time. I'm as much a stranger in another subcommittee as I would be in the legislative Committee on Post Office and Civil Service. Each one does its work apart from all others.

All members of all subcommittees are expected to behave in similar fashion in the role of subcommittee member. Three main norms define this role; to the extent that they are observed, they promote harmony and reduce conflict among subcommittees.[16] Subcommittee autonomy gives to the House norm of *specialization* an intensified application on the Appropriations Committee. Each member is expected to play the role of specialist in the activities of one subcommittee. He will sit on from one to four subcommittees, but normally will specialize in the work, or a portion of the work, of only one. Except for the Chairman, ranking minority member and their confidants, a Committee member's time, energy, contacts and experience are devoted to his subcommittees. Specialization is, therefore, among the earliest and most compelling of the Committee norms to which a newcomer is exposed. Within the Committee, respect, deference and power are earned through subcommittee activity and, hence to a degree, through specialization. Specialization is valued further because it is well suited to the task of guarding the Treasury. Only by specializing, Committee members believe, can they unearth the volume of factual information necessary for the intelligent screening of budget requests. Since "the facts" are acquired only through industry an effective specialist will, perforce, adopt and promote the Committee's style of hard work.

Committee-wide acceptance of specialization is an integrative force in decision-making because it helps support a second norm—*reciprocity*. The stage at which a subcommittee makes its recommendations is a potential point of internal friction. Conflict among subcommittees (or between one subcommittee and the rest of the Committee) is minimized by the deference traditionally accorded to the recommendation of the subcommittee which has specialized in the area, has worked hard, and has "the facts." "It's a matter of 'You respect my work and I'll respect yours.'" "It's frowned upon if you offer an amendment

---

[16] A statement of expected behavior was taken to be a Committee norm when it was expressed by a substantial number of respondents (a dozen or so) who represented both parties, and varying degrees of experience. In nearly every case, moreover, no refutation of them was encountered, and ample confirmation of their existence can be found in the public record. Their articulation came most frequently from the veterans of the group.

in the full Committee if you aren't on the subcommittee. It's considered presumptuous to pose as an expert if you aren't on the subcommittee." Though records of full Committee decisions are not available, members agree that subcommittee recommendations are "very rarely changed," "almost always approved," "changed one time in fifty," "very seldom changed," etc.

No subcommittee is likely to keep the deference of the full Committee for long unless its recommendations have widespread support among its own members. To this end, a third norm—*subcommittee unity*—is expected to be observed by subcommittee members. Unity means a willingness to support (or not to oppose) the recommendations of one's own subcommittee. Reciprocity and unity are closely dependent upon one another. Reciprocity is difficult to maintain when subcommittees themselves are badly divided; and unity has little appeal unless reciprocity will subsequently be observed. The norm of reciprocity functions to minimize inter-subcommittee conflict. The norm of unity functions to minimize intra-subcommittee conflict. Both are deemed essential to subcommittee influence.

One payoff for the original selection of "responsible legislators" is their special willingness to compromise in pursuit of subcommittee unity. The impulse to this end is registered most strongly at the time when the sub committee meets in executive session to mark up the bill. Two ranking minority members explained this aspect of markup procedure in their subcommittees:

If there's agreement, we go right along. If there's a lot of controversy we put the item aside and go on. Then, after a day or two, we may have a list of ten controversial items. We give and take and pound them down till we get agreement.

We have a unanimous agreement on everything. If a fellow enters an objection and we can't talk him out of it—and sometimes we can get him to go along—that's it. We put it in there.

Once the bargain is struck, the subcommittee is expected to "stick together."

It is, of course easier to achieve unity among the five, seven, or nine members of a subcommittee than among the fifty members of the full Committee. But members are expected wherever possible to observe the norm of unity in the full Committee as well. That is, they should not only defer to the recommendations of the subcommittee involved, but they should support (or not oppose) that recommendation when it reaches the floor in the form of a Committee decision. On the floor, Committee members believe, their power and prestige depend largely on the degree to which the norms of reciprocity and unity continue to be observed. Members warn each other that if they go to the floor in disarray they will be "rolled," "jumped," or "run over" by the membership. It is a cardinal maxim among Committee members that "You can't turn an appropriations bill loose on the floor." Two senior subcommittee chairmen explain,

We iron out our differences in Committee. We argue it out and usually have a meeting of the minds, a composite view of the Committee. . . . If we went on the floor in wide disagreement, they would say, "If you can't agree after listening to the testimony and discussing it, how can we understand it? We'll just vote on the basis of who we like the best."

I tell them (the full Committee) we should have a united front. If there are any objections or changes, we ought to hear it now, and not wash our dirty linen out on the floor. If we don't have a bill that we can all agree on and support, we ought not to report it out. To do that is like throwing a piece of meat to a bunch of hungry animals.

One of the most functional Committee practices supporting the norm of unity is the tradition against minority reports in the subcommittee and in the full Committee. It is symptomatic of Committee integration that custom should proscribe the use of the most formal and irrevocable symbol of congressional committee disunity—the minority report. A few have been written—but only 9 out of a possible 141 during the 11 years, 1947–1957. That is to say, 95 per cent of all original appropriations bills in this period were reported out without dissent. The technique of "reserving" is the Committee member's equivalent for the registering of dissent. In subcommittee or Committee, when a member reserves, he goes on record informally by informing his colleagues that he reserves the right to disagree on a specified item later on in the proceedings. He may seek a change or support a change in that particular item in full Committee or on the floor. But he does not publicize his dissent. The subcommittee or the full Committee can then make an unopposed recommendation. The individual retains some freedom of maneuver without firm commitment. Often a member reserves on an appropriations item but takes no further action. A member explained how the procedure operates in subcommittee,

If there's something I feel too strongly about, and just can't go along, I'll say, "Mr. Chairman, we can have a unanimous report, but I reserve the right to bring this up in full Committee. I feel duty bound to make a play for it and see if I can't sell it to the other members." But if I don't say anything, or don't reserve this right, and then I bring it up in full Committee, they'll say, "Who are you trying to embarrass? You're a member of the team, aren't you? That's not the way to get along."

Disagreement cannot, of course, be eliminated from the Committee. But the Committee has accepted a method for ventilating it which produces a minimum of internal disruption. And members believe that the greater their internal unity, the greater the likelihood that their recommendations will pass the House.

The degree to which the role of the subcommittee member can be so played and subcommittee conflict thereby minimized depends upon the minimization of conflict between the majority and minority party subgroups. Nothing would be more disruptive to the Committee's work than bitter and extended partisan controversy. It is, therefore, important to Appropriations Committee integration that a fourth norm—*minimal partisanship*—should be observed by members of both party contingents. Nearly every respondent emphasized, with approval, that "very little" or "not much" partisanship prevailed on the Committee. One subcommittee chairman stated flatly, "My job is to keep down partisanship." A ranking minority member said, "You might think that we Republicans would defend the Administration and the budget, but we don't." Majority and minority party ratios are constant and do not change (*i.e.*, in 1958) to reflect changes in the strength of the controlling party. The Committee operates with a completely non-partisan professional staff, which does not change in tune with shifts in party control. Requests for studies by the Committee's investigating staff must be made by the Chairman and ranking minority member of the full Committee and by the Chairman and ranking minority member of the subcommittee involved. Subcommittees can produce recommendations without dissent and the full Committee can adopt reports without dissent precisely because party conflict is (during the period 1947–1961) the exception rather than the rule.

The Committee is in no sense immune from the temperature of party conflict, but it does have a relatively high specific heat. Intense party strife or a strongly taken presidential position will get reflected in subcommittee and in Committee recommendations. Sharp divisions in party policy were carried, with disruptive impact, into some areas of Committee activity during the 80th Congress and subsequently, by way of reaction, into the 81st Congress.[17] During the Eisenhower years, extraordinary presidential pleas, especially concerning foreign aid, were given special heed by the Republican members of the Committee.[18] Partisanship is normally generated from the environment and not from within the Committee's party groups. Partisanship is, therefore, likely to be least evident in subcommittee activity, stronger in the full Committee, and most potent at the floor stage. Studies which have focussed on roll-call analysis have stressed the influence of party in legislative decision-making.[19] In the appropriations process, at any rate, the floor stage probably represents party influence at its maximum. Our examination, by interview, of decision-making at the subcommittee and full Committee level would stress the influence of Committee-oriented norms—the strength of which tends to vary inversely with that of party bonds. In the secrecy and intimacy of the subcommittee and full Committee hearing rooms, the member finds it easy to compromise on questions of more or less, to take money from one program and give it to another and, in general, to avoid yes-or-no type party stands. These decisions, taken in response to the integrative norms of the Committee are the most important ones in the entire appropriations process.

ROLE INTEGRATION

The roles of subcommittee member and party member are common to all.

Other more specific decision-making positions are allocated among the members. Different positions produce different roles, and in an integrated system, these too must fit together. Integration, in other words, must be achieved

[17] See, for example, the internal conflict on the subcommittee dealing with the Labor Department. 93 *Cong. Record*, pp. 2465–2562 passim; 94 *Cong. Record*, pp. 7605–7607.

[18] See, for example, the unusual minority report of Committee Republicans on the foreign aid appropriations bill in 1960. Their protest against Committee cuts in the budget estimates was the result of strenuous urging by the Eisenhower Administration. House Report No. 1798, *Mutual Security and Related Agency Appropriation Bill*, 1961, 86 Cong. 2d sess. 1960.

[19] David Truman, *The Congressional Party* (New York, 1959); Julius Turner, *Party and Constituency: Pressures on Congress* (Baltimore, 1951).

through the complementarity or reciprocity of roles as well as through a similarity of roles. This may mean a pattern in which expectations are so different that there is very little contact between individuals; or it may mean a pattern in which contacts require the working out of an involved system of exchange of obligations and rewards.[20] In either case, the desired result is the minimization of conflict among prominent Committee roles. Two crucial instances of role reciprocity on the Committee involve the seniority positions of old-timer and newcomer and the leadership positions of Chairman and ranking minority member, on both the full Committee and on each subcommittee.

The differentiation between senior and junior members is the broadest definition of who shall and who shall not actively participate in Committee decisions. Of a junior member, it will be said, "Oh, he doesn't count—what I mean is, he hasn't been on the Committee long enough." He is not expected to and ordinarily does not have much influence. His role is that of apprentice. He is expected to learn the business and the norms of the Committee by applying himself to its work. He is expected to acquiesce in an arrangement which gives most influence (except in affairs involving him locally) to the veterans of the group. Newcomers will be advised to "follow the chairman until you get your bearings. For the first two years, follow the chairman. He knows." "Work hard, keep quiet and attend the Committee sessions. We don't want to listen to some new person coming in here." And newcomers perceive their role in identical terms: "You have to sit in the back seat and edge up little by little." "You just go to subcommittee meetings and assimilate the routine. The new members are made to feel welcome, but you have a lot of rope-learning to do before you carry much weight."

At every stage of Committee work, this differentiation prevails. There is remarkable agreement on the radically different sets of expectations involved. During the hearings, the view of the elders is that, "Newcomers . . . don't know what the score is and they don't have enough information to ask intelligent questions." A newcomer described his behavior in typically similar terms: "I attended all the hearings and studied and collected information that I can use next year. I'm just marking time now." During the crucial subcommittee mark-up, the newcomer will have little opportunity to speak—save in locally important matters. A subcommittee chairman stated the norm from his viewpoint this way: "When we get a compromise, nobody's going to break that up. If someone tries, we sit on him fast. We don't want young people who throw bricks or slow things down." And a newcomer reciprocated, describing his markup conduct: "I'm not provocative. I'm in there for information. They're the experts in the field. I go along." In full Committee, on the floor, and in conference committee, the Committee's senior members take the lead and the junior members are expected to follow. The apprentice role is common to all new members of the House. But it is wrong to assume that each Committee will give it the same

---

[20] The ideas of "reciprocity" and "complementarity," which are used interchangeably here, are discussed in Alvin Gouldner, "The Norm of Reciprocity," *American Sociological Review* (April, 1960). Most helpful in explaining the idea of a role system has been the work of J. Wahlke, H. Eulau, W. Buchanan, L. Ferguson. See their study, *The Legislative System* (New York, 1962), esp. Intro.

emphasis. Some pay it scant heed.[21] The Appropriations Committee makes it a cornerstone of its internal structure.

Among the Committee's veterans, the key roles are those of Committee Chairman and ranking minority member, and their counterparts in every sub-committee. It is a measure of Committee integration and the low degree of partisanship that considerable reciprocity obtains between these roles. Their partisan status nevertheless sets limits to the degree of possible integration. The Chairman is given certain authority which he and only he can exercise. But save in times of extreme party controversy, the expectation is that consultation and cooperation between the chairman and the ranking minority member shall lubricate the Committee's entire work. For example, by Committee tradition, its Chairman and ranking minority member are both *ex officio* voting members of each sub-committee and of every conference committee. The two of them thus have joint access at every stage of the internal process. A subcommittee chairman, too, is expected to discuss matters of scheduling and agenda with his opposite minority number. He is expected to work with him during the markup session and to give him (and, normally, only him) an opportunity to read and comment on the subcommittee report.[22] A ranking minority member described his subcom-mittee markup procedure approvingly:

Frequently the chairman has a figure which he states. Sometimes he will have no figure, and he'll turn to me and say, "——, what do you think?" Maybe I'll have a figure. It's very flexible. Everyone has a chance to say what he thinks, and we'll move it around. Sometimes it takes a long time. . . . He's a rabid partisan on the floor, but he is a very fair man in the subcommittee.

Where influence is shared, an important exchange of rewards occurs. The chairman gains support for his leadership and the ranking minority member gains intra-Committee power. The Committee as a whole insures against the possibility of drastic change in its internal structure by giving to its key minority members a stake in its operation. Chairmen and ranking minority members will, in the course of time, exchange positions; and it is expected that such a switch will produce no form of retribution nor any drastic change in the functioning of the Committee. Reciprocity of roles, in this case, promotes continued integration. A ranking minority member testified to one successful arrangement when he took the floor in the 83rd Congress to say:

The gentleman and I have been see-sawing back and forth on this committee for some time. He was chairman in the 80th Congress. I had the privilege of serving as chairman in the 81st and 82nd Congresses. Now he is back in the saddle. I can say that he has never failed to give me his utmost cooperation, and I have tried to give him the same cooperation during his service as chairman of this Committee. We seldom disagree, but we have found out that we can disagree without being disagreeable. Consequently, we have unusual harmony on this committee.[23]

---

[21] For example, the Committee on Education and Labor, see footnote 26.
[22] See the exchange in 101 *Cong. Rec.* pp. 3832, 3844, 3874.
[23] 99 *Cong. Rec.*, p. 4933.

Reciprocity between chairmen and ranking minority members on the Appropriations Committee is to some incalculable degree a function of the stability of membership which allows a pair of particular individuals to work out the kind of personal accommodation described above. The close working relationship of Clarence Cannon and John Taber, whose service on the Committee totals 68 years and who have been changing places as Chairman and ranking minority member for 19 years, highlights and sustains a pattern of majority–minority reciprocity throughout the group.

INTERNAL CONTROL MECHANISMS

The expectations which apply to subcommittee, to party, to veterans and to newcomers, to chairmen and to ranking minority members prescribe highly integrative behaviors. We have concentrated on these expectations, and have both illustrated and assumed the close correlation between expected and actual behavior. This does not mean that all the norms of the Committee have been canvassed. Nor does it mean that deviation from the integrative norms does not occur. It does. From what can be gathered, however, from piecing together a study of the public record on appropriations from 1947 to 1961 with interview materials, the Committee has been markedly successful in maintaining a stable internal structure over time. As might be expected, therefore, changes and threats of change have been generated more from the environment—when outsiders consider the Committee as unresponsive—than from inside the subsystem itself. One source of internal stability, and an added reason for assuming a correlation between expected and actual behavior, is the existence of what appear to be reasonably effective internal control mechanisms. Two of these are the socialization processes applied to newcomers and the sanctioning mechanisms applicable to all Committee members.

Socialization is in part a training in perception. Before members of a group can be expected to behave in accordance with its norms, they must learn to see and interpret the world around them with reasonable similarity. The socialization of the Committee newcomer during his term or two of apprenticeship serves to bring his perceptions and his attitudes sufficiently into line with those of the other members to serve as a basis for Committee integration. The Committee, as we have seen, is chosen from Congressmen whose political flexibility connotes an aptitude for learning new lessons of power. Furthermore, the high degree of satisfaction of its members with the group increases their susceptibility to its processes of learning and training.

For example, one half of the Committee's Democrats are Northerners and Westerners from urban constituencies, whose voting records are just as "liberal" on behalf of domestic social welfare programs as non-Committee Democrats from like constituencies. They come to the Committee favorably disposed toward the high level of federal spending necessary to support such programs, and with no sense of urgency about the Committee's tasks of guarding the Treasury or reducing budget estimates. Given the criteria governing their selection, however, they come without rigid preconceptions and with a built-in responsiveness to the socialization processes of any legislative group of which they are members. It is crucial to Committee integration that they learn to temper their potentially disruptive welfare-state ideology with a conservative's concern for saving money. They must change their perceptions and attitudes sufficiently to view the Committee's tasks in nearly the same terms as their more conservative Southern Democratic and Republican colleagues. What their elders perceive as reality (*i.e.*, the disposition of executives to ask for more money than is necessary) they, too, must see as reality. A subcommittee chairman explained:

When you have sat on the Committee, you see that these bureaus are always asking for more money—always up, never down. They want to build up their organization. You reach the point—I have—where it sickens you, where you rebel against it. Year after year, they want more money. They say, "Only $50,000 this year"; but you know the pattern. Next year they'll be back for $100,000, then $200,000. The younger members haven't been on the Committee long enough, haven't had the experience to know this.

The younger men, in this case the younger liberals, do learn from their Committee experience. Within one or two terms, they are differentiating between themselves and the "wild-eyed spenders" or the "free spenders" in the House. "Some of these guys would spend you through the roof," exclaimed one liberal of moderate seniority. Repeated exposure to Committee work and to fellow members has altered their perceptions and their attitudes in money matters. Half a dozen Northern Democrats of low or moderate seniority agreed with one of their number who said: "Yes, it's true. I can see it myself. I suppose I came here a flaming liberal; but as the years go by I get more conservative. You just hate like hell to spend all this money. . . . You come to the point where you say, 'By God, this is enough jobs.'" These men will remain more inclined toward spending than their Committee colleagues, but their perceptions and hence their attitudes have been brought close enough to the others to support a consensus on tasks. They are responsive to appeals on budget-cutting grounds that would not have registered earlier and which remain meaningless to liberals outside the Committee. In cases, therefore, where Committee selection does not and cannot initially produce individuals with a predisposition toward protecting the Treasury, the same result is achieved by socialization.

Socialization is a training in behavior as well as in perception. For the newcomer, conformity to norms in specific situations is insured through the appropriate application, by the Committee veterans, of rewards and punishments. For the Committee member who serves his apprenticeship creditably, the passage of time holds the promise that he will inherit a position of influence. He may, as an incentive, be given some small reward early in his Committee career. One man, in his second year, had been assigned the task of specializing in one particular program. However narrow the scope of his specialization, it had placed him on the road to influence within the Committee. He explained with evident pleasure:

The first year, you let things go by. You can't participate. But you learn by watching the others operate. The next year, you know what you're interested in and when to step in. . . . For instance, I've become an expert on the ——— program. The chairman said to me, "This is something you ought to get interested in." I did; and now I'm the expert on the Committee. Whatever I say on that, the other members listen to me and do what I want.

At some later date, provided he continues to observe Committee norms, he will be granted additional influence, perhaps through a prominent floor role. A model Committee man of moderate seniority who had just attained to this stage of accomplishment, and who had suffered through several political campaigns back home fending off charges that he was a do-nothing Congressman, spoke about the rewards he was beginning to reap.

When you perform well on the floor when you bring out a bill, and Members know that you know the bill, you develop prestige with other Members of Congress. They come over and ask you what you think, because they know you've studied it. You begin to get a reputation beyond your subcommittee. And you get inner satisfaction, too. You don't feel that you're down here doing nothing.

The first taste of influence which comes to men on this Committee is compensation for the frustrations of apprenticeship. Committee integration in general, and the meshing of roles between elders and newcomers in particular, rests on the fact that conformity to role expectations over time does guarantee to the young positive rewards—the very kind of rewards of power, prestige, and personal satisfaction which led most of them to seek Committee membership in the first place.

The important function of apprenticeship is that it provides the necessary time during which socialization can go forward. And teaching proceeds with the aid of punishments as well as rewards. Should a new member inadvertently or deliberately run afoul of Committee norms during his apprenticeship, he will find himself confronted with negative sanctions ranging in subtlety from "jaundiced eyes" to a changed subcommittee assignment. Several members, for example, recalled their earliest encounter with the norm of unity and the tradition against minority reports. One remembered his attempt to file a minority report. "The Chairman was pretty upset about it. It's just a tradition, I guess, not to have minority reports. I didn't know it was a tradition. When I said I was going to write a minority report, some eyebrows were raised. The Chairman said it just wasn't the thing to do. Nothing more was said about it. But it wasn't a very popular thing to do, I guess." He added that he had not filed one since.

Some younger members have congenital difficulty in observing the norms of the apprentice's role. In the 86th Congress, these types tended to come from the Republican minority. The minority newcomers (described by one of the men who selected them as "eight young, energetic, fighting conservatives") were a group of economy-minded individuals some of whom chafed against any barrier which kept them from immediate influence on Committee policy. Their reaction was quite different from that of the young Democrats, whose difficulty was in learning to become economy-minded, but who did not actively resent their lack of influence. One freshman, who felt that "The appropriations system is lousy, inadequate and old fashioned," recalled that he had spoken out in full Committee against the recommendations of a subcommittee of which he was not a member. Having failed, he continued to oppose the recommendation during floor debate. By speaking up, speaking in relation to the work of another subcommittee and by opposing a Committee recommendation, he had violated the particular norms of his apprentice role as well of the generally applicable norms of reciprocity and unity. He explained what he had learned, but remained only partially socialized:

They want to wash their dirty linen in the Committee and they want no opposition afterward. They let me say my piece in Committee. . . . But I just couldn't keep quiet. I said some things on the floor, and I found out that's about all they would take. . . . If you don't get along with your Committee and have their support, you don't get anything accomplished around here. . . . I'm trying to be a loyal, cooperative member of the Committee. You hate to be a stinker; but I'm still picking at the little things because I can't work on the big things. There's nothing for the new men to do, so they have to find places to needle in order to take some part in it.

Another freshman, who had deliberately violated apprenticeship norms by trying to ask "as many questions as the chairman" during subcommittee hearings, reported a story of unremitting counteraction against his deviation:

In the hearings, I have to wait sometimes nine or ten hours for a chance; and he hopes I'll get tired and stay home. I've had to wait till some pretty unreasonable hours. Once I've gotten the floor, though, I've been able to make a good case. Sometimes I've been the only person there. . . . He's all powerful. He's got all the power. He wouldn't think of taking me on a trip with him when he goes to hold hearings. Last year, he went to———. He wouldn't give me a nudge there. And in the hearings, when I'm questioning a witness, he'll keep butting in so that my case won't appear to be too rosy.

Carried on over a period of two years, this behavior resulted in considerable personal friction between a Committee elder and the newcomer. Other members of his subcommittee pointedly gave him a great lack of support for his nonconformity. "They tried to slow him down and tone him down a little," not because he and his subcommittee chairman disagreed, but on the grounds that the Committee has developed accepted ways of disagreeing which minimize, rather than exacerbate, interpersonal friction.

One internal threat to Committee integration comes from new members who from untutored perceptions, from ignorance of norms, or from dissatisfaction with the apprentice role may not act in accordance with Committee expectations. The seriousness of this threat is minimized, however, by the fact that the deviant newcomer does not possess sufficient resources to affect adversely the operation of the system. Even if he does not respond immediately to the application of sanctions, he can be held in check and subjected to an extended and (given the frequency of interaction among members) intensive period of socialization. The success of Committee socialization is indicated by the fact that whereas wholesale criticism of Committee operations was frequently voiced among junior members, it had disappeared among the men of moderate experience. And what these middle seniority members now accept as the facts of Committee life, the veterans vigorously assert and defend as the essentials of a smoothly functioning system. Satisfaction with the Committee's internal structure increases with length of Committee service.

An important reason for changing member attitudes is that those who have attained leadership positions have learned, as newcomers characteristically have not, that their conformity to Committee norms is the ultimate source of their influence inside the group. Freshman members do not as readily perceive the degree to which interpersonal influence is rooted in obedience to group norms, They seem to convert their own sense of powerlessness into the view that the Committee's leaders possess, by virtue of their positions, arbitrary, absolute, and awesome power. Typically, they say: "If you're a subcommittee chairman, it's your Committee." "The Chairman runs the show. He gets what he wants. He decides what he wants and gets it through." Older members of the Committee, however, view the power of the leaders as a highly contingent and revocable grant, tendered by the Committee for so long and only so long as their leaders abide by Committee expectations. In commenting on internal influence, their typical reaction is: "Of course, the Committee wouldn't follow him if it didn't want to. He has a great deal of respect. He's an able man, a hard-working man." "He knows the bill backwards and forwards. He works hard, awfully hard and the members know it." Committee leaders have an imposing set of formal prerogatives. But they can capitalize on them only if they command the respect, confidence and deference of their colleagues.

It is basic to Committee integration that members who have the greatest power to change the system evidence the least disposition to do so. Despite their institutional conservatism, however, Committee elders do occasionally violate the norms applicable to them and hence represent a potential threat to successful integration. Excessive deviation from Committee expectations by some leaders will bring counter-measures by other leaders. Thus, for example, the Chairman and his subcommittee chairmen exercise reciprocal controls over one another's behavior. The Chairman has the authority to appoint the chairman and members of each subcommittee and fix its jurisdiction. "He runs the Committee. He has a lot of power," agrees one subcommittee chairman. "But it's all done on the basis of personal friendship. If he tries to get too big, the members can whack him down by majority vote."

In the 84th Congress, Chairman Cannon attempted an unusually broad reorganization of subcommittee jurisdictions. The subcommittee chairman most adversely affected rallied his senior colleagues against the Chairman's action—on the ground that it was an excessive violation of role expectations and threatening to subcommittee autonomy. Faced with the prospect of a negative Committee vote, the Chairman was forced to act in closer conformity to the expectations of the other leaders. As one participant described the episode,

Mr. Cannon, for reasons of his own, tried to bust up one of the subcommittees. We didn't like that. . . . He was breaking up the whole Committee. A couple of weeks later, a few of the senior members got together and worked out a compromise. By that time, he had seen a few things, so we went to him and talked to him and worked it out."

On the subcommittees, too, it is the veterans of both parties who will levy sanctions against an offending chairman. It is they who speak of "cutting down to size" and "trimming the whiskers" of leaders who become "too cocky," "too stubborn" or who "do things wrong too often." Committee integration is underwritten by the fact that no member high or low is permanently immune from the operation of its sanctioning mechanisms.

III

Data concerning internal committee activity can be organized and presented in various ways. One way is to use key functional problems like integration as the focal points for descriptive analysis. On the basis of our analysis (and without, for the time being, having devised any precise measure of integration), we are led to the summary observation that the House Appropriations Committee appears to be a well integrated, if not an extremely well integrated, committee. The question arises as to whether anything can be gained from this study other than a description of one property of one political subsystem. If it is reasonable to assume that the internal life of a congressional committee affects all legislative activity involving that committee, and if it is reasonable to assume that the analysis of a committee's internal relationships will produce useful knowledge about legislative behavior, some broader implications for this study are indicated.

In the first place, the success of the House Appropriations Committee in solving the problem of integration probably does have important consequences for the appropriations process. Some of the possible relationships can be stated as hypotheses and tested; others can be suggested as possible guides to understanding. All of them require further research. Of primary interest is the relationship between integration and the power of the Committee. There is little doubt about the fact of Committee power. Of the 443 separate case histories of bureau appropriations examined, the House accepted Committee recommendations in 387, or 87.4 per cent of them; and in 159, or 33.6 per cent of the cases, the House Committee's original recommendations on money amounts were the exact ones enacted into law. The hypothesis that the greater the degree of Committee unity the greater the probability that its recommendations will be accepted is being tested as part of a larger study.[24] House Committee integration may be a key factor in producing House victories in conference committee. This relationship, too, might be tested. Integration appears to help provide the House conferees with a feeling of confidence and superiority which is one of their important advantages in the mix of psychological factors affecting conference deliberations.

[24] Cf. Dwaine Marvick, "Congressional Appropriations Politics," unpublished manuscript (Columbia, 1952).

Another suggested consequence of high integration is that party groups have a relatively small influence upon appropriations decisions. It suggests, too, that Committee-oriented behavior should be duly emphasized in any analysis of Congressional oversight of administrative activity by this Committee. Successful integration promotes the achievement of the Committee's goals, and doubtless helps account for the fairly consistent production of budget-cutting decisions. Another consequence will be found in the strategies adopted by people seeking favorable Committee decisions. For example, the characteristic lines of contact from executive officials to the Committee will run to the chairman and the ranking minority member (and to the professional staff man) of the single sub-committee handling their agency's appropriations. The ways in which the Committee achieves integration may even affect the success or failure of a bureau in getting its appropriations. Committee members, for instance, will react more favorably toward an administrator who conforms to their self-image of the hard-working master-of-detail than to one who does not—and Committee response to individual administrators bulks large in their determinations.

Finally, the internal integration of this Committee helps to explain the extraordinary stability, since 1920, of appropriations procedures—in the face of repeated proposals to change them through omnibus appropriations, legislative budgets, new budgetary forms, item veto, Treasury borrowing, etc. Integration is a stabilizing force, and the stability of the House Appropriations Committee has been a force for stabilization throughout the entire process. It was, for example, the disagreement between Cannon and Taber which led to the in-decisiveness reflected in the short-lived experiment with a single appropriations bill.[25] One need only examine the conditions most likely to decrease Committee integration to ascertain some of the critical factors for producing changes in the appropriations process. A description of integration in also an excellent base-line from which to analyze changes in internal structure.

All of these are speculative propositions which call for further research. But they suggest, as a second implication, that committee integration does have important consequences for legislative activity and, hence, that it is a key variable in the study of legislative politics. It would seem, therefore, to be a fruitful focal point for the study of other congressional committees.[26] Comparative committee

---

[25] See Dalmas Nelson, "The Omnibus Appropriations Act of 1950," *Journal of Politics* (May, 1953).

[26] This view has been confirmed by the results of interviews conducted by the author with members of the House Committee on Education and Labor, together with an examination of that Committee's activity in one policy area. They indicate very significant contrasts between the internal structure of that Committee and the Appropriations Committee—contrasts which center around their comparative success in meeting the problem of integration. The House Committee on Education and Labor appears to be a poorly integrated committee. Its internal structure is characterized by a great deal of subgroup conflict, relatively little role reciprocity, and minimally effective internal control mechanisms. External concerns, like those of party, constituency and clientele groups, are probably more effective in determining its decisions than is likely to be the case in a well-integrated committee. An analysis of the internal life of the Committee on Education and Labor, drawn partly from interviews with 19 members of that group, will appear in a forthcoming study, *Federal Aid to Education and National Politics*, by Professor Frank Munger and the author, to be published by Syracuse University Press. See also Nicholas R. Masters, *op. cit.*, note 7 above, pp. 354–555, and Seymour Scher, "Congressional Committee Members as Independent Agency Overseers: A Case Study," this REVIEW, Vol. 54 (December 1960), pp. 911–20.

analysis could usefully be devoted to (1) the factors which tend to increase or decrease integration; (2) the degree to which integration is achieved; and (3) the consequences of varying degrees of integration for committee behavior and influence. If analyses of committee integration are of any value, they should encourage the analysis and the classification of congressional committees along functional lines. And they should lead to the discussion of interrelated problems of committee survival. Functional classifications of committees (*i.e.*, well or poorly integrated) derived from a large number of descriptive analyses of several functional problems, may prove helpful in constructing more general propositions about the legislative process.

Senate: Integrative Role in Chile's Political Development

by WESTON H. AGOR

The primary focus of this paper is "inside" the Senate, where we seek to describe and analyze how two major components of the internal distribution of influence (standing committee system and informal "rules of the game") contribute to the integration of the total Chilean political system. We define integration as the capacity to minimize conflict among component roles and subgroups by heading off or resolving the conflicts that arise.[1]

More specifically, the Senate may be visualized as a political sub-system imbedded in an environment, the most salient feature of which is a multiparty system. Because no single party normally commands a majority of the votes necessary for decision-making, the Senate serves as one arena where political parties meet, compromise, and agree on majority decisions on major legislation. But this process is complicated by the fact that although there is an enormous area of agreement among Chilean political parties on certain policy objectives,[2] there is also sharp disagreement on many others, including the means of implementation. The Senate as an institutional system is faced, then, with the organizational problem of establishing an internal structure of influence with the capability of forming majority decisions across ideologically "opposed" political parties without tearing itself apart. This centers our attention on the standing

---

[1] This definition was first used by Richard F. Fenno, Jr., in his study of the House Appropriations Committee. See Richard F. Fenno, Jr., "The Appropriations Committee as a Political System," in Robert L. Peabody and Nelson W. Polsby (eds.), *New Perspectives On The House of Representatives*, (Chicago: Rand McNally and Company, 1963), p. 80.

[2] K. H. Silvert, "The Prospects of Chilean Democracy—Some Propositions on Chile," in Robert D. Tomasek (ed.), *Latin American Politics: Studies on the Contemporary Scene* (Garden City, N.Y.: Anchor Books, 1966), p. 396.

A revised version of a paper prepared for delivery at the Sixty-Fifth Annual Meeting of the American Political Science Association, Commodore Hotel, New York City, September 2–6, 1969. Copyright © 1971 by The Free Press and Weston H. Agor.

committee system and informal "rules of the game" that enable the Senate to cope with its environment by regulating its own internal behavior,[3] and the functional relationship between these mechanisms and Chile's political system integration.[4]

Part I of this paper shows how the standing committee environment and internal norms of expertise, specialization, and consideration of the "national interest" temper and frequently offset partisanship. For example, the smallness of standing committees (five members) and the fact that sessions are closed and off-the-record encourage a friendly impersonal style conducive to a candid exchange of views and inter-party agreements. This is reinforced by committee norms and a non-partisan staff. Part II examines the Senate's informal "rules of the game" that define member and leadership roles and set minimum standards of expected behavior. We find five separate Senate norms function to reduce partisan conflict and encourage identification with national program goals: courtesy, reciprocity, institutional patriotism, legislative work, and specialization. These norms are reinforced by mechanisms of socialization and sanction. We conclude the paper by exploring how the Senate mechanisms discussed above appear to contribute to Chile's overall political system integration and relatively stable political development.

The principal data sources on which this paper is based are: in-the-field interviews (forty-three of the forty-five Senate universe, 1 ex-senator, twenty Senate staff members, 1 ex-Senate staff member, 2 Chamber staff members, officials in the Executive and the political parties); a detailed analysis of documents, committee reports, floor debates, and the work of other scholars; and extensive empirical observation of the operation of the Chilean Senate. In this paper, political parties will be abbreviated thus: National (PN), Radical (PR), Christian-Democrat (PDC), Vanguard of the People (VNP), National Democrat (PADENA), Socialist (PS), Communist (PC), and Independents (I).

I. Standing Committees: Environment and Integration

A committee system may contribute to sub-system and system-wide integration if it serves as an arena for cross-party cooperation and compromise.[5] One way to measure if a committee system performs this function is to tap senators and staff perceptions on the level of partisanship in committees versus on the

[3] This conceptual approach was first used by Richard F. Fenno, Jr., to describe the internal distribution of influence of the United States House of Representatives, and is adapted to fit the Chilean Senate. See Richard F. Fenno, Jr., "The Internal Distribution of Influence: The House," in David B. Truman (ed.), *The Congress and America's Future* (Englewood Cliffs, N.J.: Prentice-Hall, Inc., 1965).

[4] The reader may justifiably ask at this point, "How do you know that the Senate exercises influence in the total political system and is, therefore, worthy of intensive study?" The Senate's influence is treated elsewhere. See Weston H. Agor, "The Chilean Senate: Decisional Role in Chile's Political System," in Allan Kornberg and Lloyd Musolf (eds.), *Legislatures in Developmental Perspective* (Durham: Duke University Press, forthcoming).

[5] The influence and autonomy of Senate standing committees from national political parties' leadership is examined elsewhere. See Weston H. Agor, "The Chilean Senate: Internal Distribution of Influence," (Unpublished Ph.D. dissertation, University of Wisconsin, 1969).

Senate floor. Therefore, we asked both groups, "When you study a bill in committee, is there a lot of partisanship as on the floor?" All but one senator answered this question. The overwhelming majority of the senators (89 percent—thirty-eight) perceived the level of partisanship to be substantially less in committees than on the floor. Similarly, 91 percent of the staff members interviewed agreed.

A classic illustration of the capacity of the committee environment to socialize and depoliticize ideologically opposed senators was this senator's comment:

> There is still partisanship, but a lower degree of it. It's easier to overcome in committees. . . . One thing I've observed with some experience here is that the longer you stay, the more you tend to identify with a solution. The new senator arrives with strong partisan feelings; he isn't attached to the committee work. But after a few years, he becomes less partisan, more mature; he begins to reason, and the committee becomes a meeting of friends.

The end product of this process is the ability of opposing senators to work together when common goals are involved. This is revealed by one Communist Party senator's comments regarding two ideologically opposed National Party senators.

> There is often serious analysis in committees. . . . Jaramillo has voted for the interests of the workers several times in the Labor and Social Legislation Committee, and Bulnes, I know, studied hard on the 1966 Copper Bill.

Several elements linked together help encourage cross-party communication and compromise in committees. The membership is small, consisting of five senators and two staff members. Sessions are closed and considered to be off-the-record. If discussions are taped, this is solely to aid the secretary in writing the committee report, and the tapes are subsequently destroyed. There is no public gallery or press recording every comment. As a result, the dialogue is free and open, resembling more a club get-together than a formal committee meeting. Said one staff member, "There is a lot less partisanship in committees. One reason is the sessions are private. If senators know what they are saying will not go out of the room, they work a lot better together." Personal exchanges are on a first-name basis characterized by *tutuyas* (familiar *tu* versus formal use of *usted*). This climate is reinforced by the presence of a non-partisan staff. One senator gave tribute to this function, "The staff and special experts cited to appear center the theme of the discussion, and this obliges a more thorough study." Another senator concluded his analogy between committee sessions and floor debates with this comment, "The floor debates serve a public relations function; the committee is the office of work."

Serious study in committees also serves one other important function. It enables senators to build a reputation for expertise in a certain subject matter which in turn serves as a base of power—not only in committee but in the national party policy organs. Take these interview statements for example, "The real Senate work is done here in committees. This is where you get to know each other, and prove your ability," and "In committees, you see the real man—this is where you talk about the interests of Chile, and less about party."

An interesting practice of giving votes to other members is one illustration of the level of comradeship and trust *across parties* in committee. For various reasons, many senators are members of several committees simultaneously. When two of these committees session at the same hour, a senator may appear to provide a quorum, give his proxy to another member, and leave to work in the other committee. When an issue comes up for a vote, the senator who holds two will cast the one held "in trust" the same way he knows the other senator would—*even if it opposes his own vote*. What enables this system to work is the recognition that maybe tomorrow or next week, the "trustee" will want the opposition senator to reciprocate, and this principle is extended as well to the pair system on the floor.[6]

This is not to suggest that norms of partisanship are totally displaced in Senate committees. One Radical Party senator observed, "There is certainly less partisanship, but never zero. You might say there is at least twenty percent all the time." Interviews and observation indicate that the level of partisanship in committees varies by type of bill, stage of the bill (general versus specific discussion), by party, by committee, and time period.

On some key bills, the national political parties' leadership may issue orders on how their respective committee members should vote—even before the committee has a chance to review the bill. On these occasions, partisanship is accentuated. But even then it is displaced by other norms during article-by-article review.[7] For example, a Christian-Democrat senator noted that even though Radical Party Senator Bossay had orders on how to vote at the first stage of the 1968 Salary Readjustment Bill, he cooperated with the Christian-Democrat Party later to eliminate several amendments. A staff member confessed, "A lot of amendments are cut out in committees. Many are submitted to meet district or pressure group demands. But imagine, the *same* senator will take them out in committee."

Generally, committee norms of expertise and specialized study seem to predominate over partisan criteria when the content of the bill is highly technical. One staff member said, "There are two general kinds of bills, technical and partisan. When a committee goes over the former type, it works alone free from political pressure." On the latter, the displacement process is reversed, and this is accentuated by the fact that parties of the left tend to instruct their senators on how to vote more frequently than the right.

Very exploratory research also suggests that the level of partisanship may vary from committee to committee much as in the United States Congress

---

[6] For a discussion of how personal identification with the system (*i.e.*, giving each participant a stake in ensuring its persistence) provides for reduction in the intensity of partisan considerations and displacement by system attachment and support, see Ralf Dahrendorf, *Class and Class Conflict in Industrial Society* (Stanford: Stanford University Press, 1959), p. 216.

[7] Bills pass through two main stages in the Senate. The first stage is a general review centering around the question of whether or not the Senate wishes to legislate on the matter in question. The second stage (once the Senate decides to legislate) involves a detailed article by article review.

(*e.g.*, compare House Appropriations Committee to Education and Labor).[8] For example, the responsibility of interpreting the Constitution as well as the highly technical nature of most bills considered by the Constitution, Legislation, Justice, and Rules Committee cause members to emphasize norms of expertise and specialization rather than partisanship. On the other hand, many of the bills the Labor and Social Legislation Committee considers involve issues that clearly divide the political parties ideologically (*e.g.*, social security benefits, right to strike). As a result, interest group activity is more evident, and discussions tend to be more high pitched speeches than calm careful reviews. Also, circumstantial variables such as a coming election period, or animosities left as the result of a previous campaign (*e.g.*, 1965) may raise or lower the influence of one set of norms over the other. Still, as a whole, a quiet, private, and informal committee environment functions to reduce partisan conflict—or at least provide an arena where compromises can be pounded out.

II. Informal Rules of the Game and Integration

Traditionally, political parties in Chile have formed temporary blocs or coalitions large enough to insure a majority vote on legislation. During the most recent legislative period (1965–69), the Government Party (Christian-Democrat) attempted to govern by relying on other parties for support on an issue-by-issue basis rather than resorting to a formal coalition. What attracts attention is the fact that opposing political parties have cooperated with the Christian-Democrat Party in the Senate to pass major legislation. For example, the Government passed the 1966 Chileanization Copper Bill with the support of the National and Radical parties, while the 1966 Agrarian Reform Bill passed with Communist and Radical parties' votes. The 1968 Salary Readjustment Bill left the Senate with the support of *both* the National and Communist parties—polar opposites ideologically.

Evidently, ideologically "opposed" political parties are capable of dampening partisan differences sufficiently to permit actions for purposes upon which members are basically in agreement.[9] This capacity may in turn be dependent on certain "rules of the game" which set the approximate limits of expected behavior required to obtain the respect and cooperation of opposing parties' members. If this is so, tapping senators and staff perceptions as to the existence of such unwritten rules of behavior and their functions may give us empirical proof that this description is correct.

Senators and staff were asked, "Would you say there are unofficial norms, rules, expectations in the Senate, *i.e.*, certain things members must do and things they must not do if they want the respect and cooperation of fellow-members?" If the response was affirmative, they were also asked, "What are

---

[8] See Masters' comments in Nicholas A. Masters, "Committee Assignments," in Robert L. Peabody and Nelson W. Polsby (eds.), *op. cit.*, pp. 53–56.

[9] See the author's comments on policy consensus in Chile in Charles W. Anderson, *Politics and Economic Change in Latin America: The Governing of Restless Nations* (Princeton, Toronto and London: D. Van Nostrand Company, Inc., 1967), p. 197.

some of these 'rules of the game' that a member must observe?" Every senator and every staff member responding to the questions (27 percent and 95 percent of total interviewed respectively) said there were unwritten rules of the game that governed a senator's behavior. One perceptive senator said, "Seventy percent of the Senate's action is guided by informal rules. The Senate Rules are applied only when the informal ones are not observed, which is rare." A staff member concurred, "Of course there are unwritten rules. I think they are more important than the Senate Rules themselves."

NORMS THAT DECREASE CONFLICT

Courtesy—The observer is struck by the similarity of the Chilean Senate's "folkways" to those described by Donald Matthews in the United States Senate.[10] One group of norms functions primarily to reduce or set acceptable limits on partisan conflict. The first and most widely held of this group is *senatorial courtesy*. Thirty-nine (89 percent) of the senators responding specified twelve rules that define this norm. The rule most frequently mentioned was, "Don't attack other colleagues personally, nor be verbally aggressive." Related to this is the practice of avoiding reference to a colleague when he is not on the floor to defend himself. If a personal reference is unavoidable, it is expected that the senator will advise his colleague beforehand, explain the circumstances, and give him an opportunity to prepare a rebuttal if necessary. One source of particular irritation is to be misquoted by an opposition party senator. Avoiding this practice prevents the animosity that could inhibit inter-party cooperation. Similarly, if understandings or compromises are ever to be reached, senators must listen to each other, ponder the other's point of view, and be sure everyone has a chance to be heard. Accordingly, senators are expected to listen patiently while others speak—on the floor and in committee.

As in the United States Senate, a number of formal rules aid the members to approximate expected behavior. For example, senators are expected to ask the President of the Senate for permission to speak and address him rather than another senator. Senators also must address each other as "Honorable" and ask permission to interrupt a speech rather than simply break in. Take this typical example of the verbal impersonality generally maintained on the floor—even when discussing a vital issue such as the 1967 Constitutional Reform Proposal of President Frei.

> *Chadwick* (PS)—Would you permit me an interruption?
> *Aylwin* (PDC)—Charged to your time.
> *Allende* (Pres.)—With the permission of Honorable Senator Aylwin, you may have the floor, Mr. Senator.
> *Chadwick* (PS)—In the speech that Honorable Senator Aylwin is making, he mentioned in passing the law creating the Ministry of Housing. . . .[11]

Occasions such as reelection or retirement from the Senate are frequently

---

[10] Donald R. Matthews, *U.S. Senators and Their World* (New York: Vintage Books, 1960), Chapter V.
[11] *Diario de sesiones del senado, legislatura extraordinaria*, sesión 87a, February 23, 1967, p. 4264.

used to praise a colleague publicly—*across parties.* One excellent example of this practice and its linkage to Chile's democratic tradition is the retirement of several senators in 1957.

> *Amunátegui* (PL)—Senator Marín (PL) has spoken kindly of Socialist Senator Eugenio González Rojas who attends the Senate today for the last time. These kind words give prestige to the Senate and to our democracy. I think, then, that this occasion of our parliamentary life would not be complete if we didn't pay homage . . . to those other Senators who will not be with us . . . all of them fulfilled their duties with honor . . . be it on the floor, or in the active, silent, and efficient work of the committees, they served their ideas and their parties.
>
> *González, M.* (PR)—The conduct of the Senate this afternoon and in the previous session of recognizing the accomplishments of Senators who will not continue with us is a page of democratic dignity . . . that serves as an example. This is what enables us to get along together, and this is how Chilean democracy aspires and lives.[12]

Donald Matthews noted that a cardinal rule of United States Senate courtesy is that political disagreements should not influence personal feelings.[13] If we could find evidence for the existence of a similar rule in the Chilean Senate, it would indicate that an environment conducive to inter-party cooperation exists. One means of quantifying the Senate "culture" is to ask senators whether or not they get along well across parties. Senators were asked, "Would you say that senators who are members of opposing political parties get along well personally?" *Every* senator who answered (forty-three or 96 percent) felt their colleagues get along well together. One senator explained, "We sign a pact of gentlemen when we enter the Senate. You can't live fighting every minute." A second senator noted, "It is characteristic of Chilean parliamentary style that no matter how the debate goes, it does not alter personal friendships and treatment. Chile is not like other Latin American countries—hate is not strong here— we are all friends." A third added, "Yes, we are very friendly and cordial here. It is an exceptional case when senators do not get along well, and then it is because someone has an unpleasant personality, not because of their political ideas."

Many senators were schoolmates together or have served in Congress approximately the same time. Contacts outside the Senate are regular, including family cocktails or parties, and cross-party marriages are not uncommon. The product of these interpersonal contacts and family ties is a friendly and cordial atmosphere reminiscent of a private club. Indeed, one staff member pointed out, "The Senate is a club. Students from other countries who are Communists can't understand ours; they are conservative and inflexible. Here, senators are all good friends." Another highly experienced staff member agreed, "Senators know they have to live together for eight years. They have to get along in committees or other situations. The only way to live together for such a long period is to be friendly."

This is not to say that senators are always on the best of terms or that the

---

[12] *Diario de sesiones del senado, legislatura extraordinaria,* sesión 18a, April 14, 1957, pp. 525–26.
[13] Donald R. Matthews, *op. cit.,* p. 97.

norm of partisanship does not overpower the norm of courtesy periodically. For example, one Christian-Democrat senator noted that the early post-election period in 1965 was characterized by a high level of partisanship. "Things were really touchy in 1965. We felt strong, proud, and perhaps we made some mistakes as a result." He continued, "Yet, over time, we have become more friendly." Curiously, several respondents called attention to the fact that personal animosity between senators is more frequently an intra-party versus inter-party phenomenon. Well known are the personal feuds that separate Allende and Ampuero (Socialist Party) or the "two Humbertos" in the Radical Party (Aguirre and Enríquez). But, on the whole, courtesy and other norms that reduce conflict provide and maintain a culture that enables the Senate structure of influence to make decisions without tearing itself apart. Senator Von Mühlenbrock put it this way in a memorable 1967 speech, "He who yesterday was your worst enemy, tomorrow may be your best friend."[14]

Reciprocity—In view of the high level of inter-party friendship in the Senate, it is not surprising to find a widely held norm of *reciprocity* that also aids in reducing conflict. Eighty-two percent (thirty-five) of the senators responding mentioned sixteen different rules to define this norm governing several stages of legislative activity. In exchange theory terms, the norm of reciprocity prescribes that a senator should provide assistance wherever he can in full expectation that he will be repaid in kind.

Several rules govern committee work. One common rule prescribes that a regular member should temporarily step down to allow a fellow party member to watch over and vote for a bill that he has authored or that directly affects the interests of his district. A related rule is that a senator who is not a member of a particular committee should be allowed to attend sessions and even participate in the debate of a committee when a bill is of concern to him. Similarly, when a member of a committee requests that certain groups be called to testify on a bill, the president of the committee is expected to do so—even if the request comes from an opposition senator. On occasions, a member of one party may not be able to attend a committee session. If a vote is coming up that day, he will leave his "in trust" with another member. The trustee is expected to vote the same way the senator himself would have.

On the floor, a group of rules encourage inter-party cooperation to pass certain types of legislation. One rule is that senators should vote for a bill that aids another's district whenever possible. Similarly, all five senators from the same district (even if members of opposing parties) are expected to work together to draw up and pass legislation which mutually benefits their common district. A related rule calls for senators to sign a senator's petition to bring to the floor an amendment killed in committee—even if they personally oppose it then or later on the floor. For various reasons, senators of opposing parties pair votes as in the United States Congress. Breaking such an agreement is one of the most severe breaches of trust a senator can make.

This system of rules is held together by the recognition of most senators that

---

[14] *Diario de sesiones del senado, legislatura extraordinaria*, sesión 87a, February 23, 1967, p. 4281.

they may need another senator's support some day. Furthermore, if one senator upsets this system of mutual accommodation, a chain reaction may be set off that can touch the interests of each of them. For example, the Senate initiates legislation by attaching amendments on bills that the Executive has classified as urgent and that must be considered in a short period of time. Both the President of the Senate and the respective committees' presidents have the authority to rule out amendments on the grounds that they are not pertinent to the bill or are unconstitutional. But Senate norms prescribe that this prerogative be exercised sparingly and nonpartisanly. Now, if one committee president backed by a majority bloc vote begins to violate this norm, retaliation may be taken in another committee where the balance of votes is not the same. Or a floor leader may refuse to go along on a unanimous consent measure in inter-party conference.

Matthews found in the United States Senate that this game works best when senators are able to visualize legislation in national terms.[15] If we could find evidence to show that Chilean senators do have as one role orientation that of *national representative*, it would help to explain how senators appear to be able to cooperate and compromise across parties. We sought to tap the existence of this role orientation by asking, "What do you think the role of the Senate` should be in Chile's political system?" Of the twenty-nine senators responding to this question (66 percent of those interviewed), the overwhelming majority (twenty-six or 90 percent) felt the body should have as its main role that of representing the national interest.[16] Several also perceived a conflict between this orientation and that of party or district representative and indicated they resolve it on particular issues by voting for the national interest as they see it.

A survey of Senate debates supports interview response. It is significant to find, for example, Christian-Democrat President of the Senate Reyes (1965–66) calling members' attention to this passage of President Frei's first message to Congress in 1965:

There [the Senate], I learned, in grand debates, that more important than partisan positions is a spirit that is in the root of our history, and that permits us to overcome differences when national interests are involved.[17]

In another instance, Senator Videla (Liberal Party) reminded his colleagues of their national role as he stepped down from the Presidency of the Senate, "We have the obligation to contribute to the respect of and esteem for the Senate, because in this way we contribute to the future of the Nation. . . ."[18] Or take the 1961 speech of Senator Ampuero (Socialist Party), member of one of the supposedly more disciplined Chilean political parties. Opposing a change in Senate Rules that would give political party leadership greater control over individual senators, Ampuero noted that it had been traditional in the Senate

---

[15] Donald R. Matthews, *op. cit.*, p. 101.

[16] The remaining three respondents wanted either to end the Senate and form a unicameral system, or make widespread structural changes of the present arrangement.

[17] *Diario de sesiones del senado, legislatura ordinaria*, sesión 1a, June, 1 1965, p. 12.

[18] *Diario de sesiones del senado, legislatura ordinaria*, sesión 1a, May 31, 1961, p. 28.

versus the Chamber to allow a more free and open debate in search of the course of action that was in the national interest. Evidently perceiving a conflict between role orientations of a "national" versus "party" senator, Ampuero concluded:

... In the Senate it has always been the custom that each Senator, individually, has certain rights, a certain autonomy to participate in debates. In the Chamber, because of its partisan condition, political parties have had more influence as groups over the work of the legislature. Here, I repeat, the individuality of each Senator has been respected more.[19]

It is not surprising that many senators hold a national role orientation. Former President Alessandri Palma sought to incorporate in the Constitution of 1925 the requirement that senators be elected nationally, rather than regionally, and this proposal has many Senate supporters today.[20] Indeed, a reading of the records of the Constitutional Conventions of 1925 clearly show that one objective for providing partial, off-year elections of the Senate, age requirement of 35 versus 21 for the Chamber, and a term of eight versus four years was to insulate the body from short-term periodic political movements to the degree that national interests rather than partisan or personal electoral interests would predominate.[21] As Professor Guzmán, Chilean expert on constitutional law, testified before a Senate committee:

The Senate is a body of elders, that is to say, an entity where the passions are much more temperate. The institution is designed precisely to dampen the passion of the younger chamber or the Executive who is too innovative.[22]

There is, then, a widely held consensus (though not unanimous) that a senator should have as one role orientation that of representing the nation. Frequently, a conflict between this orientation and that of party or district service will be resolved in favor of the former. Herein lies the link to senators' capacity to reach cross-party compromises and make individual reciprocal agreements. As one Senate saying goes, "*Los hombres pasan, los Gobiernos caen, las instituciones quedan.*" (Men pass, Governments fall, and institutions remain.)

Institutional Loyalty—A third norm that reduces partisan conflict is that of *institutional loyalty*. Thirty-seven percent (sixteen) of the senators responding named a total of six rules that define this norm. Senators seem to take pride in the fact that the Senate and Congress as a whole have real influence in the political system versus most other Latin American countries. They are not so presumptuous as to say the Senate is the greatest legislative and deliberative body in the world, as United States Senators do, but they do make it known that it is one of the oldest and one of the most influential. They are particularly sensitive

---

[19] *Diario de sesiones del senado, legislatura extraordinaria*, sesión 15a, November 21, 1961, p. 683.
[20] José Guillermo Guerra, *La constitución de 1925* (Santiago: Establecimientos Gráficos Balcells and Co., 1929).
[21] *Actas oficiales de las sesiones celebradas por la comisión y subcomisiones encargadas del estudio del proyecto de nueva constitución política de la republica* (Santiago: Ministerio del Interior, Imprenta Universitaria, 1925).
[22] *Diario de sesiones del senado, legislatura extraordinaria*, sesión 87a, February 23, 1967, p. 4288.

about their relationship with the Executive. One staff member observed, "If there is a confrontation with the Executive, senators seem to unite no matter what their party. That's curious, isn't it?" Indeed, Senate Rules state one duty of the President of the Senate is the protection of the prerogatives and honor of the Senate.[23] Similarly, senators like to draw comparisons between the Senate and the Chamber. One senator noted, "We really work on bills here. Over in the Chamber, they have the attitude, 'pass it on to the Senate—they will review it.'" A second senator observed, "There is a lot less mutual respect in the Chamber. Look at their debates. You can hardly think. Over here, it is much more friendly and cordial. I guess we have been around longer, things come into perspective." A prolonged staff interview generated this comment:

Yes. You know, I never really thought about it, but there is a certain amount of tension between the Chambers. They are always concerned about who will preside over joint sessions. Senators have their own parking lot and a bigger staff proportionally. I think the deputies resent that. You know, come to think of it, it's interesting that joint budget committee sessions meet in the Senate rather than the Chamber. In fact, a senator always presides.

An important committee secretary related an experience that not only indicates the existence of a norm of institutional loyalty but also shows the degree to which the secretary had been socialized over the years.

When I was interviewing congressmen for my own book, Senator ———— said to me, "Why criticize the body? I know there are a lot of problems, but all in all, it's one of the best legislatures in the world." [later in interview] When Mexican congressmen come to Chile, they are amazed by the Senate's influence [said with obvious pride]. This is so, I think, because people feel it has a connection with Chile's stability and democratic tradition. That includes Frei up to a point. He is reluctant to push his powers too far.

The high degree of emotional attachment to the institution by senators and staff alike is also exhibited clearly in Senate speeches. For example, senators commemorated the one hundred and fiftieth year of Chilean Congressional history in 1961 with these passages:

Pablo (PDC)— . . . It is also certain that the power that gives character to democracy is that of Parliament. At this time, we are one of three countries in the world that can say they have a Congress with 150 years of uninterrupted institutional life. . . .[24]
Correa (PR)—In our Congress is projected the life of Chile, with its political, economic, and social differences. But all converge in an environment of mutual respect. . . . Our legislature . . . has been an impenetrable bastion of liberty.[25]
Von Mühlenbrock (PL)—Representative democracy can reside only in Congress. The sovereignty of the people can find expression only in Congress. Each party, each idea will give and find its truth there.[26]

[23] "Reglamento del senado," *Manual del senado* (Santiago: Editorial Universitaria, S.A. 1966), p. 121.
[24] *Diario de sesiones del senado, legislatura ordinaria*, sesión 14a, June 5, 1961, p. 672.
[25] *Ibid.*, p. 680.
[26] *Ibid.*, p. 684.

Even two senators of the far left could manage these tributes.

Corvalán (PC)—. . . in the past century . . . the Parliament accomplished a labor that contributed to the formation of a democratic regime, liberal, relatively advanced for this time.[27]

Tarud (I-S)—This occasion should be one of collective satisfaction, in view of the fact that Chile is the only Latin American country that has a century and one-half of continuous parliamentary life. . . .[28]

Senators' institutional loyalty is matched only by that of the Senate staff. It is traditional that senators from all political parties pay public tribute to an important staff member who is retiring. The recipient of this praise and attention normally responds with an emotional farewell that includes a recount of memorable experiences the Senate career has given him.[29] Subsequently, past and present staff members get together on periodic social occasions to rehash past events and political stories.

Of course, not every senator or staff member feels a deep loyalty to the institution. Periodically, Communist and Socialist senators have expressed a desire to form a unicameral legislature or implement other major structural changes. Others advocate moderate reforms within the constitutional framework that exists. But it is apparent that even they are frequently deradicalized and socialized into the system after a number of years of parliamentary experience. Osvaldo Sunkel writes:

It would be no exaggeration to say the left-wing parties, including the Communist Party, . . . have become incorporated into the political Establishment, and that their existence and influence depends on the maintenance of this system.[30]

NORMS THAT ENCOURAGE PERFORMANCE
OF WORK AND SPECIALIZATION

Legislative Work—A second group of norms functions primarily to encourage legislative work and specialization. The first of this group is the norm of *legislative work*. Fifty-eight percent (twenty-five) of the senators responding mentioned this norm and named ten rules to define it. Several rules apply primarily to committee work. One is that senators should try to study bills before they go to committee meetings. An ex-senator explained one evening after dinner, "I always studied bills before going to committee, and when I opened my mouth, I tried to make sure I knew what I was talking about." As in the United States Senate, overlapping committee assignments and other demands made on a senator may make it impossible to fulfill this expectation all the time. But the fact that it is a valued target to shoot for sets the tone of committee work.

Once in committee, senators are expected to dig in, discuss the bill in ques-

---

27 *Ibid.*, p. 661.
28 *Ibid.*, p. 664.
29 *Diario de sesiones del senado, legislatura extraordinaria*, sesión 12a, November 2, 1960, p. 643.
30 Osvaldo Sunkel, "Change and Frustration in Chile," in Claudio Veliz, *Obstacles to Change in Latin America* (London, New York, Toronto: Oxford University Press, 1965), p. 132.

tion, and try to come up with resolutions satisfactory to all. Jorge Tapia Valdés describes the results of this process.

The Senate is the legislative body that does most to improve legislation. Generally, it modifies totally projects sent over by the Chamber, putting articles in logical order, writing them in intelligent form, taking out unnecessary or extraneous material, and so on. . . .[31]

Senators are also expected to attend committee and floor sessions regularly. We do not have data on committee attendance, but an Office of Information of the Senate (OIS) study for the period May 21, 1965 to September 18, 1966, showed that senators attend on average 63 percent of the sessions held. This is a reasonably good performance when one takes into account other demands on their time such as district trips and periodic election campaigns.

Part of the reason Senate debates tend to be more serious and serene when compared to the Chamber is the fact that a series of rules that define the norm of legislative work exhort that a senator refrain from taking the floor when he has little or nothing to say that may shed new light on the subject at hand. Once he decides to speak, a senator generally receives more attention and overall respect if he fortifies his arguments with facts and figures, and sticks to the subject at hand.

Personal observation and an extensive reading of Senate debates convinces me that most senators take their work seriously. Since World War II, senators have devoted more and more time to their legislative careers.[32] The Senate is in ordinary or extraordinary session virtually the year around. Increasingly, senators have become concerned about the adequacy of staff support. As a result, the last decade has seen the addition of the Office of Information, professionalization of committee staffs, and the passage of legislation that enables the Senate to get the information necessary to evaluate policy proposals. Where committees sessioned only one or two days a week in 1959, personal observation during 1968 indicates that this pattern has changed markedly. The staff itself has become an active force for reform. Late in 1967, all the secretaries of the Senate committees jointly discussed methods of strengthening standing committees and improving their work methods. Subsequently, a reform project was drafted and submitted to the Senate for consideration.[33]

Specialization—As Chile has developed economically and socially over the last quarter century, legislation has increasingly covered a wider range of issues and taken on an added degree of complexity. Over the same period of time, the number of Senate committees has increased and their work loads have been augumented. A senator who sits on several committees simultaneously cannot hope to keep abreast of the developments in every one. It is not surprising then to find that 28 percent of the senators responding named rules that define a norm of *specialization.*

[31] Jorge Tapia Valdés, *La técnica legislativa* (Santiago: Editorial Jurídica, 1960), p. 31.
[32] Guillermo Bruna Contreras, *Estatuto de la profesión parlamentaria* (Santiago: Memoria de prueba, Universidad Católica, 1963).
[33] *Informe de la comisión de funcionarios de la secretaria del senado encargada de elaborar un anteproyecto de reforma del Reglamento de la Corporación,* December 29, 1967.

Members from each party are assigned to committees primarily on the basis of their knowledge, experience, and interest in the subject matter of a committee. Those senators who have several key assignments tend to concentrate on the work of two or three of them. Several senators spend two or more legislative periods (four years each) on the same committee working with the same secretary. As a result, Senators Palma, Altamirano, and Bossay become known as experts in finance matters while Senators Alessandri, Bulnes, and Aylwin are known for their competence in constitutional legislation. Caucus discussions of a bill are heavily influenced by the most knowledgeable senator on that bill, which usually is the respective committee member. Once on the floor, the president of each committee usually presents and explains the report, and each party frequently follows the lead of their member senator. Senators are expected to speak out on matters in which they have a more specialized knowledge and show deference to other senators in areas where they have little or no special competence.

Apprenticeship—It would be inaccurate to say that the Chilean Senate has a norm of apprenticeship exactly comparable to that in the United States Senate. It does not. But there are certain similarities that should be noted. Apprenticeship involves both the total congressional careers and behavior within the Senate in particular. As to the former, a typical congressional career involves several years in the Chamber followed by a transfer to the Senate. Legally, there is nothing that requires this ascent pattern. In practice, most congressmen are expected to begin their careers in the Chamber. This affords the opportunity to "learn the ropes" as well as demonstrate individual competence and judgement. Performance in the Chamber serves as one means of deciding who should be recruited as Senate candidates for each party or serve as party leaders.

Twenty-one percent (nine) of the senators interviewed mentioned rules that define a short period of watching and waiting once in the Senate. New senators appear to spend anywhere from four to six months observing and speaking infrequently, and both the Radical and Christian-Democrat parties appear to expect new members to take less desirable committee assignments while more senior senators gravitate to the top committees. Still, a seniority system does not exist in any official sense, nor is it likely to.

SANCTIONS AND SOCIALIZATION

For a norm to exist, there must be agreement or consensus about the behavior group members should or should not enact and sanctions and socialization mechanisms to produce adherence to these agreements.[34]

We have already seen that Chilean senators hold widespread agreement on at least five of the six norms we have mentioned above (courtesy, reciprocity, institutional patriotism, legislative work, and specialization). But are there formal and informal sanctions to insure that these norms are observed?

Formally, Senate Rules spell out a number of sanctions that the presiding

---

[34] John W. Thibaut and Harold H. Kelley, *The Social Psychology of Groups* (New York: John Wiley, 1959), p. 239.

officer and party floor leaders may employ. For example, the Senate norm of courtesy is defined by twelve rules. Two of these rules prescribe that a senator should not slander another or refer to him personally when he is not on the floor to defend himself. The presiding officer can meet violations with a series of sanctions ranging from ruling the offending senator out of order to the extreme of withdrawing his right to speak on the floor for a given period of time. If a particular senator or group of senators makes it a practice to violate these rules, floor leaders may retaliate by denying this senator or group's request for permission to complete an unfinished speech when their allotted floor time runs out. Or, in inter-party conference, floor leaders may refuse to place a bill this group favors on the Fast Dispatch Calendar. The possibilities are endless.

But short of these formal sanctions, are there informal social sanctions that help to keep behavior within acceptable limits? After asking senators if there were certain things members should not do if they wanted the respect and cooperation of their colleagues, we continued, "If a member does or says the things you mentioned, are there any methods that are used to encourage the member to stop doing so? What are they?" Response gives us a rich sample of the informal pressure applied. The main technique used is social ostracism. See these comments for a sample of how the members close ranks on an offender: "He stands out like a Chinaman" (*queda como chino*); "Gets the law of ice" (*la ley del hielo*); "He becomes the black eye" (*queda como el ojo negro*); "Brutal loss of prestige" (*desprestigio brutal*). In a friendly, cordial body like the Senate, the effect can be tremendous.

Another technique is to wait for the opportunity to get even. One senator described his sentiments this way. "It's an eye for an eye, and a tooth for a tooth." This may take the form of refusing a senator's motion to have his speech in the Hour of Incidental Matters published in volume for public distribution. Or, a senator might quote on the floor, "Senator ....'s statements regarding my personal character on the floor of the Senate neither add to his prestige nor that of this honorable body." Senators may even refuse to pair with the offender or vote for his amendments in committee. If the behavior persists, the senator will simply lose his colleagues' respect. One senator noted, "Well, if this kind of thing continued on very long, he would certainly lose respect. His views would be discounted, and no one would give him much attention. But we seldom ever reach that extreme."

The pressure of institutional norms combined with prolonged congressional careers appear to eventually socialize the most disruptive members into the group. One concerned Socialist Senator, Carlos Altamirano, writes:

Unfortunately, as a result of the tasks a legislator must perform and the spirit of life congress imposes, a professional congressman is created who is the antithesis and negation of what an authentic revolutionary agitator should be. This system of gradual and subtle assimilation unconsciously transforms one into support of the status quo versus being against it.[35]

[35] Carlos Altamirano, "El parlamento, 'tigre de papel,'" Suplemento, *Punto Final* (Ano II, No. 55), May 21, 1968, p. 5.

Clearly, another interpretation of this socialization process is that it produces an environment that facilitates inter-party cooperation and change, but at a pace the political, economic and social system can accomodate.

Conclusion

Chile is a pluralistic political system subject to a variety of stresses, not the least of which are competing demands by ideologically "opposed" political parties. One of the most effective ways the Chilean Senate contributes to system-wide integration is to provide an institutional environment that functions to dampen partisanship and encourage agreements and compromises *across* political parties. This not only enables majority decisions to be made (which in turn generates specific support for the total political system), but also contributes to the development of similar habits and norms throughout the total political system.

The committee system with its intermediate level of autonomy from national political parties' leadership is probably the single most important mechanism for encouraging the formation of inter-party majority agreements. Assignment of bills to specialized subject matter committees helps to break down controversies into a manageable size, and a closed door, off the record committee environment (reinforced by a highly trained nonpartisan staff) tends to dampen partisan exchanges between senators and focus attention on the means of satisfying competing demands over a given bill. Similarly, informal Senate "rules of the game" help to produce an environment that facilitates inter-party cooperation and change—but at a pace the political system can accommodate.

The Rules of the Game in the

Canadian House of Commons

by ALLAN KORNBERG

Although, as Aristotle observed, man is a social animal, in any group there exist certain norms of behavior which structure the interactions of the individual in that group so as to enable it to achieve its purposive goals and/or maintain its viability. Such norms may be formal ones which require certain types of behavior or they may be informal expectations, conventions or obligations. The latter no less than the former set forth the expectations that the group has for its members and define appropriate and inappropriate actions.

The formal rules which govern the functions of and procedures within legislative bodies have long been subjects of study of political scientists. It has been relatively recently, however, that the attention of the discipline has focused on the informal norms of legislative behavior. David Truman has pointed out the importance of these informal "rules of the game" for understanding legislative behavior:

A legislative body has its own group life, sometimes . . . it has its own operating structure which may approximate or differ sharply from the formal organization of the Chamber. When a man first joins such a body, he enters a new group. Like others, it has its standards and conventions, its largely unwritten system of obligations and privileges. To these the neophyte must conform, at least in some measure, if he hopes to make effective use of his position.

Failure to learn the ways of the legislative group, to play ball with his colleagues is almost certain, especially in a large body like the U.S. House of Representatives, to handicap the proposals in which the freshman legislator is interested and to frustrate his ambitions for personal preferment.[1]

---

[1] David Truman, *The Governmental Process* (New York: Alfred A. Knopf, 1960), pp. 343–45.

Reprinted from "The Rules of the Game in the Canadian House of Commons," *Journal of Politics* 26 (May 1964): 358–80, by Allan Kornberg, by permission of the *Journal of Politics* and the author.

The only systematic empirical investigations of these informal behavioral norms have been those carried out by Donald R. Matthews in his study of the Senate,[2] and by John Wahlke and his colleagues in their study of American State legislators.[3]

Our intentions were to determine what the rules of the game are for the Canadian House of Commons,[4] to make some meaningful comparisons of these rules with those discovered by the Wahlke group in their study, and to ascertain whether independent variables such as experience, party affiliation and so forth effect both the legislators' awareness of rules of the game and sanctions and the types of rules and sanctions they articulated. In order to carry out the first two intentions, the legislators were asked the following question:[5]

We have been told that every legislature has its unofficial rules of the game, certain things members do and certain things they must not do if they want the respect and cooperation of fellow members. What are some of these rules that a member must observe to hold the respect and cooperation of his fellow members?

Since it was assumed that the primary functions of group behavioral norms are to maintain the viability of the group and to enable it to achieve its goals,[6] it was felt that the rules of the game in the Canadian House of Commons would serve primarily three functions. These would be: (1) to expedite the flow of legislative business, (2) to channel and mitigate conflict, (3) to defend members against external criticism.

The first assumption is based on the knowledge that all democratic legislatures have had to handle an increasingly large volume of work in this century. As the positive functions of government, particularly national governments, have increased, the amount of legislation with which legislators have had to deal has increased correspondingly.[7] In Canada, every major piece of legislation introduced in Parliament is almost always commented on by the leaders and the relevant subject matter specialists of *each* of the *four* parties,[8] a practice which

---

[2] Donald R. Matthews, *U. S. Senators and Their World* (New York: Vintage Books, 1960). Matthews lists six categories of rules of the game recognized by Senators: Apprenticeship; Legislative Work; Specialization; Courtesy; Reciprocity; and Institutional Patriotism.

[3] John Wahlke et al., *The Legislative System: Explorations in Legislative Behavior* (New York: John Wiley & Sons, Inc., 1962). Wahlke and Ferguson have categorized the rules of the game according to the functions they perform. These are: Rules that promote group cohesion and solidarity; rules which promote predictability of legislative behavior; rules which channel and restrain conflict; rules which expedite legislative business; rules which serve primarily to give tactical advantages to individual members and desirable personal qualities cited as rules.

[4] This report is part of a larger statistical study carried out by the author in 1962 at which time a weighted stratified sample of 165 Members of Parliament were interviewed.

[5] This question was taken directly from the questionnaire employed by Wahlke and his colleagues in their study of State Legislators.

[6] See Dorwin Cartwright and Alvin Zander, *Group Dynamics: Research and Theory* (Evanston: Row, Peterson and Company Inc., 1953) for a complete discussion of the functions of group norms.

[7] For a discussion of the effects of the increase of the volume of legislation on the formal rules of Parliaments see Gilbert Campion, *Parliament: A Survey* (London: Allen and Unwin, 1952).

[8] The four parties in Canada fall quite naturally along the traditional left-right political continuum: The New Democrats, the party of the far Left had a House membership of nineteen; the Liberals, the party of the Left-Center had a membership of one hundred; the Progressive-Conservatives, the party of the Right-Center had a membership of one hundred and sixteen and formed the minority government for Canada's twenty-fifth Parliament; while the Social Credit, the party of the far Right had a membership of thirty.

consumes large quantities of the time in the House of Commons. The problem is further aggravated by the custom of allowing freshmen members to make at least one fairly lengthy speech during the course of a legislative session. One result of these practices, taken together with an increased work load, has been the continuous lengthening of legislative sessions since World War II. It therefore seemed reasonable to assume that some of the informal rules would encourage members to help speed the legislative process.

A democratic legislature necessarily presupposes that formal decisions will be made only after the opposition has been given a hearing and had an opportunity not only to influence the policy proposals under discussion but also to present alternative proposals. Of necessity then, democratic legislative decision-making generates conflict. In the United States this conflict is in part mitigated by the loosely disciplined parties which permit the crossing of party lines and the development of inter-party alliances. Such an arrangement is precluded by the nature of the Canadian party system. It was assumed that if conflict, a "normal" product of the democratic decision-making process which presumably is intensified by Canada's disciplined parties, was allowed to remain unchecked, it would be capable of obstructing the attainment of legislative goals and perhaps destroying the system itself. It appeared therefore, that an important function of the rules of the game in the House of Commons would be to help soften and channel conflict.

Like legislators in most countries with free speech and a free press, the Canadian legislator is a vulnerable, and sometimes an extremely attractive target for the barbs of a discontented group, or a newspaper seeking a boost in circulation by headlining a tale of supposed legislative misdeeds.[9] It was assumed that such criticism would tend to promote legislative solidarity regardless of party, and establish norms designed to discourage behavior which might bring the system and its members under attack from outsiders.

The data showed that the rules of the game in the Canadian Parliament appear to perform these three functions and in addition that they *also* appear to reinforce formal House rules, to propagate the system of disciplined parties, to mitigate intra-party conflict, to encourage members to become subject-matter experts and to perform the necessary labor required from a member of Parliament.

Canadian Perceptions of Rules of the Game

Rules listed by respondents fall into general categories: those which apply to behavior in the House itself and those which apply to behavior outside the House Chambers but within Parliament itself or to behavior entirely outside of Parliament. The following are the rules given by the legislators themselves

---

9 For example during the months of November and December when these interviews were taken, Canadian Members of Parliament came under fire in the nation's press for their conduct and performance at the NATO meetings in Paris, for their conduct during a tour of some of the new African states and for excessive drinking and absenteeism.

grouped under these two headings and further categorized according to the functions they seem to perform in the legislative system:

RULES IN THE HOUSE CHAMBER BY PRIMARY FUNCTIONS

A. *Rules to decrease conflict*   N = 57   % = 35.2
    1. No personal attacks on a member, never bring personalities into debate
    2. Don't be overly or stupidly partisan
    3. Be generous in your praise of opponents at the proper time

B. *Rules to expedite legislative business*   N = 16   % = 10.0
    1. Do not speak too often
    2. Do not speak too long
    3. Do not be a bore
    4. Do not speak without proper knowledge of the subject

C. *Rules which discourage conduct that would invite criticism*   N = 18   % = 10.9
    1. Don't curse or use improper language
    2. Always be neatly dressed, shaved, properly attired
    3. Never enter the House inebriated

D. *Rules which encourage propagation of the party system*   N = 23   % = 14.0
    1. Maintain party solidarity
    2. Don't break party ranks
    3. Don't make a speech in the House you know will offend some of your party colleagues

E. *Rules which encourage expertise and performance of labors*   N = 16   % = 10.4
    1. Do your homework before you speak, know what you are talking about
    2. Do your proper share of the work
    3. Attend House sessions, do not be absent too often

F. *Rules which reinforce respect for formal rules*   N = 7   % = 3.4
    1. Know the proper rules of debate, observe the rules of debate
    2. Extend the proper courtesies
    3. Know the correct forms of address

RULES OUTSIDE OF THE CHAMBER BY PRIMARY FUNCTIONS

A. *Rules to decrease conflict*   N = 35   % = 21.3
    1. Do not be rude or arrogant with other members
    2. Be friendly, courteous, respect other members in your relations outside the House
    3. Do not bring your partisanship out of the House, do not be partisan at social affairs, mix with everybody

B. *Rules which discourage conduct that would invite criticism*   N = 81   % = 48.9
    1. Be discrete in your comments to the press
    2. Do not pass on confidential information to the press

    3. Be honorable, honest, trustworthy, never make
another member look bad, do not get another
member in trouble with your remarks to the press

    4. Have good manners, behave yourself, act the
same way you would in any good social club

C. *Rules which encourage work*   N = 10 % = 6.2

    1. Attend party caucus, do your share of assignments,
pull your weight with your colleagues

D. *Rules which discourage intra-party conflict*   N = 10 % = 6.2

    1. Do not be too pushy, overaggressive

    2. Do not try too hard to advance yourself
over your party colleagues

Unlike the American State legislators studied by Wahlke and his colleagues, a considerable proportion of Canadian legislators seemed to perceive no rules. Fully 16.1 percent said they were not aware of any rules "in the House" and 17.4 percent were unaware of rules "outside of the House." If rules of the game are in part learned by experience the high percentage (38.7) of Freshman legislators may in part account for this large proportion of legislators who were "ignorant" of the rules. However, the data show that there are no appreciable differences among Freshman and other legislators in their awareness of the rules of the game. Another more cogent reason may have been a suspicion on the part of some of the respondents that the acknowledgment of such existing rules might be construed and reported unfavorably by the interviewer, that is, that such rules might be perceived as being underhanded, or operating to the advantage of some members. Hence they may have been reluctant to commit themselves.

Responses typical of legislators who said they were unaware of such rules:

"What do you mean, rules of the game, what rules?
I've been around here for a long time and if there are any rules I don't know of them."

or "There are no rules, none that I've ever heard of."

or "Well there may be but I'm not aware of any. I haven't really been here long enough to know. I suppose I'll learn."

or "No, no rules except that you are honest in your dealings with people."

or "No, there are no rules, but you should know the House rules."

Sanctions

Although a majority of the legislators were aware of the rules of the game, only a relatively small number were cognizant of existing sanctions to enforce the observance of the rules. In contrast to the American State legislators, all but 11 percent of whom mentioned specific sanctions available, *83.6 percent of the legislators were unaware of sanctions that could be applied in the House itself and 47.5 percent were unaware of any available sanctions outside the House.*

In response to the statement, "I imagine things would be made rather difficult for someone who didn't follow the rules?" typical responses were:

"No!"

or "I don't know of anything."

or "Not necessarily! It depends on whose toes you step on. You can be popular with the leaders and unpopular with the members or vice versa. If you're popular with the leaders, there isn't much that can be done to a guy!"

or "Maybe, but I haven't been here long enough to find out what."

or "Unfortunately, no!"

or "I don't think so! Anyone who ignores the rules is so egotistical or has such a thick skin, it's impossible to get through to him at all."

or "No. If you win big, if the party needs you, you can get away with anything. ————————————— is the biggest boor in the world but he's tolerated!"

Legislators who replied to the statement in the affirmative were asked "Can you give me some examples of those things?"

The responses again could be classified into those sanctions applied in the House Chamber and those applied outside of the House.

There were two types of sanctions applied in the House, one by the members, the other by the Speaker. Examples of the first type of sanction were:

"Yes, there are. If you get up to speak, everyone suddenly starts to leave or if they stay they heckle, laugh, hoot at you. You get the idea."

or "Yes, people will whisper and talk when you try to speak in the House."

or "He'd lose status in the House. People will rise, walk out on him when he tries to speak. They wouldn't listen, they'd jeer."

Illustrative of the second type of sanction employed were:

"Mr. Speaker has a blind eye for such people. When he gets up to speak someone gets up with him and the Speaker recognizes the other person."

or "Oh sure, the Speaker will make sure he doesn't get the floor. Then when he goes to the Speaker, he will be told off!"

or "Such people are simply ignored by the Speaker."

There were four types of sanctions employed outside the House: (1) social ostracism, (2) sanctions from the offender's party, (3) sanctions from members outside the offender's party, and (4) sanction from the constituency. The following are illustrative of these sanctions.

"Certainly. Fortunately, this type doesn't last very long. They're usually defeated. Here they simply ignore you socially. It's like anywhere else. Who's going to like you if you won't go along? You certainly aren't going to get much consideration from the party or the Ministers if you don't play ball."

or "I have watched people who have built up a pretty good political image by being a maverick. But then there comes a time when the House becomes adamant and you as a maverick get no consideration from your own party or the government. Oh, the Liberals and Conservatives have ways—no campaign funds, no patronage, keep him from the nomination. They're very adept at this."

or "You just don't invite the guy in for a drink. You don't have lunch with him, you ignore him. It's like any other social group."

or "Yes! He wouldn't have the respect of his colleagues for one thing. He'd feel it. For another he'd get no consideration from his colleagues. If he were a member of the Government he'd have real trouble getting through to certain key people."

or "He is socially kept out of it. He isn't invited to certain functions. He gets the cold shoulder. He's on the awkward squad!"

Table 1—Sanctions Employed in the Canadian House of Commons

	N.	%
Sanctions Applied in the House		
1. Sanctions from colleagues	19	11.7
2. Sanctions from the Speaker	7	4.7
Sanctions Applied Outside the House		
3. Social ostracism	53	31.7
4. Sanctions from the party	13	7.6
5. Sanctions from members	19	11.8
6. Sanctions from the constituency	2	1.3

The question arises as to why such a large percentage of the legislators either were unaware of, or stated emphatically that there were no sanctions in existence. It is suggested that there are three possible explanations for this phenomenon.

If we define a sanction as *an action which is deemed punitive or detrimental to the incumbent of the legislative position,* the key words are "deemed punitive or detrimental." In other words in order for the sanction to be effective, it must first be *perceived* by the legislator as being harmful or detrimental to him. Either through inexperience or individual personality differences, what one individual deems detrimental to him, for example social ostracism, may not be so perceived by another individual, who prefers to be left largely alone.

Another factor may be that the sanction system for enforcing adherence to the informal behavioral norms in the Canadian House of Commons may not be working effectively because of a lack of consensus about the Canadian legislator's role. That is, his party, the other legislators, and his constituents may not agree on the kinds of legislative behavior an M.P. should avoid. For example, one constituency may approve of behavior that draws the attention of the mass media to their representative because they may feel he is putting them "on the map." Another constituency, however, may feel that similar behavior on the part of their legislator should be punished by switching their support to another candidate. Similarly a member's rigid adherence to the demands of party leaders may be approved of by the members of one party, while similar actions elicit only scorn from the members of another party.

Yet another reason for failing to recognize the existence of a system of sanctions may stem from the desire of the legislator to project a favorable image of himself and the group to the interviewer. By acknowledging the existence of a system of sanctions he implicitly acknowledges that his "correct conduct" as a legislator is motivated more by an anticipation of possible punishment than by some intrinsic virtue. Similarly his loyalty to the system of which he is a part may preclude him from acknowledging the existence of what, in reality, are extra-legal measures, and which may therefore be perceived by the "outsider" (the interviewer) as being somewhat sinister or undemocratic.

The Bases of Rules and Sanctions

Wahlke and Ferguson suggest that legislators' occupations have a greater impact upon a legislator's ability to articulate rules than do either education or the demographic characteristics of the legislators' constituencies.[10] Furthermore, their data did not demonstrate that the length of a legislator's experience had any marked impact on his ability to articulate rules of the game. Since in this study not more than two of the responses were coded the analytic concern here is with legislators' ability to perceive rules and sanctions and the types of rules and sanctions they perceived, rather than with the *number* of rules that a respondent mentioned.

Table 2—Sensitivity to Rules and Sanctions by Experience

	Perceived No Rules in the House	Perceived No Rules Out of the House	Perceived No Sanctions in the House	Perceived No Sanctions Out of the House
Freshmen	18.7%	17.4%	85.5%	54.5%
"Diefenbakers" [a]	12.2	21.3	82.7	53.5
6–10 Years Service	25.4	11.9	93.2	57.7
11–16 Years Service	13.3	0.0	76.7	53.3
17 plus Years Service	13.3	13.3	63.3	66.7

[a] By "Diefenbakers," we mean those legislators who were first elected in the narrow Conservative victory of 1957 at which time Mr. John Diefenbaker became Prime Minister, and then re-elected in the overwhelming Conservative sweep of 1958.

Our data support Wahlke's finding that the length of a legislator's service had little impact upon his ability to articulate rules (if the ability to perceive rules and sanctions is considered a criterion of articulative facility). It seemed reasonable to assume that the longer the legislator's period of service in the House, the more he would be aware of the rules, and the sanctions available to enforce the rules. However, the data show that although slightly more long-service legislators than Freshmen were aware of the rules, *one quarter of all legislators who had at least*

---

[10] Our own data (not shown) offer only partial support for this finding. Although, like Wahlke, we found that differences in the demographic characteristics of the legislators' constituencies had little relation to their sensitivity to rules and sanctions, we found that differences in awareness of rules and sanctions that could be attributed to occupational differences were both insignificant and inconsistent. For example, although a higher percentage of legislators with blue collar occupations were unaware of rules outside the House than were legislators with professional or managerial occupations, the former were more sensitive than managerial types to rules in the House and more sensitive to sanctions both in and out of the House than either legislators with professional or business-managerial occupations.

six years of experience were unaware of any sanctions available in the House to enforce adherence to the rules. In addition there was a higher proportion of legislators with seventeen years or more of service than there were Freshmen legislators who were unaware of any sanctions invoked outside the House Chamber. Nor were there any really significant differences among them in the types of rules or sanctions that they perceived.

Other significant independent variables we should expect to find related to the legislators' awareness of rules and sanctions and the types of rules and sanctions to which they were sensitive are party affiliation, positions of leadership,[11] differences in education, and the legislators' positions on the conflict indices.[12]

The assumptions underlying the selection of these variables were:

1. The New Democrats, being the most politically sophisticated group of legislators,[13] would be more aware of the rules and sanctions in existence. The corollary of this would also be true, that is, the Liberal and Social Credit groups, the least politically sophisticated would be the least aware of rules and sanctions.
2. The Conservatives, the Government party, would most often mention rules that tend to expedite legislative business.
3. The New Democrats, the most party-oriented of the legislators[14] would mention rules that help propagate the party system.
4. Leaders would be more aware of rules and sanctions than those who were not leaders because of their greater political sophistication.[15]
5. Leaders would more often mention rules that mitigate intraparty conflict and that encourage legislators to work at their jobs.
6. Legislators in the high conflict categories on the constituency conflict index would be less aware of sanctions available, since they would most likely perceive sanctions coming from their legislative districts.

---

[11] All Cabinet Ministers, Parliamentary Secretaries, party and deputy-party leaders, former Cabinet Ministers, Caucus chairmen and party Whips who fell within the sample were classified as party leaders. All others were classified as non-leaders regardless of any positions held in the party organization outside of Parliament.

[12] To facilitate analysis, a number of indices were constructed which attempt to measure the effect of certain cultural and political variables on the values, attitudes and behavior of Canadian Members of Parliament. The codes for all variables were 0, 1, 2. If a respondent did not fit the description of the variable he was coded "O," if the information had not been ascertained he was coded "1," and if he fit the description, he was coded "2." Since excessively high variance together with low correlations to other items was not a factor for any of the variables employed, no special weighting was required and a respondent's position on any index was arrived at simply by summing his coded responses. The Tau Gamma rank order correlation test indicated that all correlations among the variables for each index were high enough to be judged significant. The constituency conflict index was constructed of five variables and measures the extent to which a legislator perceives conflict between himself and his constituents on goals, expectations for the legislative position, and position on certain policy issues. The four categories of the index are No Conflict, Low Conflict, Moderate Conflict and High Conflict. The Party conflict index is made up of three variables and measures the degree to which the legislator perceives himself in conflict with his party on three policy issues. The categories of the index are No Conflict, Some Conflict and High Conflict.

[13] By political sophistication we mean that the legislators had been raised in highly politicized environments, that is, their families were active politically, politics was frequently discussed at home and so forth. In addition they had held elected public and party offices at various levels before becoming candidates for Parliament.

[14] Party oriented legislators were those legislators who asserted: a) a party caucus decision was always binding; b) it is *always* necessary to vote with your party; c) one had to choose the party over the constituency in the event of conflict between the two. The Tau Gamma statistic indicated that there was a significant relationship among these variables.

[15] Data not shown.

7. Legislators with a college education, and who have been exposed to educational institutions outside of their own province would theoretically be more aware of rules and sanctions than either college educated legislators whose education had been confined to their own provinces or legislators who have less than a college education.[16]

Examination of the data confirmed some, but not all of these assumptions. With respect to party affiliation, for example (see Table 3), the New Democrats *were* the party generally most aware of the existence of rules and sanctions. However, although the Social Credit members were least aware of rules in the Chamber and sanctions outside of it, the Conservatives, rather than the Liberals, were the party least sensitive to rules and sanctions. Also, contrary to our assumption, it was the New Democrats, rather than the Conservatives who had the highest proportion of members who mentioned rules that help expedite legislative business.

Similarly, it was the Conservative and Social Credit parties, rather than the New Democrats, who mentioned rules that help propagate the party system in the legislature. The Social Credit party were almost alone in mentioning rules that function to reinforce the formal rules of debate. In addition they had the highest percentage of legislators who perceived sanctions emanating from the Speaker.[17] It would appear, therefore, that although differences in party affiliation affect the legislators' sensitivity to both rules and sanctions and the type of rules and sanctions they are aware of, these differences do not always coincide with theoretical expectations.

This was also found to be the case when we tried to explain differences in awareness and sensitivity to certain types of rules and sanctions in terms of the occupancy of leadership positions. For example, the data[18] only partially support the assumption that leaders are more sensitive to rules and sanctions than those who are not leaders. Contrary to expectations, leaders did not mention rules that discouraged intra-party conflict or encouraged members to work at their jobs more often than non-leaders.

However, a substantially higher percentage of leaders (48.7 percent) mentioned rules that tend to soften the conflict between the parties and leaders (40.5 percent) were also more sensitive to the possibility of social ostracism than were those not in leadership positions. Except for these differences, the occupancy of formal leadership positions did not appear to have an appreciable impact on this aspect of legislative behavior.

Perceptions of conflict appeared to be a more important determinant of the legislator's ability to perceive rules and sanctions. Generally, the more conflict he perceived with his district the more unaware he was of the rules (see Table 4).

---

[16] For a discussion on the relationship between education and democracy see Seymour M. Lipset, *Political Man* (New York: Anchor Books, 1963), pp. 39–42.

[17] The concern of the Social Credit group with formal rules and sanctions from the Speaker may have been related to the fact that during the first session of the twenty-fifth Parliament, a number of Social Credit members clashed frequently and sharply with Mr. Speaker. The latter actually had one of these legislators temporarily expelled from the House, an event which occurs very infrequently in the Canadian House of Commons.

[18] Data not shown.

Table 3—Relation Between Rules of the Game and Sanctions Available and Political Parties

Rules in the House	S.C.	Conserv.	Liberal	N.D.P.
Not aware of rules	21.1%	18.0%	16.1%	0.0%
Rules that decrease conflict	21.1	28.6	40.9	61.5
Rules that expedite business	9.9	10.6	6.5	23.1
Rules that discourage criticism	4.3	5.9	17.4	15.4
Rules that propagate party system	22.5	22.7	4.8	0.0
Rules which encourage expertise and hard work	0.0	14.2	11.7	0.0
Rules which reinforce formal rules	21.1	0.0	2.6	0.0
Total	100.0	100.0	100.0	100.0

(Chi Square = 218.72   D.F. = 21   P < .005)

Rules outside the House	S.C.	Conserv.	Liberal	N.D.P.
Not aware of Rules	8.5%	25.5%	13.5%	7.6%
Decrease Conflict	18.3	20.7	22.6	23.1
Discourage Criticism	60.5	41.3	49.1	69.3
Encourage Work	8.5	4.7	8.7	0.0
Discourage Intra-party Conflict	4.2	7.8	6.1	0.0
Total	100.0	100.0	100.0	100.0

(Chi Square = 63.92   D.F. = 18   P < .005)

Sanctions in the House	S.C.	Conserv.	Liberal	N.D.P.
Not aware of sanction	77.5%	87.5%	84.4%	75.0%
Sanctions from members	12.7	11.0	11.3	16.7
Sanctions from Speaker	9.8	1.5	4.3	8.3
Total	100.0	100.0	100.0	100.0

(Chi Square = 14.14   D.F. = 6   P < .025)

Sanctions Outside the House	S.C.	Conserv.	Liberal	N.D.P.
Not aware of sanctions	62.0%	48.6%	42.2%	46.2%
Social ostracism	4.2	31.0	39.6	38.5
Sanctions from party	21.1	6.3	6.4	0.0
Sanctions from members	12.7	14.1	8.3	15.3
Sanctions from constituency	0.0	0.0	3.5	0.0
Total	100.0	100.0	100.0	100.0
	(N = 23)	(N = 66)	(N = 63)	(N = 13)

(Chi Square = 66.18   D.F. = 12   P < .005)

Such legislators were also less aware of sanctions outside the House than were those in the No Conflict category. One would expect that his constituency would be a salient factor for a legislator who perceived himself in conflict with it, and his tendency to be less aware of the rules may be related to the fact that "his mind is on his district." Assuming that this is the case one would also expect him to perceive sanctions emanating from his district. However, it was the legislator on the Moderate rather than on the High position of the Conflict index who tended to perceive the possibility of district sanctions.

High conflict legislators were most sensitive to rules that decreased conflict and those which tended to maintain the party system. Conversely, *they were least aware of the rules which function to avoid criticism. Perhaps one reason they perceive themselves in conflict with their constituents is that they are more likely to behave in ways that evoke criticism from their constituents.*

A considerably higher percentage of legislators who were in conflict with their *parties* were unaware of the rules outside the House Chamber than those not in conflict (see Table 7). These legislators were also less aware of the possibility of sanctions operating outside the Chamber.

As was the case with the legislators in conflict with their districts, those in conflict with their parties also were more sensitive to rules that decreased inter-

Table 4—Relation Between Rules of the Game and Sanctions and Legislators' Positions on District Conflict Index

	No	Low	Moderate	High
Rules in the House				
Not aware	10.6%	18.9%	17.2%	18.1%
Expedite business	11.8	9.1	11.0	8.0
Decrease conflict	34.2	34.2	35.1	37.6
Discourage criticism	9.9	11.0	17.3	5.1
Propagate party-system	9.9	12.8	11.0	23.2
Encourage work and expertise	14.3	12.2	8.4	5.8
Reinforce formal rules	9.3	1.8	0.0	2.2
Total	100.0	100.0	100.0	100.0

(Chi Square = 76.45 D.F. = 21 P < .005)

	No	Low	Moderate	High
Rules outside the House				
Not aware	13.7%	15.2%	18.6%	23.2%
Decrease conflict	13.7	20.1	21.4	31.9
Discourage criticism	54.7	53.7	49.0	36.2
Encourage work	11.7	4.3	5.5	2.9
Discourage intra-party conflict	6.2	6.7	5.5	5.8
Total	100.0	100.0	100.0	100.0

(Chi Square = 60.39 D.F. = 18 P < .005)

	No	Low	Moderate	High
Sanctions in House				
Not aware	86.0	75.6	86.9	89.1
From colleagues	11.5	13.4	13.1	8.7
From Speaker	2.5	11.0	0.0	2.2
Total	100.0	100.0	100.0	100.0

(Chi Square = 30.37 D.F. = 6 P < .005)

	No	Low	Moderate	High
Sanctions outside the House				
Not aware	55.9%	48.8%	37.2%	47.1%
Social ostracism	27.3	37.2	29.0	33.3
From party	8.1	6.7	9.7	5.8
From colleagues	8.7	7.3	18.6	13.8
From constituents	0.0	0.0	5.5	0.0
Total	100.0	100.0	100.0	100.0
	(N = 48)	(N = 45)	(N = 35)	(N = 37)

(Chi Square = 46.05 D.F. = 12 P < .005)

party conflict both in and out of the House. They were also *less concerned with rules that encourage legislators to work and rules whose function is to encourage "good" behavior.* One can speculate *that their perceived differences with the party may be related in part at least to this seeming indifference to both work and good behavior.*

Another factor, the assumption that a university education and exposure to an environment which differs from the one in which a legislator is socialized would be manifested in an increased awareness of both the rules and sanctions was generally supported by the data (see Table 6). The "cosmopolitan" college graduates were more aware of the rules and sanctions in effect outside the House than were the other two categories of legislators. However their "provincial" colleagues who also attended institutions of higher learning were more aware of

Table 5—Relation Between Rules of the Game and Sanctions and Legislators' Positions on Party Conflict Index

	No	Moderate	High
Not aware	14.2%	19.6%	16.3%
Expedite business	9.5	9.2	14.0
Decrease conflict	35.5	30.4	44.2
Discourage criticism	10.9	14.0	3.5
Propagate party system	15.1	10.3	17.4
Encourage work	10.4	13.0	4.6
Reinforce formal rules	4.4	3.3	0.0
Total	100.0	100.0	100.0

(Chi Square = 45.11   D.F. = 14   P < .005)

Rules outside the House

	No	Moderate	High
Not aware	11.2	19.0	38.4
Decrease conflict	19.6	20.6	30.2
Discourage criticism	52.9	49.4	31.4
Encourage work	8.9	4.3	0.0
Discourage intra-party conflict	7.4	6.7	0.0
Total	100.0	100.0	100.0

(Chi Square = 72.48   D.F. = 12   P < .005)

Sanctions in House

	No	Moderate	High
Not aware	84.1	85.3	81.4
From colleagues	12.0	8.7	14.0
From Speaker	3.0	6.0	4.6
Total	100.0	100.0	100.0

(Chi Square = 4.90   D.F. = 4   P < .500)

Sanctions outside House

	No	Moderate	High
Not aware	42.6%	54.3%	52.3%
Social ostracism	22.7	31.5	24.4
From party	9.2	3.8	9.3
From colleagues	21.1	10.4	14.0
From constituents	2.4	0.0	0.0
Total	100.0	100.0	100.0
	(N = 92)	(N = 50)	(N = 23)

(Chi Square = 17.85   P < .025)

Table 6—Relations Between Awareness of Rules and Sanctions and Legislators' Educational Backgrounds

	College and some Education out of the Province	College in Province	No college and all Education in Province
Not aware of rules in House	6.2%	18.0%	23.5%
Not aware of rules out of House	10.2	21.1	19.4
Not aware of sanctions in House	89.8	75.5	91.6
Not aware of sanctions out of House	41.9	49.8	50.0

sanctions in effect within the House. Legislators who were not college men, aside from their lack of sensitivity to the rules and sanctions were not *markedly* different in the emphasis they placed on those rules and sanctions which they did articulate than were their better educated colleagues.[19]

Conclusions

A study of the informal behavioral norms and sanctions in operation in the Canadian House of Commons reveals that such rules appear to be functional both for the maximization of the goals of the system and for the maintenance of the viability of the system itself. Essentially the rules expedite the flow of legislation, encourage members to work hard and become somewhat expert in different areas, maintain the party system and the strength of the parties and foster respect for the formal rules of the House. Members are at the same time urged to keep their conflict and animosities within certain limits and to avoid behavior that may draw criticism to both them and the institution of Parliament. To enforce adherence to these norms, the members are made aware that deviations will provoke sanctions from other members, from colleagues in the party, from officials in the system, and even from constituents.

Some rules receive more emphasis than others. Inside the House, stress is placed on rules which mitigate personal conflict and channel it into conflict between the parties. In other words conflict is legitimized and made predictable so that the stability of the system is not threatened as it might be if conflict was personal, intermittent and unpredictable.[20]

The relatively little emphasis placed on rules that expedite the flow of legislation is surprising but probably stems from the fact that in the Canadian system the program of legislation before the House is almost entirely the responsibility of the Government. Hence, the essential responsibility for controlling both the type of legislation and the speed with which it is considered is probably also perceived as primarily a function of the government party.

Outside the House Chamber, the rules most often stressed were those which

---

[19] Data not shown.

[20] Wahlke and Ferguson found that the function of certain informal rules in the State Legislatures was to make legislators' behavior predictable. *Op. cit.*, p. 160.

encouraged the type of conduct that does not invite criticism. Such rules apparently function in two ways to maintain the viability of the system. First, by making the legislators aware of the fact that they face the criticism and hostility of "outsiders," they (the rules) serve to promote the solidarity of the group against a perceived external threat. Second, by keeping outside criticism to a minimum, demands for changes in the system by those outside it, are also kept to a minimum.

Although in articulating the rules outside the House, a smaller proportion of the legislators emphasized rules that mitigate conflict, such rules are still salient for the members. Since most of the social activities that legislators attend result chiefly from their official status as members of Parliament, they tend to interact almost as much outside, as in the House. Tensions built up in the House, which ordinarily would dissipate if legislators were not brought into continuous contact, tend to remain. Therefore, the rules require that all members are to be treated courteously, with deference and so forth. The rule requiring members not to bring their partisanship outside the House doors indicates that even "legitimate" party conflict must be restricted.

In contrast to the American Senate, relatively little attention is focused on the necessities of controlling intra-party conflict. This may arise from the fact that unlike the Senate, seniority is not a major determinant in the selection of leaders. Since members are encouraged to believe that individual ability and industry, meritorious service to the party, and not primarily seniority will result in the granting of preferred position, they are less likely to feel frustrated by the requirement of a long apprenticeship period. Consequently there is not here the same necessity for emphasizing the virtues of serving an apprenticeship, of not being overly-aggressive and of waiting one's turn, that there is in a system governed by the seniority rule.

Examination of the sanctions available to enforce compliance with the rules indicates that the sanctions were perceived as coming essentially from informal rather than formal sources. For example the most powerful and/or frequently employed sanction was the social ostracism of the offender by other members. The next most frequent sanction employed outside the House was both a formal one, in the sense that members of the opposition parties felt that they would receive little consideration from Ministers, and an informal one, in that they perceived the offender as not being able to secure understanding, help, or co-operation from the other members.

The only official sanctions that were mentioned were perceived as emanating either from the party, from the Speaker, and in a few instances, the constituency. One would assume that in a national legislature with disciplined parties, the initiative in enforcing the rules of the game would come from official sources rather than from individuals. This is not the case, it is suggested, because of the essentially extra-legal nature of the rules. Official sources can play only a limited part in securing their enforcement since the assumption by legal sources such as the Speaker, parliamentary disciplinary committees, or the heads of government departments, of too active a role in invoking sanctions might outrage the expectations of those outside the system, and endanger the system itself.

In attempting to assess the impact of different independent variables on both a legislator's awareness of rules and sanctions and the types of rules and sanctions of which he was aware, it was found that party affiliation, perceptions of conflict with party and constituency and, to an extent, the length and type of education a legislator had enjoyed seemed fairly significant. On the other hand, leadership positions, occupation and length of experience in the Commons appeared relatively unimportant.

These findings suggest that the types of rules and sanctions that a legislator is sensitive to in any particular legislative system are primarily determined by what Professor Wahlke termed "circumstantial variables,"[21] that is, variables which are transitory and are relative to a particular point in time but which may be particularly salient to the legislators being studied. For example, the data show that the Social Credit and Conservative legislators were more sensitive than were the Liberals or New Democrats to rules which promote party solidarity and propagate the party system. This is particularly interesting since the members of the latter two parties were more party oriented. Why then should a considerably larger percentage of the former two parties emphasize rules that function to promote party solidarity?

It is suggested that circumstantial variables, that is, the Conservatives' minority government position and the Social Credit's internal troubles made such rules particularly salient for them. The life of the minority Government which the Conservatives formed was continually threatened by the possibility that the opposition parties might unite against them on a vote of confidence or that dissatisfaction with the party would result in sufficient numbers of Conservatives abstaining on a vote to bring down the government. The minority position of the Conservatives may also account for their failure to articulate rules which function to expedite the flow of legislation through the House. We had expected this to be particularly important to the Conservatives since they formed the Government and the latter is charged with the responsibility for introducing most of the legislation the House will consider.[22] However as a minority Government their chances of being defeated by the opposition parties were directly related to the amount of legislation they introduced, since the more legislation they tried to push through the greater the probability that on a particular bill a coalition would form which would defeat them. Consequently rules which function to expedite the flow of legislation may have been the furthest thing from their minds at the time.

For the Conservatives, then, any informal rules which functioned to promote party unity or solidarity were particularly salient at that time while those which expedite legislation were not. This might not have been the case had the Conservatives been a majority rather than a minority Government party.

Rules that tend to promote party solidarity may have been even more important to the Social Credit group who were made up of a majority wing of twenty-six members from Quebec and a minority wing of four members from the far western provinces of Alberta and British Columbia. Even before the twenty-

21 Wahlke, *et al.*, *ibid.*, pp. 18–20.
22 *Supra*, p. 29.

fifth parliament assembled it became evident that party leader Robert Thompson would have a difficult time controlling either the Quebec wing or their ebullient leader, Real Caouette. The latter frequently issued public statements which were diametrically opposed to the "official" party policy enunciated by Mr. Thompson. Subsequent votes of confidence during the parliamentary session indicated that there were serious internal divisions within the party.[23]

Similarly, the high percentage of members from both minority parties who mentioned rules that function to discourage public criticism may have been related to the widespread criticism of the Social Credit Deputy-Leader occasioned by some of his rather intemperate remarks to the press, and by the unwanted attention the New Democrats received as a result of remarks about the new African States by one of their veteran parliamentary members.[24]

Still another finding which leads us to feel that circumstantial variables are important determinants of the types of rules articulated is the fact that not one of the respondents in the two minor parties mentioned rules which encourage expertise and hard work while 14.2 percent of the Conservatives and 11.7 percent of the Liberals articulated such rules. Since the Conservatives formed the Government and the Liberals were the only party with a real chance of displacing them, such rules were understandably important for respondents who perceive hard work and expertness in a field as a potential vehicle to a Cabinet post but less so for members of parties with virtually no chance of forming a government in the immediate future.

Finally, the emphasis placed by legislators in conflict with party and constituency on rules that function to mitigate conflict, the concern of Social Credit members with rules that reinforce formal rules and the higher percentage of their members who perceived sanctions emanating from the Speaker, reinforce the feeling that circumstantial variables which are salient to the legislator determine the type of rules and sanctions he articulates.

The findings from this study lend support for Wahlke and Ferguson's feeling that rules of the game exist in every legislature. Although there is a remarkable similarity in the types of rules articulated in the House of Commons, the American Senate, and the four State legislatures studied previously, there are also some differences, primarily the significantly higher proportion of Canadian legislators who are unaware of the rules and the sanctions available to enforce adherence to them.

Although only further studies can definitely establish why these differences should exist, we suggest that they may in part be related to the fact that the Canadian House of Commons is a parliamentary system modeled on the British.

In the American Senate and in the State legislatures studied by Professor Wahlke and his colleagues the individual legislator is much more of a "free

---

[23] As this was being written, Mr. Caouette formally disavowed the leadership of Mr. Thompson and with eleven other Social Credit members from Quebec formed a new party, Le Ralliement des Creditistes.

[24] Mr. Harold Winch's statements to the press on his return to Canada from a visit to Africa, in which he expressed alarm and concern over both the lack of democratic practices in the new African States and the racist attitudes of some African elites, received considerable attention in the national press. It was felt by some that Mr. Winch's statements were also tinged with "racism."

agent" and has considerably more opportunity to influence the output of the legislative system than in the Canadian Parliament. In the latter system the individual is much more of a "bit player" and the party as a whole the actor who plays the leading roles. Since the individual American legislator has more "to do" in helping the system attain its primary goal—the making of authoritative decisions in the form of legislation—he may be more aware of the informal behavioral norms which are related to that purpose. Another factor *may* be the relative lack of political sophistication of Canadian Members of Parliament in comparison with their American counterparts. The considerably smaller proportion of public offices available to potential aspirants in Canada as compared to the United States coupled with the rise of multi-partyism since the thirties has manifested itself in the following situation: Four parties must recruit candidates in two hundred and sixty-five districts, in which frequently two or even three of them have little chance of winning. This forces them to frequently recruit "amateurs"[25] whose chief virtues may be that they have sufficient resources to help pay part of the campaign costs and/or be able to maintain two homes on the relatively modest salaries paid Members of Parliament.[26] The fact that the least amateur of our respondents, the members of the New Democratic party were *all* aware of rules in the House while only one of them was not aware of rules outside the House offers some support for this assumption.

Much more difficult to explain is the lack of awareness of sanctions among Canadian legislators. A number of suggestions have been made as to why this should be the case, not the least important of which may be that an imperfect consensus exists there as to what constitutes a sanction. This is certainly an area which requires further empirical study.

[25] For example, 54.4% of our respondents had never held a public office before becoming a candidate for Parliament, 26.6% had never held an office in their party and 17.8% had never held either a public or a party office. In addition 34.5% were socialized in an environment almost devoid of any mention of politics and 54.8% said they did not seek the office but were recruited by the parties.

[26] At the time these interviews were taken Canadian Members of Parliament were being paid an annual salary of ten thousand dollars. Since then the salary has been increased to eighteen thousand dollars.

Committee Assignments and the

Nonconformist Legislator:

Democrats in the U.S. Senate

by WAYNE R. SWANSON

Senator Joseph Clark's well-publicized attack on the Senate Establishment in February of 1963 is of concern to political scientists for at least two reasons.[1] First, it marked that rare instance when a member of the Congress had the courage to openly condemn the ritual that most legislators simply accept as part of the unwritten rules of the legislative game. More important, the insights into legislative behavior which Clark unmasked broadened considerably our understanding of the internal operation of the Senate's "Inner Club."

The crux of Senator Clark's argument was that an Establishment, consisting largely of conservative senators from the South and West, virtually controls the assignment of senators to committees. A geographically and ideologically unbalanced Democratic Steering Committee is put in a position where, independent of the seniority rule, it can reward "cooperative" senators with favorable committee assignments and at the same time keep out of positions of influence those senators whose behavior evidences a lack of respect for Senate tradition. Implicit in Clark's speech was the notion that Senate liberals not only have the seniority rule with which to contend, but also a hostile committee-on-committees which makes it more difficult for representatives of the political "left" to move up the committee hierarchy. By exposing a portion of the behind-the-

---

[1] *Congressional Record*, 88th Congress, 1st Session. (1963). pp. 2554–67, 2664–71, 2841–46, 2848–51, 2913–25. Also reprinted in Joseph S. Clark, *The Senate Establishment* (New York: Hill and Wang, Inc., 1963).

scenes maneuvering in the Senate, Clark has provided political scientists with a testable proposition which may help to explain the type of sanction that is imposed upon those individuals who assume the role of "outsider in the Senate."[2]

The sanctions that are applied to the nonconformist in Congress provide an almost virgin field for empirical research. With but a few exceptions studies of the deviant legislator have omitted any meaningful discussion of the consequences of nonconformity.[3] The objective of the present article is to help overcome this deficiency by testing empirically the validity of Senator Clark's allegations. Are liberal Democrats in the United States Senate, particularly those liberals who fall into the nonconformist category, discriminated against when favorable committee assignments are made? To answer this question first presumes that we can point to the liberals of the Senate, and second that we can identify the prestige committees.

I

Perhaps the most systematic way to measure the ideological tendencies of congressmen has been developed by the editors of *Congressional Quarterly*. Their in-depth analysis of congressional roll call votes uncovers a rather clear distribution of ideological types. The index scores in Table 2 below were adapted from *CQ*'s annual surveys of Conservative Coalition Support to describe the ideological inclinations of forty-four Democratic members of the Senate during the Eighty-eighth Congress, the group around whom much of the scope of this article is centered.[4]

The figure for each senator represents the percentage of roll call votes for which his response was recorded that he voted with the conservative coalition.[5] The findings were computed from over three hundred selected roll calls on which the majority of voting Republicans and Southern Democrats, comprising a conservative coalition, opposed the stand taken by the majority of voting Northern Democrats. A score of one hundred would indicate complete support for the coalition, while a score of zero would register complete opposition to it. More simply, the higher the index rating, the more conservative is the voting tendency.

[2] The term is Ralph Huitt's. See his "Outsider in the Senate: An Alternative Role," *American Political Science Review*, LV (1961), pp. 566–75.

[3] See John C. Wahlke, et. al., *The Legislative System* (New York: John Wiley and Sons, Inc., 1962), pp. 152–5; Donald R. Matthews, *U. S. Senators and Their World* (Chapel Hill: University of North Carolina Press, 1960), pp. 114–7; and Malcolm E. Jewell and Samuel C. Patterson, *The Legislative Process in the United States* (New York: Random House, 1961), pp. 373–5.

[4] *Congressional Quarterly*, XVII (1961), p. 652; XIX (1963), p. 747; XXI (1965), p. 1094. Rather than simply rely on the coalition scores for one Congress, the figures for the 86th, 87th and 88th Congresses were used to compute an average coalition support score. The 86th Congress was the first for which *Congressional Quarterly* published the index. Not all Senators of the 88th Congress served in the preceding Congresses, so that the number of roll calls on which the Senator is being measured varies with his length of service in the Senate.

[5] The figures for each Senator represent a slight modification from the *Congressional Quarterly* figures. Their percentages are computed on the basis of the total number of roll calls, whether or not the individual congressman voted on all such roll calls. The coalition percentages in Table 2 were computed only on the basis of roll calls for which a Senator's response was recorded.

For the purposes of this paper the group of Democratic senators have been divided into three ideological groups. A score above sixty-five indicates a conservative voting record; those senators whose coalition support scores fall between thirty-five and sixty-four are classified as moderates; senators whose scores fall below thirty-five comprise the liberal bloc.

Of prime concern to any senator is the quality of his committee assignments. His influence in the Senate is reflected in part by his movement through the committee structure. For this reason students of Congress have attempted to group the standing committees of Congress in the order of their importance. A popular method is to rank the committees according to the aggregate number of years of service of the committee membership. The assumption is that the most important committees are staffed by the most senior members of Congress. Donald Matthews described the "committee caste system" of the Senate by comparing the patterns of shifts in membership from one committee to another.[6]

George Goodwin, Jr. has probably developed the most systematic way to measure the desirability of congressional committees. He has traced the relationship between the number of members who transfer to, and the number who transfer from each committee over a period of time. When these numbers are

Table 1—Preference Ranking of Senate Standing Committees 81st–88th Congresses[a]

Committee	Transferred To (A)	From (B)	Net Shift (A − B) (C)	No. Comm. Members (D)	Net Transf. Per Unit Membership (C ÷ D) (E)
1. For. Relations	26	1	25	122	.205
2. Finance	23	3	20	122	.170
3. Appropriations	35	6	29	192	.150
4. Judiciary	20	5	15	116	.130
5. Commerce	21	8	13	122	.110
6. Armed Services	18	5	13	122	.110
7. Agriculture	13	11	2	122	.016
8. Interior	7	8	− 1	120	− .010
9. Labor	7	12	− 5	110	− .045
10. Banking & Curr.	6	14	− 8	116	− .070
11. Public Works	9	23	− 14	112	− .125
12. Govt. Operations	7	25	− 18	98	− .185
13. Rule & Admn.	12	27	− 15	80	− .187
14. Post Office	5	29	− 24	90	− .270
15. Dist. of Col.	5	35	− 30	74	− .400

[a] Information in this table was gathered from appropriate volumes of the *Congressional Directory.* Column A gives the number of members who transferred to each committee during the 81st through 88th Congresses. (Initial 80th Congress appointments, when the new committee system went into effect, and freshmen appointments are excluded.) Column B lists the number of Senators who transferred off each committee during the same period. Column C gives the numbers who transferred on to the committee less the number who transferred off. Column D lists the total number on each committee for the period under study. Column E, which gives the net transfer per unit of membership, was arrived at by dividing Column C by Column D.

6 Matthews, *U. S. Senators and Their World,* pp. 148–49.

weighted according to the number of members on each committee, a fairly clear indication of the "committee hierarchy" can be deduced. Table 1 reports Goodwin's findings for the United States Senate.[7]

The index of committee preference is extremely useful. However, a brief note of caution should be mentioned at this point. The reader must keep in mind that each of the indices of committee preference developed thus far fails to take into consideration the fact that the interests of individual senators and the nature of their constituencies may affect their choice of committees. No two senators are alike in this respect. What might be a prize committee for one senator may be a burden for one of his colleagues. Thus an individual senator who appears to be condemned to a low ranking committee may be there of his own volition. By and large, however, it seems accurate to state that those senators who occupy the lower-rung committees on Professor Goodwin's scale are not there of their own choice, and would prefer to move on to greener pastures.

II

To fully comprehend the implications of Senator Clark's contention, a brief discussion of the "Johnson rule" and its alleged effect on the power of the Steering Committee may be helpful. Just prior to the convening of the Eighty-third Congress, Lyndon Johnson, then Democratic Floor Leader, skillfully devised a limited yet significant departure from the seniority rule. The innovation he proposed for assigning members to committees was calculated to make it possible for a member of the Senate to be assigned to a "prestige" committee during his first Congress. According to the agreement no veteran Democratic senator, regardless of his seniority, was to receive a second top committee assignment until every Democratic senator had been selected for at least one such post.[8]

The initial enthusiasm of liberals for this innovation in Senate procedure declined considerably when it became apparent that the relaxation of the seniority rule had only served to enhance the amount of discretion allotted to the Steering Committee in assigning senators to, and advancing them on, the committee hierarchy. In 1963 the fifteen member Democratic Steering Committee consisted of seven conservatives, two moderates, and six liberals. The group of conservatives held almost twice as many positions on the committee-on-committees as an ideologically balanced membership would require.[9] What

[7] George Goodwin, Jr., "The Little Legislatures: Committees of Congress" (unpublished manuscript). Note that since the Space committee is a new committee, which did not exist for the entire period under study, it has been omitted from consideration in the table.

[8] Professor Goodwin has shown that following the implementation of the "Johnson rule," the committee assignments of freshmen Senators, many of whom were liberals, did improve somewhat. See his "The Little Legislatures" (unpublished manuscript). For a revealing discussion of the implications of the seniority rule see especially George Goodwin, Jr., "The Seniority System in Congress," *American Political Science Review*, LIII (June, 1959), pp. 412–30.

[9] During the 89th and 90th Congresses the ideological makeup of the Steering Committee did change. However, conservatives and moderates still hold a majority of the positions on the committee.

Senator Clark argued and what this paper is trying to test is the notion that the non-liberals in the Senate have used their power on this committee to hold back those senators whose political views make it difficult for them to conform to accepted standards of behavior.

III

To determine the accuracy of the liberals' argument that they are frequently passed over by the Steering Committee when "prestige" committee assignments are distributed, the author first traced the progress on the committee hierarchy of all Democrats who entered the Senate after 1946 and who were still serving during the Eighty-eighth Congress (1963). (The Legislative Reorganization Act of 1946 changed the committee structure of Congress so thoroughly that a comparison of committee assignments prior to that date is somewhat meaningless.) Next, those senators in this group who had served for at least four Congresses were placed into one of the three ideological subgroups.[10]

The committee assignments for each of these senators were then converted into committee index rankings. These rankings were determined by assigning a number to each of a senator's committee assignments corresponding to that committee's rank on the preference scale in Table 1. An average committee index ranking for each senator was derived.[11]

Finally, in an effort to control for seniority by evaluating the committee assignments of senators at the same stage of their Senate careers, the committee index scores for each senator for each of their first four Congresses were compared. Thus the control group consisted of the ten conservatives, six moderates, and twenty-eight liberals for whom at least four committee index scores could be computed. Table 2 indicates both the individual index scores and the average ranking for each ideological group. The reader should bear in mind that the lower the index rating, the more favorable are the committee assignments.

Senator Clark's assertion that the conservatives move faster through the committee hierarchy is supported by the data. Democratic senators comprising the conservative wing of the party began their careers with an average committee index score of 10.6, but advanced rather dramatically to a 5.9 ranking after just four Congresses. (The fact that many conservatives in the control group were pre-Johnson rule senators explains their rather poor initial committee index score.) The rate of advancement of the moderates fell behind that of the conservatives. More significant, however, is the relative lack of progress of the

[10] Four Congresses was arbitrarily selected as a representative period of service, sufficient to generate meaningful comparisons. This group also includes those 88th Congress Senators whose fourth Congress may have occurred after 1963. Any Senator who entered the Senate after 1961 would not qualify for the control group because of his inability to meet the four-Congress criteria set by the author.

[11] For example, an assignment to the Commerce committee scored five points (because it ranked fifth in preference), while a position on the Rules and Administration Committee scored twelve points. The Senator's points were added together and then divided by the number of committees to which he was assigned (in this instance, 12 + 5 divided by 2) to get a committee index score (8.5). The lower the committee index score, the more favorable the Senator's committee assignments.

Table 2—The Advancement of Selected Groups of Senators on the Committee Hierarchy[a]

	ID score	1st	2nd	3rd	4th	TC	MC
Conservatives		10.6	7.5	6.8	5.9	22	13
Lausche	69	7.5	3.0	3.0	3.0	2	2
Smathers	75	11.0	6.5	3.5	3.5	2	2
Stennis	97	12.0	8.6	8.5	4.5	2	2
Talmadge	93	10.0	4.5	4.5	4.5	2	1
Long (La.)	65	13.0	9.0	5.0	5.0	2	1
Thurmond	96	8.7	5.5	5.5	5.5	2	2
Robertson	96	11.0	10.5	11.0	6.5	2	1
Ervin	94	8.0	7.3	7.7	7.7	3	2
Holland	93	14.0	9.0	9.0	9.0	2	0
Jordan	96	11.3	11.3	10.3	10.3	3	0
Moderates		9.8	8.5	7.8	7.4	16	8
Sparkman	55	12.5	10.5	5.5	5.5	2	2
Monroney	38	13.5	9.5	9.7	7.3	3	2
Byrd (W. Va.)	41	6.5	4.5	7.3	7.3	3	2
Anderson	35	7.5	7.5	7.5	7.5	2	0
Bible	54	9.3	9.3	8.7	8.7	3	1
Cannon	46	9.5	9.5	8.0	8.0	3	1
Liberals		9.1	8.5	8.0	7.5	68	26
A. With Major Committees							
Gore	31	13.0	13.0	6.5	1.5	2	2
Dodd	19	3.5	2.5	2.5	2.5	2	2
Pastore	13	12.7	9.5	9.5	4.0	2	2
Bartlett	17	5.5	5.5	4.0	4.0	2	2
Church	23	11.0	4.5	4.5	4.5	2	1
McCarthy	9	6.5	4.5	4.5	4.5	2	1
Hart	3	5.5	5.5	5.5	4.5	2	2
Symington	18	9.0	9.7	8.3	6.5	2	1
Humphrey	2	10.5	9.3	6.5	6.7	3	1
Mansfield	24	8.0	7.0	7.0	7.0	2	1
Long (Mo.)	18	7.0	7.0	7.0	7.0	2	1
McGee	21	4.0	4.0	7.3	7.3	3	2
Hartke	18	7.3	7.3	7.3	7.3	3	2
Metcalf	13	9.5	9.5	10.3	7.3	3	1
Pell	9	11.0	11.3	7.7	7.7	3	1
Yarborough	32	9.3	9.3	9.3	8.7	3	1
Young (Ohio)	19	9.0	9.0	8.5	8.5	2	1
Jackson	15	10.0	8.7	8.7	8.7	3	1
Burdick	13	8.5	8.5	9.0	8.7	3	1
B. Without Major Committees							
Proxmire	20	8.5	8.5	8.5	8.5	2	0
Williams (N.J.)	9	9.5	9.5	9.5	9.5	2	0
Douglas	7	9.5	9.5	9.5	9.5	2	0
Moss	16	9.5	9.5	9.5	9.5	2	0
McNamara	3	11.7	10.7	10.7	10.0	2	0
Gruening	22	10.3	10.3	10.3	10.3	3	0
Randolph	21	10.3	10.3	10.3	10.3	3	0
Clark	6	13.0	11.0	11.0	11.0	3	0
Muskie	13	11.7	11.0	11.0	11.0	3	0

[a] ID Score is the ideological index abstracted from *Congressional Quarterly's* Conservative Coalition Support surveys. The columns labeled 1–4 indicate the respective Congress for which the Senator is being measured. TC denotes the total number of Standing Committees to which the Senator was assigned during his fourth Congress. MC indicates the number of major Standing Committees on which the senator was serving during his fourth Congress.

Democratic liberals. Collectively the group of liberals began their Senate careers at a more advantageous position on the committee hierarchy than the conservatives. After just four Congresses, however, the liberals lagged noticeably behind the representatives of the political "right." One concludes that the fate of the liberal in the Senate committee structure seems to be controlled by something more than seniority.

To illustrate this important finding further we can compare the distribution of major committee assignments to each ideological group after four Congresses. For our purposes the first six committees on the Goodwin scale will be considered major committees. Their preference rankings are set apart from the lower range committees. In addition, membership on these committees would not seem to be abnormally attractive to any particular geographic segment of the country.

Table 3—Senator's Major Committee Assignments After Four Congresses, by Ideological Tendency

	Total Committees	Major Committees	Percent
Conservatives	22	13	59.1%
Moderates	16	8	50.0%
Liberals	68	26	38.2%

The results of this inquiry depicted in Table 3 are significant. After four Congresses nearly sixty percent of the total number of committee assignments of the conservative senators were to major committees. Fifty percent of the committee berths occupied by the moderates fell into this category. The liberals, however, could claim only thirty-eight percent of their assignments as major committee positions. It is worth reemphasizing that seniority cannot be blamed for the results of the preceding tests. Again, we are comparing senators at the same stage of their Senate careers.

Finally it is important to acknowledge that not all liberal Democrats have been permanently detained on the Senate's less desirable committees. Some members of the left wing of the party have done remarkably well in securing positions on major committees. Note that Table 2 set apart those liberal senators in the control group who had not received a major committee assignment after four Congresses from those who had. Students of Congress will recognize that the list of senators without major committee berths contains the names of several senators whose reputations warrant their inclusion in the group of nonconformists of the Senate. This observation leads one to believe that the tolerance for diversity that many attribute to the Senate may not extend to those individuals who are inclined to tamper with the rules and traditions that sustain the power of the Establishment.

Between January, 1961 and February, 1963 there were six resolutions that came to a vote in the Senate that put to a test issues of particular concern to the members of the Establishment.[12] Four of the resolutions dealt with the liberaliza-

---

[12] *Congressional Quarterly,* XVII (1961), pp. 564, 608. Senate Vote Numbers, 1 193, and 194. Also XIX (1963), pp. 656–57. Senate Vote Numbers 1, 5, and 6.

tion of cloture; the others related to Senator Clark's proposals to enlarge the membership of the Finance and Appropriations Committees. Not unexpectedly, the Establishment successfully thwarted the challenge on each occasion. However, the distribution of support for the Establishment on these six roll calls among the groups distinguished in Table 4 is meaningful. The near unanimous support for the "status quo" by conservatives and moderates could have been anticipated. What is most revealing is the marked discrepancy between the degree of "Inner Club" support from liberals with, and those without major committee assignments after eight years of Senate service. Liberals serving on major committees supported the Establishment at a rate nearly four times that of their colleagues who had failed to permeate the "prestige" committee barrier.

Table 4—Support for the Establishment Among Selected Groups of Senators

	Total Votes	Pro-Establishment	Percentage
Conservatives	60	56	93.3%
Moderates	36	31	86.1%
Liberals (With Major Committees)	110	47	42.7%
Liberals (Without Major Committees)	52	6	11.5%

The point to be made is that not all senators without major committee berths after four Congresses can be categorically labeled "mavericks." The reader is free to judge this for himself. However, the evidence is explicit enough to confirm the belief that those liberal senators, like Joseph Clark, who make a habit of challenging overtly the rules and traditions practiced by the Establishment, are likely to be ignored when prime committee posts are distributed. In other words, the supporters of the status quo in the Senate do have the means at their disposal to minimize the influence of the nonconformist.

IV

"Rules of the Game" in American legislatures are infrequently subject to overt challenge by the participants. John Wahlke and his associates discovered among legislators "a general acceptance of the functional utility of the rules for enabling the group to do what a legislature is expected to do."[13] In the Senate, we are told that respect for the folkways does not require that senators be in agreement on substantive issues. Many liberals joined their conservative colleagues in the group of "Senate men" without surrendering or compromising their political views. Responsibility and loyalty to the Senate consists purely and simply of a common belief that expressed differences among senators, particularly on procedural matters, should be negotiated out of public view. The rules and

---

13 Wahlke, *The Legislative System*, p. 168.

traditions of the Institution should not be attacked or disparaged on the Senate floor.

That this silence would cramp the style of the reform-minded Senator like Joseph Clark is unquestionable.[14] However, those individuals who consciously use the Senate as a forum to publicize their liberal ideals, with little regard for cherished norms, may have to pay a heavy price in terms of the potential influence that conformity would generate. As our data indicated, major committee posts come most easily to the "responsible" legislator.

[14] See Matthews' discussion of political ideology and Senate nonconformity in his *U. S. Senators and Their World*, pp. 112–14. In addition, the dilemma of the liberal congressman and a more explicit statement of "legislative responsibility" can be found in Nicholas Masters, "Committee Assignments in the House of Representatives," *American Political Science Review*, LV (1961), pp. 352–53.

Representational Role Types:
A Research Note

by NORMAN MELLER

As part of their state legislative research project, Professors Wahlke, Eulau, Buchanan, and Ferguson subjected Edmund Burke's classical phrasing of the dilemma of representation to an empirical examination.[1] Burke postulated the style of representation in terms of either-or: the legislator is either a mere spokesman for his constituents or he represents them as he believes best. The 4-state survey findings did not bear Burke out; rather, they disclosed a trichotomy, three major representational role types, with a classification of "Politico" appearing along with "Delegate" and "Trustee." The Politico expresses an overlap of both orientations, so that representative types can be conceived of along a continuum, rather than constituting two polar positions, with the Politico placed toward the mid-point. In numerical frequency, as well, the Politico type was also found to fall between the other two. Left to be determined is the universality of the 4-state formulation of representational roles.

Over the last decade I have periodically observed the evolution of legislatures functioning in the American-administered regions of the Pacific. Here are to be found a number of under-developed societies, or to employ a more informative description, distinctive cultures in transitional status adapting introduced political forms to customary political practices. These traditional practices are fundamentally premised upon the resolving of differences through the reaching

[1] John Wahlke, Heinz Eulau, William Buchanan, and LeRoy Ferguson, *The Legislative System* (New York: Wiley, 1962), 267ff; also see "The Role of the Representative: Some Empirical Observations on the Theory of Edmund Burke," this REVIEW, 53 (September, 1959), at p. 742.

Reprinted from "Representational Role Types: A Research Note," *The American Political Science Review* 61 (June 1967): 474–77, by Norman Meller. Reprinted by permission of the American Political Science Association and the author. The legislative roles and the development of the legislative process in the Trust Territory of the Pacific Islands referred to in this research note are treated at length in *The Congress of Micronesia*, published by the University of Hawaii Press.

of consensus for taking political action.[2] In 1956, when the Marshall Islands Congress in the Trust Territory of the Pacific Islands[3] was intensively studied, and in 1958 when the *Fono* (Legislature) of American Samoa was the focus for similar research, both were advisory bicameral legislatures, with lawmaking power legally residing in the executive. Both were patterned upon the model of American bodies on the mainland United States, although each incorporated nuances peculiar to its respective area. For purposes of considering representational roles, only reference to the lower houses in each is pertinent, as members of Samoa's Senate are chosen *Fa's Samoa* (by traditional ways) while the upper house in the Marshalls was nominally composed of hereditary *Iroij* and *Leiroj* (male and female nobles).[4] However, American Samoa's Representatives, as in the United States, are elected by universal adult suffrage, while the Assemblymen who sat in the 1956 Marshallese Congress owed their selection to a number of electoral devices, frequently secret election but also indirect choice by vote of the atoll councils which in turn were usually composed of *alabs* (the senior heads of families) residing on the atoll. To complete this brief sketch of the political settings of these Pacific Island areas, it need only be added that at that time neither knew political parties, and formalized pressure organizations were only just beginning to appear.

After the publication of the Wahlke survey, the 1956 and 1958 field notes were re-examined within the frame of representation there formulated, and the legislators of these two American outposts were found to fit both taxonomically and in corresponding numerical rank order within the representational roles of Trustee, Politico, and Delegate. Indeed, the same continuum could be reconstructed, with their replies nicely evidencing the lack of sharpness between the roles:

Trustee: The Marshallese legislator who categorically stated he had received no instructions from his home atoll, that he could use his own discretion in the deliberations of the Marshallese Congress, and that he was not bound to act as the atoll council might instruct him.

Politico: The Marshallese legislator who stated he could use his own discretion and did not have to follow the views of his atoll council, but who then immediately qualified it by adding, "but not always."

Delegate (shading over to Politico): "If there is [sic] any decided matters [that is, decided at the county *fono* meeting called pursuant to *Fa'a Samoan* custom] which I am against, I can say right there that I am against it. But, if my people insist, then it is my duty to bring it up before the *Fono*. If the *Fono* is not in favor of it, I will not fight for it."

Delegate (a Samoan): "If the people ask me something which I don't approve of introducing, I let it be determined by the number of villages which request it. My county consists of five villages, and if three villages think that a certain matter must be brought to the *Fono*, then I have to, even though I do not agree. . . ."

[2] See Norman Meller, "Three American Legislative Bodies in the Pacific," in Roland W. Force, (ed.), *Induced Political Change in the Pacific* (Honolulu: Bishop Museum Press, 1965).

[3] The Trust Territory of the Pacific Islands is divided into six administrative districts, of which the Marshalls comprise the easternmost. This archipelago of but 70 square miles of land, habited by 18,200 people, is scattered over some 180,000 square miles of ocean.

[4] In 1960 the Marshallese Congress was converted into a unicameral body, with *Iroij* and *Leiroj* enjoying life membership.

Unfortunately, due to data having been gathered in some cases through interpreters and also questionnaire responses requiring translation, representational
role orientations for all members of these two legislative bodies could not be
delineated.[5]

The Wahlke study, in seeking an explanation for the different representative
role orientations, and their numerical distribution, suggested "it is likely . . .
that the representative has become less and less a Delegate and more and more a
Trustee as the business of government has become more and more intricate and
technical as well as less locally centered."[6] It was therefore to be expected that in
the areas of "simple" government, like Samoa or the Marshall Islands, the
Delegate component would loom larger, if not predominate over the Trustee.
In fact, the reverse was true, but this finding was hardly conclusive, suffering
from the disadvantage of being based upon the manipulation of data amassed
without prior formulation of the existence of trichotomous representational roles
and the drafting of specific probes to test them.

Table 1—Distribution of Representational Role Orientations in Congress of Micronesia

Representational Roles	Own Role (32 members)	Constituents' View of Role (29 members)	4 State Legislatures (from Wahlke Study)
Trustee	69%	55%	63%
Politico	25	14	23
Delegate	6	31	14
	100%	100%	100%

The convening of the First Congress of Micronesia[7] for the whole Trust
Territory in July of 1965 provided the opportunity for pursuing the tentative
conclusion that these three representational roles apply equally as well to
beginning as to established legislatures, and to amass further data on the
hypothesis that they derive from the very nature of the legislative process. As a
bicameral legislating body, its members elected by secret ballot,[8] the new
Congress is comparable in composition and function to the four state legislatures
previously surveyed. It thus also afforded opportunity for extending research
beyond mere replication to determine whether the representative's own role
perception was consonant with the role he believed his constituents thought he
ought observe. In the attempt to avoid the pitfall of evoking merely formal
responses designed to please the interviewer—always a danger in Micronesia,
and as suggested subsequently, possibly constituting a methodological in-

[5] The 17 utilizable replies from the 42-member Marshallese House and the 13 responsive Samoan
Representatives of the 16 interviewed (17-member House) provided a coverage which compares well
with that reported for California in the State Legislative Research Project.
[6] *The Legislative System*, p. 281.
[7] Established by Secretary of Interior order 2882, dated September 28, 1964.
[8] In some areas, due to illiteracy, a "whisper" vote was employed.

adequacy of the whole trichotomous representational role formulation—questionnaires posing the handling of a specific problem viewed from different dimensions were completed by the Congressmen-elect in the opening morning of a pre-session training workshop under the instructions that they were thereby helping to structure the balance of the training.[9]

All twelve members of the House of Delegates and twenty-one members of the General Assembly replied to the inquiries concerning their and their constituents' views on representational roles, and all but one Assemblyman also commented on the effect upon role conception of personal or party[10] program promises to support an issue.[11] The responses clearly demonstrated that the Congressmen-elect were, if anything, more Trustee- and less Delegate-oriented than the average of the four state legislatures surveyed.

Nothing was found to substantiate the hypothesis that the Trustee representational role evolves with novelty or complexity of government. Even the Wahlke group's findings on Tennessee did not bear it out, and to explain this the authors added "it may be that 'complexity' is a function of perception, regardless of the real situation."[12] To the Micronesians the Trust Territory government and its problems appear highly intricate and technical, simple as they may seem to an American observer. Expanding government in the Trust Territory will continue to remain relatively complex, and although the Trustee's role may partially shift to that of the Politico with greater political sophistication in the area, it is difficult to conceive of a marked expansion of the Delegate role at the expense of the Trustee.

The largest single group of Micronesian Congressmen (thirteen) saw their representational role of Trustee paralleling that expected of them by their constituents, which well coincides with political reality encountered in many parts of the far-flung Trust Territory where representatives tend to be chosen for their ability to face problems beyond their constituents' ken. Only one member viewed his own role and that projected by his constituents as being a Delegate. Significantly, over half of the Micronesian legislators (fifteen of twenty-nine) indicated their role conceptualizations did not accord with those of their constituents. In part this was due to a Congressman holding to the role of Trustee while stating his constituents considered him a Politico or Delegate. But, in addition, other Congressmen voluntarily limited the scope of their roles, adopting that of Politico or even Delegate while recognizing that their constituents expected performance as a Trustee. As stated by one Delegate:

(legislator's role) "I feel that such matter should be put into full [consideration before the Congress] since it is the desire of the people—the majority—for such law to be passed. I therefore will do my best . . ." to introduce and support the measure.

(constituents' view of role) "The voters in my district place the responsibility on

---

[9] See Norman Meller, "Trust Territory," *East-West Center Today*, 6 (January-February, 1966), p. 9.

[10] Different parties ran candidates in two of the six districts.

[11] However, in a few cases replies classed as "Other," which did not fit any category, had to be eliminated.

[12] *The Legislative System*, p. 282.

me to make the wise decision . . . they expect me to put every effort to help the people . . .''

(effect of personal or party promise) "there is no difference . . . the voters of my district choose their representatives from those that they put their entire trust upon as their leaders."

Half of the Congressmen (sixteen) concurred with the Delegate quoted above in believing neither a personal promise on their part when they ran for office nor a pledge to a political party program made any difference in how they ought to conduct themselves. However, an equal number disagreed with them or entirely avoided the issue by giving a non-responsive reply (deliberately, I believe). All representational role types were found divided over the moral issue inherent in the question. It would appear that this whole area of personal and party commitment as it applies to legislative role warrants further inquiry.

Table 2—Distribution of Representational Role Orientations in Truk District Legislature (26 Replies)

Representational Role	Own Role	Constituents' View of Role
Trustee	46%	8%
Politico	31	—
Delegate	19	77
Other	4	15
	100%	100%

Coding the responses so as to fit them neatly within the trichotomous categories posited was difficult. Frequently, befitting the consensus societies of Oceania, reference was made to the judgment of fellow legislators in resolving the dilemma of representation. In view of the sense of solidarity generally engendered by membership in a legislative body, and the strength of legislative norms in determining action, this mention by Micronesian legislators of peer judgment suggests positing the values of the individual legislator, legislative norms, and constituent instructions as the three major referents for the legislator. The Politico type then becomes a catch-all for the representative who refuses to commit himself to any conceptual category.

Finally, there remains a suspicion that the Politico representational role is of entirely different nature than the Trustee and Delegate types originally projected by Burke. The polar roles are ideal types, acknowledged, legitimate, safe to disclose. The Politico role constitutes nothing more than a description of what a legislator does when he fails to follow a recognized norm. This he may be reluctant to disclose, if indeed he is cognizant that his behavior does not comply with sanctioned representational roles. An illustration is provided by the replies of Truk District[13] legislators to the same representational questions asked a month after they were posed to the members-elect of the Congress of Micronesia.

[13] The Truk District, which comprises the midzone of the Carolines, is the most heavily populated of all districts in the Trust Territory (24,500), and embraces the smallest land area.

An added factor contributing to this distribution of replies was an informal session conducted some time previously by a Trust Territory administrator in which he had stressed the right of the constituent in a democratic system to expect his elected representative to follow the constituents' instructions. Not only does the Truk District legislator's expressed response to the view of representation held by his constituents conform to this norm, but his own stated representational role perception appears to reflect this, as well.

The same reluctance to reveal non-compliance with accepted norms was earlier revealed in the 1958 interviews in American Samoa when the legislators reported transmitting to the center of government viewpoints expressed at village and county *fonos* composed of *matais* (holders of titles granted by their families) and, similarly, in post-session meetings orally informing these constituents of legislative decisions and proposed Administration actions. Parenthetically it may be added that such servicing of the communication function of legislative bodies is not synonymous with adopting a Delegate-type representative role. Queries directed to other sources revealed that in fact the practices of Samoan Representatives varied and local *fonos* were not being called in all districts reported by the legislators. Tradition required holding such *fonos* bracketing the regular legislative session, and the Samoan legislators had responded in terms of accepted behavior and past practice, rather than volunteering information regarding their current flaunting.

In Micronesia and Polynesia, where American-style legislatures with limited functions and restricted legislating capacity have been structured, a new political elite, both paralleling the chiefly elite and also comprised of those traditional leaders who have been able to make the adaptation, observe appropriate representative practices. In these transitional areas, constituent participation in self-government through introduced Western forms is more dependent upon the cues derived from the representative than would characterize more developed areas. Nevertheless, interviews revealed the same representative roles are replicated, and in corresponding rank relation, as found in the four American states surveyed by the state legislative research project. Moreover, these Pacific areas furnish the additional note that legislator specification of their role perceptions may constitute but a formal nod to legitimated roles, and that the latter may not in fact conform with role behavior. All this suggests further consideration of the nature of the three representational role types posited, and particularly that attention be turned to verifying verbalization through observed performance.

American State Legislators' Role Orientations Toward Pressure Groups

by JOHN C. WAHLKE, WILLIAM BUCHANAN,
HEINZ EULAU, and LeROY C. FERGUSON

I

In modern pluralistic political systems, the legislature is a central forum where organized interest groups articulate and express their views and press for public action favorable to their concerns. Indeed, the free representation of interests crucially affects the legitimacy of modern democratic legislatures. If interest groups were removed or prevented from influencing legislative action, the authority of the legislature would be put in jeopardy and its decisions would be found unacceptable. Yet in spite of the critical importance of the relationship between interest groups and law-making institutions, research offers surprisingly little theoretical explanation and few cumulative or comparative empirical data about this phase of the representative process.[1]

Most case studies of pressure groups do little more than describe the qualities, properties or activities of some of the pressuring groups, taking for granted

[1] Samuel J. Eldersveld, "American Interest Groups: A Survey of Research and Some Implications for Theory and Method," in Henry W. Ehrmann (ed.), *Interest Groups on Four Continents* (Pittsburgh, 1958), pp. 173–96; Oliver Garceau, "Interest Group Theory in Political Research," *Annals of the American Academy of Political and Social Science* 319 (1958), 104–12.

For discussion of some of the general problems of research, theory and conception, see also Gabriel A. Almond, "A Comparative Study of Interest Groups and the Political Process," *American Political Science Review* 52 (1958), 270–82; Alfred de Grazia, "The Nature and Prospects of Political Interest Groups," *Annals of the American Academy of Political and Social Science* 319 (1958), 113–22; W. J. M. Mackenzie, "Pressure Groups: The 'Conceptual Framework,'" *Political Studies* 3 (1955), 247–55.

Reprinted from "American State Legislators' Role Orientations toward Press Groups," *Journal of Politics* 22 (May 1960): 203–27, by John C. Wahlke, William Buchanan, Heinz Eulau, and LeRoy C. Ferguson. Reprinted by permission of the *Journal of Politics* and the authors.

the persons they press upon.[2] Such studies tend to be preoccupied with assessing the relative power of the various groups active in some particular situation and to neglect other kinds of questions political science ought to be considering: What sort of *system* is it within which groups act and become represented? How do institutional structures of this sort come into being? How do they change, or why do they not change? How does the system or structure itself facilitate or hinder performance of the representative function in the governmental process?

Questions like these direct attention to the official actors in the political process—in this case, to the activities and behavior of legislators. For, after all, the legislature is describable as an institutionalized group only insofar as relevant behaviors of legislators follow certain predictable patterns. A too-simple "group approach" to the legislative process implies an unrealistic conception of legislators' behavior and of the resultant character of the legislative process. The public policy decisions of legislatures cannot realistically be visualized as simple mathematical resultants of a given number of "pressures," each of measurable direction and strength, impinging on passively reacting legislators.[3]

Role theory provides a more appropriate and useful model. While it is not possible to develop the point exhaustively here, a few observations should be made.[4] First of all, it seems obvious that legislators' *perceptions* of pressure groups—or of any other factor, for that matter—will vitally affect the part played by that factor in the legislative process.[5] More particularly, legislators' perceptions of what constitutes legitimate or desirable or harmful activity by pressure groups or other factors, as well as their perceptions of the supposedly objective "facts" about such activity, are not random or idiosyncratic opinions held independently by each legislator individually, but are opinions intimately

---

[2] Henry W. Ehrmann, *op. cit.*, the most extensive work considering pressure groups in a trans-system context, contains a series of studies of particular countries, but not broader comparison or analysis.

Among the most noteworthy of those few studies which do deal extensively with the behavior of pressured legislators are Oliver Garceau and Corinne Silverman, "A Pressure Group and the Pressured: A Case Report," *American Political Science Review* 48 (1954), 672–91; John Millett, "The Role of an Interest Group Leader in the House of Commons," *Western Political Quarterly* 9 (1956), 915–26; and V. O. Key, "The Veterans and the House of Representatives: A Study of a Pressure Group and Electoral Mortality," *The Journal of Politics* 5 (1943), 27–40.

[3] This is one of the main criticisms voiced, for example, by Peter Odegard, "A Group Basis of Politics: A New Name for an Ancient Myth," *Western Political Quarterly* 11 (1958), 689–702. See also Robert M. MacIver's criticism of Bentley in *The Web of Government* (New York, 1947), pp. 220–21. Of course, both those criticized and the critics readily admit, if pointedly asked, that,

The politician-legislator is not equivalent to the steel ball in a pinball game, bumping passively from post to post down an inclined plane. He is a human being, involved in a variety of relationships with other human beings. In his role as legislator his accessibility to various groups is affected by the whole series of relationships that define him as a person [David B. Truman, *The Government Process* (New York, 1951), pp. 332–33].

The question is not one of recognizing such a basic postulate but of incorporating it in research and explanation.

[4] An admirable, research-oriented discussion of role theory, including a review of the relevant literature, which uses "role" and related terms in much the way they are used in this research, can be found in Neal Gross, Ward S. Mason, and Alexander W. MacEachern, *Explorations in Role Analysis* (New York, 1958), pp. 3–75, 244–57, 281–318.

[5] The point is forcibly demonstrated by Corinne Silverman, "The Legislator's View of the Legislative Process," *Public Opinion Quarterly*, 18 (1954), 180–90.

associated with what Truman has called the "influence of office"[6] and Latham has called "officiality."[7] Membership in the legislature constitutes a *status* or *position* in society. This means that people in the society *expect* certain behaviors by incumbents of that position. Legislators have similar expectations toward each other, and they all have expectations with respect to other classes of actors they encounter in doing their legislative business. The key concept to refer to these patterns of behavior associated with a given position or status in the expectations and orientations of people is *role*.

From the abstract and general principles of role theory we take the working hypothesis that legislators' conceptions of their role as legislators will be a crucial factor governing their legislative behavior and thereby affecting the access, influence or power of all groups, as well as differentiating among groups.[8] General role theory suggests that legislators' role conceptions constitute a determining factor in pressure politics at least as important as the number, size, strategy, skill or other characteristics of pressure groups themselves, the individual group affiliations and identifications of legislators, or the peculiarities of personality and personal whim of those legislators. These role conceptions can usefully be made the focal point of comparative and analytical study.

Such an approach, it should be emphasized, does not "contradict" group-focussed (or other) conceptions of pressure politics. Rather, it complements and carries them forward by linking them potentially to more general concepts and more general bodies of theory. Every hypothesis about a relation between group characteristic and group influence plainly rests upon assumptions about the behavior of the legislators supposedly reacting to the group pressures. For example, the belief that a group will have more influence if its lobbyists follow certain tactical principles rests upon assertions, sometimes quite explicit, about how legislators will react to lobbyists acting in accordance with these principles.[9] Research which tests the behavioral assumptions of group-focussed (or other) studies against the observed behavior of legislators is essential to validation of any propositions linking group power and influence to group characteristics of any sort (or any other independent variable).

---

[6] Truman, *op. cit.*, pp. 346–50.

[7] Earl Latham, *The Group Basis of Politics* (Ithaca, New York, 1952), pp. 33–40.

[8] This proposition is intimated in Truman's discussion of the influence of office and Latham's discussion of officiality. It is more directly suggested in Huitt's discussion of the way in which legislators' differing conceptions of their roles *pro* or *con* interest groups lead them to bring "competing versions of the facts" to their discussions of conflicting group demands [Ralph K. Huitt, "The Congressional Committee: A Case Study," *American Political Science Review* 48 (1954), 350]. It is the basis for empirical research in one very important instance (Garceau and Silverman, *op. cit.*), which differentiates faction-oriented, policy-oriented, program-oriented and non-generalizers' conceptions of the appropriate mode of behavior for legislators, although not formally utilizing role theory or role concepts to do so.

[9] Bertram Gross [*The Legislative Struggle* (New York, 1953), pp. 302–03] quotes the following rules set for N.A.M. lobbyists: "Avoid demagoguery before a Committee. It is resented." "Get directly to the facts. Committees are not much interested in long discussions about the trends of the time." "Don't assume a superior attitude." An often-cited rule of lobbying tactics in America, to "build up a bloc of votes in Congress to be backed with appeals from home at the psychological moment" [Stuart Chase, *Democracy Under Pressure* (New York, 1945), pp. 24–26], likewise rests obviously upon assumptions about the motivations and behavior of Congressmen.

II

Among the questions asked of some 474 legislators in four states during the 1957 legislative sessions[10] were several which make it possible to explore legislators' role orientations toward pressure groups and their agents.

A TYPOLOGY OF ROLE ORIENTATIONS TOWARD PRESSURE GROUPS

Several cautionary remarks should be made here. We are concerned with the functioning of the legislative *institution* in general, rather than with unique historical events or outcomes in the states studied. Similarly, the concern here is not with the *particular* group affiliations and identifications of individual legislators or their relative friendship or hostility toward specific groups but rather with their orientations toward pressure groups as a *generic* class of "significant others." The typology which follows has been constructed and used to suit this ultimate theoretical concern. Furthermore, rather than attempt, at this early stage of research using the role concept, to discover and describe in exhaustive detail the innumerable behaviors which add up (in the legislators' expectations) to the prevailing role conceptions relevant to pressure groups in the four state systems, attention has been restricted to what seem the most obvious areas of role orientation.

Political scientists are familiar with the doctrinal disagreement about the value of pressure politics. One view holds, as did Rousseau, that expression and promotion of conflicting private interests is inimical to discovery and promotion of the public interest; an opposing view, that of many "pluralist" theorists, holds that what is called "the public interest" is never more than the harmonization of just such partial and private interests and that organized interest groups, therefore, play an indispensable part in defining and legislating in the public interest. Legislators' views on the subject likewise differ widely. Some agree with the member who said, "Hell! We wouldn't have a government if there were no interest groups. It would be a form of anarchy if groups and parties didn't do their job." Or, as another said, when asked about the desirability of having the individual citizen participate in government directly, rather than through interest groups, "How's he going to do it 'directly'? You have to organize or go into an organization to do anything." But others agree with the legislator who said, in response to the same question, "Stop there (after the word 'directly') and you've got the whole story about our citizens and what they should do." Many legislators share the suspicion of interest groups in general expressed by the member who said, "I've heard of them all my life, but I didn't aim to fool with that, and I don't know nothing about it."

[10] 94% of the California, 100% of the New Jersey, 94% of the Ohio and 91% of the Tennessee legislature were interviewed, using a fixed schedule of questions. Interviews averaged about an hour and a half in length. For other findings of the study see the authors' "The Political Socialization of American State Legislators," *Midwest Journal of Political Science* 3 (1959), 188–206; "The Role of the Representative: Some Empirical Observations on the Theory of Representation of Edmund Burke," *American Political Science Review* 53 (1959), 742–56; "The Legislator as Specialist," *Western Political Quarterly* (forthcoming).

Table 1—Attitude of State Legislators Toward Pressure Politics

	Attitude [a]					
	FRIENDLY ⟷ HOSTILE					
Question	1	2	3	4	5	
1. Would you say that, on the whole, the legislature would work (better or worse) if there were no interest groups or lobbies trying to influence legislation? (N = 452)	41%	34%	12%	7%	6%	= 100%
2. (Do you agree that) the job of the legislator is to work out compromises among conflicting interests? (N = 462)	31%	42%	2%	12%	13%	= 100%
3. (Do you agree that) lobbyists and special interests have entirely too much influence in American state legislatures? (N = 464)	26%	34%	1%	22%	17%	= 100%
4. (Do you agree that) under our form of government, every individual should take an interest in government directly, not through interest-group organizations? (N = 458)	19%	24%	3%	19%	35%	= 100%

[a] Response categories to Question 1 were "much worse," "somewhat worse," "about the same," "somewhat better" and "much better"; to Questions 2–4, "agree," "tend to agree," "undecided," "tend to disagree" and "disagree." The most friendly responses are (1) "much worse," (2) "agree," (3) "disagree," and (4) "disagree."

It seems obvious that a legislator's reaction to the activities of pressure groups and lobbyists will vary according to such differences in evaluation of pressure politics. Legislators' generalized attitudes of friendliness, neutrality or hostility to pressure politics were therefore measured by a four-item Likert scale utilizing replies to the questions shown in Table 1. Their attitudes were found to vary as indicated in that table.[11]

It likewise seems obvious that legislators' reactions to pressure groups or lobbyists will vary with their different degrees of knowledge or awareness of group activity. The legislator who knows what the Municipal League is, what it wants, who speaks for it and when, will react differently to cues from the League

[11] The scale was constructed by awarding 4 points for the most friendly answer to a question, 3 points for the next most friendly, 2 points if undecided, 1 point if on the unfriendly side of "undecided" and 0 for the most unfriendly response. Averaging the four question-scores gives a scale-score. The power of each question to discriminate between respondents of high and low tolerance is more than sufficient, as shown by the values of Discriminatory Power obtained when the high and low *thirds* are used (actually, top 32% and bottom 35%)—a much more stringent requirement for a satisfactory scale than the usual one of at least 1.0 D.P. between upper and lower *quartiles*.

	Question Number			
	1	*2*	*3*	*4*
Mean score of upper $1/3$	3.5	3.4	3.2	2.6
Mean score of lower $1/3$	2.2	1.9	1.2	.7
Discriminatory Power	1.3	1.5	2.0	1.9

than the legislator who never heard of it and doesn't identify anyone as its spokesman. Legislators' awareness of lobbying activities was therefore measured by asking them to identify a list of lobbyists more or less active in their state legislatures during the time of interviewing.[12]

It is almost universally assumed that one important factor determining the representatives, legitimacy and authority of any given legislature is the extent and manner of its taking into account the demands of significant interest groups in its social environment. This, in turn, is no more than a reflection of the behavior of the legislators. Some members, by their behavior toward lobbyists and other group representational agents or activity, will serve to accommodate the demands of organized interest groups in the legislative process.[13] Others will serve to resist consideration or accommodation of these demands in any form. And still others, presumably attuned to other persons or factors, will play a neutral role toward such group demands.

Assuming, then, that any given legislator's behavior in this respect will depend to a considerable extent upon his general affective orientation toward pressure politics as a mode of political activity and his awareness of such activity when it occurs around him,[14] one can construct the following very simple typology of legislators' role orientations toward pressure groups:

[12] The exact wording of the question was, "Here are the names of some persons that people have told us are connected with various interest groups and lobbies. Could you tell me who each of them is or what he does?" A respondent was credited with a "correct" answer if he identified the organizational tie, the general type of interest represented, or some particular legislative measure of concern for each lobbyist listed. Names on the list had been selected to include lobbyists of varying degrees of presumed familiarity. To obtain a more precise measure, scores were weighted to give greater credit for identifying lesser-known than for identifying universally-known lobbyists.

Unlike the tolerance scores, the awareness scores cannot be compared directly across state lines, since there is no way of comparing the recognition-value of lobbyists in different systems. But corresponding quintile groups can be so compared.

Garceau and Silverman (*op. cit.*) measured several other dimensions of awareness—ability to identify selected pressure groups, and ability to recognize more than one issue on which selected groups had been active. Pre-tests indicated that the single measures based on lobbyist-recognition produced awareness scores correlating very closely with those obtained by more complex measures; the simple unidimensional measure was therefore used here.

[13] "Accommodation" does not mean "accession," although that is, of course, one form accommodation may take. Accommodation here means conscious consideration. The assumption is that persons voicing demands will far more likely accept decisions as authoritative, even if their demands are *not* accepted, if they believe the decision-makers have given them explicit consideration than if they have not. This proposition is strongly implied in J. D. Stewart's discussion of "consultation" as the characteristic form of relationship between a group and a governmental organ [*British Pressure Groups* (Oxford, 1958). pp. 3–27].

[14] These two dimensions are suggested not only in numerous general social-psychological discussions of role- and self-concepts, but also by two of the very few empirical and analytical studies of group politics. Garceau and Silverman (*op. cit.*, pp. 685*ff.*) report as the "most striking fact" discovered in their Vermont study "the extremely low level of recognition of interest group activity," and suggest that differences in legislative behavior toward groups as well as legislators' ideas about appropriate behavior toward them are associated with different levels of information about groups. Samuel H. Beer, in his analysis of operative theories of interest representation in Britain ["The Representation of Interests in British Government: Historical Perspective," *American Political Science Review* 51 (1957), 613–50], suggests a number of respects in which legislators' different conceptions of the appropriate place of interest groups (described as Old Tory, Old Whig, Liberal, Radical and Collectivist theories) imply different conceptions of how legislators should behave toward such groups or their agents. Beer singles out for special attention one facet of the legislator-group role-relationship—that involving the activity of the legislator as agent of a group (the "interested M.P.").

Table 2—Distribution of Role-orientations Toward Pressure Groups in Four State Legislatures

Role Orientation	California N = 97	New Jersey N = 78	Ohio N = 157	Tennessee N = 116	Total N = 448
Facilitators	38%	41%	43%	23%	37%
Neutrals	42	32	35	37	37
Resisters	20	27	22	40	26
	100%	100%	100%	100%	100%

Facilitators: Have a friendly attitude toward group activity *and* relatively much knowledge about it.

Resisters: Have a hostile attitude toward group activity *and* relatively much knowledge about it.

Neutrals: Either, (1) Have no strong attitude of favor or disfavor with respect to group activity (regardless of their knowledge of it),

Or, (2) Have very little knowledge about it (regardless of their friendliness or hostility toward it),

Or, (3) Both (1) and (2).

By the measures of tolerance and awareness already described each of the legislators interviewed was classified under one of these three headings. They are distributed in the four states as shown in Table 2.

The reasons given by legislators for their varying opinions about groups further describe the differences among them. When legislators were asked why they thought the legislature would work better or worse in the absence of pressure group activity, most of their responses could be coded into a comparatively few categories. These have been arranged in the order of decreasing

Table 3—Attitude-differences among Facilitators, Neutrals and Resisters as Shown by Their Appraisals of Pressure-group Activity

Most Favorable Opinion Expressed	Role Orientation [a] FACILITATOR N = 124	NEUTRAL N = 105	RESISTER N = 76
1. Groups are indispensable.	63%	39%	14%
2. Group activity is in general good, though certain "bad practices" of groups are undesirable.	23	41	46
3. Other less favorable opinions: *e.g.,* group activity may be objectionable but one ought not interfere with the democratic right to be heard; group influence is over-rated, it is not an important factor; group activity is a wholly disruptive force which ought to be eliminated.	14	20	40
	100%	100%	100%

[a] Total is only 305 because some legislators failed to give reasons when answering the question and others expressed appraisals not codable in these categories.

friendliness toward group activity in Table 3. When respondents made more than one comment, only the most favorable (highest in the table) was coded. The table shows that almost two-thirds of the Facilitators think the legislature could not get along without pressure group activity, whereas a substantial number of Resisters (40 percent) expressed much less favorable opinions. The differences are of extreme statistical significance.[15]

In spite of these very striking and consistent differences, however, it should not be overlooked that even the Resisters express fairly tolerant appraisals of group activity, some 60 percent venturing opinions (numbers 1 and 2 in Table 3) which are quite favorable. We must, in other words, recognize the fact that pressure politics has become rather widely accepted among legislators in American states.

Legislators' differences in perception of groups are not simple quantitative differences of more or less, as the initial measure of lobbyist-recognition might suggest. In responding to a question asking them to name the most powerful groups in their own state, 56 percent of the Facilitators but only 36 percent of the Resisters named only or mainly *specific organizations* or lobbyists; similarly, only 36 percent of the Facilitators but 58 percent of the Resisters referred to *broad interest aggregations* ("labor," "farmers," *etc.*). In other words, Facilitators, significantly more than either Neutrals or Resisters, tend to see groups and group activities in concrete and specific terms.[16] That Facilitators are more alert to perceive groups and group cues is strikingly indicated by the fact that, even though interviewers sought, by probing, to have all respondents uniformly name six groups in response to the question, Facilitators nevertheless named significantly more groups than either Neutrals or Resisters.[17]

Some of the grosser behavioral characteristics of the three types of legislator being described can also be explored. To begin with, assuming the validity of the role-orientation typology, one should expect to find Facilitators more ready than either Neutrals or Resisters to listen to the exhortations of pressure groups. This hypothesis is supported by the finding (see Table 4) that Facilitators named significantly more groups than did either Neutrals or Resisters when asked the question,

We've been told that there are always some groups whose advice ought to be considered, whether they happen to be powerful or not. Would you name some of these groups here in [state]?[18]

[15] $X^2 = 50.48$, D.F. $= 4$, p $< .001$; the differences are consistent in all four states.

[16] Complete data not shown. The differences are statistically significant: $X^2 = 14.9$, D.F. $= 4$, $.01 > p > .001$; the direction of difference is the same in all four states. The question was asked in the following form: "You hear a lot these days about the power of interest groups and lobbies in state politics. What would you say are the most powerful groups of this kind here in [state]?"

[17] 62% of the Facilitators named 5 or more groups, compared with 57% of the Resisters and 45% of the Neutrals. If Facilitators are compared with Neutrals and Resisters, $X^2 = 8.91$, D.F. $= 1$, $.01 > p > .001$; the differences are consistently in the same direction in all four states.

[18] X^2 for the table $= 15.96$, D.F. $= 6$, $.02 > p > .01$; X^2 for Facilitators compared with Resisters $= 11.86$, D.F. $= 3$, $.01 > p > .001$; X^2 for Facilitators compared with Neutrals and Resisters together $= 14.88$, D.F. $= 3$, $.01 > p > .001$. Again, the differences are consistently in the same direction within each state, except that Tennessee Resisters name somewhat more groups than Tennessee Neutrals (mean of 3.74 as against mean of 3.35). This finding, like the one just preceding, was wholly unanticipated, since interviewers sought to elicit a uniform number of groups from all respondents.

Table 4—Facilitators Think More Groups Worth Listening To Than Do Neutrals or Resisters

	Role Orientation		
Number of Groups Named	FACILITATORS N = 141	NEUTRALS N = 134	RESISTERS N = 108
0–1	11%	17%	20%
2–3	24	34	37
4 or more	29	27	23
"All are worth listening to" [a]	36	22	20
	100%	100%	100%
Mean number of groups named	4.17	3.50	3.35

[a] This response counted only if no more precise answer given (*i.e.*, no group named).

Table 5—Facilitators Rate Importance of Pressure Groups on Own Views of "School Needs" Problem Higher Than Do Neutrals or Resisters

	Role Orientation		
Importance Attributed to Views of Pressure Groups	FACILITATORS N = 146	NEUTRALS N = 137	RESISTERS N = 101
Very important or important	70%	57%	40%
Not very or not at all important	30	43	60
	100%	100%	100%

Table 6—More Facilitators Than Neutrals or Resisters Agree Lobbyists Give Them Valuable Help in Drafting Bills

Answer to Statement that Lobbyists Give Valuable Help in Bill-Drafting	Role Orientation		
	FACILITATORS N = 163	NEUTRALS N = 160	RESISTERS N = 120
Agree or tend to agree	63%	52%	52%
Tend to disagree or disagree	37	48	48
	100%	100%	100%

Table 7—More Facilitators Than Neutrals or Resisters Agree Lobbyists Give Them Valuable Help in Lining up Support for the Legislator's Own Bills

Answer to Statement that Lobbyists Give Valuable Help in Lining Up Support	Role Orientation		
	FACILITATORS N = 159	NEUTRALS N = 157	RESISTERS N = 115
Agree or tend to agree	78%	67%	61%
Tend to disagree or disagree	22	33	39
	100%	100%	100%

Not only do Facilitators think more groups are worth listening to than do Neutrals or Resisters; they apparently tend also to give more weight to what they hear from group representatives. At least on the problem of school needs, which was selected as a typical issue, when legislators were asked to rate the influence of several factors—committee recommendations, advice of party leaders, views of constituents, *etc.*—on their own thinking, Facilitators attributed more importance to the "views of interest groups or lobbies" than did Neutrals or Resisters (See Table 5).[19] Finally, the data provide internal evidence that at least two of the legislative behaviors one would expect to find associated with the accommodation of group interest and demands do indeed appear more characteristic of Facilitators than of Neutrals or Resisters. Tables 6 and 7 show the former to be more ready to use, or at least to admit to using, the aid of lobbyists both in drafting bills and in lining up support for bills.[20]

There is ample justification, then, for the conclusion that there are significant differences among legislators in their role orientations toward pressure groups and group agents. It is not just that they differ in tolerance and awareness of group activity—that, indeed, was assumed in constructing the typology of Facilitators, Neutrals and Resisters. The point is, important tendencies toward different patterns of behavior are associated with these basic differences in affect and cognition. The patterns are sharper for the Facilitators and Resisters, since they are attuned, favorably or unfavorably, to group behavior, and perceive, understand and react in characteristic fashion. The Neutrals, a category consisting of those who apparently fail to perceive, understand or formulate a coherent standard for judging groups-in-general, demonstrate, as one might expect, a more erratic, less distinct and consistent pattern. It is possible that each individual Neutral, at his own level of awareness or concern, behaves toward some or all group representatives in a manner that could be characterized as "role behavior," but that these patterns cancel each other out in the statistical treatment of responses. In any case, Facilitators are more likely to be aware of the nature of group demands and respond to them; Resisters to be aware of them but deliberately fail to respond; Neutrals to respond or resist, but for assorted other reasons, without caring or without knowing that a demand has been made by a group. It should be clear that these role categories do no more than classify one aspect of legislators' attitudes and behavior: they are not fixed categories of types-of-person, nor will they by any means describe all aspects of legislators' behavior. They are constructs, devised to help us explore further the working of the legislative system and, ultimately, the larger political system.

---

[19] $X^2 = 23.40$, D.F. $= 2$, $p < .001$; the differences are consistent within each state.

[20] The questions asked were, "[Do you agree to the statements], I get valuable help in drafting bills from interest groups or their agents" (Table 6), and, "Interest groups or their agents give me valuable help in lining up support for my bills" (Table 7). For Table 6, comparing Facilitators with Neutrals-and-Resisters, $X^2 = 4.71$, D.F. $= 1$, $.05 > p > .02$; for Table 7, $X^2 = 10.03$, D.F. $= 2$, $.01 > p > .001$. The differences are consistent within all four states, except that, in Table 7, New Jersey Resisters agree in greater proportions than do Facilitators, although New Jersey Neutrals agree much less.

DEMOGRAPHIC AND ECOLOGICAL CORRELATES
OF ROLE ORIENTATION TOWARD PRESSURE GROUPS

"Explanation" of the differences in role orientation described above was not an objective of this study, but the data nevertheless do suggest several comments on this problem. One would naturally expect that a variable defined generally in terms of cognition and affect, as role orientation has been defined here, would be closely related to respondents' education. If, as many educators say, education liberates the mind, eliminates excessive faith in the dogmatic truth of simple ideas, and provides increasing factual understanding of the social and physical world, then legislators with much education (and therefore greater knowledge and greater acceptance of group diversity) will more often be Facilitators than Resisters and those with comparatively little education will more often be Neutrals than either Facilitators or Resisters. As between the latter two types, less-educated persons will more often be Resisters than Facilitators. The data shown in Table 8 are consistent with all these hypotheses and are statistically significant.[21]

Role orientation is hardly a simple reflex function of education, however. It has already been shown (above, Table 2) that the four states studied differ significantly in the distribution of role-orientation types. Such differences among the states persist even if we compare only groups of comparable educational background. As Table 9 shows, there is, on the whole, at least as much variation from state to state *within* each educational level as there is *between educational levels* within any given state.[22] This suggests that "political culture"[23] is a significant variable differentiating the states' modes and styles of pressure politics. Quite possibly, norms and expectations peculiar to each state system are transmitted and circulated more or less generally among the population of that system, so that legislators, like citizens or occupants of other roles in the system, have acquired some role orientations and potential responses appropriate to their own specific legislature and state political system before they come actually to play their roles.

Some very oblique justification for such a line of reasoning is provided by the fact that role orientation is not significantly related to any of the demographic variables often discussed in behavioral research.[24] Socio-economic status, by

---

[21] $X^2 = 16.64$, D.F. $= 2$, p $< .001$. Non-college-educated includes some legislators who acquired law-school degrees without attending college beforehand, as well as some who had various non-college postgraduate work after high school (business school, night school, *etc.*). There are some intra-state departures from the pattern: California non-college-educated legislators are less likely to be Resisters than are college-educated and are more likely to be Facilitators, and college-educated Tennessee legislators are less likely to be Facilitators than to be either Neutrals or Resisters.

[22] Inter-state differences are greater than intra-state, inter-level differences when California or Tennessee is compared with either New Jersey or Ohio, but inter-level differences are slightly greater than inter-state differences when Ohio or New Jersey is compared with either of the other two states. It must be remembered that the knowledge dimension of role-orientation was normalized in the four states; for this reason the discussion here is directed toward the affective dimension, degree of friendliness (see above, note 12).

[23] For discussion of the concept of "political culture" see Gabriel A. Almond, "Comparative Political Systems," *The Journal of Politics* 18 (1956), 391–409.

[24] For a general discussion of these variables see John C. Wahlke and Heinz Eulau (eds.), *Legislative Behavior* (Glencoe, Illinois, 1959), pp. 239–72.

Table 8—More-educated Legislators Tend More To Be Facilitators and Less To Be Either Neutrals or Resistors Than Do the Less-educated Legislators

| | Level of Education | |
| | LESS THAN COMPLETED | AT LEAST COMPLETED |
Role Orientation	COLLEGE (N = 201)	COLLEGE (N = 247)
Facilitators	26%	45%
Neutrals	44	31
Resisters	30	24
	100%	100%

Table 9—Inter-state Differences in Friendliness Toward Pressure Politics Are as Great as Differences Between Legislators of Different Educational Backgrounds

| | Mean Score for Friendliness Toward Pressure Politics [a] | | | | |
Legislator's Education	CALIFORNIA N = 106	NEW JERSEY N = 79	OHIO N = 160	TENNESSEE N = 117	INTER-STATE RANGE
Less than college	2.65	3.17	3.09	3.76	1.11
At least college	2.51	2.52	2.32	3.24	.92
Intra-state, inter-level range	.14	.65	.77	.52	

[a] Scores represent quintile groups, score 1 being the most friendly, score 5 the least, on the scale described above, p. 208.

almost any index chosen, fails to exhibit such correlation: legislators with low, medium or high income fall in all three role-orientation categories with equal probability.[25] Neither their type of occupation nor their occupational status appears significantly associated with legislators' role orientation.[26] The urban-or-rural character of their county-of-residence is likewise unrelated to role orientation, as is urban-or-rural character of the places where legislators were brought up. Nor do the data show a relation between legislators' religious affiliations and their role orientations toward pressure groups. The one familiar demographic variable which does emerge significantly related to role orientation is that discussed above—education. And education, it has already been shown, fails to account for inter-state differences.

These findings hardly "prove" the suitability of "political culture" as a basic concept for the analysis of political systems, let alone prove that role-orientation is determined by such a cultural variable. But they do strongly suggest that, because the norms and expectations constituting roles in a political system are by no means wholly or directly dependent on social class, communal type, or

[25] Data not shown. Income-level measured by responses to the question, "Now, including your legislative salary, into which of these four income groups would you say your total annual income falls—(1) less than $5000, (2) $5000 to $10000, (3) $10000 to $20000, or (4) over $20000?"

[26] Data not shown. Types of occupation include Manufacturing, Construction, Mining, Transportation, Communication, Utilities, Wholesale or Retail Trade, Financial, Real Estate, Law, Other Professions, Religion, Labor, Public Service, Housewives, Miscellaneous. Occupational Statuses include Managers, proprietors and officials; Professional and technical; Clerical; Sales; Craftsmen, foremen and skilled labor; Farmers and farm managers; Housewives.

similar supposedly controlling variables, efforts should be made to describe any political system in such a way as to include political culture variables in the basic structural description.

INTEREST INCLINATIONS AND ROLE ORIENTATION

Students of the legislative process usually assume there is a relationship between legislators' personal convictions or group sympathies and their actions as legislators. In order to inquire into this relationship, legislators were classified as pro-business, pro-labor or economic neutrals. The process of classification (too complex to display here fully) involved three main steps: (1) all interest groups mentioned were classified as economic or other-than-economic, and all economic-interest groups then classified as either business, labor or agricultural; (2) each legislator's pattern of reference to each group separately was then classified as either favorable, neutral or unfavorable;[27] and, finally, (3) each legislator's interest inclination was determined on the basis of his pattern of favor, disfavor or neutrality toward the three classes of economic interest.[28]

The question is, how do such interest inclinations affect the role orientations of legislators toward interest-group activity in general? The most obvious hypothesis is that individuals who are committed to any particular interest (business, labor, *etc.*) will be less likely than individuals not so committed to look favorably upon the assertion of demands by other groups or interests, especially if those others are conflicting interests. On the other hand, because the nature of their assertion of their own interests calls attention to the group-basis of those interests, the more committed legislators will not likely be especially resistant to group activity in the abstract. From this we can infer that economic neutrals will tend more than will pro-business or pro-labor legislators to be Facilitators and tend less to be Resisters. Table 10 shows this hypothesis is significantly supported.[29]

One other feature of Table 10 deserves comment: whereas pro-business legislators tend more to be Neutrals or Facilitators than to be Resisters, pro-labor legislators tend above all to be Resisters. This suggests but by no means

[27] A group or interest could be named in three possible contexts during the interview: (1) *Group power*: Was a group named in response to the question, "What would you say are the most powerful [interest groups or lobbies] here in [state]?" (2) *Worth of group*: Was it named in response to the question, "Would you name some [interest groups or lobbies here in (state)] whose advice ought to be considered, whether or not they are particularly powerful?" (3) *Hostility to group*: Did respondent express hostility toward this same group at any time during the interview? (Interviewers recorded such volunteered indications and they were coded for all respondents and all groups.) Reference to a group in context 2 only or in both 1 and 2 were considered *favorable* references; those in context 1 only, or in both 2 and 3 (an essentially ambivalent response) or in all three contexts (also ambivalent) were considered *neutral*; and references in context 3 only or in both 1 and 3 were considered *unfavorable*.

[28] The classification exhausts the logically possible combinations of favorable-neutral-or-unfavorable references to business-labor-or-agricultural interests. "Pro-agricultural" inclinations were combined with "pro-business" while "anti-agricultural" were included with "pro-labor," since neither category contained sufficient cases for analysis, and since it seemed reasonable to assume that most contemporary interest cleavages of the sort relevant to a "conservative-liberal" distinction involve primarily the conflict between business and labor and that in most such conflicts agricultural interests side with business interests.

[29] When economic neutrals are compared with pro-business and pro-labor groups combined, $X^2 = 13.13$, D.F. $= 2$, $.01 > p > .001$; the differences in all states are consistent.

proves that American pro-labor legislators are more ideologically doctrinaire and less tolerant of pluralistic diversity than are pro-business legislators. One possible explanation is that labor-union officials or members, and presumably other persons who see the world as they do, are likely to see arrayed against them only one main group antagonist (the employer, or an association of employers), to be faced with only one, if any, competing labor organization, and, at least until recently, to feel little need to sell themselves to any consumer interest or organization. The businessman or person viewing the world as he does, on the other hand, is more likely to be exposed to a multiplicity of groups—not just antagonistic labor and target consumer groups and interests, but competing groups identical in kind with his own immediate business organization. It need hardly be emphasized, of course, that all such reasoning is at this stage highly speculative.

Table 10—Legislators Who Are Ideologically Neutral, Where Economic Interests Are Concerned, Are More Likely Than Legislators Committed to Either Business or Labor to Manifest Role Orientation of Facilitator

	Economic-Interest Inclination		
	PRO-BUSINESS	NEUTRAL	PRO-LABOR
Role	N = 239	N = 130	N = 51
Facilitator	34%	49%	26%
Neutral	36	33	33
Resister	30	18	41
	100%	100%	100%

THE POLITICAL ENTAILMENT OF ROLE ORIENTATION

General role theory holds that roles in any system are to a considerable extent engendered by the very system itself in which the roles occur.[30] Roles, in other words, are functionally specific to the system in which they are played. For example, the role of "buyer" in a market system calls for the complementary role of "seller." On such grounds one can very generally postulate that role orientations toward pressure groups are related to the functions of the political system in general and, more closely, to the functions of the legislative sub-system in particular.

Political scientists distinguish between the different functions of legislature, executive, administration and judiciary *vis-à-vis* pressure groups. As Earl Latham has said,

The legislature referees the group struggle, ratifies the victories of the successful coalitions, and records the terms of the surrenders, compromises, and conquests in the form of statutes. . . . The function of the bureaucrat in the group struggle is somewhat different from that of the legislator. Administrative agencies of the regulatory kind are established to carry out the terms of the treaties that the legislators have negotiated and ratified. . . . The function of the judge is not unlike that of the bureaucrat.[31]

[30] See especially S. F. Nadel, *The Theory of Social Structure* (Glencoe, Illinois, 1951), pp. 57*ff*.
[31] *Op. cit.,* pp. 35, 38, 39.

Even those who deny vehemently the adequacy of this view as a *complete* account of the governmental process generally admit that, insofar as *any* agency of government has the legitimate function of basing its decisions to *any* extent upon the expressed demands of organized interest groups, that function belongs more properly to legislative than to executive, administrative or judicial agencies.

If this is so and if, as it is reasonable to assume, commitment to legislative purpose increases with increasing service in the legislature, then legislators with most tenure should tend more than those with little tenure to be Facilitators. Table 11 shows that, except for Tennessee Resisters, this is indeed, the case.[32]

Table 11—Legislators With the Most Legislative Service Tend Most To Be Facilitators and Least To Be Neutrals

| | Median Number Years' Legislative Service Prior to 1957 | | | |
Role Orientation	CALIFORNIA N = 99	NEW JERSEY N = 79	OHIO N = 155	TENNESSEE N = 115
Facilitators	7.3	5.6	6.2	2.2
Neutrals	4.8	2.5	4.4	2.1
Resisters	5.3	3.8	4.6	2.4

Table 12—Experience in the Legislature Inclines Legislators Toward Facilitator Role Orientation and Away from Resister Role Orientation More Than Does Experience in Executive or Administrative Office

| | Office Held Prior to Entry to State Legislature [a] | | |
Role Orientation	EXECUTIVE OR ADMINISTRATIVE (BUT NOT LEGIS-LATIVE) OFFICE N = 84	LEGISLATIVE (BUT NOT EXECUTIVE OR ADMINISTRATIVE) OFFICE N = 105	NO PREVIOUS OFFICE N = 202
Facilitators	24%	36%	41%
Neutrals	39	43	34
Resisters	37	21	25
	100%	100%	100%

[a] At all levels of government—state, federal, local.

By the same reasoning, persons who have been active in legislative office should be more inclined to Facilitative and less to Resistant role orientations than those active in non-legislative offices. This is borne out by Table 12. The table also seems to show that persons who had *no* previous governmental experience are still more likely than are those with legislative experience to be Facilitators. But the differences here, in contrast to the differences between persons with legislative and persons with executive or administrative experience, are not statis-

---

[32] If the groups are dichotomized into those having less and those having more than the median number of years' legislative tenure in their legislature, then $X^2 = 6.14$, D.F. $= 2$, $.05 > p > .02$.

tically significant,[33] and this apparent tendency is also counterbalanced by a correspondingly greater tendency for persons with no previous governmental experience, when compared with persons having prior legislative experience, to be Resisters.

ROLE ORIENTATION AND THE LEGISLATIVE SYSTEM

It seems reasonable to suppose that the number and pervasiveness of groups in American political processes are so great that no legislator can hope to operate in disregard of them. The individual legislator can work effectively and can feel he is working effectively as a legislator only if he makes his peace with the world of pressure groups. In other words, other things being equal, the Facilitator will probably be a more effective legislator, and will feel himself to be so, than will the Neutral or the Resister.

A crude measure of legislators' effectiveness is provided by their responses to the following question:

We've been told that every legislature has its unofficial rules of the game—certain things members must do and things they must not do if they want the respect and cooperation of fellow-members. What are some of these things—these rules-of-the game—that a member must observe . . . ?

On the assumption that the more effective legislators are aware of a greater number and a greater diversity of "rules of the game," one can hypothesize that Facilitators will outrank Neutrals and Resisters in both these respects. In fact, Facilitators averaged naming 4.13 rules when answering, as compared with 3.88 for Resisters and 2.53 for Neutrals. That they likewise named rules in greater diversity is shown in Table 13.[34]

It is worth noting that the Neutrals rank lower than either Facilitators or Resisters in both measures.

It can likewise be shown (see Table 14) that significantly more Facilitators *feel* themselves to be effective legislators than do the other two types.[35] But

[33] Comparing those with executive-administrative experience and those with legislative experience, and only with respect to the Facilitator and Resister categories, $X^2 = 7.37$, D.F. $= 1$, $.01 > p > .001$. Comparing those with legislative experience (prior to state legislature) and those with no previous experience, $X^2 = 2.39$, D.F. $= 2$, $.50 > p > .30$. Comparing them only with respect to Neutral as against both other categories combined, $X^2 = 1.19$, D.F. $= 1$, $.30 > p > .20$.

[34] For Table 13, $X^2 = 11.49$, D.F. $= 2$, $.01 > p > .001$; in both cases the differences are consistent in all four states, except that Tennessee Resisters name slightly more rules than do Tennessee Facilitators. These differences are *not* merely reflections of legislators' differing educational backgrounds. In both cases (number and diversity of rules named), they are significantly greater among Facilitators, Neutrals and Resisters of the same educational level than are the differences between legislators of different educational levels (data not shown).

[35] $X^2 = 13.64$, D.F. $= 4$, $.01 > p > .001$. Tennessee Resisters have a higher efficacy sense than do Tennessee Facilitators, but they also outrank the latter in *low* efficacy sense. Efficacy sense was measured by a Guttman-type scale based on the following questions: "[Do you agree or disagree that] (1) There is so little time during a session to study all the bills that sometimes I don't know what I'm voting for or against; (2) Many of the bills are so detailed and technical that I have trouble understanding them all; (3) So many groups want so many different things that it is often difficult to know what stand to take; and (4) My district includes so many different kinds of people that I often don't know just what the people there want me to do." The results are not biased by the inclusion of the item (number 3) dealing specifically with pressure groups.

whereas Neutrals rank lowest of the three types in effectiveness, Resisters rank lowest in *sense* of effectiveness.

Another way to look at the problem of legislators' relative effectiveness is to consider other legislators' perceptions and judgments of them. It seems reasonable to assume that those most esteemed by their colleagues will have at least greater potential for influence or effectiveness than their less esteemed colleagues. On this assumption, an index of potential effectiveness was constructed from the replies by respondents in each house to three questions regarding the fellow members they considered to be "personal friends," "experts" in some legislative

Table 13—Facilitators Name (and presumably, therefore, are aware of) a Greater Diversity of "Rules of the Game"

Number of Categories [a] in Which Rules Were Named	Role Orientation		
	FACILITATORS N = 162	NEUTRALS N = 160	RESISTERS N = 119
Two or less	46%	64%	51%
Three or more	54	36	49
	100%	100%	100%

[a] The categories include rules (1) regarding predictability of behavior, (2) regarding restraint or canalization of conflict, (3) expediting legislative business, promoting group cohesion or solidarity, (4) which are tactical, primarily for the benefit of individual members, and (5) which are "personal qualities" rather than rules.

Table 14—Facilitators Have Highest and Resisters Have Lowest Efficacy Sense

	Role Orientation		
Efficacy-Sense	FACILITATORS N = 164	NEUTRALS N = 163	RESISTERS N = 119
High	43%	31%	29%
Medium	38	46	36
Low	19	23	35
	100%	100%	100%

Table 15—Facilitators Are Rated Higher Than Resisters or Neutrals by Their Colleagues (composite ratings as "friend," "respected," and "expert")

	Role Orientation		
Rating	FACILITATORS N = 163	NEUTRALS N = 164	RESISTERS N = 120
Top half [a]	53%	40%	47%
Bottom half [a]	47	60	53
	100%	100%	100%

[a] These "halves" are approximate, since tie scores made it impossible to divide some chambers exactly. Standards differed slightly between chambers with the internal distribution, but all in the top half were named by one or more members in each of the three categories, and their mentions in all three categories total six or more. None of those in the bottom half had more than eight mentions in all.

subject-matter field, and "respected for following the rules of the game." Ranking the members with respect to the number of mentions each received differentiates between those who stand out in the eyes of their fellows and those who are lost in the shuffle or (in a few instances) disliked or distrusted. This ranking of a member, be it noted, is entirely independent of his own responses to the questions, since it is a composite view of the member as seen by his colleagues. Table 15 shows that Facilitators do, in fact, rate higher with their colleagues than do Resisters and Neutrals.[36]

III

CONCLUSIONS

Several important, though tentative, conclusions are suggested by the above findings. Perhaps the most important is that the group struggle is mediated in the legislature primarily by legislators who are relatively *least* committed as advocates or agents to particular conflicting interests and who are rather conciliators among them. The emerging picture of the Facilitative legislator who is above or outside of group conflicts even while he more or less consciously defines his official role to include the accommodation of group demands adds a new dimension to the conception of government ordinarily guiding study of pressure groups. At the same time, the detection of Resisters and Neutrals warns against a too simple view of the legislative struggle as a struggle between elementary group demands. There is evidence, if such is required, that a legislature cannot forge public policy out of the raw material of naked group interests alone. Resisters are to be found in all legislatures who do not want to base public policy on such demands; even Facilitators, by standing above most groups, indicate their refusal to recognize the views of any particular groups as specially pregnant with the public interest.

On the other hand, pressure groups occupy too prominent a place in American society to permit a legislator seriously to think of doing his legislative job in complete disregard of them. What is more, the legislative function seems clearly to include the function of harmonizing and integrating group demands, so that incumbency in legislative office itself serves to shape legislators' role orientations so as to promote the group-conciliating function and the effective performance of individual legislators, probably the effective performance of the legislative system itself, depends to some extent upon legislators' acquiring such orientations.

The findings also emphasize the "autonomy" of the legislative sub-system and of the larger political system. While the differences among the four states in distribution of legislators' role orientations appear superficially to follow interstate differences in general educational level, economic status and urban-rural character of the general population, the failure of corresponding demographic

---

[36] $X^2 = 5.20$, D.F. = 2, p = just over .05. The tendency is the same in every chamber in all four states, except the Tennessee House, where Resisters are the top-rated group. If the Tennessee House is eliminated from the table, the percentage of Facilitators in the top half is increased to 55%.

characteristics of legislators to correlate with their role orientations warns us against accepting such correlations as "explanations." The fact that the Tennessee legislature is a far more informal and less "professional" legislature than those of California, New Jersey and Ohio is as important as, and is by no means directly the result of, the fact that the Tennessee population is more rural, poorer and less well educated. Whatever the causal mechanism linking such sociological variables to legislative behavior, it seems necessary to visualize a "political culture" intervening between to give to the legislative and political system of each state a characteristic structure which is more immediately significant in determining what gets done there than is the sociological composition of the population or the day-to-day specifics of pressure-group activity.

The most general conclusion, therefore, is that political science can profitably re-direct its attention to basic questions of institutional structure, mechanics and process. These questions can be properly answered by further rigorous attention to the behavior of political actors, the ultimate data for all political investigation.

LEADERSHIP

Bases of Authority in Legislative Bodies: A Comparative Analysis

by HEINZ EULAU

Authority relations are usually treated as characteristic properties of administrative or bureaucratic organizations. Though formally structured as hierarchies of superordination and subordination, authority relations in such organizations represent perplexing analytical problems involving both the identification of authority and its measurement.[1] The task of analysis is compounded in legislative bodies, where those in high formal office—presidents, speakers, and floor leaders—are either *elected* to their positions or *succeed* to office as a consequence of political manipulations which often elude the outside observer.

Little is known about authority relations in legislative bodies. There is a great deal of anecdotal information about the dictatorial speaker—"Uncle Joe" Cannon (Speaker of the U.S. House of Representatives, 1903–1911) is the prototype—or about the arbitrary committee chairman who pigeonholes whatever bills he dislikes. More systematic efforts to identify and measure power in legislative institutions through study of roll-call votes have proved difficult.[2] In the Congress, there seems to be a close congruence between formal and informal leadership, but the question—what makes for the acceptance of authority?—remains unanswered.[3]

There is reason to believe that the degree to which the decisions of legislative

[1] See Robert L. Peabody, Perceptions of Organizational Authority: A Comparative Analysis, *Administrative Science Quarterly*, 6 (1962), 461–82.

[2] See Robert A. Dahl, The Concept of Power, *Behavioral Science*, 2 (1957), 201–15; Duncan MacRae, Jr., and Hugh D. Price, Scale Positions and "Power" in the Senate, *Behavioral Science*, 4 (1959), 212–18.

[3] See David B. Truman, *The Congressional Party* (New York, 1959), pp. 94–144, 193–246.

Reprinted from "Bases of Authority in Legislative Bodies: A Comparative Analysis," *Administrative Science Quarterly* vol. 7 (December 1962): 309–21, by Heinz Eulau. Reprinted by permission of the *Administrative Science Quarterly* and the author.

leaders are accepted depends on certain "values" that serve as bases of authority being attributed to them by the rank-and-file membership.[4] Presumably, legislators are not equally credited by their peers with skill, knowledge, respect, or affection, to name just a few of such values. In so far as legislative leaders have some of these characteristics attributed to them more frequently than other legislators, their authority may be said to be rooted in such value attributions. Of course, this does not answer an important question: Do men come into positions of legislative leadership because such characteristics are attributed to them to a higher degree than to other members, or is the greater attribution of these values to them partly the result of their occupying offices invested with formal authority? Whatever the answer to this question, one should expect that the authority of legislative leaders—acceptance of their decisions—is likely to depend on their being *attributed* values to a high degree.

Three Values

Hypothetically speaking, in every legislative body authority is likely to be based on respect. Respect is a value which may be attributed unevenly: some men are given more deference than others. In legislatures, distinguished as they are from administrative structures by a strong egalitarian ethos ("each man's vote counts alike here"), respect arises out of those informal norms of behavior, "rules of the game," in terms of which legislators regulate each other's conduct[5] and which are enforced by both positive and negative incentives. Those who fail to conform are variously ostracized, censured, or punished, and they are not likely to enjoy respect. Those who excel in playing by the rules are given respect and are rewarded: their bills will have a better chance of being passed; they may be appointed to committee chairmanships; or they may be elected to positions of leadership.

The egalitarian milieu of legislative bodies, the camaraderie that comes with close personal contact, involvement in the common task, and pride in electoral survival make it easy to develop friendships (which, in bureaucratic organizations, are restricted by the status system: only those on the same level in the hierarchy, or in adjacent status positions, come into close contact in their work and associate with each other in informal settings). Friendship is a strong bond in politics, and the affections of friendship carry over into the business of lawmaking. In every legislature there are more or less cohesive groups of friends and cliques, often related to each other through overlapping memberships or secondary contacts.[6] Again, as with respect, attributions of affection are likely to

[4] This formulation is indebted to, though it also deviates from, Harold D. Lasswell's propositions about the functions of values in politics. See, for instance, Harold D. Lasswell and Abraham Kaplan, *Power and Society* (New Haven, 1950), pp. 55–62, 133–136.

[5] This has been most intensively studied in the U.S. Senate. See Donald R. Matthews, *U.S. Senators and Their World* (Chapel Hill, N.C., 1960), pp. 92–177; Ralph K. Huitt, The Morse Committee Assignment Controversy: A Case Study in Senate Norms, *American Political Science Review*, 51 (1957), 313–29.

[6] See Samuel C. Patterson, Patterns of Personal Relations in a Legislative Group, *Public Opinion Quarterly*, 23 (1959), 101–18.

be unevenly distributed. Some legislators are more widely chosen as friends than others.

Legislatures, like administrative organizations, develop and cultivate a specialization of labor in dealing with particular subjects, which has been institutionalized in the creation of standing committees. But a legislator also shows a degree of expertise that is independent of his committee assignments and that is rooted in his personal skill and training. Regardless of the committees to which they belong, some legislators are recognized as more expert than others in particular subjects by their colleagues.[7]

Values in Eight Chambers

This analysis deals with the distribution of these three values—respect, affection, and expertise—in eight chambers of four American state legislatures —those of California, New Jersey, Ohio, and Tennessee.[8] The main hypothesis of this analysis is that a greater degree of respect, affection, and expertise is attributed to legislative leaders than to rank-and-file members. If it should be found that the leaders do not differ from other legislators or, perhaps, rank below them in the values ascribed to them, it may be assumed that, unless other bases are available, their authority rests on fragile foundations. Moreover, it may be possible to identify a reserve of highly ranked legislators among the rank and file from which future leaders can be recruited.

The data on which the analysis is based were collected in an interview survey of 474 legislators in eight legislative chambers during the 1957 sessions.[9] In the course of the interview, all legislators in the sample were asked a series of questions: Whom did they consider the "most widely respected" among their colleagues? Whom did they consider their "closest personal friends?" Whom did they consider "particularly expert in their respective fields?"

In order to compare any one legislator with all others in terms of the number of nominations he received, it was necessary to develop a standard of comparison. This standard was likely to vary from one set of value attributions to the next as a function of the number of choices requested—four or five in the case of respect, five or six in the case of expertise, and an unspecified number in the case of affection (though most nominations here usually varied from none to six). As the actual number of choices could also vary within each set from one

---

[7] See William Buchanan, Heinz Eulau, LeRoy C. Ferguson, and John C. Wahlke, The Legislator as Specialist, *Western Political Quarterly* 13 (1960), 636–51.

[8] The data used in this article were collected as part of the State Legislative Research Project. For a full report of this project, see John C. Wahlke, Heinz Eulau, William Buchanan, and LeRoy C. Ferguson, *The Legislative System: Explorations in Legislative Behavior* (New York, 1962). The preparation of this analysis was made possible by a grant from the Political Behavior Committee of the Social Science Research Council and a subsidy from the Public Affairs Committee of Stanford University to Richard Duncan, who prepared a preliminary analysis of the data. None of the organizations mentioned is responsible for the analysis.

[9] In California and Ohio, 94 percent were interviewed; in Tennessee, 91 percent; and in New Jersey, 100 percent. For a short report on technical aspects of the project, see John C. Wahlke, Heinz Eulau, William Buchanan, and LeRoy C. Ferguson, The Annals of Research: A Case of Collaboration in Comparative Study of Legislative Behavior, *American Behavioral Scientist*, 4 (May 1961), 3–9.

respondent to the next, the standard had to be some measure of central tendency. Therefore, the total number of nominations in any one set was divided by the number of *potential* recipients—that is, the total number of members in a chamber. This was done on the assumption that if all actual choices were, by chance, equally distributed among all the members, the resulting hypothetical frequency of choices could serve as a standard in terms of which actual nominations could be ordered. For instance, the total number of nominations for respect in the Ohio House were 655. This figure was divided by 139, the number of members. Had the nominations been equally distributed by chance, each member would have received 4.71 choices. This hypothetical standard may serve two purposes: first, to compare the eight chambers as wholes or any subgroup in a chamber, such as the leaders and rank-and-file members; and second, to place any one member as falling above or below the standard. Table 1 presents the hypothetical frequencies (hf) for the three sets of value nominations.

Table 1—Hypothetical Frequencies of Nominations

	House				Senate			
	CALIF.	N.J.	OHIO	TENN.	CALIF.	N.J.	OHIO	TENN.
Respect	3.26	4.26	4.71	4.12	2.58	3.56	4.40	3.18
Affection	3.90	3.05	3.93	4.40	3.05	3.52	3.24	3.30
Expertise	4.96	4.94	4.62	2.62	4.00	3.52	4.95	3.60

The fluctuations within each set from chamber to chamber are probably symptomatic of different degrees of importance attached to the values of respect, affection, and expertise in the different chambers. Respect, for instance, seemed to be attributed to members more frequently in the Ohio House (hf = 4.71) than in the California Senate (hf = 2.58). Affection seemed more difficult to secure in the New Jersey House or California Senate (both with hf = 3.05) than in the Tennessee House (hf = 4.40). Expertise was less commonly attributed to members of the Tennessee House (hf = 2.62) than of the California House (hf = 4.96).

The Rank and File

How are the attributions of respect, affection, and expertise distributed among the rank-and-file memberships of the eight chambers? Table 2 shows the distributions in terms of the hypothetical frequency. It shows that the distributions do not follow a sharply pyramidal form, though the "above hypothetical frequency" groupings in no case include much more than a third of the rank and file. The largest high-ranking grouping is found in the expertise set of the Ohio Senate (37 percent), and the most exclusive high-ranking grouping characterizes the attribution of respect in the Ohio House (18 percent).

In general, Table 2 shows that the distribution of value attribution tends to be very similar in these eight legislative chambers. For instance, in the high-ranking groupings the range for respect is quite small, from 18 percent in the large Ohio House to 28 percent in the small New Jersey Senate. Although attribution of respect, as noted in Table 1, is frequent in the Ohio House, it is evidently difficult for individual members to reach a high ranking. Indeed, in the three large chambers—the Ohio House as well as the California and Tennessee Houses—inclusion in the "above" high-frequency grouping is more difficult to attain than it is in the small chambers (with the exception of the Tennessee Senate). It is plausible that there should be a relationship between the size of a chamber and the frequency with which respect is attributed: the larger a group is, the more difficult it is for an individual to be recognized as deserving respect.

Table 2—Distribution of Rank and File (in percent)

	House				Senate			
NOMINATIONS REGARDING:	CALIF. (N = 74)	N.J. (N = 52)	OHIO (N = 136)	TENN. (N = 96)	CALIF. (N = 39)	N.J. (N = 18)	OHIO (N = 32)	TENN. (N = 29)
Respect								
Above hf	23	27	18	22	26	28	25	21
Equal hf	4	4	1	8	10	5	3	10
Below hf	43	33	42	35	38	56	53	31
Zero (not named)	30	36	39	35	26	11	19	38
Affection								
Above hf	28	29	30	35	31	33	34	34
Equal hf	14	19	15	16	18	22	19	14
Below hf	51	42	48	47	38	28	44	38
Zero (not named)	7	10	7	2	13	17	3	14
Expertise								
Above hf	28	25	20	21	31	33	37	24
Equal hf	2	4	1	3	8	17	3	7
Below hf	23	25	27	22	28	17	22	28
Zero (not named)	47	46	52	54	33	33	38	41

Similarly, the range in the "above" high-frequency groupings for affection is very narrow, from 28 percent in the California House to 35 percent in the Tennessee House—a difference of only 7 percent. Affection seems to be attributed more frequently, however, than respect, as Table 2 shows.

The expertise nominations show a partly similar, partly different pattern. The difference lies in the relatively wide range of the proportions of legislators in the "above" groupings—from 37 percent in the Ohio Senate to only 20 percent in the Ohio House. The similarity lies in the apparent relationship between size of chamber and expertise attributions. As in the case of respect, nominations of expertise are made more frequently in the smaller than in the larger chambers.

A more convenient way to examine the similarities and differences between chambers and value sets is to score a legislator's total nominations with reference to the hypothetical frequency standard. For this purpose, a legislator above the hf standard was given a score of 3; a legislator whose actual nominations were equal to the hf criterion was given a score of 2; a legislator falling below the standard a score of 1; and a legislator with no nominations a score of zero. The individual scores so obtained were averaged for each value set in each chamber, yielding a simple index also ranging from three to zero.

Table 3—Value Indexes for Rank and File

Value	House				Senate			
	CALIF.	N.J.	OHIO	TENN.	CALIF.	N.J.	OHIO	TENN.
Respect	1.20	1.21	1.01	1.17	1.36	1.50	1.53	1.14
Affection	1.64	1.67	1.66	1.85	1.67	1.72	1.84	1.69
Expertise	1.11	1.07	.90	.91	1.36	1.50	1.41	1.14

Table 3 presents the index figures so obtained for the rank and file of the eight chambers. The averaged scores, it appears, fall in a range (from .90 to 1.85) below the index figure of two which should be attained if all nominations were equally distributed by chance among all potential recipients. Moreover, it appears more clearly from Table 3 that in all four legislatures (except for Tennessee in regard to respect and affection), value nominations are somewhat more widely shared in the smaller than in the larger chambers. The differences are small, but the general pattern in elective bodies such as legislatures suggests that the concentration of value attributions at the top of an institutional structure may be more characteristic of larger than of smaller organizations.

Comparison of Leadership and Membership

Whatever ideas one may entertain about the "natural history" of value attributions—whether they occurred before or after a legislator moved into a position of formal leadership—it can be assumed that in order to make effective use of the office more is needed than sheer incumbency. One should expect, therefore, that leaders as a group should receive more value nominations than the aggregate of rank-and-file members. However, each of the three values may not be equally relevant for effective authority. For instance, respect is probably more critical than affection or expertise in a leader's ability to have his decisions accepted. Without respect, leaders may not stay in office very long, no matter how many nominations they may receive in regard to values such as affection or expertise. In fact, expertise may be least relevant in this connection. It may even constitute a handicap because legislative leaders are expected to be "generalists" rather than specialists. We should anticipate, therefore, that the leadership cadres in the eight chambers will differ most from the rank and file in the share of respect they receive, less so in the share of affection, and least in the share of expertise attributions. Table 4 presents the results.

Altogether, there were 28 leaders in the high-level offices of the eight chambers, including speakers, presidents pro tem, and party floor leaders. In general, as Table 4 shows, if New Jersey is excluded, our expectations are met. Leaders differ most from members in the degree to which they are respected, then in the degree of affection shown them, and finally in the expertise attributed to them. We note one persistent exception, however, in both New Jersey chambers. Though given more respect than the members, the New Jersey leaders differ little from the members, and the differences are considerably smaller than in the other three states. In regard to affection, New Jersey Senate members actually

Table 4—Comparison of Leaders and Members

	House				Senate			
	CALIF.	N.J.	OHIO	TENN.	CALIF.	N.J.	OHIO	TENN.
Respect								
Leaders	2.16	1.50	3.00	3.00	3.00	1.67	3.00	3.00
Members	1.20	1.21	1.01	1.17	1.36	1.50	1.53	1.14
Difference	.96	2.9	1.99	1.83	1.64	.17	1.47	1.86
Affection								
Leaders	2.67	2.00	3.00	3.00	3.00	1.33	2.50	3.00
Members	1.64	1.67	1.66	1.85	1.67	1.72	1.84	1.69
Difference	1.03	.33	1.34	1.15	1.33	−.39	.66	1.31
Expertise								
Leaders	1.50	1.17	2.33	2.33	1.00	.67	1.00	2.00
Members	1.11	1.07	.90	.91	1.36	1.50	1.41	1.14
Difference	.39	.10	1.43	1.42	−.36	−.83	−.41	.86

were favored with affection more frequently than the leaders, and in the House the difference, though favorable to the leaders, is again much smaller than in the other three legislatures. In expertise also, New Jersey leaders were not credited with expertise more frequently than members.

There is a very simple explanation for the New Jersey results. In the small New Jersey chambers, all crucial procedural as well as substantive decisions are made by the majority party caucus as a body. In both chambers members of the majority party are rotated in and out of the speakership and other offices each session. Many of the members in any one session are, therefore, former speakers or former floor leaders, and they may be more influential than the incumbent officers. The wider distribution of value attributions in the data accurately mirrors these formal institutional arrangements in the New Jersey legislature. Indeed, the "deviant case" of New Jersey provides a good test of both the hypothesis and the reliability of the three value measures used in the analysis.

The results of Table 4 also suggest that expertise is not necessarily a value that serves as a base of authority. In five of the eight chambers, the differences in expertise attributions between leaders and members are either negative or very low, and in the two chambers where the difference is relatively large (the Ohio and Tennessee Houses), it is mainly due to the very low attributions given to the members. In the case of Tennessee, there is another simple institutional explanation. Tennessee legislative leaders, unlike those in the other states, are directly involved not only in the procedural but also in the substantive aspects of legislation. The floor leaders continually intervene in debates, either for or against bills, and they must have more than casual acquaintance with the content of legislation. The finding that they are named experts more than leaders in most of the other chambers seems to reflect this institutional procedure.

It is important to keep in mind that we are dealing here with aggregates of leaders rather than with individuals. In reality, there exist, of course, differences in the value attributions given to individual leaders as well. Some were nominated much more frequently than others with regard to any one of the values, but, in general, it seems that formal leaders in legislative bodies are attributed respect and affection more frequently than the rank and file. In attributions of expertise, the leaders differ much less from the membership. In fact, they do not seem to be expected to excel in a particular specialty. Moreover, as we shall see in the next section, there are among the rank and file a number of members who compare favorably with the leadership in regard to the number of nominations they receive for respect and affection.

Comparison of Leaders and Challengers

By using the hypothetical frequency standard for respect and affection, it is possible to identify those members among the rank and file who seem to "challenge" the formal leaders. These challengers may either constitute a reserve from which future leaders will be recruited by co-optation into the incumbent leadership, or they may constitute a counterelite that threatens the present leadership. Whatever the case may be, the challengers seem to be important "informal leaders" at the immediate periphery of the formal authority nucleus. They are operationally defined as those members whose nominations with regard both to respect and affection are above the hypothetical frequency standard. Their proportions in the eight chambers are shown below.

State and chamber	% challengers
Ohio Senate	9
California Senate	10
Ohio House	11
Tennessee Senate	14
Tennessee House	17
New Jersey House	17
California House	19
New Jersey Senate	22

These distributions partly confirm what is already known about the various chambers. Why the two New Jersey chambers should produce relatively large numbers of challengers has already been suggested. The relatively high proportion of challengers in the California House becomes plausible if it is recalled that, at least as late as 1957, when the study was made, party discipline was lax in the California House, where both parties consisted of fluid factions and where the speaker attained office by mobilizing a bi-partisan coalition in his support. Factionalism, too, is likely to account for the relatively high proportion of challengers in the Tennessee chambers.

In order to be able to make a meaningful comparison, the indexes of leaders and challengers were scored by the procedure described earlier, with the difference that the hypothetical frequency standard was recomputed for the leaders and challengers alone. (That is, leaders' and challengers' nominations were divided by their total number, now excluding all others.) Table 5 presents the results.

In general, comparison of the differences between the two groups shows that the formal leaders maintain their advantage over the challengers. However, in most of the positive advantages the margin is narrow. In regard to respect attributions, the New Jersey leaders in both chambers, now, not unexpectedly, come out second best; but California House leaders, too, do not have a large advantage over their challengers. In regard to affection nominations, the differences are even smaller—the largest difference being 1.25 in the Tennessee House.

Table 5—Comparison of Leaders and Challengers

	House				Senate			
	CALIF.	N.J.	OHIO	TENN.	CALIF.	N.J.	OHIO	TENN.
Respect								
Leaders	2.17	1.67	2.33	2.33	3.00	1.00	3.00	1.75
Challengers	1.71	2.10	1.53	1.19	1.75	2.76	1.33	1 00
Difference	.46	−.43	.80	1.14	1.25	−1.76	1.67	.75
Affection								
Leaders	2.00	1.33	2.33	3.00	1.00	1.00	2.00	2.00
Challengers	1.64	2.10	1.93	1.75	2.00	2.76	1.00	1.75
Difference	−.36	−.77	.40	1.25	−1.00	−1.76	1.00	.25

It would seem, then, that what facilitates occupancy of formal leadership positions in legislative bodies and gives support to the exercise of authority, more than anything else, is the respect given the incumbents of high offices by their fellow legislators. This is plausible: leaders, more than other members of a legislature, are expected to play by the rules of the game, and they are rewarded for doing so by being given respect by more of the other members than the rank and file or the group identified as challengers. Respect is probably the most distinguishing value at the base of authority in legislative bodies. Without it, authority is likely to be weak and impotent.

Conclusion

Incumbents of high formal positions in legislative bodies are attributed certain values like respect or affection more frequently than the rank and file or those members who vie with them for these values—the challengers. The data presented in the analysis cannot tell us whether high position in the legislature's informal authority structure is cause or consequence of occupancy of high formal office. They do suggest, however, that their being attributed certain values more frequently than other members is perhaps a necessary, though not a sufficient, condition for the effective exercise of leaders' authority. We may infer that as long as formal leaders are able to stay ahead of the rank-and-file members as well as of the challengers in respect attributions, they are likely to maintain their position in the structure of authority. It would seem that the attribution of values is in part facilitated by the institutional arrangements of a legislative body, but neither this alone nor formal office alone seem sufficient for effective legislative authority. Both seem to be required to generate the degree of authority without which human organizations—even such relatively democratic and egalitarian groups as legislative bodies—cannot effectively function as decision-making agencies.

Party Leadership Conferences: A Study in Swedish Parliamentary Practice

by INGVAR AMILON

The following analysis is intended primarily to provide an overview of the various forms of party leadership conferences utilized in contemporary Swedish parliamentary practices and to appraise certain tendencies in their development. . . .

Various factors have hampered attempts to probe beneath the surface of leadership conferences in Sweden. One is that such conferences are a relatively recent phenomenon. As a result they have been accorded only sporadic treatment in the scientific literature. Moreover, no basis exists in either statutory law or the constitution for convening the conferences. Instead, their forms of activity and their field of competence are regulated solely by practice. . . .

Given these circumstances, I have relied for most of my material on interviews and conversations. These included sessions with leaders of the four major parties. For their extensive cooperation I wish to thank in particular Prime Minister Tage Erlander, Professor Gunner Heckscher, Dr. Gunner Hedlund, and Professor Bertil Ohlin. I am also indebted to Jarl Hjalmarson, who consented to a written interview, and former Finance Minister Ernst Wigforss, who supplied information on leadership conferences during the 1940s.[1] . . .

---

[1] Tage Erlander served as Swedish Prime Minister from 1946 to 1969, Gunnar Heckscher was chairman of the Conservative Party from 1961 to 1965, Gunnar Hedlund became chairman of the Center (Agrarian) Party in 1949, and Bertil Ohlin was the Liberal Party leader from 1944 to 1966. Presently a provincial governor, Hjalmarson was Conservative chairman from 1950 to 1961. Ernst Wigforss served 18 years as Finance Minister (1925–1926, 1932–1949). Translator's note.

Translated from the Swedish by M. Donald Hancock. This article originally appeared as "Partiledarkonferenserna—en studie i parlamentarisk praxis," in *Statsvetenskaplig tidskrift* 66, no. 2–3 (1963): 278–86. Used by permission.

I

In Swedish parliamentary tradition informal contacts among party leaders have never been unusual. . . . On the contrary, a lively exchange of opinion among party leaders is a common sight in parliament. In the following discussion, however, such ad hoc encounters will not be considered. These "corridor conferences"—which occur when two or more party chairmen confer on more or less important matters in parliamentary stairways or corridors—do not constitute what in common parlance are called party leadership conferences. The latter encompass meetings among party leaders that occur on some kind of regular basis.

In my analysis I shall restrict myself to three principal types of leadership conferences. The first of these are the *regular leadership conferences.* A second type are *special conferences* that are convened on special notice. Finally, the most extensively discussed conferences are those held only several times each decade in which party leaders express their views or, on occasion, even reach a decision on questions that directly affect a majority of citizens. The latter type conference can be designated *major conferences.* These refer to meetings among leaders of the parties represented in the Riksdag that are intended to produce a general agreement on a certain question (or questions) and in this way to remove the issue (or issues) from partisan conflict.

The oldest of these three types of conferences are the regular leadership conferences.

II

A contributing factor, perhaps the most important, to the institution of regular conferences after the dissolution of the national four-party ministry in 1945 was that a number of problems remained in dismantling the wartime coalition. Moreover, it was not psychologically possible to disrupt abruptly the intimate contacts among party leaders that had been established during the war years.[2] The conferences provided, in short, the means to maintain contacts on an informal level. It is precisely this need for contact that is cited by contemporary party leaders as an important reason why we have leadership conferences today.

Regular conferences continued even after Erlander succeeded Per Albin Hansson as Prime Minister in 1946. That they were not considered self-evident, however, was proved when the conferences were abandoned from May to November, 1947. This disruption was likely due to the sharpened conflict among the parties that year. Since then the existence of the regular conferences has never been called into question. A change in their composition occurred

[2] In response to the outbreak of World War II, leaders of the four major parties—the Social Democrats, Center, Liberals, and Conservatives—formed a national coalition cabinet in December 1939. The coalition was dissolved in July 1945, and the Social Democrats assumed sole executive responsibility. Either alone or in coalition with the Center Party (1951–1957) they have dominated cabinet office since that time. Translator's note.

after the 1948 election when the Communists were no longer invited to attend. The reason for this step was that the Communist representation in the Riksdag was so drastically reduced that the Communists were no longer serious contenders for elections to the various parliamentary committees—a question that is included, now as then, on the agenda of the regular leadership conferences. Moreover, the political climate became more hostile for the Communists following the Prague coup earlier that year, thereby contributing to their parliamentary isolation.

During parliamentary sessions the regular leadership conferences are held every Wednesday morning at 9:30 before the full plenary body convenes at 10:00. Party leaders meet in the Prime Minister's office in the Riksdag building. Exceptions include the Wednesdays when major debates are scheduled and Wednesdays when the plenary session does not begin until 11:00. In general, the conferences do not last longer than ten to fifteen minutes, but occasionally they will continue past 10:00 and even until 11:00. If the full agenda has not been covered by then, a new meeting time will be designated.

A rigid order of business is not followed at such meetings. In practice all kinds of questions can arise, ranging from membership in the European Economic Community . . . to how expenses for a deputy's honeymoon should be tabulated. Another example was the extent to which legislation concerning the consolidation of local communes should lead to elections in the new large communes in 1963. Party leaders resolved jointly that elections should not be held in off-election years. . . .

Foreign policy issues clearly dominate discussions at the regular leadership conferences. The next most important agenda items include technical issues— for example, questions concerning parliamentary procedure—and domestic topics of varying importance.

It is of interest to note that no records are kept at such conferences or, for that matter, at any of the party leadership conferences. Thus secretaries are never present among the ten participants who usually attend each of the meetings. Only leaders of the four major parties or occasionally a substitute whom a chairman appoints in his place take part in the discussions.

Each of the three non-socialist parties is usually represented by two persons: the chairman—who is simultaneously leader of his parliamentary faction in the lower house—and the party's leader in the upper chamber. Social Democratic participants include the Prime Minister and party leaders in both houses of the Riksdag. In addition, the Foreign Minister is also a frequent participant. . . . At times other members of the cabinet such as the Foreign Minister, the Minister of Trade, and the Minister of the Interior may attend as well.

The regular leadership conferences often display purely an informative nature. They provide an opportunity for leaders to consider questions that do not require any immediate policy commitment. The conferences also provide a forum to debate issues informally that will later be decided in parliament. Although discussions are candid, they usually follow party lines. The party chairmen usually take the lead in exchanging views, with the parliamentary party leaders filling in details. . . .

III

While fairly elaborate practices have evolved regulating the regular conferences, the same cannot be said for the special leadership conferences. This term has been applied to conferences of the most divergent kinds. All that such meetings have in common is that they have been convened on special notice.

Special leadership conferences are almost always called under urgent circumstances. The impetus can be something that occurs during a plenary session of parliament. In such cases the Prime Minister can easily reach at least the Liberal and Conservative chairmen, who represent Stockholm constituencies, and usually the Center chairman as well. Should all of the party leaders not be available for a special conference, the meeting occurs among those who are present.

Opposition leaders can, of course, also clarify issues quickly by contacting the Prime Minister informally at his office or elsewhere. Special conferences of this sort are not uncommon. Informal conferences also occur frequently by telephone. . . .

Pressing matters, particularly of a foreign policy nature, have occasionally led to emergency sessions of special leadership conferences to which only the party chairmen are invited. Examples of issues that have prompted such conferences include the strengthening of air reserves in the Congo after Hammarskjold's plane was shot down and the Finland question in connection with the Soviet note of 1961.

Special leadership conferences occur in the Prime Minister's office in the Riksdag building or, if the conference is held between parliamentary sessions, in the cabinet chambers. When invitations are issued for such meetings, the Prime Minister may or may not inform the party chairmen what is on the agenda. . . .

IV

In contrast to the relatively "quiet" nature of special leadership conferences, the third type of leadership forum—the major conferences—is widely publicized. These are the sessions that have made the leadership conferences known in broader circles. They are held at the highest niveau and have taken place only a few times during the past fifteen years. The reason that such conferences are accorded such widespread attention is that they affect most Swedish citizens. Because this is the case, party leaders have convened the major conferences in an attempt to reach the broadest possible consensus on the issues involved.

Illustrations of major leadership conferences are meetings that have been held to consider the economic crisis of 1947; negotiations on the proposed Scandinavian defense community in 1948–1949; defense appropriations in the

1950s. . . ; the supplementary pension issue in 1957–1958; and the budget in the spring and fall of 1959. Most of these conferences have failed to yield any positive results, which perhaps explains why they occur so sporadically. Party leaders apparently do not wish to raise expectations that they might not be able to satisfy. Moreover, there is only a limited number of questions of sufficient magnitude to justify major conferences.

Procedures for convening major conferences do not differ significantly from those already discussed above. Party leaders confer informally to explore the extent of interest in holding a conference on a particular issue. After these preliminary feelers, the Prime Minister will take the final initiative. This practice makes it difficult to determine who was originally responsible for initiating a given conference. As far as it is possible to reconstruct past events, Prime Minister Erlander appears to have suggested the meetings in the 1940s and in 1958, while the opposition was responsible for the 1959 conference on the budget. . . .

Invitations to a major conference are issued to the party chairmen personally. Each chairman then decides whom he wishes to join him at the meeting. Usually delegations consisting of three to four persons represent each of the parties. Participants usually include the parliamentary group leaders. On occasion internal party consultations have been held on the composition of the party delegation. The number of participants has varied over the years. At the major conference on defense in 1948, only the following delegates were present: the Prime Minister, the Finance Minister, the Defense Minister, and the chairmen of each of the non-socialist parties. In contrast, thirteen persons took part in the first major conference in 1947 as well as the abortive budgetary consultations in the spring of 1959.

As in the other types of leadership meetings, debate at the major leadership conference is free. One difference is that participants in the major conferences restrict themselves largely to the principal subject of discussion. It is more the exception than the rule that additional topics are brought up for debate. . . .

Although participating ministers can be considered party delegates as well as experts, outside experts from the finance or defense departments are sometimes asked to attend major leadership conferences. Delegates will pose questions to them, and after they have provided the necessary information they leave the session. In case data provided by such experts differ from those supplied by the ministers, dramatic exchanges may occur during such presentations by outside officials. In general, however, the major conferences are conducted without major dramatics, even though greater freedom exists for a free give and take than in the parliamentary chambers where television cameras and journalists closely observe every action. . . .

All agreements reached by the party leaders are only preliminary and do not formally bind parliament in any way. Emphasizing this is the fact that the chairmen do not sign any agreement; at most a common decision constitutes a gentleman's agreement. The only exception to date was the defense agreement in 1958 which the chairmen did jointly sign. In practice no binding decisions can be reached unless the parliamentary parties are consulted.

V

Although conference delegates comprise a small exclusive circle, one should not conclude that they decide questions that they wish to keep secret from the Riksdag. It is not true—as the Communists have sometimes insinuated—that conference participants make up a clique of conspirators who are intent on devising plans behind the back of parliament about how best to reduce the latter's influence. On the contrary, one of the requisites for achieving positive results from the leadership conferences is that the parliamentary factions are kept sufficiently informed so that their members do not feel that they have been presented with a fait accompli. The question remains how this is accomplished.

In that the regular leadership conferences usually serve only informative purposes, prior meetings of the parliamentary factions are not called . . . unless the issue at stake is of major importance or time permits early discussion. Instead, party chairmen rely on preliminary contacts with those persons within their parliamentary parties who possess special competence or influence in particular questions. . . . Similarly, members of the government are informed of issues that are to be considered at the leadership conferences. The results of conferences are transmitted to both the government and members of the parliamentary parties. In important questions party leaders . . . usually report directly to those who have a special interest in what has been discussed.

Issues of particular significance—for example, those that will be considered at a major leadership conference—are debated in advance within the parliamentary party and its leadership council. . . . Conference delegates are not armed with formal instructions, but the various points of view that are expressed at such preliminary meetings are accorded appropriate weight. Liberals emphasize in particular that even minority opinions are taken into consideration. Because a major question is on the agenda, individual members of parliament are often actively involved in preparing material for the conference. This occurs when the secretary of the parliamentary party, who is responsible for compiling relevant data for the conference participants, turns to individual deputies for information. . . .

VI

After beginning as an instrument for dismantling the wartime coalition, party leadership conferences have come to fill an important need for contact and information among party chairmen. During the 1940s the regular conferences had no more practical importance than that. In general only the party chairmen and the Prime Minister participated in the regular conferences. When the conferences were expanded to include faction leaders in parliament is not known.

The growing significance of party leadership conferences was related in part to international development. Defense and foreign policy did not prove as important in the initial post-war years as they did during the 1950s. For decades Swedish political leaders have sought to elevate both issue areas above partisan controversy. Leadership conferences provided an opportunity to achieve that goal, and the opportunity was utilized accordingly.

The importance of leadership conferences also proved a function of Sweden's parliamentary situation. A review of the course of major conferences over the years reveals that they have taken place more often in periods when the opposition was strong or growing in strength and that they have occurred less frequently when the Social Democrats have dominated the Riksdag either alone or in coalition. . . .

Differing assessments among party leaders of leadership conferences as a political resource reveal the degree of importance the various chairmen accord them. All party chairmen consider them essential and emphasize that they meet a legitimate demand for information and contact. The Prime Minister maintains that they constitute a suitable channel of communication with members of parliament, . . . and stresses the role they play in facilitating parliamentary procedure. Although the chairman of the Center Party views the leadership conferences as somewhat exaggerated in importance, he accepts them as a substitute in urgent cases for the [parliamentary] foreign policy council. The leader of the Liberal Party asserts that the conferences help prevent the opposition from being by-passed in major decisions, while the Conservative chairman goes a step further and sees them as a means for the opposition to influence directly government policy. . . .

It is apparent that the party leadership conferences of the informal sort that have evolved in Swedish parliamentary practice are of considerable practical importance. They enable the parliamentary apparatus to function with greater flexibility and contribute to the smoother operation of political life.

EXECUTIVE-LEGISLATIVE RELATIONS

Presidential Leadership and Party Success

by JOSEPH COOPER and GARY BOMBARDIER

The legislative accomplishments of the Democratic Party in the 89th Congress (1965–1967) resulted in widespread acclaim for President Johnson's skill as a legislative leader and in numerous comparisons with President Kennedy that were highly unflattering to the latter. Yet the basis and significance of Democratic party success in the 89th Congress remain far from clear, especially since in the 90th Congress (1967–1969) President Johnson encountered difficulties that are reminiscent of the Kennedy years. The object of this paper is to analyze and evaluate Democratic party success in the 89th Congress. In so doing we shall focus on the House of Representatives and use the 87th Congress (1961–1963), Kennedy's only complete Congress, as a point of comparison. Thus, this paper will be centered around three basic questions.

1. Was there a significant difference between the degree of legislative success enjoyed by President Johnson in the 89th Congress and President Kennedy in the 87th?

2. If there was a significant difference, how should this difference be explained?

3. What broader significance do the elements of explanation have for understanding the present and future prospects of Democratic Party success in the House?

Kennedy and Johnson

In seeking to answer these questions we shall rely largely on an analysis of roll call votes in the 87th and 89th Congresses. However, for our purposes we

Reprinted from "Presidential Leadership and Party Success," *Journal of Politics* 30 (November 1968): 1012–27, by Joseph Cooper and Gary Bombardier. Reprinted by permission of the *Journal of Politics* and the authors.

need not consider all roll call votes, but only a selected sample that will furnish the evidence we require. Since the President as a partisan leader is the focus of our concern, we have restricted ourselves to roll call votes in which the President took a stand and a majority of one party opposed a majority of the other.[1] Of the 240 roll call votes in the 87th Congress 71 satisfy these conditions. Of the 394 roll call votes in the 89th Congress 118 satisfy them. Our sample thus is a large one. It includes approximately 30 percent of the total number of roll call votes in each Congress. In addition, both sessions of each Congress are well represented. Of the 71 roll call votes in our sample for the 87th Congress 36 occurred in the first session and 35 in the second. Of the 118 votes in our sample for the 89th Congress 63 occurred in the first session and 55 in the second.[2]

Table 1—Presidential Success

President	Victories	Defeats	% Victories	% Defeats
Kennedy	54	17	76%	24%
Johnson	107	11	91%	9%

With this preliminary discussion behind us, we are now in a position to answer our first question: who was more successful as a legislative leader in guiding his program through the House—Kennedy in the 87th Congress or Johnson in the 89th? Table 1 provides simple but convincing evidence that confirms the judgments of most Congressmen and journalists, judgments based largely on impressions of substantive or qualitative achievement such as Johnson's success in passing Medicare. Of the 71 roll call votes included in our sample for the 87th Congress Kennedy was successful in having his position endorsed on 54 votes or 76 percent and unsuccessful on 17 votes or 24 percent. In contrast, of the 118 roll call votes included in our sample for the 89th Congress Johnson was successful on 107 votes or 91 percent and unsuccessful on only 11 votes or 9 percent.

Given these findings, we can easily conclude that President Johnson did indeed enjoy a significantly higher level of legislative success in the 89th Congress than President Kennedy enjoyed in the 87th.

Party Unity and Party Success

If we turn now to our second question, two hypotheses may be offered to explain Johnson's higher degree of success.

One hypothesis would explain it as a function of a higher degree of partisan

---

[1] The authors have relied on the *Congressional Quarterly* for data on roll call votes and for identification of the cases in which the President took a stand.

[2] In the analysis which follows we have made no effort to weight votes. All roll call votes in our sample were considered to be mathematical equals both because current statistical methods for weighting votes are far from satisfactory and because the character of our objectives and findings did not make such treatment of our data essential. For the problems involved in weighting votes, see David R. Mayhew, *Party Loyalty Among Congressmen* (Cambridge, 1966), p. 7.

support for presidential programs among House Democrats. The assumption underlying this hypothesis is that due largely to Johnson's skills as a legislative leader Democratic party cohesion increased and reflected itself in a higher degree of support for presidential programs, that Johnson through shrewd use of his resources and a superb sense of strategy was able to unify his party behind him to a greater degree than Kennedy who was far less adept.

An alternative hypothesis would explain Johnson's higher degree of success as a function of the increased number of House Democrats in general and Northern Democrats in particular. We may note that the number of Democrats in the House totaled 294 in the 89th Congress and 263 in the 87th. The number of Northern Democrats totaled 194 in the 89th Congress and 152 in the 87th. The assumption underlying this hypothesis is that whatever skills Johnson displayed the critical element in his success was primarily a larger reservoir of sympathetic fellow partisans on which to draw.

Table 2—Party Cohesion and Presidential Support Mean Scores

Congress and Party	Party Cohesion	Presidential Support
Eighty-Seventh		
House Democrats	79.20%	78.03%
House Republicans	79.80%	21.38%
Eighty-Ninth		
House Democrats	79.36%	78.27%
House Republicans	81.27%	19.13%

The key to resolving this issue lies in ascertaining whether Johnson was able in fact to unite his party behind him to a greater degree than Kennedy. In order to answer this question Party Cohesion and Presidential Support Scores were calculated for our sample of roll call votes.[3] Our findings are presented in Table 2.

We can see clearly from Table 2 that the degree of party cohesion among House Democrats on issues on which the President took a stand did not increase significantly from the 87th to the 89th Congress. Nor, as we might expect, did the degree of presidential support. We may therefore conclude that increased

[3] Our Cohesion Score measures the average percentage of group agreement on roll call votes in our sample, i.e., roll call votes in which a majority of one party opposed a majority of the other and the President took a stand. It has been derived by taking the number of the group voting aye and nay on each issue, calculating the percentage in the majority, and averaging the percentages. Thus, for example, a score of 80% for Democratic members means that on the average 80% of the Democrats voting on an issue agreed or voted on the same side of the issue. Our Support Score measures the average percentage of group support for presidential positions on roll call votes in our sample. It has been derived by taking the number of the group voting for and against the President on each issue, calculating the percentage voting in support of the President, and averaging the percentages. Thus, for example, a score of 20% for Republicans means that on the average 20% of the Republicans voting on an issue supported presidential positions. It should be noted that our method of measuring cohesion differs from the method provided by the Rice Index of Cohesion. The authors, however, have preferred a measure that indicates the raw or absolute dimensions of majorities. Still, our results can easily be converted into Rice scores. See Julius Turner, *Party and Constituency: Pressures on Congress* (Baltimore, 1951), p. 26.

partisan support is not the critical variable for explaining the higher degree of success that Johnson enjoyed. Rather, the stability of the Party Cohesion and Presidential Support Scores for House Democrats plus the increase in the degree of cohesion and presidential opposition among House Republicans strongly suggest that the critical variable in Johnson's success was the increase in the number of Democrats in general and Northern Democrats in particular. In short, Johnson by maintaining the same level of support as Kennedy could win victories denied to Kennedy because he was drawing on a larger population of fellow partisans, a population in which the Northern Democrats alone could come very close to furnishing all the votes needed for a majority.

However, if our data supports choice of the second hypothesis rather than the first to explain Johnson's higher degree of legislative success, several anomalies remain to be resolved before we can be satisfied with this choice.

One anomaly concerns the increase in the proportion of Northern to Southern Democrats. We have noted previously that Northern Democrats were more numerous in the 89th Congress than the 87th. What also should be noted is that the number of Southern Democrats declined.[4] In the 89th Congress of a total of 294 Democratic members 194 were Northern Democrats and 100 Southern Democrats; in the 87th Congress of a total of 263 Democratic members 152 were Northern Democrats and 111 Southern Democrats. Thus, in the 89th Congress Northern Democrats made up 66 percent of the Democratic membership and Southern Democrats 34 percent. In contrast, in the 87th Congress Northern Democrats made up only 58 percent of the Democratic membership and Southern Democrats 42 percent. Why then did this change not result in a tangible increase in the degree of partisan support for presidential programs among House Democrats?[5] Presumably, the average Northern Democrat is more loyal or regular than the average Southern Democrat.

A second anomaly concerns the increase in the proportion of freshman Democrats.[6] In the 87th Congress 18 or 7 percent of the 263 Democratic members were freshmen. In the 89th Congress 69 or 23 percent of the 294 Democratic members were freshmen. Why then did this change not result in a tangible increase in the degree of partisan support for presidential programs among House Democrats? Presumably, freshmen are more loyal or regular than other members both because their lack of visibility and entrenchment in their constituencies tie them more closely to their party's record and because their low position in the House makes them more dependent on the favor and assistance of the party leadership.[7]

Let us deal first with the anomaly posed by the increase in the proportion of

---

[4] The authors have adopted the *Congressional Quarterly's* definition of Southern members: members from the 11 states of the Confederacy plus Kentucky and Oklahoma.

[5] The belief that Democratic party cohesion would increase as the proportion of Southern Democrats declined has heretofore found substantial support in the literature. See Raymond Wolfinger and Joan Heifetz, "Safe Seats, Seniority, and Power in Congress," 59 *American Political Science Review* 337 (June, 1965).

[6] Problems exist with regard to the definition of the freshman members in a particular Congress. The authors have defined them as members whose term of consecutive service commenced at the beginning of that Congress.

[7] See for example, David Truman, *The Congressional Party* (New York, 1959), pp. 211–17.

Northern Democrats. This anomaly suggests that some other factor must have been at work to offset the effects of the increase. The factor that immediately comes to mind is increased alienation of the Southern wing. For if the level of Northern support remained roughly the same, a material decrease in the level of Southern support could well offset the increase in the proportion of Northern Democrats.

In order to test this hypothesis we have calculated Presidential Support Scores for Northern and Southern Democrats in the 87th and 89th Congresses. In addition, we have used the Index of Likeness to calculate Likeness Scores for Northern and Southern Democrats in the 87th and 89th Congresses.[8] In both cases we have relied on the sample of roll call votes used throughout this paper. If our hypothesis of increased Southern alienation is correct, our Likeness Scores should show increased dissimilarity in voting patterns between Northern and Southern Democratic House members. Our Presidential Support Scores should both reflect the effects of increased dissimilarity and indicate that it is unidirectional. That is to say, they should indicate increased alienation of the Southern wing by showing a material decrease in the level of Southern support and little or no change in the level of Northern support.

Our findings confirm our hypothesis. The Index of Likeness provides scores of 67.11 for Northern and Southern Democrats in the 87th Congress and 61.85 for Northern and Southern Democrats in the 89th Congress, a decline in likeness of 5.26 points. As for presidential support, the scores for Northern Democrats were 90.56 percent in the 87th Congress and 90.76 percent in the 89th Congress. In contrast, the scores for Southern Democrats were 60.75 percent in the 87th Congress and 54.03 percent in the 89th Congress.

If our hypothesis of increased Southern alienation accounts for the fact that the increase in the proportion of Northern Democrats had little effect on the level of Democratic support for presidential programs, it does not account for the lack of effect of the increase in the proportion of freshmen Democrats. Moreover, in seeking to resolve this anomaly we shall also shed additional light on the first anomaly. We may remember that Southern alienation was able to offset the effect of the increase in the proportion of Northern Democrats because the level of support among Northern Democrats did not increase. Now, as Table 3 indicates, Northern freshmen accounted for all of the increase in the number of Northern Democrats as well as most of the increase in the number of Democratic freshmen. Thus, the problem of why the level of Northern Democratic support for presidential programs did not rise as the proportion of Northern Democrats increased is to a large extent simply an element of the more general problem of why the level of Democratic support for presidential programs did not rise as the proportion of Democratic freshmen increased. In both cases the logic of expecting an increase rests in large part on the presump-

[8] The Index of Likeness measures the degree of similarity in voting behavior between two groups. It is derived by calculating the percentage of each group on one side of an issue and subtracting the difference from 100. The higher the score the greater the similarity or likeness. Thus, our Likeness Scores have been derived by subtracting the difference between the percentage of Northern and Southern Democratic aye votes on roll call votes in our sample from 100 and averaging the results. See Turner, *op. cit.*, p. 36.

tion that freshmen Democrats would give the President and party leadership a higher degree of support than more senior Democrats.

Here as elsewhere we can resolve the issue we have posed by using our sample of roll call votes to calculate Presidential Support Scores. Table 4 presents such scores for freshman and non-freshmen Northern and Southern Democrats in the 89th Congress.[9]

Table 3—Freshmen as Percentage of Northern and Southern Democrats

	Total	Freshmen	% of Freshmen
Eighty-Seventh Congress			
Northern Democrats	152	12	7.89%
Southern Democrats	111	6	5.40%
Eighty-Ninth Congress			
Northern Democrats	194	58	29.89%
Southern Democrats	100	11	11.00%

Table 4—House Democrats—Eighty-Ninth Congress Mean Presidential Support

Blocs by Region and Status	Support Score
All Northern Democrats	90.76%
All Southern Democrats	54.03%
Non-freshman Northern Democrats	90.64%
Non-freshman Southern Democrats	52.79%
Freshman Northern Democrats	91.03%
Freshman Southern Democrats	64.06%

Given our findings in Table 4, we can easily understand why the increase in the proportion of Democratic freshmen did not raise Democratic support for presidential programs in the 89th Congress to a significantly higher level than that attained in the 87th Congress.

As far as Northern Democratic freshmen are concerned, the group that represents the bulk of the increase in freshman Democrats, their support for presidential programs was simply not so much higher than the support provided by more senior Northern Democrats that it could materially affect the level of

---

[9] In calculating Support Scores for Northern and Southern Democratic freshmen, the authors have used a different method of calculation than the one employed heretofore. See *supra*, note 3. Instead of calculating support percentages for individual issues and averaging the results, we have calculated support percentages for individual members and averaged the results. Since we have restricted ourselves to votes actually cast by members in calculating their support percentages the scores obtained by this method are equivalent to the scores that would be obtained by our former method. And in the case of freshmen it provides a more convenient method for handling the data presented in the *Congressional Quarterly*. One more point should be noted. The scores for non-freshmen Northern and Southern Democrats have been derived arithmetically on the basis of the scores of all Northern and Southern Democrats, the scores of Northern and Southern freshmen Democrats, the percentage of Northern and Southern freshmen Democrats, and the percentages of non-freshmen Northern and Southern Democrats.

Northern Democratic support. Nor is this surprising. On the one hand, non-freshman Northern support was itself extremely high and difficult to exceed to any substantial degree without approaching complete or total obedience to presidential wishes. On the other hand, freshman Northern Democrats despite their increase in number still represented only about 30 percent of the total number of Northern Democrats which diluted the effect of any increment in support they provided. As far as Southern Democratic freshmen are concerned, they did provide a significantly higher level of support than more senior Southern Democrats. Still, their level of support was not high enough to offset the diluting effect of their small number. Indeed, it lagged far behind the level of support provided by freshman or non-freshman Northern Democrats. Thus, their higher level of support had no great effect on the level of Southern support.

As a result, the influx of Northern and Southern Freshman Democrats in the 89th Congress neither increased the level of presidential support within these blocs nor the overall level of presidential support among House Democrats to any significant extent over the levels attained in the 87th Congress. Indeed, in the case of the Southern wing the level of presidential support declined significantly. And this fact indicates the true importance of the increase in the number and proportion of freshman Democrats. Since the overwhelming majority of these freshmen were Northerners, the primary effect was to increase the proportion of Northern Democrats which in turn served to stabilize the overall level of presidential support among House Democrats despite the decline in Southern support.

Trends and Prospects

Thus far we have dealt with two of the three questions we posed at the beginning of this article. Let us conclude by turning our attention to the third and last: what broader significance do our findings have for the future prospects of Democratic party success in the House?

Several of our findings are very suggestive: the fact that the level of Northern Democratic support for presidential programs did not increase despite the increase in the number of Northern Democrats; the fact that the level of Southern Democratic support declined; and the fact that the number of Southern Democrats declined.

Now it seems likely from our analysis that the level of Northern Democratic support for presidential programs is not amenable to being influenced materially by increases in the number of Northern Democrats. However, our study does not reveal whether the decline in the level of Southern Democratic support and the number of Southern Democrats is a persistent feature of recent Congresses or merely an idiosyncratic feature of the 87th and 89th Congresses.

To settle this issue we have assembled data bearing on these points in Tables 5 and 6. Table 5 indicates that the decline in the number of Southern

Democrats has been a persistent feature of recent Congresses. Although no steady or prolonged material decline in the number of Southern Democrats occurred in the first four decades of this century, from 1945–1966 the number has declined from 117 to 100 or about 15 percent.[10] Moreover, the 90th Congress (1967–1969) witnessed a further substantial decline. Of the 248 Democrats in the 90th Congress 157 were Northern Democrats and only 91 were Southern Democrats. We may conclude that over the past two decades there has been a steady trend toward reduction in the number of Southern Democrats, that by the mid-1960's the cumulative effect has been substantial, and that this trend shows no sign of abating.[11]

Table 5—Decline in Number of Southern Democrats Seventy-ninth Through Eighty-ninth Congresses

Congress	Total No. of Democrats	No. of Northern Democrats	No. of Southern Democrats	No. of Southern Republicans
79 (1945–47)	243	126	117	5
80 (1947–49)	188 [a]	73	115	7
81 (1949–51)	263	145	118	4
82 (1951–53)	234	118	116	6
83 (1953–55)	213 [a]	102	111	9
84 (1955–57)	232	122	110	10
85 (1957–59)	234	124	110	10
86 (1959–61)	283	172	111	9
87 (1961–63)	263	152	111	9
88 (1963–65)	259	154	105	14
89 (1965–67)	294	194	100	19

[a] Democrats in Minority.

As far as Southern Democratic support for presidential programs is concerned, we are handicapped both by the lack of cumulative data and by the fact that the Democrats did not control the Presidency from 1953 to 1961. However, what we are essentially interested in is change in the degree of party loyalty among Southern Democrats when a Democratic President serves as the party chief, as the definer of party programs. Thus, if we can establish that the degree of partisan support among Southern Democrats has declined in recent Congresses, we can also infer that Southern support for the programs offered by Democratic Presidents has also declined.

In this regard we may turn to the *Congressional Quarterly*. The *Quarterly* has calculated Party Unity Scores on a consistent basis for House members since 1955. Such scores for Southern Democratic members for the years from 1955 through 1966 are presented in Table 6. It should be noted that these scores differ from the Cohesion Scores we have heretofore presented in this article since they measure the average percentage of group agreement simply on issues in

[10] At ten-year intervals from 1900 to 1940 the number of Southern Democrats totaled 90, 102, 112, 104, and 117.

[11] It should also be noted that the decline in Southern Democrats has been due primarily to replacement by Republicans, not loss of seats through reapportionment. See Table 5. In the 90th Congress the number of Southern Republicans rose to 28.

which a majority of one party opposed a majority of the other. In contrast, our Cohesion Scores are confined to issues on which the President took a stand as well. Nonetheless, though the *Quarterly's* scores provide a less intense measure of party loyalty and can be expected to be somewhat lower than our scores, they provide a readily accessible set of scores that can be relied upon to indicate both the general level of partisan support and trends in partisan support.[12]

Table 6—Southern Democratic Party Unity Mean Scores, 1955–1966

Year	Party Unity
1955	63%
1956	66%
1957	65%
1958	58%
1959	71%
1960	52%
1961	58%
1962	57%
1963	61%
1964	55%
1965	48%
1966	42%
Average 1955–59	64.6%
Average 1960–64	56.6%

Table 6 indicates that Southern support for Democratic party programs has declined steadily and substantially over the past decade. Moreover, evidence exists that strongly suggests that, as in the case of the decline in number, the decline in support is part of a trend that began before 1955. Julius Turner has pointed out that in the 1920's and early 1930's the Southern Democrats were the most loyal element in the party. He notes, however, that in the late 1930's a split of significant proportions developed between the Northern and Southern wings of the party which greatly affected the level of Southern support. Thus, Party Unity Scores calculated by Turner indicate that the score for Southern Democrats dropped from 92.9 percent in 1930–31 to 79.3 percent in 1937 and 70.5

---

[12] There are two reasons why the *Quarterly's* Party Unity Scores can be expected to be lower than our Cohesion Scores, though both are measures of the average percentage of group agreement. First, cohesion or unity is normally higher on issues in which the President takes a stand. These are usually the more important partisan issues and presidential involvement contributes to pressure for regularity. Second, the *Quarterly's* Party Unity Scores are computed by calculating the percentage of the time each individual member votes with a majority of his fellow partisans on issues in which a majority of one party opposes a majority of the other and averaging the results, rather than by calculating the percentage of the group in the majority on each issue and averaging the results. This in itself is not important since if all factors are equal both methods would produce the same result. However, in calculating percentages for individual members the *Quarterly* does not base its percentages on votes actually cast, but on the number of possible votes; whereas our Cohesion Scores are based on votes actually cast. Thus, the *Quarterly's* scores can be expected to be lower since they penalize failure to vote. In addition, it should be noted that these same factors have a similar effect on the relation between the *Quarterly's* Party Unity Scores and our Presidential Support Scores. Here too the former can be expected to be lower than the latter. See notes 3 and 9 *supra*.

percent in 1944.[13] We may conclude, then, that the decline in the number of Southern Democrats over the past several decades has been accompanied by a decline in the degree of Southern party loyalty.

Given all this, three points of broad significance become clear. First, though Democratic Presidents and the House Democratic party leadership have had considerable difficulty enacting party programs over the past several decades, they are likely to have even more difficulty in the immediate future unless they can consistently maintain the number of Northern Democrats at a level that significantly exceeds the average level of the past. To illustrate the point let us establish an average Democratic controlled Congress for the period from 1945 through 1964. Such a Congress would have 139 Northern Democrats and 112 Southern Democrats. Let us also assume an average Southern Democratic Party Unity Score of 65 percent on the presumption that it would be at least this high since Turner's findings as well as our findings in Table 6 strongly suggest that Southern scores in the 1940's and early 1950's were significantly higher than in the early 1960's.

Now compare this Congress with the 89th Congress. In that Congress there were 100 Southern Democrats and their average Party Unity Score per session was 45 percent. Thus, whereas in our representative past Congress the leadership on the average could gather 73 Southern Democratic votes on party unity issues, in the 89th Congress it could gather only 45—or 28 less. If we assume that the Northern Democratic Party Unity Score in the 89th Congress (about 80 percent) is within 5 points plus or minus of the average score for Northern Democrats in the years from 1945–1964 and also assume that the Republican Party Unity Score in the 89th Congress is not materially lower than the average score for Republicans in the years from 1945–1964 (and both of these are fair assumptions given the evidence that does exist), this means that the House Democratic party leadership in the 89th Congress needed another 26–44 Northern Democratic members or a total of 165–183 Northern Democrats to be roughly in the same position as in our representative past Congress which contained only 139 Northern Democrats.[14] Moreover, it means that the leadership needed substantially more than 165–183 Northern Democrats to do substantially better than in our representative past Congress. For on the more controversial

---

[13] See Turner, *op. cit.*, pp. 78 and 128–43. Turner's definition of Southern members differs in one regard from the one we have employed. He does not include Kentucky as a Southern State. Still, this difference is too slight to have any substantial effect. For additional information on the split in the Democratic Party in the late 1930's see James T. Patterson, *Congressional Conservatism and the New Deal* (Lexington, 1967).

[14] The Republican Party Unity Score in the 89th Congress was 69%, whereas the average for Congresses in the period 1955–64 was 70.6% and the range from 66–73%. Unfortunately, no Northern Democratic Party Unity Scores are available in the *Congressional Quarterly* for any year up to 1965. Still, it is highly probable that the Northern Democratic Score in the 89th Congress is within 5 points plus or minus of their average score for Congresses over the past several decades. To be sure, there were far more Northern Democrats in this Congress than the average number in Congresses from 1945–1964. Nonetheless, a five point difference is a considerable one and our Cohesion and Support Scores in the 87th and 89th Congresses indicate that the degree of Northern Democratic party loyalty is relatively impervious to increases in number. We should also note that if the Northern Democrats' score in the 89th Congress was about the same as the average score for Congresses from 1945–1964, then the additional number of Northern Democrats required would be 35 or a total of 174.

issues support falls below average levels. Thus, we may note that even in the 89th Congress which contained 194 Northern Democrats some important Democratic party programs were won by margins of only 5–10 votes, e.g., rent supplements and minimum wage increases.

Second, assuming that the degree of Northern Democratic support for party programs does not materially increase and the degree of Republican opposition does not materially decrease, if Democratic Presidents and the House Democratic party leadership in the immediate future cannot consistently maintain the number of Northern Democrats at a level significantly higher than the average level of the past, we can expect Northern Democratic discontent with the leadership strategy followed by Democratic Speakers in the past several decades as well as their inclination to challenge continued reliance on this strategy to increase.

The characteristics or features of this strategy extend back into the 1920's and the 1930's, but they have been fully developed and employed only subsequent to the split in the Democratic Party that occurred in the late 1930's. Its chief architect was Speaker Sam Rayburn (D-Tex.), but the strategy has been continued with only slight modification by Speaker John W. McCormack (D-Mass.). The Rayburn strategy is essentially one designed to placate Southern Democrats and to avoid any aggravation of existing divisions in the party. Thus, it has three basic characteristics: avoidance of formal party decision making mechanisms such as caucuses, steering committees, policy committees, etc.; reliance on personal appeals, contacts, and influence; and within extremely broad limits tolerance of party irregularity.[15]

Northern Democratic discontent with this strategy has grown steadily over the last decade or so and is now quite strong. The most concrete manifestation has been the creation of the House Democratic Study Group in the late 1950's and its subsequent activities by way of mobilizing and deploying Northern Democratic forces in floor struggles over important bills, seeking changes in the rules and mechanisms of both the formal and party organizations, and opposing candidates for important committee vacancies who have low or only mediocre records of party loyalty.[16] The founders and leaders of the Study Group have felt that the party leadership's informal, personal, and permissive approach has impaired the prospects for party success by providing an inadequate organizational basis for mobilizing party strength and by failing to take sufficient care to insure that key vantage points in the formal structure will be responsive to a majority of the party. Nor is it surprising that Northern discontent has grown. The motivating cause has been increased dissatisfaction with the degree of Democratic party success in the House. But underlying this cause is the fact that the Rayburn strategy is one that has been increasingly less adapted to cope with the party situation in the House as the number and degree of support of Southern Democrats has declined.

---

[15] See Charles Clapp, *The Congressman: His Work as He Sees It* (Washington, 1963), pp. 285–320.
[16] See Clapp, *op. cit.*, pp. 323–28; Richard Bolling, *House Out of Order* (New York, 1965), pp. 54–58; and Kenneth Kofmehl, "House Democratic Study Group," 17 *Western Political Quarterly* 256 (June, 1964).

Thus, we can expect Northern Democratic discontent to grow even stronger in the immediate future if the Democrats fail to consistently maintain the number of Northern Democrats at a level sufficient to offset the decline in the number and degree of support of Southern Democrats. For the result of such a failure will be even less party success in the immediate future than in the past several decades which in turn will spur Northern Democratic discontent. On the one hand, given a decline in success from levels that were not satisfactory previously, the benefits of continuing to placate the Southern wing will appear even smaller to Northern Democrats. On the other hand, since a decline in the level of party success combined with a decline in Southern support will highlight the importance of the sheer number of Northern Democrats, Northern Democrats will be disposed to press even harder for changes in leadership strategy designed to increase the prospects for electoral success in the North, e.g. the projection of a more intense and consistent liberal image through creation and use of a policy committee, violation of the seniority rights of disloyal Southerners, etc. Indeed, if the frustrations Northern Democrats have experienced over the past several decades increase, even a determined effort by the Study Group to disrupt the established path of leadership succession and take over the Democratic Party in the House by electing one of its own cohorts to the Speakership would not be surprising when the need to replace McCormack arises.

Third, and last, if Democratic Presidents and the House Democratic party leadership do have greater difficulty enacting party programs in the immediate future than in the past several decades, the causes of increased obstruction should not be attributed to the venality of Congressmen or the incompetence of the party leadership.[17] If the Democratic party leadership has erred in continuing to apply old maxims to a situation in which they are increasingly inappropriate, no dramatic or quick improvement will result from adopting a new strategy. Similarly, if the House in the immediate future resists, delays, or waters down important Democratic programs to an even greater extent than in the late 1940's, 1950's, and early 1960's, this will not come about because Congressmen are intent on the frustration of majority will or the public interest. Indeed, it would

---

[17] The chances of a decline in Democratic party success in Democratic controlled Houses in the immediate future are good, even if we hold Democratic control of the Presidency constant. As our analysis in the text has indicated, by the mid-1960's the Democratic party leadership needed in excess of 165 Northern Democrats to be roughly in the same position as in our representative past Congress which contained only 139 Northern Democrats and it is likely that the problem will be aggravated by further declines in the number and degree of support of Southern Democrats. Yet the ability of the Democrats in upcoming Congresses to compensate for past and future declines in Southern support by consistently attaining levels of Northern Democratic membership in excess of 165 appears highly questionable. Excluding the 89th Congress as atypical, the average number of Northern Democrats in the House in the 87th, 88th, and 90th Congresses has been 154. This represents a substantial increase over the average number in Democratic controlled Congresses in the late 1940's and 1950's. Nonetheless, the possibilities of additional gains appear more limited. Excluding the 89th Congress, the average number of Republican marginal seats in the 1960's is smaller than in the Democratic controlled Congresses of the early 1950's. In addition, whereas the average number of Republican marginal seats in Democratic controlled Congresses in the early 1950's was substantially larger than the average number of Democratic marginal seats, the difference has withered. The average figures for the 1960's, again excluding the 89th Congress, are 41 marginal Republican seats and 37 marginal Democratic seats. Finally, a portion of the marginal Republican seats are in the South, e.g., about 15 percent in the 90th Congress, and if reclaimed will not add to the total of Northern Democrats.

be comforting if the causes of obstruction did lie in such simple matters as incompetence or malevolence. However, they do not. Rather, the problem lies in the fragility of the majorities that have controlled the House in the past and the present inability or unwillingness of the Nation to place in the House on any consistent basis a coherent and determined majority dedicated to the passage of new and advanced forms of social legislation.

Problems of Parliamentary Democracy in Europe

by KARL DIETRICH BRACHER

The Dilemma

The phrase "crisis of parliamentarism" is nearly as old as the phenomenon of modern parliamentary democracy. It is closely bound up with the deeply rooted social and intellectual transformations in which the process of emancipation—first with a liberal, then with a socialistic stamp—broke the framework of constitutional government based on privileged estates, and in which the principle of full representation and participation of all citizens in a parliament chosen in a general and equal election was carried out. This development reached its critical peak after World War I. For the concept of parliamentary democracy the moment of apparently complete victory over the autocracies of old Europe signified at the same time the beginning of a structural crisis which particularly affected the newly created parliamentary democracies of Europe and which aided the strongly antiparliamentary dictatorial movements toward a quick rise.

With the exception of Czechoslovakia and Finland this crisis quickly displaced and destroyed all new parliamentary democracies: in Russia and the Baltic states; in Poland, Hungary and the Balkan countries; in Italy, Germany and Austria; in Spain and Portugal. Everywhere in this area the parliamentary system seemed to prove itself unworkable; almost nowhere did it seem capable of absorbing the political and social tensions of the "age of the masses" in a democratic order that was both stable and flexible. The transition from the old liberal parliamentarianism of well-to-do individuals (*Honoratiorenstaat*) to egalitarian party-state parliamentarianism led to serious functional disturbances

Reprinted by permission from *Daedalus*, Journal of the American Academy of Arts and Sciences, Boston, Massachusetts, 93, no. 1 (Winter 1964).

even in the tradition-bound older democracies of Europe. In England, to be sure, it was possible to absorb the effects of these disturbances by thorough-going changes in the system of parliamentary rule; in France the Third Republic was able to sustain itself, but only with difficulty. Even in the Scandinavian countries, spared by the World War and apparently sheltered against the European crises, minority governments were often only provisionally able to contain the tensions; even they scarcely provided a proof of the workability of the parliamentary system.

The second postwar epoch of the European parliamentary democracies is of course significantly different from this first crisis period, which ended in the catastrophe of another world war. On the one hand it was still confronted with those basic problems of democratic structural change which the nineteenth century had laid in the cradle of European parliamentarianism. But on the other hand conditions had deeply changed, giving a new profile to the attempts at reconstruction or new construction of parliamentarianism in western Europe after 1945. On three levels these new perspectives were opened.

1. *Constitutional:* The experience of the twenties and thirties directed attention to possible precautionary measures and modifications in the parliamentary system for the protection of its substance and its efficiency. The West German "chancellor democracy" and even more the half-parliamentary presidential regime of the Fifth Republic in France are examples of this attempt at a limitation of parliamentarianism.

2. *Sociological:* At the same time the process of realignment and leveling of society—the product of the radical changes of the war and postwar period, a tendency away from ideologizing and toward pragmatizing of the parties—fostered the concentration of parties and finally the approach to a two- or three-party system, which was strengthened and hastened by constitutional and technical electoral provisions. West Germany was the most strongly affected by this process, in the course of the immigration and absorption of well over ten million displaced persons. But the tendency characterized much too simply as "Americanization" of party and parliamentary life was strong in the rest of Europe as well. This development seemed to simplify the formation of an administration and an opposition, to clarify political alternatives and to allow the parliamentary process to become less hindered by the formation of ideological fronts.

3. *Foreign Affairs:* The decisive phase of European political change at the end of the forties was marked by an increasingly firm opposition to the dynamics of Soviet Russia's European politics. The American politics of restraint, the Marshall Plan, the establishment of NATO placed western Europe within the framework of a broader international cooperation. It opened aspects of a supranational integration which could have an incomparably more lasting effect on the internal politics and structure of the European states than the League of Nations had once had. The idea and the weight of a European and Atlantic community formed, first of all, a kind of protection for the new parliamentary democracies; insofar as they were still limited by powerful groups hostile to democracy—as in the case of France and Italy with their strong Communist parties—the growing interdependence meant a supplementary support.

The starting conditions for the "new Europe" thus seemed more favorable than in 1918. The attempt at a self-limitation of sovereignties had taken the place of a confusion of national ambitions, which at that time had made the rise and triumph of nationalistic dictatorial movements possible. The East-West conflict seemed to outweigh the internal explosive forces of national parliamentarianism. In the foreground stood the overlapping problems of political cooperation, economic and military networks, and the overcoming of the colonial age. In the face of such problems intrastate tensions tended to diminish in sharpness and importance or at least to recede to a deeper level of confrontations more specific and more suited to compromise. Such a prognosis seemed especially plausible from the German point of view. Had not Germany immediately after the occupation joined, as the Federal Republic, the European and Atlantic politics of alliance, within whose frame the West German parliament system could develop and stabilize itself almost without hindrance? Indeed, the experience of a parliamentary democracy operating with political and economic success was something entirely new in the history of German political thought, which had learned from the catastrophes of 1848, 1918 and 1933 to identify parliamentary politics with crisis and collapse.

But these positive perspectives reflect only the external, superficial image of the reconstruction period. They say nothing about the real stability and functional capability of the reconstituted parliamentary democracies of western Europe. Upon closer inspection it has quickly become apparent not only that the old problems of parliamentary politics continued to exist unsolved under the double protection mentioned, but also that the new conditions of the post-war period, with their revolutionizing consequences in the economic, social and intellectual areas, necessarily led to new crises of adjustment in the political system. It became a question whether and how, in the light of the changes cited, the individual parliaments would be able to carry out their role—which was still conceived in the classical sense of control and "decision-making"—in the actual practice of national politics. The increasingly complicated network of the modern industrial state confronted them with a dismaying array of new problems for which political common sense and the old parliamentary practice no longer seemed adequate. These problems threatened to undermine the competence and decision-making ability of the individual member of parliament, to strengthen at the cost of parliament the power of committees, experts and the bureaucracy of the executives and to lead toward an undermining of the parliamentary system of government from within.

As a result a series of surprisingly similar basic questions came to the fore in all of the western democracies. Is a parliament as such still capable, under such circumstances, of exercising an effective control of politics, not even to mention active participation in the formulation of political desires? Further, is it possible any longer to defend the submission of complicated economic, social and military decisions, which demand precise planning, to the tedious discussion procedure of technically incompetent large assemblies, considering that the deliberations of a small circle of committee experts are simply repeated in these sessions? And under these circumstances is it at all possible to continue upholding the classical basic principle of parliamentarianism—to combine democratic representation and the correct decision of all questions—or does not the parliamentary process become reduced to a formality in the face of the incompetence of the mass of the representatives?

A further consideration derives from the fact that precisely the supra- and international network of those technical decisions transcends the capacities of the national parliaments and at the same time must impose sensitive limitations upon them. The development of European institutions has demonstrated in recent years what a great effect this consideration has had in shifting politics from the parliamentary level to that of administration and bureaucracy. A European bureaucracy of a new character has gained a decisive advance upon the parliamentary organs in those institutions; the supranational formation of politics has been shifted extensively to an extra- or superparliamentary area of competence handled by experts and governments; in the face of this power the merely advisory function of the European "parliaments," which moreover have possessed only a derivative legitimation, not a direct one through direct European elections, has had little effect.

In view of these problems our diagnosis of parliamentarianism in western Europe will consider the following elements. We shall inquire about the model, the reality and the structural transformation of "classical" parliamentarianism, which has also been the point of departure for the parliamentary democracies of postwar Europe. We shall analyze the most important factors and arguments that form the basis of this structural change. What are their consequences: the transformation or the decline of parliamentary politics? Last, we shall endeavor to ascertain what efforts toward reform, substitute forms and future perspectives can be recognized within the national and supranational framework. Although the examination will proceed from Germany to the particular conditions of the various countries, attention will be devoted principally to the typical instances of those problems which today more than ever bear a general European character, both in positive and in negative regards.

Structural Transformation of Democracy

The "crisis of parliamentarianism" figured, immediately following World War I, as the central theme of countless conferences of the Interparliamentary Union—in Washington, Ottawa, Geneva, Paris, Prague and Berlin. The discussion probed deeply into essentials. It dealt with the actual and necessary adjustment to the new European situation; it vacillated between a modernization or a limitation of parliamentarianism. At the same time it became increasingly clear that parliamentarianism had undergone an actual structural transformation which also needed to be put into effect constitutionally and institutionally.

Indeed the language of the constitutions and of their interpreters—insofar as it referred to the original model of the "classical" parliamentarianism, developed according to the idealistically elevated English pattern—was so far from reality that it appeared to be more and more fictitious. Whereas constitutional theory held to the concept of the independent member of parliament, responsible only to his conscience, in reality the representative found himself to be working within a network of social and political ties, a network which had become increasingly dense with the complication of modern industrial society and with the organizational consolidation and increase in importance of parties and organized interest groups. The result was that the member of parliament, contrary to the postulates of the constitutions, was subjected increasingly, whether consciously or unconsciously, to an "imperative mandate" by party interests and other joint interests. His role as representative of the people as a whole had thereby become unreal. The classical-liberal form of representative parliamentarianism gave way to a parliamentary democracy determined by plebiscite and party politics, a democracy which also brought about far-reaching changes in the process of forming political opinion and the function of the parliament as an organ for decision and control.

The interrelationship of this "structural transformation of democracy" (Leibholz) with modern party history has meanwhile been thoroughly analyzed. After World War II some of the European constitutions tried to give the new reality its due—though only in a makeshift way and rather incidentally—by dedicating a few articles to the role of the parties and their structure. Probably the most prominent instance of this was in the Basic Law of the Federal Republic of Germany, the West German constitution of 1949, in which (contrary to the Weimar Constitution) not only is the participation of the parties in determination of political policy emphasized, but their democratic structure and their agreement with the ordinances of the constitution are also specifically required. To be sure the old postulate of representative democracy was also preserved. The deputies are considered the "representatives of the people as a whole, not bound to specific commissions and directions, and subject only to their consciences" (Art. 38); thus they are supposed to be free of the "imperative mandate" to which they are in fact so thoroughly bound by the manner of nomination of candidates, electoral modes, parliamentary practice and party coercion.

The whole tension between theory and practice continues in these introverse stipulations. In other European countries the situation appears to be scarcely any different. In the merely laconic, usually meaningless reference to the parties there still prevails that "conspiracy of silence" (Loewenstein) with which the constitutions hold to the fiction of partyless parliamentarianism and the super-party parliament member. This is true of the Italian constitution (Art. 49) as well as of the French constitutions of the Fourth and Fifth Republics, even though the beginnings of a transformation are visible and in the practice of constitutional interpretation there is a growing attempt to give the political reality of party democracy its due. It is expected that this reality will be taken into account still more thoroughly by the new Swedish constitution, which has been in preparation for years with the authoritative participation of political science.

There is, however, a further aspect of that structural change which, although so far it has enjoyed less attention, has a more fundamental, comprehensive significance than the constitutional-political reform of the relationship between party, parliament and government. This is the expansion of the organized interest groups on the one hand and of public administration on the other hand. The consequence of both is that "unpolitical" experts and superparty planning confront the parliament's claim to power of decision and control with an increasing claim to primacy, attempting to undermine or even displace the parliament. The reasons for this development are as various as they are obvious. They lie in the need for continually improved, rational organization and planning in a complex, highly differentiated, sensitive society which can no more afford mere improvisation and dilettantism than can modern economics and industry.

But at the end of this development, which opposes to the political process of parliamentary democracy the greater effectiveness of the "unpolitical" experts, the objectively planning and rationally functioning, specialized bureaucracy in state and society, there appears the frightful image of a mere technocracy, a rule by the managers and functionaries, which would evade control and the entire realm of democratic-parliamentary decision-making. Thereby the balance of power would be seriously disturbed and a new form of dictatorship would be coldly brought into being. It is this opposition between highly specialized expertise and the principle of democratic participation that appears as the central structural problem of all western parliamentary democracies. To be sure this dilemma is also by no means new, however sharply it confronts us today on all sides.

Bureaucratization and specialization, no less than liberal and social emancipation movements, accompanied the development of parliamentary democracy at an early stage and continue to do so to an increasing degree. They have governed its forms and at the same time complicated them. The development of the apparatus of government has meant more than an expansion of its political function. It has fostered the rise of the modern professional bureaucracy, which especially in nineteenth-century Germany was most closely tied to the continuation of absolutistic and authoritarian-official (*obrïgkeitsstaatliche*) elements in the structure of state and society. This became especially apparent after the establishment of the Weimar Republic, which tried, with the army and the state bureaucracy, to incorporate the great, allegedly indispensable supports of political continuity into the new order of parliamentary democracy—an attempt which is known to have been a huge failure. The collapse of the first German democracy was to a considerable degree a result of the unsolved tension between parliamentary and bureaucratic-authoritarian elements of structure; this tension was already prepared for in the dualism of the Weimar Constitution; it finally ended with the victory of a bureaucratic presidial dictatorship and its pseudo-democratic manipulation and subjugation by Hitler.

To be sure, the cause for this was not simply a faulty construction of the constitution. Rather, the problems of the first German republic showed how unavoidable was a clarification of the relation between the conflicting elements. Max Weber had already recognized at the end of World War I the tendency toward bureaucratization and expertise in the leadership of the state as a dominating sign of the age; according to him there remained only the choice between bureaucratization and dilettantizing. Later Karl Mannheim saw our "period of social change" to be essentially determined by the fact that great "strains" arose "out of the contiguity of the principle of competition and the principle of regulation and planning," strains which could be solved only by a system of "planning for freedom."

This problem certainly did not apply exclusively to the democracies. The authoritarian and totalitarian regimes were also unable to solve the strain, even after eliminating the parliaments; it continued to exist almost undiminished in the dualism of state and party, especially visible in the "Third Reich." And finally it became apparent in postwar France and Germany how great an importance is possessed by the continuity and the growing weight of the elite of experts in organized interest groups or unions and in state bureaucracy as opposed to the politically-parliamentary dynamics. Only recently it was once more pointed out, by Maurice Duverger, that the bureaucracy of experts in France plays a stabilizing role that alone makes government possible. The Fifth Republic deduces from this fact the consequence—albeit a disputed one—of a restriction of parliament, which ultimately aims at a *gouvernement de legislature* in which the parliamentary and the presidial systems would be merged. This, however, could be the end of real parliamentarianism and the victory of rule by executive mandate with a plebiscitary façade.

In West Germany, which with controversial arguments held to the continuity of the political apparatus beyond the period 1933–1945, the development proceeded somewhat differently. Here the "chancellor democracy" commanded a continually growing governing and steering apparatus whose complication and indispensability in the modern bureaucratic state works against a change of government. Now that it has outlasted several parliamentary periods this apparatus is far superior in technical knowledge to the parliamentary agencies of power, which in the Bonn system are curtailed anyway. In addition there is the fourteen-year duration of the political constellation, which is modified only by the federalistic structure. Here the danger of instability of the government is averted at the cost of disempowering the parliament, whose capacity for control becomes inferior to the claim to expert knowledge and the stability of the political apparatus. The head of the government himself was able, thanks to his constitutionally assured position and to the special authority of Adenauer as Chancellor and party head, to extend the executive power far into the parliament, which then converts his will into laws prepared for him by the government bureaucracy.

In both cases, even though by different courses, the consequence of the unsolved strain is a tendency toward authoritative remodeling of parliamentary democracy. Of course in both cases the concrete form owes much to a personal element. It may not outlast de Gaulle and Adenauer. But the development itself would scarcely be thinkable without the factual and structural problems which lie at the basis of the crisis of parliamentarianism in the industrial and mass state of the twentieth century.

Between Crisis and Reform

In the following survey we shall try therefore to summarize the most important points of view and arguments which characterize the critical discussion of parliamentarianism in Europe.

In the representative system the direct contact with the will of the people is lost, since in the large modern state the parties of rank have become mass parties, and elections based on personality have become impersonal, machine elections. One consequence is the stronger demand for plebiscitary arrangements, which correspond to a more general tendency toward "supraparty" ties. Just recently de Gaulle, who set the Fifth Republic on this course, criticized the lack of such arrangements in the Bonn democracy. All the recent experiences indicate, however, that they are feasible only in the smaller framework of a direct democracy (such as Switzerland still is), if the danger of uninformed demagogy or even of a new autocracy is to be avoided.

The prestige of the members of parliament has fallen precipitously since they no longer have to resist an autocratic principality and are enjoying a career that is almost without risks. To the public they seem to be dispensable: a constitutional state and a functioning government are already insured by good organization and efficient development of the political apparatus.

The organization of parliamentarianism, originally created for political problems, is not suited to deal with the penetration of economic and social problems into the concerns of government. Law-making has extended its boundaries considerably. It embraces almost all areas of social existence and it makes too great demands on the abilities of the members of parliament, both technically and temporally. The results are extended periods of session and necessary specialization. The participating citizen is replaced by the professional politician, who himself becomes a bureaucrat, a functionary, without having the experience and the specialized training of the state official.

Thus the continual broadening of functions of the state threatens traditional parliamentarianism, which is thereby alienated from its real function and fragmented in its effectiveness. On the other hand, a limitation of the extent of parliamentary control, especially in the economic area, has proved fatal, the more complicated the economic and social organism of the modern state has become and the more it has called for coordination and planning. But one is confronted with the facts that the state is seldom a capable entrepreneur and that the parliament is not a good organ of control for economic undertakings, especially since in this case it will transfer its prerogatives to a great extent back to the political bureaucracy. A system of decentralization scarcely offers the satisfying solution either. Federalism can of course unburden parliamentarianism, given the appropriate historical premises (as in Germany or Switzerland) by disseminating responsibility and control more broadly. But thereby coordination and planning become more difficult and complicated.

As the expansion of the state places too great demands on the abilities of the members of parliament, it at the same time lowers their position and the importance of their activity. An elected representative cannot, by the nature of the thing, be equal to the many-sided detailed problems with which society and bureaucracy confront him. The fact that he has to make pronouncements and decisions and exercise control in these matters, as if he were an expert, contributes to the lessening of the prestige of parliamentarianism in the eyes of the public and makes the member of parliament himself vulnerable, insecure and resigned in the face of the real or alleged specialists inside and outside of the political institutions. It also does not help to make his activity more attractive to the really suitable persons. At the same time that technical and political competence is concentrated in a minority within the parliamentary parties, the representative becomes dependent on an apparatus of reporters and specialists, and parliamentary debate is reduced to a mock struggle in the foreground behind which work those anonymous and nonresponsible apparatuses upon which the member of parliament is dependent to a great extent in technical matters.

The consequence is not only a weakening of the parliamentary debates but also that loss of substance and interest which has become characteristic for the greater part of parliamentary activity, with the exception of the few debates over matters of principle; this is also especially true of that domain particularly proper to parliament, which has become so complicated—household politics. The attendance in the parliament chamber is often meager; the parties function as mere voting machines; their activity seems to the critical public to be an expensive waste and complication; derogatory remarks against the conduct of parliament, whether they come from the government and the bureaucracy or from the interest groups, fall upon fruitful ground; finally, the institution itself is no longer taken seriously and it is overridden wherever possible and led into error. Overtaxed in its assignments, the parliament limits itself to topics that have an effect on the elections and abandons important decisions in practice to the planning and formulating bureaucracy. Thus their roles are often exactly reversed. Lawgiving is transferred to the apparatus of administration and parliament loses its authority to a quasidictatorship of the executives. Finally the will of the experts triumphs over the parliamentary art of submitting technical decisions to political decision and control; the decisions have already been made.

The structural transformation into the party state has sharpened these problems still more. The advance determination of decisions in the party committees so extensively binds the parliamentary member, whose parliamentary existence rests upon the party's favor, that even without express party coercion his parliamentary flexibility is extremely limited. Discussion, the basic element of democracy, no longer takes place chiefly on the parliamentary level but in the preparliamentary area of party politics, and largely to the exclusio₁ of the public. Parliamentary decisions are prefabricated there and become a mere matter of form, since the voices are previously counted; the minority, that is usually the opposition, is left with mere resignation—until the next election—or with increasing anger, which can become intensified to enmity toward the regime itself, to a revolutionary mood. Old and new attempts to put an end to this development—for instance by prohibiting the "imperative mandate"—are of course condemned to failure. But the consequences can be lessened, above all under two conditions: by the loosening effect of decentralization and federalism and by a greater flexibility and elasticity of the parties themselves if they are no longer strictly bound to certain classes and programs and if there is a continuation of the process of leveling and pragmatization, which is so characteristic for the postwar development, especially that of Germany. On the other hand, here as in Italy and other countries the phenomenon of the "Christian party" has been thwarting this process and has added a new chapter to the European history of the (ideological) "Weltanschauung" parties.

The selection and education of the members of parliament is not holding pace with the complication of political tasks. Even the process of selecting the candidates seems inadequate from this point of view. The central dilemma of modern parliamentarianism becomes apparent here. A strong influence of the central party leadership is the only guarantee for the nomination of objectively suited, specialized candidates for parliamentary and party work; but this method endangers precisely that immediate contact with the constituency which seems to be possible only by way of local electoral committees, through a decentralized party organization. The technical question of the electoral system is secondary to this. The point of view of the continental backers of the majority election, in so passionately supporting the reform of parliamentarianism by a "personality election," is still oriented to the older model of parliamentarianism. However, empirical observations in England have confirmed that with the change from prestige democracy to party democracy, the elections have also changed from personality elections to party elections regardless of the electoral system.

It is felt especially urgent, therefore, that the representatives to parliament be better informed and equipped. An advance technical examination of the candidates, such as has been called for again and again, can be neither politically justified nor technically realized; it seems impossible to set up suitable standards. On the other hand, an expansion of the apparatus for information and assistance is under way everywhere. Assistants, experts, forces of aid of all sorts are to see to it that the balance of power between the government apparatus and the parliament, which is supposed to control the government apparatus, does not become too unequal in the conduct of affairs. But precisely this may give rise to another problem. A second big apparatus is created which is scarcely less subject to the tendencies of bureaucratization than is the government apparatus. Such a bureaucratization of parliamentarianism once more calls up, only on a different level, the old danger that the member of parliament is overridden by or becomes dependent upon extraparliamentary, nonresponsible experts. The collaboration of government officials, experts and members of parliament in committees of experts does increase the possibilities for objective information and controls, but it also considerably complicates the course of government and committee activity and in addition confuses the executive and legislative competences. One way out is the formation of commissions of experts in the government, as they are used in England with some success; thereby the technical knowledge of the organized interest groups is drawn especially into economic and social planning. But that does not essentially foster either a solution of the control problem or the reactivation of parliamentarianism as a whole; it only shifts, and probably sharpens, the tendencies to "expertocracy."

In all of this it is the ponderousness of the parliamentary system that is especially exposed to criticism. The first principle of modern government and economy, the principle of rationality and effectiveness, is apparently contradicted by the existence and practice of the parliaments so strikingly that the critics question not only their ability to function but also their justification for existence. Important decisions—as in Germany a new penal law, the social reform or the party law expressly required in the constitution—and also a plethora of detailed tasks are often postponed over several periods of sessions or remain entirely unsettled. For the greater part of the representatives the sessions mean up to 90 percent idle time; for the public they mean a waste of valuable working power. This too scares many a qualified person away from the parliamentary career. Therefore recommendations have been put forward again and again for the technical rationalization of parliamentary procedure, which is still in the state it was in the eighteenth and nineteenth centuries. For example, time-wasting sessions might well be curtailed by the exchange of opinion and voting in writing or by telephone, extensive use of electric brains and other methods. But there are still narrow limits set to the simplification and shortening of the procedure. It is precisely the nature of the parliamentary system, as distinct from and contrary to bureaucratic procedure, to achieve a more comprehensive basis and sharper control of political decision through more extensive proceedings.

The idea of a second chamber of experts to bridge the gap between expert knowledge and political power has been playing a significant role right up to the present. Made up on the basis of technical suitability and professional grouping from the various provinces of economic and social life, such a "parliament of experts" could contribute as an auxiliary organ of the parliament and government to the objectification of the political process. To be sure, it has proved an insolvable difficulty to decide in what way and according to what key such an institution could be recruited. All previous attempts have also either run aground in useless technical discussions, as in the economic council of the Weimar Republic, or have been misused for the purpose of deposing the parliamentary system by authoritarian regimes, as in Mussolini's *stato corporativo* and similar institutions in Greece, Poland, Austria and Portugal in the thirties. In France since 1945 and especially in the Fifth Republic the idea of an economic council has been institutionalized; but this coincides again with a threat to parliamentary democracy.

Theoretically the auxiliary function of such an agency, which makes it possible to incorporate technical-economic expertise into the political process, should be hailed as a support of parliamentarianism. But the practical realization of it appears to be incomparably more difficult than the formation of commissions and councils, which according to the English example of the royal commissions and committees would have to bridge expert knowledge and politics and simultaneously curb and channel the pressure of interest groups.

A chamber of professionals and experts seems to be not only historically discredited but also a danger in the present. The interest groups' influence on politics, which is already almost too strong, would have in such a chamber an additional vehicle and instrument. Therefore as a guarantor of objectivity it would be scarcely better qualified—indeed, its members would be still more subjectively tied to particular interests than the members of parliament, who have to represent various interests at once and therefore are more predestined for a comprehensive manner of making decisions. The primacy of politics is also indispensable in all matters of technical decision.

An especially weighty argument of the critics is finally the lack of stability of parliamentary governments. This was especially true of the unbridled parliamentarianism of the period between the wars. The twenty-one administrations in the fourteen years of the Weimar Republic were a frightening example. Even after World War II the French Fourth Republic exhausted twenty-five administrations in the space of thirteen years. It is true that the rapid change of cabinets was mitigated by the fact that often there were only minor shifts in the personnel component. But without a doubt, not only the total triumph of Hitler (and the assent of broad circles in Germany) but also the more moderate victory of de Gaulle over parliamentary democracy are to be ascribed in no small way to discontent about the discontinuity of parliamentary state politics. This discontinuity has been particularly consequential in periods of economic and political crises, which have needed the more far-sighted objective planning and persistent execution of a course of consolidation to a greater extent. Parliamentarianism appears to be not only a particularly cumbersome but also an unreliable form of government which, because it is entirely bound up with the transitory present, is incapable of demanding unpopular sacrifices for more far-reaching politics from a short-sighted "will of the people."

Thus the tendency of European democracy is toward a modification of the parliamentary system of government. Its particular goal is to lengthen the duration of periods of government and to render more difficult the overthrow of cabinets and the dissolution of parliaments. This of course has always implied the danger of lessening or even blocking political dynamics, the flexibility and capability for decision of the political forces. The rigidifying chancellor democracy of Adenauer and the psuedo-presidential regime of de Gaulle are examples of this problem, which can result in the undermining and displacement of a lively parliamentarianism rather than in reform. There are various forms of this modification. The Fifth Republic has established a dualistic system, which runs on two tracks by placing representative and plebiscitary execution of the popular will in a parallel position and thus producing a peculiar system of balance in which finally the presidial-plebiscitary element dominates. From the German point of view this recalls all too vividly the faulty construction of the Weimar Republic; a decision for genuine presidential democracy or for the restitution of parliamentary democracy will not be avoidable when the present special form is no longer protected by the peculiar phenomenon of de Gaulle.

But the forms of modification in the Bonn democracy are also disputed.

Undoubtedly an astonishing stability of the political constellation has been brought about by the elimination of splinter parties by the 5-percent clause, by the officially privileged position of the parliament parties by state financing, by hindrances put in the way of the overthrow of government by the "constructive vote of lack of confidence"; at the same time the dissolution of parliament is impeded, owing to a weakened position of the federal president. But the other weaknesses of parliamentarianism enumerated above have appeared all the more prominently. And more particularly the government, the bureaucracy and the interest groups, protected by the stable parliamentary conditions, have achieved such a great weight that many clear-sighted critics characterize the Bonn democracy as an actual government by bureaucracy and interest associations. This parliamentary democracy also will not have to stand its test until the moment of a change of administration; the end of the Adenauer era leaves many questions open, even though it seems to be less dramatic than the transition to the post-de Gaulle era.

This summary of the critical points in European parliamentarianism, as incomplete as it is, nevertheless indicates the central significance of the inquiry into the relation between politics and technical knowledge with regard to the future of European parliamentary democracy. This problem should now be pursued first in the national, then in the supranational, contexts.

Perspectives toward a Solution

Three main directions are taken in the attempts to solve—without a loss of democratic substance—the sharpened conflict between parliamentary politics and technical planning in the expanding industrial state of present-day Europe. The first direction is pursued especially in England and in the Scandinavian countries. It is the attempt to democratize the growing phenomenon of specialists and experts by making it useful and at the same time bringing it under control within the framework of, or in association with, the apparatus of government. This attempt proceeds from the insight that the activity of the interest groups cannot be separated from the political process and abandoned or consigned to a fictitious neutrality of the experts. In England the development of the royal commissions and similar institutions is significant in this line and at the same time poses a counterbalance to the rule of an isolated state bureaucracy. To be sure, new problems are created by the expansion of such commissions, which advise the government and administration in economic, social and cultural-political questions with technical competence, but also with their own interests prevailing. The importance of the experts has been fostered, the "anonymous empire" (S. Finer) of interest groups becomes institutionalized, but the parliaments' loss in substance has progressed further while the cabinet system, which is founded on parties and the administrations, has grown stronger.

A second course proceeds by way of the attempt *to submit parliamentarianism itself to the tendencies toward technology and rationalization* which have led to the advance of the expertise-and-planning system. This course has been pursued most decisively in France by means of the unburdening of the parliament (which of course also means its loss of importance), and by means of the institutionalizing of the system of expertise in large planning commissions. Another variation of this "rationalization" of parliamentarianism is the progressive shifting of technical decisions from the plenum to the commissions of the parliament, as is especially characteristic of the German development. The plenum retains little more than the sanctioning of the decisions that the members of the commissions bring before it. Therefore the selection and incorporation of the experts into the parliamentary party groups becomes the principle content of parliamentary activity. Here too the "rationalization" results in a loss of substance and significance of the actual parliamentary discussion. The system of *hearings*, which could steer this development, is lacking in the European parliamentary democracies with the exception of the Swiss democracy, which has a different form. Substitutes such as the interrogation hour of the Bonn system, in which the ministers must answer critical questions before parliament, are hardly sufficient, although in some cases (as the Spiegel affair) it proved quite important. But the basic principle remains in danger—the principle that decision is the prerogative of the politically responsible, elected officials of the parliament and of the government, and that it is not to be relegated to the bureaucracy or to the experts, with or without an interest-group slant.

All the more important are the efforts toward a new delimitation of the altered functions of parliament, government, administration and the organized interest groups which are undertaken in view of this dilemma. Their premise is that in view of the general tendency to bureaucratization the future of democracy depends upon whether objectivity and expertise can also be exercised outside of bureaucratic areas of organization. A clear separation of political decision (parliament) and technical planning (bureaucracy) is not possible; it would finally lead to the hypertrophy of the administrative state, to the victory of the hierarchy of officials over open democracy. To equate bureaucracy with expertocracy could appear as the tempting solution to the problems. But it contains serious dangers; it implies an evasion of democratic control and creates a new gap between the state and the citizens; it sharpens their dependence and helplessness in the face of the political-social process and degrades them to subjects facing a highly specialized, uncontrollable network of rule without comprehension. The result could be indifference and resignation; the political answer could become an erroneous reaction such as that of 1933 in Germany, if in place of a political solution to the problems a bureaucratic one were to prevail.

It is indisputable that the number of the actual decision-bearers in the modern state is becoming steadily smaller and the tendency toward rule by experts is becoming steadily harder to control. Thus the future of democracy depends all the more on whether it becomes possible to open up new ways for the citizens to participate in political and social affairs and thus to rise above the role of mere observers. Parties, organized interest groups and self-rule offer possibilities to create a counterweight against the threatening depolitization; an improved political education seems to be its precondition. This is true at the same time for the expert in the planning and steering committee. His "democratization" and control is most likely to become feasible if every kind of monopoly and hierarchy of the agencies of competence is avoided and if room is made for the principle of free competition in the sense of competition for achievement.

The basis for all attempts at solving the problem is therefore the insight that there must be no necessary opposition between expert knowledge and politics, between expertise and democracy. The primacy of politics must be maintained. The question is only what place parliamentarianism is to retain here, in what form it is to be brought into accord with the changed conditions of modern state, social, economic and military politics. The parliament and the parties which support it still have the double function of first working for contact and conjunction between the various areas of expertise, interests and politics, thereby guaranteeing the openness, readiness for compromise and competition; and second of control of technical counseling and technical planning, re-examining them in the discussions between administration and opposition and relating them to concrete political reality.

For both tasks—the uniting of political determination and technical planning on the one hand; the critical examination of the interest associations and also those of the experts on the other hand—the European democracies now as before need parliamentary institutions that are capable of functioning. We have indicated what possible modifications are being discussed and also to some extent realized to reduce the disadvantages and crises of parliamentarianism and to consider the structural changes of society and state. These modifications are resulting everywhere—not only in France—in a limitation of the "classical" parliamentary rule. But at the same time they aim at an intensification and rationalization of parliamentarianism in its indispensable functions. Improvement of the channels of information, expansion of the system of commissions, more conscious policy in the selection of their own experts on the part of the parliamentary parties and incorporation of the specialists into the work of the parliament are the means of this rationalization. Its goal continues to be to work as a clearing house and counterweight to the technical claims of the bureaucracy of government as well as of interest groups, and to provide the comprehensive impetus for the primacy of political decision.

This is particularly applicable to the new problems that have been brought forward by the international network and the creation of *supranational* institutions. Today an isolated view of intrastate parliamentarianism is no longer possible. It is superseded by the comprehensive question as to how the separation of politics and planning, of democracy and expertocracy can be bridged in the sphere of the European network, and partly also in the Atlantic network. Here too only an inadequate political control by the governments confronts the forward-moving, expanding bureaucracy of administrators and specialists. Commissions and ministerial councils of the European economic community incorporate this tendency as do the other European administrative offices. And here too the parliamentary institutions have remained far behind. As qualified as some of their members are and as favorable as the supranational exchange of thought is, European parliamentary institutions have little actual weight as long as they lack legitimation through direct European elections and as long as they carry out only insignificant advisory functions. Here too it must be recognized that technical planning needs political planning and control if it is to be both effective and democratic.

The danger of self-satisfied expertocracy is heightened still more by the economic and technical successes of cooperation on the level of bureaucracy. The collapse of negotiations between the Common Market and England fits into this complex. If England can be counted as a model of a parliamentary democracy that has succeeded in adjusting to the changed conditions without a breach of the basic principles, then England's inclusion would without doubt shift the politics of European unification from the bureaucratic level to the parliamentary level. Therein—and not only in a French claim to leadership—lies one of the reasons for the resistance of de Gaulle, who may fear the disturbing effect of such tendencies on the economic-technical development of the European cooperation. But therein also lies the reason for the all too long hesitation of England, which regards with mistrust the reciprocal effect on the tested institutions of its own political system.

Not only in Italy and the Benelux countries but also in Germany these political aspects of the problem—along with the economic and military ones—have in the meanwhile come into such prominent awareness that the French standpoint appears considerably isolated. The Fifth Republic is considered a special case, not a model for the solution of the problems of European parliamentarianism. Precisely at a moment in which a Europe of reduced sovereignties is considering its strengthened role in the world, a retreat into national, or even regional, small-European isolation has become unthinkable. This is not only a question of economic and military potential. It is still more a political question. The danger that threatens the European democracies externally because of their geographical position, and internally still more because of the multifariously broken tradition of their parliamentarianism, also has not been averted by their rapid reconstruction. In the search for security and necessary reform the European states need not only close association among themselves but also with the Anglo-Saxon democracies, which command the strongest traditions and experiences in the art of the adjustment of a firmly established parliamentarianism to the new conditions of the industrial world.

Conclusion

While there are striking parallels and similarities in the appearance and problems of parliamentarianism in present-day Europe, the differences between the national forms of its realization still seem very great. In Germany, the experience of the Weimar Republic and the causes of its fall form the exit-point for all discussions about the relation of parliament, government and bureaucracy. The pseudo-presidential experiments of 1930–1933, which led to the dictatorship of Hitler, seem to justify the widespread mistrust against all attempts to minimize the position and function of parliament in favor of bureaucracy. In France, under the impact of the failure of classical parliamentarianism in the

Fourth Republic, the experiences influencing public opinion and discussion support a very different view, almost contrary to the German version of a parliamentary party state. While in both of these cases, however, the main tendency goes toward a modification of parliamentary democracy, in Italy the older type of a multi-party system still prevails, confronted with the classical problems of a parliament which is split up in many political groups hardly able to form stable coalitions.

Such profound differences in the domestic scene of the European states must be considered if the prospects of coordination and integration of the national systems into a "new Europe" are examined. Besides strong remnants of the past —including very different experiences—it is a question of how to combine strong government and executive authority with effective control, which has led to individual solutions of the problems of parliamentarianism; decentralization and federalism—as traditional in Germany—are further elements of difference. The quest for European integration may as well complicate these problems as it tends to neglect them. It is also for such reasons that the position of a European parliament as a legislative body seems still very uncertain.

If the relation between parliament, government and bureaucracy demands new answers on the national as on the supranational level, this applies even more to the role of parties, interest groups and expert commissions within the institutional framework of parliamentary democracy. Beyond all national differences, two main tendencies are discernible: the growing importance of pressure groups, tending even to a *Verbande-Staat*; at the same time, the decline of ideological parties. This process, to be sure, is modified by the existence of strong Christian parties which may work as integration factors in a biconfessional society, as in Germany; but it may simultaneously block the tendency to open two-party systems, as does the unbroken strength of Communist parties in Italy and France.

In summing up, the development of democracy in western Europe, showing so many different traits and tendencies, has posed many new questions. On the level of domestic politics, there are as yet no common answers in terms of a "new Europe." This will be the future task of interstate compromises which may result in the creation of a European parliament. In spite of the experiments of the French Fifth Republic, however, the substantial form of European governments has remained that of parliamentary democracy, though modified: a fundamental change in the direction of a presidential system seems outside of all possibilities. On this point, the difference between Europe and the United States, whose peculiar political system seems not fit for export, remains a reality which in its importance for European and Atlantic politics should not be overlooked.

The Politics of Legislative Monarchy:
The Iranian Majlis

by JAMES A. BILL

The study of legislative systems has been unusually resistant to the forces of change that continue to transform the study of politics. Configurative, formal-legal, ethnocentric, and static emphases still characterize much of the scholarship on legislatures. The search for deep behavioral patterns and persistent power processes within legislatures has only begun to be implemented in a broadly comparative setting. The drive to relate legislatures to the fundamental issue of modernization remains embryonic despite the burgeoning literature concerning this issue. Partly because of this, legislatures and their formal-legal structures are often considered as positive symbols of political development. Such assumptions have followed easily from analysis that has for decades dwelled almost exclusively upon Western democratic legislative systems.

By analyzing a non-Western legislative system located within a less developed, Islamic society, this study attempts to introduce a new perspective into the investigation of legislative politics. Traditional assumptions concerning legislatures will be examined through the prism of the Iranian Majlis. The patterns and processes that mark Majlis politics will be related specifically to the challenge of modernization.[1]

---

[1] The Iranian constitution is one of the dozen oldest constitutions still in effect in the world. Born in an environment of violence and upheaval that marked Iranian politics at the turn of this century, it reflected a fundamental attempt to check the powers of absolute monarchy. The documents composing this constitution, which has been in effect since 1906–1907, have never been basically revised. Patterned closely after the Belgian Constitution of 1831, they stress very strongly the development and organization of a National Consultative Assembly, or Majlis.

The Fundamental Law of December 30, 1906 consists of fifty-one articles describing the organization, duties, authority, and procedure of this assembly. According to this law, the Majlis has the right and duty to perform the following activities: to examine and discuss in complete security and confidence whatever it considers in the interests of the country and the nation (Article 15); to approve

A description of the formal and constitutional dimensions of the Majlis would explain relatively little about the intricacies of Iranian politics. The constitution that blueprinted the legislative organization developed as a direct result of pressures generated by a hated and decrepit ruling dynasty (the Qajars), a century of foreign intervention and interference, deep divisions between social classes that polarized poverty and affluence, and an influx of revolutionary ideas spawned by continually increasing contact with the West. The constitution was granted grudgingly and reluctantly by the last kings of a dynasty surrounded by vacillating flatterers and threatened by an enraged population. Its provisions concerning a National Assembly were viewed as a temporary concession that could never become permanent because the pendulum of power was bound to swing back to monarchy.

The continuity of parliamentary structures and constitutional strictures extend shakily through a stormy half-century that has left deep scars upon the Iranian legislative process. The Majlis has survived the vicissitudes of two world wars and the dramatic rise and struggle for supremacy of a new dynasty.[2] Confrontations and conflicts have sporadically erupted to the surface of Majlis politics as the parliament building has been bombed, legislative sessions arbitrarily dismissed, and deputies physically threatened by mobs. At a deeper and more persisting level, however, the Iranian legislative process has been marked by a shifting struggle and enduring tension that reflect the key patterns of Pahlavi politics.

The Iranian Majlis has existed as a potential force of competitive opposition to the executive power wielded by the shah and his cabinet. It was born in this role and has sporadically threatened to curtail sharply the monarchical prerogative. Twentieth century Iranian political history can be divided into four periods according to the shifting exigencies of Monarch–Majlis tension. The Majlis was in the ascendance between 1906–1926 and again during 1941–1953,

---

necessary laws (Article 16); to regulate and adjust financial questions and the budget (Articles 18–20); and to authorize the granting of concessions and the conclusion of treaties (Articles 23–24). Besides these rights, the Supplementary Fundamental Law of October 8, 1907 provided the Majlis with the power to ensure ministerial responsibility (Articles 60–61). The National Consultative Assembly was to be the mechanism whereby "every individual in the realm has the right to participate in approving and overseeing the affairs of the country." For an up-to-date translation of the Iranian constitutional documents, see Abid A. Al-Marayati, *Middle Eastern Constitutions and Electoral Laws* (New York: Frederick A. Praeger, 1968), pp. 1–43.

The Iranian legislative system is constitutionally composed of two houses, the National Consultative Assembly and the Senate (the *Majlis-i Shawra-yi Milli* and the *Majlis-i Sina*). The senate or upper house never existed until 1949 and has been of little importance in the political system. It has existed as a house of reward and retirement for elderly personalities who have loyally served monarchy and dynasty and, thus composed, as a constant check against the lower house. Half of the sixty-member senate are direct appointees of the shah. The Majlis, in contrast, has been an integral and relatively persistent part of contemporary Iranian politics.

According to the original election law, Majlis deputies were to be elected in situations where the supervisory election councils were to be representative of six classes: clerics, nobles, landlords, businessmen, tradesmen, and farmers. A new election law that took effect in 1963 replaced the noble and landlord classes by workers and peasants. Women are also now eligible to elect and be elected to the Iranian legislature. The term of membership has traditionally been two years, but this was extended to four years in 1957. At that time also, the size of the Majlis was expanded from 136 to 200 deputies.

[2] The Pahlavi dynasty dates to 1925 when Riza Khan crowned himself shah. His son, Muhammad Riza Shah, has ruled since 1941 when his father abdicated due to the Allied occupation of Iran.

while monarchical forces prevailed 1926–1941 and 1953–1969. The first two decades of Majlis existence marked a period in which the legislature played an important role in terminating the rule of an entire dynasty. Strong vocal forces in the first five Majlises were raised against the existence of monarchy in general as well as against particular kings. The Sixth to the Twelfth Majlises, which existed between 1926–1941, met in the shadow of Riza Shah who deliberately and successfully relegated the legislative body to a position of humble subservience. With the forced abdication of Riza Shah in 1941, the Majlis again became a center for opposition to the monarchy. It was not until the fall of Musaddiq in 1953 that the monarchy was able to regain complete control of the legislative branch. Since this time, the Majlis has existed at the sufferance of the king, who has shaped its composition and has engineered the construction of its sociopolitical ideology.

Despite the fluctuations outlined above, the general story has been one of legislative impotence and executive strength.[3] The Majlis has never successfully and systematically been able to impose its will upon the shah and it has seldom been able to influence even cabinet behavior.[4] Legislative subordination has been due primarily to the following two considerations: (1) The monarch has generally maintained direct control of the processes of selection and election of Majlis deputies; and (2) during periods of executive weakness the Majlis has been unable to grasp the initiative owing to internal division and fractionation. During the two periods when the monarchy was seriously besieged by challenging social forces (1906–1926, 1941–1953), the Majlis membership was splintered into many competing and conflicting groups. The staggering forces of monarchy intensified and exploited these divisions until they were able once again to regain firm control in the political arena.[5] The legislative process in Iran has been wrapped around the person of the shah whose centrality has invested Majlises with the peculiarities that shape these institutions.

The following patterns and characteristics of the Majlis have played a crucial role in helping preserve and reinforce traditional Iranian political patterns:

1. Strong executive control of legislative recruitment processes.
2. Persisting formal-legal procedures publicizing monarchical legitimacy and popular participation.

---

[3] This fact is increasingly and satirically reflected in the Iranian press. The cynical attitude adopted toward the Majlis can be seen in the following two stories. In 1968 the Tehran biweekly *Khvandaniha* discussed Iranian deputies' understanding of political concepts such as "parliamentary immunity." In 1966 a particular Majlis representative was crossing from Afghanistan to Iran during the cholera epidemic. When officials attempted to vaccinate him, he shouted: "You can't do that to me. I have immunity!" In 1969 the magazine *Tawfiq* carried a drawing portraying the following exchange between the speaker of the Majlis and the prime minister. *Majlis speaker:* "You sent us 90 kilos of government bills and the Majlis approved all 90 kilos without the slightest change." *Prime minister:* "Majlis? What Majlis?"

[4] For the best analysis of Majlis-cabinet relations, see Leonard Binder, *Iran: Political Development in a Changing Society* (Berkeley and Los Angeles: University of California Press, 1962), pp. 107–17.

[5] For empirical support for this point, see E. Abrahamian, "The Failure of the Iranian Aristocracy," paper delivered at the Conference on the Structure of Power in Islamic Iran, University of California, Los Angeles, June 26–28, 1969.

3. Institutional elasticity derived from personal and informal intra-Majlis decision-making processes.
4. Legislative continuity and traditional control enhanced by exceptionally pervasive patterns of overlapping membership.
5. Inbuilt capacities for the absorption of system-challenging complaints as well as for the coöptation of system-challenging individuals.

Monarchical control over the legislature can be most dramatically documented by reference to the many cases of direct executive intervention. Key examples include the Constituent Assemblies called and packed by Riza Shah in 1925 and by Muhammad Riza Shah in 1949. These Assemblies convened when an embattled monarchy bypassed the Majlis in a way that permanently weakened the legislative process. In the 1949 case, the shah was given the right to dissolve the Majlis whenever he wished and a senate was instituted. The latter was to be legally bound to the person of the shah even more closely than the Majlis and would therefore exist as a legislative insurance policy against possible Majlis intransigence.[6] Although there have been numerous examples of this kind of overt influence, the monarchy has been able to control the Majlis most consistently through its direction of the recruitment process.

Beginning with the Sixth Majlis during the Riza Shah period, Majlis representation was completely controlled by the king. At the beginning of each legislative period, the monarch's handpicked prime minister submitted a list of names to his majesty. The latter would cross out the names he objected to. The prime minister then sent the list to the Ministry of Interior and new elections would be announced. The slate handed down by the prime minister with the shah's approval never lost an election. One study of the Riza Shah period summarizes this procedure as follows: "The most successful members of the Majlis were those who most admired the shah and the Pahlavi organization. They were also secret police agents who reported the secrets and discussions of their associates."[7] During this period, "only those who submitted themselves to the shah and his agents led a decent life."[8]

The present shah operates in much the same manner as his father, and the 1963 and 1967 election procedures are cases in point. Each member of the Twenty-first and Twenty-second Majlises had to manipulate his way through the following screen. First, substantial sums of money had to be paid in order to gain party membership while additional fees were involved in assuming candidature for the Majlis. In the case of the 1967 elections, all candidates had to join a party according to the instructions of the shah. Second, any Majlis hopeful required an important connection or broker who would present the individual's case not only to the party's leaders but to the shah as well. In the 1963 elections, for example, the most important figures of this kind were Ahmad Nafisi and Hasan 'Ali Mansur. Nafisi was mayor of Tehran and presided over the Congress of

---

[6] This pattern of establishing a senate as a checking mechanism against the potentially more radical lower house is of broad comparative significance. Other developing, non-Western societies in which this has been the case include Malaysia and the Philippines.

[7] *Sharq-i Tarik*—The Dark East (Tehran, 1942), p. 141. In Persian.

[8] *Ibid.*, p. 143.

Free Men and Women, which nominated the parliamentary candidates. Mansur was the head of the "Progressive Center" Majlis faction, which later became the Iran-i Nuvin Party.[9] Third, all Majlis aspirants have had to be thoroughly investigated and approved by the Secret Police. The latter has been very active in the recommendation and disqualification of candidates. Finally, an individual might succeed in maneuvering through all the above entanglements only to be vetoed by the shah. There have been many cases in recent years where this king has crossed out would-be candidates in much the same manner as his father had done in the 1930s. The king, then, stands as the final barrier and allows only proved and loyal personages to pass. This process molds the Majlis into a force possessing built-in malleability for executive control.

The Pahlavi monarchs and political elites have consciously struggled to protect and preserve the existence of the Majlis in Iranian society. The public presence of this institution strongly suggests limited monarchy and popular political participation. As such, the Majlis stands as a conspicuous symbol that is strategically available to confront those who would challenge the legitimacy of the system. It exists as an instrument of justification for the policies of the executive. Thus, Leonard Binder perceptively writes that "the traditional classes have a vested interest in the maintenance of conventional institutions. . . ."[10] The formal accoutrements of legislative politics, such as party identification, electioneering, public debate, and parliamentary procedures, are given wide exposure by the elite-controlled press. Riza Shah, who ruled Iran as a virtual dictator, consistently supported elections and preserved legislative activities. The present king describes the Majlis as "the cradle of the Constitution,"[11] and he writes that the Iranian "great step forward" occurred because "we had blended the Western principle of parliamentary democracy with the Persian monarchical tradition."[12] Partly by clothing the exercise of political power in a legislative garb, the Iranian shahs continue to rule in an era when kingship is a dangerous and dying occupation.[13]

The strong tradition of personal and informal politics that infuses Iranian society was not threatened by the appearance of an institutional parliamentary group specifically designed as a center for political debate and decision making. Quite to the contrary, the Majlis has tended to strengthen the traditional patterns of secrecy, cliquishness, insecurity, personalism, and informality. From earlier analysis, it is clear that the very recruitment process for Majlis member-

[9] Nafisi was charged with corruption and arrested in December 1963. Mansur was assassinated in January 1965.

[10] Binder, *Iran*, p. 274.

[11] Mohammad Reza Shah Pahlavi, *The White Revolution* (Tehran: Imperial Pahlavi Library, 1967), p. 86.

[12] Mohammad Reza Shah Pahlavi, *Mission For My Country* (London: Hutchinson and Co., 1960), p. 166.

[13] Even in the West, this distorted legitimizing function of legislatures has not been entirely unnoticed. Frank E. Myers, for example, writes: "Emasculated legislatures permit the corporate state to function smoothly in a way implicitly at odds with liberal theory even while liberal theory may receive rhetorical endorsement." See Myers, "Social Class and Political Change in Western Industrial Systems," paper prepared for delivery at the 65th Annual Meeting of the American Political Science Association, New York City, September 2–6, 1969, p. 16. See also, Gabriel A. Almond and G. Bingham Powell, Jr., *Comparative Politics: A Developmental Approach* (Boston: Little, Brown and Co., 1966), pp. 137–38.

ship rests upon a highly ascriptive methodology of maneuver. Even more important, however, are the decision-making patterns that emerge in the Majlis itself. The formal legislative framework masks a fluctuating and fractionating network of personal cliques, and it is here where decisions are made and business is transacted.[14]

The Iranian Majlis represents a fine example of personal, informal politics because of the high degree to which these processes have been institutionalized in the legislative arena. In the Majlis, these cliques have come to be called "fractions" (*firaksiyunha*), and parliamentary politics are in fact fraction politics. A leading Iranian statesman and scholar has called these types of informal groups *shikastahbastahha* ("those that shatter and re-form") because of their amorphous, fragmented nature.[15] This is a system of "fractions without parties" where groups do not "have any permanence or durability and live their short lives haphazardly."[16] The committee system and party system, for example, are dominated and shaped by the personal politics of the fraction. Committees are basically formal legislative sub-settings where the members of informal fractions compete and bargain. Political parties (which have usually been created from above in Iran) are fleeting collectivities that exhibit all the characteristics of fractions or personal cliques.

Fraction membership, like party or even committee membership, is constantly changing as deputies jockey for more secure positions. Informal group politics enables individuals to shed group attachments with a minimum of effort. This is an important consideration in societies where the whims of authoritarian leaders and powerful executives are persistently shifting. Political survival often rests upon personal favor, and this dictates a minimum of entangling group loyalties and a maximum of personal contacts. Informal groups such as fractions flourish in such an environment.

A parliament building and procedure fail to disguise the fact that Iranian legislators are securely woven into the traditional sociopolitical fabric. Most decisions are made outside of the Majlis. Major decisions, of course, are made by the political executive represented by the shah and cabinet members. Even minor decisions, however, are arrived at outside the Majlis. They are usually made in informal groups and cliques meeting in clubs, gardens, and homes and then are announced in the Majlis setting. One elderly statesman and veteran of five Majlises writes that "most fractions tend to meet outside of the Majlis in the homes of the individual members. They make their decisions concerning bills, proposals, speeches, and committees before each particular meeting."[17] Thus, although the Majlis actually operates as the mouthpiece for decisions made in executive-influenced personal cliques, it is presented as a popular, well

---

[14] For a detailed study of informal groups and personal politics in Iran, see James A. Bill, "The Plasticity of Informal Politics: The Case of Iran," paper prepared for delivery at the Conference on the Structure of Power in Islamic Iran, University of California, Los Angeles, June 26–28, 1969.

[15] Dr. Rizazadah Shafaq, *Khatirat-i Majlis va Dimukrasi Chist?*—Majlis Memoirs and What is Democracy? (Tehran, 1955), p. 58. In Persian.

[16] *Ibid.*

[17] 'Ali Mu'ayyad-Sabiti, "Chahardahumin Dawrah-yi Qanunguzari—The Fourteenth Legislative Period," in *Dunya—1342* [A Persian Almanac—1963], p. 141.

organized, independent, and formally effective institution. In this way, the Majlis buttresses the elitist and ascriptive processes of traditional politics.

Another mechanism that has reinforced these processes has been the constant appearance of the same deputies in various legislative periods. A fifty-year analysis of Majlis representation encompassing the Second through the Nineteenth Majlises (1909–1960) reveals the strength of this pattern. During this eighteen-Majlis period, twenty-seven individuals sat in *at least* half of the Majlises. Some 100 deputies were present one-third of the time. Approximately 60 percent of the deputies served more than one term in the Majlis. The pervasiveness of this overlapping and interlocking membership is particularly

Table 1—Majlis Representatives Whose Fathers Have Also Been Deputies (In Percentages)

Legislative Period	1	2	3	4	5	6	7	8	9	10	11	12	13	14	15	16	17	18	19	20
Deputies	—	—	2	6	7	8	8	7	8	10	9	7	10	14	16	15	9	21	21	15

Table 2—Majlis Representatives Whose Fathers Have Also Been Deputies in the Three Constitutional Periods (In Percentages)

Constitutional Period	Deputies
First (1906–1926)	3
Second (1926–1941)	8
Third (1941–1963)	16

Source: Zuhrah Shaji'i, *Nimayandigan-i Majlis-i Shawra-yi Milli dar Bistuyik Dawrah-yi Qanunguzari—* The Representatives of the National Consultative Assembly During the Twenty-One Legislative Periods (Tehran, 1965), p. 246.

documented by figures concerning district representation. During these fifty years, one out of every four deputies elected to two or more Majlises came representing different districts. An important case in point is Shaykh 'Ali Khan Dashti who represented Savah in the fifth, seventh, and eighth Majlises, Bushihr in the sixth and ninth Majlises, Damavand in the thirteenth Majlis, and Tehran in the fourteenth Majlis. Forty deputies who sat in two Majlises represented a different district each time.[18] This trend can also be seen in terms of the numbers of deputies whose fathers have also held membership in the Majlis. Tables 1 and 2 reveal the steadily increasing percentages in this regard, until in the decade between 1953–1963 (eighteenth to twentieth Majlises), one of every five deputies who sat in the Majlis was the son of a former deputy. Table 2 indicates that the percentage of such membership has consistently doubled from one constitutional period to the next. A leading Iranian Majlis scholar explains this pattern as follows: "The offspring of deputies enjoy the probability that they will attract

[18] This information has been based on statistics provided in Zuhrah Shaji'i, *Nimayandigan-i Majlis-i Shawra-yi Milli dar Bistuyik Dawrah-yi Qanunguzari*—The Representatives of the National Consultative Assembly During the Twenty-One Legislative Periods (Tehran, 1965), pp. 291–381. In Persian.

the confidence of the state authorities and influential groups and for this reason they enter the Majlis more easily."[19]

The preservation of the traditional political system is also furthered by a significant legislative tension-relieving function. The Majlis stands as both a formal and informal depository for the complaints of the Iranian people. Formally, the Majlis Complaints Committee receives thousands of petitions each year. Informally, each deputy represents a tribunal of appeal to a network of personal friends, acquaintances, neighbors, and relatives. This allows a relatively small but potentially disruptive number of individuals to present their demands at a high level in the system. Although many such demands are never effectively acted upon, the fact that they are heard tends to siphon off explosively confined frustration.

More significant, perhaps, is the system's capacity to absorb and coöpt threatening individuals and opposition leaders. This coöpting function "gives the opposition the illusion of a voice without the voice itself, and so stifles opposition without having to alter policy in the least."[20] The Majlis is an extremely important part of this process because it is able to absorb relatively large numbers of actual and potential system-challengers. Table 3 indicates the occupational status of the representatives to the twenty-one Majlises. Traditionally, the Majlis has been dominated by landlords and clerics. Such social forces harbored a commitment to the ongoing social structure and political system, while at the same time occasionally challenging the right of one particular family to direct that system. Thus the Majlis existed first, as an institution packed with individuals dedicated to the preservation of traditional political *patterns*, and second, as an enticement to coöpt those who would challenge the right of the Pahlavis to direct those patterns. During the six-decade lifespan of the Majlis, 62 percent of its membership has been composed of landlords and clerics.[21]

With the coming of the 1950s and 1960s, the traditional Iranian political system has been confronted by a fundamentally new challenge—a professional middle class.[22] The members of this class have increasingly refused to accept the long standing social structure and political patterns, and their disruptive discontent was first documented in the dramatic rise and appeal of the Communist-oriented Tudah Party and the highly nationalistic Musaddiq movement. The political elite's response to this threat is partially documented in the Majlis where a higher and higher percentage of the membership has been drawn from professional middle-class ranks. Table 4 reveals how the professional-technical group has grown while the cleric class, for example, has declined through the three constitutional periods. By the Twenty-first Majlis, almost one-fourth of

---

[19] *Ibid.*, p. 245.

[20] James S. Coleman, *Community Conflict* (New York: The Free Press, 1957), p. 17 as quoted by Peter Bachrach, "Nondecision Making and the Urban Racial Crisis," paper prepared for delivery at the 65th Annual Meeting of the American Political Science Association, New York City, September 2–6, 1969, p. 4.

[21] This figure has been arrived at on the basis of statistics provided in Table 3.

[22] James A. Bill, "The Social and Economic Foundations of Power in Contemporary Iran," *Middle East Journal* 17 (Autumn, 1963), 400–18.

Table 3—Occupations of Majlis Representatives During the Twenty-one Legislative Periods[a] (In Percentages)

			Occupation				
Legislative Period	LANDLORD	MERCHANT TRADER	GOVERNMENT EMPLOYEE	CLERIC	PROFESSIONAL TECHNICAL	PRIVATE INDUSTRY	LOWER CLASS
1	21	41	23	20	7	5	0
2	30	9	46	24	19	2	0
3	49	7	47	31	12	5	0
4	45	9	55	23	9	1	0
5	49	4	51	24	15	2	1
6	52	7	48	23	12	2	2
7	56	12	44	17	9	1	2
8	59	15	42	10	13	1	1
9	55	20	42	9	16	2	1
10	54	19	37	8	19	1	1
11	59	18	35	6	2	2	1
12	58	18	32	6	21	2	1
13	59	18	30	6	23	2	1
14	57	13	37	8	21	2	0
15	56	15	49	4	19	1	0
16	57	13	50	2	19	3	0
17	49	9	46	11	19	3	0
18	60	18	40	2	17	2	0
19	59	11	52	0	19	3	0
20	58	8	48	1	22	2	1
21	35	12	69	0	21	16[b]	6[c]

[a] The figures in this table total well over 100 percent per Majlis because certain representatives practiced several occupations.

[b] With the Twenty-first Majlis, the industrial aristocracy first appeared as a category. The statistics for this period reveal that five deputies were "capitalists, industrial shareholders, factory owners, . . ."

[c] This 6 percent includes nine workers and two peasants.

Source: Shaji'ī, *Nimāyandigān-i Majlis-i Shawrā-yi Millī,* pp. 180, 267.

Table 4—Occupations of Majlis Representatives During the Three Constitutional Periods (In Percentages)

	Constitutional Period		
Occupation	FIRST 1906–1926	SECOND 1926–1941	THIRD 1941–1963
Landlord	39	57	57
Merchant-Trader	15	16	13
Government Employee	44	39	46
Cleric	24	11	4
Professional-Technical	12	17	19
Private Industry	3	2	2
Lower Class	0	1	0

Source: Shaji'ī, *Nimāyandigān-i Majlis-i Shawrā-yi Millī,* p. 180.

Majlis membership had been engaged in professional-technical occupations, whereas the clerics were completely unrepresented. According to Table 3, 69 percent of the Twenty-first Majlis membership was composed of former government employees. These were virtually all middle-ranking bureaucrats who had been land reform officials and members of the new middle class. The government and professional-technical employees together accounted for a majority of Majlis membership.

These interrelated patterns of recruitment control, legitimizing emphases, personally informal decision-making, overlapping membership, and persistent coöptation have invested the Majlis with an extraordinary capacity to preserve traditional sociopolitical processes in Iran. In the first place, these intralegislative patterns are congruent with those that mark the social and political systems in general. They overlap and interlock with similar patterns that prevail in the royal family, the cabinet, the party organizations, and the civil and military bureaucracies.[23] Second, by embodying these processes, the Majlis is able to preserve itself as a central political institution in Iran. This in turn allows it to preserve and propagate the very patterns it embodies. The implications of this kind of legislative mechanism for the processes of modernization in Iran are of profound import.

The mere existence of a legislature has come to suggest national progress and political modernization. In Iran, for example, it reflects increased participation and institutionalization—the two developmental indices most frequently stressed by political scholars.[24] Yet, the Majlis has been an important force preserving traditional political patterns and buttressing the position of a powerful monarch. It has functioned in the context of an archaic social class structure and has been instrumental in the persisting existence of this structure. The Majlis has maintained itself in a political system where strong executive-monarchical forces continually extend direct, personal, informal, and ascriptive control. This situation suggests that watchwords of modernization such as participation and institutionalization must be carefully reassessed and discriminately redefined.

The study of legislative politics demands profound and comparative re-examination. By analyzing the experience of non-Western legislative systems, one is led to suggest a number of unorthodox propositions concerning the role of legislatures in a changing society. Genuine participation and deep political institutionalization are not necessarily advanced by legislative bodies. Legislatures can instead promote misrepresentation, under-representation, and pseudo-representation. Legislatures can serve as instruments that subtly impede change and preserve patterns of oppression and repression. Western-styled legislatures grafted on to the political systems of non-Western cultures, for example, reflect an illusory picture of legitimation and modernization. Legislative bodies thus become forces of reaction that build additional staying power into crumbling social and political systems. By concealing traditional patterns with the mask of considered modernity, legislatures raise the cost of modernization and the price that will inevitably have to be paid for system transformation.

[23] See Norman Jacobs, *The Sociology of Development: Iran as an Asian Case Study* (New York: Frederick A. Praeger, 1966) and Bill, "The Plasticity of Informal Politics."

[24] See, for example, Samuel P. Huntington, *Political Order in Changing Societies* (New Haven: Yale University Press, 1968).

Legislative
Decision-Making

PARTY AND CONSTITUENCY INFLUENCES

Voting in State Senates: Party and Constituency Influences

by HUGH L. LeBLANC

State legislatures are held accountable to the people through electoral processes based on geographical boundaries. No matter what roles he plays in the legislative process and regardless of whether a district can or should be represented,[1] the legislator seeking an additional term must convince the voters of his constituency that he should be returned to office.

The study which follows was prompted by the belief that electoral accountability is more rationally ordered when party serves as a short-hand term to orient the voter in his electoral choices and a reference group, immediate or not,[2] for the legislator in his voting decisions. The presumption is the familiar responsible party argument. Party responsibility in turn, some evidence suggests, is fostered under a competitive party system where the constituencies that elect the candidates of one party are reasonably homogeneous and recognizably different from the constituencies that elect the candidates of the other party.[3] The extent to which the constituency conditions supposedly favorable to party responsibility are actually met in the states and correlate with legislative divisions

---

[1] The best study of legislative roles is John C. Wahlke *et al. The Legislative System* (New York: John Wiley, 1962), particularly Part IV. Pp. 287–88 discuss the difficulties of representing a district.

[2] For a discussion of the diffuse effects of party, see Fred I. Greenstein and Elton F. Jackson, "A Second Look at the Validity of Roll Call Analysis," *Midwest Journal of Political Science*, Vol. 7 (1963), pp. 161–63.

[3] See the discussion and studies cited in Thomas A. Flinn, "Party Responsibility in the States: Some Causal Factors," *American Political Science Review*, Vol. 58 (1964), pp. 60–71.

Reprinted from "Voting in State Senates: Party and Constituency Influences," *Midwest Journal of Political Science* 13, no. 1 (February 1969): 33–57, by Hugh L. LeBlanc by permission of the Wayne State University Press and the author. Copyright © 1969 by Wayne State University Press.

is little known.[4] Accordingly, the purpose of this study is to investigate the links to be found between party and constituency characteristics and roll call votes in state senates.[5]

Data Sources

Data for the roll calls were compiled from a single session of each of 26 state senates. Inasmuch as a broad coverage was thereby insured, states were selected in large measure by the availability of their senate journals in the Library of Congress. No Southern states were included, however, because party competition was a major focus of the paper.

The session year studied was either 1959 or 1960, the later year if the senate met in regular session, to coincide as nearly as possible with the collection of census data. Population shifts otherwise might have marred the usefulness of an analysis of constituency influences on senate voting.

The decision to study only state senates was dictated in part by their smaller size in comparison to lower houses. Collection of roll call data thus was made easier. Of more significance, however, was the greater likelihood that constituency data for senatorial districts could be compiled from accessible census materials. Small-sized representative districts in metropolitan areas would have posed almost insuperable problems of data collection.

Roll calls selected for study in each senate satisfied one of two levels of conflict. The more inclusive test accepted for analysis all roll call votes of the session in which at least 10 percent of those voting dissented from the majority position. A second more rigorous test extracted only those roll calls in which party majorities stood in opposition to one another.

Each of the bills contested by the two sets of roll calls was classified for more detailed study according to functional area as follows: appropriations, education, election administration, health and welfare, judicial and legal, labor, legislative organization and procedures, local subdivisions, natural resources, business regulation, state administration, taxation and revenue, and transportation and motor vehicles.

The choice of constituency variables to compare to roll call votes was limited by the comparability of data compiled from published and unpublished census tracts and *The City and County Data Book*.[6] Stated as percentages of their respective groupings in each of the senatorial districts, the variables were: nonwhite population; foreign stock population; persons with five years and under

[4] See the two articles by Norman Meller, "Legislative Behavior Research," *Western Political Quarterly*, Vol. 13 (1960), pp. 131–53 and "Legislative Behavior Revisited: A Review of Five Years' Publications," *Western Political Quarterly*, Vol. 18 (1965), pp. 776–93. Of particular significance is the limited use of multi-variate analysis to link constituency characteristics to roll calls.

[5] This study is a revision of a paper delivered at the Southwestern Political Science Association Annual Meeting of 1967. I was assisted in its preparation by a grant from the Washington *Evening Star* to The George Washington University. The assistance of The George Washington University Computer Center is also gratefully acknowledged.

[6] Census tract data were made to conform to data published in *The City and County Data Book* because the latter were applicable to more senate districts in more convenient form.

schooling; persons with high school education and better; families with under $3,000 income: families with $10,000 income and over; unemployed workers; unemployed male workers; workers employed in non-durable manufacturing; workers employed in durable manufacturing; sound homes with all plumbing facilities; owner occupied homes; and the Democratic vote when available for presidential electors, 1960, and governor and state senator for years appropriate to the legislative past under investigation.

Difficulty was experienced in collecting constituency data for those senatorial districts drawn within county boundaries. The data (other than voting variables) could be obtained only by totaling figures from census tracts that lay within each senate district. If census tracts were carved out so as to avoid crossing district lines, the problem was merely that of tedium. If census tracts overlapped senate boundaries, a more serious problem was posed. It was here decided no great violence would be done to the data by including within a senatorial district any census tract that lay more than half within the district boundary since: (a) the constituency variables were all stated in percentage terms and (b) census tracts are drawn to represent homogeneous areas.

Intra-party Cohesion and Inter-party Conflict

The Rice index of cohesion is often rendered useless as a test of party strength in state legislatures because of the inflationary effect of the large number of unanimous and near unanimous roll call votes.[7] Party cohesion was impressive in some state senates, however, when the test was applied to roll calls marked by a 10 percent or more disagreement vote (Table 1). Some overstatement of party effectiveness is yet possible, particularly if the divisive roll calls clustered about the 10 percent cut-off figure. More convincing evidence that party is a rallying force was the rise in the mean level of party cohesion in most senates when party majorities were aligned against each other (Table 1).[8]

Although party cohesion was related to party opposition votes in state senates, it was not a direct function of the narrowness of control of the majority party (Table 1).[9] The Rhode Island senate was almost evenly divided and each vote was a closely fought test of party strength. Yet the party division within the Utah senate was even closer and roll calls found many straying across party lines. Nor did parties with a dominant majority necessarily turn inward to contest

[7] A discussion of the strengths and weaknesses of roll call analysis can be found in Lee F. Anderson *et al.*, *Legislative Roll Call Analysis* (Evanston: Northwestern University Press, 1966) Ch. 1, and David B. Truman, *The Congressional Party* (New York: John Wiley, 1959), pp. 10–14. For a discussion of party as a reference group and a summary of roll call studies treating state legislatures, see Malcolm E. Jewell and Samuel C. Patterson, *The Legislative Process in the United States* (New York: Random House, 1966), pp. 416–26.

[8] Reflecting partially, of course, the arithmetic involved in computing the index.

[9] Wiggins concluded from a study of six sessions of the Iowa legislature that although party balance was of marginal significance as a determinant of the frequency of party voting, it was positively related to variations in cohesion of the parties. Charles W. Wiggins, "Party Politics in the Iowa Legislature," *Midwest Journal of Political Science*, Vol. 11 (1967), pp. 86–87.

Table 1—Conflict and Cohesion in 26 State Senates, 1959 or 1960

	Number of Senators		GUBER-NATORIAL PARTY	Number of Bills		Mean Index of Cohesion Democrats		Mean Index of Cohesion Republicans		Mean Index of Likeness	
	DEMS.	REPS.		ALL DIV.[a]	PARTY OPP.	ALL DIV.[a]	PARTY OPP.	ALL DIV.[a]	PARTY OPP.	ALL DIV.[a]	PARTY OPP.
California	27	13	D	219	37	58	48	59	57	79	48
Connecticut	29	7	D	6	3	94	90	78	67	42	6
Delaware	11	6	R	188	116	68	84	77	87	37	14
Idaho	27	17	R	161	49	50	58	55	62	70	40
Illinois	24	34	R	274	74	45	75	75	63	56	31
Indiana	23	27	R	243	124	65	65	60	68	56	34
Iowa	18	32	D	241	94	66	69	60	60	66	35
Kansas	8	32	D	82	29	55	49	80	82	63	34
Kentucky	30	8	D	64	25	48	51	51	59	66	45
Massachusetts	23	16	D	158	117	72	78	67	77	37	23
Michigan	12	22	D	142	82	73	81	72	75	46	22
Missouri	26	8	D	57	20	45	49	62	63	67	44
Montana	38	18	R	164	60	66	54	59	56	71	45
Nevada	7	10	D	29	8	55	70	56	43	73	43
New Hampshire	6	18	R	66	41	58	63	35	38	60	49
New Jersey	7	13	D	13	6	79	85	65	90	50	12
New York	24	34	R	64	45	68	76	81	88	35	18
Ohio	20	13	D	305	210	81	83	61	71	39	23
Oregon	19	11	R	219	64	59	55	59	64	69	40
Pennsylvania	22	28	D	260	213	78	82	85	90	25	14
Rhode Island	23	21	R	12	12	99	99	96	96	3	3
South Dakota	20	15	D	162	72	60	67	61	67	59	33
Utah	12	13	R	46	12	50	41	61	53	74	53
Vermont	8	22	R	80	32	63	63	38	41	66	48
Washington	35	14	D	181	90	59	60	71	78	55	31
West Virginia	23	9	R	86	46	73	85	58	73	48	21

[a] Includes all roll calls in which at least 10 percent of those voting dissented from the majority position.

issues of public policy. Kansas Republicans and Connecticut Democrats, for example, maintained party ranks with impressive solidarity despite lopsided majorities.[10]

No interstate pattern was found that related cohesion to the majority or minority status of the senate parties. The senates were almost evenly distributed between those in which the majority party achieved greater cohesion and those in which the minority party was more united. The relative level of unity obtained by the parties was seemingly unaffected by their control of the office of governor. Neither the majority party nor the minority party was identified by greater relative unity significantly more times when it controlled the governorship than when it was not similarly advantaged. Such conditions might have proved important if viewed historically within a state but were left untested by our cross-sectional analysis.[11]

The degree of party conflict found in state senates appears related to levels of urbanization and industrialization within a state.[12] An unprecise test of this relationship is to compare measures of party conflict to measures of urbanization and industrialization in Spearman rank-difference correlations. The percentage of a state's population living in SMSA's was used as an index of urbanization rather than the percentage residing in urban places. Because the Census definition of the latter includes all incorporated cities of 2500 population, it does not reflect as well contemporary urban living. The measure employed for industrialization was the percentage of the work force engaged in occupations other than agriculture, fisheries, and forestry.[13] Because percentage figures do not convey absolute size, they may not convey accurately the stage of industrial development within a state. Until a certain threshold is reached, the actual numbers employed in industrially related enterprises may have greater political significance than the relative numbers so engaged. Nevertheless, the measure does suggest some degree of economic diversity which might be politically relevant. The correlations presented in Table 2 confirm a relationship between party conflict and indices of urbanization and industrialization, particularly when the index of likeness is used as the test of party conflict.

The California senate was easily the outstanding exception to the relationships suggested by Table 2. Despite its large cities and industries, California has never exhibited high partisanship in its politics. Regional conflict, equal representation of counties in the senate, and a tradition of political non-partisan-

[10] In explaining party cohesion Duane Lockard emphasized the organizational strength of Connecticut parties in *New England State Politics* (Princeton: Princeton University Press, 1959), Ch. 9; Jewell and Patterson noted the coincidence of increased cohesion and increased use of the caucus in Kansas, *op. cit.*, p. 425.

[11] Malcolm Jewell reached essentially the same conclusion in his study of eight state legislatures, *op. cit.*, p. 791. A study showing gubernatorial influence on legislatures is Sarah P. McCally, "The Governor and His Legislative Party," *American Political Science Review*, Vol. 60 (1960), pp. 923–42.

[12] Among the first to offer statistical verification of this thesis was Malcolm Jewell, "Party Voting in American State Legislature," *American Political Science Review*, Vol. 49 (1955), pp. 773–91; see also Jewell and Patterson, *op. cit.*, pp. 422–26 and Austin Ranney, "Parties in State Politics" and Thomas R. Dye, "State Legislative Politics" in Herbert Jacob and Kenneth N. Vines (ed.), *Politics in the American States* (Boston: Little, Brown, 1965), pp. 67–70, 153–57.

[13] This was the measure used by Thomas R. Dye in *Politics, Economics, and the Public* (Chicago: Rand McNally, 1966). See pp. 29–30.

ship given recognition in the practice of cross-filing all help to explain the low level of party conflict in its senate. Although other states did not fit comfortably into the pattern, they did not display California's consistent departure from the hypothesized relationship in all of the comparisons made; that is, states whose ranking in urbanism did not closely match their ranking in party conflict displayed a better relationship between their rankings in industrialization and party conflict, and so on. Although the correlation coefficients suggest much unexplained variance, one is led nevertheless to speculate that a complex social and economic structure associated with advanced industrialization provides a base for parties whose constituencies are divided broadly along class-status lines. Differences between the parties then arise in part from their response to their separate constituencies and to matters of their own self-interest in roll call votes.

Table 2—Spearman Rank-Difference Correlations Comparing Measures of Party Conflict and Measures of Urbanization and Industrialization

	% of Population in SMSA's	% of Work Force Employed in Occupations other than Agriculture, Fisheries, and Forestry
Percentage of Divisive Roll Calls with Opposing Party Majorities	.21[a]	.52
Mean Index of Likeness	.45	.61

[a] Not statistically significant at .05 level.

Regional historical influences might also be important in explaining variations in levels of party conflict. No state senate in which party opposition votes constituted a majority of divisive roll calls or whose index of likeness for divisive roll calls was 50 or below came from west of the Mississippi. No state east of the Mississippi, excluding the one-party or modified one-party states of New Hampshire, Kentucky, and Vermont, had a higher index of likeness than any states west of the Mississippi. One obvious difference between East and West that has political relevance, apart from the greater concentration of urban-industrial states east of the Mississippi, is in the size and saliency of the ethnic vote. The influx of immigrants into the urban centers of the East and Midwest in the decades surrounding the turn of the century produced a distinctive brand of politics marked by policy postures derived from the "immigrant ethos" and political organizations based in the big city machine.[14] The effects of this political style linger on and help to emphasize partisan political behavior in those regions. On the other hand, more sparse settlement of the West and the egali-

[14] The ethos theory was originally stated by Hofstadter and elaborated by Banfield and Wilson; see Raymond Wolfinger and John Osgood Field, "Political Ethos and the Structure of City Government," *American Political Science Review*, Vol. 60 (1966), p. 306. Although Wolfinger and Field concluded in their study that structure and policies of local governments are related to regional differences and are not a function of ethnicity, they suggest that "certain regional historical experiences related to the influx of immigrants and the responses to their needs" may help to explain the development of particular political forms (p. 320).

tarian influence of the frontier may have relieved the newly arrived from organizing politically as a defensive measure against established groups and fostered an individualism that eschewed partisanship in politics.

Partisanship and Issue Areas

To determine if party voting was associated with particular types of issues, the 10 most partisan bills, determined by the index of likeness, and the 10 most divisive bills, ignoring partisan stand, were recorded for each of the senates. It was thought that the most severe examples of each type of legislative conflict might be more revealing of the role of party than an examination of all divisive bills. At least it would show the types of issues that pressed the parties to unite against their opposite numbers and the types of issues in which the parties were least able or concerned to maintain ranks. Measures which produced the sharpest partisan contest in state senates conformed only partially to orthodox thinking that links party voting to socio-economic issues and matters of party self-interest[15] (Table 3). The summary of most partisan roll calls shows only a

Table 3—Summary of Lists of Ten Most Partisan and Ten Most Divisive Bills by Issue Categories, 26 State Senates, 1959 or 1960

	Most Partisan Lists		Most Divisive Lists (Ignoring party stand)		N
	NO. OF STATES REPRESENTED	NO. OF BILLS LISTED[a]	NO. OF STATES REPRESENTED	NO. OF BILLS LISTED[a]	
Taxation and Revenue	17	74	18	32	400
State Administration	17	55	18	42	360
Appropriations	16	71	12	18	280
Legislative Organization	14	54	10	18	161
Labor	14	53	12	18	212
Judicial and Legal	14	23	19	37	286
Election Administration	13	29	6	6	97
Local Subdivisions	11	25	15	22	393
Regulation of Business	9	18	19	37	357
Education	9	17	11	14	192
Transportation and Motor Vehicles	9	14	8	15	227
Health and Welfare	6	10	6	9	116
Natural Resources	4	4	4	6	104

$r_s = .54$ (comparing most partisan and most divisive lists)[b]

a The number of bills does not sum to 260 because of ties for the tenth rank. Parties in Pennsylvania, Ohio and Delaware, for example, recorded zero indexes of likeness on a total of 184 roll call votes.

b The rankings were determined by the number of state lists in which an issue appeared. In case of a tie, the number of bills recorded in an issue category determined rank.

15 Jewell and Patterson states that party cohesion "is more likely to appear if the measure fits into one of three categories: (1) issues involving the prestige and fundamental programs of the administration, (2) social and economic proposals for welfare programs or the regulation of business or labor-issues associated with the 'liberal-conservative' dichotomy, (3) issues involving the special interests of the parties or legislative organizations and procedures." *Op. cit.*, p. 430. See also Thomas R. Dye, *op. cit.*, pp. 186 and 187.

comparatively limited number of bills relating to health and welfare and business regulation issues. The number of partisan contests over diverse judicial and legal bills was surprising because substantial issues of civil or political rights seldom were involved. On the other hand, party-serving bills classified as election administration, legislative organization, and state administration predictably aroused partisan loyalties, as did revenue, appropriation, and labor issues which likely involved a governor's or a party's program commitments.

There were few discernible patterns in comparing the lists of partisan issues. Bills that dealt with natural resources were among the more partisan issues in 4 state senates, all of the West. Health and Welfare bills achieved high partisan ranking only in large industrial states. Labor bills appeared more frequently on the lists of urbanized-industrialized states but were also among lists of Kansas, Iowa, Montana, and Missouri. No other issue categories were obviously associated with either the degree of partisanship, the level of industrialization or the regional location of a state.

A comparison of the issue categories that produced the highest partisan contests with those that divided senates closely but along other than party lines reveals a surprising similarity (Table 3). However, a further examination showed that the individual bills that produced the closest roll call votes seldom were the same as those that divided the parties most sharply. Because party strength in most senates was unevenly distributed, a substantial duplication could have occurred only if party ranks had been regularly maintained.

The Spearman rank-difference correlation between the summaries of the most partisan and most divisive lists was .54. The greatest dissimilarity occurred in three issue categories. Election administration and legislative organization issues aroused struggles between parties rather than clashes that split parties internally; this was to be expected since they are characteristically partisan measures. Business regulation was a more intriguing exception. Not only was it absent from most lists of highly partisan issues, which we have commented on earlier, but it ranked near the top of divisive issues handled by senates when partisan stand was ignored.

When party conflict within issue categories was measured by the index of likeness the rank order of partisan issues differed from the standings based on each state's list of 10 most partisan bills (cf. Tables 3 and 4). Issues of judicial and legal affairs fell to the lower half of the list of partisan subjects, suggesting a particularized character to those bills with partisan appeal that was not revealed by our classification. Issues of party self-interest (election administration and legislative organization) moved to the head of partisan topics, displacing measures that more likely involved programmatic commitments (appropriations and taxation and revenue). Still conspicuous by their absence from upper ranking were the issue categories of business regulation and health and welfare.

Much the same issue categories were found to be contested along party lines in senates of both high and low levels of partisanship (Table 4).[16] The more

---

[16] The senates were divided into equal groups by levels of partisanship as measured by the index of likeness.

Table 4—Conflict and Cohesion in Divisive Roll Calls of 26 State Senates by Issue Categories, 1959 or 1960

	Mean Index of Likeness						Mean Index of Cohesion					
			MOST PARTISAN SENATES [a]		LESS PARTISAN SENATES [a]		ALL SENATES		MOST PARTISAN SENATES [a]		LESS PARTISAN SENATES [a]	
	ALL SENATES	N		N		N	Dems.	Reps.	Dems.	Reps.	Dems.	Reps.
Election Administration	38	97	20	60	55	37	78	66	89	75	68	59
Legislative Organization	38	161	21	88	57	73	73	70	87	85	57	53
Labor	43	212	24	127	58	85	67	79	73	87	63	57
Taxation and Revenue	50	400	35	211	64	189	63	68	71	77	55	59
Appropriations	51	280	32	156	68	124	70	69	82	74	59	66
State Administration	51	360	40	188	61	172	68	63	74	72	61	55
Transportation and Motor Vehicles	58	227	42	128	75	99	57	62	63	72	50	51
Local Subdivisions	61	393	47	212	74	181	64	58	72	65	58	53
Judicial and Legal	62	286	52	139	72	147	61	58	69	63	55	53
Education	63	192	57	94	74	98	65	57	69	64	61	51
Health and Welfare	64	116	52	76	79	40	55	66	59	65	49	67
Regulation of Business	64	357	57	185	72	172	58	57	61	59	55	54
Natural Resources	75	104	68	38	80	66	55	59	56	51	54	64

$r_s = .87$ (comparing most partisan and less partisan)

$r_s = .50$ (comparing Democrats and Republicans, all senates)

[a] The senates were divided into equal groups by the index of likeness.

partisan senates differed from the less partisan mainly in the scope and intensity of conflict, that is, more bills provoked party battles in the more partisan senates and party lines were more sharply drawn. The Spearman rank-difference correlation between the issue categories of the two senate groups was .87.

Democratic voting was compared to Republican voting in the several issue categories by means of the index of cohesion (Table 4). That party cohesion generally improved with party opposition votes has already been noted. Thus one might infer that the same issue categories would produce the highest cohesion for both parties although on opposite sides of the question. Such an inference is generally correct despite some dissimilarities (Republican senators were more cohesive than Democratic senators in labor and health and welfare issues, less cohesive in issues of election administration). No striking differences are revealed by comparing senates of high and low levels of partisanship.

A further examination was made of individual bills which produced the lowest cohesion in each of the parties to determine if Democratic senators split badly over the same bills as Republican senators. This was not the case, a discreteness suggestive of partisan influences. However, when the bills were grouped by issue categories, the differences were lost. The issue categories that badly divided Republicans differed little from those that proved most troublesome to Democratic senators.

Senate Voting and Constituency Variables

We have shown thus far that partisanship in state senates varied by states and with issues. We turn now to the question of whether party voting reflected constituency factors, since such a relationship, if established, would tend to support the hypothesis that partisanship is caused in part by the response of each party to the more or less distinct constituency that provides its durable support.

It is understood, of course, that constituency influences on legislative voting are sometimes difficult to disentangle from party influences and the dictates of the legislator's own conscience or convictions.[17] Often the several influences reinforce one another.[18] Thus an individual of liberal convictions is politically involved in the Democratic party for that reason and, as the Democratic party's candidate for senator, is victorious at the polls in a constituency conventionally

[17] Compare Warren E. Miller and Donald E. Stokes, "Constituency Influence in Congress," *American Political Science Review*, Vol. 57 (1963), pp. 50–51. According to Miller and Stokes, three requirements must be met to insure constituency *control*: ".... the Representative's votes ... must agree substantially with his own policy views or his perceptions of the district's views, and not be determined entirely by other influences ...:"; ".... the attitudes or perceptions governing the Representative's acts must correspond, at least imperfectly, to the district's actual opinions"; and "the constituency must in some measure take the policy views of candidates into account in choosing a Representative." The fact of electoral accountability, however, could cause a legislator to vote his constituency whether or not the voter understood or weighed policy alternatives; and a legislator could vote his constituency by relying on external influences (party) if party and constituency pressures were reasonably congruent.

[18] See Loren K. Waldman, "Liberalism of Congressmen and the Presidential Vote in Their Districts," *Midwest Journal of Political Science*, Vol. 11 (1967), p. 83.

associated with Democratic party success—perhaps a racially-mixed, low income, urban constituency, heavily populated with industrial workers. In voting to increase workmen's compensation payments, the senator could be said to vote his convictions, his party's program, and his constituency. When there is a congruency among legislator's attitude, party tradition, and constituency characteristics, it seems to me, the precise reference point for the legislator's vote is of minor consequence to the question of accountability.

Although in my judgment legislative-constituency relations are more logical when a party's legislative record mirrors its electoral majority, legislative voting may still be linked meaningfully to constituency characteristics even though party voting is infrequent. It is the absence of demonstrable legislative constituency relations that causes apprehension. One may, of course, view the legislative system as a decisional body confronted by the complex issues of modern-day society whose choices either cannot or should not be linked to the artificial boundaries of legislative districts.[19] Yet the voter here is deprived of basic references to guide his electoral choices. In the face of survey research, one cannot be sanguine about voter perception of issues unrelated to party or constituency interests.

To test for constituency relationships, the voting record of each senator in all party opposition votes was compared to selected variables of his constituency in both simple and multiple regression equations. The constituency variables were stated in percentage figures (see above). The dependent or predicted variable was a voting index constructed for each senator from the proportion of times he voted with the Democratic party majority. The index ranged from zero to 100, with a score of zero indicating complete opposition to the Democratic party majority, and a score of 100 indicating perfect loyalty to the Democratic party. The coefficient of correlation that was computed measures the linear relation between the constituency variables and the voting indexes of the senators for each state.

The single best predictor of legislative voting among the variables tested proved to be the votes cast in election contests in 13 states (Table 5).[20] Considering only those among the 13 with complete election statistics, voting in either gubernatorial or presidential elections together ranked as the best predictor more often than voting in state senatorial elections.[21] Moreover, with but a single exception, when either presidential or gubernatorial voting was the best predictor, the two strongly inter-correlated but not with senate voting—that is,

---

[19] See Wahlke et al., *op. cit.*, pp. 303–04. One should not forget, however, that state-wide laws have local impact. A district does not have to be represented *per se* but can be viewed as part of the whole.

[20] For a discussion of electoral margins and their effect on party voting, see Jewell and Patterson, *op. cit.*, pp. 438–39 and the sources they cite. Our regression equation measured only a linear relation between popular voting and legislative voting and did not control for "typicalness" of district. Flinn has noted that the relationship between electoral plurality and legislative behavior in Ohio is non-linear, that once a certain threshold is reached, vote margins no longer operate to affect party loyalty. *Op. cit.*, p. 67.

[21] The correlations between presidential voting and legislative divisions are all the more interesting because the legislative sessions occurred prior to the presidential election measured. On the other hand, gubernatorial elections were selected that placed a governor in power during the legislative sessions under study and coincided with the elections of one-half of the senate bodies.

Table 5—The Relationship Between Individual Constituency Variables and Support of the Democratic Party Stand in Party Opposition Votes of 23 State Senates, 1959 or 1960[a]

	% OF POPULATION		% OF PERSONS 25 AND OVER		% OF FAMILIES EARNING		LABOR FORCE			% OF HOMES		DEMOCRATIC % OF		
	Non-white	Foreign stock	with 5 years schooling and under	with High School Diploma & over	under $3,000 Income	$10,000 income and over	Unemployed	Employed in Non-durable Manu-facturing	Employed in Durable Manu-facturing	Sound with Plumbing	Owner Occu-pied	Sena-torial Vote	Guber-natorial Vote	Presi-dential Vote
California	.32	-.01	.11	.15	.01	-.16	.14	.04	.01	-.18	-.24	.06	.15	-.05
Connecticut	.37	.49	.51	-.59	.46	-.51	.46	.16	.07	-.44	-.43	.53	N.A.	N.A.
Illinois	.36	.23	.35	-.39	.02	-.04	.29	.30	.04	-.08	-.36	.55	N.A.	N.A.
Idaho	-.19	.25	.00	-.28	.34	-.33	.26	-.49	.29	-.44	-.16	N.A.	.27	.21
Indiana	.06	.25	N.A.	N.A.	.09	-.20	.18	.26	.10	-.15	-.10	.60	.62	.50
Iowa	.33	-.10	-.32	-.47	-.25	.23	.19	.27	.26	.10	.28	.28	.58	.53
Kansas	.05	-.27	-.35	-.49	.19	-.17	.47	.26	.20	-.16	.22	.30	.30	.20
Kentucky	-.16	.19	-.13	-.02	-.15	.18	.04	.11	.06	.19	.14	N.A.	N.A.	N.A.
Massachusetts	.23	.37	.28	-.27	.21	-.22	.11	.13	.01	-.28	-.41	-.28	N.A.	N.A.
Michigan	.37	.70	.42	-.07	-.03	.17	.51	.46	.17	.29	-.23	.79	.77	N.A.
Missouri	.01	.24	-.17	.23	-.31	.13	-.05	.24	.24	.25	-.03	.15	N.A.	N.A.
Montana	-.16	.14	-.04	.16	-.29	.21	.25	.04	N.A.	.30	.11	N.A.	.40	.28
New Hampshire	.13	.68	.41	-.36	-.30	.10	.51	.34	-.45	.50	-.27	N.A.	.21	.58
New York	.45	.47	.59	-.12	.28	-.21	.07	.28	-.44	-.06	-.66	.82	N.A.	N.A.
Ohio	.15	.45	.12	-.13	-.30	.29	.31	.14	.27	.26	.32	.70	.65	.52
Oregon	.40	.31	.03	.07	-.54	.31	-.48	.17	.00	.25	-.25	.43	.68	.74
Pennsylvania	.46	.47	.41	-.11	.16	-.14	.29	.27	-.10	-.04	-.39	.85	.77	.71
Rhode Island	.12	.72	.12	-.41	-.08	-.11	.29	.31	.45	.15	-.09	.78	.66	N.A.
South Dakota	-.11	.00	-.06	.08	.17	-.11	.13	.02	-.24	-.03	.00	N.A.	.57	.49
Utah	.06	-.17	.41	.02	.27	-.52	.28	.13	-.13	-.28	.11	.30	N.A.	N.A.
Vermont	.51	.13	.35	.08	-.31	.47	.26	.04	-.32	.57	.01	N.A.	N.A.	N.A.
Washington	.14	-.04	.15	-.15	.06	-.38	.18	.25	.27	-.02	.10	.20	.55	.58
West Virginia	.49	.00	.40	-.12	.08	.05	.23	-.32	-.26	-.08	-.40	.23	.61	.60

a Because of the small size of their senates, Delaware, Nevada, and New Jersey were excluded from the multiple regression analysis and no print-out was obtained of the simple correlation coefficients of their independent variables. In separate runs comparing only voting variables to legislative divisions, Delaware showed correlations of .23, .46, and .38 for senatorial, gubernatorial, and presidential voting respectively; Nevada, -.03, .17, and .32; New Jersey, .28, .26, and .56. In interpreting the table, it should be remembered that the correlations are not based on a sampling of either constituencies or roll-call votes and therefore the statistical problem of a normal distribution does not arise.

senate voting had significantly less predictive power than either of the other two variables. On the other hand, when senate voting was the best predictor, the three voting variables were better inter-correlated, although presidential voting was the weakest predictor.

One surmises that the reference provided by national party labels in presidential elections is more clearly perceived by the voters in some states than the labels provided in state senate contests, and that this perception of the meaning of national party affiliation reasonably approximates the senator's perception of the objectives of his state party as reflected in his legislative voting. That gubernatorial voting was a consistent predictor of senate roll calls (either predicting best or correlating well with the best popular voting predictor) might be attributed to two facts: (1) the greater visibility of gubernatorial politics compared to state legislative politics and, similar to presidential contests, a better orientation of the voter; and (2) the possibility that the governor's electoral margin within a senatorial district cues the senator on the necessity of supporting the administration program out of a concern for electoral security.[22]

Significantly, one of the popular voting variables was the strongest link to legislative voting in nine of the 11 more partisan senates.[23] Alternatively, popular voting in only three of the 11 less partisan senates was linked more closely to electoral margins than to other constituency factors. The inference is that where partisanship is significant, the party label is important as a common reference for both legislative divisions and popular voting.

If party does not provide a reference for his vote and, particularly, if a senator is impressed by the admonition of the legislative hornbook to vote his constituency, factors other than partisan strength within his district should affect his legislative decisions.[24] This presumption was tested in two ways. Social and economic variables were grouped with election statistics in a multiple regression equation to determine if they would strengthen the correlation with legislative voting. Then election statistics were dropped from the equation to determine constituency relations unencumbered by electoral preferences.

The addition of social and economic variables clearly improved the correlation with senate voting in 17 of the 21 states examined (cf. Tables 5 and 6). In six of the 17 states, social and economic factors actually displaced voting as a predictor as the multiple regression analysis followed a program of discarding the independent variable contributing the least to the combined correlation until a significance level of .10 was attained for each variable. In 11 states, social and economic variables strengthened the multiple correlation but as a complement

[22] Although inferring state patterns from congressional practice is risky business, Waldman found the size of the presidential vote in congressional districts affected the Congressman's voting record. *Op. cit.*, pp. 73–85.

[23] Voting in presidential elections in New Jersey, where legislative partisanship is high, is also probably the best predictor of legislative divisions in that state. See footnote to Table 5.

[24] See Duncan MacRae, Jr., "The Relation between Roll Call Votes and Constituencies in the Massachusetts House of Representatives," *American Political Science Review*, Vol. 46 (1952), pp. 1046–55; Thomas R. Dye, "A Comparison of Constituency Influences in the Upper and Lower Chambers of a State Legislature," *Western Political Quarterly*, Vol. 74 (1961), pp. 473–80; John G. Grumm, "A Factor Analysis of Legislative Behavior," *Midwest Journal of Political Science*, Vol. 7 (1963), pp. 336–56; and Thomas A. Flinn, *op. cit.*

Table 6—The Relationship Between Combined Constituency Variables and Support of the Democratic Party Stand in Party Opposition Votes of 23 State Senates

	ALL CONSTITUENCY VARIABLES			ONLY SOCIO-ECONOMIC VARIABLES	
	No. of Election Variables[a]	No. of Socio-Econ. Variables[a]	Multiple Correlation Coefficents	No. of Variables[a]	Multiple Correlation Coefficients
More Partisan Senates[b]					
Connecticut	0	5	.73	5	.73
Illinois	1	1	.55	3	.55
Indiana	2	0	.70	3	.50
Massachusetts	0	4	.66	4	.66
Michigan	1	4	.91	5	.86
New York	1	1	.83	4	.76
Ohio	1	6	.89	6	.86
Pennsylvania	1	1	.85	2	.64
Rhode Island	1	2	.81	6	.80
Washington	1	3	.69	3	.60
West Virginia	2	5	.82	5	.72
Less Partisan Senates[b]					
California	0	3	.45	3	.45
Idaho	1	3	.68	4	.67
Iowa	2	2	.70	1	.47
Kansas	0	5	.67	5	.67
Kentucky	–	–	–	6	.58
Missouri	0	3	.46	3	.46
Montana	1	3	.59	3	.48
New Hampshire	2	2	.87	5	.81
Oregon	1	2	.82	2	.65
South Dakota	1	1	.62	4	.54
Utah	0	4	.74	4	.74
Vermont	–	–	–	4	.84

[a] The program used discarded independent variables contributing the least strength to the multiple correlation until each reached a significance level of at least .10. The multiple R was significant at least to the .01 level in every state but Kentucky, Missouri and South Dakota where it tested to the .05 level.

[b] Because of the small size of their senates, Delaware, Nevada, and New Jersey were excluded from the multiple regression analysis. No election figures were available for Kentucky and Vermont at the time the program was run. Other state analyses included election statistics for at least one office. See Table 5.

to the voting variables. Only slight improvement in predictive ability was achieved by adding to the voting variables in the remaining four states.[25]

When constituency variables other than election statistics were compared to senate voting in a multiple regression analysis, a linear relation was found to exist, significant at least to the .01 level in twenty of the twenty-three states examined, and significant to the .05 level in the remaining three states (Table 6).[26]

[25] For these four states, one may conclude that non-voting variables did not add independently to the multiple correlations but one cannot state they showed no relation to legislative divisions.

[26] Compare to Dye who found in Pennsylvania "no significant relationship . . . between the party cohesion displayed by senators and either their margin of election or the socio-economic composition of their districts." Thomas R. Dye, *op. cit.*, p. 479.

The amount of variance explained by the socio-economic variables ranged from a low of twenty percent in California to seventy-three percent in Michigan and seventy-four percent in Ohio.

The predictive power of constituency variables is associated with the level of partisanship in state senates. The Spearman rank-difference correlation between the multiple regression coefficients (comparing all constituency variables to senate voting) and the mean indexes of likeness for the state senates was .51. This was better than the rank-difference correlations found when the multiple regression coefficients were compared to measures of industrialization and urbanization. Even when election variables were excluded, the multiple cor-relation coefficients were slightly better related to the mean indexes of likeness of the state senates than to measures of urbanization and industrialization within the states. Table 7 shows the relationships.

Table 7—Spearman Rank-Difference Correlations Comparing the Predictive Power of Constituency Variables with Measures of Party Competition, Urbanization, and Industrialization

	Mean Index of Likeness	*% Residing in SMSA's*	*% Employed in Occupations other than Agriculture, Fisheries and Forestry*
Predictive power of all constituency variables	.51	.09 [a]	.38
Predictive power of socio-economic variables only (excludes voting)	.46	.06 [a]	.44

[a] Not statistically significant at .05 level.

One may infer from the above that socio-economic interests of constitu-encies are more likely perceived as differentiated by senators from the more industrialized states who are inclined to vote their constituencies. This often results in party votes. However, the senator frequently perceives his constituency in terms of the voting strength of his party as well as its socio-economic charac-teristics and thus gains an additional reference for his legislative vote. Where this is the case, partisan voting in state senates is more pronounced and legislative-constituency relations are the strongest. Thus the average amount of variance explained by all constituency variables in the roll call votes of the eleven most partisan senates was 60 percent, the eleven less partisan senates, 41 percent.

The socio-economic factors that appeared most often as reliable predictors of legislative voting in the 11 more partisan senates were the percentages of foreign stock (8 states) and non-white (6 states), both positively linked to support of the stand taken by a majority of Democratic senators. Families earning income of $10,000 or better correlated negatively with Democratic voting in four states, but positively in Ohio and West Virginia. Because senators in Ohio stand election county-wide, it is possible that the family income correlation is spurious. One might guess that factors of urbanism, not tested, are the genuine indicators. Low income areas of mountain Republicanism coupled with traditional Democratic dominance in the relatively high income cities may account for the positive correlation in West Virginia.

Estimates made (where possible) of the strength each independent variable contributed to the multiple correlation coefficient confirmed the predictive power of the foreign stock variable in the more partisan senates (Table 8). The percentage of non-white population also lent important strength to the multiple correlations and, with a single exception, in the same states where the percentage of foreign stock was significant. In only West Virginia and Washington of the more partisan grouping was neither variable important. The percentage of families earning income of $10,000 or more accounted for more than 90 per cent of the explained variation in the Washington senate, while the percentage of persons with five years schooling and under accounted for two-thirds of the explained variance in the West Virginia senate.

Less homogeneity and more ambiguity characterized the relation of constituency factors and legislative voting in the less partisan senates. No single factor in the regression analysis predicted consistently in more than three states. For seven of the 12 independent variables examined, both positive and negative correlations were found in different senates. Nor did estimates of the contribution made by independent variables to the multiple correlations reveal recognizable patterns (Table 8). The percentage of families earning under $3,000 income explained more variance than any other independent variable, but it correlated negatively with the Democratic party stand in two states, positively in two, and was scarcely significant in one.

Although constituency variables generally related less well to voting in senates of lower partisanship, impressive correlations were found in some. In those states with strong senate-constituency relations, the national image of the parties was weakly reflected. Kansas and Utah were the closest to the national model in that senators who opposed the Democratic party stand were elected from the higher income constituencies (Kansas and Utah) and the better educated constituencies (Kansas); while senators who supported the Democratic party stand were elected from the more poorly educated constituencies (Utah). The more impressive correlations, nevertheless, were found in New Hampshire and Vermont, whose parties were imperfect copies of their national counterparts. In Vermont, for example, opposition to the Democratic party stand came from senators who were elected from constituencies of low income families (probably Republican farmers) and constituencies with a higher percentage of workers employed in durable manufacturing, while constituencies with a high percentage of homes classified as sound by the Bureau of Census elected senators who supported the Democratic party majority. Regardless of the pattern, strong constituency-legislative vote relations coupled with weak party cohesion suggests that political parties have not capitalized on constituency differences. Yet a political realignment may be difficult if the state has a tradition

Table 8—Estimates of the Contribution of Individual Variables to the Explained Variance in Party Opposition Roll Call Votes in 18 State Senates, 1959 or 1960

Percentage of Variation Explained By Individual Variables[a]

	% of Variation Explained by Multiple Correlations	% OF POPULATION Non-white	% OF POPULATION Foreign Stock	% OF PERSONS 25 AND OVER with 5 Years Schooling & Under	% OF PERSONS 25 AND OVER High School Diploma & Over	% OF FAMILIES EARNING under $3,000 income	% OF FAMILIES EARNING $10,000 Income & Over	% of Male Workers Unemployed	% OF LABOR FORCE Unemployed	% OF LABOR FORCE Employed in Nondurable Manu.	% OF LABOR FORCE Employed in Durable Manu.	% OF HOMES Sound with Plumbing	% OF HOMES Owner Occupied
Illinois	30	11	6		(−)13								
Indiana	26		11			(−) 8							
Michigan	73		43	2					21	6	5		
New York	57	13	27		(−) 3	(−) 9	(−) 8						
Pennsylvania	41	20	21										
More Partisan Senates													
Rhode Island	64	3	55			(−) 1	(−) 2			2			
Washington[b]	35					(−)32	3			7			(−) 2
West Virginia	52			36	(−) 5	2	(−) 2						(−) 7
Less Partisan Senates													
California	20	11				(−) 1	(−) 9						
Idaho	45		(−)10	(−)22	(−)23	18				(−)17			
Iowa	22												
Kansas[b]	45	(−) 2				(−) 7	(−)10						
Montana	23	(−) 4				(−)10			10			9	6
New Hampshire	66					5			18	17	(−)18		
Oregon	41					(−)33							
South Dakota	29	(−)10		12		10			9				
Utah	54					(−)32	(−) 3			6	(−)17	4	(−) 8
Vermont[b]	71					(−)26					(−)17	30	(−) 9

[a] The estimate of contribution for each variable is the product of its beta-weight times r. The limitation of this method is that the product must be positive. Thus no estimates were possible for Connecticut, Massachusetts, Ohio, Kentucky and Missouri. See J. P. Guilford, *Fundamental Statistics in Psychology and Education* (New York: McGraw-Hill, 1965), 4th ed., p. 400. A negative sign enclosed in parentheses before a percentage figure indicates a negative correlation of the variable with the stand taken by a majority of the Democratic party.

[b] Does not sum perfectly because the beta-weight times r product for one variable shows a small negative value.

of non-partisanship or if the voters are strongly attached to a party whose historical role has made it a symbol of state or regional solidarity in pursuing national objectives.[27]

Summary

The findings which follow must be interpreted with the usual caution. Only a single session year was studied in each state, and a limited time dimension can distort. Implicit in the selection of constituency data was the belief that legislative divisions would reflect class-status or economic issues; other data might have yielded stronger correlations with legislative voting. The analysis was fundamentally quantitative in character; yet a few issues, because of their transcendent importance, might have supplied a better gauge of legislative behavior. Withal, the data offer a useful beginning to a comparative analysis of state legislative behavior.

1. Political parties undoubtedly influenced voting behavior in most state senates, but in varying degrees. Party cohesion was not related directly to the balance of party strength in senate chambers but did improve with party opposition votes. No interstate pattern was found to suggest that the relative level of cohesion displayed by the parties in a state senate was linked to their majority or minority status or to control of the governorship.

2. Party voting in state senates was most obviously linked to states of the East and Midwest characterized by relatively advanced stages of urbanization and industrialization.

3. Party-serving measures of legislative organization and election administration divided senates along party lines most frequently; but revenue, appropriation, and labor bills also produced sharp partisan contests in many states. Business regulation and health and welfare issues ranked relatively low as partisan topics. The more partisan-minded senates differed from the less partisan-minded not so much in the type of issue which produced partisan votes as in the frequency and intensity with which they were contested.

4. The relative level of cohesion shown by senate Democrats in the issue categories was similar to the relative level of cohesion shown by Republicans on the opposite sides of the issue categories. The parties rarely displayed their poorest cohesion over the same bills.

5. A senator's support of the stand taken by a majority of the Democratic party showed a stronger linear relation to the voting strength of his party than any other single variable tested. In some states, voting in presidential or gubernatorial elections was a better predictor than voting for state senators. The linear relation was strengthened in most states by the addition of social and economic variables.

6. Voting in the 11 most partisan-minded senates displayed stronger average correlations with constituency variables than voting in senates of lesser partisan-

---

[27] See V. O. Key, Jr., *American State Politics* (New York: A. A. Knopf, 1956), pp. 20ff.

ship. Senate-constituency relations in the partisan senates reflected the national image of the Democratic party as the party supported in constituencies of racial and ethnic minorities, the low income, and the poorly educated rather than in constituencies of high income and superior education. Foreign stock and non-white populations were impressively linked to legislative voting in some of the industrial states east of the Mississippi.

7. Voting in the 12 least partisan senates exhibited more limited and more ambiguous relations to constituency variables. Not only did fewer variables predict consistently, but the more impressive correlations agreed poorly with popular notions of who supports our political parties.

To place the foregoing in the context of the initial premise which prompted this study: It is probably true that legislative partisanship is encouraged when party and constituency factors are interlocking variables influencing roll call votes. One might argue further that the successful marriage of party and constituency provides the linkage between legislative divisions and constituency characteristics required of responsible political parties. Yet those who pin their hopes of a rationally ordered system on the conditions of responsible parties being met must have cause for apprehension. It may be the case that our present party politics, conceived in the era of the New Deal and nurtured through Fair Deal, New Frontier, and Great Society, is inadequate in describing the political divisions within the states today. Partisanship is not finely drawn in states west of the Mississippi and perhaps never has been. Although the urban eastern half of the country is more comfortable with a New Deal model of politics, even here the significance of party struggles may be questioned. Measures affecting the self-interest of parties rank at the top of partisan contests. Health and welfare and business regulation measures, issues conventionally associated with our party politics, apparently incite less partisan controversy than before. One may wonder too whether the legislative divisions linked so strongly to the foreign stock in several states of the Midwest, Middle Atlantic and lower New England are a function of associated socio-economic character-istics or of ethnic kinship alone. This questioning does not imply that party is wholly inept in performing its brokerage role between people and their govern-ment. It does suggest a concern for the continued saliency of party as a reference group in face of an increasingly younger electorate and a new leadership whose partisan attachments are not built from the same emotional commitments as those whose political loyalties were formed in the decade of the thirties.

CDU Deviancy in the German Bundestag

by GEORGE L. RUECKERT
and WILDER CRANE

The Christian Democratic Union with its Bavarian wing, the Christian Social Union, achieved a majority of members in the German Bundestag which was elected in 1953 and thus became the first German party ever to obtain a majority in parliament. To a large extent, its success was an indication of Chancellor Adenauer's popularity and his ability to bring together diverse elements of German society. However, this diversity of the CDU/CSU has led to lower cohesion in its parliamentary delegation than has been the norm in German politics.

There were 167 roll-call votes during the 1953–57 period of the Bundestag.[1] The CDU deputies were unanimous on 44 of these roll-calls, many of which were foreign policy issues. Twenty-two roll-calls may be regarded as free votes. On 101 roll-call votes, the caucus determined a party position but some deputies abstained or voted against their own party. On an issue concerning equal rights for men and women the deviations resulted in a roll-call defeat for the CDU.[2] On other issues the deviations made the CDU dependent on support from members of other parties to obtain a roll-call victory. These deviants violated what the Germans call caucus compulsion (*Fraktionszwang*). Such action is unusual in German parliamentary practice and, in fact, occurred only five times within the Social Democratic delegation in the entire 1953–57 period.

---

[1] These statistics differ somewhat from those presented in the excellent article by Gerhard Loewenberg, "Parliamentarianism in Western Germany: The Functioning of the Bundestag," *American Political Science Review*, LV, 1 (March, 1961) 87–102. Loewenberg derived his roll-call data for the second Bundestag from the Socialist Party publication *So haben sie abgestimmt!*, *Register und Tabellen der namentlichen Abstimmungen in Bundestag* (2. *Wahlperiode*) 1953–57, Herausgegeben vom Vorstand der SPD, Bonn, 7/57, whereas the roll-call data for this study are derived from the official *Verhandlungen des deutschen Bundestages* (2. *Wahlperiode*).

[2] 206. *Sitzung*, p. 11783 C.

Reprinted from "CDU Deviancy in the German Bundestag," *Journal of Politics* 24 (August 1962): 477–88, by George L. Rueckert and Wilder Crane. Reprinted by permission of the *Journal of Politics* and the authors.

Explanations of the usual high cohesion in German parliamentary delegations often involve assertions that civil servants, who comprise a large group in the Bundestag, can be relied on to be docile followers of the party line. Now that some deviancy in the CDU has been noted, explanations for this deviancy have included assertions that deputies from single-member districts are more likely to deviate than deputies elected by proportional representation and assertions that Protestant deputies may deviate from the position of a predominantly Catholic party. This study is an empirical test of these assertions.[3]

Single-Member Districts vs. P.R.

A prevailing notion about the effect of electoral systems on internal party structure is that representatives elected in single-member districts are more likely to assert their independence from their parties than those elected under a system of proportional representation. It is alleged that those elected in single-member districts will be more subject to constituency pressures and thus will be more likely to deviate from their parties than those dependent on party officials for their positions on election lists. Duverger and others state this notion as a general principle of politics,[4] and some writers on German politics have alleged that the representatives from the single-member districts in the Bonn Republic are more concerned about their districts and less concerned about their parties than were the P.R. representatives in the Weimar Republic.[5]

West Germany's current electoral system provides a unique controlled laboratory experiment for testing this generalization.[6] Approximately one-half of the members of the German Bundestag are elected in single-member districts and the other half from proportional representation lists drawn up in the ten states of the Federal Republic.[7] Because those already elected in single-member

---

[3] This study is restricted to the 236 members who served the entire four year term. It does not include those who began but did not finish the term, the replacements, those who entered the Bundestag when the Saar rejoined Germany in 1957, or those who were elected by other parties and joined the CDU caucus during their terms. While data on these members have been compiled and their votes on roll-calls tabulated, they cannot be included in a study based on the entire four-year session.

[4] See Maurice Duverger, *Political Parties; Their Organization and Activity in the Modern State* (translated by Barbara and Robert North; Wiley, New York, 1954) pp. 264–65 and Robert Neumann, *European and Comparative Government*, 3rd ed., (McGraw; New York, 1960), p. 721. Duverger writes: "In a single-member constituency system in which the elections have an individual character and the constituencies look rather like strongholds devoted to the man rather than to the party label, the local position of the elected representatives is very strong and the party caucuses cannot do much against them; they must continue to provide the support of the party lest they lose the seat. Individual subordination is very slight. On the other hand when there is list-voting, in which the party becomes essential, and in which the support of its caucus can determine success or defeat, this subordination is much greater. The clearest sign of the subordination of the deputy to the party remains the voting discipline . . ." Neumann states succinctly: "P.R. increases party discipline while all kinds of single-member districts tend to weaken it."

[5] See, for example, James K. Pollock, "The Electoral System of the Federal Republic of Germany —A Study of Representative Government," *American Political Science Review*, XLVI (December, 1952) p. 1065.

[6] F. A. Hermens' life-long campaign for single-member districts has been conducted without the benefit of such a controlled laboratory test. See, for example, his recent effort, *The Representative Republic* (University of Notre Dame Press, Notre Dame, 1958) pp. 201–10.

[7] Explanations of the German election system may be found in U.W. Kitzinger, *German Electoral Politics: A Study of the 1957 Campaign* (Oxford University Press, Oxford, 1960), pp. 17–37; and James K. Pollock, ed., *German Democracy at Work* (University of Michigan Press, 1955) pp. 79–103.

districts are taken into consideration in determining the distribution under proportional representation, the CDU delegation has considerably more single-member seats than P.R. seats. Nonetheless, there were enough CDU members elected on proportional representation to conduct a meaningful study.

As Table 1 indicates, CDU members who were elected on proportional representation were considerably more deviant than those elected in single-member districts. Since this result is so clearly at variance with the prevailing notions in the contemporary literature, further tests were made to locate other factors which might account for this unexpected result.[8] Every other factor which had been coded was held constant, and the P.R. members were always more deviant than the district members. These other factors were age, sex, occupation, education, religion, political experience, legislative leadership, external party leadership, and interest group leadership. Table 1 alone dispels the myth that P.R. members are more likely to be loyal to the party, but further analysis suggests that there are factors in German politics which induce P.R. members to be more deviant than their district colleagues.

Table 1—Deviancy of CDU Bundestag Members Categorized According to Nature of Election Districts

Number of Deviations	Single-Member Districts (N-168)	State P.R. Lists (N-68)
0	42%	21%
1–3	42	51
4 or more	16	28
	100%	100%

Civil Servants

The high cohesion of German parliamentary delegations is also commonly explained on the basis that they include many civil servants. Common German practice allows civil servants to stand for election to the Bundestag, take part in political campaigns, and retain their posts if unsuccessful. If elected to the Bundestag, civil servants can retire on pension and then apply for reinstatement on the active list when they cease to be members; this arrangement has resulted in a large number of civil servants in German parliamentary delegations. A common assumption is that these technicians by nature and training prefer administration and adjudication over politics and hence tend to be docile followers of the party line.[9]

---

[8] This result would not be so unexpected by those who have come to recognize the confusion of Burke's analysis which equates district orientation with serving as a mere delegate. See Heinz Eulau *et al.*, "The Role of the Representative: the Theory of Edmund Burke," *American Political Science Review*, LIII, 3 (September, 1959) pp. 742–756.

[9] This assertion has been clearly expressed in the writings of Professor Herbert J. Spiro. See, for example, Herbert J. Spiro, *Government by Constitution* (Random House, Cambridge, Massachusetts, 1959) pp. 287–88; and Herbert J. Spiro, "The German Political System" in Sam Beer and Adam Ulam, ed., *Patterns of Government* (Random House, New York, 1958) p. 374.

Here again an elementary statistical calculation dispels a prevailing myth. Table 2 indicates that civil servants are in fact more deviant than non-civil servants. The subsequent breakdown of all occupational groups in Table 6 indicates that civil servants are exceeded in their deviancy only by those who

Table 2—Deviancy of Civil Servants in the CDU Bundestag Delegation

Number of Deviations	Civil Servants (N-39)	All Others (N-197)
0	23%	38%
1–3	59	42
4 or more	18	20
	100%	100%

listed labor as their occupational backgrounds. Further analyses of the ten roll-call votes on which the greatest number of CDU M.P.'s deviated suggests that their occupational status may be more important in understanding the legislative voting behavior of civil servants than their alleged non-political technical status, for they tended to deviate with labor against business and farmer domination in the party.[10]

Religion

German history from the Thirty Years' War through Bismarck's *Kulturkampf* to the present has been characterized by a Protestant-Catholic religious cleavage frequently marked by violence. The CDU, although its origins go back predominantly to the Catholic Center Party, has attempted to bridge this long-standing rift by soliciting Protestant support and by nominating Protestant candidates. However, Catholics clearly predominate in the party to the extent that one possible explanation for deviancy in the parliamentary delegation is religious cleavage. Many writers have explicitly commented on the serious problem for party cohesion represented by the CDU's unusual interconfessional religious composition.[11]

Whatever these religious differences may be, Table 3 indicates that deviancy

[10] This seems to bear out Herz's observation that "they (German civil servants) are strongly in favor of acting as a pressure group themselves in competition with the other social and occupational interests represented in parties and parliaments." See John H. Herz, "Political Views of the West German Civil Service," in H. Speier and W. P. Davison, *West German Leadership and Foreign Policy*, (Rand Corporation, Evanston, Illinois, 1957) p. 114.

[11] The potential danger of party disintegration inherent in the interdenominational composition of the CDU is stressed especially strongly by German authors. See, for example, Rudolf Wildenmann, *Partei und Fraktion* (Verlag Hain, Meisenheim, 1955) pp. 61–62; and Walter Dirks, "Die Christliche Demokratie in der deutschen Bundesrepublik" *Frankfurter Hefte*, (1 Jg., Heft 9, 1953) pp. 672–75. However, most authors share the view that the interconfessional Christian approach toward social problems is presently a stronger cohesive force in the party than divisive element.

Table 3—Deviancy of CDU Bundestag Members Categorized According to Religion

Number of Deviations	Catholics (N–144)	Protestants (N–92)
0	33%	39%
1–3	47	42
4 or more	20	19
	100%	100%

in the parliamentary delegation cannot be explained by the dissatisfaction of the Protestant minority. On the contrary, the table reveals that Catholic M.P.'s were more deviant than Protestant M.P.'s.

Leadership Status

Having dispelled some prevailing myths about German legislative behavior, this study also makes an attempt to develop some hypotheses about party loyalty and deviancy.

An obvious expectation is that party leaders in the legislative body would be more loyal than backbenchers. Table 4 indicates that this expectation is confirmed by statistical evidence by demonstrating that ministers and presiding officers were most loyal. However, this table also reveals the consequences for party loyalty inherent in the German committee system under which committee chairmen and vice-chairmen are not necessarily members of the executive committee of the party caucus.[12]

Another expectation in politics is that persons who are leaders of the external party organization are more loyal to the party than those who are

Table 4—Deviancy of CDU Bundestag Members Categorized According to Leadership Status in Parliament

Number of Deviations	Presiding Officers (N–3)	Ministers (N–12)	Caucus Leaders (N–31)	Committee Chairmen and Vice Chairmen (N–20)	Backbenchers (N–170)
0	67%	67%	42%	30%	32%
1–3	33	33	48	55	44
4 or more	0	0	10	15	24
	100%	100%	100%	100%	100%

[12] Committee chairmen who were also caucus leaders, i.e., members of the caucus executive committee, are included in the caucus leader category in Table 4. Committee chairmen in the Bundestag are selected by the Council of Elders ("Aeltestenrat"), a group of fifteen deputies chosen by the political parties according to their strength in the assembly. The opposition is awarded some chairmanships, and thus vice chairmanships have been included in this table in those circumstances in which the chairman of the committee was not a member of the CDU.

Table 5—Deviancy of CDU Bundestag Members Categorized According to Leadership Status in External Party Organization (Membership on Party Executive Committees)

Number of Deviations	National (N–18)	State (N–34)	State — Local or Only Local (N–53)	Non-Leaders (N–131)
0	44%	35%	26%	38%
1–3	50	41	55	41
4 or more	6	24	19	21
	100%	100%	100%	100%

simply elected on the party's ticket. Table 5 confirms this expectation for members of the national party executive committee, but it indicates that party officials in the lower echelons of the organization feel no greater compulsion for party regularity in the parliament than those who do not hold positions in the external party organization.

Occupation and Interest Group Leadership

Table 6, which classified deviancy in the CDU according to occupational origins, seems to provide the basis for the most credible hypotheses about German legislative behavior as well as to explain why some prevailing notions are not accurate. This table indicates that, aside from those professional politicians who are difficult to classify in any other occupational category, businessmen are most loyal to the party, followed by farmers, while laborers are the most deviant occupational group. This table thus suggests, without proving it, that business groups exercise the strongest influence in determining the party's position on those domestic issues on which deviancy occurs. It suggests further that farm groups wield important influence in determining party policy. On the

Table 6—Deviancy of CDU Bundestag Members Categorized According to Occupational Origins

Number of Deviations	Politicians[a] (N–15)	Business (N–58)	Professional[b] (N–45)	Miscellaneous[c] (N–15)	Farmers (N–34)	Civil Servants (N–39)	Labor (N–30)
0	73%	47%	40%	33%	32%	23%	17%
1–3	27	45	44	40	47	59	30
4 or more	0	8	16	27	21	18	53
	100%	100%	100%	100%	100%	100%	100%

[a] Politicians include fifteen members who have devoted their lives so exclusively to politics that it is difficult to classify them in any other occupational category. Adenauer, with his long tenure as mayor and now chancellor, would be an example.

[b] Professionals include attorneys, physicians, professors, etc.

[c] This category includes nine housewives as well as those for whom no definite occupations can be determined from their official biographies.

other hand, labor representatives, who share common economic interests with the SPD, presumably enter the CDU primarily because of their Catholic faith, but sometimes deviate from a business-dominated party to vote with the working-class Socialist Party. The importance of this voting pattern is indicated by the fact that seven of the ten issues on while deviancy was greatest were economic issues, principally labor and social welfare.

The hypothesis that CDU voting behavior is principally based on economic factors may also explain why Protestant deviancy in a predominantly Catholic party is so low. Table 7 indicates that labor representatives in the CDU delegation are almost exclusively Catholic, while Protestant members of the CDU delegation include a much higher percentage of businessmen and farmers than is true in the case of Catholics.

Table 7—Occupations of CDU Bundestag Members Categorized According to Religion (Farm, Labor, and Business)

Occupations	Catholic (N–144)	Protestant (N–92)
Labor	19%	2%
Farmers	12	18
Businessmen	24	36
Others	45	44
	100%	100%

While these data support hypotheses concerning the importance of occupational background and economic interests as explanations of CDU voting behavior, they do not provide evidence for explanations of higher deviancy of P.R. members than district members. Here one can only go beyond the data to suggest hypotheses which would require further testing. It appears to the authors that CDU leaders have attempted to balance their party's legislative representation by using their proportional representation lists to include members who could not be elected in single-member districts.[13] These P.R. members apparently represent interests which are not so strong among the party's voters as those interests whose representatives can be elected in single-member districts. Indications of this pattern would include such impressionistic evidence as the following: in rural Bavaria a higher percentage of those labor members elected were on P.R. than in industrial North-Rhine Westfalia or in Baden-Wuerttemberg. (It is further interesting to note that labor members from Bavaria were less deviant than labor members from North-Rhine Westfalia or Baden-Wuerttemberg).

German parties have a built-in system of interest group representation which involves a clear-cut allocation of certain parliamentary seats to representatives

[13] On this point see Klemens Kremer, *Der Abgeordnete* (Isar Verlag, Munich, 1956), p. 25. In addition, Karl Loewenberg, *op. cit.*, p. 89.

of interest groups.[14] Official biographies of Bundestag members reveal that, whatever their occupational origins, many are professional officials of interest groups. Table 8 indicates that the deviancy of these interest group officials is consistent with the similar occupational patterns indicated in Table 6.

Table 8—Deviancy of Interest Group Leaders in CDU Bundestag Delegation (Farm, Business, Labor)

Number of Deviations	Business (N–41)	Farm (N–28)	Labor (N–43)
0	44%	39%	14%
1–3	49	54	37
4 or more	7	7	49
	100%	100%	100%

It seems plausible that these interest group representatives would regard their respective economic organizations as more important reference groups than the party organizations which provided them with parliamentary seats. This hypothesis could be tested only by the systematic interviewing techniques which Wahlke and his associates have used with American legislators,[15] but it now appears to the authors to be the most plausible hypothesis to test.

Beyond its report on roll-call data, this study also suggests something about the nature of the CDU/CSU Party. Although business and farm interests predominate, a genuine effort has been made to establish a majority party in which other groups, including labor, are represented. The price which the party has had to pay for these attempts has been a greater tolerance in legislative voting than has generally characterized German parliamentary behavior. This observation leads to the speculation that, if the SPD hopes to make gains beyond those registered in 1961, it must also broaden its base of support and be prepared to tolerate some deviation.

[14] The exceptional degree to which the deputies of the major German parties are identified with different interest groups is emphasized in Karl Deutsch and Lewis Edinger, *Germany Rejoins the Powers* (Stanford Press, Stanford, 1959) p. 91. Rupert Breitling, *Die Verbaende in der Bundesrepublik* (Hain Verlag, Meisenheim, 1955) pp. 136–137 stresses that this procedure results in mutual advantages for both the interest groups and the political parties.

[15] John C. Wahlke *et al.*, *The Legislative System: Explorations in Legislative Behavior* (John Wiley and Sons, New York, 1962).

MAJORITY-MINORITY RELATIONS

Majority vs. Opposition in the French National Assembly, 1956–1965: A Guttman Scale Analysis

by DAVID M. WOOD

Introduction

A series of significant developments in French politics has recently touched off speculation about the possibility that a major transformation of the structure and behavioral patterns of the system of political parties is taking place.[1] The most salient developments from 1958 until 1967 can be briefly listed: (1) the unprecedented longevity of governmental coalitions throughout the entire span of life of the Fifth Republic (only one Government overthrown in eight years); (2) the near single-party majority attained by the Gaullist UNR in the November, 1962 elections; (3) the ability of five major non-Gaullist parties to coalesce their forces behind only two candidates opposing General de Gaulle in the December, 1965 presidential election, with the resulting necessity for a second ballot; (4) the subsequent merging of forces on the moderate left and the

---

[1] The debate among French observers has centered around the possibility of a two-party system emerging. See *Le bipartisme est-il possible en France?* (Paris: Association Française de Science Politique, 1965). Opinion in this colloquium was weighted toward caution. However, momentarily in the wake of the March, 1967 legislative elections, writers foreseeing a two-party system were having their inning: Alfred Fabre-Luce, "Giscard ou Mendès," *Le Monde* (March 17, 1967), p. 7; Maurice Duverger, "Vers le Dualisme," *Le Monde* (March 19–20, 1967), p. 9. It is an assumption of the present article that considerable *simplification* of the party system can take place without a two-party system necessarily resulting.

Reprinted from "Majority versus Opposition in the French National Assembly, 1956–1965: A Guttman Scale Analysis," *The American Political Science Review* 62 (March 1968): 88–109, by David M. Wood. Reprinted by permission of the American Political Science Association and the author.

moderate right into combinations[2] bent upon coordinated efforts in the March, 1967 legislative elections; (5) the successful construction of a Gaullist electoral alliance limiting the number of official Gaullist first-ballot candidates in each constituency to one; (6) the electoral agreements between the Communists and the moderate left *Fédération* permitting only one candidate of the left to remain in the race in any constituency on the second ballot; and (7) the tendency of voters to reward the united fronts of the outgoing Gaullist majority and the consistent leftist opposition and to penalize the relatively small and ambiguous center force, the *Centre Démocrate*.[3]

These developments seem to add up to two fundamental changes in the nature of the French party system between 1958 and 1967: (1) The number of effective major parties has been reduced from at least six to no more than five.[4] (2) All but one of the major parties can now be identified as a loyal majority partner or a consistent opponent,[5] whereas only two, the Gaullist UNR and the Communists, could be so identified with confidence in the wake of the November, 1958 legislative elections.[6] It has really been only since the 1965 Presidential election that these developments have taken place at a level visible to all but the closest students of the French political scene. Yet before then there already existed one salient fact which distinguished political party behavior under the Fifth Republic from that under the Fourth: government stability. Even during the First Legislature[7] of the Fifth Republic (1958–1962), when no single party was close to having a majority of the seats in the National Assembly, no Government was toppled by the Assembly until nearly four years had elapsed, a record for longevity until then unsurpassed in the history of republican France. Majority cohesiveness was already apparently a reality more than five years before a coherent majority coalition faced the electorate in 1967. Could it be said that a fairly simple majority-opposition division already existed in the Assembly early in the Fifth Republic? Were the voting patterns at that stage appreciably less complex and more predictable than those of the Fourth Republic? Did the legislative election of 1962 effect an abrupt change in the alignment of parties in

[2] *The Fédération des Gauches Démocrates et Socialistes* (left-center) and the *Centre Démocrate* (right-center).

[3] For an incisive account of the 1967 legislative elections see François Goguel, "Les élections législatives de mars 1967, "*Revue française de Science politique,* 17 (June, 1967), 429–67.

[4] The figure "six" for the number of effective major parties in 1958 is rather arbitrary. The following are considered to rate that characterization: the Communists, the Socialists, the Radicals, the MRP, the Gaullist UNR, and the Independents. What is striking, however, is that there has been a clear reduction in the number of splinter parties that have to be taken into account. In 1958 there were an additional four or five parties that had to be reckoned with, locally at least. By 1967 only two could by any stretch of the imagination be considered significant: the *Parti Socialist Unifié* on the left and the *Alliance Républicaine* on the right. For 1958 see Philip M. Williams and Martin Harrison, "La Campagne pour la referendum et les élections legislatives," in Association Française de Science Politique, *L' Etablissement de la Cinquième République: Le Referendum de septembre et les élections de novembre 1958* (Paris: Armand Colin, 1960), pp. 21–59.

[5] In the election campaign the five major parties were grouped as follows: majority—UNR and *Républicains Indépendants*; opposition—Communists and *Fédération des Gauches*; ambiguous—*Centre Démocrate*.

[6] Although most of the seven parties identified as "major" for 1958 voiced their support for the policies of General de Gaulle, there was no identifiable majority coalition as there was in 1967.

[7] The term "Legislature" refers to the span of service of a given set of National Assembly deputies from one election to the next, as the term "Congress" refers to a given two-year term of office of members of the U.S. House of Representatives.

the Assembly by giving one party a near majority, or did that election merely accentuate trends already in existence? It is the purpose of this article to shed light on these matters by analyzing voting patterns and trends in the French National Assembly during the period 1956 to 1965, a period which spans the last years of the Fourth Republic and most of the Fifth Republic years up to the present writing. Guttman scale analysis[8] is used as a means of establishing the essential voting patterns that existed during these years and of enabling comparison between the three legislatures elected during that time span, those of 1956, 1958 and 1962.

The use of Guttman scaling in this article may be differentiated from its uses by other students of legislative roll calls whose studies have come to the author's attention.[9] According to the authors of a handbook for legislative roll call analysis, Guttman scaling has been utilized for three purposes: "the characterization of roll calls; the characterization of the voting behavior of individual legislators; and the characterization of the voting behavior of groups of legislators."[10] All three are subsidiary purposes of the present study; but a more fundamental purpose is to characterize three whole legislative bodies and compare them with one another.[11] In order to do this the samples of roll call votes taken for each Legislature have been subjected to the empirical method of scale-searching outlined recently by Duncan MacRae, Jr.[12] In this method no a priori classification of items (roll calls) is made aside from that applied originally in the selection of the sample. The items in the sample are compared with one

---

[8] In addition to the standard fountainhead essay, Louis Guttman, "The Basis for Scalogram Analysis," in Samuel A. Stouffer *et al.*, *Measurement and Prediction*, Vol. IV of *Studies in Social Psychology in World War II* (New York: John Wiley & Sons, Inc., 1966), pp. 60–90, see Duncan MacRae, Jr., *Dimensions of Congressional Voting* (Berkeley and Los Angeles: University of California Press, 1958); and H. Douglas Price, "Are Southern Democrats Different? An Application of Scale Analysis to Senate Voting Patterns," in Nelson W. Polsby, Robert A. Dentler and Paul A. Smith (eds.), *Politics and Social Life* (Boston: Houghton Mifflin Co., 1963), pp. 740–756.

[9] A useful listing of such studies may be found in Lee F. Anderson, Meredith W. Watts, Jr., and Allen R. Wilcox, *Legislative Roll Call Analysis* (Evanston, Ill.: Northwestern University Press, 1966), pp. 120–21, footnote 14.

[10] *Ibid.*, p. 90.

[11] At this level of generality we move away from the initial objectives for which Guttman scaling was devised and first applied to legislative bodies: attitude measurement. The scale has been viewed in earlier studies as a kind of yardstick measuring various degrees to which roll calls express certain underlying attitudes: e.g., George M. Belknap, "A Method for Analyzing Legislative Behavior," *Midwest Journal of Political Science*, 2 (November, 1958), 377–402; and David M. Wood, "Issue Dimensions in a Multi-Party System: The French National Assembly and European Unification," *Midwest Journal of Political Science*, 8 (August, 1964), 255–76. Most students have recognized that the legislative vote is likely to involve a more complex choice situation than the response to a survey question (e.g., Lee F. Anderson, "Variability in the Unidimensionality of Legislative Voting," *Journal of Politics*, 26 (August, 1964), 568–85), and they have therefore paid considerable attention to the relationships that can be found between the positions of legislators on the scales and (1) the various groups, organized and categorical, to which legislators belong or (2) certain properties of the constituencies they represent: e.g., Duncan MacRae, Jr., "Roll Call Votes and Leadership," *Public Opinion Quarterly*, 20 (Fall, 1956), 543–58; Leroy N. Rieselbach, "The Demography of the Congressional Vote on Foreign Aid, 1938–1958," this REVIEW, 58 (September, 1964), 577–88; Samuel C. Patterson, "Dimensions of Voting Behavior in a One-Party Legislature," *Public Opinion Quarterly*, 26 (Summer, 1962), 185–200; Lee F. Anderson, "Individuality in Voting in Congress: A Research Note," *Midwest Journal of Political Science*, 8 (November, 1964), 425–29. In attempting to characterize an entire legislative body in Guttman scaling terms, I hope, among other things, to make evident the possible applications of the tool in *comparative* study, whether cross-national or cross-state.

[12] Duncan MacRae, Jr. "A Method for Identifying Issues and Factions from Legislative Votes," this REVIEW, 59 (1965), 909–26.

another in pair-wise fashion to ascertain whether or not they satisfy some measurement criterion of pair-wise fit. The matrix of pair-wise coefficients is examined to determine what is the largest possible sub-set of items that can be found wherein each pair of items satisfies the fit criterion employed. This sub-set is then extracted from the sample and the remaining items (if any) are subjected to the identical procedure to determine what is the second largest sub-set; and the procedure is repeated as many times as are necessary to characterize every one of the items in the sample as belonging to some sub-set of one item or more.

Studies which have employed this procedure for roll call analysis have frequently found that the largest scale to emerge is heterogeneous in terms of the substance of the issues before the legislators and is considerably larger than the next largest to emerge. Often the smaller scales are more homogeneous in content.[13] This suggests the existence of a dominant alignment of legislators ranging from strong supporters to strong opponents of the existing Government. Only under the stimulus of issues about which the executive leadership is indifferent or which evoke strong loyalties of (for example) a sectional or religious nature that transcend positions *vis-à-vis* the Government, is there likely to be a different alignment emerging, one that will be characteristic only of certain types of issues and not of others. This is particularly likely to be the pattern in a parliamentary system, since many of the votes on substantive issues are treated by the Government as matters of confidence and legislators must take into account the consequence of their votes for the life or death of the Government. It can be argued, therefore, that during the life of a single coalition in a multi-party parliamentary system we should expect to find a single dominant heterogeneous scale encompassing the bulk of at least the more important votes taken, especially those regarded as votes of confidence.

An exception to the above would be a case in which a Government, in order to persist, must hover between two alternative majorities, consisting of a common element of reliable supporters and two mutually exclusive supplementary elements. In such a case one would find two major scales emerging, neither one of them dominant, less heterogeneous than in the normal case but more so than is usually true of the smaller exceptional scales. Whatever the number of dominant scales, however, the legislative body could be divided into three types of legislators according to their positions on the dominant scale or scales: a sub-set of consistent supporters, a sub-set of consistent opponents, and a sub-set of intermediate legislators, now supporting the Government, now opposing it. For any given scale it would be possible to establish lines of demarcation between the types at the points along the scale cut by the confidence vote most positive for the Government and the confidence vote giving it the least support. If more than one scale emerges with confidence votes the ranks of the consistent supporters

---

[13] MacRae's findings fit this pattern for the Democrats in the House of Representatives, but the results for the Republicans are mixed: *ibid.*, 922–23. See also William O. Aydelotte, "Voting Patterns in the British House of Commons in the 1840's," *Comparative Studies in Society and History,* 5 (January, 1963), 134–63; Duncan MacRae, Jr., "Intraparty Divisions and Cabinet Coalitions in the Fourth French Republic," *Comparative Studies in Society and History,* 5 (January, 1963), 164–211; and Loren K. Waldman, "Liberalism of Congressmen and the Presidential Vote in Their Districts," *Midwest Journal of Political Science,* 11 (February, 1967), 73–85.

and opponents are likely to shrink to the advantage of the intermediate type, since the consistent deputies will have to be consistent on all scales or else be counted among the intermediates. As a final ground rule, should a single scale be found encompassing more than one Government, as might happen in a legislature such as the National Assembly of the Fourth Republic, which was unable to sustain any single Government during the entire period between elections, it is regarded as the alignment pattern of a single coalition which, though stable in structure itself, could not sustain a stable Government. This might happen if a group of intermediaries held the balance of power between a frozen group of consistent supporters and a frozen opposition, maintaining its support for a given Government only up to a point, but then withdrawing it, only to serve once again as the key "swing" group for the succeeding Government.

Employing the above assumptions and technique, study has been undertaken of the three legislatures between 1956 and 1965 in order to answer two questions: (1) Has there been a trend during this time toward a less complex, more unidimensional voting structure in the Assembly?[14] (2) Have the consistent supporters and opponents increased as a proportion of the Assembly at the expense of the intermediate element? If there was indeed a trend toward a simplified majority-vs.-opposition voting structure in the Assembly before 1965, the answers to both questions should be positive. In the Scandinavian multiparty parliamentary systems majority and opposition coalitions are fixed at the

[14] Two votes can be considered to share the property of unidimensionality if they divide up the legislative body into only three of the four possible sub-sets shown in the following fourfold table:

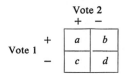

So long as one of the four cells is unoccupied, unidimensionality prevails, although if the unoccupied cell is either a or d, it will be necessary to reverse the signs of one of the items to make the items fit the conventional scale model: Anderson, Watts and Wilcox, *op. cit.*, p. 92:

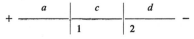

Here cell b is unoccupied and the deputies are divided by votes 1 and 2 into three sub-sets, with those in the center (c) having voted negatively on vote 1 and positively on vote 2. By extension, more than two votes would be perfectly scalable if each of the possible pairs among them exhibited pairwise perfection.

Clearly such perfection in human behavior is unattainable. Some measure of scalability must be used allowing a certain minimum of non-scalar behavior (i.e., a few deputies in the c cell in the above example). Before the pairwise method of scale-finding was introduced an overall measure of scalability, called the coefficient of reproducibility (cr), was used, permitting a certain percentage of "errors of reproducibility" (non-scale votes) scattered throughout the scale: see Guttman, *op. cit.*, p. 77. With the pairwise method MacRae recommends the use of Yule's Q, a correlation coefficient designed for four-fold tables: "A Method for Identifying Issues and Factions from Legislative Votes," *op. cit.* I am impressed by the necessity to measure correlation as well as reproducibility, but prefer a measure which combines the two standards, as ϕ/ϕ max rather neatly does. See Edward E. Cureton, "Note on ϕ/ϕ max," *Psychometrika*, 24 (March, 1959), 89–91. This measure provides for a comparison between cells b and c, which Q does not. The author is indebted to Mr. Joel S. Rose for demonstrating to him the applicability of the ϕ/ϕ max coefficient. By pegging ϕ/ϕ max at the .7 level it was found that no pair of items was admitted to a scale at less than the .94 level of cr for any of the scales of the three legislatures studied. The overall cr's for the five scales analyzed are presented in footnote 36, *infra*.

outset of the Legislature and generally remain in force throughout its life.[15] All members of the legislative body may be counted either as consistent supporters or consistent opponents. Since groups of legislators seldom exchange roles with one another during the Legislature, unidimensionality (albeit a rather uninteresting variety) prevails. While France has not yet reached this limit, the question at hand is whether or not, prior to the Presidential election of 1965 which constrained the parties to assume more overt positions as majority or opposition elements,[16] trends were in existence which moved the National Assembly closer to a pure majority-opposition confrontation than had been the case during the waning years of the Fourth Republic.

The 1956–1958 Legislature

The data utilized in this article are most of the roll calls (*scrutins*) mentioned in *L'Année politique*, the French political yearbook, for the years 1956 to 1965, inclusive.[17] These total 83 for 1956–58, 65 for 1959–62, and 47 for 1962–65. The three legislatures will be analyzed in chronological order, with general comparisons between the three appearing in the concluding section.

The 83 votes for the Third (1956) Legislature of the Fourth Republic are taken from a total universe of 972 taken up to and including the investiture of Pierre Pflimlin as Premier on May 13, 1958.[18] The votes have been classified in terms of the substance of issues involved. These are rather rough categories

---

[15] See Stein Rokkan, "Norway: Numerical Democracy and Corporate Pluralism," and Nils Stjernquist, "Sweden: Stability or Deadlock," in Robert A. Dahl (ed.), *Political Oppositions in Western Democracies* (New Haven: Yale University Press, 1966), pp. 70–146. When compared to the British two-party model, the Scandinavian multi-party systems fall short of a thoroughgoing majority-opposition confrontation. Stjernquist characterizes the Swedish opposition parties' tactics thus: "in election campaigns, the English approach; in parliament and elsewhere, collaboration with the government in order to influence the political decision-making as much as possible": *ibid.*, p. 137. But the dualism is still present, at least in elections, whereas, until 1967, it was non-existent in France. Maurice Duverger has recently stated the thesis that present-day "centrism" in France (i.e., the joining of the centers against the extremes) is nearly unique to France among present-day European countries: *La Démocratie sans le Peuple* (Paris: Editions du Seuil, 1967), pp. 129–32.

[16] Unlike a legislative election, a presidential election forces the parties to choose between a small *finite* number of individual candidates rather than an indefinite number of potential coalitions. With de Gaulle as one of the candidates, parties in the center of the spectrum either had to fall in behind him or support an active, critical opponent. For accounts of the pre-election soul-searching experienced by the parties see William G. Andrews and Stanley Hoffmann, "France: the Search for Presidentialism," in William G. Andrews (ed.), *European Politics I: The Restless Search* (Princeton, N. J.: D. Van Nostrand Company, Inc., 1966), pp. 104–138; and Georges Suffert, *De Defferre à Mitterand: La Campagne présidentielle* (Paris: Editions du Seuil, 1966).

[17] *L'Année politique, économique, sociale et diplomatique en France,* 1956–1965 (Paris: Presses Universitaires de France, 1957–1966). MacRae used roughly the same criterion for identifying important votes in his study of the National Assembly in the Fourth Republic. For his persuasive justification, see *Parliament, Parties and Society in France* (New York: St. Martin's Press, Inc., 1967), pp. 339–41. Only the votes for which *pour* and *contre* totals were given in the "Politique intérieur" section of the yearbook were used in the present study. Several votes with excessive numbers of absences and abstentions were omitted, as were all votes in which more than 90 per cent of the deputies voting positively or negatively voted the same way. Deputies' votes were tabulated from Journal officiel de la République française, *Débats parlementaires, Assemblée Nationale,* 1956–1965.

[18] Seven votes were mentioned in *L'Année politique* for the weeks immediately following the Pflimlin investiture (#974, #977, #986, #989, #990, #993, and #1000). These votes were omitted from the study by my oversight. They include the investiture of General de Gaulle and the granting to him of "pleins pouvoirs."

whose purpose is primarily to make it more evident at a glance whether the various scales obtained are relatively homogeneous or heterogeneous in content:

Category	Symbol	Number of Votes
North Africa	N	20
Budget	B	11
Government (general)	G	9
Social welfare	S	8
Europe	Eu	6
Church-state	Ch	4
Economic policy	Ec	4
Political	Po	4
Constitutional revision	Co	3
Military	M	3
Education	Ed	2
Veterans	V	2
Agriculture	Ag	1
Energy	En	1
Foreign policy	F	1
Housing	H	1
Labor	L	1
Overseas possessions	O	1
Procedural questions	Pr	1

North African votes for the most part concerned the Algerian War, a dominant issue in the Legislature. One vote concerning the Suez crisis of 1956 and two relating primarily to Franco-Tunisian relations in 1958 are also included in the category. Government questions involve debates on general policy surrounding motions of confidence or interpellations. However, confidence motions and interpellation resolutions that are specific to a particular issue are included in the appropriate substantive category. Political votes concern electoral system reform and questions of the eligibility of newly elected deputies after the January, 1956 legislative elections.

Party identification of the 615 individuals who were members of the National Assembly for all or part of the 1956 Legislature is best accomplished by adhering to the *groupes parlementaires* formed within the Assembly for purposes of internal organization. Fragmentary groups not appreciably different from others belonging essentially to the same political "family" are combined with the latter in the following analysis for purposes of simplification. Eleven such groups are identified below roughly as they sat from left to right in the Assembly chamber:

Official Designation	Name Employed in This Study
Groupe communiste	Communists
Groupe socialiste	Socialists
Union démocratique et socialiste de la Résistance	UDSR
Républicains radicals et radicals socialistes	Valois Radicals
Groupe radical-socialiste	Morice Radicals
Rassemblement des Gauches républicaines	Faure Radicals
Républicains Sociaux	Gaullists
Mouvement républicain populaire	MRP
Indépendants et Paysans d'Action sociale	Independents
Groupe paysan	Peasants
Union et Fraternité française	Poujadists

The Morice Radicals are included only in the analysis of the latter part of the Legislature. Their defection from the main body of Radicals (the Valois Radicals) occurred in October, 1956.

Essentially two dimensions emerge from scale analysis of the 1956 Legislature. Use of the scale-finding procedure outlined above produced five separate sub-sets of the 83 items, grouping 51, 28, two, one, and one items respectively.[19] The two largest sub-sets were then subjected to scale analysis.[20] The items in the 51-item scale (Scale A) are analyzed in terms of the categories of votes represented. The votes are listed in the order in which they appear on the scale, beginning with the smallest percentage voting for the position supported by the Government.[21]

The second-largest scale (Scale B) contained 28 items.

The most striking feature of these scales is the clear-cut difference between them in the times when the votes were taken. Whereas the median votes for Scale B (#104 and #105) were taken on May 2, 1956, that for Scale A (#691) was taken on September 25, 1957. Aside from two rather untypical Scale B votes taken in September and October, 1957 (#682 and #692),[22] the overlap between the two scales encompasses only twelve votes, taken between July 11 (#210) and November 19 (#303), 1956. With the exception of this interim period, therefore, it can be said that there were two time-spans during the 1956 Legislature, one from January to June, 1956, and the other from November, 1956 to April, 1958, in each of which there was a single dominant dimension characterizing all or most of the votes taken during the period. In the first of these timespans all 21 votes taken were found to fit on the same scale (Scale B). In the second period, 45 of the 50 votes included in the study for the period were encompassed by the dominant scale (Scale A). For approximately 23 of the 28 months covered in the study virtual unidimensionality prevailed.

Two additional differences between the scales should be noted: (1) The heavier concentration of confidence votes toward the negative end of Scale A than is the case for Scale B indicates that governments found their majorities more precarious during the time period covered by the former. In the median

---

[19] A special computer program was written in Fortran by Mr. Joel S. Rose to find scalable sub-sets in the prescribed fashion. This overcame the almost insurmountable complexities involved in trying to find the largest scalable sub-set from an 83 × 82/2 matrix.

[20] The four non-scalar votes for the Legislature (with substantive categories in parentheses) were #211 (Eu), #840 (Po), #841 (Po), and #972 (G). Only #972 was a confidence vote; it was the investiture vote for the Pflimlin Government. The brace of "Political" votes comes the closest to a small homogeneous scale of any of the sub-sets. Both votes relate to electoral reform.

[21] Roll calls were originally coded according to the criterion that the side on which members of the Government voted should be considered "positive" and the other side "negative." For the two Fifth Republic legislatures, with members of the Government no longer doubling as deputies, the side of the motion supported by the majority of the Gaullist UNR was taken as the positive side. The computer program included a feature whereby pairs of items were flagged if they would scale with the reversal of signs of one of them, thus making it possible to catch items for which the sign criterion was inappropriate. One item (#692) was actually added to Scale B (1956) in this fashion. All of the various types of absences and abstentions by which the *Journal Officiel* classified deputies were combined into a single residual code category.

[22] Both were motions which tended to rally the left and center of the Assembly against the right, an untypical occurrence after late 1956, since the left was usually divided in the period covered by Scale A.

Scale A (1956)

Scrutin	Type	Date	Scrutin	Type	Date
880	Co	Mar. 12, 1958	387	F	Dec. 20, 1956
693*	G	Oct. 28, 1957	420	Eu	Jan. 22, 1957
971	N	Apr. 15, 1958	212	Eu	July 11, 1956
571*	G	May 21, 1957	823	N	Feb. 11, 1958
690*	N	Sept. 26, 1957	655*	N	July 19, 1957
772*	V	Jan. 16, 1958	701	N	Nov. 12, 1957
365*	V	Dec. 10, 1956	846*	M	Mar. 7, 1958
366*	B	Dec. 10, 1956	522	Ag	Mar. 6, 1957
714*	Ec	Dec. 5, 1957	687	N	Sept. 26, 1957
807	N	Jan. 31, 1958	227*	M	July 28, 1956
777*	N	Jan. 22, 1958	873	Ec	Mar. 10, 1957
813	M	Feb. 4, 1958	401	B	Dec. 27, 1956
582*	Ec	June 24, 1957	694*	G	Nov. 5, 1957
942	Co	Mar. 21, 1958	265	N	Oct. 31, 1956
396	B	Dec. 26, 1956	745	B	Dec. 16, 1957
704*	Ec	Nov. 19, 1957	304	B	Nov. 20, 1956
963	N	Mar. 27, 1958	307	B	Nov. 21, 1956
710*	N	Nov. 29, 1957	210	Eu	July 11, 1956
709*	N	Nov. 29, 1957	254*	G	Oct. 25, 1956
367*	B	Dec. 10, 1956	609	Eu	July 4, 1957
364*	B	Dec. 10, 1956	850	Ed	Mar. 8, 1958
884*	Co	Mar. 18, 1958	317	Ed	Nov. 27, 1956
778	N	Jan. 22, 1958	681	N	Sept. 25, 1957
623	Eu	July 9, 1957	608	En	July 2, 1957
748*	B	Dec. 19, 1957	242	G	Oct. 5, 1956
574*	G	June 12, 1957			

Asterisks denote motions of confidence or investiture votes.

Scale B (1956)

Scrutin	Type	Date	Scrutin	Type	Date
105	S	May 2, 1956	11	N	Feb. 7, 1956
692*	G	Oct. 18, 1957	119*	S	May 5, 1956
34	Ch	Feb. 24, 1956	239	B	Aug. 2, 1956
19	Ch	Feb. 17, 1956	37*	L	Feb. 28, 1956
272	Ch	Nov. 8, 1956	103*	S	May 2, 1956
255	Ch	Oct. 26, 1956	120*	S	May 5, 1956
52	N	Mar. 9, 1956	152*	S	June 8, 1956
10	Po	Feb. 7, 1956	6*	G	Jan. 31, 1956
9	Po	Feb. 7, 1956	157	O	June 19, 1956
104*	S	May 2, 1956	682	N	Sept. 25, 1957
151*	S	June 8, 1956	54*	N	Mar. 12, 1956
220*	B	July 25, 1956	56*	N	Mar. 12, 1956
2	Pr	Jan. 25, 1956	53*	N	Mar. 12, 1956
163*	S	June 21, 1956	303	H	Nov. 19, 1956

confidence vote[23] in Scale A (#709) 200 deputies voted against the Gaillard Government; only 108 deputies voted against the Mollet Government in the median confidence vote of Scale B (#103). (2) The two scales differ somewhat also with respect to the nature of the issues involved in the confidence votes. One-half of the Scale B confidence votes involved the Mollet Government's Old Age Fund proposal. This issue, in fact, provided that Government with most of its more difficult confidence motion situations in the early months of its existence. North African confidence votes are prominent in both scales, but it is note-worthy that they were among the least critical of those in Scale B and provided some of the most troublesome, and even disastrous, situations among those in Scale A. Veterans' votes are found only in Scale A, and they were clearly among the most dangerous for governments to face.

The explanation for the scalar pattern outlined above becomes quite evident when the alignment of parliamentary groups on the two scales is examined. Of the 52 possible classes (0 through 51) which individuals could occupy in a 51-item scale, deputies were found in 29 in Scale A. Since many of these classes were occupied by one or a very few members, neighboring classes were combined in such a way that no remaining class, original or combined, would contain less than two percent of the 615 deputies.[24] As a result of the combining 11 classes remain for Scale A. The group distribution among the classes is listed in Table 1.

[23] This refers to the median confidence vote in the order in which confidence votes are arrayed in the above table listing Scale A votes.

[24] The procedure for collapsing scale categories departs from that suggested by MacRae in "A Method for Identifying Issues and Factions from Legislative Votes," *op. cit.* The method used here proceeds from the assumption that, in a parliamentary legislative body, the vote on a given scale which most clearly characterizes a sub-set of legislators is the one at which it first votes against the position advanced by the Government. Thus, as we move from the positive to the negative side of a deputy's voting pattern on the scale, he will be scored according to the point at which the first negative vote that can be deemed scalar appears. This follows the conventional pattern if there are no errors or abstentions on the margin. Thus:

$$(1) \quad - - - - - + + + + +$$

is scored as 5, as is

$$(2) \quad - - - - - + + + - +$$

Errors on the margin pose problems for any scoring convention. The way to mentally "sweep an error under the rug" is to pretend that the vote is what it should have been to conform to the pattern. But what of the following kind of pattern?

$$(3) \quad - - - - + - + + + +$$

Here the problem is whether to treat the marginal + as a − or the marginal − as a +. Under the assumption prevailing in this study we attach greater significance to the negative vote. Thus the + is converted to a − and the deputy scores 4. (Incidentally, deputies are given no score if they have more than 10 percent errors or more than 40 percent absences and abstentions.) Absences and abstentions on the margin are treated as if they were positive votes, since the vote against the Government is deemed the "harder" alternative. Thus,

$$(4) \quad - - - - - 0 + + + +$$

is scored as 5.

Given the importance attached to the first negative vote, we can identify each class on the scale by the vote which separates it from the next most positive class. If a class contains less than two percent of the deputies we must choose whether to combine it with the class to its positive side or with that to its negative side. To resolve this problem the "identifying vote" for the small class is compared with each of its neighbors to see which pair yields the higher ϕ/ϕ max coefficient. Pairs of items with the higher coefficients are combined as are the classes of deputies identified with them. I do not recommend the use of these conventions for other kinds of studies. The particular purpose of the present study—measurement of majority and opposition voting—seemed to warrant it.

Table 1—Scale A (1956)

Class	Group Composition	Cutting Point
10	96 Socialists 21 Valois Radicals 8 UDSR 1 Morice Radical 3 Faure Radicals 1 Gaullist 72 MRP 2 Others —— 204 Total	
9	1 Valois Radical 3 Morice Radicals 2 Faure Radicals 16 Independents —— 22 Total	#880 (March 12, 1958), Triboulet amendment to Constitutional revision report tending to limit number of occasions where confidence and censure motions can apply: 281–211
8	4 Morice Radicals 2 Faure Radicals 10 Independents 1 Peasant —— 17 Total	#971 (April 15, 1958), Government motion to postpone debate on Franco-Tunisian relations (unofficial confidence motion: Gaillard Government falls): 255–321
7	13 Independents 3 Peasants —— 16 Total	#571 (May 21, 1957), Motion of confidence regarding Government fiscal project (Mollet Government falls): 213–250
6	3 Morice Radicals 3 Faure Radicals 4 Gaullists 10 Independents —— 20 Total	#690 (September 30, 1957), Motion of confidence regarding Government project on Algerian institutions (Bourgès-Maunoury Government falls): 253–279
5	3 Gaullists 10 Independents —— 13 Total	#772 (January 16, 1958), Confidence motion posed against agenda propositions of Conference of Presidents, especially relating to veterans' allowances: 253–233
4	1 Gaullist 12 Independents —— 13 Total	#366 (December 10, 1956), Confidence motion regarding budget for Posts, Telegraphs and Telephones: 228–204
3	1 Valois Radical 2 Faure Radicals 6 Independents 3 Peasants 1 Other —— 13 Total	#813 (February 4, 1958), Postponement of debate on organization of Army: 322–248

Table 1—continued

Class	Group Composition	Cutting Point
		#884 (March 18, 1958), Confidence motion regarding adoption of dispositions revising Constitution of 1946: 282–196
2	9 Valois Radicals 1 UDSR 3 Gaullists 4 Independents 1 Peasant 2 Others	
	20 Total	
		#304 (November 20, 1956), Opposition to previous question in debate on Financial project for 1957: 187–382
1	6 Peasants 30 Poujadists	
	36 Total	
		#210 (July 11, 1956), Priority of Government *ordre du jour* in Euratom interpellation debate: 389–181
0	149 Communists 1 Peasant	
	150 Total	

Scale A reveals a solid combination of Socialist and MRP deputies supporting the three governments whose lives spanned the period covered by the votes in the scale. UDSR support was near-perfect, and the governments could count upon them over 60 percent of the Valois Radicals. Opposition, on the other hand, came from the Communists, the Poujadists, most of the Peasants, and some of the Independents, Gaullists and Valois Radicals (those who supported the position of Pierre Mendès-France). In between were ranged the Morice and Faure Radicals and the remainder of the Gaullists, Independents and Peasants. Since the reliable supporters of the Government did not constitute a number sufficient to assure a majority, this intermediate element held the balance of power in the Assembly throughout the entire period from late 1956 to the Spring of 1958.

The alignment of deputies on Scale B bears some resemblance to that of Scale A, but there are also important differences, as Table 2 reveals. In the early months of the Legislature the majority elements included the Communists as well as the Socialists, the UDSR and part of the Valois Radicals (this time including the supporters of Mendès-France, who was still a member of the Government throughout most of this period). But the MRP deputies were at best sometime supporters, although their support was generally forthcoming on confidence motions. The Poujadists were in opposition, as were a somewhat larger number of Independents and Peasants than were in opposition in the Scale A period. Valois and Faure Radicals, Gaullists, and many of the Independents are ranged in between, although because of the support of the sizeable Communist bloc, the Government did not, strictly speaking, need the intermediate votes to retain its majority. The Communists were not regarded as part of the Government's official majority, however. In fact the Mollet Government at this time regarded itself as a "minority Government" which charted its own

Table 2—Scale B (1956)

Class	Group Composition	Cutting Point
9	148 Communists 92 Socialists 1 UDSR 8 Valois Radicals 1 Other ——— 250 Total	
8	1 Communist 1 UDSR 18 Valois Radicals ——— 20 Total	#105 (May 2, 1956), Boisdé amendment to Old Age Fund bill: 263–290
7	2 Socialists 10 UDSR 15 Valois Radicals 1 Gaullist 1 Other ——— 29 Total	#692 (October 18, 1957), Pinay investiture (unsuccessful): 198–248
6	2 UDSR 2 Valois Radicals 2 Gaullists 62 MRP 5 Others ——— 73 Total	#52 (March 12, 1956), Arrighi amendment to bill authorizing special powers in Algeria: 278–305
5	5 Valois Radicals 2 Faure Radicals 5 Gaullists 7 MRP 1 Independent ——— 20 Total	#104 (May 2, 1956), Paquet counter-project to Old Age Fund bill: 178–369
4	1 Valois Radical 9 Faure Radicals 4 Gaullists 5 Independents ——— 19 Total	#163 (June 21, 1956), Confidence motion on National Solidarity bond bill: 314–123
3	2 Faure Radicals 26 Independents ——— 28 Total	#239 (August 2, 1956), Supplementary budget for 1956: 286–130
2	25 Independents 7 Peasants ——— 32 Total	#6 (January 31, 1956), Mollet investiture (successful): 420–71

Table 2—continued

Class	Group Composition	Cutting Point
		#54 (March 12, 1956), Confidence motion on
1	19 Independents	project authorizing Algerian economic expansion
	2 Peasants	project: 451–72
	1 Poujadist	
	22 Total	
		#303 (November 19, 1956), *Loicadre* on construc-
0	1 Gaullist	tion: 490–59
	4 Independents	
	2 Peasants	
	40 Poujadists	
	1 Other	
	48 Total	

course and relied upon the good sense of the centrist groups to prevent a situation wherein the Government must rely upon the Communists' votes to survive.[25]

As events in the Algerian War pushed the Mollet Government more and more toward a policy which the center-right of the Assembly could support, the Communists and the Mendèsist Radicals began to cool toward Mollet and the Socialist leadership. This incipient left opposition became more selective in voting during the summer and early fall of 1956 (the period when votes are found falling on either scale). Finally, in the wake of the Suez crisis and the Hungarian revolt, the Communists turned to systematic opposition. Soon the Mendèsists were voting fairly consistently against the Government and Mollet was talking as if a "new contract" existed (implicitly with the MRP, the dissident Radicals, and perhaps even some of the Gaullists and Independents).[26]

A comparison of the positions of deputies on scales A and B, presented in Table 3, will facilitate the identification of types of deputies according to the threefold classification advanced at the outset of the article (consistent supporters, intermediates, and consistent opponents). Note that deputies who are unclassifiable for one of the scales because of excessive absences or non-scalar votes cannot be included in the table. On each scale there are two cutting points which define the outer limits of tolerance of members of the Assembly. They are the cutting points which fall closest to the confidence votes in each scale wherein the largest and smallest number of deputies respectively supported the Government. For Scale A the cutting point between classes 8 and 9 is vote #971. Though not officially a confidence motion, it was regarded as such by the Gaillard Government, which fell as a consequence of the adverse vote. It can be considered the most negative confidence vote on the scale for any of the three governments whose lives Scale A votes spanned.[27] The least negative confidence vote on the scale is #254, the closest cutting point to which is that between classes 1 and 0.

25 See *L'Année politique*, 1956, pp. 4–22.
26 *Ibid.*, pp. 80, 97–99.
27 #693, immediately to its negative side, was the unsuccessful second investiture attempt of Guy Mollet, thus not a confidence vote for an active Government.

Table 3—Comparison of Scales A and B (1956)

	9	8	7	6	5	4	3	2	1	0
10	92 Soc. 5 V.R.	8 V.R.	1 Soc. 5 UDSR 5 V.R. 1 Other	2 UDSR 1 V.R. 1 Gaul. 61 MRP	1 V.R. 1 F.R. 7 MRP	1 M.R. 2 F.R.				
9			1 M.R.		2 M.R.	3 Ind.	2 F.R.	2 Ind. 10 Ind.		
8			3 M.R.		1 F.R. 1 Ind.	1 F.R. 1 Ind.	2 Ind.	2 Ind. 1 Peas.	3 Ind.	
7						1 Ind.	5 Ind.	5 Ind. 2 Peas. 1 Other		
6			1 Gaul.	1 M.R. 1 Gaul.	1 M.R. 1 Gaul.	3 F.R.	3 Ind.	4 Ind.	3 Ind.	
5					1 Gaul.	1 Gaul.	4 Ind.	4 Ind.	2 Ind.	
4						1 Gaul.	2 Ind.	1 Ind.	5 Ind.	3 Ind.
3					1 V.R.	2 F.R.		2 Ind. 1 Peas. 1 Other	2 Ind.	1 Peas.
2		3 V.R. 1 UDSR	4 V.R		1 Gaul.			1 Ind.	2 Ind. 1 Peas.	1 Ind. 2 Oth.
1									30 Pouj. 6 Oth.	
0	146 Com.	1 Com.								1 Peas.

However, Class 1 is populated by Poujadist and ex-Poujadist deputies who actually abstained on vote #254 and who consistently refused their support to any Government on any confidence motion. Hence it is preferable to move up the scale to the cutting point between classes 1 and 2, which falls closest to the second most positive confidence vote on the scale, #694, the vote on which the Gaillard Government was invested. Below this line of demarcation are the deputies who were consistent opponents to all governments throughout the period covered by Scale A. Above the line between classes 8 and 9 are the consistent supporters of all three governments. For Scale B the counterparts are the cutting point between classes 0 and 1 and that between classes 5 and 6.[28]

Above Class 8 on Scale A and to the left of Class 5 on Scale B are found the consistent supporters of all governments during the entire Legislature. Below Class 2 on Scale A and to the right of Class 1 on Scale B are the consistent opponents. In the remaining occupied cells are the intermediate deputies, those who supported one or more governments up to a point or who supported one or

[28] #104 is chosen for the dividing line between the consistent majority and the intermediates rather than #692, which is the unsuccessful investiture attempt of Antoine Pinay.

two governments consistently but not all three. Below are listed the deputies belonging to each type, grouped according to party affiliation:

Consistent Supporters	Intermediates	Consistent Opponents
93 Socialists	147 Communists	1 Peasant
7 UDSR	1 UDSR	30 Poujadists
19 Valois Radicals	9 Valois Radicals	6 Others
1 Morice Radical	8 Morice Radicals	—
1 Gaullist	12 Faure Radicals	37 Total (7%)
61 MRP	7 Gaullists	
1 Other	7 MRP	
———	74 Independents	
183 Total (37%)	6 Peasants	
	4 Others	
	———	
	275 Total (56%)	

The key to the Legislature is to be found in the intermediate category. Lacking a majority of consistent supporters governments were forced to choose between two mutually exclusive combinations determined by the inclinations of different kinds of intermediate deputies. A majority of the left could be obtained by collaborating with the deputies in the lower left hand corner of the table (Communists and Mendèsists). But the moment a Government sought to pursue a course of action which these left elements could not approve, it was forced to the right, where there were not enough reliable deputies to put together a lasting majority. All three governments fell as a result of the defection of deputies toward the upper right corner of the table, deputies in Scale A classes 6, 7 and 8 who had generally opposed the Mollet Government during its early months. All three classes were weighted heavily with Independents, the most prominent intermediate group other than the Communists. Quite clearly the balance of power which governments of the center-left faced during the period from late 1956 until the Spring of 1958 was held by deputies whose coloration was well to the right of center.[29]

[29] The interpretation of the 1956 Legislature advanced here does not differ significantly from MacRae's intra-party scale analysis of the National Assembly in the Fourth Republic. See *Parliament, Parties and Society in France: 1946–1958, op. cit.,* pp. 157–78. *Inter-*party scale analysis does seem to bring out two features more clearly: (1) the sharp break in voting alignments occurring in late 1956; and (2) the unidimensional pattern extending through 2½ governments from late 1956 to April 1958. MacRae does note differences in scalar patterns for both the "Moderates" (Independents and Peasants) and the "Radicals" (Valois Radicals and UDSR) as between the early and late parts of the Mollet Government. He sees the cut-off point for his Radicals, however, as being in the Spring of 1957, rather than in late 1956: *ibid.,* pp. 171–73. Yet, in December, 1956, a substantial proportion of the Mendèsists voted against three confidence motions on the budget (#365, #366, and #367), although they were not yet joined by Mendès-France himself. (Indeed his three positive votes on these motions were non-scalar with respect to the rest of his voting pattern and made it impossible to give him a score.) This break-away behavior by a significant group of Radicals on motions of confidence certainly must have meant a basic re-positioning of deputies within the party by late 1956.

Beyond very general statements it is difficult to compare MacRae's results with those for this study for three reasons: (1) Scale analysis is more sensitive to slight variations in individual voting patterns within individual parties than within the Assembly at large, since individual inconsistencies are counterbalanced in the latter by the monolithic consistency of large parties like the Communists

The 1958–1962 Legislature

North African issues played an important role again in the 1958 Legislature, as the Algerian crisis continued to plague the French political system. However, several other issue areas shared equal time in the Assembly, as can be seen in the following list:[30]

Category	Symbol	Number of Votes
North Africa	N	10
Procedural questions	Pr	10
Agriculture	Ag	9
Budget	B	9
Church-state	Ch	8
Overseas possessions	O	5
Government (general)	G	4
Military	M	4
Social welfare	S	3
Constitutional revision	Co	1
Economic policy	Ec	1
Veterans	V	1

Procedural questions are, for the most part, votes taken on the new rules of procedure adopted by the Assembly at the outset of the Legislature. North African votes include, among others, four dealing with extremist activity in both Algeria and Metropolitan France and the measures taken by the Government to curb it.

Only six *groupes parlementaires* existed in the Legislature, partly as a result of the rules change which elevated the minimum number of deputies eligible to constitute a *groupe* from 14 to 30. In the following list the names used for purposes of this study ignore the fact that several of these groups are marriages of convenience of a number of parties and isolated individuals:

---

and the Socialists. (2) Since he could only employ roll call votes on which the party was divided internally, MacRae's sample of votes consulted for any given party was likely to be smaller than that used here for the Assembly as a whole and unlikely to be at all representative of it. (3) MacRae endeavored to reduce roll calls to nearly dichotomous items by interpreting abstentions as either positive or negative votes, or by creating two items out of one, interpreting the abstentions first as + votes and second as − votes. This certainly makes for a more rigorous pre-condition to scaling than is true of the procedure used in the present study, wherein abstentions were ignored in the original pairing and in the eventual *cr* calculation. However, I feared that an arbitrary assignment of abstentions to the + or − side would distort the pattern of majority and opposition voting for a string of items. Admittedly, however, in the procedure used here distortion occurs in the scoring, where it is also necessary to interpret abstentions as + or − votes. I consider this method (see footnote 22, *supra*) less arbitrary than MacRae's *for the purpose of capturing the relative positions of deputies vis-à-vis the Government*, which was not MacRae's central purpose. For MacRae's scaling procedures see *ibid.*, pp. 339–52.

[30] The 65 votes examined are from a total of 196 taken during the Legislature.

Official Designation	Name Employed in This Study
Groupe socialiste	Socialists
Union pour la Nouvelle République	UNR
Républicains populaires et Centre démocratique	MRP
Entente démocratique	Radicals
Unité de la République	Algerians
Indépendants et Paysans d'Action sociale	Independents

Several smaller party units remained outside these formations for all or part of the four year period, being unable to constitute *groupes parlementaires* for want of 30 members. Most notable of these were the Communists, whose ranks had been reduced to ten through the impact of the electoral law, which had replaced proportional representation with the second ballot plurality system. Since they are easily identified, the Communists will be treated hereafter as if they were an official group.

Scale analysis of the 65 items reveals the striking finding that there was a more complex multidimensional voting pattern in the First Legislature of the Fifth Republic than in the last Legislature of the Fourth Republic. Three distinct scales were pulled out, numbering 36, 11 and five items. Only the first two will be analyzed, since they contain votes on motions of censure while the third scale does not.[31] The 36-item scale (Scale A) is analyzed below in terms of the categories of votes represented:

Scale A (1958)

Scrutin	Type	Date	Scrutin	Type	Date
151	Ag	Oct. 12, 1961	84	Ag	May 19, 1960
153	Ag	Oct. 18, 1961	27	Pr	June 3, 1959
196*	Co	Oct. 4, 1962	17	Pr	May 28, 1959
66	B	Dec. 17, 1959	188	Ec	June 21, 1962
112	M	Oct. 18, 1960	120	B	Nov. 13, 1960
191*	G	July 16, 1962	78	Ag	May 12, 1960
130*	M	Dec. 6, 1960	116	B	Oct. 27, 1960
177	B	Dec. 11, 1961	73	Ch	Dec. 23, 1959
122*	M	Nov. 22, 1960	7	Pr	Jan. 21, 1959
179	B	Dec. 12, 1961	72	Ch	Dec. 23, 1959
185	G	Apr. 21, 1962	32	Ch	July 1, 1959
113*	M	Oct. 24, 1960	33	Ch	July 1, 1959
36	Pr	July 21, 1959	14	S	May 14, 1959
80	Ag	May 18, 1960	70	Ch	Dec. 23, 1959
9	Pr	Apr. 28, 1959	34	Ch	July 2, 1959
76*	Pr	May 5, 1960	28	N	June 10, 1959
46	B	Oct. 29, 1959	1	G	Jan. 16, 1959
58*	G	Nov. 27, 1959	71	Ch	Dec. 23, 1959

[31] Of the five votes on the third scale, three deal with procedural questions (#5, #10 and #18) and two concern agriculture (#30 and #195). For speculation as to the meaning of this juxtaposition, see David M. Wood, "The Shifting Bases of Legislative Majorities in the French Fifth Republic: A Guttman Scale Analysis," paper delivered at the 1966 meeting of the Midwest Conference of Political Scientists, Chicago, April 30, 1966. The 13 non-scalar votes are widely distributed among substantive types. Three are budget votes (#63, #165 and #166), two deal with North Africa (#74 and #184), two with social welfare measures (#99 and #100), two with agriculture (#106 and #109), one with procedure (#3), one with overseas territories (#77), and one with veterans (#118). One of the North African votes (#184) was a censure motion. It differed in voting distribution from that of the main 1958 scale (see Table 4, *infra*) only in the inversion of position of some of the Algerian and Independent deputies toward the negative end of the scale.

Altogether, 55 percent of the total number of items appear on the scale. The percentage is higher for the first half of the Legislature: 58 percent of the votes taken during 1959 and 1960 appear on the scale (72 percent for 1959 alone) as opposed to 47 percent of the votes for 1961 and 1962. This distribution is not as strikingly skewed as that for the 1956 Legislature, however. More arresting is the fact that the higher numbered votes (i.e., those taken later in the Legislature) tend more than the lower numbered votes to fall at the negative end of the scale, indicating a tendency for support for the Government to fall off as the Legislature progressed. An examination of the dates of the seven motions of censure will reinforce this impression.

Of the eight classifications having four or more of the original 64 votes, only two, North Africa and Overseas possessions, are under-represented among the votes in the scale. Of the five remaining, three (Procedural questions, Agricultural and Budget) are fairly evenly distributed along the scale from the positive to the negative end, whereas two are weighted more heavily toward one end of the scale or the other. Military issues proved to be relatively troublesome for the Government, while Church-state questions accounted for six of the ten most positive votes.

The second scale identified (Scale B) reveals noteworthy differences in content from Scale A. As the following listing shows, all 11 of the votes are of the North Africa and Overseas possessions types:

Scale B (1958)

Scrutin	Type	Date	Scrutin	Type	Date
121	N	Nov. 15, 1960	89	O	June 9, 1960
172	N	Nov. 30, 1961	162	N	Nov. 9, 1961
87	N	June 1, 1960	102	O	July 20, 1960
161	N	Nov. 8, 1961	104	O	July 20, 1960
190	N	July 5, 1962	103	O	July 20, 1960
187*	N	June 5, 1962			

Since the question of the independence of overseas possessions was involved in both kinds of votes, Scale B can be characterized as quite homogeneous in substantive content. However, the time element is also important in distinguishing this scale from Scale A. All of the Scale B votes occurred after 61 percent of the Scale A votes; and the median Scale B vote in time (#121) was taken later than 72 percent of the votes constituting Scale A. Thus the second dimension became an important factor only toward the end of the Legislature. Still, it did not erase the dominant dimension of the early months of the Legislature as had happened in the 1956 Legislature. The votes on Scale A (1958) are differentiable from those on Scale B more in substantive content than in time. The Scale A dimension continued to be the most prominent dimension in the second half of the Legislature, but it cannot be said that unidimensionality prevailed at any time during the four-year period.

Table 4 exhibits the most prominent alignment of deputies in the Assembly

Table 4—Scale A (1958)

Class	Group Composition	Cutting Point
9	169 UNR 5 MRP 3 Algerians 3 Independents 11 Others 191 Total	
8	15 UNR 3 Radicals 5 Independents 3 Others 26 Total	#151 (October 12, 1961), Agriculture price project: 173–270
7	5 UNR 14 MRP 2 Radicals 2 Algerians 26 Independents 4 Others 53 Total	#196 (October 4, 1962), Motion of censure on constitutional revision: 280 *pour*
6	1 UNR 12 MRP 1 Radical 13 Independents 27 Total	#191 (July 16, 1962), Motion of censure in budget debate relating to *force de frappe* and European policy: 206 *pour*
5	6 UNR 5 MRP 21 Algerians 15 Independents 5 Others 52 Total	#179 (December 12, 1961), Final vote on Financial Law, overriding Senate objection: 307–192
4	1 Radical 3 Algerians 24 Independents 1 Other 29 Total	#36 (July 21, 1959), Assembly rules of procedure: 294–126
3	1 MRP 1 Algerian 11 Independents 13 Total	#76 (May 5, 1960), Motion of censure for President's refusal to convoke extraordinary session: 122 *pour*

Table 4—continued

Class	Group Composition	Cutting Point
2	5 MRP 3 Radicals 1 Algerian 5 Independents 1 Other 15 Total	#46 (October 29, 1959), Fiscal reform project: 380–95
1	4 MRP 6 Radicals 2 Independents 2 Others 14 Total	#27 (June 3, 1959), Assembly rules of procedure: 427–91
0	10 Communists 44 Socialists 11 Radicals 65 Total	#32 (May 18, 1960), Amendment to Social Promotion project specifying application to private institutions: 441–73

during the 1958 Legislature. The table shows that, aside from the UNR, the Communists and the Socialists, the parliamentary groups were widely divided internally *vis-à-vis* the Government. Aside from a few renegades who actually departed from the party in the late stages of the Legislature (those in classes 5, 6 and 7), the UNR members solidly supported the Government. Communists, Socialists, and most of the Radicals were consistently in opposition. For most of the votes in the scale the Government enjoyed a comfortable majority, but important test votes beginning in May, 1960 showed that the support for the Government among the MRP, the Algerians and the Independents was not altogether reliable (see classes 3 through 6). Finally, in the censure vote on October 4, 1962, the Government lost the support of a key group dominated by the MRP and the Independents (Class 7). With this vote the Government's support was reduced to a minority of the Assembly, comprising the UNR itself and a handful of other deputies (see classes 9 and 10).

Table 5 presents the essential information for Scale B. On the Algerian policy of General de Gaulle, as it began to move perceptibly toward acquiescence in Algerian independence, the Government could count upon massive majorities consisting of the disciplined parties on the left and the bulk of the UNR and MRP deputies in the center of the spectrum. Opposition came from the Independents and Algerians, as well as from a few MRP and Radical deputies and UNR defectors (the deputies identified as UNR in classes 0 through 3, plus some of those labelled "Others"). Hence, while retaining its strong base of support in the center of the spectrum, the Government compensated for its loss of right-of-center support on Algerian questions by attracting the solid support of the

Table 5—Scale B (1958)

Class	Group Composition	Cutting Point
6	10 Communists 42 Socialists 155 UNR 36 MRP 6 Radicals 4 Others ——— 253 Total	
5	8 UNR 3 MRP 1 Radical 1 Algerian ——— 13 Total	#121 (November 15, 1960), Request for suspension of detention of Pierre Lagaillarde: 201–219
4	2 UNR 7 MRP 15 Radicals 24 Independents 1 Other ——— 49 Total	#172 (November 30, 1961), Amendment to budget bill making local force in Algeria integral part of French armed forces: 218–280
3	9 UNR 2 MRP 9 Radicals 7 Independents ——— 27 Total	#87 (June 1, 1960), Request for suspension of Lagaillarde detention: 165–268
2	1 UNR 4 MRP 1 Radical 1 Algerian 15 Independents 3 Others ——— 25 Total	#161 (November 8, 1961), Credits for Algeria: 332–138
1	3 UNR 4 Radicals 8 Algerians 12 Independents 6 Others ——— 33 Total	#89 (June 9, 1960), Project approving Independence Agreements with Mali Republic: 355–68
0	1 UNR 13 Algerians 35 Independents 11 Others ——— 60 Total	#102 (July 20, 1960), Project approving agreements with Central African Republic, Congo (Brazzaville) and Chad: 384–62

Communists and Socialists. The latter two groups, however, did not extend their support beyond the questions covered by votes on Scale B.

The comparison of scales A and B (1958) in Table 6 shows that there is very little correlation between them, considerably less than between the two 1956 scales. Deputies are scattered more widely among the cells, leaving only 31 percent of them unoccupied, as against 59 percent for the 1956 scales. Consistent supporters of the Government are found above Class 7 on Scale A, having refused to vote the fatal motion of censure of October 4, 1962, and to the left of Class 1 on Scale B. All but ten of the deputies to the left of Scale B Class 1 refused to vote for the motion of censure of June 5, 1962, condemning the Government's Algerian policy, the only censure motion on the scale. None of these ten is found above Class 7 on Scale A. Consistent opponents of the Government are found below Class 3 on Scale A and to the right of Class 2 on Scale B. The cutting point between Scale A classes 2 and 3 (#46) is the closest on the scale

Table 6—Comparison of Scales A and B (1958)

	6	5	4	3	2	1	0
9	139 UNR 4 MRP 7 Others	5 UNR 1 Other	2 UNR 1 MRP 1 Ind.	6 UNR 1 Ind. 1 Other	1 Alg.		
8	8 UNR 2 Rad.	3 UNR	2 Ind.	2 UNR 2 Rad. 1 Ind.			
7	11 MRP 1 Other	1 Rad.	2 MRP 12 Ind.	1 Rad. 2 Ind.	3 Ind.	4 Ind.	2 Ind. 1 Other
6	7 MRP	1 MRP	2 MRP 1 Rad. 3 Ind.		1 UNR 4 Ind.		2 Ind.
5	1 MRP		1 MRP 2 Ind. 1 Other	2 MRP	3 Ind. 1 Other	1 UNR 5 Alg. 1 Ind. 1 Other	12 Alg. 7 Ind. 5 Others
4			1 Rad.		4 Ind.	1 Alg. 2 Ind.	11 Ind. 2 Others
3	1 MRP					3 Ind.	1 Alg. 5 Ind.
2	3 MRP			1 Rad. 1 Ind.	1 MRP	1 Rad. 1 Alg. 2 Ind. 2 Others	4 Ind.
1	2 MRP 1 Rad.		1 Rad.	2 Rad.	2 MRP		1 Ind. 2 Others
0	10 PC 42 Soc. 1 Rad.		7 Rad.				

to the least troublesome censure motion faced by the Government (#58 of November 27, 1959). The remaining deputies on the chart are the intermediates. The following listing shows the distribution of the three types:

Consistent Supporters	Intermediates	Consistent Opponents
165 UNR	10 Communists	1 Radical
5 MRP	42 Socialists	1 Algerian
4 Radicals	2 UNR	7 Independents
1 Algerian	36 MRP	4 Others
5 Independents	17 Radicals	—
9 Others	19 Algerians	13 Total (3%)
—	71 Independents	
189 Total (46%)	12 Others	
	—	
	209 Total (51%)	

Here it can be seen that the Government enjoyed the support of a near majority of the Assembly in the face of all of the major issues which generated censure motions. Needing only a small percentage of votes to round out the majority, the Government had potentially available to it a large pool of intermediate deputies upon whom to draw for support on particular votes. The only danger to the Government was the uniting of the intermediates against it, and, given the heterogeneous nature of the intermediate pool, this could happen only as a result of the accumulation of a variety of specific complaints. In fact this did occur during the course of the period 1960 to 1962. First procedural disagreements, then military policy, then Algeria, then Europe, and finally constitutional revision peeled away elements of the Government's majority.[32] Had General de Gaulle not decided to change the mode of Presidential election, or had he followed a more orthodox means of revising the Constitution, the Government's life might have been prolonged through the continued support of the Class 7 deputies on Scale A. But this would have meant a different strategy for the next legislative elections, and very likely a less successful one from the Gaullist standpoint.[33]

The 1962 Legislature

The legislative elections of November 1962 produced a Legislature with a decidedly Gaullist coloration.[34] The UNR could count on a stable majority resting upon its own near-majority numbers and about 30 *Républicains Indépendants* (ex-Independent supporters of Finance Minister Valery Giscard d'Estaing). Apart from these defectors to the Gaullist camp, the Independent group

[32] Careful analyses of voting trends on censure motions during the 1958 Legislature appear in Jean-Luc Parodi, *Les rapports entre le Législatif et l'Exécutif sous la Ve République* (Paris: Fondation Nationale des Sciences Politiques, 1962); and Macridis and Brown, *Supplement to "The De Gaulle Republic"* (Homewood, Ill.: The Dorsey Press, Inc., 1963), pp. 58–61.

[33] See Andrews and Hoffman, *op. cit.*, pp. 88–98.

[34] A good capsule description of the re-alignment following the 1962 elections is to be found in *L'Année politique*, 1962, pp. 140–41.

was eclipsed by Gaullist opponents, and the MRP was seriously hurt as well, although it was still able to field a parliamentary group with the help of a few former Independents and members of the *Entente Démocratique* who were unwilling or unable to join the Radicals in their new formation, the *Rassemblement Démocratique*. On the left, the Radicals, Socialists and Communists all increased their strength in the elections. The *groupes parlementaires* in the 1962 Legislature were as follows:

Group	Main Element
Groupe communiste	Communists
Groupe socialiste	Socialists
Union pour la Nouvelle République	UNR
Rassemblement démocratique	Radicals
Centre démocratique	MRP
Républicains indépendants	Independents (Giscardiens)

The 1962 Legislature comes the closest of the three examined to true unidimensionality. Of the 47 votes studied for the period December, 1962 to November, 1965, 45 fit a single scale![35] Thus a single dominant alignment existed for the entire first three years of the Legislature.[36] The original sample of 47 items necessitates a restatement of the categories used to identify the kinds of issues involved:

Category	Symbol	Number of Votes
Budget	B	8
Military	M	7
Political	Po	5
Foreign policy	F	4
Administrative	Ad	3
Economic policy	Ec	3
Housing	H	3
Justice	J	3
North Africa	N	3
Agriculture	Ag	2
Education	Ed	2
Government (general)	G	2
Labor	L	2

The category labelled "Political" includes items dealing with the reorganization of municipal elections and the policy respecting political broadcasts on the state-

---

[35] There was a total of 254 votes taken during the four-year period studied. The two non-scalar votes are #75 (housing) and #234 (North Africa). Neither was a motion of censure.

[36] As an additional indicator of the high degree of unidimensionality, the 1962 scale has the highest overall coefficient of reproducibility of the five scales examined here:

Scale		cr
1956	(A)	.976
1956	(B)	.988
1958	(A)	.970
1958	(B)	.977
1962		.993

owned radio and television facilities. The three Justice votes deal with the project establishing a State Security Court to replace the extraordinary military tribunal created during the Algerian crisis. Administrative votes involve the reorganization of the Paris region and the budget of the Ministry of the Interior.

The following list sets forth all of the 45 items included in the above-mentioned scale, beginning with the item with the smallest positive percentage:

1962 Scale

Scrutin	Type	Date	Scrutin	Type	Date
50	H	Oct. 9, 1963	24	J	Feb. 13, 1963
51	H	Oct. 9, 1963	33	B	May 29, 1963
44	H	July 19, 1963	2	Ag	Dec. 18, 1962
226	N	Oct. 25, 1965	28	B	May 8, 1963
104	Po	May 28, 1964	68	M	Nov. 7, 1963
43	L	July 17, 1963	111	Ad	June 11, 1964
57	N	Oct. 28, 1963	58	F	Oct. 29, 1963
118	Po	June 18, 1964	241	B	Oct. 28, 1965
94	Po	May 21, 1964	159	B	Nov. 9, 1964
11	J	Jan. 4, 1963	115	Ad	June 12, 1964
193	M	May 6, 1965	65	Ed	Nov. 6, 1963
146*	G	Oct. 27, 1964	41	L	July 17, 1963
153	Ag	Nov. 5, 1964	235	Ed	Oct. 19, 1965
87	Po	May 20, 1964	1	G	Dec. 13, 1962
238	F	Oct. 20, 1965	70	B	Nov. 9, 1963
239	Ad	Oct. 25, 1965	237	M	Oct. 21, 1965
15	J	Jan. 11, 1963	78	B	Dec. 6, 1963
203	M	May 26, 1965	23	B	Jan. 25, 1963
161	M	Dec. 2, 1964	197	Ec	May 13, 1965
242	Ec	Nov. 5, 1965	160	Ec	Nov. 26, 1964
35	F	June 13, 1963	36	F	June 13, 1963
106	Po	May 28, 1964	3	B	Dec. 18, 1962
162	M	Dec. 2, 1964			

The ordering of votes on the scale shows no evident trend toward either greater or less support for the Government during the course of the three year period. Note that support for the Government's budget was relatively high throughout the period, while housing policy and the Government's position on political matters and North African affairs received relatively weak support.

Table 7 gives the group distribution for the scale. In comparison with the scales for the two preceding legislatures, groups on this scale are quite compact and, except at its lower end, tend not to overlap to any great degree. The distribution of groups is quite similar to that for Scale A (1958) if account is taken of the realignment that took place in the center of the spectrum in the wake of the 1962 election. The arrangement for the 1962 Legislature differs from the bi-dimensional pattern of the 1958 Legislature in the absence of the deputies on the right-hand side of Scale B (1958), who had opposed the Government's Algerian policy. This element was virtually unrepresented in the new Legislature. Of the 74 Metropolitan deputies in classes 0 and 1 of Scale B (1958), only nine survived the 1962 legislative elections.

Table 7—1962 Scale

Class	Group Composition	Cutting point
11	146 UNR 3 Rép. Ind. 1 Other —— 150 Total	
10	55 UNR	#50 (October 9, 1963), Laurin amendment to Tinguy amendment to Housing Construction bill: 148–310
9	11 UNR	#51 (October 9, 1963), Tinguy amendment to Housing Construction bill: 250–210
8	17 UNR 1 Other —— 18 Total	#44 (July 19, 1963), Amendment to Financial project to suppress credits for state-supported building societies: 228–224
7	28 RI 2 Others —— 30 Total	#226 (October 25, 1965), Request for special commission to study indemnification of repatriated Frenchmen: 237–225
6	13 Centre Démoc. 3 RI 3 Others —— 19 Total	#118 (June 18, 1964), Third reading of Municipal Councillors' bill: 257–206
5	26 CD 1 Other —— 27 Total	#242 (November 5, 1965), Project approving Fifth Plan: 283–184
4	13 CD	#68 (November 7, 1963), Military Expenses article of Financial project: 297–160
3	13 Rassemb. Démoc.	#41 (July 17, 1963), Previous question opposed to project regarding strikes in public services: 146–315
2	12 RD 2 CD 1 Other —— 15 Total	#78 (December 6, 1963), Text of Financial law proposed by mixed commission: 316–139
1	2 Communists 3 Socialists 6 RD 2 Others —— 13 Total	#160 (November 26, 1964), Project regarding Fifth Plan: 353–120
0	39 Communists 64 Socialists 7 RD —— 110 Total	#3 (December 18, 1962), First part of Financial law: 321–113

Table 7 can be used to determine the distribution of deputy types. The only censure motion voted on during the period (#146) will serve as the dividing line between consistent supporters and the rest of the Assembly. The closest cutting point is that separating classes 6 and 7. Thus the consistent supporters are those above Class 6 on the scale. The consistent opponents can be demarcated by the initial vote of approval received by the Pompidou Government at the outset of the Legislature (#1).[37] This falls closest to the cutting point between classes 2 and 3 on the scale. Thus the consistent opponents are those below Class 3. Intermediates are those between classes 3 and 6, inclusive. Below are listed the compositions of the three types for the 1962 Legislature:

Consistent Supporters	Intermediates	Consistent Opponents
229 UNR	13 RD	41 Communists
31 RI	52 CD	67 Socialists
4 Others	3 RI	25 RD
—	4 Others	2 CD
264 Total (56%)	—	3 Others
	72 Total (15%)	—
		138 Total (29%)

The most striking feature of this distribution, is, of course, the comfortable majority of consistent supporters enjoyed by the Government. Although the intermediate pool was markedly reduced relative to the previous legislatures, the Government had no need of the less reliable type of support. Further comparison of this distribution with those for the other legislatures is undertaken in the concluding section.

Conclusion

The principal concern of this article has been to ascertain empirically whether or not the apparent trend toward a simplified majority-opposition confrontation in French politics has been evident over the last decade at the level of legislative behavior. Two criteria have been employed to measure trends in voting behavior in the National Assembly: (1) the degree of unidimensionality in voting patterns, and (2) the distribution of role types among deputies according to the three-fold typology outlined in the opening section. Concerning the first criterion, analysis of voting patterns for the three legislatures studied leads to a rather ambiguous answer. Using the strict standards of unidimensionality employed in Guttman scaling, the most unidimensional pattern has been found for the most recent of the three legislatures studied. However, it cannot be said that a consistent trend in the direction of unidimensionality has been found. Whereas more than one dimension was discovered in the voting patterns of both the first and second

[37] There is no requirement for an investiture vote in the 1958 Constitution. Nevertheless, the vote on the Premier's policy statement can be regarded as an expression of the degree of support existing at the outset of the Legislature for the particular Government which Pompidou headed.

legislatures in chronological order, it is possible to divide the time-span of the earliest Legislature (1956) into two sub-periods, in each of which there was substantial unidimensionality. From late 1956 until the Spring of 1958 the degree of unidimensionality was very nearly as great as that found for the first three years of the most recent Legislature (1962). In the intervening Legislature (1958) a mildly multidimensional pattern was found. Thus, at first glance, there seems to have been no clear-cut trend.

If, on the other hand, we were to adopt a less rigorous conception of dimensionality, a somewhat different answer might emerge. In both the 1956 and the 1958 legislatures governments found themselves facing less an opposition than two alternative sets of partners, each seeking to influence policy (especially regarding North Africa) in a distinct direction and to prevent the alternative element from sharing in power. While left-right terms have been used sparingly in this article, there can be no question that, in the traditional parlance of French politics, the governments of these two legislatures were governments of the center; the two dominant dimensions of each legislature involved voting cooperation of the center supporters of the governments with the right against the left on one dimension and with the left against the right on the other. The central base of support shifted noticeably to the right as a result of the 1958 elections, which decimated the ranks of the left parties and swelled the ranks of the MRP, the Independents and especially the Gaullists.

By the 1962 Legislature, however, the far right, which had included in its ranks the only consistent opponents in the two preceding legislatures as well as the fringe supporters of the center-right voting alignments, had virtually dropped out of the picture. Suddenly the Gaullists found themselves on the right-hand side of the party spectrum in the Assembly.[38] The single dimension which emerged in that Legislature reflected the fact that the Gaullists had no real alternative set of voting partners and opponents. The roles of the various parties had become frozen. To a large degree, of course, the new situation reflected the fact that the Algerian question had virtually disappeared from French politics. Once again a single prevailing structure of roles and expectations could develop in the Assembly, there being no transcendent issue which could disrupt the existing set of commitments. When the voting patterns are viewed in this more

---

[38] The Gaullists themselves object to the "rightist" label, and their voting behavior in the 1956 and 1958 legislatures certainly strengthens their claim to "centrist" status. Unfortunately for their claim, if not for their majority status, they emerged from the 1962 elections with nothing but thin air to their right. The *Républicains Indépendants* were the least right-of-center of the old Independents, and the *Centre Démocratique* was predominantly composed of MRP, or center, deputies. All three groups (UNR, RI and CD) could be said to occupy roughly the same ideological space: from dead center to moderate right. To be sure, de Gaulle's foreign policy puts the Gaullists to the left of center on the spectrum, but their outlook on the Constitution, with emphasis upon a strong executive, is traditionally a right-wing position in France. Thus, the extremes of their "ideological profile" go beyond those of the other two parties; but, if it were possible to devise a multi-dimensional measure of ideological position, it is likely that the UNR would be close to the other two parties, at least in a measure of central tendency. The impressions of the author are drawn from interviews in Paris with candidates of the "Fifth Republic" alliance and the *Centre Démocratique* during the campaign for the March, 1967 legislative elections, as well as from examination of campaign statements of the party leaders appearing in *Le Monde* during the campaign. A useful pre-election compilation of party positions on the primary issues of the moment is to be found in *Le Dossier politique de l'Electeur français* (Paris: Editions Planète, 1967).

general, less technical, sense it becomes clear that, while there was not a consistent trend toward unidimensionality between 1956 and 1965, the kind of unidimensionality that prevailed in the period 1962–65 was considerably more conducive to a simplified majority-opposition confrontation than that prevailing between 1956 and 1962.

The contrast between the 1962 Legislature and its two immediate predecessors becomes all the more apparent when the percentage distributions of deputy types in the three legislatures are compared:

	Legislature		
Deputy types	*1956*	*1958*	*1962*
Consistent supporters	37%	46%	56%
Intermediates	56	51	15
Consistent opponents	7	3	29
	100%	100%	100%

Only in 1962 do we see the beginnings of a real opposition in the National Assembly. Although it is still overpowered by the cohesive majority, it is possible to point to a single area of the political spectrum and identify it as the Opposition, even though it was still in the 1962–65 period a delicate plant, divided between three parliamentary groups and lacking a single leader.[39] Prior to 1962 we see governments threading a dangerous course between two actively hostile

[39] It is possible to hazard an assessment of the distribution of deputy types at the outset of the 1967 Legislature. An estimate can be made from the analysis of votes for the first censure motion of the Legislature appearing in *Le Monde*, May 23, 1967, p. 9. By assuming (1) that the members of the group *Progrès et Démocratie* (primarily the *Centre Démocrate*) who voted for the motion are intermediates, (2) that members of the two left groups, Communists and *Fédération des Gauches* are consistent opponents, (3) that deputies who did not vote for the motion are consistent supporters; and using their earlier scale scores to classify the isolated deputies who voted for the motion, one arrives at the following distribution:

Supporters	Intermediates	Opponents
200 UNR, etc.	38 CD, etc.	73 Communists
3 CD, etc.	1 Other	121 FGDS, etc.
42 RI	—	2 Others
5 Others	39 Total (8%)	—
—		196 Total (40%)
250 Total (52%)		

(One isolated deputy voting for the motion, who was not a member of the 1962 Legislature, is not included in this break-down.) Here we see the further advance of the opposition and the further decline of the intermediates, with the growth trend of the majority being halted and somewhat reversed. Despite the last development, however, it is striking to note the 7 percent increase in the combined strength of the majority and opposition at the expense of the intermediates.

Too much stock should not be placed in these figures as predictive of what the character of the new Legislature will be. The characterization of the Communists as consistent opponents may not withstand the test of events if the Assembly faces any foreign policy issues. As early as April, 1966 a censure motion advanced by the Socialists attacking de Gaulle's NATO policy failed to get the support of the Communists, thus joining the two ends of the 1962 scale against the middle: see *L'Année politique*, 1966, pp. 34–37. This should be sufficient warning, incidentally, that the "1962 scale" characterizes only the first three years of the 1962 Legislature and not necessarily the entire four, the year 1966 not having been examined.

part-time oppositions. However, the Gaullist influx in 1958 decisively altered the stalemate situation that had prevailed between 1956 and 1958. The Government now had enough reliable support that it could afford to choose among potential voting partners from the intermediate ranks. This made it possible for a solution to the Algerian problem to be achieved without a complete break-down of the parliamentary mechanism.

The Algerian War thus can be seen as a factor of transcendent importance to an understanding of French politics during the period under consideration. The nature of its impact was different at different times, however. In 1956 it made for inflexibility and stalemate. In 1958 it generated events which were to result in a much more flexible and mobile system. And in 1962 its conclusion resulted in a considerable simplification of the system. To be sure, other factors contributed to these results: the personality of General de Gaulle, the institutional changes of the Fifth Republic, as well as more problematical long-term developments, such as the decline of localism in French politics in the face of the increasing importance of national leadership under the influence of the mass media, and the reputed decline of ideology in Western Europe, especially on the left side of the political spectrum. But the Algerian War was the catalyst which brought the more immediate factors to life and which conditioned the expressions which the longer-term trends would take. Whether, on balance, it hastened or retarded the appearance of a more simplified majority-opposition confrontation cannot be ascertained from the data reviewed here. The difficulty with longitudinal analysis of French politics is that it is virtually impossible to find a "normal" period sometime in the recent past with which to compare more recent developments.

The Minority Party and Policy-making
in the House of Representatives

by CHARLES O. JONES

Considerable attention has recently been focused on political oppositions in democracies. A recent book examines oppositions in various Western countries[1] and a journal called *Government and Opposition* was founded in 1965.[2] The significance of the role of an opposition in democracies does not have to be stressed. It is generally accepted.

What of the role of the opposition in the United States? Robert A. Dahl notes that one must use the plural when speaking of opposition in this country since, "a distinctive, persistent, unified structural opposition scarcely exists in the United States . . . it is nearly always impossible to refer precisely to "the" opposition, for the coalition that opposes the government on one matter may fall apart, or even govern, on another."[3]

While it is true that "the" opposition is not institutionalized as a definite cohesive, persistent, distinctive group in American politics, it is also true that there has usually been an identifiable minority party in Congress. Though it does not always oppose the majority, and cannot be expected to be synonymous with "the" opposition very often, it does persist. Despite handsome invitations to disband—in the form of successive defeats at the polls—a sizeable number of congressmen, senators, and congressional candidates continue to call themselves Republicans and to organize as such in Congress.

This study focuses on the range of strategies, including various forms of

[1] Robert A. Dahl (ed.), *Political Oppositions in Western Democracies* (New Haven, Conn.: Yale University Press, 1966).

[2] The first issue of *Government and Opposition* was published in November, 1965.

[3] In Dahl, *op. cit.*, p. 34.

Reprinted from "The Minority Party and Policy-Making in the House of Representatives," *The American Political Science Review* 80 (June 1968): 481–93, by Charles O. Jones. Reprinted by permission of the American Political Science Association and the author.

opposition, available to the minority party in congressional policy-making. Specific attention will be paid to the Republican party as a minority party in the House of Representatives for two reasons: (1) to limit the scope of the article and (2) because the Republican party is the contemporary minority party. The major questions to receive attention are: What are the principal policy-making strategies of the minority party? What political conditions determine the range of strategies available to it in any one Congress? The major thesis is that there are various types of minority parties when classified by the range of strategies available to them for participating in policy-making. Some minority parties are extremely weak and ineffectual, others have significant sources of power available to them. The role of the minority party in Congress is not a single, consistent role over time. It varies considerably depending on a number of external and internal conditions.

Political Setting for the Minority Party in Congress

There are certain relatively stable factors in the American political setting which are of importance in determining the role of the minority party. Notable among these are, of course, federalism, representation, and the separation of powers—all three of which tend to decentralize the political party structure. While distributing power between a central unit and sub-units, federalism also distributes elective offices throughout the land. Parties exist to fill these offices and therefore organize where elections take place. The representation system is based on the land mass of states for the Senate, population for the House, and a combination of the two for the Electoral College. Separation of powers in and of itself allows for only a minimum of coordination at the national level for the majority party and almost none at all for the minority party. Thus, decentralization and lack of cohesion may be taken as "givens" when analyzing American political parties.

The role of the minority party is also determined by the role of Congress in national policy-making. In general, Congress has the primary function of legitimating one course of action, designed to solve a public problem, over another. The legitimation process is ultimately one of some type of majority rule and therefore policy to be legitimate must be traced to a numerical majority. Thus, if a course of action is to be legitimated in Congress, it is necessary for political leaders to consider the majority-building prerequisite. The output of the legitimation process may be called policy and normally it is the result of compromise. Note that reference is made to a legitimation "process." There is considerably more involved in this process than voting on legislation. The final vote is merely the manifestation of success, or lack of it, in building a majority. By legitimation process is meant all those activities to collect a majority which go on in Congress (and specifically in the House for this study).

This process of legitimation is not simply one of ratification of what the executive proposes. The executive is, indeed, a major source of proposed courses of action but there are many other sources too—interest groups, constituents, state and local public officials, members themselves. The process of building a majority involves considerable bargaining. The results of this process may bear only slight resemblance to any one of the courses of action originally proposed—whether from the executive or elsewhere.

There are a number of strategies which may be employed by the minority party in the majority coalition-building process in Congress—depending on the political conditions at the time. A minority party which is severely restricted by political conditions may only be able to *support* the majority party or offer *inconsequential opposition* to the majority-building efforts of the party in power. A minority party which has a President in the White House will have the opportunity of *participating* in majority coalition-building efforts. A minority party which is favored by political conditions may have a range of strategies available—e.g., *consequential partisan opposition*, employed to defeat majority party efforts; *consequential constructive opposition*, where the minority party counters with its own proposals; *innovation*, where the minority party initiates its own proposals and attempts to build a majority in favor; *cooperation*, where the minority works with the majority on a particular problem; *support*, as mentioned above; or *withdrawal*, where the minority party is divided on an issue and can find no basis for agreement.

What are the political conditions which may determine the range of strategies for the minority party? Conditions both inside and outside Congress may be significant. I have identified four "external conditions" and four "internal conditions" which seem to have important effects.

The general temper of the times is the first external condition to consider. Is there a domestic or international crisis which dominates policy-making? Or is there relative calm? To what extent has there been expressed a national mood for action in Congress and the executive? Since there are no simple, scientific measures of this condition, I will have to rely on fairly crude estimates of the temper of the times. The second external condition is the relative political strength of the minority party outside Congress (see Table 1). Is the party strong or weak nationally among the voters? in the states? in the White House? The third external condition is national party unity. Obviously a disunified party will be preoccupied with party matters to the exclusion normally of an active role in congressional policy-making as a party.

A fourth external condition is presidential power. A President with a variety of sources of power would normally limit the range of strategies of the minority party whereas a President with only limited sources of power would normally allow more flexibility.[4]

The first of the internal conditions is procedure in the House. Generally speaking procedure is relatively stable but minor changes occur frequently and major changes have occurred in the House in 1910–1911, 1946–1947, and 1961–1965. Such changes may have an important effect on the minority party. A second internal condition is the size of the margin enjoyed by the majority party over the minority party. A third condition is that of majority leadership and organization,

[4] I rely to a great extent on Richard E. Neustadt's analysis of presidential power contained in *Presidential Power: The Politics of Leadership* (New York: John Wiley, 1960).

Table 1—Various Combinations for the Two Parties Sharing Dominance of the House, Senate, Presidency, and National Voter Preference, 1900–Present

Com- bination	Democrats Control	Republicans Control	Occurring In
1	NPI, PR, HO, SE	—	1933–47, 1949–53, 1961–67 (24 yrs)
2	NPI, PR, SE	HO	
3	NPI, PR, HO	SE	
4	NPI, PR	HO, SE	1947–49 (2 years)
5	NPI	PR, SE, HO	1953–55 (2 yrs)
6	NPI, SE, HO	PR	1955–61 (6 yrs)
7	NPI, HO	PR, SE	
8	NPI, SE	PR, HO	
9	PR, HO	NPI, SE	
10	PR, SE	NPI, HO	
11	PR	NPI, HO, SE	1919–21 (2 yrs)
12	PR, SE, HO	NPI	1913–19 (6 yrs)
13	SE, HO	NPI, PR	
14	SE	NPI, PR, HO	
15	HO	NPI, PR, SE	1911–13, 1931–33 (4 yrs)
16	—	NPI, PR, SE, HO	1909–11, 1921–31 (20 yrs)

Key: NPI—National Party Identification of Voters (Survey Research Center Concept)
  PR—Presidency
  HO—House of Representatives
  SE—Senate

and a fourth is minority party leadership and organization. Of particular interest is the ability, style, and sources of strength of both sets of leaders and the nature of the organization relied on.

The Minority Party in Four Congresses

I have selected four congresses to illustrate the various political conditions which can set the range of strategies for the minority party. These four—the 63rd (1913–1914), 73rd (1933–1934), 85th (1957–1958), and 87th (1961–1962)—represent widely differing situations for the Republicans as a minority party in Congress. The first two (63rd and 73rd) illustrate the minority party in its most restricted role, the third (85th) illustrates one of those ambiguous policy-making situations where the minority party has a President in the White House, and the fourth (87th) is an example of greater flexibility for the minority party.

RESTRICTED MINORITIES—63RD AND 73RD CONGRESSES

As noted in Table 2, the differing political conditions in 1913 and 1933 placed serious limitations on the alternative strategies which could be practically employed by the minority party. Of major importance in 1913 was the disunity of the Republican Party. Though the Republican Party was presumably the majority party in terms of voter preference in the nation,[5] the Democrats won

---

[5] Of course, there were no voting behavior surveys for this period. Based on election returns, I am assuming that the Republican Party was the majority party in terms of voter party identification.

Table 2—Political Conditions and Range of Minority Party Strategies in Four Selected Congresses

	EXTERNAL CONDITIONS				INTERNAL CONDITIONS				
Congress	Temper	Maj-Min Combination [a]	Min. Party Unity	President	Procedure	Margin	Majority Party Leadership	Minority Party Leadership	Type of Minority Party by Range of Strategies
63rd (1913–1914)	No Dominant Crisis Mood for Action	12 (Ambiguous)	Weak	Strong (Wilson)	Major Changes	Large	Strong	Weak	Restricted
73rd (1933–1934)	Dominant Crisis Mood for Action	1 (Unambiguous)	Moderate	Strong (Roosevelt)	No changes	Large	Weak	Weak	Restricted
85th (1957–1958)	No Dominant Crisis Mood Unclear	6 (Ambiguous)	Moderately Strong	Weak (Eisenhower)	No Changes	Small	Strong	Weak	Participating
87th (1961–1962)	No Dominant Crisis Mood Unclear	1 (Unambiguous)	Strong	Moderate Strength (Kennedy)	Minor Changes	Medium	Weak	Strong	Flexible

[a] See Table 1 for explanation of combinations.

control of both houses of Congress and the White House (combination 12, Table 1). The result was that Woodrow Wilson had sources of power not ordinarily available to a minority party President. He could capitalize on the disunity of Republicans and the fact that, though there was not a specific domestic or international crisis which dominated politics, there was a mood of dissatisfaction.[6] Arthur S. Link described it as follows:

The election of 1912 marked the culmination of more than twenty years of popular revolt against a state of affairs that seemed to guarantee perpetual political and economic control to the privileged few in city, state, and nation. The uprising that came so spectacularly to a head in the first years of the twentieth century—the progressive movement—was the natural consummation of historical processes long in the making.[7]

Such sources of strength are formidable but they could be reduced somewhat by internal political conditions favorable to the minority party. This was not the case in 1913, however. As noted in Table 2, the internal conditions also favored Wilson and the Democrats. There had been major procedural changes in the House of Representatives in the two preceding congresses which could also be traced to the divisions in the Republican party. As will be noted below, the reduction of the power of the Speaker had the effect of forcing the Democratic party leadership to develop new techniques for building majorities. They proved themselves adept at doing so—without having to rely on minority party support. Further the Democrats were blessed with a wide margin in the House in 1913—290 to 127. To that date, no party had ever had such a comfortable House margin.

Majority party leadership and organization in the House in the 63rd Congress were both strong and effective. With the diminution of the Speaker's power, and the rejection of collegialism and personalism as leadership styles,[8] it was natural that the House would have to go through a period of democratization. Certainly Speaker Champ Clark could not expect to wield power equal to that of his immediate predecessor, Joseph G. Cannon. At the same time, there were 290 Democrats in the House—a great many of them freshmen—who had to be led, and there was a President in the White House who wanted action. The pattern of leadership and organization that the Democrats developed in the House as a response to this situation is one of the most fascinating in the history of the modern Congress.

Speaker Clark was almost perfectly suited to the conditions of the moment. An affable, personable, and beloved member, Clark is quoted as saying in the 61st Congress, "Although I am going to be Speaker next time, I am going to

---

[6] Woodrow Wilson was not the kind of man to ignore the opportunity. He had expressed himself on the need for a stronger executive in his book, *Congressional Government* (New York: Meridian Books, 1956, first published in 1885). To him, the president had merely been a branch of the legislature (see p. 173).

[7] Arthur S. Link, *Woodrow Wilson and the Progressive Era* (New York: Harper, 1954), p. 1.

[8] These are terms used by Randall B. Ripley in *Party Leaders in the House of Representatives* (Washington, D.C.: The Brookings Institution, 1967).

sacrifice the Speaker's power to change the rules."[9] He referred to himself as "Dean of the Faculty." Randall B. Ripley classifies him as a "figurehead" Speaker.[10] Clark's majority leader, however, was Oscar W. Underwood—the brilliant Congressman, later Senator, from Alabama. Underwood also served as Chairman of the powerful Committee on Ways and Means and therefore of the Democratic Committee on Committees. He became the principal Democratic leader in the House.

Underwood capitalized on the inevitable period of democratization following Cannon's demise by relying on the caucus as a policy-setting group. Though the evidence on Underwood's techniques is still scanty, it is possible to describe the procedure which developed. Following the introduction of major bills, and their assignment to committees, the Democratic caucus would meet to debate the legislation—sometimes for two weeks. A vote would be taken, making the bill a party measure. Unless they excused themselves, Democrats were bound to vote for the bill and to vote against all amendments except those supported by the party leaders. The bill would then be brought before the appropriate committee, hearings held if the Democratic leadership so desired, and sent to the House floor for debate.[11] The Republicans played a very minor role in these proceedings, and they often expressed their frustrations. For example, Sereno E. Payne (New York), ranking Republican on the Committee on Ways and Means and former majority leader under Speaker Cannon, made the following statement in the minority report on the Underwood Tariff: "In this statement we shall not attempt to analyze this bill or to criticize it in detail. *Our acquaintance with it is too brief to permit this.*"[12] The minority report on the Federal Reserve Act expressed the same frustrations.

The undersigned regret that when the Committee on Banking and Currency met finally to consider H. R. 7837 they found the majority members of the committee so *bound by their caucus action that they could not consider amendments* to the bill which, if adopted, would have eliminated its unsound and questionable provisions.

Such changes . . . are fundamental and vital. The majority members of the committee refused to favorably consider them on the ground that they involved matters of Democratic party policy settled *by the caucus.*[13]

---

[9] Quoted in Chang-wei Chiu, *The Speaker of the House of Representatives Since 1896* (New York: Columbia University Press, 1928), p. 303.

[10] Ripley, *op. cit.*, Ch. 2. The other categories of leadership style relied on by Ripley are "collegial" and "personal."

[11] Various sources may be relied on for a more complete description of this procedure. See Chiu *op. cit.*; George R. Brown, *The Leadership of Congress* (Indianapolis: Bobbs Merrill, 1922); Paul D. Hasbrouck, *Party Government in the House of Representatives* (New York: Macmillan, 1927); Arthur S. Link, *Wilson: The New Freedom* (Princeton: Princeton University Press, 1956); Wilder H. Haines, "The Congressional Caucus of Today." this REVIEW, 9 (November, 1915), 696–706.

[12] U.S. Congress, House, Committee on Ways and Means, House Report No. 5, 63rd Cong., 1st sess., 1913, p. lv (emphasis added).

[13] U.S. Congress, House, Committee on Banking and Currency, House Report No. 69, 63rd Cong., 1st sess., 1913, p. 133 (emphasis added). It is not suggested that all legislation passed without incident in the House. For example, the Tariff bill and Federal Reserve bill both were controversial within the Democratic Party. Once the principal issues were resolved in the party, and between Democratic congressional leaders and President Wilson, however, major bills passed the House by large margins.

Even with all of these disadvantages, it is conceivable that the minority party's options could be increased simply due to the strength, imagination, and style of its leaders. Unfortunately for the House Republicans in 1913, they could not expect to rely on this source of power either. They were led principally by old-guard leaders—all of whom had supported Cannon in 1910 during the speakership fight. The minority leader was James R. Mann of Illinois—an interesting, rather enigmatic figure in House politics. He was closely identified with Cannon and won the minority floor leadership post in 1911 because the old-line Republicans still maintained a majority in the House Republican Party. Mann was apparently precise, humorless, and brilliant in his own way—a sort of "thinking man's H. R. Gross." He seemed to be a transitional figure for the House Republicans—not very well liked among his colleagues and charged with the responsibility of holding the party together until they recaptured control of Congress. It is noteworthy that when the party did gain a majority in the House in 1919 Mann was defeated for the Speakership by Frederick H. Gillett of Massachusetts.

This combination of external and internal political conditions effectively neutralized the House Republican Party. Republicans were limited to *inconsequential opposition*. That is, they opposed the principal aspects of Wilson's program but could do little more than try to have amendments accepted, attempt to have the legislation recommitted, and then oppose final passage. Only if the Democrats were seriously split on some issue could the Republicans expect to play a significant role. These instances were extremely rare.[14]

House Republicans were equally impotent during the 73rd Congress but for different reasons (see Table 2). The economic collapse of the nation was the dominant condition and it worked to the advantage of the Democrats. In 1928, the Republican Party had firm control of Congress, the White House, and the nation. In 1932, the Democratic Party was unquestionably the majority party (combination 1 in Table 1). The 1932 presidential election is classified as a "realigning election" by the Survey Research Center,[15] since major shifts were occurring in voter preference between the two parties. Indeed, even some congressional Republicans failed to support Hoover in 1932. The resulting effect of these external conditions was to provide President Roosevelt with a virtual "blank check" by the public in the 1932 election. He had more impressive sources of power than almost any President in history.

What of the internal political conditions? Did they act to blunt the thrust of presidential leadership sustained by crisis? Several did in later Roosevelt congresses, but in the 73rd Congress there were few roadblocks. There were no major rules changes, but the existing rules were made to serve the President.

[14] One such instance was the legislation to repeal the exemption to American coastwide shipping under the Panama Canal Act of 1912. Speaker Clark and Majority Leader Underwood opposed President Wilson on repeal but, with some Republican support, Wilson was able to build a majority without their endorsement. See Link, *Wilson: The New Freedom;* and James M. Leake, "Four Years of Congress," this REVIEW, 11 (May 1917), 252–83.

[15] Angus Campbell, *et al., The American Voter* (New York: John Wiley, 1960), Ch. 19; and Philip Converse, *et al.,* "Stability and Change in 1960: A Reinstating Election," this REVIEW, 55 (June, 1961), 269–80. See also, V. O. Key, Jr., "A Theory of Critical Elections," *Journal of Politics,* 17 (February, 1955), 3–18.

Major legislation was sometimes processed in a matter of days. The Democratic margin over Republicans was 198 seats—313 to 117. This was the largest margin for either party in history, though new records would be set in the 74th (219 seats) and the 75th (244 seats) Congresses.

For the most part, of course, majority party leadership in the 73rd Congress was in the White House. It was probably fortunate for the Democrats that there was strong presidential leadership, the margins were large, and the mood was for action. Neither the Speaker, Henry T. Rainey of Illinois, nor the Majority Leader, Joseph W. Byrns of Tennessee, were strong leaders. Randall B. Ripley classifies Rainey as a figurehead who was conservative in his use of power.[16] He classifies Byrns in the same way when Byrns became Speaker in the 74th Congress. The Democratic Whip for the 73rd Congress was Arthur H. Greenwood of Indiana.[17]

If Democratic party leadership in the House was weak, Republican party leadership was weaker. Gone was the strength of Nicholas Longworth of Ohio and John Q. Tilson of Connecticut, who led the House during the Coolidge and Hoover Administrations. The minority floor leader in the 73rd Congress was Bertrand H. Snell. Snell, a staunchly conservative businessman from upstate New York, was never very effective as leader in his eight years as minority leader (though it must be said that he led under extremely difficult circumstances). The Whip was Harry L. Englebright of California.

Given these circumstances, it is not surprising that the minority party in the 73rd Congress varied between the weak strategies of *support* of the majority coalition-building efforts of the President and *inconsequential opposition.* The emergency was there, the President had won an overwhelming mandate to proceed with whatever proposals he thought necessary, and the Republican party had little if any claim to public support. House Republicans could only add a voice to the consensus which served to legitimize unprecedented legislative actions.

The classic instance of Republican support came very early in the first session. The Emergency Banking bill was introduced, debated, and passed in both houses on March 9, the opening day of the 73rd Congress. Majority Leader Byrns asked for and got a unanimous consent agreement to limit debate to 40 minutes *even though members had not seen the bill.* Minority Leader Snell expressed the hope that Republicans would not object to this procedure.

The house is burning down, and the President of the United States says this is the way to put out the fire. And to me at this time there is only one answer to this question, and that is to give the President what he demands and says is necessary to meet the situation.[18]

The bill passed by a voice vote.

[16] Ripley, *op. cit.*, Ch. 2.
[17] The caucus apparently proved useful in canvassing opinion and organizing the great numbers of new Democrats. See E. Pendleton Herring, "First Session of the 73rd Congress," this Review, 28 (February, 1934), 65–83. The Democratic caucus minutes for this period are available in the Library of Congress.
[18] *Congressional Record*, 73rd Cong., 1st sess., March 9, 1933, p. 76.

No other legislation in the first session would go through the House with such ease. But the process by no means returned to normal. House Democrats pushed through legislation at a record pace by relying on closed rules which restricted amendments. A total of ten closed rules were employed during the first session, compared to an average of two such rules a session for other Roosevelt Congresses. As Lewis J. Lapham, in his detailed study of the House Committee on Rules, has noted: "Hardly a single important bill having to do with the economic recovery program of the president was considered by the House except under the restrictions imposed by a so-called gag rule."[19] Despite these tactics—so dreaded and heavily criticized by the minority—sizeable numbers of Republicans supported the legislation.

During the second session of the 73rd Congress, House Republicans were considerably less supportive of Roosevelt's efforts. They assumed the slightly more aggressive strategy of *inconsequential opposition*. For example, with the reciprocal trade bill, they issued a minority report which listed 24 separate reasons why Republicans could not support the bill. House Republicans rarely issued minority reports in the first session. When the bill reached the floor Allen T. Treadway (Massachusetts), ranking Republican on the Committee on Ways and Means, served mild notice that Republicans would offer less support in the future.

> . . . in making critical remarks I wish to say that they are in no way reflections on the personality of the President of the United States. I hold the President in the very highest esteem. I have voted with him as far as I could, consistently with my conscience, in his program of recovery; but I claim that when our stern convictions differ from those of the President of the United States, there is but one course for us to pursue. . . .[20]

Treadway's remarks were very circumspect, however, and, it might be added, of no great concern to the President. Roosevelt had a sizeable and dependable majority without Republican support.

The 63rd and 73rd Congresses represent very unusual minority party situations. In both instances, political conditions were such that the minority party could rely on only a very narrow range of strategies in congressional policy-making. House Republicans in both congresses had an immediate, internal party problem—that of survival as a political party.

Yet there are important differences between these two situations for the minority party. As noted in Table 2, the Republicans in 1913 had one potential source of power which was not available in 1933—they were presumably still the majority party nationally. In 1913, the salient condition determining the restriction on the minority party was disunity. Therefore, it was within the power of the minority party to make the adjustments necessary to correct this condition. If successful, the restrictions on the minority party in Congress could well be temporary. If unsuccessful, the party could well disappear as a major

[19] Lewis J. Lapham, *Party Leadership and the House Committee on Rules* (unpublished Ph.D. dissertation, Harvard University, 1954), p. 52.

[20] *Congressional Record*, 73rd Cong., 2nd sess., March 23, 1934, p. 5262.

party. Thus, there were important stakes in seeking a rapprochement. Given the characteristics of the American party system this reunion might best be accomplished by less aggressive behavior on both sides. That is, the party might accomplish a partial healing by just "holding on"—insuring that the divisiveness not go further and that those disagreements which did exist not be advertised so broadly. For the most part, this is precisely what happened.

In 1933, however, the Republicans did not have it within their power to produce remedies. Events were out of control, as far as the minority party was concerned. The party had to stand aside and hope that, by some miracle, the situation would change. It did not. Of the two situations, that during the 73rd Congress is clearly the most undesirable from the point of view of the minority party since it signals a long period when the minority party can expect to play only the most limited role in policy-making.

A PARTICIPATING MINORITY—85TH CONGRESS

As is noted in Table 1, the American electoral system makes possible very ambiguous political situations. One such is illustrated by the 85th Congress. President Dwight D. Eisenhower was reelected by a very large margin in 1956 but the Republican Party was unable to capture control of either house of Congress. Thus, the minority party in Congress was faced with conflicting demands and expectations—enacting the President's program while opposing congressional Democratic leadership.

Since the margins in both the House and Senate were narrow (33 seats in the House, 2 in the Senate), there were three conditions—one external, two internal—which could have resulted in a strong role for the minority party in Congress (see Table 2 for a summary of conditions). The first of these, the external condition, would be a President with a number of sources of power other than a majority in Congress. President Eisenhower did have one such source of power—his phenomenal popularity among the public. There were several factors which prevented Eisenhower from turning this advantage into success in policy-making, however. First, there was no all-engaging crisis or general mood for action which would rally all legislators to support the President. Second, it was unlikely that a man of Eisenhower's background would have the necessary skills for majority coalition-building in these circumstances (an asset for him at the polls but not in negotiating for majorities in Congress).[21] Third, it seems that the President did not see the need for legislation in many areas and therefore did not press hard for its enactment. Thus, for the very reasons that he did have personal popularity, it was unlikely that he would try to capitalize on this advantage.

The internal conditions which might have strengthened the minority party would be weak majority party leadership combined with strong minority party leadership. If House Democratic leaders had been inept—unable to control their majority—and House Republican leaders had been exceptional negotiators, it is conceivable that the minority party would have been highly successful in building

[21] See Neustadt, *op. cit.,* pp. 163–64.

majorities for a Republican program. Unfortunately for the minority, the reverse was the case during the 85th Congress.

In the House, the Democrats were able to rely on Sam Rayburn as Speaker and John W. McCormack as Majority Leader. Rayburn was serving his 22nd term as a member of the House and his seventh full term as Speaker. Though Rayburn apparently lost some of his characteristic alertness in later Congresses, he led his party with strength in the 85th Congress. Rayburn approached the perfect model of the effective Speaker of the House of Representatives. He knew the rules and how to use them, he maintained contact with all of the various wings of the House Democratic party, and he was very protective of his procedural majority—sensing when he may have gone too far with any member. He also retained a fine sense of compromise, and relied on techniques of leadership which emphasized party unity.

McCormack was serving his 15th full term in the House and his ninth term as the second-ranking leader in his party—seven as Majority Leader, two as Minority Whip. Though generally considered to be more partisan than Rayburn, McCormack had proved himself to be a very durable, and generally well-liked, leader.

Rayburn and McCormack did not rely on either the caucus or a steering committee. They maintained a relatively efficient whip system as a formal system of communication (led by Carl Albert, Oklahoma, in the 85th Congress) but both relied more heavily on informal methods of contact than on the formal whip system. Both leaders avoided calling caucuses to set party policy, fearing the effects of such meetings on party unity.

House Republicans were not so fortunate in getting strong leadership. They were led by Joseph W. Martin, Jr., of Massachusetts. Martin certainly was experienced in leading House Republicans—he had done so since the 76th Congress. As contrasted with his long-time friend, Sam Rayburn, however, Martin was losing control over his party. He had lost contact with many of the younger members and his health was failing. Evidence for this appeared in convincing form in the 86th Congress when Martin was defeated for the minority leadership post by Charles A. Halleck of Indiana.

Like Rayburn, Martin relied on "personalism" as a leadership technique. But he was never as successful as Rayburn. It seemed as though conditions in the Republican Party (e.g., less sectional diversity) favored greater use of party caucus and committee action than for the Democrats. Republicans were generally more unified and could gain publicity from such meetings. Martin, however, continued to rely on a coterie of advisers. Halleck was one of these in earlier times but Martin had grown to distrust him. Leslie C. Arends, Illinois, served as his Whip and while performing adequately, Arends took a narrow view of his function as Whip.

Thus, House Republicans had rather uninspired leadership in the 85th Congress. Martin's greatest source of strength was his friendship with Rayburn. But many young members considered this friendship more harmful to the party than helpful. They wanted to establish a more positive image for the party and were frustrated with the leadership of Martin, Arends, and ranking committee members like Clarence Brown (Ohio). These dissatisfied members were to make many changes in the House Republican Party in ensuing years.[22]

The range of strategies for the House Republican Party in the 85th Congress was almost as restricted as that during the 63rd and 73rd Congresses. House Republicans *participated* in majority coalition-building. The President would be expected to count his own party first in building majorities and rely on House Republican leaders to assist him in getting the necessary Democratic votes to enact his policies. Given the weakness both of the President and the House Republican leaders, however, it is reasonable to distinguish between *weak* and *strong* participation. The former, of course, characterized the House Republican Party in the 85th Congress.

The range of strategies for the minority party could be expected to be somewhat broader if a particular proposal became more identified with the House Democrats. Thus, if the Democrats were successful in altering the president's legislation to a considerable extent, then House Republicans would be free to adopt a number of strategies—oppose the legislation, substitute their own proposal, support the Democratic version, etc. Further, if the President compromised with the Democrats without House Republican concurrence, or despite their objections, the range of strategies would be increased. It is obvious that majority coalition building under these conditions requires considerable finesse—particularly if the issue is significant and controverisal. The policy-making result in the 85th Congress was often confusion, ambiguity, and stalemate.

There were instances during the 85th Congress when the two parties worked together to pass legislation—with the Republicans forming the principal basis of support. For example, the Civil Rights Act of 1957 was characterized by bipartisanship at every stage of the process. On the other hand, there were cases when a presidential proposal divided House Republicans. Efforts to unify Republicans risked the loss of needed Democratic support. Efforts to gain Democratic support further divided Republicans. The President had a mixed record on such issues. On reciprocal trade and national defense education, he and his party leaders were able to build a coalition sufficiently large for passage. On federal aid to education, he was not only unsuccessful in doing so, but apparently had some doubts about the bill himself.[23] And who can know how many proposals were never even made due to the ambiguity of the congressional situation? The president himself was discouraged following the first session: "I am tremendously disappointed that so many of these bills have not been acted on, and in some cases, not even have held hearings."[24] The editors of the *Congressional Quarterly* summarized the second session: "Adjournment of the 85th Congress . . . brought to a close a second session as remarkable for what it didn't do as for what it did do."[25]

---

[22] For a discussion of the frustrations of House Republicans under Martin's leadership, see Charles O. Jones, *Party and Policy-Making; The House Republican Policy Committee* (New Brunswick, N. J.: Rutgers University Press, 1964), Ch. 2.

[23] See Neustadt, *op. cit.,* p. 75.

[24] Quoted in *Congressional Quarterly Almanac,* Vol. 13, 1957, p. 87.

[25] *Congressional Quarterly Almanac,* Vol. 14, 1958, p. 57.

Quite clearly, the external and internal conditions which existed in the 85th Congress resulted in a most confusing policy-making situation. For the most part the House Republican party was limited to a participating strategy in majority coalition-building. Thus, as with the 63rd and 73rd Congresses, the minority party had a restricted range of strategies available. As distinct from those two Congresses, however, the minority party was considerably more involved in congressional policy-making during the 85th Congress.

A FLEXIBLE MINORITY—87TH CONGRESS

The combination of conditions which characterized the 87th Congress provided a greater range of strategies for the minority party than the other three congresses examined here. President Kennedy's view of the presidency was in the tradition of Wilson and Roosevelt, but he did not have their sources of strength. There was no all-pervasive crisis to dominate national politics in 1960, Kennedy's margin over Nixon was extremely narrow, congressional Republicans had increased their numbers in both houses over 1958, Republicans were generally unified, and Democrats were plagued with a measure of disunity (see Table 2 for summary of all conditions). Kennedy's greatest sources of power seemed to be his energy in producing new ideas, and renovating old ideas, for solving public problems, and the fact that so little had been accomplished in the 86th Congress. In Neustadt's terms, he was able most to rely on "the expectations of those other men regarding his ability and will to use the various advantages that they think he has."[26] President Kennedy took a very broad view of the presidency:

Whatever the political affiliation of our next President, whatever his views may be on all the issues and problems that rush in upon us, he must above all be the Chief Executive in every sense of the word. *He must be prepared to exercise the fullest powers of his office—all that are specified and some that are not.*[27]

With the exception of a procedural change in the House, internal conditions also tended to favor the minority party. As noted above, for the first time since 1952, Republicans increased their numbers in the House of Representatives. The Democrats still had a commanding majority—263 to 174—but with probable Democratic disunity on some measures, the Republicans could expect some success in building negative majorities so as to defeat the President's proposals. The President was successful in effecting a procedural change of some significance. The House Committee on Rules had become an anti-administration device and could be expected to cause considerable procedural difficulty for the President's program. In a major power struggle between Chairman Howard W. Smith and Speaker Rayburn, Rayburn won (with the critical support of 22 Republicans) and the Committee on Rules was enlarged by three members. Though enlargement did not result in the Committee's loss of power and independence, it did represent a major defeat for those who had relied on it to

[26] Neustadt, *op. cit.*, p. 179.
[27] Quoted in the *New York Times*, January 15, 1960, p. 16 (emphasis added).

curb the majority and merely opened the door to other, more drastic reforms.[28]

The House party leadership situation in the 87th Congress was almost the reverse of that during the 85th Congress. The Republicans were much stronger, the Democrats much weaker. Rayburn, McCormack and Albert continued to lead the Democrats but the long-time Speaker was apparently losing his touch. As one senior Democrat put it:

Rayburn died at a propitious time. During the last three to five years, things were getting out from under his control. And during the last two years people really had no idea, but it was distressing to sit there with his group of about 15, and see him trying to grapple with bills like the foreign aid bill when he had lost his touch.[29]

McCormack was elected Speaker after Rayburn died in November, 1961.

The Republicans changed leadership in 1959. Joe Martin was in poor health and had grown away from many of the party's younger members. The 1958 election, in which House Republicans lost 47 seats, served as a catalyst for change. The new minority leader, Charles A. Halleck of Indiana, was less a friend of Rayburn and was considered more partisan than Martin had been. Though he was not the first choice of many House Republicans who had pressured for a change in leadership, they generally considered him superior to Martin.[30] As it turned out, he was to serve as interim leader only—until the insurgents could muster enough support to get a more preferred candidate elected.[31] At the time that Halleck was elected, House Republicans also reorganized their party. The most significant change was to separate the floor leadership and Policy Committee chairmanship posts. This change was made at the insistence of the insurgents. Though the reorganized Policy Committee by no means satisfied those House Republicans who desired more vigorous and imaginative policy leadership, it did give them somewhat more access to leadership decision-making and served to unify the party.

The first point to establish in analyzing policy-making in the 87th Congress is that a minority party with several sources of power is "consequential" in policy-making. Thus, what the House Republicans did during the 87th Congress, the strategy they adopted on a particular piece of legislation, was often important to the outcome. Further, the very fact that they could mount consequential opposition became important in majority coalition building. Put another way, to the extent that the minority party has flexibility in choosing strategies, the majority party's role in policy-making is limited.

[28] There are a number of excellent studies of this struggle. See Robert L. Peabody and Nelson W. Polsby (eds.), *New Perspectives on the House of Representatives* (Chicago: Rand-McNally, 1963), Chs. VI and VII; William R. MacKaye, *A New Coalition Takes Control: The House Rules Committee Fight of 1961* (New York: McGraw-Hill, 1963); Neil MacNeil, *Forge of Democracy: The House of Representatives* (New York: McKay, 1963); James A. Robinson, *The House Rules Committee* (Indianapolis: Bobbs-Merrill, 1963). See also my "Joseph G. Cannon and Howard W. Smith—An Essay on the Limits of Leadership in the House of Representatives," *Journal of Politics,* 30 (August, 1968). It should be noted that further changes were made in 1965 to reduce the power of the Committee.

[29] Personal interview with a senior House Democrat, June, 1963.

[30] For details, see Jones, *op. cit.,* pp. 27–42.

[31] See Robert L. Peabody, *The Ford-Halleck Minority Leadership Contest, 1965* (New York: McGraw-Hill, 1966).

In the 87th Congress, House Republicans had a number of options at different stages of the legislative process. They could simply oppose that which was offered by the majority party (partisan opposition), they could counter with their own proposals (constructive opposition), they could support proposals (support), they could cooperate in developing policy (cooperation), they could initiate proposals of their own (innovation),[32] or they could simply not take a party position (withdrawal). As would be expected, a consequential minority potentially can be involved in policy-making during all stages of the legislative process—and various options may be available at each stage. It must be recognized, however, that there are separate minority party leaders—usually the ranking minority members of the committee or subcommittee—during the early stages of legislation. They may or may not consult the House minority leadership in developing strategies. Thus, it is conceivable that the minority party, through its various leaders, may actually employ different strategies at different stages.[33] By their very nature, one would expect that the cooperative and innovative strategies would be employed during the early stages of the legislative process (notably subcommittee and early committee action); partisan and constructive opposition, withdrawal, and support, during the later stages (final committee action and floor action).

It is not possible in this article to provide illustrations of all of the various combinations mentioned above. Only a few examples of the range of possibilities can be offered. There were many bills in the 87th Congress which illustrated *partisan opposition* by the minority party. In some cases, unified partisan opposition found enough support among Democrats to defeat the legislation. Thus, the federal aid to education bill in 1961, the attempt to establish a Department of Housing and Urban Affairs in 1962, and the first farm bill in 1962, all were defeated by the combination of a cohesive minority and defecting Democrats. The total House Republican vote on these three bills was 20 in favor and 480 against (an overall index of cohesion of 92).[34]

In other cases, House Republicans offered *constructive opposition* on the House floor following unsuccessful efforts in committee to have their proposals adopted.[35] That is, efforts were made on the floor to amend the legislation and/or recommit it with instructions to accept Republican changes. One such effort—on the Area Redevelopment Act of 1961—was inconsequential. Many House Republicans defected to vote against recommital and for the bill. Other efforts came close to victory. The recommital motion on the Omnibus Housing Act was defeated 215 to 197 and on the Tax Reform Act the recommital

---

[32] Theodore Lowi argues that innovation is a principal function of the minority party in Congress. See "Toward Functionalism in Political Science: The Case of Innovation in Party Systems," this REVIEW, 57 (September, 1963), 570–83.

[33] This is always true of the minority party; but in more restricted situations, the party's options are limited throughout the legislative process. It also should be pointed out that there is considerable legislative and representative behavior by minority party congressmen which is simply not attributable to party membership.

[34] Relying on Stuart Rice's index of cohesion: *Quantitative Methods in Politics* (New York: Knopf, 1928).

[35] It should be noted that "constructive" means that the Republicans were offering an alternative. That alternative may well have been "destructive" from the point of view of the President.

motion was defeated 225 to 190. House Republicans were actually successful in substituting their pared-down version of a minimum wage bill on the House floor in 1961—an important defeat for the Kennedy Administration. The President recovered, however, by a victory in the Senate for his bill. The Conference Committee adopted the Senate bill and their report was approved by the House only because 33 Republicans supported the President.

There were many other patterns of strategy during the 87th Congress. On the important Trade Expansion Act of 1962, there was considerable Republican *cooperation* and *support* during the formative stages of the legislation in the Committee on Ways and Means. The legislation split the House Republican Party, however, and many conservative Republicans opposed the bill. Due to this division, no Republican position was adopted. The minority party "withdrew" on this legislation. The House Republican Policy Committee took no position—allowing members to vote as they wished. The results showed 80 House Republicans in favor, 90 opposed.[36]

The Communications Satellite Act of 1962 is an example of *cooperation* in the formative stages followed by *support* on the House floor. The Manpower Development and Training Act of 1962 is an example of *innovation* followed by *support* on the House floor. The Subcommittee on Special Projects of the House Republican Policy Committee had conducted a general study of employment in the United States. One section of the study dealt with manpower retraining. Many of the recommendations contained in this study eventually found their way into the Manpower Development and Training Act.[37]

There are many other examples which could be given—in this Congress and in the first session of the 88th Congress (where, prior to the assassination, the minority party also had a rather wide range of strategies).[38] The point has been established, however. Conditions were such that the minority party had a range of strategies available in the process of majority coalition-building in the House.

Summary and Questions

The principal thesis of this article has been that the minority party's role in the process of majority coalition-building in the House of Representatives is by no means a consistent role over time. External conditions (temper of the times, minority party strength, minority party unity, and presidential power) and internal conditions (procedure, the margin, majority party leadership and organization, and minority party leadership and organization) determine the range of strategies available to the minority in congressional policy-making. As illustrated by four congresses, the range of strategies varies from the limited

[36] For details on the Republican dilemma on this legislation, see Jones, *op. cit.*, pp. 126–34.
[37] *Ibid.*, pp. 65–66.
[38] For evidence on the 89th Congress, see Robert L. Peabody, "House Republican Leadership: Change and Consolidation in a Minority Party," unpublished paper delivered at the 1966 Annual Meeting of the American Political Science Association, Statler-Hilton Hotel, New York City, September 6–10.

number available in the most restrictive minority party situations to the large number available in the flexible minority party situations. A number of these strategies are identified and discussed.

There are several important questions raised by this research which require separate analysis. For example, what are the functional consequences for policy formulation and policy administration of these various types of minority parties? It can be hypothesized that if the minority party has available a wide range of strategies, then both policy formulators and policy administrators will take into account minority party interests and views when performing their respective tasks. A consequential minority party may have a definite effect on the policy-making process. If an issue divides the majority, policy formulators may have to court minority party votes; the minority may be developing alternative proposals which become attractive to those affected by a policy problem and thus these proposals may be taken over by the majority party; minority victories in defeating the President may force executive policy formulators to rethink a proposal; minority party research into administration of policy may result in new legislation; and the general expectation that the minority party will oppose with strength and has certain rights, which are protected, to criticize presidential proposals, may induce caution, precision, and careful consideration in policy formulation and administration.

A second major question relates to minority party goal achievement. Do individual strategies in congressional policy-making contribute to the realization of the principal minority party goal of majority party status? If the minority party has a wide range of strategies available, does that result in victory at the polls? On the surface, it appears that the data confirm what every student of Congress knows—electoral success is related to a wide variety of factors, of which the range of policy-making strategies available is relatively minor.[39] In this century the Republicans as a flexible minority have scored impressive gains in the next election (1942, 1946, 1952), scored only slight gains (1962), and lost ground (1944). The greatest victories for Republicans in this century, in terms of net gain of seats, have followed congresses in which the minority party was severely restricted (1914, 1938, and, to a lesser extent, 1966). Republicans as a participating minority in the House have never gained in the next election (1912, 1956, 1958).

If electoral success does not follow from a more active role for the minority party in majority coalition building, a rather anomalous situation results. Minority party leaders are generally expected to rely on strategies which presumably will be rational in terms of the overall party goal of majority party status. Yet the impact of their actions on whether the minority party in fact becomes the majority party may be of very little consequence.

A third major question asks: What of the other combinations of variables not discussed here? Are there other types of minority parties when classified by the strategies available? A cursory examination of the congresses in this century suggests that the categories identified here are generally serviceable. But, as was

---

[39] For a general discussion of the opposition party in governmental decision-making, see Anthony Downs, *An Economic Theory of Democracy* (New York: Harper and Row, 1957), especially Chapter 4.

indicated in the discussion of the differences between the 63rd and 73rd Congresses, a great many refinements can and should be made. Thus, for example, some restricted minorities have little immediate prospect of a greater range of strategies. Clearly, there are degrees of restrictedness and flexibility. Further, it is perfectly conceivable that a participating minority may have a strong, rather than a weak, President in the White House. And what of those rare instances when both parties are in the minority in Congress—one in each house? The two congresses of this type in this century, the 62nd and 72nd, represented highly abnormal policy-making situations wherein the majority party nationally was in the process of being deposed.

This research suggests many other questions as well. Are there differences between the minority parties of the House and Senate in any one Congress? Preliminary analysis indicates that there are. Does the analysis provided here apply to the Democratic party as a minority party? Does it apply to a large number of congresses? What happens to a minority party which fails over a long period of time to achieve majority party status? To what extent are goals of individual members functional or dysfunctional for achieving the party's goal? To what extent is "party" important at all in the formative stages of legislation? These and other important questions must be answered if we are to understand the role of political parties in Congress.

Epilogue

Epilogue

Some Priorities for Future Research

by M. DONALD HANCOCK
and HERBERT HIRSCH

We wish to conclude this venture with an inventory of some future research priorities. As the selections in this volume testify, the existing literature on legislative behavior is rich and varied. Organized according to the categories of system analysis, the published material and original essays we have compiled can provide a suitable basis for cross-national comparisons of legislators and legislative processes. Yet the current state of research, as well as the system concept itself, reveals serious shortcomings when measured against the new requirements of contemporary political inquiry.

Just as domestic and international politics are marked by previously unforeseen forms of revolutionary upheaval, modern scholarship confronts a crisis of relevance and methodological adequacy. With the rise in advanced political systems of such militant protest groups as the student and Black Power movements, the end of ideology illusion of the 1950s has been displaced by new forces of ideology controversy. Simultaneously, the erosion of bloc cohesion in both East and West and quickened aspirations for national self-determination in former colonial territories have initiated a potentially profound transformation of the international political system.

These changes in both the domestic and international political environments have directly challenged the efficacy of modern political analysis. Having successfully waged a struggle against "traditional" scholarly tenets for greater theoretical sophistication and methodological precision, behavioralists throughout the Western scholarly community have now encountered major limitations inherent in the principles as well as the methods of the prevailing "behavioral persuasion."

Specifically, the positivist emphasis on "prediction as a basis for testing the validity of scientific theories . . ."[1] has proved largely fallacious. In light of the sharp discontinuities in domestic and international politics in recent years, the inadequacy of simple projections from the present into the future is clearly revealed. Because of their preoccupation with middle-range theories that assume continuity and a high degree of sociopolitical stability, most Western scholars have been unable to anticipate the major changes that are now occurring throughout the contemporary world. Moreover, the theoretical orientation of modern positivism—restricted as it is to such projections—has led many social scientists to deprecate important empirical evidence that might otherwise help account for processes of continuing sociopolitical change.[2]

Within the relatively specialized field of legislative behavioral research, these limitations of theory, method, and data are all too readily apparent. As salutary as recent attempts to employ systematic theory in the study of legislative behavior have been, most prevailing theoretical approaches fail to advance the avowed predictive capacity promised by positivism. Studies of legislative supports that do not take into consideration the possible disintegration of public support, for example, are unlikely to tell us very much about future directions of political change. Limitations on the scope of data—e.g., the omission of the possible effects on legislative processes of new groups functioning outside the established political framework—have likewise restricted the relevance of even the most recent studies of legislative behavior.

Hence a first priority for the further pursuit of legislative research must be, in our opinion, a basic reassessment of the role of theory as both a tool of prediction and a basis for the selection of data. What is required is not the abandonment of the positivist underpinnings of modern behavioralism but the incorporation of alternative theoretical models that can help make scholarship more sensitive to forces of contemporary change.

A necessary step in such a theoretical reorientation is to adopt a dynamic view of politics in place of the system maintenance bias of most existing approaches. As James A. Bill's essay in this volume on the legislative system of Iran suggests, studies of political modernization provide a possible basis for such a perspective. Involving processes of enhanced control by man over his physical, social, and individual environments through the application of advanced technical and scientific knowledge, modernization is by definition a dynamic concept.[3] Political systems may modernize to the extent that they acquire greater economic, social, and political capacities to meet demands placed on them by the international and domestic environments and to the extent that political par-

[1] Gideon Sjoberg, M. Donald Hancock, and Orion White, Jr., *Politics in the Post-Welfare State: A Comparison of the United States and Sweden* (Bloomington, Indiana: Carnegie Seminar on Political and Administrative Development, 1967), p. 2.

[2] *Ibid.*, pp. 2–4. For an expanded treatment of the limitations of behavioralism and structural-functionalism as tools of prediction, see "Epilogue" in M. Donald Hancock and Gideon Sjoberg (eds.), *Politics in the Post-Welfare State: Responses to the New Individualism* (forthcoming).

[3] Especially incisive treatments of the modernization concept include Dankwart A. Rustow, *A World of Nations* (Washington, D.C.: The Brookings Institution, 1967); C. E. Black, *The Dynamics of Modernization* (New York: Harper & Row, 1966); and Manfred Halpern, "A Redefinition of the Revolutionary Situation," *Journal of International Affairs* 23, no. 1 (1969): 54–75.

ticipation is extended to an increasing number of citizens. Conversely, systems may regress into conditions of what Samuel Huntington describes as "political decay."[4]

If selectively applied to the study of legislative behavior, the modernization concept can yield important insights into the effect of political change on legislative functions. As one of the co-editors of this volume posits in another context, political systems can be classified along a pre-industrial, industrial, and post-industrial continuum of modernity.[5] The major variables in determining the level of modernity in a given system are its degree of industrialization, its utilization of technology, and prevailing patterns of collective-individual relations.

Politically, the third variable is the most significant. In pre-industrial systems the capacity of the individual to determine his own environment is sharply proscribed by the claims of the collectivity for subservience to traditional mores, religious beliefs, and time-sanctioned forms of authority. In industrializing systems the autonomy of the individual is similarly restricted—in this case by the necessity for disciplined social action to achieve or sustain modernizing goals. Only in the post-industrial phase of modernization—in which the primacy of production yields to the primacy of distribution—can the individual attain meaningful capacity to assert effective freedom of choice and hence control over his individual environment.[6]

What must be emphasized is that legislative functions vary according to the attainment of given levels of modernity. To the degree that legislatures effectively control executive-administrative behavior, they provide a key index of political modernity. Hence on the level of descriptive analysis the modernization concept can help provide a cogent basis for classifying rule-making structures according to their scope of control relative to other aspects of the political environment. More important from the view of a dynamic or processional analysis of politics is the realization that the transition to post-industrial society is likely to yield new—perhaps radically different—relations between the collectivity and the individual. As a result, legislative functions as we know them today may undergo significant transformation. Whereas differentiated rule-making structures have performed indispensable functions in integrating diverse sociopolitical and economic interests during the historical phase of industrialization, they may become counter-productive in the post-industrial quest for greater individual freedom *vis-à-vis* the group. Alternatively, national and state legislatures might become largely honorific bodies in the post-industrial state as effective rule-making authority is transferred to a decentralized network of community and corporate power structures. Whatever the outcome of post-industrial modernization in a given political system, the substitution of a dynamic view of politics for the present emphasis on system maintenance can heighten the social scientist's

[4] Samuel Huntington, *Political Order in Changing Societies* (New Haven: Yale University Press, 1968).

[5] Hancock and Sjoberg, *Responses to the New Individualism.*

[6] We do not mean to suggest that this will inevitably take place. Advancing technological change also makes possible new forms of suppression.

awareness of the range of conceivable sociopolitical options that the future might hold.

A closely related priority in undertaking processional analysis is the need, as we indicate above, to construct new theoretical models that can facilitate prediction. If the prevailing tendency among modern behavioralists to assume a high degree of continuity from the present into the future restricts the capacity of social science to anticipate possible discontinuities, alternative approaches must be sought. An especially promising analytical model is provided by counter system analysis.

As propounded chiefly by Gideon Sjoberg, the counter system is a theoretical construct based on dialectical analysis.[7] Sjoberg argues with Mara and Sorokin that all social systems—including sub-systems such as bureaucracies as well as larger political systems such as the modern industrial-welfare-state—encompass inherent contradictions that become increasingly exposed as the system reaches maturity. Such contradictions may serve in turn as major stimuli for the emergence of anti-systems (such as total or partial ideologies) that can be the harbingers of revolutionary change. At a minimum, anti-systems—by challenging the dominance of established values, status systems, and political processes—are likely to initiate system change by provoking the dominant élites to respond with measures ranging from repression of the anti-system to modifications of the social system to meet its criticism. To avoid the extremes of repression and revolutionary violence that emerging contradictions in the advanced industrial-welfare systems might generate, Sjoberg advocates that social scientists construct logical counterparts to existing reality—i.e., counter systems—that might point to ways in which conflict can be effectively resolved or at least diminished.[8]

Counter system analysis does not provide the means to predict the future in any literal sense, but it does offer important advantages over the theoretical limitations of existing forms of political analysis. By focusing more of his attention on emerging sociopolitical contradictions, the social scientist can acquire a better understanding of processes of contemporary political change. Through the construction of logical counter systems, he can more effectively judge the possible consequences of such changes for future forms of political behavior.

Applying the modernization concept and counter system analysis to the study of legislative behavior will require, as a third priority of research, a broadened universe of data. Conventional aspects of legislative analysis remain important. More, not less, attention must be paid to such vital considerations as roles, legislative supports, integration, and decision processes. Yet changes in the broader political environment of legislative bodies necessitates the simultaneous study of new factors—such as the rise of the extraparliamentary opposition in Western Europe and North America—that may increasingly impinge on con-

---

[7] Sjoberg, Hancock, and White, *Politics in the Post-Welfare State*, pp. 2–4. A more detailed presentation of counter system analysis is provided in Gideon Sjoberg and Leonard Cain, "Negative Values, Counter System Models and the Analysis of Social Systems," in Richard Simpson and Herman Turk (eds.), *The Sociology of Talcott Parsons and George Homans* (forthcoming).

[8] For an illustration of counter system analysis, see Orion White, Jr., "The Dialectical Organization: An Alternative to Bureaucracy," *Public Administration Review* 29 (1969).

temporary legislative functions.[9] What, for example, are the implications of radical demands for "direct democracy" for the viability of existing representative structures? To what extent do recent attempts by some legislators to go outside the legislative structure to mobilize popular support for particular issues suggest a significant trend for the future?[10] By expanding systematic inquiry to include such questions, the student of legislative behavior can more readily assess the changing role of legislative processes in the modern world.

Finally, we believe that studies of legislative behavior must become more genuinely comparative. The distinction between "American" and "comparative" politics is growing increasingly obsolete, sustained more by the force of custom than any by rational division of labor. To generalize intelligently about political behavior, however, it is necessary to test hypotheses in a broader context than simply the experience of a single national system or sub-system thereof. It is unrealistic to expect students of American politics to acquire the essential linguistic skills and foreign experience that would enable them to become well versed in comparative political analysis or to require scholars of comparative politics to become equally conversant with American politics. What we can and do advocate is that students of legislative behavior endeavor to utilize functionally equivalent categories in their research to facilitate cross-national comparisons. In addition, collaborative efforts between domestic and comparative specialists can usefully serve to promote more comprehensive knowledge of legislative processes in a variety of settings.

[9] A "theory of extraparliamentary opposition" is presented in Johannes Agnoli and Peter Brückner, *Die Transformation der Demokratie* (Frankfurt am Main: Europäische Verlagsanstalt, 1968).

[10] A case in point is Senator Gaylord A. Nelson's public campaign against pollution and chemical-biological weapons. See Gaylord A. Nelson, "Our Polluted Planet," *The Progressive* 33, no. 11 (November 1969): pp. 13–17.

INDEX